After the Deportation

An estimated 160,000 people, a mix of résistants and Jews, were deported from France to camps in Central and Eastern Europe during the Second World War. In this compelling new study, Philip Nord addresses how the Deportation, as it came to be known, was remembered after the war and how deportation memory from the very outset became politicized against the backdrop of changing domestic and international contexts. He shows how the Deportation generated competing narratives – Jewish, Catholic, Communist, and Gaullist – and analyzes the stories told by and about deportees after the war and how these stories were given form in literature, art, film, monuments, and ceremonials.

PHILIP NORD is Rosengarten Professor of Modern and Contemporary History at Princeton University. His publications include *France 1940: Defending the Republic* (2015) and *France's New Deal: From the Thirties to the Postwar Era* (2010).

Studies in the Social and Cultural History of Modern Warfare

General Editor

Robert Gerwarth, *University College Dublin*

Jay Winter, *Yale University*

Advisory Editors

Heather Jones, *University College London*

Rana Mitter, *University of Oxford*

Michelle Moyd, *Indiana University Bloomington*

Martin Thomas, *University of Exeter*

In recent years the field of modern history has been enriched by the exploration of two parallel histories. These are the social and cultural history of armed conflict, and the impact of military events on social and cultural history.

Studies in the Social and Cultural History of Modern Warfare presents the fruits of this growing area of research, reflecting both the colonization of military history by cultural historians and the reciprocal interest of military historians in social and cultural history, to the benefit of both. The series offers the latest scholarship in European and non-European events from the 1850s to the present day.

A full list of titles in the series can be found at:
www.cambridge.org/modernwarfare

After the Deportation

Memory Battles in Postwar France

Philip Nord

Princeton University

CAMBRIDGE
UNIVERSITY PRESS

CAMBRIDGE
UNIVERSITY PRESS

University Printing House, Cambridge CB2 8BS, United Kingdom

One Liberty Plaza, 20th Floor, New York, NY 10006, USA

477 Williamstown Road, Port Melbourne, VIC 3207, Australia

314–321, 3rd Floor, Plot 3, Splendor Forum, Jasola District Centre, New Delhi – 110025, India

79 Anson Road, #06-04/06, Singapore 079906

Cambridge University Press is part of the University of Cambridge.

It furthers the University's mission by disseminating knowledge in the pursuit of education, learning, and research at the highest international levels of excellence.

www.cambridge.org
Information on this title: www.cambridge.org/9781108478908
DOI: 10.1017/9781108781398

First published 2020

Printed in the United Kingdom by TJ Books Ltd, Padstow Cornwall

A catalogue record for this publication is available from the British Library.

ISBN 978-1-108-47890-8 Hardback

For Erin and Tina

Contents

Figures

Acknowledgments

I am indebted to many friends and colleagues whose advice and criticism have made this a better book than it would otherwise have been. I want to thank first of all those who read the manuscript in part or in whole: Alice Conklin, Emma Kuby, Michael Gordin, Arnaud Orain, Daniel Sherman, and Daniel Zemel. They have tried to rescue me from error and to help me clarify what I wanted to say. To Carolyn Dean, who worked her way through the text more than once, bringing a judicious and caring intelligence to the challenge of improving it, I express a special thanks. I have had the opportunity to present my work in a variety of venues, and the feedback that resulted made a difference on more than one point. I am grateful to the people who invited me to speak and to audience members who posed questions that led me to think more critically about my work. It is a pleasure to name them: David Abraham, Stephen Aron, Paul Cohen, Richie Cohen, J. P. Daughton, Vincent Duclert, Albert Friedes, Krista Goff, Dimitri Gondicas, Michael Gordin, Jeff Horn, Marc Lazar, Michael Miller, David Nasaw, Iris Rachamimov, Paul-André Rosental, Sandrine Sanos, Jerrold Seigel, Moshe Sluhovsky, David Troyansky, Yael Sternhell, and Keith Wailoo.

Many obstacles came up along the way, and when I needed help with a question, a fact, or an archive, there were friends and colleagues on hand to steer me in the right direction: Bridget Alsdorf, Claire Andrieu, Antoine de Baecque, Edward Baring, Annette Becker, Jean-François Chanet, Martin Conway, Sarah Gensburger, Philippe Gumplowicz, Sudhir Hazareesingh, Eric Jennings, William Jordan, Piotr Kosicki, Susan Pennybacker, Guillaume Piketty, Renée Poznanski, Anson Rabinbach, Paul-André Rosental, Michaël de Saint-Cheron, Emmanuel Szurek, Jean-Charles Szurek, Thomas Trezise, Claire Zalc, and Froma Zeitlin. I hesitate to single anyone out for special mention in this connection, but in two cases I would be remiss were I not to do so: one a colleague here at Princeton, the second one just starting a career in France. They are David Bellos and Simon Perego. I have learned enormously from both of them.

For four years, I served as director of the Davis Center for Historical Studies at Princeton. "Belief and Unbelief" and "In the Aftermath of Catastrophe" were the chosen themes of the Center's discussions during my tenure of service. I profited immeasurably from these exchanges and want to thank all involved: Nicole Archambeau, Pamela Ballinger, David Barnes, Adam Beaver, Susan Carruthers, Simeon Evstatiev, Jennifer Foray, Pierre Force, Pierre Fuller, Peter Gordon, Atina Grossmann, Katja Guenther, Jochen Hellbeck, Dagmar Herzog, Brandi Hughes, Matthew Karp, Marie Kelleher, Benedict Kiernan, Emma Kuby, Sophie Lunn-Rockliffe, Katherine Luongo, Rebecca Nedostup, Arnaud Orain, Stefania Pastore, Caterina Pizzigoni, Jared Roll, Moshe Sluhovsky, Julia Smith, Victoria Smolkin, Louis Warren, Yael Sternhell, and Max Weiss.

I have had occasion to teach some of the material dealt with in this book. Instructors invariably learn from the instructed. My case is no exception, and so I'd like to thank those students, graduate and undergraduate, who have also been my teachers: Sarah Barnette, Zoë Buonaiuto, Constanza Dalla Porta, Emily Downey, Nikolaus Hofer, Rafi Lehmann, Molly O'Brien, and Charlotte Werbe.

It takes contributions of many kinds to make a book like this possible. My wife Deborah and I made a memorable trip to Izieu, which would not have happened without the good offices of Marion Vivier and Dominique Vidaud. Véronique Chabrol shared with me memories of her father, Paul Flamand. I had difficulty tracking down some of the images for this book, but I succeeded thanks to the interventions of Simon Texier and Susan Woodland. Throughout, I have benefited from the help of archivists who were unfailingly generous with their time and assistance: Xavier Aumage; Father Robert Bonfils, S. J.; Dominique Hiéblot; Guy Krivopissko; Karen Taïeb; and Vladimir Trouplin. At the very end, when the moment came to find a publisher, Michael Watson of Cambridge University Press took charge of the manuscript and, with thoughtfulness and tact, sped it on its way. To all of these, I owe a debt.

But my deepest debt is owed to my family: to my mother, Del, who sat me down as a boy to watch the Eichmann trial when portions of it were aired on American television; to family members who are no longer here, my father, Henry, my mother-in-law, Gayola, and my brother-in-law Jeremy; to family who sustain me as I write these words, my sons Joseph and David, my daughters-in-law Erin and Tina, and, of course, my beloved Deborah; and to future family members, may they live long and prosper, who are yet to be born.

Abbreviations

AADJF	Amicale des anciens déportés juifs de France
ACOL	Archives de la Chancellerie de l'Ordre de la Libération, Paris
ADIR	Association nationale des anciennes déportées et internées de la Résistance
AFL	American Federation of Labor
AIU	Alliance israélite universelle
AJC	American Jewish Committee
AJ-C	Amitié judéo-chrétienne de France
AN	Archives nationales, Paris
ANFROM	Association nationale des familles de résistants et d'otages morts pour la France
APFCJ	Archives de la Province de France de la Compagnie de Jésus, Vanves
ATD	Aide à toute détresse
BNF	Bibliothèque nationale de France, Paris
CCIF	Centre catholique des intellectuels français
CDJC	Centre de documentation juive contemporaine, Paris
CFLN	Comité français de libération nationale
CGQJ	Commissariat général aux questions juives
CHDG	Comité d'histoire de la deuxième guerre mondiale
CICRC	Commission internationale contre le régime concentrationnaire
CIF	Comité des intérêts français
CRIF	Conseil représentatif des Israélites de France
EDC	European Defense Community
EU	European Union
FFDJF	Les Fils et les Filles des Déportés juifs de France
FLN	Front de libération nationale
FNDIR	Fédération nationale des déportés et internés de la Résistance

FNDIRP	Fédération nationale des déportés et internés résistants et patriotes
FSJU	Fonds social juif unifié
IDHEC	Institut des hautes études cinémathographiques
IMEC	Institut Mémoires de l'édition contemporaine, Caen
MNPGD	Mouvement national des prisonniers de guerre et déportés
MOL	Musée de l'Ordre de la Libération, Paris
MRAP	Mouvement contre le racisme, contre l'antisémitisme et pour la paix
MRN	Musée de la Résistance nationale, Champigny-sur-Marne
PCE	Partido comunista de España
PCF	Parti communiste français
RDR	Rassemblement démocratique révolutionnaire
SFIO	Section française de l'Internationale ouvrière
SHD	Service historique de la Défense, Division des archives des victimes des conflits contemporains, Caen
STO	Service du travail obligatoire
TEC	Travail et Culture
UGIF	Union générale des Israélites de France
UNADIF	Union nationale des Associations de déportés, internés et familles de disparus

Introduction

An estimated 160,000 persons were deported from France to camps in Central and Eastern Europe during the Second World War; 76,000 of these were Jews. Of the rest, a rough half, 41,000 or so, were résistants. The Jews did not survive the ordeal: a mere 2,500 returned. Résistants and others fared better – 47,500 came back – but the toll was still a terrible one.[1] The figures are an eloquent reminder, if one is needed, of the lethalness of the German camp system. Nonracial deportees had a somewhat better than fifty-fifty chance of coming out alive. For a Jew, transport to the East amounted to a death sentence. Embedded in the numbers is also an assumption: that the story of the Deportation, as the French call it, was double.[2]

Résistants and Jews alike were herded onto trains and shipped eastward, but the fate that awaited them was not the same, and a vocabulary has been invented to characterize the difference. David Rousset was arrested for Resistance activities in 1943 and packed off to a series of camps, Neuengamme and Buchenwald the most infamous among them. He had an insider's knowledge of the Nazi carceral archipelago and lived to write about it, publishing *L'Univers concentrationnaire* in 1946. The text was one of the first of its kind, an analysis of the camp phenomenon understood as an alternate reality, a system with an infernal logic all its own.[3] The term caught on and, translated as *concentrationary universe*, has even migrated into English. Jews do make an appearance in Rousset's oeuvre, but they are marginal to the story he has to tell.

So, what vocabulary was available to talk about what had happened to *them*? The jurist Raphael Lemkin coined a new word for just that purpose in 1944, *genocide*.[4] In November of the next year at the Nuremberg trials, a Nazi official, Wilhelm Höttl, cited the figure of six million murdered Jews.[5] Among themselves, Yiddish-speakers referred to the destruction of European Jewry as a *Hurbn*, or catastrophe, the most recent in a long history of misfortunes that dated all the way back to the destruction of Solomon's Temple in 587 BCE. In 1947, the *Cahiers sioniens*, a Catholic periodical with an interest in Jewish conversion, lamented "the appalling holocaust of an entire people," borrowing a term from the Greek, *holocaust*, that signified a burnt offering.[6] Jews themselves were not averse to using the term. Léon Poliakov employed it, albeit sparingly, in *Bréviaire de la haine. Le IIIe Reich et les juifs* (1951), the first historical study of the destruction of Europe's Jews in any language.[7] The uncertainty of the signifier, the recourse to neologisms and foreign languages to name it, says something about the incomprehensibility of the phenomenon it purported to denote. How hard was it then, and still now, to grasp the Holocaust in all its enormity?

The Deportation then was two stories rolled into one, that of the concentrationary universe and of its yet more monstrous doppelgänger, the Holocaust. Daunting as it was to speak about such matters, people made the endeavor nonetheless. Survivors felt duty-bound, if not compelled, to try: to honor fallen comrades and dead family members, to exorcise the pain, to confront a world all too comfortable in its forgetfulness or incomprehension. There were artists of all kinds, moreover, whether survivors or not, who were equally determined to join in and to speak even at a remove of trials they may not have known firsthand, because the subject was too urgent and portentous to ignore. The result was a corpus of work that was varied and substantial – indeed, enormous in the case of France. It included histories, novels, poetry, movies, paintings, monuments, ceremonials. That outpouring, and the stories that were made out of it, is the subject of this book.

Insofar, that is, as the outpouring was intended for the public consumption of Francophone audiences. I will not discuss, except in passing, private or family memory, nor France's "Yiddish public sphere."[8] French-speaking France is the center of attention, which is not to say that the world beyond will be absent. Africa, the Caribbean, and Latin America make appearances, and global events too impinge on the discussion: the Cold War, France's war in Algeria, and the Arab–Israeli War of 1967, to cite some of the most important ones. The way the Deportation was thought about in France, of course, did not develop in isolation. The issues at stake were reflected on elsewhere – in Israel, Germany, and the United States – and the French paid attention, reacting against foreign examples as well as learning from them. So, while this is a national history, it is set in a global context.

Now, it's not as though these issues have never been written about before. Historians debate when and how the concentrationary paradigm, so dominant in the immediate postwar decades, lost ground over time to the Holocaust story. Film historians, literary critics, and the like debate the possibility of representing the unrepresentable and the means that artists, undeterred by the challenge, devised to do so. What I propose to do is to combine both approaches: to analyze the ebb and flow of the stories told about the Deportation and at the same time to engage with the "how" of such storytelling – the repertoire of images and narrative techniques that survivors and artists mobilized to give form and meaning to what they had to say. It is my hope, of course, that the subject I have taken on, how the Deportation was remembered and memorialized in France, will appear in a new light as a result.

Deportation Stories

Historians as a rule home in on one story or the other, that of the concentrationary universe or of the Holocaust. As they do, they often posit an implicit relationship between the two, one that is sequential in nature. Two major ways of thinking about this sequential relationship have developed.

The more venerable of the two – indeed, it has now attained the status of received wisdom – is cast as a from–to narrative. According to this way of thinking, the concentrationary story came first and held sway for decades. It took time, by contrast, for Holocaust consciousness to incubate, but when at last it did, it cast its erstwhile rival into the shadows. The motion then is from one story to the next or, so far as the Holocaust is concerned, from silence to voice.

On this understanding, there were not many in the war's immediate aftermath for whom the calamity visited on the Jews was a burning preoccupation. Among Jews themselves, a general amnesia prevailed as a traumatized community set about rebuilding and carving out a place for itself in a nation under reconstruction. Amateur historians of the Holocaust existed, to be sure, but they were just that, amateurs isolated on the margins of academia and little attended to. As for survivors, they hesitated to speak, all the more so in the face of a lingering, postwar anti-Semitism, and they were just a handful of people in any case.[9] No, it is said, what the general public was primed to hear and what they were indeed fed on were stories of the Resistance, of heroes and martyrs who had died in deportation or, cheating death, had come back haloed in glory. These men and women had staked all for the greater good, and the epic of their sufferings was a redemptive one, just what France – and Europe – needed in the aftermath of the *Nazizeit*.[10] The myth of the Deportee, a universal figure who emblematized the wartime tribulations of the nation as a whole, enabled the French to wash clean the sins of the past and to turn toward a brighter future based on principles of liberty and justice.

This "regime of memory," of course, did not last forever, but came unraveled in the 1960s and 1970s.[11] The exact timing varies depending on the account, but there is no doubting what took its place: the long-repressed story of the Holocaust, repressed no more. And make no mistake, this story was a Jewish one, related by Jews, not least of all by Jewish survivors who at last found a voice. These men and women, now entering middle age, dredged up terrible memories of an ordeal unlike any other, one that was unprecedented and unique. They had been the targets of a vast, murderous enterprise whose primary objective was the extermination of men, women, and even children, the very symbols of innocence, all killed not for acts committed but for the "crime" of being Jewish. The crystallization of Holocaust consciousness relegated to the wings the concentrationary paradigm, an experience of eclipse that not all Resistance deportees accepted with equanimity.

There is, however, a second way of thinking about this "reversal of memories,"[12] one less insistent on an initial repression of Holocaust remembrance. This school of thought, the second of the two mentioned above, is of more recent vintage. It does not take Jewish silence or the uncontested reign of the concentrationary paradigm as its point of departure. It maintains, rather, that Jews had in fact something to say about the fate inflicted on them and that they went about saying it right from the outset . Yiddish-speaking Paris mourned its dead, gathering every year at the Bagneux Cemetery in the city's near suburbs to recall loved ones swept away in the Nazi genocide.[13] In 1943, even as the Holocaust was in full swing, Jews convened in Grenoble to found what is today known as the Centre de documentation juive contemporaine (CDJC), which set itself the task of compiling a record of what had happened and was still happening to France's Jewish community. The CDJC relocated to Paris after the war and continued its efforts, building an archive and a monument.[14] Nor was it just among themselves that Jews talked. Take the Finaly Affair as an example. During the war, the Finalys, a Jewish couple later deported and murdered, had confided their two sons to a Catholic religious order for safekeeping, which in turn confided them to a caretaker. Relatives came looking for the boys after-wards, but the caretaker did not want to yield them up and arranged for their baptism in the hopes of enlisting the Catholic Church hierarchy as an ally and accomplice. A ferocious custody battle ensued that made national headlines in 1953, requiring the intervention not just of the courts but of high officials, secular as well as religious, to resolve.

Add in on top of this the era's literary production, and the claim that Jews maintained silence begins to look more and more like mythmaking. Anne Frank's diary was translated into French in 1950, and it caught the public's imagination in France, much as it did elsewhere. A slew of books soon followed, among them André Schwarz-Bart's *Le Dernier des Justes* (1959) and Anna Langfus' *Les Bagages de sable* (1962), both winners of the prestigious Prix Goncourt. Schwarz-Bart's novel concluded with the protagonist, Ernie Levy, entering a gas chamber at Auschwitz. Langfus' is a post-catastrophe story that evokes the melancholia of a Polish-Jewish woman survivor who relocates to France after the war, where she tries and fails to start life anew. It was not just a discerning few who read such novels. *Le Dernier des Justes* was a best seller. So too was Jean-François Steiner's *Treblinka*, a fictionalized rendering of a Jewish extermination camp revolt, published in 1966, which not only sold well but stirred a major public controversy.

Silence about the Holocaust then was never all-pervading. Yet even partisans of this new line of thinking concede that something did indeed change in the twentieth century's fin de siècle. There had always been a public for the story of the Holocaust, but now it widened. The CDJC had acted with decorum but not so later generations of Jews who grew ever more vociferous and assertive. And the authorities, once uninterested, began for reasons of their own to take an interest at long last, a process that culminated in 1995 when President Jacques Chirac issued a public acknowledgment of the French state's role in the genocide of the Jews. Holocaust consciousness thus expanded, spreading like an inkblot or, better, bounding forward in quantum leaps.[15]

These two models of memory – from silence to voice, from small beginnings to official sanction – share elements in common. The destination remains the same, with a new paradigm, that of the Holocaust, taking the place of an older, concentrationary one. Most often, the transition is rejoiced in. France's Jews had at long last made themselves heard, bringing non-Jews along the way to an awareness of the singular nature of European Jewry's fate. On occasion, however, a note of regret is sounded. As the Holocaust took center stage, older, soberer norms of memorialization went by the boards. What took their place was a dogged insistence on Jewish particularity, a particularism that was said to be confining to Jews (*wasn't there more to Jewish life than the Holocaust?* many Jews asked themselves) and at times grating to the general public, now laboring under a "surfeit" of memory.[16] No doubt, the bygone talk of heroes and martyrs smacked of mythmaking, but was such mythologizing, many wondered, any worse than all the clamor about victimhood?

Opinions may vary about how to characterize the rise of Holocaust consciousness, but not about the fact of it. There is also agreement about the centrality of hinge moments in speeding the process along. Partisans of the silence-to-voice model have pointed to 1961 and 1967 as critical turning points.[17] Adolf Eichmann, an architect and executioner of Hitler's Final Solution, was captured by Israeli agents and placed on trial in Jerusalem in 1961. Israel went to war with its Arab neighbors in 1967. These events, it is claimed, each in its way, galvanized French Jews to break their silence and speak out about the Holocaust. The quantum leap model also has its moments of inflection. In 1963, *Le Vicaire*, a French translation of Rolf Hochhuth's play, *Der Stellvertreter* (*The Deputy* in English), was staged in Paris. It indicted the Vatican's willingness to look away while European Jewry was massacred, and, as might be expected in a France still largely Catholic, the drama caused an uproar, rousing the general public – never inattentive – to yet heightened awareness of the Holocaust. A series of prosecutions in the 1980s and 1990s compelled the French state in its turn to sit up and take notice. Klaus Barbie, the Gestapo chief in Lyon during the Occupation, was extradited from Bolivia in 1983, placed on trial four years later for crimes against humanity, and convicted. Paul Touvier, a member of the Milice, Vichy's political police, had directed the murder of seven Jewish hostages during the war. He was arrested in 1989 and sentenced to life imprisonment in 1994. These trials were not the only ones of their kind, moreover, but dramatic high points in a spate of proceedings that mesmerized the public and drew French officialdom into the Holocaust's gravitational pull. As the twentieth century came to a close, the murder of the Jews had thus become an affair of state, with Chirac's 1995 declaration adding an exclamation point of recognition to a fact already established.[18]

One last point of commonality has to do with the role of generational change in raising Holocaust consciousness. Jews who had known the traumas of the genocide from experience hesitated to speak of them or, when they did, they spoke in muted tones, but not so their children. It may have been an identitarian quest that spurred on the young or an identification with the self-assertive Israeli Jew. Whatever the reason, a rising generation made the difference. Its youthful energies propelled a silenced or muffled story into the public limelight, a development that also had an impact on the Holocaust generation itself, inciting them at long last to speak up and bear witness.[19]

In the pages that follow, I won't question that the concentrationary paradigm has lost the preeminence it once enjoyed or that the Holocaust story *grosso modo* has supplanted it. What I will question is whether the concentrationary regime of memory was ever as cohesive a phenomenon as the name implies. It was more like an overarching canopy that sheltered a range of narratives, sometimes in competition with each other, sometimes not. Communists had an understanding of what the deportation experience had been all about, and it was not the same as the

Gaullists', the two camps vying with each other in recurring memory battles that spanned a quarter century. The non-communist Left joined in the fray, as did Catholics, and Jews too, for that matter. Amidst the general cacophony, there were also cordial interactions, the multiple narrative voices at moments singing in (relative) concert. There was dialogue too, above all between Catholics and Jews, which in time helped to win the latter, never silent, a more sympathetic hearing in the court of public opinion. It should not be thought, moreover, that the Jews themselves spoke in a singular voice. What we now think of as *the* Holocaust story was not one articulated at a stroke in all its detail. Rather, it was adumbrated across decades of research and reflection, its narrative arc changing as the historical context changed. The history of deportation memory then is not an either/or proposition, but something more complex, polyphonic, and, as far the Jewish part of it is concerned, emergent.

That word, emergent, is a tip-off that this will not be a history of the silence-to-voice variety. Jews in my view were neither silent nor unlistened to in the first postwar decades. Yet, vocal as they were, they sounded but one note among many, and the other voices were more forceful still. The situation would change over time, and so this history, as a number before it, will have to tackle the vexed question of how to account for the transformation.

I will emphasize processes over turning points. Generational shift will play a central role in my analysis, as it has in many others, but with some provisos. The Holocaust consciousness that crystallized in the 1960s and 1970s was not the brainchild of baby boomers alone, but of a movement of opinion stirred by men and women sometimes a little older – the Klarsfelds, for example: Beate, who was born in 1939, and Serge, who was born in 1935. What needs underlining, moreover, is the political context in which the generational shift took place, the era of 1968, which shaped both the content of the new Holocaust consciousness and the militant practices of those who advocated for it. I will also examine a second process, interfaith dialogue, which has been less often addressed in the literature on the Holocaust.[20] Catholics, like the Thomist philosopher Jacques Maritain, professed an understanding of the camps that acknowledged the Jewish tragedy, incorporating it into a Christian, salvific framework. The Jews' sacrifice, horrific as it was, had helped humanity advance on the path toward redemption. Jews like the historian Jules Isaac proffered an alternative account, one that assigned the Catholic Church an accomplice's role in the Holocaust as the purveyor of anti-Semitic teachings that paved the way for Nazi criminality. The two sides entered into a vigorous, painful debate, which began right after the war and did not subside until the mid-1960s (if even then). Such exchanges catapulted what both sides had come to call the Holocaust into French public consciousness.

Rejecting the silence-to-voice story arc raises yet one further issue that will have to be addressed at the appropriate moment. The conviction that there was a general refusal to face up to the Holocaust in the immediate postwar decades was once conventional wisdom, and it was deeply held. Were the partisans of this view just plain mistaken? What I will try to demonstrate by way of an answer is that, while indeed mistaken, they had reasons nonetheless, often good ones, for thinking as they did.

The Dilemmas of Representation

For critics of literature, film, and architecture, however, such histories of ebb and flow, such distinctions between concentrationary and Holocaust memory, are not the heart of the matter. Something unspeakable took place in the camps, and many people, survivors or not, felt an imperative to speak about it all the same. The result was a significant body of work, some of it testimonial, some of it creative, all of it in one way another at grips with problems of representation that were that much more challenging given the monstrous novelty of the subject at hand, the camps. There were issues of believability first of all. What had transpired in the camps was so outside the norm, it seemed scarcely possible to convey the nature of the experience in a way that was at once convincing and adequate to the extremity of it all. There were ethical issues as well. The murdered were owed a debt of respect, which seemed to militate against stylistic indulgences that showed off the author's technical skills to the detriment of the memory of the dead.

Survivors and artists wrestled to find ways to address these dilemmas, and what critics have done is to analyze and catalogue these "solutions," in crudest terms sorting them into two broad categories. The first is most often characterized as "realist." It makes use of representational techniques, simple and unadorned, that highlight the facts of the matter without inventions or flourishes that might stretch credulity or draw attention away from those who had suffered. For artists and memorialists in the second group, the realist approach was deemed inadequate. Presentation of the facts might persuade readers or viewers of the camps' existence, but mere facts did not suffice to communicate what camp life itself had really been like. It was all so fantastical, so surreal, that it was essential to bring the public's imagination into play by whatever means necessary, realist or not. Whether that exhausts the range of representational possibilities remains to be seen, and I will return to the question over the course of this book.

For the moment, I will content myself with pointing out a puzzle. Historians have proposed two regimes of memory, concentrationary on the one hand, Holocaust-centered on the other. Yet for critics, and some of the very best, no such distinction seems to exist. For them, it's all about the Holocaust, so understood as to encompass every form of expression about the camps. Thus, in a classic work about film and the Holocaust, Jean Cayrol and Claude Lanzmann are treated side by side. In yet another classic, this one about the Holocaust in literature, Jorge Semprun and Elie Wiesel are discussed together.[21]

Yet, do they really all belong together? Jean Cayrol was deported to the Gusen concentration camp as a résistant. He later collaborated with the filmmaker Alain Resnais in the making of *Nuit et Brouillard* (1956), one of the first documentaries about the camp phenomenon and an innovative work in formal terms as well. Claude Lanzmann, a résistant himself though never a deportee, also made a film about the camps, *Shoah* (1985). Yet, Lanzmann didn't like it when movie houses programmed *Nuit et Brouillard* and *Shoah* on the same bill. The films didn't deal with the same subject, he claimed, a point Resnais himself was willing to concede.[22] Jorge Semprun was a communist résistant who finished the war a detainee at Buchenwald. He wrote a book about the train-ride to the camp, *Le Grand Voyage* (1963), and much later another one about camp life itself, *L'Écriture ou la vie* (1994). It so happened that Elie Wiesel also spent time in Buchenwald, and in fact, the two men were liberated at the same moment. Wiesel, of course, is world famous as the author of *La Nuit* (1958), an eyewitness account of life and death at Auschwitz, where he had been deported in 1944. In the face of the advancing Red Army, the Germans evacuated the camp, driving its inmates westward, which is how Wiesel finally wound up at Buchenwald – the Little Camp at Buchenwald, that is – a quarantine facility transformed at the very end into a hell hole for Jews in extremis, which is what Wiesel then was. The two men, Semprun and Wiesel, had the opportunity in later years to converse together about Buchenwald, Auschwitz, and the Nazi camp system, and they arrived at a shared conclusion: that Wiesel's wartime experience and Semprun's had not been the same.[23] Were Lanzmann and Wiesel, both Jews, monopolizing the Holocaust for themselves? Then why did Resnais and Semprun yield the terrain without a fight? The answer to this question is that Jewish experience *was* in fact sui generis, distinct from that of résistants. In which case, what justification remains for lumping the two together?

It is tempting to acquiesce to this line of critique and, therefore, to commit to prying apart the two regimes of memory and to treating them as separate entities. Not all stories about the camps are Holocaust stories.

There are in fact variants (as will be seen) in which Jews play no role at all or at best a secondary part and sometimes even a negative one. It would seem to be the wisest policy then not to mix together materials that are so distinct.

That's not the course of action that will be pursued here. For when it comes to matters of representation, concentrationary art and literature and their Holocaust counterparts do indeed bear a family resemblance to one another. After all, they both deal with an experience of extremity: what it was like to be deported – rounded up, crowded into trains, and conveyed to a Nazi camp. Little wonder then that they ended up drawing on a common stock of images. That of the cattle car is one obvious example, that of barbed wire another. Little wonder too, and for much the same reason, that they experimented with narrative forms and techniques of a sometimes radical newness. It is productive then to consider the two together, but it is critical at the same time to treat them, not as the varied expressions of a single Holocaust story, which is the usual practice, but as instantiations – related but not identical – of a more encompassing phenomenon, the art and literature of the Deportation.

What such a perspective will bring into sharp relief is just how pervasive the memory of the Deportation was in postwar France and in fact how insistent it has remained down to the present day. It made its presence felt everywhere and did so with an unrivaled expressive imagination. I don't believe the claim is overblown. Consult a list of the best documentaries ever made. It won't be strange to find among the top twenty Resnais and Cayrol's *Nuit et Brouillard* and Lanzmann's *Shoah*, not to mention Jean Rouch and Edgar Morin's *Chronique d'un été* (1961) and Marcel Ophuls' *Le Chagrin et la pitié* (1969), all French films that evoked the Deportation, sometimes taking it head on, sometimes coming at it obliquely. Whether it's in fact accurate to label all four *documentaries* is a matter that will be discussed below. In the final analysis, what is most striking about the French case is how vital and creative, not to say contentious, the public debate about the Deportation and its meanings proved to be. The question of why France was the site of such contentious creativity is one in its own right, and I will return to it in the conclusion.

These preliminary remarks set the agenda for what is to follow. It is clear where to begin: at the war's end, when camp survivors began to straggle back to France and the first images of the camps themselves, photographs and newsreels, alerted a shocked public as to what the Deportation had been like. When to end is less obvious. Lanzmann's *Shoah* gave the Holocaust a new name, which caught on in France as elsewhere. Chirac's 1995 speech recognized the French state's investment in the Shoah as a counter-image to all that the France of today aspired to be. That then is where I will wind up, in the mid-1990s. This is not to say that history came to a halt at the end of the last century, just that a certain understanding of the Holocaust/Shoah crystallized at that time, casting into partial eclipse older narratives about the Deportation, once so important, but now themselves a dimming memory.

So, let us begin then at the beginning, just after the war, when Communists made a determined and for a short while successful bid to proprietorship of the deportation story and what it meant.

Part I

Heroes and Martyrs

1   Le Parti des Déportés

The Parti communiste français (PCF) never doubted that its militants made greater sacrifices in the battle for France's liberation than anyone else. To be sure, Charles de Gaulle had provided leadership, but he led from London. On French soil, it was the Communists who had been out front, bringing the fight to the enemy from early on. In August 1941, a party militant, Pierre Georges, killed a German officer at the Barbès-Rochechouart metro stop in Paris. Not two months later, in October, a party commando gunned down a second German officer in the port city of Nantes. This time, the Germans took hostages, executing forty-eight of them, including twenty-seven at the sand quarries of Châteaubriant. Most of the Châteaubriant martyrs – that was the Party's chosen term for them – were Communists, among them the seventeen-year-old Guy Môquet, who left behind a letter of farewell to his parents and younger brother, which, in its simplicity of phrasing and expressions of devotion to family and cause, retains the power to move to the present day. The Party was proud of its contribution to the Resistance, adopting the nickname "*le parti des 75,000 fusillés*." The figure is inflated, but that is beside the point. The Germans shot, hanged, and murdered many thousands, and among the executed, the *fusillés*, the PCF counted more than its fair share.

The Party's martyrology, however, included a second category of victim no less critical to its self-perception, the deportee. It took time for the figure of the deportee to gain in prominence. In the first months after the war, the PCF was more focused on bruiting its Resistance exploits. It had to contend after all with a de Gaulle still very much on the scene who was not about to let Communists steal a march on him when it came to claiming the legitimating mantle of the Resistance. But the General left office in January 1946. Camp survivors in the meantime had begun to return to France and to organize, and the largest deportee organization of all, the Fédération nationale des déportés et internés résistants et patriotes (FNDIRP), maintained close ties to the Party. The FNDIRP's leading personalities were a pair of onetime

Buchenwald inmates, Marcel Paul and Colonel Frédéric Manhès, the former a senior party member, the latter a fellow traveler.[1] Internal party rivalries, moreover, helped out the deportee cause. The PCF's general secretary, Maurice Thorez, spent much of the war in the Soviet Union and felt rivalrous with comrades like Charles Tillon, who had remained on home soil to take part in the armed struggle. Thorez maneuvered to sideline Tillon and at the same time to contain talk of Resistance heroism that might empower competitors.[2]

So it was that the PCF made itself into, not just the *parti des fusllés*, but also the *parti des déportés*, fashioning in the process a communist understanding of what the camp experience had been all about. Communists built a narrative that gave meaning to the Deportation, a story with heroes and villains that also helped to orient believers in the political present. The anti-fascist struggle was not over and done with, but ongoing, and it was essential to know who fascism's heirs were in the postwar world.

It should not be thought, moreover, that the communist narrative was always recounted in the didactic accents of the right-thinking ideologue. When it came to representing the Deportation, artists, whether party members or sympathizers, experimented. The socialist realist mode had its exponents, but there were others – Robert Antelme, for example, or Pablo Picasso – who invented alternative forms, less heroic in cast, starker in their depiction of pain and desolation. Such experiments did not always sit well with party officials, who preferred uplift to tragedy. Antelme left the PCF in 1950, and Picasso took a step back from party activism in the mid-fifties though never to the point of rupture. There was a moment in the postwar years, however, when the PCF was content to constrain but not to suffocate, and artists working within a communist idiom found the room to fashion a vocabulary of representation that pointed in new directions.

Memory Battles[3]

In the first months after the Liberation, the PCF and de Gaulle dueled over how to remember and commemorate the sacrifices of the war years. The dispute revolved in part around space, around identifying and laying claim to sites sacred to Resistance memory. But it also had to do with who deserved recognition, whether soldiers like General Leclerc de Hautecloque, de Gaulle's brother-in-arms and the liberator of Paris, or communist *fusillés*. Each side advanced its own slate of heroes and martyrs. Deportees, as we shall see, had a place in this tit for tat, but they were not in these early years the main object of either protagonist's commemorative attentions.

De Gaulle made the initial thrust. He paid a visit on All Saints' Day 1944 to Fort Mont-Valérien, a site just west of Paris used by the Germans during the war as a place of execution for hostages and résistants. A photo from the day shows him standing among a small group, paying respects before a planting of chrysanthemums laid out in the shape of a Cross of Lorraine.

The Communists, of course, did not intend to be outdone. The Front National, a Resistance organization under party influence, sponsored a demonstration on the first Armistice Day after the Liberation, November 11, 1944. The cortege gathered at the Arc de Triomphe. De Gaulle, though present and head of government, was confined to a secondary role.[4] This salvo was followed the next May by a commemoration grander still. The Party's May Day event in 1945 brought out a throng of marchers, and the parade was led by contingents of Buchenwald and Ravensbrück survivors garbed in the gray-and-blue striped uniforms they had worn in the concentration camps. On the 27th, a little more than three weeks later, deportees were not just featured participants but the principal honorees. There was a march to the Mur des Fédérés in Père-Lachaise Cemetery in northeast Paris to remember their sacrifice. This was hallowed ground to the PCF. Here it was that the Party's revolutionary forebears had made a last stand in 1871 in the waning days of the Paris Commune. Not far from the wall were buried two figures who loomed large on the Party's roster of the great and the good, the pacifist writer Henri Barbusse and Paul Vaillant-Couturier, onetime editor-in-chief of the communist daily L'Humanité, who had died an early death in 1937. Under the wall's shadow then, a crowd congregated in May 1945. The deportees in the audience, many dressed in the "striped pajamas" of the camps, struck up a song, the "Chant des déportés," also known as the "Chant des marais." It was the composition of German political prisoners who had been sent to the Börgermoor work camp to dig peat in the early days of the Third Reich. It had gone on to migrate beyond German borders, surfacing in multiple translations – English, Spanish, and French – and in the process achieving international distinction as a deportee anthem.[5]

Deportees then were a presence at party events at Père-Lachaise, but when it came time to erecting monuments on the site, it was the *fusillé* and not the deportee who was accorded first recognition. In October 1944, a provisional monument was raised at Châteaubriant in an ecumenical ceremony that included prominent non-communists. The following July, the remains of eight of the Châteaubriant martyrs, including the body of Guy Môquet, were removed to the communist corner of Père-Lachaise. Then in November 1945, once again at Père-Lachaise and just next to Barbusse's grave, a plot was prepared for seven of the Party's elected officials from the Paris region, all *fusillés*.[6] Gabriel Péri, a storied figure executed at Mont-Valérien, was among them. Louis Aragon, a party poet, had dedicated a poem to Péri, *La Rose et le réséda*, but it was Péri's letter of farewell, penned while awaiting execution, that did most to elevate him to legendary status. In it, he expressed an undimmed conviction "that Communism is the youth of the world and that it is preparing tomorrows that sing," and that phrase, "the tomorrows that sing," would in time enter into the book of party phrases as a poetic summing up of communist aspiration.

For all such efforts, the PCF faced stiff and ongoing competition from de Gaulle, who was still in power and still full of fight. In 1945, he staged a commemorative exercise of his own, far more imposing than anything the PCF had yet conceived. The first post-Liberation Armistice Day had been a communist-led affair, but not so the second. De Gaulle's minister in charge of repatriation, Henri Frenay, conceived a spectacular ceremonial, and the General gave him the go-ahead to execute the plan. In the Great War's aftermath, it had been possible to identify a single figure, the Unknown Soldier, who was designated to stand in for all the war dead. In the Second World War, however, there had been so many ways to die, not just in the trenches, but as a combatant in de Gaulle's Free French Army, as a résistant, or as a deportee. Frenay decided to represent all these categories, assembling the remains of fifteen men and women who had sacrificed their lives for France over the course of the war: nine soldiers, three résistants, and three who had died in deportation. On the evening of November 10, 1945, the bodies of the fifteen were conveyed to the Hôtel des Invalides, where they lay in state. From there, they were removed the next morning to the Arc de Triomphe for the main event, presided over by de Gaulle, who delivered a brief speech to a vast crowd of assembled officials and onlookers. This was followed by a military parade, and then that evening, in a solemn nighttime ceremony, the dead were transported to Mont-Valérien for burial in one of the fort's casemates. This was a provisional arrangement, however, and plans were laid to organize a national subscription to erect a more permanent marker.

There is much to say about the occasion and what it revealed about de Gaulle's understanding of the war and its place in French history, but that's for later. For the present, what matters is the anti-communist tenor of de Gaulle's Armistice Day. The ceremony in all its phases gave pride of place to the regular army. The interior Resistance, although not slighted, was cast in a supporting role. As for the résistants and deportees who were singled out for acknowledgment, not one had belonged to the communist Francs-Tireurs et Partisans, among the most combative of all the armed Resistance forces. Last of all, there was de Gaulle's speech. "It is essential," the General remonstrated, "that we agree to unite fraternally in order to heal a wounded France. Fraternally! That is to say, in silencing absurd quarrels so that we might march on the same road, at the same pace, singing the same song!" The intent of the General's exhortation was not hard to decipher. It behooved the PCF to abandon its fractious ways and accept its place in a Gaullist-led patriotic front.[7]

In the months that followed, de Gaulle acted to tighten his grip on the Mont-Valérien site. June 18 occupied a special place on the Gaullist calendar. It was on that day in 1940 that the General, speaking from London, had issued his celebrated call to arms, enjoining the French to carry on the fight against the Germans. The first June 18 after the Liberation – June 18, 1945 – was marked by a military parade on the Champs-Élysées, followed by a more modest ceremony at Mont-Valérien. The next year, however, the emphasis was altered, with Mont-Valérien now assigned the more prominent part. De Gaulle was no longer in power (he had resigned from office in January), so this event was a semiprivate affair. There was no parade, and no representatives of state participated, although the government did provide financial and logistical support. Gaullist loyalists themselves orchestrated the ceremonials with Compagnons de la Libération taking the lead. The Compagnons were members of a chivalric order created by de Gaulle during the war to honor comrades who had distinguished themselves in the fight for France's liberation. So it was then that the Chancellor of the Order, Thierry d'Argenlieu, opened the June 18, 1946 proceedings with a visit to the Tomb of the Unknown Solider under the Arc de Triomphe. He lit a torch from the eternal flame, which was afterwards carried to Mont-Valérien. There, it was used to light a second flame, this one at the casemate containing the remains of the fifteen heroes laid to rest the preceding November. De Gaulle entered the crypt alone while a moment of silence was observed by the small crowd in attendance, mostly former résistants and Free French veterans.[8]

In the wake of such proceedings, it might have looked like a division of sacred space was under way, with Père-Lachaise reserved for the PCF and Mont-Valérien for de Gaulle. The situation was more complicated than that, however, for the Communists too felt they had a claim on a piece of Mont-Valérien. The so-called *clairière des fusillés* was an open plot of land inside the fort's walls that the Germans had converted into an execution ground. Starting in 1946, the Association nationale des familles de fusillés et de massacrés de la Résistance française, presided over by Gabriel Péri's widow, organized once-a-month pilgrimages to the clearing to lay flowers, and every All Saints' Day there was a more formal remembrance ceremony, with speeches by luminaries of the communist Resistance. Colonel Manhès spoke in 1946 and Charles Tillon in 1947. In 1948 and 1949, the government forbade speechmaking inside the fort's walls and the following year stationed police to make sure the order was enforced.

The Party's foothold at Mont-Valérien then was contested, but so too for that matter was de Gaulle's. After de Gaulle departed office, the ministry in charge of veterans' affairs passed to Laurent Casanova, a senior member of the PCF. Casanova took advantage of the opportunity to cancel the national fund-raising campaign to erect a memorial at the Mont-Valérien crypt site.[9]

It was not just over sacred space that Gaullists and Communists clashed, but also over what kind of Resistance hero was most deserving of official acknowledgment. The Gaullists gloried in the military exploits of Free France, and that elevated Leclerc into a leading candidate for such accolades. He was the one, after all, who had commanded the armored column that entered Paris in August 1944, a decisive moment in the city's liberation. The war not long over, there was talk, it seems, of raising a monument to Leclerc. Nothing came of it until some years later, but the very idea was vexing to Communists.[10]

In July 1946, with rumors swirling about a Leclerc memorial, party officials debated how to respond. Why not, one proposed, memorialize the résistants who had done the real fighting in August 1944, rather than de Gaulle and the military men he surrounded himself with?[11] Just such a memorial was in fact in the making, and the figure singled out for special party honors was none other than Pierre Georges, better known by his nom de guerre, Colonel Fabien. Fabien's biography was compelling. He was of modest origins, had volunteered in the Spanish Civil War, and fought in the Resistance and in the liberation of Paris. What's more, he had gone on to command a military unit, the Fabien Brigade, which campaigned alongside Patton's Third Army and General de Lattre de Tassigny's First Army to drive the Germans out of France once and for all. It was in Alsace on the nation's German frontier in fact that Fabien had been killed in December 1944, in a mine blast that also claimed the lives of five fellow soldiers.[12]

Fabien was a source of party pride from the very first. He was buried in a plot at Père-Lachaise in January 1945. That August, the Place du Combat, a square in Paris's Xe arrondissement, was renamed, in his honor, the Place du Colonel Fabien. The next year, a campaign was mounted to build a monument to him. There was some thought of situating it on the Place du Colonel Fabien, but in the end a Père-Lachaise location was fixed on within sight of the Mur des Fédérés. A flier circulated announcing a competition for the monument design, and it made plain just why Colonel Fabien's memory mattered. He symbolized, the flier explained, "in such a remarkable way the heroic struggle of our people against fascism. An armed struggle begun on Spanish soil that was carried forward on our own." A committee was subsequently formed to oversee the competition, advised by a panel of artists that included Aragon, the poet Paul Éluard, and Picasso, every one of them a party member.[13]

The final design, all in cement atop a concrete base, had a rugged power. There was little decoration apart from a shallow bas-relief on the sarcophagus in front, a depiction of France with the head of Marianne in Phrygian cap superimposed. It had been decided to memorialize not just Colonel Fabien but also three of the officers who had died with him, and all were identified by name and rank. Each, moreover, was represented by a portrait carved in the cement, with simplified features but detailed enough to allow a measure of individuation (the design committee had solicited photos from the families of the bereaved to help the sculptor out).[14] This was a military monument in a new key, simple and stark, that validated the revolutionary patriotism and square-jawed determination of the four men buried there.

The memory battles of these first postwar years might have ended in a draw at Mont-Valérien, but not so at Père-Lachaise, where the Party laid claim to one plot after another. As it did so, the cemetery's northeast corner, the so-called 97th division, was converted into a veritable outdoor Pantheon,[15] a burial site for the PCF's most revered heroes and martyrs. Deportees took part in memorial events at the cemetery, but they were not as yet themselves the targets of memorialization. That would soon change. The initiative came, not from the Party itself, which had other commemorative preoccupations, but from allied organizations like the FNDIRP and the patchwork of amicales (associations), in effect survivor groups, which found a common home under the FNDIRP umbrella.

The FNDIRP

Under the Occupation, Vichy had created a network of mutual-aid centers, centres d'entraide, to provide material and moral comfort to returning prisoners of war. The war once over, the network was expanded to handle the flood of returnees of all kinds, deportees included. Communists were effective in colonizing the centers, which federated at the Liberation, giving rise to the Fédération nationale des centres d'entraide des déportés et internés politiques. In 1945, the federation turned into the Fédération nationale des déportés et internés politiques and then the year following into FNDIRP proper.[16]

The FNDIRP was by far the largest of all the postwar deportee organizations, claiming in December 1946 a membership upwards of 100,000.[17] The reasons for its success were multiple. First of all, there was the quality of the federation's leadership. It's not just that the principals were Communists, often quite senior in the party hierarchy. They also had solid experience running things. Marcel Paul was a trade union organizer who had done a stint as minister of industrial production in de Gaulle's postwar provisional government, with Colonel Manhès working alongside as a member of Paul's ministerial staff. And the FNDIRP's general secretary, Maurice Lampe, had seen service as Laurent Casanova's chef de cabinet during the latter's term as minister of veterans' affairs.

Over and above that, Paul and Manhès were undeniable Resistance heroes, and on this score, their Buchenwald experience was crucial. The SS had devised a clever and crushing scheme to rule over concentration camp populations. They held sway at the top, but a buffer of intermediaries, charged with executing SS orders and maintaining camp discipline, stood between them and the mass of camp inmates. These kapos, block elders, and the like were often recruited among common criminals, identified by the green triangles they wore. Such an arrangement spared the Nazi overlords intimate contact with the run of camp prisoners; it created an inmate hierarchy that in effect divided the inmates among themselves; and it gave sanction to the brutal impulses of the criminal element, ensuring a regime of terror that served the Nazi appetite for order and sadism, all the while maximizing the misery of the prisoners.[18]

In a few camps, however, Buchenwald most prominent among them, inmates had organized and leveraged the influence that organization afforded to maneuver postings for so-called politicals (identified by red triangles) in the critical middling ranks of the camp chain of command. At Buchenwald, it was the longest-serving generation of inmates, in effect German Communists, who took the lead in organizing. The French contingent, though, also made a contribution. In 1944, a Comité des intérêts français (CIF) was set up, and Marcel Paul and Colonel Manhès both belonged. The CIF represented a range of political currents, but Communists were the dominant element, and Paul was named to act as the CIF's liaison with his German counterparts. Prisoner organization had a double objective: to find ways to scale down the cruelty of the camp's disciplinary regime and to prepare a Resistance offensive. To this latter end, weapons and ammunition were stockpiled in preparation for a future camp revolt, and in the spring of 1945, that moment came. As American tanks were seen approaching the camp, the prisoner leadership gave the green light for an insurrection. Armed inmates opened fire, and the SS guards fled the scene.

Just imagine how the Buchenwald insurrection must have looked to French communist hagiographers. A party stalwart, Marcel Paul, had taken charge of organizing the Buchenwald Resistance, and that Resistance had in turn pulled off an astounding feat, the camp's self-liberation. In fact, it was German Communists, not the CIF, who steered prisoner organization, and it was they who gave the signal for a rising in the spring of 1945. The signal, moreover, came late in the game. The SS, informed that American forces were near at hand, had already begun to evacuate. Those remaining behind in due course spotted US tanks on the horizon. The SS were also fired on by prisoners and at this point decamped. There were no inmate casualties. That said, the Buchenwald story, even stripped of its mythmaking elements, was a powerful one. Paul and Manhès had militated in the camp resistance, and there had indeed been a prisoners' revolt, even if it was not the most decisive factor in effecting the camp's liberation.[19] These were the men, crowned in Resistance glory, who represented the FNDIRP's face to the public.

The FNDIRP held a second trump. It was open-armed in a way other deportee organizations were not. It did not accept into its ranks common criminals, but otherwise it extended a welcoming hand to all deportees and internees: politicals, of course, but also racial deportees (i.e., Jews), and anyone who, whether by design or error, had been swept up in the Nazis' repressive dragnet. The FNDIRP's principal organizational competitor, the Fédération nationale des déportés et internés de la Résistance (FNDIR), was more restrictive in its recruitment, insisting on Resistance credentials as a condition of membership. Thus, to the extent Jewish survivors had an official voice in the first postwar years, it was articulated via the FNDIRP or one of the FNDIRP's affiliated amicales.

The FNDIRP styled itself a federal organization, as indeed it was. From the very beginning, survivor associations gathered under its aegis: the Amicale de Mauthausen, the Amicale de Neuengamme, the Amicale de Ravensbrück, the Amicale d'Auschwitz, and the Amicale des anciens déportés juifs de France (AADJF). It's worth taking a moment to say a word about the last two organizations. Both were formed in 1945. The former was composed of Francophones, ninety percent of them Jewish, although its leadership, which came from PCF ranks, was more mixed. The amicale's president and vice-president, Maurice Honel and

Marie-Claude Vaillant-Couturier, were party members of note, he of Jewish background and a former deputy, she not Jewish at all but Paul Vaillant-Couturier's widow and from 1946 a serving member of the National Assembly.[20] The AADJF represented a different constituency, Jewish camp survivors from Auschwitz and elsewhere, who were often foreign-born and Yiddish-speaking. Its founder and guiding spirit, Henry Bulawko, was no Communist but a Marxist Zionist who had militated in the youth organization Hashomer Hatzair. Bulawko, however, had more than a little experience navigating in party waters. During the war, he had served as a liaison between Hashomer Hatzair and the armed communist Resistance. Arrested and sent to Drancy, a transit camp in the Paris suburbs, he helped to set up a communist collective there. And in 1950, Bulawko took part in founding the Mouvement contre le racisme, contre l'antisémitisme et pour la paix (MRAP), a peace organization that hewed to the party line in the era's Cold War debates and that, indeed, housed its headquarters in a building occupied by the Party itself.[21]

Nor was the FNDIRP's inclusiveness just a matter of membership access. It was also reflected in the federation's policy position concerning deportee benefits. This was a contentious issue when it came up for legislative debate in 1948. The National Assembly ended up adopting a pair of bills settling the matter, the first in August and the second the next month. The August bill dealt with résistants who had been deported or interned. It was not easy to obtain state recognition for such honored status, but recognition once obtained, the beneficiary was assigned a military rank and awarded the appropriate pension. The September law defined a second category of victim, a residual grouping that included deportees dispatched to the camps for racial reasons or for subversive activities. This meant Jews and many Communists, that is, those who had been captured and deported qua Communists.[22] Charlotte Delbo, for example, fell into the latter category. She was a member of a communist women's organization and, during the war, worked as a clandestine operative. The Gestapo arrested her in 1942 and deported her to Auschwitz. She survived, but on return was refused classification as a résistante under the 1948 legal regime. It was not just that the slight was rankling, but that it had material consequences. Survivors who had been deported as Jews or as subversives were treated as civilians, second-class victims in comparison to the soldiers of the Resistance and so did not merit the same generous level of benefits. Communist officials, and the FNDIRP too, were adamant in opposition to the dual-status regime, insisting on the establishment of one status for all. A party circular laid out the position of the communist delegation in the National Assembly. All "victims of Nazism," it asserted, deserved equal respect.

The document went on to protest the inadequacy of pensions for the widows of murdered militants (citing Mathilde Péri as an example), a stinginess all the more deplorable when the government of the day was lavishing such vast sums "to sustain the 'dirty war' in Indochina and [to] prepare, under the direction of US governing elites, a new war against the Soviet Union."[23]

The inclusiveness debate was reopened in 1951, though this time it was not the status of nonpoliticals but of self-styled "labor deportees" (*déportés du travail*) that was at issue. In 1943, under German pressure, Vichy had set up the Service du travail obligatoire (STO). This was a labor draft, and the unlucky conscripts, a total of more than 730,000 over the course of the war, were dispatched to the Reich to work in Germany's war industries. Returnees coveted the status of deportee, but in 1951, the National Assembly, on the urging of FNDIR among others, enacted legislation, stipulating that STO conscripts did not qualify for the designation. As late as 1978, the main pressure group that lobbied on behalf of STO conscripts was refused the right to use the word *deportee* in its title. For official purposes, the Fédération nationale des déportés du travail, as it was known to its members, had to employ a different name.[24] The PCF, as might be expected, made the cause of the labor conscript its own. It brought the matter up in parliamentary debate. A monument was raised to *déportés du travail* in the party corner of Père-Lachaise. Marie-Claude Vaillant-Couturier maintained an ongoing correspondence with a constituency organization representing labor conscripts that revealed just how much the injustice of the situation was galling to party militants. Fritz Sauckel had run Hitler's slave labor program and had been sentenced to hang for it at Nuremberg. He had committed a capital offense, so why, militants wanted to know, were Sauckel's victims judged so unworthy of consideration?[25]

When it came to speaking for deportees, for all of them and not just for the heroic kernel of résistants, no one spoke with a more embracing or forceful voice than the PCF and the FNDIRP. The FNDIRP indeed made a commitment to unity central to its appeal. The very first issue of the federation's newspaper, August 1, 1946, reported on a commemorative ceremony at Compiègne, the site of the Royallieu transit camp. The article was authored by a Jesuit father, Michel Riquet, who reminisced about the camp, remembering with emotion Père Jacques' "interminable palavers" with "his communist friends" and the red choir that was conducted by a priest from the Creuse. Aragon dedicated *La Rose et le réséda* to Gabriel Péri but also to Honoré d'Estienne d'Orves, a naval officer and practicing Catholic who, like Péri, had been executed at Mont-Valérien.[26] The poem's opening lines, "He who believes in heaven/He who does not," invoked the brotherhood of the Resistance, united by a bond that brought together believer and unbeliever alike. The poem was a much-cited favorite not just among résistants but among deportees as well. The camp experience was to them what the trench experience had been to the generation of the Great War, a crucible of fraternity.[27]

The Communist Pantheon

The PCF did not want for heroes and martyrs, but who it celebrated and how changed over time. Colonel Fabien and Guy Môquet always remained key personalities, but the party pantheon expanded to encompass new figures, deportees like Marie-Claude Vaillant-Couturier, who had survived at Auschwitz, and Danielle Casanova, who had not. The pantheon expanded in a second sense as well. The 97th division at Père-Lachaise, home to the graves of the Party's most venerated fusillés, saw the erection, starting in 1949, of a battery of monuments honoring not so much the sacrifice of named individuals as the collective suffering of the myriad men and women who had died in the camps without sepulcher. Even as the ranks of the Party's exalted dead swelled, so too did the repertoire of formal means employed to depict them become more varied. For the heroicized male, the realist mode remained the norm, but to deal with women and the anonymous dead, artists cast about for alternatives. That alternative might be traditionalist and Christianizing, as it was for the Party's female martyrs, or experimental and abstract as it was for the anonymous dead. But either way, the Party proved itself, at least for a passing moment, open in surprising ways to aesthetic variety.

The PCF became a mass party in the thirties, and it experienced a rebirth of growth after the war, thanks in part to a concerted effort to build up its youth and women's branch organizations.[28] When it came to proposing role models to such targeted constituencies, Guy Môquet and Colonel Fabien were obvious choices. They came from humble backgrounds, the former a son of La Chapelle, a working-class neighborhood in northern Paris, the latter a baker's apprentice. Môquet had declared himself a Communist as a mere child (it helped that both his parents were communist elected officials). Colonel Fabien started out as a boy scout but then switched over in his teens to the Jeunesses communistes. What made the duo stand out was the revolutionary zeal they embodied, a zeal all the more remarkable in militants so young. Môquet was likened to Bara, a child hero of the French Revolution, "who preferred to die for the Republic rather than to shout 'Long live the King!'" As for Colonel Fabien, it was said that he had fought like a latter-day Marceau, a reference to François Séverin Marceau, one of the youngest generals to rise through the ranks in the era of the French Revolution. What exemplary deaths they had died: Môquet before a firing squad without shedding a tear and Colonel Fabien at the front, arms in hand.[29]

Môquet's final hours in particular bore telling and retelling. There was first of all the soon-to-be famous letter. When Môquet's body was brought back from Châteaubriant in July 1945, it lay in state at the town hall of the XVIIe arrondissement before transfer to Père-Lachaise. A crowd of six thousand, including Môquet's parents, gathered to pay respects, and a party militant read out Môquet's farewell text to the assembled mourners.[30] A thumbnail biography that appeared a year later in the party-sponsored comic book *Le Vaillant* reproduced the letter in full. The accompanying text wound up with an account of the young teen's last moments. The twenty-seven Châteaubriant *fusillés* were killed in batches of nine. Môquet figured in the second group, which, it seems, broke into "La Marseillaise" as it was trucked to the execution site. Among the group was Dr. Maurice Tenine, who reproached the German firing squad for taking the life of a boy so young. "Shut up, Tenine," Môquet is supposed to have interjected. "I'm no less courageous than you and will know how to face death as well as anyone!"[31] A draft manuscript of a party biography of Môquet proposed a different account of the young teen's final words: "Leave it alone, Tenine … I'm just as much a communist as you." That phrasing didn't make it into the published edition, which pared down much of the party militancy of the earlier draft, but a trace remained nonetheless. The version of the biography that was actually published told of the singing of "La Marseillaise," but it also recounted how the first contingent of prisoners as they faced the firing squad cried out "Long live France, long live the USSR, down with Hitler."[32] Môquet was first and always a French patriot. He and the men who died with him were also firm Communists, a fact that might be muted where youthful audiences were concerned but never erased altogether.

It was not just men and boys who fought the anti-fascist fight, though, but women too. The female anti-fascist was not a martial figure in quite the same way as her male counterpart. She was represented as a sufferer who cared for others even as she agonized herself. Take the cases of Marie-Claude Vaillant-Couturier and Danielle Casanova. On January 24, 1943, a trainload of prisoners departed the Compiègne station en route to Auschwitz. The two hundred and thirty on board were women, and the majority of these were Communists, Vaillant-Couturier and Casanova among them. A Polish prisoner escaped from the camp in July, bringing word of what had happened to the French women.

The news was broadcast from Britain over Radio-Londres, and in the hexagon, Communist Party publications relayed the information in printed format. Under a pseudonym, François la Colère, Aragon published a poem in October with the clandestine publishing house Éditions de Minuit that opened with the verse: "Ausschwitz [sic], Ausschwitz [sic], oh bloody syllables." It then went on to name the unfortunates who had fallen into Nazi hands, singling out Vaillant-Couturier for a special mention: "It is you whom I salute in this worst of hours,/Marie-Claude, intoning as I do, hail Marie."[33] In the postwar, the Party's women's publication, *Filles de France*, picked up where Aragon's Hail Mary left off. Vaillant-Couturier was transferred in August 1944 to Ravensbrück, which was liberated by the Red Army the following spring. She did not repatriate right away, but stayed on into the summer to tend to the sick and debilitated. The magazine published more than one piece on her selflessness, but it was also at pains to bring out the strength that underlay the woman's angelic exterior. In February 1946, it featured a story on Vaillant-Couturier's testimony at the Nuremberg trial, the survivor, "so fragile and so blonde," squaring off in an unflinching face-to-face with the thuggish Hermann Goering.[34] Vaillant-Couturier was a latter-day Mary, but also a woman of steely resolve.

Danielle Casanova was no different. She was treated as part militant, part saint, though it was more often Casanova's sacrificial character that was highlighted. Before deportation to Auschwitz, Casanova was held at the Romainville internment camp. Vaillant-Couturier was there too, and she related how the prisoners, to bolster morale during a dismal Christmas season, staged a revue, a series of tableaux telling the story of France across the ages. In such company, scenes from the Revolution and the Paris Commune were de rigueur, but there was also a tableau on Jeanne d'Arc, the militant Jeanne, not the martyr burned at the stake. The role was played by Danielle Casanova, and when she declaimed a speech about driving the foreigner out, the audience of soon-to-be deportees caught its breath.[35] Casanova, though, was as much angel on the hearth as soldier of France. A dentist by training, she was posted to a position of privilege at Auschwitz, working in the infirmary. It was said that she would sneak out after hours to look after the sick and to bring them stolen medicines. Casanova earned the love of her fellow inmates. She was everyone's big sister, but such devotion came at a price. On a visit to the camp sick bay, the dreaded Revier, she contracted typhus and was swept away.[36]

A biography of Casanova by Simone Téry was published in 1949. The book had the PCF's blessing, the author (herself a Communist) making the rounds of communist women's groups to do readings and sign copies.[37] Yet there is no mistaking that this was a hagiographical text as much Christian as communist in tone. To be sure, it respected the formulas of the militant's bio. Casanova came from modest Corsican roots. At dental school in Paris, she had been recruited into a communist student organization (by Dr. Tenine, as it happened), there meeting her life partner, Laurent Casanova. As a young militant, she had made her mark, helping to found a women's organization, the Union des jeunes filles de France. Once Téry's story moves to the camps, however, it takes a more Christianizing turn. Téry describes the train trip to Auschwitz as the beginning of Casanova's "Calvary" and the camp itself as a "Gehenna." Even more revealing is Téry's recounting of Casanova's deathbed scene. She sings "La Marseillaise" and the "Internationale," on key "by a strange miracle" for the first and only time in her life, and when news of her death reaches her home in Corsica, "the church bells rang out in every village."[38]

Marie-Claude Vaillant-Couturier was a revered figure. As for Danielle Casanova, she was not so much reverenced as canonized. There is scarcely a red suburb that does not boast a rue Danielle Casanova.[39] Perhaps most telling of all is Boris Taslitzky's painting *La Mort de Danielle Casanova* (1950). Taslitsky was a lifelong Communist, best known for unembroidered images of camp life sketched while a prisoner at Buchenwald. There is little of realism, however, in Taslitzky's rendering of Casanova's demise. This is a Deposition from the Cross in a camp setting, with Casanova cast as a modern-day Christ (see Figure 1.1).

Figure 1.1 Boris Taslitzky, *La Mort de Danielle Casanova*, oil on canvas, 1950, 194 × 308 cm. Donation Boris Taslitzky, coll. Musée de l'Histoire vivante, Montreuil (France)

When it came to the camp memorials at Père-Lachaise, however, Christian iconography figured not at all. These were secular monuments, denuded of the crosses and conventional symbols of funereal solemnity that ornamented the surrounding graves. This is not to say that they were blank and inexpressive. In fact, they spoke twice over, first through a newly minted vocabulary of signs invented to capture something of the unprecedented horror of the camp experience and second through the uses to which they were put as sites of gathering, mourning, and political point scoring.

The dedication of the 97th division to deportee memory began in June 1946. The Amicale d'Auschwitz arranged to have an urn of ashes brought back from the camp to Père-Lachaise. A monument was erected three years later, designed by Françoise Salmon, herself an Auschwitz survivor (see Figure 1.2). It was an unusual structure, a tall, rectangular block of volcanic rock from which emerged a wraithlike figure with an

Figure 1.2 Auschwitz Memorial, Père-Lachaise Cemetery, Paris, 1949

Figure 1.3 Ravensbrück Memorial, Père-Lachaise Cemetery, Paris, 1955

outsized head.[40] A Neuengamme memorial went up the same year. The design was more conventional, representing a woman kneeling behind a stele on which her left arm rested, with a memorial plaque affixed to the front. Then came the Ravensbrück monument in 1955 (see Figure 1.3). It was not a statue but something more symbolic, a pair of bound hands emerging from flames below. The Mauthausen memorial came next in 1958, and it was a mix of figuration and symbol (see Figure 1.4). The stylized, zigguratlike staircase was meant to conjure the flight of steps that ran up from the bottom of the Mauthausen rock quarry, and in fact, the stone portion of the monument was sculpted from Mauthausen granite. Deportees had to carry rocks up these steps, and the monument includes a bronze sculpture of one such figure, skeletal and bent over beneath the weight of the burden he carries. The whole was anchored on a triangular base with a triangle of stone situated at the foot of the staircase, an

Figure 1.4 Mauthausen Memorial, Père-Lachaise Cemetery, Paris, 1958

evocation of the identifying triangles all camp prisoners were made to wear. But for skeletal figures, it was the Buchenwald-Dora monument, designed by Louis Bancel, that stood out (see Figure 1.5). It was inaugurated in 1964 and depicts a grouping of three deportees, all emaciated, one holding up a second who has collapsed, while a third stands tall. There were more monuments to come, all of them situated within a short distance of one another in Père-Lachaise's northeast corner, creating a memorial ensemble that was and remains both impressive and affecting.

For present purposes, the ensemble prompts three orders of reflection. The first has to do with representation. Auxerre was the site of the very first deportation memorial unveiled in April 1949, just two months before the Auschwitz monument at Père-Lachaise. It set off a polemic. The Auxerre memorial was not so different in design from its soon-to-be Père-Lachaise counterparts, featuring as it did five figures, three

Figure 1.5 Buchenwald-Dora Memorial, Père-Lachaise Cemetery, Paris, 1964

half-clothed, all gaunt, their bodies expressive of the tortures they had endured. It was clear, nonetheless, that they had not been broken in spirit. A reviewer for *Le Monde* complained that the monument was lacking in grandeur, but the sculptor, Henri Lagriffoul, stood up for himself. "Our critic," he shot back, "would he have wanted vengeful gestures, winged victories, and avenging swords?"[41] The martial symbolism of the war memorial, the reassuring allegory of the *monument aux morts*, these were not the fitting accoutrements for a shrine to deportees. What was needed was a new vocabulary, simple, even abstract, and it was that new vocabulary that visitors to the deportee corner at Père-Lachaise found on display. The interred urn of ashes, the triangle, the bound hands, the emaciated body wracked in pain: such signs stood in for the deportation experience as a whole and gave passersby a clue, however allusive, as to what the deportees themselves had suffered through.[42]

The deportation memorial then was meant to challenge viewers with an evocation of awfulness, not to console them in the accustomed or conventional manner. That did not mean, however, that the body in agony, tormented by human cruelty, was supposed to be the final word, that there was no possibility of consolation at all. This is my second order of reflection. The enlarged head on the Auschwitz memorial, its creators explained, was intended to symbolize the triumph of the spirit, even as the flesh wasted away. Of Bancel's trio of deportees, it was said that they expressed not just the misery but also the "solidarity of the camps" and the indomitability of the deportee who remained unbowed even in the most extreme hardship (one hand of the erect deportee is clenched in a fist).[43] Lest the stones fail to speak with sufficient eloquence, there were inscriptions attached to get the point across. Paul Éluard contributed a pensée to the Auschwitz memorial that concluded with the lines: "When there's killing no more, they will be avenged/Justice's sole wish has as its echo life." There were two inscriptions on the Mauthausen memorial. One seconded Éluard's aspiration toward a more pacific tomorrow: "May their sacrifice help to bar the way to oppression and open humanity's path toward a better future of friendship and peace among nations." A second spoke of the "the blows of the SS" and of the deportees' "combat for France's independence." For the Buchenwald-Dora monument, Aragon composed a quatrain that invoked both the dehumanizing depths of the deportees' pain and "the courage and devotion" that had enabled them to remain men. It all added up to a powerful message. The deportees had suffered and died, but not in vain. They stood up against Nazi barbarism, and the deportee spirit gave promise of a brighter world to come with France – indeed, all humanity – restored to itself, blessed by a lasting peace among nations.

These were not in any explicit way communist memorials, even though they lay amongst the graves of party luminaries and bore inscriptions authored by the Party's most illustrious poets. Yet one more point remains to be made, for there were moments when the Party's voice did speak loud and clear. In June 1946, at the time the urn of Auschwitz ashes was moved to Père-Lachaise, five orators addressed the assembled mourners: a representative of the AADJF, Marie-Claude Vaillant-Couturier, Frédéric Manhès, Georges Cogniot (editor of *L'Humanité*), and Laurent Casanova. On the occasion of the seventh anniversary of the transport of the ashes, Marcel Paul spoke. Two former deportees were in evidence, distinguishable by their striped uniforms, displaying portraits of Ethel and Julius Rosenberg, who had just then been executed. When the Buchenwald-Dora monument was inaugurated in 1964, there was Paul once more, this time talking about the Buchenwald revolt and the urgency of peace and disarmament.[44] The Party had its causes, and the deportee monument was a place, not only to grieve, but also to make the Party's case.

The PCF did not forget Colonel Fabien and Guy Môquet, but alongside the Resistance hero, a new figure emerged in the party pantheon, the deportee. The deportee, however, posed a problem: how to communicate pain in a way that did not rule out all hope. That's in part why the Buchenwald insurrection was such a favored theme. From suffering was born resistance and all its regenerative possibilities. In aesthetic terms too, the Buchenwald uprising created fewer difficulties. The derring-do of the armed inmates lent itself to heroic renderings in the socialist realist mode, and in fact, Taslitzky, a versatile artist, depicted the subject in just such terms in a series of paintings and watercolors executed in the early 1960s. The composition is always the same, a wedge of insurrectionaries on the move, brandishing weapons. One notable feature of the deportation experience, however, was that it was not just a male but also a female experience. When it came to women deportees, a different language of representation was employed, hagiographical and, indeed, Catholic in cast. In sacrifice too, there was redemption. Yet a third representational key was struck in the deportee quadrant at Père-Lachaise. Here, the artists strove to devise a new vocabulary, neither realist nor religious, but made up of signs and symbols that worked as stand-ins for an experience of inexpressible torment. Yet even at Père-Lachaise, the new, expressive mode worked within certain limits. The Communist Party promised tomorrows that sing, and the deportee monument did not belie that promise but, in the end, willy-nilly, confirmed it.

Deportation and the Limits of Representation

There were two artists, however, who pushed the boundaries of what the Party could tolerate: Pablo Picasso and Robert Antelme. Picasso joined the PCF in 1944. He was an anti-fascist Spaniard and a longtime friend of Paul Éluard, ideological and personal links that drew him into party circles. It is as a friend of peace that Picasso, the communist militant, is best remembered. He attended the Congrès mondial des Intellectuels pour la Paix in Wrocław, Poland, in August 1948 as part of a French delegation that included Éluard and the painter Fernand Léger, also a party member. Not long afterward, Aragon paid Picasso a studio visit. Thumbing through the artist's prints, Aragon came on a pigeon. "Here's our poster," he is supposed to have said, "the dove of peace!" The image was soon mocked up as a poster and used to advertise the Congrès mondial des Partisans de la Paix, which convened in 1949 in Paris. Picasso's peace dove, of course, had, in various instantiations, a long career ahead of it.[45] But Picasso was not all sweetness and light. He could be hard, on the enemies of peace above all, and to the party stalwart in the early 1950s, peace had no greater enemy than the United States. In 1952, Picasso signed a petition protesting America's (alleged) use of bacteriological weapons in Korea.[46] The year before he had painted *Massacre en Corée*, its composition modeled on Goya's *The Third of May 1808*. Goya's canvas had depicted a Napoleonic firing squad gunning down Spanish civilians. In Picasso's, the parties involved were not specified, but it was unambiguous who they were. The victims were Korean innocents, their killers anti-communists, whether American or South Korean soldiers.

Most remarkable of all, though, was Picasso's so-called peace temple. Here were treated at one and the same time the themes of war and peace with all the complexities a great artist could bring to bear. Picasso moved to the south of France after the war, settling in Vallauris, not far from the Mediterranean coast, in 1948. The painter's longtime rival, Henri Matisse, had begun work designing a Dominican chapel in nearby Vence, and Picasso, not to be bested, envisioned a temple of his own. He found a site, a Cistercian chapel fallen into disuse, and obtained permission from the communist-run Vallauris town council to refurbish it. He set to work in 1952, completing the panels covering the left and right side walls in 1954 and the panel for the nave three years later.[47] The right wall-panel was titled *La Paix* and depicted an arcadian scene of picnickers and nude women frolicking to the panpipe. The left wall-panel, titled *La Guerre*, was a more complex image, a paladin of justice on one end, bearing a shield with the dove of peace upon it, blocking the advance of a band of black, silhouetted warriors. The warriors are led by a charioteer, holding a bloody knife in one hand and a basket of hideous bugs – a not too subtle reference to bacteriological warfare – in the other. As for the nave panel, its design is elemental: four human figures, representing all the races of the world, touch hands and reach upward toward a dove (once again) haloed in a gold disk. The ensemble is amazing on many counts. Picasso, as no other artist, had looked hard at the darkness of the twentieth century, and here the darkness is again, this time with an allusion, not to Franco's Spain as in *Guernica* (1937), but to Cold War America. He conjures a pagan, Mediterranean alternative and a promise of human reconciliation under the sign of peace. Yet that sign – the haloed dove – and its placement high in the chapel nave cannot but bring to mind the dove of the Holy Spirit. Picasso's was a secular vision, but one anchored in a deeply Catholic sensibility.

Think of the darkness of the twentieth century, and it is impossible not to think of the camps. Picasso, who did not recoil from themes of pain and violence, did not recoil from this one either. Sources report that the painter helped out the fund-raising efforts of the Amicale d'Auschwitz, contributing artwork to be raffled off.[48] In 1955, for the amicale, he sketched a pen-and-ink drawing, *Dix Ans après*, to commemorate the tenth anniversary of the liberation of Auschwitz. It was a minor work, representing the head of a male deportee in striped uniform with a sunken face and shaved head, but the FNDIRP set enough store by the image to reproduce it as the frontispiece to a 1967 FNDIRP-sponsored photo album that told the history of the camp experience in pictures. There was a concluding image as a well, a line-drawing by Léger of a pair of arms clothed in deportee stripes, reaching through barbed wire toward the sun.[49] Expositions on the deportee experience were a feature of the 1950s art scene, and it was standard practice to include a work or two by Picasso.[50]

The ink drawing of the deportee head may have been a work of secondary importance, but not so *Le Charnier* or, in English, *The Charnel House* (see Figure 1.6), a large-format grisaille painting that Picasso began work on in 1944 and completed the following year. There is some disagreement as to the nature of the piece's connection to the Deportation. It has been claimed that Picasso drew direct inspiration from the photos and newsreels of the camps that had begun to circulate in postwar Paris. The communist art critic Pierre Daix tells a somewhat different story. According to him, it was massacre and death Picasso wanted to paint, fueled first of all by memories of the Spanish Civil War. Picasso was worried, though, that the Party might take umbrage at a picture more about "mourning" than victory and so called in Daix to take a critical look. The critic was himself just returned from Mauthausen, where he had been an inmate, and the image he saw overwhelmed him. Daix knew what it was like to live among mounds of cadavers, and there on canvas, Picasso had been able to communicate the shock of the experience, even though he had had no firsthand or even secondhand knowledge of it. Picasso was accepting of Daix's reading and, according to the critic, not in the least astonished that he, as an artist, had been able to anticipate in imagination the awful reality of the camps.[51] Whatever the actual source of the painter's inspiration, contemporaries had no doubt what the subject matter of *Le Charnier* was: the horrors of the Deportation.

As for the painting itself, the grisaille technique, the violence of the image, and jagged edges of the execution call to mind nothing so much as Picasso's *Guernica*. The Spanish Civil War and the camp experience, in

Figure 1.6 Pablo Picasso, *The Charnel House*, 1944–1945. Digital Image © The Museum of Modern Art/Licensed by SCALA/Art Resource, NY

Picasso's imaginary, as in the PCF's, were not discrete but linked phenomena. Picasso's painting, moreover, made its own contribution to the emergent iconography of the Deportation. Note the bound hands thrusting up from the pile of bodies and the flames rising from the right-hand side, both foreshadowings of the Ravensbrück memorial at Père-Lachaise. The scene itself – a murdered family of three, mother, father, and infant, their twisted bodies stacked up under a table with a still life on top – has been described as a Massacre of the Innocents, a New Testament reference that makes sense in light of Picasso's Catholic susceptibilities. There is a note of militancy sounded as well, for one of the bound hands is a clenched fist. Yet overall, and Picasso knew it himself, at least as Daix tells the story, the painting was about loss. There were hints of transcendence, whether through faith or resistance, but what left the most enduring impression was the carnage.

Picasso's anxieties about the painting's reception were not misplaced. An exhibition titled *Art et Résistance* was mounted in February 1946 at Paris' Musée national d'art moderne under the sponsorship of the communist-linked Amis des francs-tireurs et partisans. Jean Cassou, a future director of the museum, curated the show, and he was a remarkable figure in his own right: an arts official under the Popular Front who had been persecuted by Vichy, gone underground, and then spent time in jail for Resistance activities. Such were the patrons and such the venue where Picasso's *Le Charnier* was first displayed. The next June, it was Boris Taslitzky's turn to address the public, this time in a private one-man show. The exhibition included a large-scale painting of camp life, *Le Petit Camp à Buchenwald*, a horrific, garish *danse macabre*-like composition of skeletal figures. The contrast could not have been starker, and in the party debates that followed, Picasso's unheroic and doleful imaginings came in for criticism both at home and abroad.[52] In August 1948, as noted, Picasso attended the Wrocław peace conference, where he was the target of a disagreeable whispering campaign, denigrating him as a decadent bourgeois. Some years later, Picasso was taken to task again, this time over his memorial portrait of Stalin, published in March 1953 on the cover of the PCF literary organ, *Les Lettres françaises*. The image was categorical in its modernism and made no effort at all either to glamorize or to glorify the just deceased dictator. The socialist-realist painter André Fougeron seized the occasion to lash out at Picasso's sterile formalism. In the uproar that ensued, Picasso had fewer backers than in the past. Aragon, the editor at *Les Lettres françaises*, was on the block himself; Éluard had died the year before (and was buried facing the Mur des Fédérés at Père-Lachaise); and Thorez, convalescing in the wake of a stroke, was out of the picture. In the end, the Party could not bring itself to part with an asset so valuable as Picasso, and Picasso, ever the anti-fascist, could not bring himself to leave the Party. The relationship between the two, however, was never the same again.[53]

Picasso's art pushed the limits of what the Party was able to abide. Aesthetics were at issue too in Robert Antelme's fractious relations with the PCF. Antelme was a résistant, a member of François Mitterrand's Mouvement national des prisonniers de guerre et déportés. He ended up a deportee himself in June 1944. At the war's end, Mitterrand, by then a veterans' official, was making the rounds of just-liberated camps, and a member of Mitterrand's entourage came on an Antelme near death. Mitterrand saw to it that his erstwhile comrade received the care he needed and was repatriated. Antelme moved into an apartment on the rue Saint-Benoît near Saint-Germain-des-Prés along with his wife, Marguerite Duras, and friend Dionys Mascolo (who was also Duras's lover). Duras had joined the PCF in 1944, and her two partners followed suit in 1946. Antelme did not prove himself a conventional party militant, however, and soon landed in trouble. In the spring of 1948, he and a group of friends agitated in party ranks for greater freedom of cultural expression. There was a place for avant-gardism, they argued, notwithstanding the Party's prevailing commitment to socialist realism. Picasso and Éluard were approached about the matter but refused to associate themselves. Laurent Casanova, at the time the Party's arbiter of taste in cultural matters, made it plain that writers had just so much latitude when it came to experimentation and no more. It's not clear how Antelme felt about the reprimand at the time, but a year later, a snitch, said to be the Spanish writer and camp survivor Jorge Semprun, reported on a conversation he had heard at the Café Bonaparte (just down the block from the rue Saint-Benoît). In it, Antelme was supposed to have had a good laugh with cronies at Casanova's expense. Then in November 1949, the so-called Rousset Affair erupted. David Rousset, yet another camp survivor and a one-time Trotskyist, proposed creation of a panel to investigate concentration camps in the Soviet Union. He solicited Antelme's participation. Antelme was not one to forget the bonds born of the camp experience; Rousset and he were friends; and so Antelme agreed to take part, all the while protesting that he had no intention of slandering the USSR. He remained as convinced as ever, he expostulated, that capitalism was humanity's greatest enemy. Such caveats, however, didn't help. Antelme was expelled from the Party, and Duras and Mascolo resigned in solidarity. He took the trouble, nonetheless, to explain to party officials why he had acted as he did, and the Party offered to take him back, but Antelme wasn't interested, and that was that.[54]

Antelme was not a conventional militant, nor was the book he wrote, *L'Espèce humaine*, a camp memoir of the sort a conventional militant might write. It was first published in 1947 to little fanfare. A second edition came out two years later, this time garnering attention as well as a literary prize. The version with which today's readers are familiar did not appear until 1957 under the Gallimard imprimatur. The power of the book resides in part in the quality of its prose, hard-edged and unflinching. Antelme did not eschew all literary effects – this isn't reportage – but he was not obvious about it. The result, in the words of Edgar Morin, a friend, was "a masterpiece of literature with the literature stripped away."[55]

In important respects, Antelme's account does in fact conform to the communist vision. Antleme's narrator (like Antelme himself) is an atheist, an internationalist, and an adept of the class struggle. The Party, however, did not scruple to wrap its message in the language and imagery of Christianity. The internationalism it espoused was the internationalism of the Buchenwald uprising, comrades from all nations fighting shoulder to shoulder. And the class struggle, as the Party saw it, was a heroic enterprise, muscular proletarians taking the course of History into their own hands. None of this was for Antelme, who refused heroics and high emotion in favor of a more hard-boiled picture of the camp experience.

Let's start with religion. It is Good Friday in the Gandersheim work camp. A prisoner takes out a Bible. This might be an occasion for pathos or an adaptation of Christian imagery to party purposes, but that's not the path Antelme takes. Good Friday, he writes, is "The story of a man, nothing but a man, the cross for a man, the story of a single man." The repetition hammers home that Jesus is human and nothing but. Not only that, he is a human abandoned. Antelme begins to cite Christ's words on the cross, "My Father, why hast thou –" but then cuts short the plea and winds up the passage with two fragments: "Screams of children who are being suffocated. Silence of ashes spread across a plain."[56] Antelme could be brutal on the subject of Christianity. As he told friends in Paris, "Every time someone speaks to me of Christian charity, I answer back, Dachau."[57] Antelme's camps are a space of bleakness and abandonment.

The misery is not altogether unrelieved, however. There are the consolations of internationalism, of a comradeship that knows no boundaries. Antelme's vision of internationalism, however, is more personal and down-to-earth than combative or heroic. German is the language of the camps, and in the mouths of the Nazi overlords, it is a language of cruelty and abuse. No opportunity is missed to let the inmates know that they are shit. Yet, the German tongue, twisted as it has become, still has the power to communicate brotherhood. The narrator has been put to work on a factory floor. A civilian is in charge, a Rhinelander, who without gesture or expression utters a single, monitory word, "*Langsam*" (slowly), and later the two will exchange a handshake. Further on, Antelme finds himself on a frigid day side by side with a conscientious objector, a Jehovah's Witness. The CO turns to him, states with the utmost simplicity, "*Das ist ein schön Wintertag*," and together they take in a moment of beauty. Last of all, there is the book's finale. Antelme is in Dachau now. American troops have just liberated the camp, and he is able at long last to indulge in a smoke. He shares a cigarette with a Russian prisoner. "*Wir sind frei*" (we are free), remarks the narrator. The Russian looks at him, extends a hand, and formulates a one-word reply, "*Ja*." On this note of affirmation, the book concludes.[58] There are no heroics here. The Cause and the Resistance are not evoked. Fraternity is born of a word or simple gesture, not of the class struggle.

On the matter of class itself, Antelme at times makes all the right noises. The Nazis are masters and the camp inmates their slaves.

The camps themselves are a kind of capitalism in miniature, squeezing every ounce of energy from the wretched deportees, the ultimate proletarians. Yet Antelme's deportees are not the proletarians of party myth. They neither plot nor agitate, but struggle to survive and persist in the struggle even in the most extreme deprivation. The book's opening line – "I went to piss" – lets the reader know from the outset and in unvarnished terms that the camp world is one of the most basic needs. And in extreme need, at that moment when a desperate clinging to life is all that remains, humanity is revealed to itself. In much camp literature, the garbage-eater is a symbol of despair, someone who has passed beyond the limits of the human. Not so in *L'Espèce humaine*, where he is understood as a figure of resistance. The SS want to deprive him of life, but he will not yield and hangs on. It is the weakest who tell us what is most fundamental about ourselves. This is in its way a humanist message – we are all poor, bare, forked creatures – but it is not one of uplift and redemption.[59]

The Deportation and Cold-War Politics

The Deportation mattered to the PCF, and more so over time. Artists with communist affiliations took the theme head on, propelling the Party to the forefront of the postwar cultural scene (with aesthetic consequences that the Party did not always embrace). The Deportation mattered in a second sense as well. The PCF had a grand story to tell about the twentieth century, and the Deportation occupied a strategic place in it. That narrative identified heroes and villains. The heroes were deportees and those who carried forward the work they had begun, fighting back against Nazi barbarism. The villains were the Nazis and their postwar heirs, for there should be no mistake: though Nazi Germany had been defeated on the battlefield, fascism lived on, Nazism's mantle of oppression now assumed by others. Deportees were motivated to speak out on such matters, bringing to bear the special moral weight conferred upon them by what they had gone through. In all these respects, the Deportation took on added layers of meaning, and that meaning was political in ways that redounded to the credit of the Party and the policies it espoused.

The Party's grand narrative is the place to begin. The Bolshevik Revolution had opened a new era in human history. Capitalism meant to stifle the baby of hope in its cradle, and fascism was the instrument devised for the purpose. That's why the Spanish Civil War – the first clash in what was destined to become a continent-wide civil war pitting fascists against anti-fascists – counted for so much in the communist scheme of things. Colonel Fabien's service in the International Brigades was not just an incidental fact, but an essential building block of the legend constructed around him. The communist quadrant in Père-Lachaise contained four kinds of monuments – to the Party's great and good, to the *fusillés*, to deportees, and to veterans of the Spanish Civil War.

The Spanish Civil War was but a preliminary to the yet more horrendous reckoning with Nazi barbarism, and that barbarism was nowhere more in evidence than in the camp system, the ultimate expression of what fascism was all about. Picasso, as noted, was a member of the French delegation to the Wrocław Peace conference in 1948, and he took the occasion to pay a visit to Auschwitz-Birkenau.[60] Pierre Daix was also a member and at the congress attended the screening of a fiction film about Auschwitz-Birkenau, *La Dernière Étape*, written and directed by camp survivors Wanda Jakubowska and Gerda Schneider. The movie had been filmed at Birkenau itself, recruiting its cast among former inmates, and its opening sequences are unforgiving in their depiction of the hardships of camp life. Daix's reaction was unforgiving in its own way. He proposed a series of equations – fascism equals the camps equals Wall Street:

The camps are not a world apart, but the logical consequence of the fascist world. [...]
There is a concentrationary world that has survived the Nazi camps. Its capital places are no longer called Berlin, Rome, Tokyo, Auschwitz or Mauthausen, but Madrid, but Athens, but Santiago, Chile.
And those today, on Wall Street or in the White House, who assume its heritage, also assume its methods.[61]

Edgar Morin made a similar point, although with more subtlety, in a review of *L'Espèce humaine* published in the FNDIRP newspaper. "The truth of the camps," he wrote, "it's the truth of the world we live in, but exasperated, laid bare."[62] It couldn't have been plainer. The camp system did not represent some bizarre state of exception but rather the essential nature, without cloaking or mystification, of the wider world – fascist and capitalist – in which it was embedded.

Fascism, then and now, menaced world peace, but the cause of humanity, happy to say, had its champions: the PCF and the Soviet Union. The PCF had given proof of its grit and patriotism in the Resistance, and it had done so no less in the Deportation. Marcel Paul said of the Buchenwald insurrection: "To speak of the liberation of Buchenwald is to speak of the deportation as a whole."[63] What lessons then did the Buchenwald experience have to teach? Marcel Paul's papers contain a heroicizing biography, which paints him as the uprising's planner and Colonel Manhès as its commander.[64] As we have seen, this was stretching the truth. The French, nonetheless, did contribute two battalions to the fight, one named after General Marceau, the second after the Jacobin revolutionary Saint-Just, and the choice of names is significant. Communism and love of country were not antithetical. For the FNDIRP, the claim was built into its very name. That "P" stood for "patriotic," and the organization's paper, *Le Patriote résistant*, made clear which of the two terms, patriot and résistant, came first.

Loyalty to France did not, however, preclude other commitments. The Red Army had sacrificed beyond measure to liberate Europe from the fascist scourge, but that was not all the Soviets had done. Daix saw *La Dernière Étape* in Poland in 1948. The FNDIRP organized a screening later that year in Paris, and the film then made the rounds of the city's film club circuit. The movie, shot on site, had a compelling authenticity, and its images were destined for reuse. There is a scene of a transport train pulling into the Auschwitz-Birkenau railhead on a foggy night, which Alain Resnais would borrow for *Nuit et Brouillard*. The American filmmaker Leo Hurwitz released a concentration camp documentary of his own in 1956, *The Museum and the Fury*, which also made use of extracts from Jakubowska's fiction film.[65]

There was more than authenticity to Jakubowska's movie, however. *La Dernière Étape* tells the story of a women's barracks at Auschwitz-Birkenau. The group includes a Jewish woman, Marta Weiss, who had been deported with her family. The family is murdered on arrival, but Weiss is not because she knows German and is useful as a translator. Otherwise, the inmates are mostly politicals, and it is easy to discern the politics they embrace. A message is smuggled in early on from Stalin assuring the camp inmates that he knows of their privations and will make the Nazis pay. News of Stalingrad prompts the women to singing and dancing … and to thinking about organized resistance. A Russian woman doctor, self-possessed and fearless, makes the first gesture. An international commission pays a visit to inspect the camp, and she blurts out in German as they pass by how the inmates are really treated. The delegation departed, she is tortured to death, trussed up strappado and tormented with hot irons. The prisoners have reason to fear, as the Soviet army approaches, that they will all be liquidated, and they hatch a plan to get the word out so that the world will know. Two inmates contrive to escape, Marta and a male comrade, and pass the word to a resistance cell with a radio transmitter. Both are recaptured, and Marta is destined for the scaffold. In the final scene, she stands on the gallows, hands bound. The hangman, a fellow prisoner, slips a knife to her, and she slits her wrists. As she expires, Soviet planes fly overhead; the Russian army is near; and the Germans flee.

As the movie lurches from authenticity to melodrama, the political points pile up. The Soviet Union knows and cares about what is happening; communist prisoners take the lead getting the camp resistance up and running; and, perhaps most important of all, it is the Red Army that liberates Auschwitz. There is even a dash of French patriotism thrown in. A truckload of French women inmates is carted off for execution, and as they depart, one beseeches the prisoners left behind to tell how she died. Then all the French together intone "La Marseillaise."

Love of France and its revolutionary past, the spirit of resistance, and gratitude to the Soviet Union: for FNDIRP members, or most of them, these were not distinct and competing sentiments but part of a single, coherent package. A fraction of FNDIRP members existed that didn't share such sentiments, that felt Rousset had a point, and that objected to the organization's pro-Soviet bias. The FNDIRP sent a telegram of congratulations to Stalin in 1949 in honor of his seventieth birthday. A number of members deemed the gesture a violation of the organization's pledge to nonpartisanship, but the FNDIRP leadership had an answer to all such criticisms. Marcel Paul reminded the membership that it was the Red Army that had rescued Europe and that none of them would be alive today but for its sacrifices. Louise Alcan – a member of the Amicale d'Auschwitz and editor of its bulletin, *Après Auschwitz* – published an article in *Le Patriote résistant* under the title, "Glory to our liberators." So why then begrudge Stalin a word of congratulations? What Auschwitz survivor could ever forget what he, what she owed to the Soviet Union?[66]

In the communist narrative, a dual patriotism – to France and to the USSR – was not a mésalliance but a legitimate union consecrated by the Deportation, by the experience of resistance in deportation, and by Soviet rescue. That marriage affirmed, it was clear where the FNDIRP, indeed, all right-thinking anti-fascists were bound to stand on the issues of the Cold War.

They stood first of all for peace. The Amicale d'Auschwitz deputed a delegation of three to attend the 1949 world peace conference in Paris. The next year, the World Peace Council, presided by French physicist and PCF-member Frédéric Joliot-Curie, issued the Stockholm Appeal, which called on all nations to forswear nuclear weapons, condemned in the appeal's words as "instruments of intimidation and mass murder of peoples." Both the Amicale d'Auschwitz and the FNDIRP signed on.[67]

Atomic weapons threatened peace, and so too did a rearmed Germany. *Le Patriote résistant* published an appeal in 1947 authored by former political prisoners, damning the Marshall Plan as a spur to "the rebirth of German militarism." The United States wanted a newborn West Germany to rearm. The French government was unenthusiastic and sought to craft an alternative, proposing the creation of a European Defense Community (EDC), a continent-wide army made up of national units but under the command of an international authority. Germany might have an army, but one that did not answer to German superiors. Such an accord was in due course negotiated, and it came up for debate in France's National Assembly in 1954, where it was rejected. The Marie-Claude Vaillant-Couturier archive contains a file on the matter, including a flier calling for a mass demonstration against the EDC to coincide with the January anniversary of the first trainload of communist women deported to Auschwitz. The Amicale d'Auschwitz itself, Louise Alcan acting as an intermediary, shot off a letter to Vaillant-Couturier, protesting against the EDC – much as the Marshall Plan had been protested against – as a boost to the "rebirth of German militarism."[68]

It was the German rearmament debate that first prompted Robert Merle to write *La Mort est mon métier*, a fictionalized account of the life of Rudolf Höss, the camp commandant at Auschwitz. The book represented an early attempt, one of the first of its kind, to plumb the mind of the perpetrator, and Merle had good material to work with: the dossier, including an extensive psychological profile based on face-to-face interviews, compiled in connection with Höss's testimony at the Nuremberg trials, plus information on camp life culled from the archives of the Centre de documentation juive contemporaine.[69]

Several points bear making about Merle's text in the present connection. The first one has to do with Merle himself. He set to work writing the novel in 1950 (it was published in 1952), catalyzed by the threat of a remilitarized Germany and the public's seeming indifference to the prospect. Merle was at the time a new recruit to the Left. He joined the PCF eventually, but in the early fifties was more at home in fellow-traveling organizations like MRAP than in the Party itself. There were comrades who judged Merle too heterodox, but not Aragon. In Aragon's view, if the writer saw things as the Party did (and he did when it came to Germany and the cause of peace), then that made him orthodox enough.[70]

There were indeed elements in Merle's analysis that might well appeal to the communist way of thinking. Merle's Höss (named Rudolf Lang in the novel) was raised in a punishing Catholic household. In the family bathroom, an engraving of Satan was pinned on the inside of the door facing the toilet seat. Höss/Lang encountered the image on a second occasion in adult life, this time in the form of a hideous anti-Semitic caricature in the Nazi newspaper *Völkischer Beobachter*, and from that moment on he became a fanatic anti-Semite. Christianity lay at the heart of Nazism's monstrous racism, but Höss/Lang was not just some religious primitive. He was also very much the modern manager, who ran Auschwitz like a factory. He thought it "unworthy of a great industrial nation" to dispose of bodies in a ditch and advocated crematoria as a more efficient solution.[71] Most of all, Höss/Lang was a German. Merle's book opens with an evocation of the authoritarian home Höss/Lang grew up in, a world of punctuality, cold water, and open windows on frosty days, ruled over by an exacting father descended from a long line of military officers. It ends with Höss/Lang marching to the gallows, counting the steps as he goes. Obsessive discipline and reflexive obedience to orders, these are what made mass murder possible, and they are qualities inbred in the German character. The implication is clear: it would be an act of madness to place weapons in the hands of such men ever again.

Merle's novel is topical in another way. Höss/Lang is captured and incarcerated in a Nuremberg prison. An American officer asks him why he committed the crimes that he did, and the following exchange ensues (Höss/Lang is writing in the first person):

> I focused on the technical side of my task.
> I added:
> – A little like a pilot who drops bombs on a city.
> He [the American officer] replied in an angry tone:
> – A pilot has never annihilated an entire people.
> I thought about that and I said:
> – He would do it, if it was possible, and if he was given the order to do so.[72]

Remember that the Stockholm Appeal was launched just as Merle sat down to write. Nuclear weapons, it had declared, were weapons of mass murder. So, who was it that had made first use of the bomb, who was the potential mass murderer in the postwar world, and who by that token was Nazism's inheritor? The answer to all three questions was one and the same: the United States.

The Rosenberg case provided an opportunity to nail down the association. In November 1952, Bulawko's AAJDF dispatched a telegram to President Truman, pleading with him to spare the lives of the "two innocents." It did not identify the Rosenbergs as innocent Jews, but the point was implicit, given the source of the telegram. Then, after the execution, a mass meeting of commemoration was convened with Colonel Manhès seated on the podium. The event took place at the Vélodrome d'hiver. This was the very spot where the French police had concentrated thousands of Jews arrested in the infamous anti-Semitic roundup of July 1942. *Le Patriote résistant* reported on the meeting under the headline, "It's Nazism that killed the Rosenbergs."[73]

America dropped the bomb; it was the driving force behind German rearmament; and it had killed the Rosenbergs. There was the menace of a new barbarism on the horizon. It came from the United States, and there were deportees aplenty on hand to lend what moral clout they wielded to the argument.

What's Left Out

For all the talk about the Rosenbergs, it was never stated explicitly that they were Jews, which raises the question of what the communist narrative left out. There are two items that need dealing with in this connection: the anti-Semitic dimension of the Deportation, of course, but also the awkward period between France's defeat in 1940 and Hitler's invasion of the Soviet Union in 1941. The PCF's lodestar, the USSR, was on good treaty terms with Hitler in those years, but what about the PCF itself? Did it just sit on the sidelines and toe the Soviet line, thereby belying its oft-repeated postwar claim that it was always France's staunchest bulwark against fascism?

The Party, it happens, was not silent on either issue. It argued first of all that it had been active in the fight against fascism almost from the beginning. De Gaulle had gotten the Resistance started, broadcasting the June 18, 1940 appeal, summoning the French to keep up the fight despite Pétain's bid for an armistice, but the PCF had not been far behind. Party chiefs Maurice Thorez and Jacques Duclos circulated a tract on July 10 entitled "Peuple de France." The text rehearsed the party line still in effect – that the Second World War was an imperialist war – but then went on to lambaste Vichy as a regime of reaction. Once the war was over, the "Peuple de France" text came in for a reworking. *L'Humanité* published a purported facsimile on December 12, 1947. The facsimile had in fact been doctored to redirect the thrust of the original document. The altered text remained anti-Vichy in tone, but now it was also anti-Nazi, its animus against the Occupier highlighted by a call to resistance. In this form, the tract was touted as the PCF's answer to de Gaulle's "Appel du 18 juin."

Indeed, in two respects, the Communists had even outdone the General. De Gaulle returned to power in June of 1958. The next month, an article in *L'Humanité* took a dig at the General's Resistance credentials. He had acted while abroad, and the audience he addressed was composed of "military men and technicians." The Party's "Appel du 10 juillet," by contrast, had been issued on French soil, and better still, it had appealed, not to a select few, but to the nation as a whole. The awkward years, in the Party's accounting (with a little help from a doctored text), were not so awkward after all, but a moment when the organization began to gather its strength for a fight that was redoubled in the wake of Hitler's assault on the Soviet Union.[74]

What then about the special fate of the Jews in deportation? This was not a theme, it turns out, that communist discourse shied away from. In Jakubowska's *La Dernière Étape*, Marta Weiss's entire family is sent to their deaths in the film's opening sequences. Merle's whole book takes on the subject of Auschwitz as an extermination center, and there's never any doubt that it's Jews who were being annihilated. In the first issue of *Le Patriote résistant*, Colonel Manhès made reference to Jews "hunted down like poor beasts – both by the boches and by Vichy."[75] The 1967 FNDIRP album includes a section on Auschwitz that in fact overestimates how many Jews were killed in the camp, citing a figure of three million when the actual number was closer to one million, still a staggering total.[76] At the unveiling of the Auschwitz memorial at Père-Lachaise in 1949, Laurent Casanova eulogized all who had died at Nazi hands: those who had perished "because they loved their country" and those "because they were Jews." A representative from the Grand Rabbinate was present at the event, and a grand rabbi was also in attendance at the inauguration of the Mauthausen monument in 1958. Nor was what happened at the Vél d'hiv forgotten. Every year, starting in 1946, Henry Bulawko's AADJF organized a commemorative ceremony on the spot, including prayers for the dead recited by a rabbi. At the 1963 ceremony, the Israeli ambassador Walter Eytan was also present.[77]

Jews were not erased from the deportation story, not at all, but it is critical to understand the exact role they played in it. Three examples will help to clarify the matter. In 1947, British authorities in Palestine applied force to turn back a boatload of Jewish survivors of the Nazi genocide on their way to what was soon to be the State of Israel. This was the *Exodus* Affair (so named after the vessel at the center of the face-off), and French deportee organizations had no doubt where right and justice lay. The Amicale d'Auschwitz sided with the *Exodus* passengers. Boris Taslitzky understood the fight as part of a larger struggle. The war had ended, but fascism remained on the prowl, and there to prove it were events "such as the Exodus tragedy, such as the lynching of blacks, such as the deportation of Vietnamese workers in France to penal colonies in Indochina, which really do exist just as the Nazi camps once did."[78]

The second example has to do with the theatrical version of Anne Frank's diary, and how it was received. The production opened in Paris in 1957 at the Théâtre Montparnasse-Gaston Baty (there's an irony here as Baty, a celebrated theater director, had been something of an anti-Semite himself). It played to packed houses, the audiences reportedly moved to tears. Controversy had bubbled around the drama in the United States. Frances Goodrich and Albert Hackett had handled the dramatization of the diary, making changes along the way that down-played the text's Jewish content. The intrigue turned, rather, on the sharp-minded adolescent's complicated relations with her family and a budding romance with a fellow teen, Peter Van Daan, also in hiding with the Frank family. This is the stuff of many a young girl's life. In the penultimate scene, the Franks' place of concealment – the annex – is betrayed and all its inhabitants arrested, the Franks along with four others quartered with them, the three members of the Van Daan family and Dr. Dussel, a dentist. The arrest is not shown on stage, just the panic of the principals as they hear the clomping of boots and the barked orders of the German commando come to take them away. This is followed by a final scene, which winds up on a note of unearned hopefulness. Anne's father, Otto, has survived deportation and returns to the annex. He lets the audience know that he learned just the day before of Anne's death at Bergen-Belsen (she died of typhus), and the play's last words are spoken off-stage by Anne: "I believe, I continue to believe in spite of everything, that people are really good at heart."[79] Needless to say, that's not how the diary itself ends. The play's minimization of the protagonists' Jewishness, its focus on the life and loves of a typical teenager (however untypical she was), and its concluding message of hope stirred many in the United States to anger, none more than Meyer Levin, who had done so much to promote the American translation of the diary and who had written a dramatization himself that was rejected by Otto Frank. Levin complained of the universalization of Anne Frank's life and fate. In the context of French deportee experience, however, this was just the quality that appealed. *Le Patriote résistant* published an enthusiastic review and cited approvingly the director's appraisal of the play's moral: "Not a particu-larist message focused on the problem of the Jews, for example. No, a message more general, more human. The Jewish problem is not the only one. You've seen what's happened recently to blacks in America."[80]

Last of all, there is the example of the Eichmann trial. Adolf Eichmann, of course, was a senior SS officer, Hitler's man in charge of implementing the Final Solution. He had escaped to Argentina after the war and remained there until 1960, when he was abducted by Israeli agents and brought back to Jerusalem for trial, which took place the following year. Journalists, including Hannah Arendt and, for the French newspaper *Libération*, Madeleine Jacob, gathered from around the world to cover the proceedings. For Arendt, Eichmann was the faceless bureaucrat, but not so for Jacob, who found him a "monster in the purest state." What upset her about the trial was how it particularized the evils of Nazism, for "[in] particularizing Jewish suffering, the responsibility of the system that engendered it is covered over. Eichmann's crimes are the crimes of fascism, of which anti-Semitism is just one aspect." *Le Patriote résistant* cited all this approvingly and added an observation or two of its own to underscore Jacob's point. Fascism had indeed continued into the postwar era, and the proof? "The swastikas of Alabama" and Chancellor Adenauer's choice of national security advisor, the infamous Hans Globke, who had had a hand in crafting the anti-Semitic Nuremberg Laws of 1935.[81]

The communist narrative of the war made a place for the destruction of European Jewry. The Final Solution, however, was not a story in itself but part of a bigger one, the anti-fascist struggle, the fight against Nazi barbarism and its militarist and racist postwar avatars, the Federal Republic of Germany and the United States.

Historians have observed how the figure of the deportee was sacralized in the postwar decades, converted into an emblem of Occupation-era pain and deliverance.[82] The PCF and its partners worked hard to achieve just such an end, paying homage and tending to the needs of the thousands who had passed through the fires of the Nazi camp system. The Party's concern was both genuine and interested. The honor paid to the deportee was real, and it took more than one form: books, monuments, paintings, movies. To be sure, much of this was cast in the standard heroic mold: the deportee, however crushed in body, still stout in spirit, sustained by comrades and ever ready to fight the good fight with whatever energy remained. On occasion, the story of deportee suffering came embellished with a Catholic, redemptive gloss. Yet, in critical instances – in the deportee corner of Père-Lachaise, in the work of Picasso and Antelme – there was a search for a new vocabulary to express mourning and fathom the darkness of abjection. The PCF itself, though, never lost sight of the deportees' political possibilities. They gave living proof of the Party's patriotic commitment and deep-rootedness in France's revolutionary past. The camps themselves were understood as expressions of what capitalism, stripped of all its mystifications, was all about. Deportees, moreover, were there as ever-present reminders to keep up the anti-fascist struggle. The deportee stood as a symbol of past resistance and a promise of resistance to come against the fascists and racists of today. By such means, the deportee experience was not just sacralized but weaponized and impressed into front-line service in the Cold War.

The PCF, of course, did not own the memory of the Deportation. Gaullists were on the scene and fought the Communists to a draw over control of Mont-Valérien, but they then retreated from the field of battle. A resurgence of Gaullist memory would come, but not until the General's return to office in 1958. As for Jews, they were not inactive, as will be seen presently, but for the moment, it was the Party that had the patent on Auschwitz. One historian, indeed, the pioneer in the field, has written of a communist "confiscation" of Jewish memory.[83] Thanks to hard battling, the Communists gained the upper hand in the memory wars of the immediate postwar period. It did not take long, however, for their near monopoly on the deportation experience to come under challenge, and it was that renegade Trotskyist, David Rousset, who led the charge.

2 The Concentrationary Universe

L'Univers concentrationnaire is the title of David Rousset's classic dissection of the concentration camp experience. It was published in 1946, not long after he had returned from Reich territory, where he had spent years as an inmate in a series of *Lager*s (camps). The volume became a standard reference work for all subsequent studies of the subject and made its author a figure of repute in the deportee community.

That would change in 1949 when Rousset issued an appeal for an inquiry into the existence of concentration camps in the Soviet Union. The call detonated an explosion that fragmented the organizational universe of camp survivors. The communist-oriented FNDIRP splintered, giving birth to a new group, the Union nationale des Associations de déportés, internés et familles de disparus. UNADIF in turn made common cause with FNDIR, the two organizations forming a new institutional bloc, more mainstream in political orientation and no longer guided by the party vision of what the camp phenomenon had signified.

Yet if the party vision lost its monopoly, what kind of competition did it now face? A materialist, often Marxist-inflected understanding of the camps as an extension of capitalism and its grinding production-mindedness still retained a hold. That was in fact Rousset's own interpretive point of departure (although he would complicate it in due course). Rousset's innovation was to tar the Soviet Union with the same productivist brush he had used on the Nazis. The PCF made the case that fascism was just liberal democracy stripped of its hypocritical mystifications, "laid bare" in Edgar Morin's striking phrase. Rousset proposed a different pairing, not fascism and liberal democracy, but fascism and Communism, bound in a common authoritarianism whose purest expression was the labor camp – in Russian, the *Gulag*. Rousset himself is said to have been the first to introduce the word into the French language. In the Gulag, as in the *Lager*, wringing productive labor from the inmates was the primary goal, an objective pursued with a terrible, bureaucratized cruelty. From here, it was a short step to totalitarian theory, one that Rousset took, although he never elaborated on the concept with the acuity of English-language theorists like Hannah Arendt, who remained little known in France until the 1960s.

The new institutional nexus was generative not just of new understandings but also of new forms of representation. The UNADIF-FNDIR alliance was well connected in the corridors of power, and in the 1950s, when the state began to think about constructing a deportee memorial, it was to UNADIF-FNDIR that it turned for advice and assistance. The result of the collaboration was a commemorative ensemble, designed by the architect Bertrand Monnet and sculptor Lucien Fenaux, that was completed in 1960 on the site of the former Nazi concentration camp of Natzweiler-Struthof in Alsace. The word *ensemble* is well-chosen, for the memorial consisted in three parts: a cemetery for deportees, a towering monument more than forty meters in height that was abstract and modernist in conception, and the preserved remains of the Natzweiler-Struthof camp itself. To know what a camp was, readers might consult Rousset, but to see for themselves firsthand, they needed no more than to take a train to Strasbourg and then travel by bus to Natzweiler-Struthof, never leaving France in the process.

The effort to represent the concentrationary universe and to recreate for the uninitiated what a real camp was like was not left to artists alone, but carried forward by academics, who brought to the subject a documentary zeal all their own. Memoirs of the deportation experience proliferated in the postwar years, eyewitness accounts written by survivors determined to bear witness. There was at the same time an emergent impulse to adopt a more methodical approach, to collect testimony and documents that would permit a systematic, scientific account. The ethnologist Germaine Tillion rallied to Rousset in 1949 and took the additional step of participating actively in Rousset's actual Gulag investigations. Tillion was an academic by training, a student of Marcel Mauss and Louis Massignon. She had been deported to Ravensbrück for Resistance activities in 1943 and while still there had begun to gather and organize information, putting together a veritable "university course" on the camps, which she did not hesitate to share with any inmates willing to listen.[1] On her return, she made it her business to communicate what she had found out to the French public at large, publishing *Ravensbrück* in 1946, an analysis of the Ravensbrück camp and its functioning. As fresh material accumulated – the trial testimony of camp officials, the release of new archives, additional eyewitness accounts – Tillion expanded and republished the text, not once, but twice, first in 1973 and then again in 1988. Rousset's *L'Univers concentrationnaire* was a think piece, pithy, even visionary. He had also written a more expansive account of the camps, *Les Jours de notre mort* (1947), but this was a novel. Tillion's approach, by contrast, was neither interpretive nor narrative but analytic, drawing on an accumulation and sifting of evidence.

Tillion was not the only one in the field, however. Educator though she was, she did not publish under the auspices of the university. This was the accomplishment of Olga Wormser-Migot, who defended and published a doctoral thesis on *Le Système concentrationnaire nazi* in 1968. Wormser-Migot, the daughter of a Menshevik exile, was closer to the communist world than Tillion was. She counted a sister who was an active PCF member, and she herself welcomed neighborhood party members into her apartment for cell meetings.[2] Such fellow traveling, however, came to an end no later than 1956, the date of the Soviet invasion of Hungary. Wormser-Migot's dissertation was not the first to deal with the traumas of the Deportation. Michel Borwicz had defended a thesis in 1954, examining texts left behind by Nazi execution victims, a sample that included deportees, both Jewish and non-Jewish, as well as résistants imprisoned in France.[3] Borwicz's doctorate, however, was a work of sociology, not of history, and the camps were not the prime focus. For a historical approach to the concentrationary universe, Wormser-Migot's thesis, late as it was, was the first of its kind in France.

The onset of the Cold War fractured communist hegemony in the deportee community, and the breakup proved a productive one. Rousset's version of totalitarian theory was an invitation to think of the Deportation not just as an experience specific to the war and the anti-fascist struggle, but as a more generalizable phenomenon. The camp as a form and the concentrationary universe as a system were both transferable technologies, monstrosities hatched by the Nazis, but adaptable to authoritarian climates elsewhere.

David Rousset

Rousset is remembered as an analyst of the camp phenomenon who later turned hard-core anti-communist. That's a fair thumbnail sketch, but it does not do full justice to the complexities of the man's life and work.[4]

Rousset's leftism was genuine enough. He read Leon Trotsky's *History of the Russian Revolution* as a young man, an encounter that converted him to the Trotskyist cause; he even had occasion to meet Trotsky in person during the latter's sojourn in France in the early thirties. Resistance activity and deportation widened Rousset's political horizons. After repatriation, he still hankered for a continent-wide socialist revolution, but no longer saw the Trotskyist Fourth International, with its rigidity of thinking and sectarian ways, as a suitable vehicle for the purpose. Rousset instead fell in with a cluster of like-minded friends, among them Maurice Nadeau, a onetime Trotskyist himself. The group gathered in the editorial offices of *La Revue internationale*, which Rousset characterized as a "an extreme left publication."[5] In its pages, starting in December 1945, he began serializing installments from *L'Univers concentrationnaire*. Less than two years later, Rousset had made the move from letters to politics, teaming up with Jean-Paul Sartre in November 1947 to launch an appeal for a neutralist Europe, socialist and democratic, that would be committed to maintaining its distance from both superpower blocs. The appeal evolved into an organization, the Rassemblement démocratique révolutionnaire (RDR). Sartre was much taken with Rousset, who was dynamic and full of argument. Sartre's journal, *Les Temps modernes*, excerpted a second Rousset publication, *Les Jours de notre mort*, and Sartre himself, who hosted a radio show for a brief period in the postwar years, devoted a spot to Rousset.

The partnership soon soured, however, in large part because Rousset had begun to take sides in the Cold War. The RDR needed funds, and Rousset turned to American organized labor for help. He knew the American Federation of Labor man in Paris, Irving Brown (who also worked for the CIA), and the contact opened doors in New York, where Rousset visited in the hope of soliciting money from trade-union officials.[6] This was not neutralism as Sartre understood it, and he pulled away, first from Rousset and then from the RDR itself, which he quit in October 1949. The organization foundered. As for Rousset, he was back in the headlines before the year was out, calling for an investigation into the Soviet Gulag.[7]

In some respects, Rousset's trajectory – from Trotskyist to Cold Warrior – is a familiar one, but two additional biographical points bear making, which bring into relief aspects of Rousset's work less often remarked on. He was first of all a voracious reader with literary aspirations of his own. He counted friends among France's literary avant-garde – Marguerite Duras, for example, a pioneer of the New Novel. Nadeau was a comrade-in-arms from Trotskyist days but also a literary critic, publisher, and author of a full-length and still useful study of the Surrealist movement. *Les Jours de notre mort*, of course, was billed as a novel. One more observation along these lines, a small one, but nonetheless telling as to Rousset's predilections: he named his son "Stephen" after Stephen Dedalus, a protagonist of James Joyce's *Ulysses*.[8] The second point has to do with religion. Rousset was a Protestant by birth and not just any Protestant, but a Darbyist. Darbyism was an evangelical, Scripture-based sect, and though

Rousset left the faith, he remained steeped in biblical culture. As a Protestant, Rousset felt he had a special kinship with members of other minority religions, Jews in particular.[9] That may not be so apparent from a reading of Rousset's published work, but there's no doubt that he enjoyed good working relations with the Centre de documentation juive contemporaine (CDJC). In 1948, Rousset published *Le Pitre ne rit pas* (*The Clown Doesn't Laugh*), a document collection that burlesqued the mad cruelties of Nazi thinking and practice. He culled much of the material from the center's archives, helped out by a CDJC researcher, Léon Poliakov. Rousset had a chance to return the favor. The CDJC let go of Poliakov in 1951, who for "three or four years" thereafter found himself in financial difficulties. He was kept afloat thanks to Rousset, who hired Poliakov on as a secretary and all-purpose amanuensis.[10]

Politics, literature, and the Bible: these were Rousset's touchstones, and they shaped not just how he lived, but also how he wrote about the camps. So, let's start with the politics. Rousset's account of the origins of the camp system recapitulates the common wisdom of the era's anti-fascist orthodoxy.[11] The Depression had struck fear in Germany's middle classes, terrified at the very real prospect of proletarianization. Fear led to scapegoating and to lynch law, and the camps were just that, lynch law executed on an industrial scale.[12] So the Germans alone were not to blame, but capitalism and the class struggle, which lay behind it all. As for the victims, the Jews had no doubt been subjected to an appalling fate, singled out for humiliations more vicious than those heaped on other categories of camp prisoner. Rousset had the warmest praise for the work of the CDJC, which had undertaken to assemble documentation on the genocide of the Jews. He noted, however, how the CDJC's archive had mutated over time. Focused at first on "the purely Jewish aspect of our problems," it then evolved, driven by "its own internal logic," to encompass all aspects of the concentrationary system, or, in Rousset's words, "the situation of the modern slave in its entirety."[13] The principals in Rousset's concentrationary drama – Germans and the Jews – were not compelling in their particularity, but as incarnations of larger forces at work, capitalism and the industrialized form of bondage it gave rise to.

The real force of Rousset's analysis, however, does not reside so much in its conventional critique of capitalist modernity as in its analysis of camp life on the ground. Politics are in play here too (though not politics alone), as oppressors and oppressed battle it out, the former grinding away at the inmates' sense of self, the latter finding strength or, at least, strength enough to survive in a collective effort of resistance.

The *Lager* system, on Rousset's accounting, was a vast bureaucratic machine designed to pulverize inmates, isolating them in order to dominate them. All classes, all ages, all nationalities were piled together pell-mell, a veritable Babel of humanity. The SS anointed the criminal element, the green triangles, to rule over the chaos, and rule they did, through random acts of extreme violence. But violence was not the sole instrument of governance. Kapos had privileges to distribute – extra rations, less-onerous work assignments – which were much-coveted goods in a universe of hunger and exhaustion. Prisoners jockeyed for what pitiful advantages there were, kowtowing, proffering bribes and services, and the pervasive corruption that resulted added to the insanity and what Rousset called "the total disaggregation of the individual." [14]

Order-obsessed though the Germans were, the camp system they created had a lunacy to it, and Rousset found a descriptor to convey that quality of dementia, *ubuesque*. The reference here is to a stage character, Ubu, invented by turn-of-the-century playwright Alfred Jarry. The character debuted in 1896 in *Ubu roi*, a Macbeth-like tale of Ubu's blood-spattered rise to kingship, overthrow, and subsequent machinations to regain power. Ubu is Macbeth-like, except that Jarry's "hero" is also a grotesque, a comic monster who is arbitrary, infantile, and greedy, flouting in ways at once shocking and ridiculous every convention of decent language and behavior. To Rousset, there was indeed an Ubu-like "tragic buffoonery" to the camps. He prefaced the first chapter of *L'Univers concentrationnaire* with a quote from Jarry; he characterized the camp system as an "Ubu-God" lusting for sacrifice; and to the camp system's overlord of overlords, Heinrich Himmler, he applied the epithet *clown*.[15]

It is Himmler who is the strutting, straight-faced clown-in-chief of Rousset's *Le Pitre ne rit pas*, presiding over an absurd universe that would be ludicrous were it not so horrible. The collection includes a document, an August 1941 letter addressed to a regional prefect from a Vichy official charged with implementation of the regime's anti-Semitic policies. Vichy has undertaken to draw up a census of all Jews, and the official deploys a crazed logic to explain why Catholic priests, if of Jewish ancestry, had to present themselves to be counted:

If Pontius Pilate had ordered a census of the Jews, Jesus Christ himself would have obeyed; the humblest of his servants on earth must therefore submit to the law's commands, especially when there's nothing vexatious about them and also because humility is a Christian virtue.[16]

The document is an exercise in mad logic, dragooning Christ's example and Christian virtue into the service of racial persecution. It is also indicative of Rousset's theological sensibilities. He titles one chapter, "*Les ubuesques*," but many more have biblical referents: "*Dieu a dit qu'il y aurait un soir et un matin*" ("And God called the light Day, and the darkness he called Night. And the evening and the morning were the first day," Genesis, 1:5); "*Il existe plusieurs chambres dans la maison du Seigneur*" ("In my Father's house are many mansions," John, 14:2); "*À quoi sert à un homme de conquérir le monde*" ("For what is a man profited, if he shall gain the whole world," Matthew, 16:26). These are not just learned allusions, but revealing of Rousset's understanding of Nazism as a theological system. To the Nazis, political opponents and racial inferiors were so many "heretics," embodiments of "Evil," destined for destruction in an "apocalyptic fire." But the miscreants had to atone first, and that was the raison d'être of the camps. They were machines to squeeze labor out of the Nazis' enemies, no doubt, but they were more than that: "high places of expiation" where the chastising hand of the SS overlord, "the justiciary priest," as Rousset describes him, did not just inflict pain but prolonged it to make the sinner pay.[17]

Yet soul-crushing as the Nazi camp regime was, prisoners did not lack completely for resources to fight back. There was humor, first of all, a gallows humor that armored inmates against the maniac absurdities of camp life. Anything, in fact, that helped to keep the mind alive made a difference. Rousset, in collaboration with fellow Buchenwald inmate, the novelist and littérateur Benjamin Crémieux (who would not survive), put together a conference series. All manner of material was treated: history, sport, travel, whatever would frustrate Nazi designs to strangle the mental life of prisoners.[18] Yet far and away the inmates' most potent weapon was solidarity. In *Les Jours de notre mort*, Rousset does not hide his admiration for the iron resolve of the German politicals. What a contrast with the French, who were looked down on by other nationalities as so many petit-bourgeois chauvinists with a weakness for intellectualizing and pontification.[19] On the matter of solidarity, though, it is the Jews who come off worst in Rousset's estimation. He tells the story of a band of just-deported Hungarian Jews marching into camp, arms raised in the fascist salute in a desperate and vain effort to curry favor with the Nazi bosses. Jews had a reputation as feeble reeds, prone to snitching; indeed, to every form of baseness, cannibalism included. They even fought among themselves, "their dreadful misery" just exacerbating the mutual animosity.[20] It was the German detainees who knew how to stick together and to make others line up behind them with a ruthlessness that fascinated and impressed Rousset.

What the German politicals had going for them was not just the common bond of language and an all-too-Germanic sense of discipline.

Les Jours de notre mort bills itself as a novel, but it is just as much a think piece full of argument among politics-minded prisoners about how best to fight back against the Nazis. On this point, there should be no doubt: the politics in question are the politics of the revolutionary Left. Much of the book takes place in Buchenwald. The politicals, German Communists in the main, have taken over the organization of prisoner life, employing a mix of brute force and corruption to elbow aside the criminal element. Preparations for a prisoner uprising are set in motion, and the Buchenwald revolt hovers on the horizon. In the meantime, the political elite makes sure that its friends are awarded the best work assignments and its enemies, the worst. Some inmates get packages from home. A system is set up to distribute the contents: a portion to the recipients, but a portion as well to comrades in need. The Nazis want to assemble trainloads of detainees slated for deportation to the East; they turn to prisoner officials to draw up the lists, and the politicals make sure that it's unreliable elements who are shipped off to an almost certain death. For traitors and rats, justice is on the spot and summary. They are murdered then and there. It's a brutal world, and Rousset's characters quarrel at length over the morality of it all, but there's no question in the end what the final verdict is. The rights of private property and of the individual have to go by the board as obstacles to survival. Solidarity, even enforced solidarity, afforded the collectivity of prisoners a measure of protection against the diabolical arbitrariness of the camps' criminal element and the SS. It made possible resistance and, as the moment of liberation approached, revolt. More than that, the bitter lessons that camp life taught held out the promise of a better future for Europe, indeed, for all humankind. A deportee remnant, hardened in the fires of deportation, knew what was needed, "a socialist United States of Europe."[21]

As important as the socialist tomorrow was to Rousset, however, politics did not get the last word. *Les Jours de notre mort* concludes with an almost religious exaltation of inmate solidarity and of its redemptory example. What the deportees had achieved, as Rousset phrased it, was "a triumph well beyond ourselves for the collectivity of all men. Never did we give up fighting, never did we disavow who we were. Never did we blaspheme against life."[22]

Rousset had made himself into a public personality in late-1940s France. He had published two major works on the camp experience and a third, *Le Pitre ne rit pas*, on Nazism. The texts anatomized how the machinery of the camp system worked and did so in a prose rich in allusion, both literary and religious. Not least of all, Rousset evoked the possibility of a better world born out of the camps, one that drew sustenance from the spirit of solidarity and resistance germinated in the dung of camp life.

Now to Rousset's 1949 bombshell. He was not the first to bring up the subject of the Soviet camp system. In 1946, a high-ranking Soviet defector, Victor Kravchenko, had published an exposé, *I Chose Freedom*, detailing the full spectrum of Soviet crimes. It was translated into French the next year, prompting the PCF's literary organ, *Les Lettres françaises*, to sue Kravchenko for defamation. Kravchenko won at trial – the verdict was rendered in April 1949 – but for most people on the intellectual Left, all the attendant hullabaloo did little to shake their pro-Soviet sympathies. What moral standing did Kravchenko have after all, a turncoat who had handed himself over to American authorities?

That November, however, when Rousset raised the specter of the Soviet Gulag, he was not so easy to dismiss, all the more so given how Rousset's appeal was couched. True, it was published in a right-wing venue, *Le Figaro littéraire*, but Rousset made clear that he had a different kind of audience in mind, addressing the text "to former deportees" and designating a half-dozen by name, among them Robert Antelme and the journalists Louis Martin-Chauffier and Rémy Roure. Rousset made just as clear, moreover, what he was accusing the Soviet Union of: constructing a "concentrationary universe" of its own, not identical to the Nazi camp system in all respects, but like it in its exploitation of "corrective labor" for economic advantage. The Gulag, as Rousset represented it, was no mere excrescence on the Soviet body politic, but an integral part of it that had metastasized into an "economic trust" of gigantic proportions. The subject needed looking into, and there was no group better suited to the task than former deportees, who knew all too well what a real concentration camp was and how it operated. It was Nazism's former victims who were best qualified to conduct an investigation into the Soviet Union's "crimes against humanity." [23]

The appeal stirred an uproar. There had been tensions in FNDIRP ranks surrounding the organization's seventieth birthday telegram to Stalin. Rousset's proposal brought them to a boil. The FNDIRP, of course, rejected it out of hand, and a spate of high-profile departures then followed. The FNDIRP's vice-president, Father Michel Riquet, resigned. A number of ex-FNDIRP members were afforded an opportunity to explain themselves in the pages of *Le Monde*, Rémy Roure's newspaper, and they did not hold back, framing what they had done as a reaction to the FNDIRP's "crypto-communism."[24]

All the to-do did not slow the realization of Rousset's plans to assemble an investigative body. A Commission française d'enquête contre le régime concentrationnaire was set up in January 1950, which was followed by the creation later that year of an international organism, the Commission internationale contre le régime concentrationnaire (CICRC), based in Brussels. These efforts resonated with elements in France's deportee community. FNDIR, as might be expected, lent its support, and so too did the Association nationale des anciennes deportées et internées de la Résistance (ADIR), the most important organization of women camp survivors. Geneviève de Gaulle Anthonioz (General de Gaulle's niece), Anise Postel-Vinay, and Germaine Tillion all belonged. Tillion was in fact named to the Commission d'enquête and later to the CICRC's French delegation, on which she served alongside Martin-Chauffier.[25]

The communist world did not remain idle in the face of such challenges. *Le Patriote résistant* excoriated Riquet et al. as "secessionists,"[26] and *Les Lettres françaises* lit into Rousset's appeal as a tissue of lies, a fabrication based on fabrications. The allegation earned the journal's editors – Pierre Daix and Claude Morgan – a lawsuit. Now it was they who were charged with libel, and the plaintiff, of course, was none other than Rousset.

The trial did not last long, running under two months, from November 1950 to January 1951, and it ended in a guilty verdict, with Daix and Morgan obliged to pay a fine and print a retraction. What made the event noteworthy was the range of evidence Rousset marshaled. He received help pulling together the documentary dossier from Poliakov and Elinor Lipper.[27] The former had lasted out the Occupation in France on the run from the Nazis; the latter had spent eleven years in Kolyma, a Soviet labor camp in the Arctic Circle. A number of eyewitnesses were called on to testify as well, and there was one, Grete Buber-Neumann, who spoke with a particular authority, having had personal experience of both the Nazi and Soviet camp systems. She was a German Communist (and Martin Buber's onetime daughter-in-law) who had fled to the Soviet Union after Hitler's accession to power and there been caught up in the machinery of the Stalinist purges. She was interned in a Soviet labor camp and then, in the wake of the Nazi-Soviet Pact of 1939, handed over to the Nazis, who deported her to Ravensbrück.

The Rousset controversy marked a turning point in deportee affairs. The PCF had to that point exercised a tight grip on the interpretation of deportee experience, a position of authority it used to line up deportees on the Soviet side in the Cold War. Rousset, however, turned the tables. The camps, as he read them, remained the expression of a capitalism run rampant, but another layer of meaning was added on. They were also the consequence of a productivist, labor-exploiting logic that was not at all alien to the Soviet way of thinking – indeed, quite the contrary. Rousset thus thrust the Communists in the dock alongside the Nazis, both discredited as totalitarians.

Organizations

It wasn't just communist ideological hegemony that was broken up in the wake of the Rousset appeal. The constellation of deportee organizations also came in for a reconfiguring, and the FNDIRP found itself pushed to the side as a consequence. It remained a force to contend with but no longer occupied the high ground, and communist deportees in the process found themselves more and more on the defensive.

At the level of the amicale, there had been smoldering tensions even prior to the Rousset affair. ADIR offers a case in point. In the immediate postwar years, Communists and non-communists had gotten along. Marie-Claude Vaillant-Couturier, a member of the communist-leaning amicale de Ravensbrück, also served on the ADIR executive committee, which was non-communist in its majority. In 1946–1947, the Allies convened a tribunal in Hamburg to sit in judgment of Ravensbrück camp officials. The Amicale de Ravensbrück and ADIR both nominated Germaine Tillion, no party member herself, to attend the proceedings as an observer. Such relative comity, however, soon broke down. In 1948, Czech Communists seized power in the so-called Prague coup, arresting loyalists of the ousted Beneš regime, including three Ravensbrück survivors. ADIR wrote to the Czech communist authorities and pleaded for mercy, prompting Marie-Claude Vaillant-Couturier to resign from the ADIR executive committee. Two of the three Ravensbrück survivors were sentenced to prison terms, and one was executed.[28] That same year, Anise Postel-Vinay published a pair of articles in ADIR's press organ, *Voix et visages*, recalling the anguished choices that the camp's inmate leadership had had to face when doling out such privileges as lay in their control. It had been hardest of all for non-communists, she wrote, who valued the individual in a way that the Communists, ever ready to sacrifice the one for the many, did not. Vaillant-Couturier sent in a letter of remonstration, protesting that Communists too had known pangs of conscience.[29] Then came the Rousset appeal, and the ADIR leadership made it a point of pride that its executive committee had voted "unanimously among those members present" to work with Rousset.[30]

The same kind of tug-of-war went on within the Amicale de Dachau. The presiding figure at the amicale was Edmond Michelet, a first-hour résistant deported to Dachau in 1943. Michelet was a practicing Catholic whose moral rigor and force of personality had propelled him into the front ranks of the camp's prisoner leadership. Repatriated after the war, he was elected to the National Assembly in 1945 as a Christian Democrat and then went on to serve a stint as defense minister in de Gaulle's provisional government. In light of Michelet's religious and political convictions, it will come as no surprise that he sided with Rousset in 1949, and it was a choice that earned him the enmity of the Amicale de Dachau's communist minority, who waited on an opportunity to unseat him. In 1950, Michelet declared himself favorable to an amnesty for Maréchal Pétain, and it was then that the minority made its move. Michelet managed to beat back the insurgency, addressing his adversaries in terms that made crystal clear what he thought was stake: "We will not allow you – you and your friends – to take over the Amicale de Dachau in order to turn it into an instrument of your totalitarian designs."[31]

In the world of amicales, the Rousset appeal led to a scaling back of communist influence, as the examples of ADIR and the Amicale de Dachau attest. The appeal also prompted the creation of an altogether new deportee federation, the Union nationale des Associations de déportés, internés et familles de disparus. It was founded in 1950, and Father Riquet was the man who took the initiative. UNADIF, like the FNDIRP, welcomed all comers. It also made a claim to nonpartisanship, which didn't prevent it from entering into close partnership with FNDIR, an organization a good deal less hesitant about wearing its political colors. FNDIR's president, Léon Mazeaud, was a jurist and a Gaullist, and Mazeaud's two right-hand men, Eugène Thomas and Michelet, sat in the National Assembly. The former was a socialist and the latter a Christian Democrat who in 1947 rallied to de Gaulle's Rassemblement du peuple français. So, for all its professions of apoliticism, UNADIF, through its FNDIR ally, situated itself squarely in the anti-communist camp. That camp would in short order generate a memory politics of its own, potent enough to outcompete the PCF on terrain the Party had once considered its special preserve.[32]

The Struthof Monument

UNADIF did not confine itself to representing the interests of deportees, but also became involved early on in the business of keeping deportee memory alive. The deportee memorial at Natzweiler-Struthof in Alsace was inaugurated in July 1960, and the person who presided at the monument's unveiling was Charles de Gaulle, returned to power just two years before. The monument, however, was not a product of the Gaullist Fifth Republic, but of the regime that preceded it. It was the brainchild of Fourth Republic administrators, working in collaboration with the deportee community, and on the deportee side of the partnership, it was the UNADIF-FNDIR nexus that played the key role.

In the wake of France's defeat in 1940, Alsace was annexed by the Germans. The SS established a network of mountainside camps in the region to quarry stone. Natzweiler-Struthof or "Struthof," for short, was the hub of it all, and over the course of the war fifty thousand inmates drawn from across the continent passed through the gates of the Struthof camp complex.[33] Although most were not French, many were, a number that included illustrious figures of the armed Resistance such as General Aubert Frère, who died there, and General Charles Delestraint, later executed at Dachau. The camp, moreover, was located on native soil, seized by the Reich during the war but restored afterward to the *mère-patrie*. The locale then had a symbolic power that made it an ideal choice for a deportee memorial.

The process took time, however. At the war's end, Struthof was turned over to the Ministère d l'Intérieur, which converted the premises into an administrative internment center. That facility was closed in 1949, although families of deportees still came to lay wreaths or bouquets. The Amicale de Natzwiller-Struthof (in French, that's how Natzweiler is spelled) kept an eye on the property to protect it against vandalism, but otherwise the site fell into disrepair. The prefect of the Bas-Rhin later that year brought the situation to the attention of the prime minister, Henri Queuille, who in turn instructed the minister of veterans' affairs to take the situation in hand.[34]

A series of meetings ensued, and a plan of action began to take shape. Struthof was classified a historic monument in 1950, and a gassing facility, located a short distance from the camp proper, was awarded the same status a year later. As for the site itself, the Ministère des anciens Combattants had one overriding desideratum. It was responsible for the repatriated remains of French men and women who had died in deportation, and it soon fixed on Struthof as a suitable place to lay them to rest. The Ministère de l'Éducation nationale named Bertrand Monnet, a government architect, to take charge of the project, and by July 1953, he had devised a scheme satisfactory to all involved. Struthof was situated on a sharp incline, and at the summit, Monnet envisaged a cemetery and, in close proximity, a monument. The monument's design was as yet unspecified, but it was meant to be imposing, visible from far and wide. The vestiges of the camp itself, the watchtowers and eleven still-extant barrack houses, extended down the slope below. Four of the barracks, two at the bottom and two at the top, were slated for preservation, the rest for demolition. There remained the question of how to fund the project, a matter settled in October when it was decided to launch a public subscription and to appoint a National Committee to handle the fund-raising.[35]

State officials meanwhile took action to clarify the lines of authority. The National Committee was conceived of as an umbrella group with a large membership. It was intended to be representative of the deportee community in its entirety, with an eye to enhancing its ability to appeal to donors. The hands-on management of the project, however, was invested in a second, more compact body, the Executive Commission, placed under the direct authority of the Ministère des anciens Combattants. The members of the former were appointed in 1953, and of the latter the next year.

UNADIF delegates made up far and away the largest contingent on the National Committee, accounting for fourteen of its forty-three members. All of UNADIF's senior officers were named: its president, two vice-presidents (Father Riquet among them), and secretary-general. Add in members of affiliated organizations like FNDIR, and the tally rises to nineteen. The FNDIRP, important as it was, received just four slots. The balance of the committee was made up of clergy (Cardinal Maurice Feltin, Pastor Marc Boegner, and Rabbi Jacob Kaplan), two officers of the Amicale de Natzwiller-Struthof, and a sampling of government officials. It was all too obvious that the communist wing of the deportee movement had been snubbed, and the Communists knew it. FNDIRP representatives, it seems, abstained from participating in the committee's deliberations, an absence conspicuous enough to be remarked on at the time.[36]

And on the Executive Commission, the FNDIRP was not represented at all. The commission's honorary president was the minister of veterans' affairs, André Mutter, a one-time résistant and man of the classic Right. The actual running of the body was confided to Georges Degois, a customs official and former deportee, who was a UNADIF vice-president. He was assisted by six officers: three government officials (Louis Houy, Alexandre Mattei, Richard Pouzet); two UNADIF members (General Frère's widow and Berthe Thiriart); and the Amicale de Natzwiller-Struthof's president, Dr. Léon Boutbien. In the late 1940s, Boutbien had backed Rousset's RDR. By 1954, however, when he was named to the Struthof Executive Commission, he had moved on to join France's socialist party, the Section française de l'Internationale ouvrière (SFIO), which he represented in the National Assembly.[37]

Non-communists oversaw development of the Struthof site, and so it's worth querying whether that fact had any impact on the memorial's

Figure 2.1 Struthof Memorial, Alsace, 1960

actual design. The answer is not clear-cut. Monnet's blueprint called for a monument massive in scale, and he enlisted a sculptor, Lucien Fenaux, to help out. The Executive Commission did not like the idea of a sculptural element and for sure did not want one that smacked of realism, but the Monnet/Fenaux team found a way to allay such concerns. They drew up a plan for a curved, flame-shaped edifice constructed of concrete and sheathed in a high-quality, marblelike stone. On the inside was incised the figure of an emaciated deportee, ascending skyward (see Figure 2.1). It was an abstract, nonrealist form, and Boutbien, for one, was pleased with the stylization.[38]

The monument's symbolism was not difficult to unpack. The deportee had suffered in the flesh but was resurrected in spirit, rising beyond the miseries of camp life, "the sole escape route possible for the detainee," as Monnet put it to a journalist from *Le Monde*.[39] The Executive Commission was highly satisfied with the Monnet/Fenaux scheme.

Figure 2.2 Struthof Commemorative Stamp, 1956

It had from the outset entertained issuing a commemorative stamp to help publicize the project and in 1956 received the go-ahead from the Ministère des Postes, Télégraphes et Téléphones. The image selected was Fenaux's emaciated deportee (see Figure 2.2).[40] The FNDIRP did not have the connections to issue a stamp, nor the wherewithal to erect a structure, such as this one, forty meters in height. Yet there is also much about the Struthof monument that calls to mind the deportation memorials clustered in the communist quadrant of Père-Lachaise: the use of concrete, the stylized, skeletal figure of the deportee, the theme of the spirit's ultimate triumph over matter.

That said, the Struthof monument was conceived to express patriotic and republican commitments in ways that its Père-Lachaise counterparts were not. Father Riquet was an old soldier, a veteran of the Great War, and he wanted the Struthof necropolis laid out like a military cemetery, each grave marked by a stone in a shape – a cross, a Jewish star – that signaled the deportee's religious affiliation.[41] The proposition was accepted, and so too a Boutbien proposal relating to the design of Monnet's towering stone flame. The structure was wrapped around a circular space, half enclosing it. Boutbien had the idea to orient the monument such that the open end faced toward France, the figure of the incised deportee thus looking out onto the land that had nurtured him. An inscription was carved into the spiraling interior wall of the flame. The Struthof Executive Commission debated its content and agreed on a phrase that echoed the motto etched onto the pediment of the Pantheon. The Pantheon inscription read, "To great men, a grateful fatherland;" Struthof's, "To the heroes and martyrs of the deportation, a grateful fatherland." So it was on this spot in July 1960, enfolded in the love of a thankful nation, that the remains of an unknown deportee were buried, this commemorative gesture calling to mind not so much the Pantheon as the Tomb of the Unknown Soldier at the Place de l'Étoile. Indeed, the deportee's final resting place was marked with an inscription, "Here lies an unknown deportee," which was an adaptation of the device "Here lies an unknown soldier" that adorned the unknown soldier's gravesite beneath the Arc de Triomphe.[42]

The Struthof monument, for all its modern design elements, was woven into a memorial fabric that extended back to the Great War and beyond. But more than that – and this was perhaps the memorial's most original aspect – Struthof was a museum – in fact, a museum twice over. In 1965, Pouzet inaugurated an exposition on the deportation experience, housed in one of the preserved barrack blocks. It included artifacts from Mont-Valérien and Châteaubriant as well as from the Vélodrome d'hiver and Drancy.[43] The collection was not that impressive, consisting of borrowed materials and reproductions. The real museum, though, and this one *was* impressive, lay out of doors. Here, the visitor had an immediate encounter with a genuine concentration camp and all the elements that went into the making of one. There were blockhouses, barbed wire, and an ensemble of four barracks, among them one at the top of the site that accommodated the museum and one at the bottom containing the camp crematorium. In between loomed a gallows, situated on a flat space where prisoners once gathered to witness the execution of their unfortunate comrades. There were also two out-of-camp sites. One, just beyond the gates, was located on a sloping plain, in camp days gardens that the SS had fertilized with the ashes of incinerated inmates. It was marked by a so-called Lanterne des morts, several meters high and always lit. Further away was the second site, the camp gas chamber. It was a smallish affair, but a gas chamber nonetheless.

This vast outdoor museum told of the martyrdom of the deportees and of the cruelty of the Nazis who hanged, gassed, and burned them, contriving to profit even from their corpses.

Struthof was not a politicized monument in a way that was deeply divisive. It was a modern memorial, stylized in design, which, its massive scale apart, would not have been out of place in the 97th division of Père-Lachaise. To be sure, the harkening to national commemorative tradition no doubt left more than one party comrade cold, but overall the site's accent on patriotic sacrifice was of a sort to comfort deportees from many political horizons, Communists included. Struthof's pedagogical ambitions were its most original feature. Rousset had sketched the contours of the concentrationary universe, and Struthof gave flesh to the image, transforming what was written on the page into three-dimensional form. At the same time, there was no invitation to camp visitors to reflect on any concentrationary system, Soviet or otherwise, beyond the Nazi one that lay before them. The memorial ensemble might not be one that Communists themselves would have conceived, but it wasn't in any explicit way designed against them.

This is not to say, however, that the Struthof memorial was inclusive in all respects. Most of the camp's inmates had been foreigners, and a number had also been Jews, including several score who perished in the camp gas chamber. To these victims, the site, national and patriotic in conception, accorded little or no acknowledgment.[44] Then, once again, there were the Communists. They might not have profound reason to object to the memorial per se, but the site was not always a welcoming one to them. I'll begin with a minor point. Communists played next to no role in fund-raising. As noted, the FNDIRP was a marginal presence on the National Committee that was tasked with the job. The archives indicate one occasion when the FNDIRP took part in the solicitation of funds. In 1958, it helped to organize a raffle. But that's all. The Amicale de Natzwiller-Struthof, which sold postcards, accomplished just about as much.[45] And the Réseau du souvenir, a UNADIF spin-off, did a lot more. It organized a gala evening event, a "Veillée du Souvenir," on the tenth anniversary of the liberation of the camps. The Palais de Chaillot was the chosen locale, and the program featured movies and music, including a cantata, "Le Château du feu," composed for the occasion. Darius Milhaud, who had spent the war in exile in the United States, did the composing, working from a poem by Jean Cassou. All the proceeds went to the construction of the Struthof memorial.[46]

Communists were not of the sort to accept marginalization without pushback. Time and again, they tried to use the memorial for political gatherings. In March 1957, the Union des femmes françaises, a PCF affiliate, planned a demonstration at the site to protest the naming of General Hans Speidel, once a high-ranking member of the Wehrmacht brass in occupied Paris, as commander of NATO forces in central Europe. General Frère's widow got wind of the plan and made sure the memorial was closed down for the day. It was not so easy, however, to bar the FNDIRP from the camp. FNDIRP members in fact made regular pilgrimages to Struthof. On a couple of occasions in 1960, the pilgrimages spilled over into rallies, complete with "regrettable speeches," or so it seemed to the Struthof Executive Commission. It petitioned the Ministère des anciens Combattants to petition in turn the local prefect to enforce a respectful silence on the premises. Religious ceremonials were permissible, the prefect decreed, but no noisy rallies. This didn't stop the FNDIRP from organizing future marches to the memorial, but it did place strict limits on what could be said and done.[47] Of no less importance, there was the ceremonial inauguration of the site itself, a grand and moving event that made no room at all for communist participation.

That fact, significant as it was, was overshadowed by another one, General de Gaulle's presence at the unveiling. This was not, however, a planned-for eventuality but, rather, the result of happenstance. In April 1957, the memorial project had advanced far enough that the Executive Commission began naming contractors. There were hopes that construction might be completed the following year, and it was then that the commission began to give some thought to inaugural proceedings. The president of the Republic, René Coty, was invited to officiate, and he agreed, but these plans soon fell apart. The Fourth Republic collapsed, and on top of that there were building delays that postponed the unveiling into 1960. A solution soon presented itself, however, in the ever-providential figure of General Charles de Gaulle. Boutbien had a chance encounter with Pierre Koenig, a former commander of the armed Resistance, who had gone on to a political career in the 1950s as a Gaullist deputy from the Bas-Rhin. Koenig informed Boutbien that de Gaulle was willing to preside at the unveiling; negotiations followed; and a date was at last agreed upon, July 23, 1960. De Gaulle then was brought in at the last moment.[48] He had no hand in shaping Struthof's design. His participation did, however, have an impact on the inaugural solemnities, imparting to them a martial tone very much in the Gaullist vein.

The main event, the unveiling, took place on July 23, a Saturday, but there was also a burial ceremony the night before that culminated in the entombment of the unknown deportee. This was overseen, not by de Gaulle, but by the minister of veterans' affairs, Raymond Triboulet. Proceedings began at 9:30 PM with the minister's arrival. A poem by Dr. Boutbien was read, and then the remains of the unknown deportee, accompanied by an honor guard of torch-bearing comrades, were carried up from the foot of the camp, as a chorus intoned the Resistance anthem, the "Chant des Partisans." The interment of the coffin was followed by prayers for the dead, offered up by representatives from all four of France's major religions. Taps was then played and a moment of silence observed, the ceremony's finale punctuated by a singing of "La Marseillaise."[49]

The unveiling proper took place the next morning. This was a grander event, but still brief and closely scripted. De Gaulle arrived at the campsite by car and was greeted by the commanding officers of the region, Natzwiller's mayor, and Triboulet. The General toured the camp, stopping at the bottom to visit the crematorium and to preside over the awarding of decorations. He pinned the insignia of a Grand Officer of the Légion d'honneur on Boutbien, both men decked out in their military uniforms. This was followed by a parade of troops, after which the General marched up the slope alone to the cemetery, returning afterward to the monument site itself, where the elongated figure of the deportee was draped over with a huge tricolor flag. De Gaulle, flanked by two of his ministers, Edmond Michelet and Pierre Sudreau, both camp survivors, uncovered the monument. There had been plans for a squadron of jet planes to fly past at just that moment in a Cross of Lorraine formation. In the event, just a single jet roared low overhead, creating what was still an impressive effect. De Gaulle observed a moment of silence and then turned to work the crowd.[50]

It's the orchestration of the Saturday morning interment that is most striking in all this, enshrining as it did a Gaullist vision of the war years. The day's ceremonials did not just celebrate patriotic sacrifice, which was natural, but the military side of the story. It almost did so under the sign of the Cross of Lorraine, but not quite.[51] Boutbien had a significant part to play in the proceedings (on Friday evening too). UNADIF was also a presence: among the invitees, but also in the person of its vice-president, Roland Teyssandier, who, like Boutbien, was awarded a decoration. It was de Gaulle, however, who stole the show, appropriating a monument designed by others for purposes of his own. As for the once hegemonic FNDIRP, it seems to have been left out entirely. Communists might try to use the space as a launching pad for demonstrations and pilgrimages, but it was an uphill battle in the face of an unaccommodating Gaullist state.

Réseau du Souvenir

The Réseau du souvenir has been mentioned in passing as a helpmate in the Struthof fundraising effort. Yet it was also an independent actor that crafted a memory politics of its own no less significant than UNADIF's.

The Réseau began life in 1950. It was known then as the Commission du souvenir, and it was a UNADIF subsidiary. Father Riquet belonged, as did Paul Arrighi, a lawyer and camp survivor, and Annette Lazard, the widow of a deportee, Christian Lazard, who had died at Auschwitz. Commission members went knocking on doors, soliciting advice on how to proceed. It was in this context that Annette Lazard came calling on Henri Michel, a historian and former résistant. Since 1946, Michel had directed a research commission charged with gathering documentation on the history of the Occupation. He knew anyone and everyone with an investment in the subject, and he shared what he knew with the Commission du souvenir. The commission set about building up a network of supporters and then in May 1952 struck out on its own, constituting itself as the Réseau du souvenir. Arrighi served as president, Riquet and Lazard as vice-presidents, and Michel as secretary-general. The executive committee included a number of familiar faces from the pro-Rousset camp: Edmond Michelet, Rémy Roure, and Germaine Tillion.[52]

The Réseau du souvenir was a small organization, never numbering more than a few thousand, and it was a tight-knit one. Arrighi and Father Riquet had shared a straw mattress their first night at Mauthausen. The Jesuit father was later transferred to Dachau, where he crossed paths with Michelet, the very embodiment of "the splendor of the Christian layman," as an admiring Riquet later said of him.[53] Thanks to excellent political connections, the Réseau du souvenir was also in a position to make things happen. In the spring of 1953, Riquet drafted a resolution calling for the establishment of a national day of remembrance to honor France's deportees. He lined up endorsements from representatives of all of France's major religions. Arrighi asked Michelet, at the time a senator, to submit the proposal to the National Assembly, which Michelet did, and it passed without debate in early April 1954. So came into being the Journée nationale de la Déportation, observed the last Sunday of every April from that year down to this.[54]

The Réseau du souvenir proved just as effective when it came to museum work and publishing. Henri Michel and a young researcher, Olga Wormser-Migot, were the pivotal figures here. In December 1951, Michel's commission on the Occupation fused with a second research body to give rise to a new organism, the Comité d'histoire de la deuxième guerre mondiale (CHDG), with Michel himself at the helm. With funding from the Réseau du souvenir, he set up a subcommittee on the Deportation and went about staffing it. He recruited Olga Jungelson (soon to be Olga Wormser, then Olga Wormser-Migot) in 1952, and the choice was an inspired one. Although not a former deportee herself, Wormser-Migot did have hands-on knowledge of the Nazi camp system. As a staff member at Henri Frenay's postwar veterans' administration, she had been sent to Germany to assist in the repatriation of French deportees, traveling to Bergen-Belsen and later as far east as the Auschwitz and Majdanek camps in Poland. Wormser-Migot, moreover, was a woman of intelligence and energy, who brought an imaginative zeal to the subject – the Deportation – that was to become a lifelong passion. In 1954, just two years into her new job, she, seconded by Michel, mounted a museum exhibition on the theme and published a book, *Tragédie de la Déportation*; Michel was involved in this enterprise too though he was not the prime mover. The Réseau du souvenir was on the scene throughout, providing financial support and, in the case of *Tragédie de la Déportation*, making a concerted effort to see that it was read and reviewed.[55]

The exhibition, titled *Résistance, Libération, Déportation*, opened in 1954 and was timed to coincide with the tenth anniversary of the Liberation of Paris. It seems that students were the target audience, given the venue chosen, the Musée pédagogique on the rue d'Ulm. Films related to the exhibition's subject matter were screened: René Clément's *La Bataille du rail*, Roberto Rossellini's *Rome, Open City*, and Wanda Jakubowska's *La Dernière Étape*. Objects from the concentration camps were also put on display, including a suite of Taslitzky drawings. The overall effect was impressive and moving. ADIR's house organ praised "the piety, the seriousness, the intelligence" of the show, and another newspaper remarked on its "reliquary aspect": "People come there not as visitors but as pilgrims."[56] The exhibition did not have a religious message to convey, but it provoked viewers to react in religious terms.

In the case of *Tragédie de la Déportation*, the religious language was not just the reviewer's, but built into the book's very design. The volume was made up of excerpts from survivor accounts. Camp literature was already so plentiful that it was possible to construct an ideal-type of what camp life had been like, broken down into a sequence of core experiences, beginning with arrest and deportation and ending in death or liberation. The editors then coated this structure with a Christian overlay. In the book's introduction, they likened the Deportation to a modern-day Passion: "The reader will trace in this work, stage by stage, the stations of the cross that the deportees traveled." This helps to account for the editors' particular choice of chapter headings, beginning with "First Station: Transports" and ending with "Final Station: Death."[57]

One of the book's central preoccupations was why certain inmates held on while others succumbed, and on this point too, the language of faith inserted itself. Wormser-Migot and Michel included a passage from Léon Mazeaud's memoir on the deportation experience. The camps were designed to degrade, Mazeaud explained, and it was no easy task to hold up in such circumstances. "There existed in this hell, however," he went on, "exceptional beings. Those who had a faith, an ideal. A political or religious ideal, Communists and Christians for the most part." That was in fact Wormser-Migot's and Michel's own general conclusion. Intellectuals melted down in the white heat of the camp inferno, they noted, but not "Christians, Communists, and a few rare men steeped in humanism." It was persons such as these who performed acts of unrequited goodness, who respected the dignity of the human person, and who took comfort in moments of beauty, however few and far between. By such gestures, they remained free men and withstood the storm.[58]

There was a consistency then to the volume's interpretive line. The Deportation was in identifiable aspects the same for all, and character played a role in survival, above all character fortified by strong convictions that nourished the spirit of resistance.

The Jewish experience, of course, did not fit this paradigm. A special fate was reserved for Jews – extermination – and faith, however deeply felt, made no difference. Wormser-Migot and Michel, it needs to be said, did not avoid the issue entirely. They included a selection from the camp memoir of Georges Wellers, an Auschwitz survivor and CDJC member, and from Poliakov's *Bréviaire de la haine*. François Mauriac too was excerpted. He was a Catholic writer, but one with an all too vivid memory of what had happened to Jews in France during the Occupation years. In a wartime text, from which Wormser-Migot and Michel cited, Mauriac wrote of Jewish children "torn from their mothers, piled into cattle cars, such as I saw them on a somber morning at the gare d'Austerlitz."[59] There was no denial of Jewish suffering or of what happened to the Jews once deported. The Soviet war correspondent Vasily Grossman had written an account of the liberation of the Treblinka death camp, published in 1944. That account was also excerpted in *Tragédie de la Déportation*, with a footnote to help readers identify the site in question: "[An] extermination camp located in Poland, which operated through 1942, date when Auschwitz became a model *Vernichtungslager* (extermination camp)."[60] Wormser-Migot and

Michel themselves brought the subject up one more time in the volume's final pages, noting that the Deportation had taken the lives of eight million people, three-quarters of them burned in camp crematoria "for the crime of being Jews."[61]

The men and women of the Réseau du souvenir knew full well what had happened to the Jews, and they didn't mean to hide the facts. In 1951, as Annette Lazard made the rounds to line up backers for the memory project she was embarked on, she arranged to meet with a CDJC delegation headed by Isaac Schneersohn, the CDJC's founder. Schneersohn was direct: the Nazis had murdered six million Jews, and almost all those who had died at Auschwitz were Jewish. He then paid homage to the citizens of France who, "in spite of their government, managed clandestinely to save 1 Jew in 3," and concluded with an offer of support and cooperation.[62] The Réseau du souvenir did not seize the extended hand, but the CHDG did. It published a scholarly journal, the *Revue d'histoire de la Deuxième Guerre mondiale*, and in 1956, the review dedicated a special issue to the wartime fate of the Jews. It obtained help from Poliakov and from Joseph Billig, a CDJC researcher, who was also the first person to publish a documented examination of Vichy's anti-Semitic policies.[63]

The Réseau du souvenir's account of wartime events did not ignore the Jews, nor were Jews forgotten when it came time to market *Tragédie de la Déportation*. Lazard wrote to Edmond Fleg, a well-known Jewish man of letters, asking him to arrange a notice in *La Revue de la pensée juive*. Arrighi petitioned the Israeli embassy for help in circulating the book to the Israeli press. The embassy demurred, proposing instead that Arrighi contact Israeli journalists in Paris and work through them. The name and address of Elie Wiesel (correspondent for *Yedioth Ahronot*) were supplied. Even when the target of the marketing campaign wasn't Jewish, the racial theme was not far removed. Arrighi sent a copy of *Tragédie de la Déportation* to Cardinal Montini, the future Paul VI, explaining to His Eminence why he might be interested in the book's subject: because "your name is synonymous with tolerance and the fight against the racial idea in any form."[64]

The Rousset Affair reconfigured the organizational landscape of the deportee community. A non-communist counterpole to the FNDIRP took shape, centered on the FNDIR-UNADIF axis. Additional support came from Michelet's Amicale de Dachau, the women survivors gathered around ADIR, and the Réseau du souvenir's expanding memory network. This was a powerful and well-connected assemblage, in a position to effect change. The Journée nationale de la Déportation, the rue d'Ulm exhibition, Wormser-Migot and Michel's *Tragédie de la*

Déportation, and, of course, the Struthof memorial were the first fruits of such labors. In the process, a new kind of understanding of the deportation experience began to take form. Jews were not excluded from the story, not at all, but enormous as their pain had been, they remained ancillaries in a narrative whose center of gravity lay elsewhere. The mechanization and productivist logic of modern civilization had made possible a new kind of domination, which found its ultimate expression in the concentration camp. The Nazis had invented the machinery that made the camp experience the hell that it was, but they did not hold a patent on it. The practices and techniques involved were available for use wherever there was a will to break the human spirit, and the Soviet Gulag was proof of that. But there also existed people with a different kind of will, the will to resist, and they bore up, even under the crushing weight the Nazis heaped upon them. It was a sense of solidarity that made them strong, a commitment to others born of deep religious or ideological belief. That accent on solidarity made it difficult, even for the most sympathetic like Rousset, to talk about what happened to the Jews – themselves, it seemed, so lacking in solidarity – without a judgmental callousness. That accent on faith made it difficult, even for non-Christians like Wormser-Migot, to talk about the agony of the camps without recourse to the imagery of the Crucifixion.

Tillion and Wormser-Migot

That narrative, however, was not set in stone. Scholars like Tillion and Wormser-Migot never ceased to reflect on the meaning of the camp experience, writing tomes about it in an effort to bring academic rigor to a subject that the public had first come to know through the survivor account. In so doing, they refined the totalitarian model Rousset had handed down, in Wormser-Migot's case helping to ring changes on it that cleared the path for an understanding that moved beyond Rousset's own. Such refinements, of course, were not arrived at in a vacuum, the immaculate products of pure thought. There was a political context that shaped them, and that context was war in the Maghreb. France, from 1954, was embroiled in a no-holds-barred struggle to retain possession of Algeria, and in pursuit of that objective had recourse to methods – mass internment and torture – that are now all too familiar features of so-called asymmetrical warfare. This was not a subject of indifference to deportees, victims themselves of such techniques, and they were distressed by it. *Was colonial France so different from Nazi Germany?* they asked themselves. Tillion and Wormser-Migot rejected the proposition, but the point is that they felt duty-bound to address the issue, to think about contemporary events and about Algeria in terms of what they had experienced or knew of the Nazi camp system.[65]

Germaine Tillion began to accumulate information about the camps while still a prisoner at Ravensbrück. She calculated how much it cost to keep an inmate alive and the profit that a prisoner's labor generated, figures that enabled her to arrive at a rough estimate of the camp's net income. Personal experience and on-the-scene research, however, were just a starting point. As the Second World War neared its end, the Swedish Red Cross took many liberated Ravensbrück inmates into its care and recorded testimony from a number of them. Tillion made use of the collection, and, of course, as an ADIR official, she had access to eyewitness accounts from fellow ADIR members. Tillion valued such testimony – these women had been comrades after all – but she did not take the survivor's word as gospel. Some witnesses were more reliable than others, and it was the researcher's duty to separate the wheat from the chaff. There were other sources, apart from victim accounts, to help round out the picture. The Nuremberg trials of 1945–1946 generated a trove of documentary evidence, and Tillion was present as an observer at the Hamburg trial of the Ravensbrück camp command.

Tillion never let up when it came to accumulating evidence. She published a brief account of the Ravensbrück camp in 1946 but did not stop there. As fresh material became available, she revised the text twice more, and, thus, over time what had begun as an extended article developed into a weighty work of scholarship.

In most respects, though, Tillion's interpretive frame remained unchanged throughout. Germany's turn to Nazism, as she saw it, was at root the result of an over-rapid modernization. A nation saturated with Prussian militarism had plunged headlong into the industrial world. The smash-up of the Great War left the Germans rudderless, in a state of prostration, which the Nazis exploited to bootstrap themselves into power. It was a conjunction then of economic dislocation and political crisis that opened the door to Hitler.[66] On the matter of the camps, economics also had a part to play. These were cash-generating enterprises, a fact Tillion knew all too well, having done the bookkeeping herself. That Himmler owned the land on which Ravensbrück was built, a telling detail Tillion learned while still an internee, clinched the analysis. He was the "hierarchical and stock-holding boss" of a vast corporation that ground profits out of slave labor. An "ingenious capitalist," Himmler contrived to increase cash flow by renting out prisoners to toil in nearby businesses, and Tillion cited in evidence the example of Siemens, the German electricity and communications giant, which had set up a factory right next door to Ravensbrück.[67]

Tillion recognized, of course, that the Nazi camp system was a complex phenomenon. It had been devised to warehouse the Reich's enemies and make a profit out of them. But it also existed to effect the extermination of all European Jewry. That fact had been driven home to Tillion during the war by a group of Czech prisoners who had been transferred from Auschwitz to Ravensbrück. They told Tillion of "the systematic annihilation of Jews by gassing." Tillion's own postwar research, moreover, persuaded her that the Nazi *Lager* system was composed of two kinds of camps, one for labor and a second for mass murder.

Yet both, Tillion was determined to argue, were governed by the same logic. As an inmate, she had noted that exhausted prisoners, no longer capable of useful labor, were selected for relocation to the East in so-called "black transports." These were proof that the labor and extermination camps were connected. In the labor camp, prisoners were worked to death on the spot or, once worn out, sent to certain death at an extermination camp. At the extermination camps, death came with greater speed, but in the final analysis, all prisoners faced the identical fate, whether as victims of extermination through labor or of extermination tout court. And always the Germans made sure that they reaped a profit. Living bodies were set to work, and bodies slated for extermination were turned to fertilizer. With a mania for order all too German, every victim, both the quick and the dead, was made to yield a cash dividend.[68]

Tillion's perpetrators were fanatics and racists, but first and foremost they were money-grubbers. The prisoner world, by contrast, represented an antithetical set of values: friendship, art, and solidarity. Tillion had fallen ill at Ravensbrück, sick enough to harbor thoughts of giving up on life, but she did not let go. Chance events helped her to survive, and so too a vitalizing fury to tell the story of what the Germans had done. But above all, it was the affection and succor afforded by a tight-knit circle of friends that in the final analysis rescued her. That saving friendship, Tillion believed, was most keenly felt among women prisoners, who were more open to expressions of affection than their male counterparts and less divided by politics.[69]

Art too provided a boost. The camp command meant all prisoners to work. Those without particular skills were classified as *Verfügbaren*, occupants of a general labor pool, available for whatever job, however wretched or demeaning, that came along. This was Tillion's standing. She had some success dodging assignments, and even when assigned, schemed to do as little as possible. Tillion tells of one occasion when she and a group of fellow inmates were charged with unloading trains. Her comrades, sympathetic to her work-shy habits, gave her a break, hiding her in a packing crate. Tucked away, Tillion set to work on the libretto of an operetta, *Le Verfügbar aux enfers*, an account of camp life as it might look to a visiting ethnologist. The title was borrowed from Jacques Offenbach's *Orphée aux enfers* (*Orpheus in Hell* in English) and the tunes from a variety of classical and popular sources, but the humor, black and mordant, was all Tillion's own.[70]

Creation was a way to hold it together, indeed, to fight back against the dehumanizing pressures of the camp experience. The solidarity born of a shared Frenchness, by contrast, was a more ambivalent asset. Tillion acknowledged the common wisdom among camp inmates: that the French were individualistic and intellectualizing and that these qualities made them unsuited – "unadapted" was the word she used – for the rigors of camp life. Yet, Tillion wasn't prepared to let the matter go at that. The French, she countered, bridled at SS discipline as if by instinct, because they had an inbred sense of what liberty meant. They treated one another without brutality and never ratted out comrades. So, the French may have been riffraff (*racaille*), but they were freedom-loving riffraff, and patriots too. Tillion recalled the nighttime ritual at her Ravensbrück barracks block. After lights out, one inmate would call out "France," eliciting a collective exclamation from the rest: "will live!"[71] What a contrast with other nationalities, who were thuggish or subservient or who, like the "Jewish pseudo-people" – and here she reprised a stereotype familiar from Rousset – lacked any sense of solidarity at all.[72]

It was Tillion's mix of direct knowledge and scientific expertise, her critical understanding of the system and its victims, that made her such a desirable recruit for Rousset's CICRC. She knew what a camp was and how it fit into a regimen of totalitarian rule, and she was not so philo-Soviet as to close her eyes to what the Soviet Union had done. Quite the contrary. Already before the war, Tillion had been told of the Ukrainian famine of 1932–1933 by one of her dissertation supervisors, Marcel Mauss. She was informed about the Gulag as well, having learned of it, while still a prisoner at Ravensbrück, from fellow inmate Grete Buber-Neumann.[73] Tillion then was well disposed to the CICRC's project and geared to take a prominent part in its activities. In 1951, Rousset staged a mock trial in Brussels. The Soviet Union was called to account, accused of running a concentrationary regime. Rousset cast himself as prosecutor, and Tillion played the number-two role, acting as judge (one of four).[74] The verdict rendered was "guilty." Imagine the jubilation of the non-communist deportee press when the Soviet avant-garde journal, *Novy Mir*, published Alexander Solzhenitsyn's *One Day in the Life of Ivan Denisovich* in 1962. Rousset, Tillion, and others had pressed the case against the USSR way back at the beginning of the fifties, meeting hostility and resistance all the way. Now, at last, there was confirmation, originating from within the Soviet Union itself, that they had been right all along.[75]

The Algerian war, however, nagged at the good conscience of anti-totalitarians like Tillion. Like many French ethnologists and social scientists, she had cut her professional teeth doing fieldwork in French North Africa. The war then was a matter of pressing professional concern, but it was more than that. Tillion was an ex-deportee, a status that implicated her in multiple and complex ways in the Algerian conflict.

First of all, it was as a former deportee that Tillion came to write *L'Algérie en 1957*, a classic social science account of how Algeria had landed in its then present-day predicament. She was commissioned in 1956 by ADIR comrades to report on the "Algerian tragedy," which she did, publishing a pair of articles about it in *Voix et visages*. Tillion had a good deal more to say on the subject, so much so that ADIR decided to assemble a brochure. The demand for the brochure in turn proved so great that the entire venture was turned over to a professional publishing house, Jérôme Lindon's Éditions de minuit.[76]

The story Tillion had to tell was one of incomplete modernization. Two civilizations had come into contact in North Africa: France's own, which was modern, and Algeria's, which was archaic. Modernity brought with it many advantages: the cash economy, literacy, and scientific medicine; yet such goods were at times Janus-faced. Tillion cited as an example modern medicine, which, with its life-saving antibiotics, rescued many from an early death but as a consequence triggered a demographic explosion among Algeria's all too reproductive rural populations. The *bled* did not have the wherewithal to absorb all the new bodies, and so the excess was released into Algeria's coastal towns. But these were men and women raised in backwardness, "unadapted" to the demands of the modern city, and so, far from prospering in their new surroundings, they sank into a life of shantytown idleness and parasitism. Tillion coined a word to describe such downward mobility, "*clochardisation*," which she understood to be the root cause of all Algeria's contemporary difficulties. Grim as the situation was, however, there were solutions: birth-control education, which would at one and the same time empower women and brake population growth, vocational training to prepare men of all ages for work in a market economy, and significant developmental investment to create jobs. France alone had the means and the motivation to make such a financial commitment, and so its ongoing engagement in Algerian affairs was vital for all, but most of all for Algeria itself.[77]

Tillion favored a federalist relationship between France and Algeria, not national independence, which she took to be a dodge, a way for both sides to sidestep the real, underlying issue, *clochardisation*. Sartre, as might be expected, had little patience with Tillion's analysis. France's presence in Algeria, as he saw it, was not the consequence of fortuitous events but of an expansionist, exploitative impulse. Tillion did not address the critique (*what answer to it was there?*) but did mock Sartre's partiality for terrorist violence. The weak were better served, she felt, not by outbursts of rage but by reform that alleviated misery, and as a camp survivor, she felt that she had a special sympathy for what Algeria's downtrodden were living through. Indeed, she saw in *clochardisation* a less extreme form, a less rationalized and profit-squeezing variant, of *le système concentrationnaire* itself.[78]

Yet what if France had erected a concentrationary regime of its own in Algeria? What if France tortured and interned as it went, much as Nazi Germany had done in the Second World War? Tillion did not evade such questions. The CICRC in April 1957 voted to conduct an inquiry into the existence of camps in Algeria. Rousset contacted the French prime minister's office, which agreed to provide the CICRC access to internment facilities. France itself was now on trial, and for that reason the official three-member CICRC delegation was composed of non-French nationals. It traveled to Algeria, however, chaperoned by two French observers, Louis Martin-Chauffier and Germaine Tillion.

For Tillion, the expedition was momentous many times over. The CICRC's investigations were harrowing, uncovering evidence that French authorities did in fact make extensive use of torture, a discovery that left Tillion "shattered."[79] Then there was Tillion's encounter with a Front de libération nationale (FLN) militant, Saâdi Yacef. He sought her out as a person of goodwill. They had a clandestine meeting in the Casbah, and he proposed a grand bargain: that the FLN cease terrorist acts, provided the French government stopped torture and executions. Tillion communicated the offer to France's prime minister, Maurice Bourgès-Maunoury, via the intermediary of André Boulloche, a résistant and camp survivor like Tillion herself.[80]

Not much good came of any of this. The CICRC report, issued in July 1957, acknowledged serious abuses, but exculpated France on the principal charge. Internment camps in Algeria did not require prisoners to work. They were an emergency measure, an ad hoc response to terrorism and rebellion, and so they did not constitute an essential, endemic feature of French rule. France in a word maintained camps, but not a concentrationary system. As for Yacef's peace initiative, French authorities in Algeria took no note of it, and France's war of counterinsurgency continued with unabated ferocity. Yacef himself was captured in September and put on trial for terrorist acts. Tillion became involved, supplying written testimony to defense counsel that spoke of Yacef's good-faith negotiating efforts. Defense counsel leaked the document, which was published in *L'Express*, but Yacef was convicted even so and sentenced to the guillotine. This was in the fall of 1958, however, and de Gaulle was now back in power. He knew of Tillion's intervention and, moved by it, commuted Yacef's sentence to life imprisonment.[81]

The Existentialist Left scorned Tillion's Algerian stance. In September, three members of the *Les Temps modernes* editorial board met over dinner: Simone de Beauvoir, Jacques-Laurent Bost, and Claude Lanzmann. It was in the aftermath of an anti-Gaullist demonstration broken up by a police charge, and the company, all of whom had taken part, were still in a state of agitation. Tillion's trial testimony came up for discussion, and the trio agreed it was a "pile of crap (*saloperie*)."[82] Tillion knew that the middle position she had staked out – refusing FLN terror on the one hand and torture on the other – was anathema to the Sartreans. She also knew that she was not alone in her views, that she had like-minded friends, among them Albert Camus, with whom she remained in regular contact during this period. "I had all of his Paris phone numbers," as she put it to an interviewer in 2000. In that very same interview, she was questioned about the relationship between the two major experiences that shaped her public life, Ravensbrück and Algeria, to which she had a terse and unequivocal reply: "They are consubstantial."[83]

Olga Wormser-Migot published her dissertation in 1968. As the thesis's title, *Le Système concentrationnaire nazi*, attests, she started from the same premise as Tillion, and Rousset too for that matter. The Nazi camps constituted a system. She then steered the discussion in a different direction, however, away from economic explanations toward ideology. The end result was not an affirmation of the totalitarian essence of the Nazi camp regime, but of its ultimate uniqueness.

Wormser-Migot worked from documents rather than from testimony. She was interested in how the Nazi concentrationary regime functioned, and she relied on the record left behind by the perpetrators to tell her what she wanted to know. The archive made clear to her, as it had to Tillion, that two parallel camp systems existed, one in the East for Jews and one in the West for the Reich's political enemies. Once again, for Wormser-Migot as for Tillion, these parallel lines drew together over time. Wormser-Migot tracked a first step in the convergence to 1942, a date that was fateful for Jews and non-Jews alike. In January, at Wannsee, the Nazis decided on how to implement the Final Solution. That next April, the regime also rethought its policies vis-à-vis non-Jewish camp inmates. Its objective, until then, had been to sequester its adversaries and to exploit their labor power. From April 1942, however, politicals were slated for death as well, not through gassing as in the East, but through overwork – "extermination through labor," in that by now well-worked phrase.[84]

Yet, even as the distinction between the eastern camp network and its western counterpart collapsed, on one point the gulf between the two remained as yet unbridged. As Wormser-Migot read through the archive, she found meager evidence of gas chambers in the West. To be sure, the SS had erected a small gassing facility at Struthof. In February–March 1945, a facility was also erected at Ravensbrück, which operated briefly and sporadically. But that was all. The camp system took an exterminationist turn in 1942, but the method of extermination was not the same and never would be in the West as it was in the East.[85]

In the end, however, this distinction too broke down. As the war reached its denouement, the westward progress of the Red Army brought the process of convergence to a cataclysmic finale. Jews not yet murdered were transferred to the West, where they were mixed in with political deportees. The fates of both groups were now conjoined in a horrific, murderous climax, as disease and starvation ravaged populations already thinned out by gassings and overwork, a process that did not stop until Nazism's final defeat on the battlefield.

Wormser-Migot's analysis had resemblances to Tillion's. There is the same emphasis on system and the common fate over time of politicals and Jews, but the similarities go no further. For Wormser-Migot, it was ideology rather than profits that determined the turning point of 1942. The Nazis believed "a priori" in the subhumanity of their victims; they wanted to intern enemies but also to claim for themselves, for the SS elite and the German *Volk* alike, a living space cleansed of inferiors. Wormser-Migot drew on Hannah Arendt's work to provide analytical backup, citing, not from *The Origins of Totalitarianism* (1951), but from an article, "Social Science Technique and the Study of Concentration Camps," which had appeared the year before in *Jewish Social Studies*. Crimes, as a rule, Arendt had argued, had a utilitarian purpose, but not so Nazi crimes, which were unprecedented and defied all reason. They were motivated, as Wormser-Migot put it, by "ideological nonsense." In the camps, the Nazis, "monstrous unlettered Ubus," had created a "universe of the Absurd," and in employing such terms, Wormser-Migot departed from Arendt to return to a vocabulary invented by Rousset.[86]

Wormser-Migot's findings, however, pointed to a conclusion that was far different from Rousset's. The concentration camp was a movable apparatus, as Rousset saw it, of use to totalitarians of all kinds, whether Nazi or communist. To Wormser-Migot, it was an ideology-fueled phenomenon, criminal in its essence, and nothing comparable to the Nazi camp system's exterminatory machinery had ever existed before or since in human history. Keep in mind, however, that what made the system unique was not its special targeting of Jews for extermination, but its determination, from 1942 on, to kill *all* inmates, Jewish or not.

Wormser-Migot was not caught up the way that Tillion was in soul-searching about the Algerian War, but she was well aware that the interpretive position she had staked out had implications for those debates. For if the Nazi camp system was in fact sui generis, then it was unlike any other, be it Soviet or French, "whatever might be the excesses of colonialism."[87] Yet, if the Nazi camps were so unique, did that mean that the perpetrators themselves – the German people – bore a unique responsibility? Wormser-Migot hedged on this issue. It was unjust to claim, she wrote, that no one but the Germans had the criminal imagination to invent the camp system, but then she concluded: "One can only note that the system assumed dimensions in Germany and a murderous efficiency unknown in other situations and in other places."[88]

The publication of Wormser-Migot's thesis stirred a public controversy, but it was not what she had said about the uniqueness of the Nazi camp system or the German people's burden of responsibility that caused the uproar, but what she had said about the gas chambers. Mauthausen survivors knew from experience that the Nazis had equipped the camp with a gas chamber, just as Ravensbrück survivors knew that Ravensbrück's gassing facility was more than an incidental phenomenon. ADIR was so upset about the matter that it deputed Germaine Tillion to intervene, and she did not lack for motivation. Tillion's own mother, Émilie, had died by gassing at Ravensbrück. Wormser-Migot took a drubbing in the exchange that ensued. She was in error after all. But she still remained a figure of mark in the deportee community, shunned by some, but still admired by others, among them Michel Borwicz and the writer and camp survivor Charlotte Delbo.[89]

In the immediate postwar years, thanks to the FNDIRP, the PCF enjoyed a position of preeminence in the deportee community. Leftists of all stripes had for a period sheltered within the federation's capacious embrace, but Rousset's 1949 lightning bolt blasted that world open, sending fragments flying every which way. For many breakaways, it was not always easy to part company with the PCF, let alone with the USSR, but by 1956 even holdouts like Wormser-Migot had done so. Nor was it easy to shake off the productivist mindset, so hard-wired into the left-wing thinking of the era, and indeed, Rousset and Tillion never fully did.

What they did do was to demonstrate that the camps were a portable technology suited to the purposes of authoritarian regimes of more than one kind. The camp as a form and as a system had in fact resurfaced in the Soviet Union, driven by the same imperative that governed the Nazi concentrationary regime, the impulse to wring productive labor out of inmates. There was a word to describe the common bond that the Nazis and Soviets shared, and that word was *totalitarianism*. The camp universe, from this perspective, was totalitarianism's identifying trait, a synecdoche for the system as a whole, and for that very reason, it was essential to be able to identify what a real camp, the system's fundamental building block, looked like.[90] Hence all Rousset's and Wormser-Migot's attention to itemizing the concentration camp's component parts: the barbed wire, the barracks, the blockhouses, and hence all the care invested in restoring the camp grounds at the Struthof Memorial site.

The Algerian War threatened to complicate matters for the deportee mainstream, although in the end it did not. Revelations about the existence of French-run internment camps compelled ex-deportees to wonder whether France, once the homeland of the Resistance, had not itself become a perpetrator of atrocities. Tillion faced the question without flinching. She acknowledged French crimes, but still maintained that there was a distinction between what the Nazis and Soviets had done and what the French were doing. Wormser-Migot too rejected the colonial parallel, concluding instead that the Nazi camp system had been one of a kind, dedicated to an exterminationist project that no other camp system shared in.

The camps, of course, were not just a system but also an experience, a form of life or of death-in-life endured by tens of thousands of deportees, and on this point too non-communists had their own way of looking at things. To Communists, what mattered most was the anti-fascist fight. Wormser-Migot and Tillion, by contrast placed the accent less on heroic struggle than on solidarity and pain. Who stuck together, and who held on? How did the body and spirit stand up under duress? The Communists understood themselves as unswerving antiracists who spoke up for Jews much as they did for America's blacks. The place of Jews in the non-communist scheme of things was more ambivalent. Wormser-Migot struggled toward an understanding of the specificity of Jewish experience, while Rousset and Tillion were less sympathetic, finding Jewish camp inmates wanting in collective sentiment and self-respect.

On matters of aesthetics and form, however, the differences between the two camps were less pronounced. To be sure, non-communists bandied about literary references – to Camus, Jarry, Solzhenitsyn – that were not congenial to their communist confreres. They had novel pedagogical objectives as well, which motivated them to find ways to help an uninformed public understand and identify what a genuine concentration camp looked like. And they were also pioneering when it came to academic work, crafting serious document-based studies of the camp system. But there are striking similarities too. Communists and non-communists borrowed from the same stock of Christian images to convey suffering and transcendence; they sounded similar patriotic notes; and they embraced a common modernist aesthetic, stripped down and stylized, to convey the stark brutality of camp life.

For aesthetic experimentation of a bolder sort, the UNADIF-FNDIR axis is perhaps not the place to look. But where then, if at all? One of Rousset's onetime comrades was poet and novelist Jean Cayrol, a Gusen survivor who had been a member in good standing of the FNDIRP. He resigned in answer to Rousset's 1949 appeal. Cayrol, however, did not accompany Rousset down the path to totalitarian theorizing, but charted an original course. It was one that trailblazed a memory project of a new kind, entailing the invention of alternative aesthetic means to carry it out. To get a glimpse of the contours of that project, a good place to start is with a closer look at Cayrol himself.

3   Monster with One Eye Open

No one, on Jean Cayrol's accounting, had a corner on the camp form. Planned, bureaucratized brutality wasn't the apanage of the Nazis or the Soviets, of this or that political regime. All modern societies had the potential to become concentrationary, or, as he put it in a letter to David Rousset: "All nations are in a pre-concentrationary situation."[1] The camps were an immanent feature of modernity itself, a sleeping monster that had been brought to awful awakening in the Nazi era and might yet be awakened again.

The totalitarian states had camps, but so too did others, not least of all France itself. Cayrol wrote the scenario for *Nuit et Brouillard*, a documentary on the Nazi camps directed by Alain Resnais, which was released in 1956. Both Cayrol and Resnais made plain that the movie was intended as a *"dispositif d'alerte"* or notice of warning. It was not just an evocation of bygone horrors, but a caution against a recrudescence of such cruelties in the present day. France was then engaged in a merciless war to maintain its sovereignty in Algeria, and it was that war and its racist violence that Cayrol and Resnais had in mind when they filmed *Nuit et Brouillard*.[2] They were not aware at the time that France had constructed a network of detention centers to warehouse Algerian independence fighters apprehended in the struggle, but they became aware of the fact soon enough and, in light of that knowledge, invited a post-facto reading of *Nuit et Brouillard*, not just as an implicit critique of colonial repression, but also as one of France's own implication in the concentrationary enterprise.[3]

David Rousset and Germaine Tillion refused the parallel between Nazi wartime conduct and France's "war without a name" in Algeria. Not so Cayrol and Resnais, and they were far from alone. Jean Rouch and Edgar Morin, the former an anthropologist and moviemaker, the latter a sociologist, collaborated on *Chronique d'un été*, a self-styled experiment in *cinema vérité* filmed in 1960 and released the next year. The chronicle is an investigation by experiment-minded social scientists into how the French lived at the dawn of the sixties, but midway through, there is a shift in tone. A dinner scene depicts a heated discussion among guests seated around a table still strewn with the debris of a meal shared in common, and the subject is the Algerian war and what to do about it. This scene is soon followed by another that in like manner mixes conviviality and serious talk. The setting is the Café Totem on the terrace of the Musée de l'homme, and the participants, many of them familiar from the dinnertime debate, are reflecting on events in the Congo, just then descending into postcolonial civil war. One of the company, a young woman named Marceline, has a number tattooed on her forearm, and Morin inserts himself into the action, asking what the tattoo means. Raymond, a young Ivoirian friend of Rouch's, replies that he has seen such tattoos before in a film, and a second member of the group names the film as *Nuit et Brouillard*. So there it is once more, the brutalities of decolonization paired with an evocation of the concentrationary universe.

This dual concern crops up yet again in the oeuvre of Charlotte Delbo. Delbo was the author of the concentration camp trilogy *Auschwitz et après* (*Aucun de nous ne reviendra*, 1965; *Une Connaissance inutile*, 1970; *Mesure de nos jours*, 1971), and she thought of herself, much like Resnais, as an artist. Delbo's work, in its concision and stripped-down prose, in its unsparing depictions of human vulnerability, calls to mind Robert Antelme's, but there are important differences. In part, that's because Delbo wrote in a woman's voice, recovering a range of gendered experiences unavailable to Antelme. In addition, by the time she began to publish on the camp phenomenon, Delbo had been out of the Communist Party ecosystem for some time. She had been a *militant de base* in the 1930s and a party aide during the Occupation. At Auschwitz, however, she lost faith, disillusioned by the "privileged" situation of party hierarchs like Marie-Claude Vaillant-Couturier. It was harder for her to give up on the Soviet Union, but she did that too in the wake of the Soviet invasion of Hungary in 1956. Such sentiments of disaffection are evident everywhere in Delbo's writings, but even as an ex-Communist, she remained committed to the Left, and there is no better proof of that than her resolute opposition to the war in Algeria. Jarring references to the war are scattered here and there in *Auschwitz et après*, and indeed the war itself was the subject of Delbo's very first publication, *Les Belles Lettres* (1961).

In such works, the relationship between past and present is far from a simple one. The Deportation, of course, has lessons to teach contemporaries, and "Never again!" is prime among them, but the train of thought at times travels in the opposite direction, present-day reflections on colonialism dredging up memories of the Nazi camps. There was a movement to and fro between the two sets of experiences, a complex affinity that Michael Rothberg has called "multidirectional memory."[4]

Such is the line of analysis pursued in this chapter, but with two addenda and a caveat. As much as Algeria mattered to the artists in question, other issues mattered too. Resnais' filmography illustrates the point. After *Nuit et Brouillard*, he went on to make a series of feature-length films – *Hiroshima mon amour* (1959), *Muriel* (1963), and *La Guerre est finie* (1966) – all of them touching on controversial issues, past and present. *Muriel*, to be sure, featured an Algerian theme. But *Hiroshima mon amour* dealt with the bomb and the Occupation, the latter handled with a breathtaking iconoclasm. The same may be said of *La Guerre est finie*, a demystifying assessment of the ongoing struggle against Franco's dictatorship in Spain. Resnais' oeuvre was multidirectional all right, but the memory package he was working with encompassed a lot more than the Deportation–Algerian War duo. The same was true of the others: of Rouch and Morin, who after all first conceived *Chronique d'un été* as an inquiry into the discontents of postwar consumer society, and of Delbo as well, whose *Auschwitz et après* made allusive reference, not just to Algeria, but also to the United States' War in Vietnam.

It's obvious just how close this memory agenda was to that of the PCF, but it was not identical. Resnais, Cayrol, Morin, and Delbo, though less so Rouch, all came to align themselves with the non- or ex-communist Left. From that perspective, they had a bone to pick with the Party. The communist aesthetic line was too suffocating. The Party refused to confront the reality of the Gulag. Worst of all, it followed a wait-on-the-masses line during the Algerian war, a policy of prudence exasperating to a non-communist Left that was choking on the urgency of the anticolonial struggle. Multidirectional memory, in this instance, was not a free-floating entity, but one anchored in an identifiable political milieu close to the PCF but in critical tension with it.

Now for the caveat: the artists under consideration, all of them, from Cayrol and Resnais on down, understood themselves as chroniclers of the concentrationary universe. Their subject was the Deportation in general, not the Holocaust as such. Jews figured from time to time in the stories they had to tell – Delbo in particular handled the subject of the Jews' fate with an exceptional sensitivity – but they were a sideshow to the main event, which was an analysis of the camp phenomenon and its crushing impact on the inmates, whether Jewish or not, caught up in its toils.

This then is the world Cayrol leads us into. It is one populated by filmmakers and writers preoccupied with devising the formal means to capture the dysfunctions of contemporary life. It is a world of fierce left-wing commitments, anticapitalist and anti-imperial, yet also one unconstrained by the rigors of party discipline. And it is a world haunted by the camps, understood as a memory ever resurfacing and as an emblem of the concentrationary possibilities of modernity itself.

Nuit et Brouillard

The story of the making of *Nuit et Brouillard* starts with Olga Wormser-Migot and Henri Michel's rue d'Ulm exhibition on the Deportation. Film producer Anatole Dauman paid a visit that set him to thinking about a documentary treatment of the subject. He recruited Wormser-Migot and Michel as technical consultants and then set about looking for a filmmaker. The choice fell on Resnais, who had built a reputation as a provocative and original documentarist, but Resnais was reluctant to say yes, convinced that the job was better suited to a genuine deportee. That anxiety was assuaged when Jean Cayrol was enlisted to assist with the scenario.

Cayrol was a former camp inmate, and it helped that Resnais and he were already on good terms. Resnais was friends with fellow filmmaker Chris Marker, an habitué of the offices of Paul Flamand's publishing house Le Seuil. Cayrol was also a regular, and it was at Le Seuil head-quarters on the rue Jacob that Resnais and Cayrol first met, Marker acting as matchmaker. A mutual admiration developed that would deepen over time. Marker helped to advance the project in a second respect. Resnais' movies to date had made creative use of original music to add drama to the documentary image, and Marker felt he had just the man to score Resnais' new film: Hanns Eisler. Marker got help persuading Eisler to take on the job from Vladimir Pozner, a Russian émigré who had worked at MGM and the US War Department before relocating in the 1950s to the Eastern bloc. Eisler agreed to join in, and now all the principals were in place. There was even a provisional title: *Résistance et Déportation.*[5]

The team that worked on *Nuit et Brouillard*, as the film later came to be known, occupied a political space situated right at the borderlands between the communist and non-communist Left. Eisler stood squarely on the communist side. He had fled Germany after Hitler's rise to power and, following a complicated itinerary, made his way to Hollywood. In Cold War days, the House Un-American Activities Committee set its sights on him as "the Karl Marx of music," and it was then that he resettled in East Germany.[6] He went on to compose the East German national anthem, "Auferstanden aus Ruinen" ("Risen from the Ruins"), and when he died, he was buried in an East German cemetery close to an old friend (and for a period fellow Hollywood exile), Bertolt Brecht. As for Wormser-Migot, she was never a card-carrying Communist, but more of a fellow traveler and one at that who, by the time *Nuit et Brouillard* was made, had already begun to rotate out of the Party's sphere of influence. It is worth mentioning in this connection how the film was financed, a portion of the funding coming from the French government, a portion from communist Poland. Resnais, Wormser-Migot, and Michel in fact traveled to Poland in the fall of 1955 to gather material and met with a well-disposed interlocutor, Wanda Jakubowska, who supplied them with clips from Polish and Soviet newsreels.[7]

Like Eisler and Wormser-Migot, Resnais tacked to the Left. He was a Breton from a conservative Catholic background who, during the Occupation years, attended the Vichy-created film school, IDHEC. The end of the war found him in the Latin Quarter, and like many of the era's left-bank cinephiles, he gravitated toward the grassroots arts alliance, Travail et Culture (TEC), founded in September 1944. TEC had a complicated pedigree. A number of its founding members, TEC president Pierre-Aimé Touchard among them, had had a brush or more with Vichy-era institutions, but, disillusioned, they turned away from the regime, a number of them heading into the Resistance. Whatever the antecedents of its most senior personnel, TEC itself, as one adherent remembered it, was a "left-wing thing."[8] This was the organization Resnais was drawn to. Chris Marker belonged as well, as did André Bazin, soon to distinguish himself as a film critic, which prompts speculation that TEC's leftism might not have been its sole draw for Resnais.

Touchard, Bazin, and Marker were, all three, associated not just with TEC, but also with Emmanuel Mounier's *Esprit*, a periodical that in matters of faith advocated a Catholic spirituality with an accent on youth and renewal and that in matters of politics inclined more to the Soviet side than to the American in the era's Cold War struggles. *Esprit* was published by Le Seuil, whose editor, Paul Flamand, was also a TEC member.

Spiritualizing currents coursed through the Latin Quarter world Resnais frequented in the immediate postwar years. He himself had given up on organized religion, but that didn't mean he remained unmarked by the Catholic world he had grown up in. He described himself as a "mystical atheist," the kind of nonbeliever who was spellbound on hearing by chance the radio broadcast of a sermon delivered in accompaniment to morning Mass. And via Cayrol, he became involved in a never-realized project entitled *La Vie du Christ*. Cayrol wrote the scenario and lined up Resnais for the direction. They wanted an authentic setting and heard tell of a village "untouched for two-thousand years" where

Aramaic was still spoken. Cayrol, it seems, wanted the actors themselves to speak Aramaic, but never found anyone to translate the script, and the collaboration fell through.[9] Resnais did make one film, though, with a religious leitmotiv, *Van Gogh* (1948). This was a short subject, an eighteen-minute treatment by one artist of another's life, and the Van Gogh that Resnais evoked was a man of exalted faith in quest of the absolute. Van Gogh's last years were spent in Auvers, where he painted a *Pietà* (1889). The image was singled out in Resnais' documentary and lingered over. The camera never reveals the painting whole but crops it, concentrating on the hands, Mary's right and Jesus's left, and on Christ's broken body. The viewer is thus invited to draw a parallel, Van Gogh's agony mirroring Christ's own.

These are just fragments of evidence, but together they point to a Resnais who was far from tone-deaf in matters of the spirit. As for Resnais' politics, he was not one to make programmatic pronouncements, but he did speak through his movies. In this connection, two early short subjects deserve our attention: *Guernica* (1950–1951) and *Les Statues meurent aussi* (1953). The first treats the story of the Luftwaffe's bombing of a Basque town during the Spanish Civil War. It uses a range of images from Picasso's oeuvre with primary emphasis on the artist's eponymous painting. Resnais never quite shows the work in its entirety, but homes in on one portion of it or another – the wailing mother, the terror-stricken horse – to convey the horror and violence of the event, the effect heightened by the dissonances of Guy Bernard's score. The script, read in voice-over, was written by Paul Éluard, and it does not pull punches. These are images, the narrator explains, born of a world under fascist assault, and they cry out an unyielding "no to oppression." The film ends on an irenic note, however, with a shot of a Picasso statue. It is the sculpture of a man, the narrator tells us, carrying a lamb in his arms and "in his heart a dove," an allusion to Picasso's dove of peace, a token of humanity's hope for a future without war.

As *Guernica* testified to Resnais' anti-fascism, so did *Les Statues meurent aussi* to his anticolonialism. The film was commissioned by *La Présence africaine*, a journal of the African Diaspora founded by the Senegalese intellectual Alioune Diop. Resnais worked on the film with Marker and the cinematographer Ghislain Cloquet, and the result was a remarkable and imaginative reflection on the fate of "*l'Art nègre*" in an era of colonialism. Resnais had now mastered a documentary style all his own that combined voice-over, music, and the filmed image, each treated in a signature manner. The voice-over was more declamatory than conversational and the score more jarring than lyrical. When it came to the images, Resnais did not just photograph static objects, but panned over them, the camera's movement imbuing the artwork, which was the film's principal concern, with contour and vitality.

Les Statues meurent aussi was as noteworthy for its content as for its technique. There were two parts to the story that Resnais had to relate. The first turned on colonialism's abstraction of African art from its sacred context, an aestheticization of the object that drained it of life. Hence the film's title: statues also die. Yet colonialism, even as it destroyed one form of art, gave rise to another. The African Diaspora stood up for itself, devising new modes of expression, new modes of defiance: jazz, boxing, and the black laborer's struggle. As with *Guernica*, *Les Statues meurent aussi* wound up with an aspirational entreaty: that the two cultures delineated, European and African, might, in a spirit of equality, recognize the common humanity that they shared.

The film received a mixed reception. It won a major award, the Prix Jean Vigo, but French censors forbade its general release. Resnais himself had this to say about the matter: "At first it was not our idea to make a film against colonialism. But we have naturally been led to ask certain questions that provoked the ban of the film."[10] This was the man – a leftist of anti-fascist and anticolonial convictions – Dauman recruited to make *Nuit et Brouillard*.

What then of Cayrol? It's a fact often overlooked, but he too was a man of the Left. Cayrol was deported to Mauthausen for Resistance activity and assigned to quarry work in a slave labor commando at nearby Gusen. The experience almost killed him (it did kill Cayrol's brother, who was "burned" – Cayrol's word – in a camp crematorium). Cayrol was forever grateful to fellow inmates who had looked after him when he was on the verge of death and made a point of thanking two by name, Hans Gruber and Père Jacques, both priests. He also had a kind word for a communist mutual-aid group, which made sure that he was fed when too exhausted to look after himself.[11] Cayrol returned from the camps seared, a rebel against war and all its manifestations, from the camps themselves to Hiroshima. It's no surprise then to find him among the ranks of Paris protesters, "with an insult on his lips," when General Ridgway came to town in 1952, the American general accused of deploying bacteriological weapons against the North during the Korean War. It's no surprise again that he was such a partisan of Gary Davis, an American bomber pilot in the Second World War turned peace activist. Davis, remorseful for what he had done, renounced his US citizenship and became an advocate of global government, issuing world passports to hundreds of thousands of like-minded dissidents, including Edward Snowden (Davis did not die until 2013).[12] He was a huge favorite among Parisian intellectuals, Cayrol among them.

It is not as a rebel for peace, however, that the postwar Cayrol is best remembered, but as a poet and author of a searching essay on the camp experience, *Lazare parmi nous* (1950). There should be no confusion: this Cayrol is a believing Catholic who understood what happened at Mauthausen-Gusen and the scars that ordeal left on him in Christian terms. Cayrol, as he told it, had led a double life in the camps. There was first of all the life of the everyday, hallucinatory and nightmarish, when "the Beast" stalked.

But, harsh as the Beast's rule was, inmates found ways to push back, to live another life, a second one, more human. In 1946, Cayrol published a collection, *Les Larmes publiques*, which concluded with a poem dedicated to Père Jacques, who had made "Christ to smile" even in the cruel confines of the Gusen camp. The poem (and the volume) ended with a couplet evoking God's abiding and protective love: "My God, you are there, calm and near to me/a tree that shelters against the tempest."[13] Faith fortified the inmate against the waking nightmare that was the routine of life in the camps.

Poetry helped too. Cayrol, like Tillion, wrote while a deportee – in Cayrol's case, verse; all the poems were addressed to "my beloved." These were lost when camp life came to an end, then later found and published as a collection under the title *Alerte aux ombres*. The cycle of poems finishes with one dated April 1944, in which Cayrol imagines himself united once more with the woman he loves, the two reposing in a garden as dawn breaks. They are welcomed by a young man, half naked, and it is evident who the young man is. Together the couple draw open a curtain, not just on the new day, but "on the ultimate marvel of the world:/a man fallen from the Tree and from the Cross/ hands joined/in the ineffable smile of his poverty/ and of his plaint."[14] Visions of Eden and of Christ sustain an inviolate self in the misery of the camps.

It was not just in poetry that inmates found respite, but also in dreams. After the war, Cayrol wrote at length about "*les rêves concentrationnaires.*" The prisoner asleep, as he saw it, was for a fleeting instant "elsewhere," in a space undefiled by the persecutor. There were saving moments in such dreams, blasts of strong color that cried out, summoning up the divine within and, in the dreamer turned visionary, a recollection of "man's invincible forces."[15]

The camp inmate, once liberated, did not cease to dream, but now his dreams turned dark. The sleep that in camp days had brought intimations of the divine brought the survivor endless replays of horrors endured. The ex-inmate then continued to lead a double existence. In the camps, he had gone through the day-to-day in a trance, living a second life – a life of faith, poetry, and dreams – in his head. In the aftermath, the day-to-day had the appearance of normality, but at night the survivor was pursued by memories of the death he had lived through. Like Christ, he bore all the stigmata of suffering, his flesh torn by thorns, his mouth forever agape, not to form words, but to cry out. Unlike Christ, however, the survivor's passion had not yet ended, for, though resurrected, he still walked among men, a zombie, a Lazarus.[16] There were writers and artists to tell of the Dantesque torments of camp life, and Cayrol named them: Antelme, Picasso, Rousset. But who was there to speak of the disquietude of the Lazarean hero? This was a more daunting challenge, but Cayrol had a nominee for that job too, Albert Camus.[17]

All the principals involved in the making of *Nuit et Brouillard* boasted a left-wing pedigree. It was Resnais and Cayrol, though, who took the creative lead. Resnais, as in previous documentaries, made sure that the music served the images, a priority Eisler accommodated. As for the script, Wormser-Migot drafted a series of treatments, structured along the same lines as *Tragédie de la déportation*, but Cayrol wrote the final version (with help from Chris Marker), turning Wormser-Migot's step-by-step historical approach into something more spiritualizing.[18] It was Cayrol's poetic prose read aloud in voice-over that did so much to create the film's distinctive haunting and melancholy tone. It was at this juncture, moreover, that the film's name was changed. *Résistance et Déportation* was discarded in favor of *Nuit et Brouillard*, a title borrowed from a volume of poetry Cayrol had composed on return from the camps, *Poèmes de la nuit et du brouillard* (1946).[19] The film was completed in 1955 and released the following year.

It was a remarkable movie, the product of a collaboration between two friends of kindred sensibility, men of the Left inclined to a universalizing spiritualism. Yet, just because the documentary's makers were men of the Left, does that mean perforce that the movie they made was a left-wing one?

It's important not to overstate the claim, but politics, as we have seen, mattered to Resnais and Cayrol, and that in turn mattered to the kind of movie they created. The very decision to film a documentary about the camps was a fraught one. Film-world Communists worried that Resnais' movie would stoke the public's suspicions about the existence of camps in the Soviet Union – don't forget that the Rousset affair was not that long in the past – and one had a word with Resnais about the matter, proposing a solution: "So, listen: stop by and we'll rewrite the commentary with you." Fellow director, Louis Daquin, who was also a Communist, stood up for Resnais, and the Party backed off.[20]

Party critics were right, however, in suspecting that Resnais had present-day concerns in mind that were of a charged, political nature. An interviewer queried Resnais in 1984 as to what *Nuit et Brouillard* had been all about. He answered in the simplest of terms: "the whole point … was Algeria."[21] What Resnais wanted to communicate in the film was that the concentrationary past was not over and done with. He didn't intend to make the film equivalent of a "*monument aux morts*," which commemorated Nazism's victims even as it closed the books on a horrific chapter in the history of human wrongdoing with a reassuring cry of "*Plus jamais ça.*" "Never again" did not have the same connotation in the 1950s that it has today. Then, it was a catchphrase much favored by deportee organizations, the FNDIRP first and foremost, and Resnais, insofar as he disavowed the slogan, signaled his determination to make a movie that obligated viewers to think not just about the deportee experience, but about the present, indeed, about the future.[22]

Resnais, ever the experimentalist, invented the formal means to express what counted to him most. *Nuit et Brouillard* alternates between then and now, mixing black-and-white footage from the past with color shots of camp sites in the present. The past is made up of stills, newsreels, and the occasional borrowed clip (from Jakubowska's *La Dernière Étape*), and the images Resnais fixed upon have now become iconic: the photograph of the little boy, hands up, arrested in the wake of the Warsaw Ghetto uprising; the mounds of eyeglasses, shoes, suitcases, and human hair piled up at Auschwitz; and the bulldozing of corpses for mass burial by British troops after the liberation of Bergen-Belsen. There was a huge killing machine at work, the voice-over tells the audience, designed for the annihilation of camp inmates, but not before they had been made to work. Death and productivity were the watchwords of the concentrationary universe, and the film breaks down the camp's apparatus of profit-generating destruction into its component parts, much as Wormser-Migot had done in *Tragédie de la déportation*.

Resnais filmed on the spot at Auschwitz, using Eastmancolor rather than Agfacolor, a choice that brightened the here-and-now and sharpened the contrast with a past wrapped in the gray hues of memory. But he did not want to keep the spectacle of horror that the past unfolded at too great a distance. Time and again, he selected shots of inmates facing into the camera: a Roma girl peeking out from inside a boxcar, the fear-stricken look of an inmate in a camp identification photo, the terrified stare of a dying man laid out on a camp bunk. The concentrationary past reaches out to the viewer with a death-transfixed gaze.

Nor is the present itself constructed as an oasis of safety. Resnais' camera moves through the geography of the camp in long, meditative tracking shots. The architectural elements of the site are still intact – the blockhouses, barracks, and barbed wire – albeit now overgrown with weeds. The past the movie conjures up still has the power to freeze us with its gaze from beyond the grave, but maybe, we are invited to reflect, the present is different. Perhaps time has done its work. Are these after all no more than ruins? It is here that Cayrol's text intervenes to orient the work of reflection. The camp monster, we are told, is not dead but merely sleeps, "one eye always open." There are torturers still "among us … lucky kapos, officials who got away, unidentified informers." Who are we then to find new hope, "as if the concentrationary plague admitted of a cure, we who pretend to believe that all this has to do with one time and one place, and who don't think to look around us, and who don't hear the unending cry."[23] With this, the film ends.

It is not hard to detect the Lazarean accents in Cayrol's final peroration. The invocation of plague is a veiled reference to Camus who, in Cayrol's estimation, understood as well as anyone the anguish of a life lived in the shadow of death.[24] And that cry without end is an expression of the camp survivor's – in fact, of Cayrol's own – unrelieved pain, but also of the pain of all who still suffer in an unjust world. The voice that Cayrol's commentary fashions, however, does not shout in anger.[25] The narrator speaks with a quiet restraint, letting the images do most of the talking, and when he does speak up, it is in tones, not of hate, but of a rueful sadness. Bazin, who knew Cayrol well, characterized *Nuit et Brouillard* as "a film of gentleness and tenderness, a film of pity."[26] François Truffaut pushed the analysis further: "*Nuit et Brouillard*, it's the deportation as seen and told by Christ … in my opinion."[27] More than a little of Cayrol's Christian sensibility had indeed made it into the film.

Critics of the movie regretted that it stirred up wartime enmities now best forgotten, but they missed the point. This was how Cayrol answered such charges. *Nuit et Brouillard*, he wrote in *Le Monde*, "tells of an adventure that implicates not just the Nazis, *la douce Allemagne*."[28] The images weren't meant to soothe but "to redden the faces of army brass everywhere, of police everywhere." No nation was innocent, not Germany, not France. The Nazis' victims, moreover, came from all walks of life, from every corner of Europe, and the voice-over commentary in *Nuit et Brouillard*, listed them, starting with "Burger, German worker," then followed by "Stern, Jewish student from Amsterdam, Schmulzki, Warsaw merchant, Annette, Bordeaux high-schooler."[29] Wormser-Migot's draft scenario for the film had included a reference to the Final Solution, but Cayrol edited it out. He never explained why, but a clue is provided in an article he published in *Les Lettres françaises*.

Resnais and he, Cayrol explained, had conceived of *Nuit et Brouillard* as a warning: "In the indifferent sky of these arid images, there are clouds, menacing, always in motion, of an eternal racism." Racism, Cayrol implies, has a long history and many targets, the Jews just one among them. It's not that anti-Semitic persecution is unworthy of attention, but what happened in the past must not obscure what is happening today, when bigotry's prey is not the Jews but Algerians. "Don't forget," Cayrol concludes, "that our country is not exempt from the racist scandal."[30]

Nuit et Brouillard is a documentary about the Deportation, a collaborative effort by artists of independent Left persuasion with an anticolonial objective in mind. It has often been mistaken for a film about the extermination of European Jewry. It is not that. No doubt Jews, Serge Klarsfeld among them, saw themselves in the movie on its first release. That's because Jews *were* a presence in the film.[31] To be sure, the word *Jew* is used just once in Cayrol's commentary. But the Vél d'hiv also gets a mention, and there are shots of people identifiable as Jews because of the telltale six-pointed star they wear. Indeed, under the impact of what he had learned researching in Poland, Resnais shifted the center of gravity of his narrative eastward, away from Buchenwald and Mauthausen – for many political deportees the ideal type of the Nazi concentration camp – toward Auschwitz-Birkenau, where the Jewish dimension of the story was all but impossible to elide. So, the Jews were there in the film for anyone who cared to see. They were not, however, the focus of attention.[32] Nor was capitalism. To be sure, the Nazi obsession with productivity was not scanted, but as with the fate of the Jews, it was treated as one piece of a larger puzzle. Bigotry, backed by the police and the military and armed with all the weapons of modern technology, from barbed wire to poison gas: *voilà l'ennemi*, and it's an enemy, *Nuit et Brouillard* reminds us, which has not faded into memory.

Many decades later, fellow filmmaker Claude Lanzmann reproached Resnais for not making more of the extermination of the Jews, the subject of Lanzmann's own cinematic masterpiece *Shoah*. Resnais' response was succinct: "Yes, he's right."[33] Then again, it was the Deportation, as it was understood in the mid-fifties, and not the Holocaust, that was Resnais' theme.

That's why the deportee community embraced the film with such unalloyed fervor, its anticolonialist subtext notwithstanding. It is well known that *Nuit et Brouillard* met with official opposition, from the French censorship office first of all. In its original version, the movie featured the figure of a police officer on guard at a French-run internment camp, Pithiviers. The officer's headgear, a kepi, left no doubt that he was a Frenchman, and the censor wanted the scene removed. Resnais negotiated this hurdle on his own, obscuring the officer in shadow while retaining a shot of the Pithiviers camp (also mentioned by name), a solution that proved satisfactory to all concerned. When it came to dealing with objections from the West German embassy, however, Resnais had to rely on outside help. The film was entered into competition at the 1956 Cannes Film Festival. Festival rules stipulated that movies offensive to the sensibilities of any participating nation were liable to removal from the program. Well, West German diplomats found *Nuit et Brouillard* objectionable and made representations to that effect to the French government, which had the film yanked. The FNDIRP let out a predictable howl: this was what came of making friends with the West Germans. The Réseau du souvenir adopted a more diplomatic tack, organizing a delegation to engage the government official in charge; a letter was also written; and such maneuvers obtained the desired result. *Nuit et Brouillard* was not reentered in the competition, but it was shown *hors festival* "under the patronage of the Ministère des Affaires étrangères and of the Secrétaire d'État à l'Industrie et au Commerce." Better still was the date selected for the screening, 29 April, the very day that the third annual Journée nationale de la Déportation was observed.[34]

This was a triumph for the Réseau du souvenir, which in subsequent months did all in its power to promote *Nuit et Brouillard*, drumming up favorable reviews, arranging screenings for deportee organizations, and featuring the movie at deportee events like the May 1957 Rennes arts exposition *Résistance-Déportation*. For non-communists in the deportee community, this was their movie, expressive as no other of their shared ordeal.[35] Critics at the time well understood that Resnais and Cayrol had current-day concerns. The film did not console but prompted discomfort, not just because of the upsetting images, but because it touched a raw nerve in an anxious nation still riven by colonial war. None of this, however, proved a deterrent to the warm reception that the film was accorded by ex-deportees.

Resnais and Multidirectional Memory

In the years that followed the release of *Nuit et Brouillard*, Resnais' preoccupation with the Algerian war did not abate, just the reverse. He was always on the lookout for a medium that would allow him a more direct confrontation with it. Yet, even as Resnais wrestled with Algeria, other interests crowded in – the atomic bomb, the fight against Francoist dictatorship. And through it all, despite a widening portfolio of militant commitments, the memory of France under Occupation (and of the

Deportation) continued to consume Resnais, present problems ever summoning up images of a past impossible to shake off.

For a moment post-*Nuit et Brouillard*, Resnais contemplated an adaptation of Daniel Anselme's 1957 novel, *La Permission*, and it's clear why, obsessed by Algeria as he was, the book appealed to him.[36] Anselme tells the story of three conscripts on a holiday season leave in Paris. They're back from Algeria and will return once the leave is over. In the meantime, they wander the city in a state of anger and despair, consigned to a miserable fate even as those around them celebrate. Their peregrinations include a dinnertime visit to the home of the youngest of the three, Laurent. It's in a working-class, communist neighborhood, the streets and squares named for the likes of Gabriel Péri and Danielle Casanova. The parents are warm, down-to-earth people, but the dinner company includes a less sympathetic figure, a Communist Party official who is didactic and ponderous. Algeria comes up for discussion, and the official counsels patience and the necessity of slow-building action, which prompts an explosion from Laurent: "And what about us lot, then? He was shouting: Our youth is being wrecked."[37]

This film was never made, leaving Resnais still in search of a way to engage with the Algerian crisis. The issue ate at him, so much so that he was prompted to a rare act of public militancy. In September 1960, he signed the celebrated "Manifeste des 121," an antiwar petition published in the magazine *Vérité-Liberté*. The document asserted the right of French draftees to refuse to serve, and it was signed by leading lights of France's cultural avant-garde: Surrealists, Existentialists, writers of the New Novel, and cineastes of the New Wave.

Not two years later, Resnais began shooting *Muriel ou le temps d'un retour*, as it is known by its full title, a project that at last provided him the avenue of expression he was seeking. The story is set in Boulogne-sur-Mer in the fall of 1962, a Channel port that had been the scene of fighting during the Second World War. The city has now been rebuilt, and Resnais' camera makes much of its bustling newness. Yet, behind the façade of consumerist France, memories of war simmer: memories of the Second World War, of course (there are shots of vestiges of German coastal fortifications), but also and above all of the war in Algeria. For one of the protagonists is Bernard, the stepson of an antique furniture dealer. He's a strange and disturbed young man just back from a tour of duty in Algeria, and he's an amateur filmmaker. Bernard has assembled a short on his North African experience, a soldier's travelogue with shots of scenery and wartime buddies, which he screens for an acquaintance. As he does, he recounts an event from the war, the story of a young woman tortured with cigarette burns and beaten to death by French soldiers.

Bernard, it seems, was present at the scene, and he gives the woman a name, Muriel. Then a chance encounter brings him back into contact with an army mate, Robert, a cynical and seductive character who was the ringleader of the group that murdered Muriel. Robert tries to pressure Bernard back into the cruel camaraderie of the war years, but he balks and ends up gunning down Robert. He bolts Boulogne-sur-Mer toward an uncertain future, and on that note the movie draws to a close.

One more observation about the movie needs making. *Nuit et Brouillard* had been a treatment of the Deportation, scarred with oblique references to the Algerian war, but in *Muriel*, the relationship is reversed. Here, the Algerian war is preeminent, and it is the Deportation that lingers on the margins. Remember that Cayrol authored the screenplay, and then think about the "impossible return" that the film's title speaks of. Is it just Algeria that Cayrol, the camp revenant, has in mind? How about Bernard, for that matter, who bears more than a passing resemblance to Cayrol's idea of the Lazarean hero, a survivor bearing up under memories of an unspeakable past?

It was not just Algeria that nagged at Resnais' imagination. He took up the subject of the atomic bomb in *Hiroshima mon amour* (1959) and that of the Spanish Civil War in *La Guerre est finie* (1966). The deportation experience did not figure in a prominent way in either film, and yet in both, as in *Muriel*, the Deportation hovered, a spectral presence.

In the case of *Hiroshima mon amour*, the deportation connection is easy to spot. This was the first film Resnais made after *Nuit et Brouillard*, and it was commissioned by the same producer, Anatole Dauman. Dauman envisioned a documentary on the atomic bomb, but that's not what he got.[38] The reason for that has in part to do with Resnais' collaborator on the project, Marguerite Duras, who scripted the screenplay. Duras was an ex-party member, once married to and now divorced from the camp survivor Robert Antelme, and it merits a mention how Resnais ended up partnering with her in the first place. He had tried working with Chris Marker but hit an impasse. Dauman proposed the novelist Françoise Sagan as an alternative, and it was then that Resnais thought of Duras, author of *Moderato Cantabile*, a New Novel he had read and admired. Resnais didn't know Duras, however, but was able to make contact through a mutual acquaintance, none other than Olga Wormser-Migot.[39]

On the matter of the movie itself, it was a risk-taking venture in many ways, avant-garde in theme as well as in execution. It was shown at Cannes in 1959 but not included in the regular prize competition, lest it offend American sensibilities.[40] The subject was the incineration of Hiroshima after all, and the film does not spare the viewer awful scenes that document the toxic effects of atomic radiation on the human body. Yet the movie is also the story of a love affair, which interlaces material on the bomb with scenes of erotic intimacy, a juxtaposition built into the movie's very title. The principals are a Japanese man and a French actress come to Hiroshima to make a peace movie. Both are married to other people, and both are weighed down by memories of the war. He was a soldier from Hiroshima, stationed away from his hometown when the bomb that reduced his entire family to ash was dropped; she had a relationship with a German soldier, an Occupier – the film does not make it easier for audiences by specifying that he was a "good German" – and after the Liberation she is punished for it. [41]

There is much here to shock the conventional, 1950s moviegoer, first of all the film's depiction of lovemaking, naked bodies intertwined, between an Asian man and a European woman. Even more daring is the film's sympathetic treatment of a romance, set in wartime France, between a French woman and a German soldier. Resnais raises the stakes yet higher, by implying a parallel between the French woman's fate and that of concentration camp inmates. At the Liberation, her head is shaven, and her family confines her to a basement. There she claws the walls, bringing to mind a scene from *Nuit et Brouillard* that depicts a gas chamber ceiling scored by the nails of suffocating victims desperate to escape.[42] And as in *Nuit et Brouillard*, Resnais experimented in film technique, using flashbacks to explore how present-day gestures and events conjured up scenes from a supposedly buried past.

La Guerre est finie has no thematic connection to the Deportation, but note who Resnais' collaborator on the film was: Jorge Semprun, a camp survivor. The fact of Semprun's participation poses an obvious question: How was it that the two men came to work together, Resnais the leftist dissident and Semprun the Communist, who at last sighting was supposed to have snitched on Antelme to PCF higher-ups? In two key respects, the Semprun of the mid-1960s was no longer the obedient party militant he had been in the early postwar years. First, he was no longer a Communist. He had joined the Partido comunista de España (PCE) as a teenager in 1942 and was deported to Buchenwald two years later for Resistance activities. There Semprun took part in the communist-led Buchenwald uprising, which helps account for the depth of his party loyalties. Yet that attachment flagged with time. In 1956, the PCE chief in Paris, Santiago Carrillo, sent Semprun on a mission to the Eastern bloc to argue with party officials, among them Dolores Ibárruri (better known as La Pasionaria), on a point of party strategy. To no avail. Then in 1961, Semprun was dispatched to Madrid on an underground assignment. It was futile work, and it seems that he spent as much time writing as agitating. A reading of Solzhenitsyn's *A Day in the Life of Ivan Denisovich* two years later brought Semprun to a turning point. The text made such an impression in part because one of the novel's minor characters, Klevshin, had, like Semprun himself, spent time in Buchenwald. For Klevshin, however, the end of the war did not spell liberation but transfer to the Gulag, an itinerary, even if fictional, that leveled Semprun's already crumbling party faith. He was excluded from the PCE three years later.[43]

In the meantime, Semprun had become an author, a second major change in life course. All that time as a clandestine operative in Madrid had not in fact been wasted. Semprun set to work on a fictionalized account of his own concentrationary experience, which was published in French in 1963 under the title *Le Grand Voyage*. It tells of a prisoner's train ride en route to a concentration camp and of events that took place before and after. The convoy passes through Trier, German territory, where it is pelted with stones by a young boy who abuses the prisoners with shouts of "*Schufte*" and "*Bandieten*." The incident prompts the narrator, Gérard, to a boldface profession of faith: "He threw a stone at us because it was necessary for the alienated and mystified society in which he had grown up to throw a stone at us. For we are the potential negation of that society, of that historically conditioned apparatus of exploitation which is today the German nation." Such rhetorical boiler-plate leaves no doubt as to Semprun's communist politics. On the whole, though, he uses more subtle means to make known where he stands. In one telling vignette, it is evening, and the heat in the overcrowded transport has become unbearable, causing prisoners to collapse and rousing a dangerous panic. Yet, as Semprun writes, "there is always someone who rises out of the mass of anonymous voices to say what needs to be done." An unknown comrade instructs the others to urinate into an empty jam jar and then soak rags in the piss. Chilled by the night air, the rags become cold compresses, effective in reviving those who have fainted. The quick thinking of the ordinary man, the solidarity of the mass, these are the qualities that save the situation and, more than that, portend a better world in the future, a "classless society."[44]

There are moments in the text, however, when Semprun strikes a less orthodox note. The narrator is a Spaniard, and not for him the usual gestures of French patriotism. He recalls the return to France after the camp's liberation and how the prisoners, as the French border was crossed, broke into a joyous "Marseillaise," but he would not take part. The *patrie* was an overrated thing. As miserable as Gérard's train ride is, moreover, he knows that it is yet more miserable for others, for Jews who are tight-packed in a way politicals are not. Jews are indeed an inescapable presence in the novel. Gérard is oppressed by a nightmarish memory of a group of Jewish children, just arrived at the camp, set upon and shredded by SS dogs. Then there is Gérard's comrade in the Resistance, Hans. He is Jewish and is killed fighting a rearguard battle that will allow others to escape. He explains to a comrade why he has chosen a path that will lead to certain death. "I don't want to die a Jew's death," he says, meaning by that the passive death of a victim.[45] One last story: Semprun's narrator survives the camps, and like Semprun himself, becomes an underground operative. The story is recounted by the train-riding narrator as a flash-forward. It is set in Franco's Spain sometime after the war, and Alfredo, a friend of the narrator, has been captured. Will Alfredo be able to withstand torture? The narrator remembers an earlier moment when Alfredo and he had talked over a book together, Henri Alleg's *La Question* (1958), an exposé of France's use of torture in the Algerian War. They had wondered how they would hold up under physical pressure, and now Alfredo is being put to the test. In a single scene, three sets of experiences are compressed: the Deportation, the Algerian War, and the fight against Spanish fascism.[46]

It was an ensemble of commitments bound to appeal to a man of the independent Left like Resnais, and even more appealing must have been the book's overall design. The story of the train ride is told in an unfolding present, but there are also scenes from before and after. The convoy's ultimate destination is unknown to the prisoners, though a farmer in a scene set in the postwar reveals it to have been "Buckenval." Throughout, the camp-bound narrator toggles back and forth in time as events and the associative work of memory prompt him. The narrative strategy is self-consciously Proustian, and indeed, the narrator spends his first night on the train trying to reconstruct Proust's *Du Côté de chez Swann*.[47]

For Resnais, an artist of memory, this must have settled the matter. He read *Le Grand Voyage* and was so taken with it that he approached Semprun in 1964 about working together. They discussed Greece and Vietnam as possible subjects and then hit on the Spanish Civil War.[48] The film that resulted, *La Guerre est finie*, represented a long good-bye to a memory-charged past, a farewell to Communism. Resnais, as ever, experimented in formal terms, using flashbacks but also flash-forwards to suggest the possible consequences of one or the other course of action. The hero is Diego, a middle-aged Spanish militant, played by Yves Montand (himself once close to the PCF). It's never stated that Diego is a PCE member, nor that the Paris-based committee he answers to is a PCE committee, yet he is and it is. The committee wants to send Diego to Spain to agitate for a revolutionary general strike, but he knows the *rapports de force* there, having crossed in and out more than once, and he knows that the Party's strategy is misguided. What to do? Diego's political crossroads is coincident with a romantic one. He is married, but his wife doesn't know that he's involved in clandestine work. He meets up with a cell of young revolutionaries who imagine that planting bombs is the revolutionary gesture par excellence, and he has a sexual encounter with one of them. Diego is no party puritan, and Resnais' film in its mixing of politics and eroticism is no party film.[49]

Diego in the end finds a way forward. He renews affections with his wife, telling her about his secret life, and then returns to Spain, not to do the Party's revolutionary bidding, but, in Semprun's own words, to pursue "a strategy of mass struggle, pacific."[50] It is a tough-minded choice that might well cost Diego his life (there are hints that the Spanish police are onto him), but it is a mature one made by a man who has settled accounts with the past. The struggle for a better future goes on, but the Spanish Civil War is over.

For Resnais, as for all his collaborators, the memory of the Deportation was not a stand-alone phenomenon but a link in a chain that extended back in time to the war in Spain and forward to the war in Vietnam. They all knew the party line on such matters – Duras and Semprun after all had been Communists themselves – but they had moved on. That moving on, moreover, had an aesthetic dimension. Not for Resnais, or for any of the others, the conventions of socialist realism or the pathos of heroic action. Their heroes were nonheroes, weighed down by memory, and their time was nonlinear, the past ever erupting into the present, present circumstances ever calling to mind the past. Yet even as they turned away from Communism, they remained men and women of the Left: critical of a political status quo that buried a troubled history beneath an avalanche of consumer goods and that conducted a war in Algeria that conjured disturbing associations with the Nazi camp system.

Edgar Morin and Jean Rouch: *Chronique d'un été*

A critique of consumer society was just what Edgar Morin had in mind when he teamed up with Jean Rouch to make *Chronique d'un été*. The two men had crossed paths at an ethnographic film festival in Florence in 1959. Morin had published on the Hollywood movie industry and its role in generating images of the happy life to sustain the unhappy denizens of a postwar world where assembly-line production had drained work of all meaning. That's why he was at the festival. He profited from the opportunity to propose to Rouch, already a well-known ethnographic filmmaker, a joint venture, a documentary study not of faraway peoples but of their own "tribe," the Parisians.[51] Rouch, an adventurous spirit, was intrigued, and the two men had no trouble lining up a producer, the always enterprising Anatole Dauman.

The working title of the project, *Comment vis-tu?* or *How do you live?*, was evocative of Morin's sociological concerns. He understood the late 1950s as a moment of transition. Modern times had elevated "happiness" to a primordial value, and the postwar world had created a panoply of means to achieve that most desired of ends: mass consumerism and leisure, backstopped by the largesse of the welfare state. Hollywood had its part to play in the scheme, tendering promises of a happy ending to one and all, its stars embodying an untrammeled freedom that mere mortals might dream of but never attain. This model, however, had reached a dead end. Morin is not explicit as to why, though the ever greater fragmentation of the work process has something to do with it. What is certain is that he spotted symptoms of a "crisis of happiness" everywhere. They were manifest first and foremost in the movies: in the breakdown of the Hollywood dream factory, whose stars (Liz Taylor, for example) no longer lived lives of airbrushed bliss, and in Hollywood's loss of monopoly control over film markets as newcomers like the New Wave filmmakers rose up in challenge. Mass culture, at least of a certain kind, was losing its grip, and people took refuge in private utopias, in the home and the vacation resort. The cinema in turn reflected the change, homing in on the problems of "the couple," erotic or otherwise, instead of stardom and glamor.[52] Well Morin might want to know how Parisians were managing to find their way in this new order of things.

It was not sociological concerns alone, however, that Morin brought to the project with Rouch. During the war, Morin had joined the PCF and entered into Resistance work. It was at this juncture that he jettisoned the surname he was born with, Nahoum, a Sephardic Jewish name, in favor of a nom de guerre, Morin. The Party assigned him to infiltrate the Gaullist Mouvement de Résistance des prisonniers de guerre et déportés, which later transformed into the Mouvement national des prisonniers de guerre et déportés (MNPGD), led by François Mitterrand. Morin militated in the MNPGD alongside Dionys Mascolo, who in turn introduced him to Marguerite Duras and later, after the war, to Robert Antelme, just returned from the camps. They all became fast friends, and indeed, for a period, Morin lived in Duras and Antelme's rue Saint-Benoît apartment. He was present, moreover, at the Café Bonaparte roast of Laurent Casanova, which resulted in Duras and Antelme's parting of ways with the Party. Morin himself was spared.[53]

So, the war for Morin ignited a double commitment, to Communism and to the deportee experience, and the two were interconnected, although over time that relationship grew more fraught. At the Liberation, Morin conceived the idea of mounting an exhibition to expose the French public to the horrors of the Hitler regime. He came up with a title *"Crimes hitlériens"* and he had a rough idea of what he wanted to achieve: an evocation of the camps, something similar, as he later wrote, to what Resnais and Cayrol had achieved in *Nuit et Brouillard*. Duras and Mascolo were recruited to help out, as was a well-connected party official, Jacques Billiet, who maneuvered to grab control of the enterprise. Billiet wanted to rename the exposition "German crimes," but was thwarted. He also recommended tapping Soviet archives for evidence, which proved to be a mixed blessing. The Soviets were helpful with photographic materials, but they also provided "documentation" about the Katyn massacre that laid blame for the mass execution of Polish officers in 1940 on the Nazis when, in fact, it was the Soviets who had been responsible. By the time, the exhibit opened in June 1945, Morin and his friends, fed up with the way Billiet pushed them around, had pulled out.[54]

That didn't stop Morin from taking up a position on the editorial board of *Le Patriote résistant* or from siding with the Party during the Rousset Affair in 1949. He didn't doubt that the Soviet Union maintained work camps, but to speak about the matter was to strengthen the hand of the United States, still, in Morin's estimation, humanity's most dangerous enemy. Anyhow, there were more urgent problems to deal with than the Gulag. What Morin really wanted to know about were the lives of working people and colonial subalterns forced by the bourgeois world to live, as he put it, *"en situation concentrationnaire."*[55] That's what Rousset should have been investigating.

Morin's party commitment was, nonetheless, starting to erode. He was shaken by the show trial of Laszlo Rajk in Hungary. Rajk, a dedicated Communist with a Jewish wife, was charged as a Titoist spy, found guilty, and executed in 1949. Jean Cassou, a good friend of Morin's, made a trip to Yugoslavia that same year and returned persuaded of the justice of the Titoist cause, above all in the face of Stalinist bullying. He wrote about the experience in *Esprit*, and for Morin, Cassou's critique of Soviet totalitarianism carried weight. Then came the Café Bonaparte imbroglio and Antelme's exclusion from the Party. Morin, as we have seen, escaped the same fate, but it was clear that he sympathized more with the heterodox ways of *la bande à Antelme* than with the party hierarchy, and that made him a comrade under suspicion. In 1951, he published an essay in *L'Observateur*, a journal of independent opinion scorned by right-thinking Communists, and that was enough to get him tossed out at long last. The year 1956 sealed the separation. There was an uprising in Hungary and factory revolts in Poland. In a gesture of solidarity with the Polish workers' rebellion, Morin traveled to Warsaw the year following, joined by Antelme, Mascolo, and Claude Lefort (a key member of the editorial collective at *Socialisme ou barbarie*). That was not the sole purpose of the trip, however. Morin had just seen Resnais and Cayrol's *Nuit et Brouillard*, and he and the others made a point of visiting Auschwitz during their stay.[56] The Party had involved him in deportee affairs, and it was a commitment that did not wither, even as he parted company with the Party itself.

Deportee networks also had a hand in shaping Morin's stance on Algeria. He had been a high-school classmate of Henri Salem, better known as Henri Alleg. Alleg's *La Question* hit Morin hard, "right in the face" as he put it. He execrated the Algerian War from an early date, but the position he staked out was not a conventional one. Partnering with Mascolo and Antelme once again, he organized a Comité d'action des intellectuels contre la poursuite de la guerre en Afrique du Nord in 1955 (Resnais also belonged). At the same time, Morin rejected the FLN's strategy of armed struggle, and this landed him in trouble with Sartre, who was a staunch partisan of violent methods. Then, Morin did not sign the "Manifeste des 121." He opted instead to circulate a petition that advocated for "a negotiated peace." Even worse than that, the ci-devant Communist Morin was willing to listen to David Rousset, when Rousset, through the intermediary of Cassou, approached him about lining up the Comité d'action's endorsement of a CICRC initiative to investigate the existence of concentration camps in Algeria. Nothing came of the démarche, but it was proof enough to many on the Left that Morin, however much opposed to the war, was not opposed in the right way and kept bad company into the bargain.[57]

As it happened, Jean Rouch did sign the petition that Morin circulated. He had lost faith in France's imperial enterprise a long time before. Rouch had trained as an engineer and in that capacity was sent to Niger in French West Africa during the Second World War. He fell afoul of the colony's pro-Vichy administrator, who sized him up as a Gaullist and banished him to Dakar.[58] Rouch, a Gaullist? He described himself as an anarchist who preferred Bakunin to Marx, but he was not an anarchist of the bomb-throwing sort. As an engineering student in the late 1930s in Paris, Rouch had fallen under the spell of Surrealism, resonating to the movement's preoccupation with dreams and wonders. He also took courses at the Musée de l'homme and felt the pull of anthropological study as practiced by Marcel Griaule, a specialist on the Dogon people of

Mali. The two passions were interlinked. "For me," as Rouch phrased it, "de Chirico's paintings were connected with the Dogon landscape."[59] The mysterious was what Rouch sought after, and he discovered it in Africa, laid out in plain sight, and he would discover it in Europe too, though there the poetry had to be dug out, hidden away as it was in the folds of a technology-minded civilization.

Rouch found a way to marry the divergent interests that seemed to pull him in such different directions. After a wartime stint serving in the Free French Army, he took a degree in anthropology, writing a thesis on the religion of the Songhay peoples of Niger and then embarking on a series of studies, first of African ritual practices and then of migration patterns. Along the way, he bought a cheap secondhand camera, taught himself filmmaking skills, and began to record the marvels Africa had to offer up to the eye of a knowledgeable and sympathetic observer with a taste for the surreal.

The result was a trio of remarkable films: *Les Maîtres fous* (shot in 1954, released in 1955); *Moi, un noir* (shot in 1957, released in 1959); and *Jaguar* (shot over an extended period from 1957 to 1964, released in 1967).[60] The framing of all three is similar. Africans have left Niger in search of adventure, a better life, or both in the continent's coastal cities, Accra on the Gold Coast (present-day Ghana) in the case of *Les Maîtres fous* and *Jaguar*, Abidjan on the Côte d'Ivoire in that of *Moi, un noir*. The city is a place of modernity, indeed, of colonial modernity. Cars rush through the streets; construction is underway everywhere; and advertising posters trumpet Rolex watches and the most recent movie releases. This is also a world in political flux as European rule gives way to national independence, as the imperial ceremonials evoked in *Les Maîtres fous* are replaced in the later films by election-day scenes and, as in Accra, by a shot of a party parade with banners proclaiming long life to the revolution. Rouch's male protagonists, fresh from the bush, have to negotiate a difficult transition from the familiar rhythms of country life to the disorienting bustle of "mechanical civilization," as the narrator of *Les Maîtres fous* describes it. It is not an easy task. City work is grueling, casual labor in the main loading ships and trucks. Rouch in fact presents the challenge that his migrant protagonists face as a problem of adaptation, echoing Germaine Tillion's own research on the pauperized populations of North Africa's coastal towns.

It's not *clochardisation*, however, that captures Rouch's imagination, but the optimism and creativity of the newcomers. *Les Maîtres fous* is about the invention of new religious forms – in this instance a spirit possession cult – that help newcomers exorcise the ills born of big-city living. In *Moi, un noir*, the film's two protagonists, avatars of a "youth wedged between tradition and machinism, between Islam and alcohol," dream of better things – a wife, a house, a car. Some of the dreaming is just that, pure fantasy, and Rouch's heroes have, indeed, been marked by commercial film culture down to the names they have chosen for themselves. One calls himself Edward G. Robinson, the other Eddie Constantine (an American actor who made his career in Europe). On Saturday nights and Sundays, however, with the grind of the workaday world behind them, they set out to live a "waking dream," joining in a range of leisure activities from a co-ed trip to the beach to attendance at a boxing match to joining in a dance contest, which express the joy and high spirits of youth. Indeed, in *Jaguar*, it is a whole new kind of urban cool that is created.[61] In the movie, a herdsman, a fisherman, and a public scribe head to town. They mean to go just for a season to see what city life is like and then to return. The scribe, Damouré, has a little education, and he does well for himself. He purchases sunglasses and city clothes. He takes to walking the streets with a little swagger, a cigarette in his mouth. And he enjoys the admiring looks of the city girls. As Damouré tells us himself in voice-over, he has become a Zazou man; he is "Jaguar." The film ends with the trio back home once again, bringing with them a hard-won worldliness that excites the admiration of fellow villagers. They are, in the words of the narrator, "the heroes of the modern world."

The way the movies are made says something about the nature of the heroism Rouch wanted to explore. *Les Maîtres fous* is a documentary, a mix of footage and commentary, that purports to represent and interpret a ceremonial event; but not so the later films. They have a narrative arc that tells a story of personal growth as city ways are navigated and adopted. There is a narrator who occasionally intervenes to explain what is happening, but most of the talking is done by the protagonists themselves. Rouch shared his footage with Damouré and the others, inviting them to improvise their own voice-over scripts to accompany the images he had filmed. The movies that resulted then were collaborative efforts, "ethno-fictions," in which black Africans had a chance to speak for themselves and to take part in crafting their own history. That history was not political.[62] There is an election sequence in *Moi, un noir*, and Edward G. Robinson and Eddy Constantine both declare that they have no intention of casting a ballot, disdaining collective action in favor of the pursuit of individual happiness. Rouch maintained ultimate control of the film editing process, and in this sense, the collaborative dimension, significant as it was, was more one-sided than might at first appear.[63] Still, this was ethnographic filmmaking of a new kind, one that cast Africans as heroes and gave them voice as they confronted the challenges of life in the decolonizing city with an exuberant creativity.

The filmmaking technique, moreover, was inspirational, at least for the up-and-coming filmmakers of the New Wave like Jean-Luc Godard, who was taken with *Moi, un noir* in particular.[64]

Rouch took up one more film project before joining forces with Morin, *La Pyramide humaine* (shot in 1959–1960, released in 1961). The movie carried forward Rouch's investigations into the possibilities of ethnographic filmmaking both in theme and in cinematic technique. He himself wrote the scenario, telling the story of a mixed-race high school class in Abidjan. In the beginning, the Africans and Europeans sit on opposite sides of the classroom, and beyond the classroom's walls they don't interact at all.

In Rouch's tale, these racial barriers are broken down. The more progressive-minded on both sides agree to socialize outside of school, doing what young people do: playing guitar together, kicking around a soccer ball, and going out to a dance. Nadine is an attractive European teen, new to Africa, and she is a flirt who encourages the attentions of two of the white teenagers, Alain and Jean-Claude, as well as two of their black counterparts, Baka and Raymond. Nadine's friend Denise, who is black, is the voice of wisdom, helping to clean up the emotional mess that Nadine leaves in her wake. Along the way, the whites learn about the apartheid regime in South Africa; there is discussion of the daily slights that blacks are subjected to in the Côte d'Ivoire; and blacks and whites together debate whether what the French are doing in the Côte d'Ivoire is any different from what the British and Dutch have done in South Africa. Through such interactions, the students come to lay aside suspicions and prejudices. They learn, as the narrator's voice assures us, "to get to know one another." There is a hinge moment in the process, a classroom scene midway through the film. The students now are intermingled, and they listen together as a poem is read, Paul Éluard's "La Pyramide humaine," from which the movie takes its title.

Poetry, music, dance: these are the antidotes to the poison of racism, and moviemaking also has its part to play. Rouch cast the film with students from an actual Abidjan lycée and in an early scene shows himself sitting down with them, first the whites and then the blacks, telling them that he just wants them to play themselves. *La Pyramide humaine* is in effect an exercise in role-playing, a psychodrama, which does not just enact a story but has a real-life impact on the "actors" who are engaged in it.[65] What matters is not just what happens in front of the camera, but what happens "around the film." The movie's final shot frames four of the principals – Alain, Denise, Nadine, and Raymond – strolling together on a Parisian boulevard, now fast friends in a way impossible to imagine had Rouch's movie never been made.

There is a contrived quality to *La Pyramide humaine* and a naïve hopefulness to its conclusion. Even so, how many films were there that confronted squarely the racism born of empire and that did so with such invention? In addition to that, the connections between a number of the participants did not evaporate when the filming was concluded but lasted on beyond, at least for three of them – Nadine, Raymond, and Landry – who would all reappear, still friends, in Rouch and Morin's *Chronique d'un été*.

Chronique d'un été was a joint investigation into the state of France as a new decade began. It blended the concerns of the two principals involved, Rouch and Morin, in ways that were always imaginative, if not always compelling. The film is divided into three parts plus a coda.

The first part opens with man-in-the-street interviews, as passersby are asked whether they're happy or not. This line of inquiry proves to be unfruitful, as the responses are perfunctory and uninformative. The focus then shifts to a day-in-the-life study of Angelo, an autoworker at Renault, and the film captures the regimentation and noise of life in a modern factory. There were complications shooting some of the sequences, as Renault did not welcome Rouch and Morin's intrusions, and in fact Angelo ended up being fired.[66] It may not have helped his cause that he was a voluble personality and a self-professed revolutionary. Interspersed with the Angelo sequences are interviews with couples who talk about the pleasures and difficulties of living together. These are interior scenes, shot inside apartments. The Gabillons, Simone and Jacques, speak of bedbugs and meaningless work. Jean-Pierre and Marceline speak about the impending collapse of a relationship that has grown tense. All four are acquaintances of Morin's. Gabillon was a former deportee and a member of the FNDIRP. Marceline Loridan (later Loridan-Ivens) was a woman of fiery temperament who had been in and out of the PCF. She was also a concentration camp survivor, and at one point, as Jean-Pierre and she are filmed, Rouch's camera pans down from her face to zero in on the numbered tattoo on her forearm. As for Jean-Pierre, his full name is Jean-Pierre Sergent, and he was a student who had earlier been involved in the Réseau Jeanson, an underground network that funneled funds to the FLN, a network named after its principal figure, Francis Jeanson (an acolyte of Sartre's). There is also material on immigration in the film's first part. The Ivoirian Landry talks about racism in France, and Marilou, an Italian woman employed in the offices of the *Cahiers du cinéma*, talks about feelings of loneliness and isolation, all the while in a state of near emotional breakdown. Rouch and Morin's interlocutors are appealing people, but life on the whole is not easy for them. Work is unfulfilling; living together has its ups and downs;

and immigrants face difficulties, which the easygoing Landry seems up to dealing with, but not the distressed Marilou. The movie never states outright that the milieu under the microscope is a left-wing one, but that's what it is, the protagonists to varying degrees in revolt against France's established order.[67]

That becomes more explicit in the film's second part, which consists of three sequences. In the first, a dinnertime debate is filmed. Rouch and Morin are themselves in the frame alongside members of the film crew, and the topic is Algeria. The young are exercised on the subject – Marceline, Jean-Pierre, and Régis – and well they might be, for universal conscription is the law of the land, and Jean-Pierre and Régis are of an age to be called up. In the event, Rouch and Morin edited down the sequence for fear of incurring the censor's ire. Marceline remembers one exchange that did not make the cut, that of a young man – she doesn't specify whom – fielding a question about the draft. Asked what he would do if called to the colors, he responds: "If I'm called up, I'm deserting."[68] It's easy to imagine Sergent saying this, or Régis too for that matter, whose full name was Régis Debray, at the time a left-wing student but soon to be Che Guevara's comrade-in-arms in Bolivia.

The Algerian sequence gives way to a second, this one set outside the Musée de l'homme, and the action at the outset is focused less on Algeria than on race relations in France and events in the Congo. Rouch's friends – Nadine, Raymond, and Landry – are all present, and the crowd is a young one. A question comes up: Do young Africans feel solidarity with all black struggles? Marceline interjects herself into the debate, affirming that she feels just such solidarity whenever the fate of Jews is at stake, and then Morin intervenes. What's that number on Marceline's forearm, he asks, a question no one seems able to answer. Marceline begins to explain; Raymond adds that he knows about concentration camps from a movie; and Régis supplies the movie's title, *Nuit et Brouillard*. The assembled know what the allusion signifies. A tense quiet follows, as Nadine begins to cry.

The next and third sequence shows Marceline, walking first across the Place de la Concorde and then through a gallery at Les Halles. It is August 15, the Feast of the Assumption, and both locales, on normal days so busy, are eerily deserted. Marceline is speaking to herself, and she recalls her family's deportation to "Pitchipoi," a nonsense name invented by internees at Drancy to designate the unknown destination that awaited them in the East. That destination was Auschwitz-Birkenau, and Marceline goes on to remember a chance encounter there with her father. They talk. An enraged SS man beats her into unconsciousness, and yet her father still manages to slip her an onion, a gift of untold value that he came by God knows how. Marceline concludes her monologue with an expression of grief. She returned, and her father did not.[69]

The Marceline scenes are remarkable not just for their content and intense feeling, but also for the way they are filmed. Marceline is on the move, and so too is Rouch's camera. The documentarist did not use a dolly but a car, the cameraman, lightweight apparatus in hand, standing up through the sunroof and shooting from there. The car itself was pushed, to eliminate engine sounds. It was one thing to eliminate unwelcome noise, but it was another to find a way to record Marceline's murmurings, even as she was filmed at a distance. Rouch devised a solution. In the Place de la Concorde shot, Marceline carries a tape recorder hidden beneath her raincoat, and in the next scene, it is secreted in large handbag. In both instances, a microphone, hidden from view, was attached to her lapel, and she spoke into it as she progressed. This was moviemaking of a new kind and one that relied on a combination of new technologies: lightweight cameras, a portable recording device, and the lavaliere mic.[70]

The subject matter of all this invention happened to be the Deportation. Not the Holocaust? Marceline after all was a Jew who had been sent to Auschwitz and lost a father to the genocide. Yet, remember the reference earlier in the movie to *Nuit et Brouillard*. Marceline, in a later interview, talked about what she was thinking as her monologue about Auschwitz was filmed. Lines from *Hiroshima mon amour* kept coming to mind, she reported, and she had to keep pushing them down.[71] *Chronique d'un été* was made in the shadow of Resnais' work, and just as Resnais' partner Jean Cayrol understood the Deportation not as a Jewish experience but as an artifact of modernity itself, so too did Rouch's partner Edgar Morin. Marceline Loridan, moreover, felt much the same way. For years, she kept a reproduction of a Picasso painting in her apartment, an ever-present reminder of what she had experienced in the camps. "The cries of *Guernica*," as she put it, "I saw them at Birkenau."[72] The Spanish Civil War was not a Holocaust referent, but it did loom large in the imaginary of the anti-fascist Left. Not just that: *Chronique d'un été* asked viewers to reflect on whether happiness was possible in contemporary France, and Marceline had an answer ready to hand that spoke volumes about what Auschwitz-Birkenau meant to her. As she told Rouch and Morin:

Can one be happy in a country where police terror, torture, racism, and arbitrariness reign? I am all too familiar with racism, having suffered it myself, and I know that there is no basic difference in the way that Algerians are treated in France compared with my Jewish situation during the war, except maybe a difference in degree, which lies in the absence of crematoriums, that's all.[73]

The tension, built up over the course of the political debates, crescendos with the Marceline scenes. After that, the film winds down. Rouch didn't like so much political talk and insisted upon injecting an element of adventure. Part three of *Chronique d'un été* follows the protagonists, Landry in the lead, to a vacation spot on the Mediterranean, Saint-Tropez. In a reversal of roles, the African Landry is now the anthropologist, and the French at play are his subjects. The material is lighthearted and nowhere near as gripping as the preceding sequences.

This is followed by a coda. Rouch and Morin screen what they've filmed for the participants, who in turn think about how true to life the film's portraits of themselves are. Then, last of all, Rouch and Morin are filmed, pacing up and back along a corridor of the Musée de l'homme. They ruminate on the nature of truth, how it might be discovered, and how elusive it proves to be in the end. A voice-over at the beginning of the film had advertised it as an exercise in *cinéma vérité*, and it is clear at last what the term connotes. It refers in part to the range of techniques employed to get at the truth: real-life people playing themselves, improvisation, psychodrama, the camera in the street, and so on. But it refers above all to the idea that truth itself is not just an objective, but a problem.

Chronique d'un été has been interpreted as a portrait of the baby-boom generation, of young people not that many years removed from the events of May 1968. It was that, but also something more. It caught an independent Left milieu at a moment of transition, a milieu that even as it spun away from Communism still spurned the temptations of consumer society and refused above all to maintain a prudent silence in the face of imperial violence. Yet, the most salient point for present purposes was that it was a milieu haunted by the camps, a haunting that colored in fundamental ways how its inhabitants interacted with the present-day world around them. The film itself garnered the international critics' prize at the 1961 Cannes Film Festival, the same honor that had been bestowed on Resnais' *Hiroshima mon amour* two years before.

Charlotte Delbo

Charlotte Delbo tracked an almost identical trajectory. She too knew something about the communist milieu. Delbo claimed never to have been a card-carrying party member, but in prewar days she had been active in the Party's youth branch, and she was married to a party man, Georges Dudach (executed by the Nazis in the spring of 1942). The train convoy that transported Delbo to Auschwitz in January 1943 carried 230 women on board, a preponderance of them Communists.

The experience of deportation, however, soured Delbo's relations with France's party chiefs, and Khrushchev's Twentieth Party Congress speech in 1956, detailing Stalin's crimes, dispelled whatever illusions still lingered about the Soviet Union itself.[74] Delbo spent the postwar decades working for actor-director Louis Jouvet and for the United Nations in Geneva, and then in the sixties she began to publish. She debuted with *Les Belles Lettres* in 1961, a book-length collection of letters and commentary on the Algerian War. The letters were written by others, the commentary – acerbic and often angry – by Delbo herself. It took four more years before she at last addressed the subject of the Deportation. First came *Aucun de nous ne reviendra*, an Auschwitz memoir that she had drafted in 1946 and sat on for almost two decades. A few months later, she published *Le Convoi du 24 janvier* (1965), a prosopographical portrait of the 230 women in Delbo's deportation cohort. The protagonists are sketched in one by one in alphabetical order, with tables at the back providing information on their education, occupation, political affiliation, and so forth. There is an entry for Delbo herself, of course, but under her married name Charlotte Dudach. After that came the deluge of 1970–1971, a reprint under the Éditions de minuit imprimatur of *Aucun de nous ne reviendra*, plus two follow-up volumes, *Une Connaissance inutile* (1970) and *Mesure de nos jours* (1971); the three books were packaged together as a concentration camp trilogy with the title *Auschwitz et après*.[75] The trilogy was the most personal of Delbo's works, a raw, intimate evocation of the camp experience and its aftermath, unforgiving in its handling of what happens to the body – to a woman's body – under extreme circumstances.

There has been a revival of interest in Delbo's oeuvre in recent years, which is as much to say that for a preceding period it was less well-known than it deserved to be. There are reasons for this. Delbo was not well integrated into the deportee community. She had burned her bridges with the Party, of course, and her ties with the non-communist Left, though real, were tangential. As the war drew to a close, Delbo had been transferred from Auschwitz to Ravensbrück, where she got to know Geneviève de Gaulle, Anise Postel-Vinay, and Germaine Tillion. Internment had ruined Delbo's health, and, once liberated, it was in an ADIR-run facility that she convalesced.[76] Delbo then moved on. A link to the world of deportee memory was reestablished when she set to work on *Le Convoi du 24 janvier*. In need of documentation, she turned for help to the Amicale d'Auschwitz and to Olga Wormser-Migot, with whom she had maintained an ongoing relationship.[77] Delbo's voice was a marginal one, and this at a time when competing voices, Gaullist and Jewish, were growing louder. The Gaullist penchant for grand ceremonials (more on

this in a later chapter) left Delbo cold. For Jewish deportees, she manifested a remarkable solicitude absent from so much of the work done by
politicals. Yet, Delbo was not a Holocaust writer but a political herself
who, much like Resnais and Cayrol, thought about the Deportation in
"multidirectional" terms, as a lens for understanding other, but to her
mind, related forms of suffering. She was a universalizer, and this was a
position in retreat in the late 1960s.

Delbo's work may have been out of phase, but it is extraordinary all the
same, first of all, for its formal properties. In the world of the camps, as
Delbo constructs it, time is well-nigh suspended. Experience is broken
down into moments – vignettes – that do not succeed one another in any
intelligible chronology. The vignettes themselves are interspersed with
poetry, and the language employed throughout is elemental and spare.
Sentences are disjointed, and elliptical. *Aucun de nous ne reviendra*, the
first volume in Delbo's trilogy, features one fragment early on, a dialogue
between a French political prisoner and a second woman, described this
way: "She doesn't have an F on her chest. A star." The political, never
identified as Delbo, encourages her interlocutor to keep on fighting,
which meets with a resigned response:

> Why ... Why struggle because we must all ..."
> She finishes with a hand gesture. Rising smoke.[78]

In a sequence of images – the star instead of the F (a signifier of French
nationality), a hand gesture, the smoke rising – the fate of Jews in the
camps is evoked. Indeed, the unspoken and what the reader is to make of
it lie very much at the heart of Delbo's art. Her poems are compressed,
written in free verse with lines of unequal length, a number of them made
up of just a few words. Each poem, however brief, occupies a full page,
the printed words framed in a vast white expanse, leaving it to the reader
to fill in the blankness.[79]

In matters of theme, Delbo does not always strike out in new directions. She makes the claim, much as Cayrol did, that art has the power to
redeem. After an initial period of incarceration at Auschwitz, Delbo is
sent to Raisko, an Auschwitz satellite. This was a labor camp, and the
conditions, awful as they were, were less lethal than at Auschwitz itself.
The women in Delbo's bunk feel a breath of new life and decide to stage
a play, Molière's *Le Malade imaginaire*, which one of them is able to
reconstruct from memory. Others join in, and the collective effort buoys
everyone involved, reawakening a world of imagination that Auschwitz
had stifled. Later, now transferred to Ravensbrück, Delbo strikes a
bargain with a Roma woman who has come into possession of an object
Delbo covets, a copy of *Le Misanthrope* (Molière once again). She barters

a ration of bread for the text. At supper, Delbo's barracks mates learn of the swap and prevail on Delbo to read to them as they eat.[80] Each woman in return gives up a portion of her own ration so that Delbo won't go hungry, art and camaraderie going hand in hand.

Camaraderie among women is indeed one of Delbo's most heartfelt preoccupations. It is a leitmotiv in much deportee literature – just think of Tillion – but Delbo handles it with a special poignancy. It is roll-call time on a frozen winter morning at Auschwitz, and Delbo's lungs flap like "laundry on a wash-line." Overcome by vertigo, she collapses. A close comrade, Viva, summons her back to life with a stern entreaty: "Stay strong. Get up." The voice is commanding but also maternal, and Delbo responds, retaking her place "in the poor communal heat that our contact creates." The warmth, physical and emotional, that the group bond affords is in the end what sustains Delbo. Elsewhere, she tells of a moment on a ditch-digging commando when she finds herself alone. A deep despair sets in. The kapo orders her to rejoin her comrades, but even so, the sense of hopelessness persists. A good friend, Lulu, steps in: hide behind me, the narrator is instructed, and have a cry. Lulu's goodness and the flow of Delbo's tears – "as if I cried against my mother's bosom" – are restorative.[81]

The persona Delbo limns in the Auschwitz trilogy is not a heroicized figure, but a vulnerable being ever up against the body's limits. Antelme wrote about the camp inmate's unrelenting hunger. Delbo evokes the torture of an unslaked thirst, when the mouth goes dry and the tongue leaden, when words no longer form and delirium looms.[82]

In many ways, Delbo followed in the footsteps of others – Cayrol, Tillion, Antelme – but there are just as many in which she headed out into uncharted territory. For one thing, the bodies Delbo writes about are female, and she is blunt about the matter. Starvation reduces breasts to folds. Hair is shaven off from head to toe, and beauty vanishes along with. So too modesty, for the camp is a world in which all are stripped bare, in which mothers are made to appear naked before their daughters. Yet hair does not stop growing. On a work commando outside the Raisko camp, the kapo allows the prisoners a moment to wash up in a nearby stream. For the first time in three months, Delbo removes her undergarment, heavy with caked diarrhea. The hair on her pubis has started to come back, and it too is crusted in shit. "[I] had a hard time," she writes with characteristic frankness, "disentangling it."[83]

Delbo was a late entrant into the lists of deportation writers, and that too was consequential for what she chose to write about. Delbo tracked the lives of her camp comrades deep into the postwar. They are survivors in a double sense, not just of the camps, but also of reentry into "normal" life. By the sixties, when Delbo records their experiences, they have been home for decades, and it is all too evident how scarred they still remain. The survivor body is in a state of ongoing breakdown. The circulatory system doesn't work, the lungs wheeze, and the heart beats in irregular rhythms. Then there are the unhealed psychological wounds. The women have nightmares, of course, and bouts of anxiety. Some feel that they have died in the camps, and that life *après Auschwitz* is just so much playacting. They fight back, grasping at normality, starting families, but they are always susceptible to fatigue and to melancholy, which drain away their joie de vivre. The survivors find shelter and comfort in one another's company, but the comfort is temporary and unconnected to the realities of the postwar scene. Delbo's portrait of life in the aftermath is one of loss and sadness, tempered by the tenderness she feels for old comrades and by the deep bonds that former comrades still feel for one another.[84]

That same tenderness infuses Delbo's handling of Jewish experience. Recall Rousset's and Tillion's hard words on Jewish inmates' lack of solidarity. Delbo, by way of contrast, tells of an encounter with Esther, a Jewish woman, assigned to the *Effekts* commando, the work detail in charge of sorting through personal items seized from Jews on arrival at the camps. The narrator remarks on the beauty of Esther's teeth, and the next day Esther brings her a toothbrush and toothpaste. It's an act of generosity, left unexplained, as is so much else in the vignette. Why Esther enters into the narrator's life is never accounted for, nor her just as sudden departure.[85] Jewish figures like Esther are everywhere in Delbo's oeuvre – the first volume of the Auschwitz trilogy is composed of forty-three fragments, eleven of them touching on Jewish themes – and they are subjects of unvarying empathy and concern. In *Mesure de nos jours*, the final volume, Delbo includes a fragment entitled "Ida." It is not stated in so many words that Ida is Jewish, but she knows Yiddish, is made to wear a star, and has been deported via Drancy. More remarkable still, the story is told in the first person, Delbo imagining herself as a Jew, speaking in a Jewish woman's voice.[86] As in so much deportee literature, Delbo's Auschwitz trilogy includes a Christmas scene, "The Stuffed Bear," and even in the midst of holiday celebration, Delbo does not forget the Jews' special fate. French inmates are celebrating Christmas Eve with Polish comrades, and the women find ways to beautify them-selves. There is a tree, singing, and an exchange of gifts. Delbo's friend Madeleine receives a stuffed bear, the title animal, and the narrator then explains how the creature found its way into Auschwitz, clutched in the arms of a little Jewish girl. She left it, the narrator explains in the story's final lines, "with her clothes well folded, at the entrance to the shower.

A prisoner from the heaven commando, as we call those who work in the crematoria, found it among the clothes piled in the shower's antechamber and bartered it for some onions."[87] This is typical Delbo, terse, elliptical, and hard-hitting, the poignancy of the Christmas tableau punctured by evocation of a Jewish child gassed into oblivion.

The claim has been made that politics don't figure much in Delbo's deportation writings, and to the extent that they do, that they are treated in a roundabout, allusive manner.[88] Fair enough, but that isn't true for the publications that bookended Delbo's literary career, *Les Belles Lettres* and the posthumous *La Mémoire et les jours* (a compilation of essays published in 1985, just after Delbo's death). The former pulls no punches in its criticisms of the Algerian War; the latter takes aim at a range of dictatorial regimes from Franco's Spain to the Soviet Union. When all the evidence is added together – the explicit material and the less explicit – a consistent political picture emerges. Delbo nursed a deep-felt grudge against the PCF, and yet at the same time she remained unshakeable in her anti-imperialism and opposition to any form of authoritarianism, convictions that were firmly anchored in the bedrock of her own camp experience.

Le Convoi du 24 janvier includes portraits of Danielle Casanova and Marie-Claude Vaillant-Couturier, both revered figures in the PCF's pantheon of deportee heroes. Delbo, however, does not give them the hero's treatment. Casanova, as a camp dentist, had enjoyed advantages. She was not shorn as the other prisoners were, and she ate better. Yes, she died, but the result, in Delbo's acid phrasing, was "the only good-looking cadaver ever seen at Birkenau." Delbo was even less generous to Vaillant-Couturier, yet one more well-fed comrade, who had enjoyed the comparative benefits of a privileged posting in the Auschwitz sick bay. Then in the postwar, Vaillant-Couturier had the nerve to boast how little camp life had changed her. No doubt Vaillant-Couturier had had an easier reentry than most, a chagrined Delbo reflected, but that was because she returned to an intact family and to a lover, Pierre Villon, who, unlike Delbo's own husband, had managed to survive.[89]

It just made matters worse the way the Party was all too quick to freeze out comrades it suspected as turncoats. In *Mesure de nos jours*, Delbo tells the story of Jacques, a communist deportee rumored to have sold out to the enemy. The misery of the survivor's life is compounded in Jacques' case by soul-numbing isolation. The Party eventually learns that it has made a mistake, and Jacques is rehabilitated, but the experience of shunning has marked him: "I can't look on the comrades the same way as before," he remarks, and that was very much how Delbo felt herself.[90]

The Party's temporizing attitude on the matter of the Algerian War just intensified her animus. The PCF expressed disapproval of the "Manifeste des 121." The masses, officials explained, were lacking in a mature antiwar consciousness, and so the time was not yet right for the Party to take direct action. That was a poor excuse, as Delbo saw it. *Les Belles Lettres* included a missive from one Madame F.B. It was all well and good, the letter writer expostulated, for the Party to wait on mass consciousness to ripen, but what would have happened had would-be résistants done the same in 1940?[91]

Rousset's 1949 appeal had stirred a still pro-Soviet Delbo to anger, but over time she arrived at a different view. *La Mémoire et les jours* concludes with a fragment on Kolyma. In it, Delbo takes a hard swing at the Soviet Union as a whole, describing it, using Solzhenitsyn-like imagery, as a vast continent strung across with "an archipelago of leprous islets, cursed places with blockhouses and barbed wire."[92]

Yet, Communism's errors and crimes did not convert Delbo into an antitotalitarian apologist for the Western bloc status quo. She remained an unrelenting critic of imperialism, and of French imperialism first and foremost. *Les Belles Lettres* includes a letter from the novelist Georges Arnaud, who did not restrain himself. What France was doing in Algeria, he charged, was tantamount to genocide. Delbo herself was not prepared to go so far. France maintained a *Lager* system of its own, all right, and she cited as an example the prisoner detention center at Larzac in the Aveyron, which came equipped with all the identifying traits of a real concentration camp. Even so, Delbo acknowledged, Larzac was no machine for mass murder. It was no Auschwitz, a distinction, however, that afforded her little consolation, if any at all.[93]

Les Belles Lettres was a polemical work, and so it's not surprising to encounter in it harsh-toned accusations, but similar sentiments filter into Delbo's Auschwitz trilogy, and the reader experiences them like a slap in the face. Delbo recalls a moment in La Santé prison not long after her arrest. Four inmates are taken out for execution, and the prisoners remaining behind belt out "La Marseillaise" from their cell windows in a gesture of solidarity. Delbo winds up the fragment with a newspaper clipping, dated August 1960, which tells of an "Algerian patriot" who was marched to the guillotine in Montluc prison sustained by "the singing of all his comrades." Later, there's an extended vignette on the evacuation westward of Auschwitz prisoners in the face of the Soviet army's advance. Delbo witnesses acts of kindness: a brutal SS officer helps a comrade, Carmen, lace up her boots; on a train, Slovenian SS men offer Delbo a cigarette. Once again, the fragment concludes with a postwar reference, this time to Lieutenant William Calley, the US officer who, as Delbo put it, "massacred one hundred and nine Vietnamese" at My Lai. Killer though he was, Calley had also, it seems, adopted and cared for an orphaned Vietnamese.[94]

Delbo's work is suffused with politics from beginning to end, and it's clear enough what kind of militant she understood herself to be. She did not side with the PCF, nor with the Soviet Union, nor with anti-totalitarians à la Rousset. Those who stood up against the concentrationary universe, French résistants and Algerian patriots, these were Delbo's comrades-in-arms. She knew what awaited them, humiliation and death, and it is less about their heroism that she writes than about their vulnerability and naked humanity. And while Nazism and the Algerian War stand at the core of Delbo's story, hers is a grander epic than that, extending back in time to the Spanish Civil War and forward to the war in Vietnam.[95] She is every bit as "multidirectional" as Resnais and the others, and from the same perspective.

That perspective has points in common with the communist way of looking at things. On both accounts, the Spanish Civil War is a watershed event and Picasso's *Guernica* an aesthetic touchstone. Fascism itself is an unprecedented evil, and the concentration camp its exemplary expression. And France's imperial wars (as, later, America's war in Vietnam) made all too evident that the concentrationary impulse was still at work in the world, abetted by the hard-driving greed of industrial capitalism. Such commonalities don't require deep explanation; so many of the artists who championed this view had once been Communists themselves or dwelled on the edges of party life.

Yet, there were differences as well, and these grew more acute over time. The PCF equivocated on Algeria, while the men and women of the independent Left demanded immediate action, and a number of them in fact committed themselves to clandestine work on behalf of the Algerian Revolution. To be sure, Spain still mattered, but what counted now was not conserving the mythic memory of a war long past. That war was over, and the anti-Franco struggle had evolved into a fight more down-to-earth and practical. Then there was the Party's position on aesthetics, its preference for the heroic posturing of socialist realism, and concomitant rejection of all art that smacked of bourgeois formalism. The writers, social scientists, and moviemakers discussed here, by contrast, were without exception invested in formal experimentation, looking to Camus, Proust, Solzhenitsyn, and Surrealism for inspiration and working side by side with authors of the New Novel and cineastes of the New Wave. The creative oeuvre that resulted was remarkable: two masterpieces, Resnais and Cayrol's *Nuit et Brouillard* and Delbo's Auschwitz trilogy, and a rough-cut gem, Rouch and Morin's *Chronique d'un été*.

All three works have a theme in common – the Deportation – but it is not dealt with as the PCF dealt with it. For the Party, the camp phenomenon was an expression of capitalist exploitation stripped of its mystifications, and it was a lurking possibility in all capitalist societies. This may have been a point of departure for many on the independent Left, but in time they came to see the camps in a different light. The camp was a mobile form, adaptable to the purposes of authoritarian regimes of all kinds. It might well recrudesce in American guise, but it did so in other guises as well, Soviet and, not least of all, French. The hard-driving greed of industrial capitalism was part of the story, but so too the assembly-line efficiency of modern technology and the ambitions of the Leviathan state. From this angle, it was not just the United States and capitalism that stood accused, but modernity itself. The concentration camp was a permanent and ever-looming virtuality of contemporary life, a sleeping monster with one eye open.

4   The Triumph of the Spirit

Catholics took part in the Resistance, which meant that Catholics, along-side militants of the secular Left, found themselves among the deported. Paul Arrighi, Edmond Michelet, and Father Michel Riquet, all encoun-tered before, are cases in point. Such men left a record of what they had experienced – Edmond Michelet, for example, who authored a classic deportation memoir, *Rue de la Liberté* (1955). As we will see, he was just one among many to speak out. Such narratives touched on some of the same themes treated in more secular texts, but framed them in religious terms. In the process, a Christian understanding of the Deportation's meaning was crafted, accenting the pain of sacrifice, but even more the triumph of the spirit and the ultimate reconciliation of all humankind in the name of love and forgiveness.

Catholics sponsored construction of a monument that bodied forth such ecumenical aspiration, the Mémorial des Martyrs de la Déportation on the Île de la Cité, inaugurated in 1962. The memorial is not a Christian edifice in any obvious way, but it was the Réseau du souvenir – Arrighi, Michelet, and Riquet in the lead – that selected the site behind Notre-Dame de Paris and made sure that the monument was built. The architect they chose for the job, Georges-Henri Pingusson, was an ardent Catholic himself, at that very moment engaged in a program of church construction. The memorial that resulted was understood by all as an emanation of the spirit. Janet Flanner for one (she was the *New Yorker*'s Paris correspondent at the time) was reminded of nothing so much as a wayside shrine where the weary pilgrim might take a moment to repose and reflect.

The memorial has been criticized for its effacement of Jewish experi-ence, and the critique is not wrong.[1] The architecture and inscriptions speak of deportees, making no mention of Jews or the specificity of what had happened to them. Yet, it's not as though the memorialists of the Catholic Deportation were altogether silent on the subject. Michelet and Riquet were enemies of anti-Semitism who resisted Nazi persecution of the Jews. Yet, more than that, as Christians, they understood Jews to occupy a special place in God's design for humankind's salvation. They had been singled out to play a role, and the agonies endured in the Holocaust were but one more terrible confirmation of that fact. What that role might be as yet surpassed human understanding, hence Michelet and Riquet's common use of the phrase, "mystery of Israel," when talking of Jewish martyrdom. In so doing, they borrowed from the lexicon of a man they both knew and admired, the Catholic philosopher Jacques Maritain. Maritain in turn had been marked by the Holocaust, interpreting it as an apocalyptic event that inaugurated a new era in humanity's progress toward redemption. The return of Jews to Zion and the establishment of the State of Israel were certain proofs that God was taking an active, molding hand in human affairs.

From this angle, the Catholic response to Jewish suffering was part cry of compassion but also part appropriation. The "Christianization of the Holocaust" is a term invented to characterize such appropriations, and it has its uses. French Catholics battened onto the figure of Anne Frank, turning her into a martyred innocent, a lamb of God whose sacrifice might yet bring warring nations together. They also used the Holocaust to argue about the Church's own responsibilities and future direction, never more so than in the commotion raised by Rolf Hochhuth's *Der Stellvertreter* (1963). The play, an indictment of Pope Pius XII's silence in the face of the Holocaust, was translated into French that same year and performed at the Athénée theater in December, igniting a controversy that pitted Catholic against Catholic.

The notion of a Christianization of the Holocaust, however useful as it might be, hides as much as it reveals. Jews did not stand idly by as Catholics argued among themselves, but joined in the debate, giving rise to a productive exchange that was less about appropriation than about working toward a mutual understanding. It is perhaps best to leave an assessment of that exchange for a later moment. For the present, let's start with how Catholics attempted to come to terms with the Deportation and with the distinctive role of Jews in the story.

Prayer, Visions, and Holy Days

In so many respects, the Catholic experience of the camps was not sui generis. There was a deep yearning to escape into books and dreams, and the problem of solidarity was, for Christians as for secular inmates, a source of concern. It helped to have deep conviction to survive, but strength of character was not enough. No one held on without the aid and comfort of comrades, and for the consolations of comradeship French Catholics turned first (though not only) to their countrymen.

They were as ardent patriots as their nonpracticing confreres, just as liable to break into "La Marseillaise," just as concerned about the precarious place of the French, all too near the bottom in the camps' nation-based hierarchies of power.

Yet to all such issues, Catholics brought a set of religious resources that set them apart. Geneviève de Gaulle was incarcerated at Fresnes prison prior to deportation to Ravensbrück. There she found comfort, taking communion from the prison chaplain and reading through a packet of books sent by an unnamed source. The books? The Bible, of course, and writings by the Catholic authors Charles Péguy and Paul Claudel. On arrival at the camps, SS guards confiscated all printed matter, but that didn't prevent the circulation of smuggled texts. Père Jacques, for instance, deported to Mauthausen-Gusen, was the recipient of a gift package from Polish prisoners: a breviary, a Missal, and a copy of the early-modern devotional classic, *L'Imitation de Jésus-Christ*. Father Riquet also had a memory of books in circulation. On deportation, he was sent first to Mauthausen and then to Dachau, where in the fall of 1944, the Nazis decided to gather clergy from across the concentration-ary universe in a single priests' bunkhouse. In that company, Riquet came upon a reading that brought joy to his heart, a copy of Maritain's 1936 masterwork, *Humanisme intégral* (1936).[2]

There were dreams and visions too to hearten the soul in distress. Riquet shared a straw bed at Mauthausen with a military man. Together, each evening, they recited the litany. So many places back home had shrines consecrated to the Virgin: Chartres, Puy, Lourdes, and the men invoked each one, praying for a sign of mercy. They revisited France from end to end in the process and drifted off to sleep, Riquet dreaming of "a chapel illuminated by a thousand candles" and of himself embraced in its radiant light.[3] Geneviève de Gaulle was vouchsafed a vision. She wrote a short essay about her experience in the camps after the war and then ceased to write on the subject until half a century later, when, in 1998, she published *La Traversée de la nuit*. In that text, she remembers a harrowing moment from her camp past. The SS, for unspecified reasons, had isolated her from the other prisoners, and she expects to be executed at any moment. She is allowed out in an enclosed courtyard on a snowy day and then, closing her eyes, in a state of despair, is seized by an interior illumination. There is a lake in a dark wood, and she feels herself about to let go, about to fall in, but an unseen "vigorous hand" restrains her, and at that very moment the words of the Salve Regina, with its invocation of the "mother of mercy, our life, our sweetness," surge up from the depths of memory and recall her to life.[4]

There was an "elsewhere" for Christians, but that other place was not an aestheticized space but a religious one. As for the here and now, the bedrock of survival was faith. It was not the critical-minded intellectual who resisted best the stresses of camp life but the believer, "the man who had committed his life, the man of faith," as Arrighi put it.[5] Louis Martin-Chauffier recalled a young Catholic doctor at Neuengamme who radiated a "supernatural joy" that sustained him and brought hope and love to all around, Martin-Chauffier not least of all, whose own flagging faith was rekindled. Belief was in part a matter of individual conviction and practice. Indeed, for the incarcerated, individual prayer took on a special and deeper significance. It was "a soothing balm," as Michelet wrote home from Fresnes: "It's only in a jail cell that one truly prays."[6] That's how it felt in prison. In the actual camps, the intensity of the experience was redoubled. Geneviève de Gaulle supplicated God's mercy, trying as she did to imagine Christ's long night at Gethsemane as he prayed to God, the Father, in a state of anguish about the suffering that awaited him.[7] The prisoner found solace in prayer, and she knew, in a way most free people could not, what prayer meant to those despairing souls who felt abandoned, even as Christ himself had felt forsaken in the Garden of Olives and again on the Cross.

The inner light of faith gave comfort, and that comfort-giving work was sustained in communion with other believers. The word *communion* is an apt one. Michelet's memoir tells of a layman who carried the host to a sick and dying priest at Dachau, Father Dillard. Father Riquet would have done so, but Dillard was in sickbay where priests, healthy ones, were unwelcome. The layman is described as a latter-day Tarcisius, a reference to a third-century Roman youth who, while carrying the Holy Sacrament, was martyred by a pagan mob. That anonymous Tarcisius, Michelet's son later revealed, was Michelet himself, who bore repeated witness in the camps to the power of the Eucharist and the "inexpressible comfort" it afforded to the sick and dying.[8] Needless to say, it was not just the sick and dying to whom communion mattered.

Catholic accounts of the Deportation abound in vignettes of improvised Masses. The site is a humble one, the camp laundry or the wash-house, and the materials are scrounged up: a table serving as an altar and a handkerchief as an altar cloth, a tomato tin standing in for the ciborium and an aluminum cup for the chalice. The wine and bread have been supplied by sources unidentified, and then there is the officiant himself, a priest, even a bishop dressed in prison stripes.[9] The setting called to mind the days of the first Christians, when Mass was celebrated in the catacombs. There was a "compelling majesty" to such scenes, as the faithful gathered not far from the smoking crematorium to watch, as one priest phrased it, "the deportees' host, heavy with so many tortures, so many slow deaths, become the Victim of Calvary."[10]

That sense of coming together in Christ's presence, which was what Mass was all about, was heightened on holidays. Secular deportees, as we have seen, valued Christmas as a moment of respite and good fellowship. How much more did the day mean to believers, to Geneviève de Gaulle for example, alone in her cell, hearing from a distance her comrades sing "Stille Nacht, heilige Nacht." She was moved by the music to a forgiving reflection on the meaning of Christ's sacrifice, a life laid down for all God's creatures – for all of them without exception – from "the most miserable among us" to "the cruelest of the SS."[11] Then add in the Mass on top of a holiday. A Polish prisoner recalled an Easter service at Gusen. Père Jacques officiated at a barracks Mass as prisoners stood guard. The assembled, on their feet, were quiet and thoughtful, the meditative mood turning to tears as Jacques in his camp uniform raised the Eucharist. It is with these words that the Polish prisoner's account concludes: "Jesus Christ is present on the altar. He is therefore with us and among us."[12]

There is Père Jacques again, a presence in himself. Catholic deportees, like Communists, had leaders to look to, not party cadres, but saints, clerics, and laymen who set a Christian example. Father Riquet looked to Saint Joan for strength, the imprisoned and martyred Joan, "poor daughter of France," whose final word on the burning pyre was "Jesus." Edmond Michelet looked to the Virgin, whose grace transfigured sorrow and lifted the burden of hatred from angry hearts.[13] But how many prisoners in turn looked to *them* as men of the spirit, saints in prisoner's garb! Michelet worked in a disinfection commando. It was an ungrateful job to which he dedicated himself unstintingly, earning the respect of a communist comrade who acknowledged in him a latter-day Saint Vincent de Paul. It was Saint Paul tout court that Monseigneur Gabriel Piguet made fellow inmates think of. Piguet was the most senior French cleric deported, and there he was, a prisoner of faith like Paul the Apostle, a prelate of the Church sharing in Christian humility the misery of camp life with the humblest of prisoners.[14] The most venerated figure of all, however, was Père Jacques himself, and for good reason. Jacques was indefatigable in the service of others. He found time to take confession just after morning coffee and before the day's work began, and in the evening, he gathered the faithful around to recite the rosary. Nor were the services Jacques tendered spiritual alone. He shared bread with the hungry. Worshipful Polish prisoners made him gifts, which he redistributed to French comrades. He even attempted to construct a primitive welfare system, organizing inmates in groups of four, each assigned a sick or malnourished comrade to care for. Jean Cayrol had the most tender words for Père Jacques, remembering an evening the two men had spent together. It was the feast day of Thomas Aquinas, and in the saint's honor, they regaled themselves with black bread spread with camp margarine. They then prayed, and "thanks to the intimacy of the Cross," Cayrol discovered "an oasis of peace" amidst the degradations of the Gusen hell.[15]

Catholic conviction armed the inmate twice over against Nazi cruelty. The camps, conceived under "the sign of the Beast," were a diabolical construct, designed to break down the human spirit. Yet, even in that inferno, thanks to faith, God was present. He may have been no more than a visitor, like Jesus himself who, as recounted in the Apostles' Creed, descended to hell between the Crucifixion and Resurrection, but he was there. The divine presence in turn opened a path, however narrow, to redemption. In most cases, the Nazis' schemes to degrade worked all too well. But not in all, for there were men, lifted up by faith, men like Père Jacques, who rose above the muck to blazon "the incredible possibilities of the human soul."[16]

This was the great lesson that Father Riquet took away from the experience of deportation. He had many occasions to speak of what he had lived through, and on one of them, he recalled the train trip that had taken him to Mauthausen, in the company of well over a hundred other men, all crammed together naked in a cattle car. It happened to be that Good Friday fell in the midst of the journey. A priest, not Riquet himself, called for a moment of silence, and then all assembled recited Our Father and Hail Mary together. There they were, stripped down to "the most perfect poverty," as Saint Francis of Assisi himself had been stripped down. However terrible the camps, Riquet concluded, such trials uplifted more than one inmate, leading him on a "spiritual ascent" toward God's embrace. [17]

The concentrationary experience then had a meaning. It was an episode, the latest, in a millennial battle between belief and unbelief that dated back to biblical times. The Nazis were unbelievers who mocked the inmates' faith as Jesus had been mocked by his Roman jailers. A Polish priest, Father Garecki, recounted how he was ridiculed as "black Shit" by a Gestapo officer and threatened with torture: spikes under the fingernails but assuredly not, the officer sneered, into hands and feet as that might allow the victim to imagine himself a successor to Christ. On arrival at the camps, priests were subjected to all manner of humiliations, spat upon as charlatans and magicians, their religious objects seized and trampled underfoot as guards promised to heap punishment on any and all who even so much as made the sign of the cross.[18]

Little wonder that Catholic inmates thought of themselves as primitive Christians, heirs to the persecuted believers who practiced their faith underground as in the days of the Emperor Diocletian. Or that they understood themselves as reenacting the Gospel story with inmates cast as the Man of Sorrows and their Nazi tormentors as Pilate's Roman minions. There were even references to the Hebrew Bible. All that toting of rocks and stone, whether at the Mauthausen quarry or elsewhere, called to mind nothing so much as the slave labor performed by the ancient Hebrews under pharaoh's lash.[19]

The Left, communist and non-communist alike, interpreted the concentration camp as an economic mechanism and the struggle against it as an anticapitalist one. The perspective was a tempting one, but Catholics insisted above all on the primacy of the spiritual. It was to safeguard the spirit that they battled, and what they battled against was not so much capitalism – or even fascism – as a cruel, monstrous modern-day paganism.

Much as the Left's fight against fascism continued even after the war's resolution, so too was the Christian's struggle ongoing. Part of that struggle was conducted in the spirit of "Never again": never again torture, never again a concentration camp system. It's not surprising for that reason to find former deportees like Martin-Chauffier and Michelet speaking out against torture as the violence of the Algerian War crescendoed. Waterboarding and the like were Gestapo tactics, and it was unbearable to camp survivors that the France they had sacrificed for should make such free use of the selfsame techniques.[20] That's also why Martin-Chauffier and Riquet enlisted with such alacrity in Rousset's anti-totalitarian crusade. Riquet in particular was pointed on the subject. He was revolted by the "pharisaical" pronouncements of party comrades, justifying the dispatch of millions to "the *frozen tundra*," there to suffer, as he phrased it, "the same Calvary that was ours" in Hitler's camps.[21] Paul Arrighi, Riquet's good friend from Mauthausen days, died in 1975, and Riquet wrote a reminiscence of him. The two men had arrived at Mauthausen on a Saturday night, spending the wee hours together waiting out of doors. The next day, they were marched up to the camp for the inevitable first shower, a rite of passage for all new inmates, espying as they did the morning star. It was Easter, and that vision, a reminder of Christ's resurrection, braced them for the travails to come. In like manner, Riquet concluded, Christian faith fortified prisoners the world over, enabling men like Solzhenitsyn, as it had enabled Riquet himself, to withstand the degradations of "the concentrationary universe."[22]

Making a reality of the hard lessons that camp life taught meant not just standing up against a repeat of the cruelties inflicted there, but building up a new spirit of human fellowship, a version of the brotherhood of prisoners, yet writ large. One of Père Jacques' great virtues was his determined ecumenicalism. He was a brother to one and all, Communists included, which in fact prompted Polish prisoners to worry that he was too red. Jacques had a ready answer to such suspicions, reminding his Polish friends that the Good Word was intended as much, if not more, for doubters as it was for the faithful. The fraternity between those who believed and those who did not was a topos dear to Communists, of course, but it was no less so to Catholics. Toward the war's end, a typhus epidemic swept through Dachau, almost carrying Michelet away. His memoir tells of a Communist, a member of the disinfection commando, who, in a gesture of friendship, volunteered to attend chapel on Michelet's behalf as he convalesced. Martin-Chauffier had two comrades at Neuengamme, a docker and a hairdresser, both party militants. They made an embarrassed confession to him one day: that they said prayers for Martin-Chauffier every evening. Neither man survived the war, both dying as unbelievers. The two never knew God, Martin-Chauffier observed with regret, but he wound up the vignette on a different, more hopeful note, expressing the heartfelt conviction that God knew them.[23]

The onset of the Cold War put paid to such manifestations of Christian/communist fellow feeling, but Catholic hopes for a redeemed humanity did not falter. In the late fifties, Geneviève de Gaulle Anthonioz (she married after the war) paid a visit to Noisy-le-Grand, a bidonville in the eastern suburbs of Paris. She was shepherded around by Father Wresinski, who was the shantytown's inspirational leader. The misery of the encampment made de Gaulle Anthonioz think of Ravensbrück, a revelation that sparked a lifetime's vocation. She made the cause of Noisy-le-Grand's inhabitants her own, forming an organization in 1961 – Aide à toute détresse (ATD) – to help them out and to help them help themselves. The camps had taught de Gaulle Anthonioz that God's love embraced one and all, that the most cruelly abused were her sisters and brothers: Jews, Roma, garbage-eaters, and, yes, even the prostitute and bread thief who had stolen from her back in camp days.[24] Catholic camp survivors, indeed, did not hesitate to extend the hand of brotherhood to erstwhile enemies in the name of Christian reconciliation. The preface to Michelet's *Rue de la Liberté* was supplied by none other than Germany's Christian-Democratic Chancellor, Konrad Adenauer. In 1964, Father Riquet traveled to Berlin to attend a ceremony at the old Reichstag in memory of the July conspirators,

Wehrmacht officers executed in the wake of a failed 1944 plot to assassinate Hitler.[25]

Riquet felt it was the camp experience itself that predisposed him to such gestures of fellowship. In the 1930s, as a young Jesuit, he had taken part in international youth conferences organized under the auspices of Pax Romana. He experienced that feeling of cross-national solidarity again in Mauthausen. As he later wrote, there among inmates drawn from all over, he came to know and to love Europe as never before. Transfer to the priests' block at Dachau changed nothing. The other clergymen felt as he did, and together they worked to impart more enduring form to a nascent sentiment of Europeanness, creating a Ligue internationale de fraternité sacerdotale. Father Riquet wrote about it to Jacques Maritain after the war. In the fires of the camps had been forged a "Christian humanism," a new hope for the continent, and Riquet dreamed of France taking the lead in bringing that redemptive message to Europe as a whole.[26]

Catholic camp survivors fashioned an understanding of the camp experience all their own. Theirs was a story of sacrifice and redemption, populated by saints living and dead. The Catholic inmate had transcendental intercessors, the Virgin and Christ himself, and they had living shepherds to guide them, none more venerated than Père Jacques. Prayer, confession, the cycle of Holy Days, but above all the practice of the Mass sustained the spirit, even as the camps ground the body down. Yet the experience, insane as it was, had a sense to it. A new paganism was waging war on Christianity, and the Christian, however beleaguered in the flesh, had spiritual weapons to fight with, Scripture not least of all, which was cited time and again. Scripture, moreover, was a capacious thing, embracing the New Testament from the Gospels to the Book of Revelation and the Hebrew bible as well. The end result was not despair but hope for a better future, for a reconciliation of all in Christian forgiveness and for the construction of a new Europe.

Le Mémorial des Martyrs de la Déportation

These were not mere words. Catholic deportees were determined that the memory of the camps endure and that the promise of reconciliation embedded in that memory be made real. Father Riquet stood at the forefront of these endeavors, but he did not stand alone. He was seconded by Paul Arrighi and Edmond Michelet, the three together constituting the backbone of the Réseau du souvenir, which was responsible for erecting one of the most compelling of all deportee memorials, the Mémorial des Martyrs de la Déportation, located just behind

Notre-Dame Cathedral at the eastern tip of the Île de la Cité. The monument is not thought of as having a religious message to convey, but in light of the religious commitments of the principals involved, this is just the reading that I would like to propose.

In the immediate postwar years, Father Riquet staked out a position as the premier spokesman of the Catholic Deportation. That he was a FNDIRP vice-president, until the 1949 rupture that is, accounts in part for his high profile, but just in part. Riquet first came to public attention in a major way in July 1945. Religious authorities organized a grand outdoor Mass on the esplanade of the Palais de Chaillot to mark the return of all the miserable souls who had been forced to spend the war away from the national homeland: deportees, prisoners of war, and the like. A huge cross was erected, six to seven meters high, and in its shadow gathered a crowd of 150,000. Cardinal Emmanuel Suhard presided over the event, and the papal nuncio, Monsignor Roncalli (the future Pope John XXIII), was also present. Priests circulated in the crowd, giving communion to an estimated 40,000 persons. It was Father Riquet who was chosen to deliver the concluding homily, and he did so in his camp prisoner's uniform (see Figure 4.1). The message he communicated was a simple one. He insisted on the comradeship in Christ that had sustained prisoners in deportation, reciting the final words of one who had died in Riquet's own arms. "Never," the man had whispered to the priest, "have I felt God so close to me." "Remember the ties of friendship that bound us in the camps," Riquet entreated the assembled crowd, and, in Christ's name, let us love one another: "So be it."[27]

The drama of the occasion and Riquet's performance (he was reputed to have an exceptional voice) made an impression on Cardinal Suhard. The Cardinal was also archbishop of Paris and, in that capacity, on the lookout for an Easter speaker. He believed that he had found his man in Riquet, and so from 1946 into the mid-fifties, the Jesuit father was called on to deliver a cycle of six sermons at Notre-Dame Cathedral each holiday season. These were broadcast over the radio, reaching an audience said to number in the millions. One listener was Pierre Brisson, editor-in-chief of Le Figaro, and he in turn was impressed enough to offer Father Riquet a regular byline in his newspaper.[28]

Father Riquet's growing stature made him the go-to man whenever the memorialization of Catholic deportees was in question. The so-called Chapelle de la Déportation, inaugurated in 1953 at the Église Saint-Roch in downtown Paris, may be cited as a case in point. The project was initiated three years earlier by Irène de Lipkowski, president of the UNADIF-affiliated Association nationale des familles de résistants et d'otages morts pour la France (ANFROM).[29] Lipkowski felt an urgent

Figure 4.1 Father Michel Riquet at the Palais de Chaillot, Paris, 1945.
Photo by -/AFP via Getty Images

need for a religious site to commemorate the martyrs of the Deportation and arranged to have ashes brought back from the camps for that purpose. The ashes, contained in urns, were transported to the chapel and blessed in April 1953, and it was Father Riquet who was called in to pronounce the benediction.[30] Four years later, the urns were immured in a marble wall, inscribed with the words of Saint Francis of Assisi: "Lord, make me an instrument of thy peace." Geneviève de Gaulle Anthonioz and Chancellor Adenauer were both on hand for the event. The Deportation, as Christians like Riquet (and de Gaulle Anthonioz) conceived it, was an instrument, not of division, but of reconciliation.

It will be recalled from a preceding chapter that Catholics, like Michelet, had been active in the creation of a national Deportation Day of Remembrance. Father Riquet played a behind-the-scenes role in the enterprise, and he made a further contribution, helping to bring on board a prestigious recruit in the person of playwright and poet Paul Claudel. Even prior to the consecration of the Deportation Chapel, it had become the practice to commemorate the Deportation's Catholic martyrs there every spring. One such observance took place in April 1952. Father Riquet was present, as was Claudel on Riquet's invitation. The playwright was moved by the event and moved again when he learned that the rue de la Victoire synagogue had conducted a similar ceremony that very same day to commemorate Jewish deportees. An upwelling of fraternal emotion prompted Claudel to pen an extraordinary open letter to the grand rabbi of Paris. It was not long ago, he wrote, that the blood of Jewish and Christian martyrs had been mingled in the camps of the Deportation. Claudel well understood the heavy weight of Jewish sacrifice. The Israelites, as he called them, using the formal French word for Jews, had contributed by far the largest portion to "that enormous holocaust ... whose odor for all eternity will never cease to rise to the nostrils of the Lord of heaven and earth." Would it not be fitting, he asked, in light of such common suffering, that the living join hands in united prayer and that a day be set aside for the purpose? Annette Lazard of the Réseau du souvenir paid Claudel a congratulatory visit just days later to enlist him in the Réseau du souvenir's campaign to create a Journée nationale de la Déportation.[31]

That project came to fruition in 1954, and much as Claudel had imagined, the solemnities of the day came over time to intermingle Christians and Jews. "Over time" is the operative phrase, because the first Journée nationale de la Déportation was not an ecumenical affair. The ceremonials began on Saturday at UNADIF headquarters. An urn of ashes collected from the camps was transported from the site, accompanied by an honor guard of ANFROM and FNDIR personalities, to the

Ministère des anciens Combattants. The next morning, it was conveyed to Notre-Dame, then to the Arc de Triomphe, and last of all to its final resting place in the casemate at Mont-Valérien.[32] In future years, this ritual pattern was readjusted, and the new scheme became religious and ecumenical in just the way Claudel had hoped for. Now the ceremonials began on Friday night at the rue de la Victoire synagogue with representatives of deportee organizations in attendance. On Saturday, morning services were held at the Église Saint-Roch, followed by Sunday Mass at Notre-Dame and, in parallel, a commemorative event at a Protestant Church. Also on Sunday, mourners paid an afternoon visit to Mont-Valérien for a brief moment of sober reflection. A torch of remembrance was involved in the ritual, following a prescribed itinerary: on Saturday, it was conveyed from the Église Saint-Roch to the Ministère des anciens Combattants for a nighttime vigil, and then late on Sunday it made its way up the Champs-Élysées from the George V intersection to the Arc de Triomphe.[33]

Anise Postel-Vinay turned out for the event for the first time in 1960. She hadn't felt up to it before. Father Riquet, Postel-Vinay noted, spoke at services at both the Église Saint-Roch and Notre-Dame, but it was what he had to say at the former that left the most lasting impression. Riquet talked of the yellow star Jews had made to wear, conjuring mournful memories and calling to mind to each and every one present, the "personal blows to dignity of which he had been the victim or worse, the impotent witness."[34]

Father Riquet was an apostle of reconciliation who reached out to Germans as he reached out to Jews, and it was that ecumenical spirit that presided at the Église Saint-Roch's Deportation Chapel and at the Journée nationale de la Déportation. It is well worth asking, however, whether the Île de la Cité memorial was conceived in a similar spirit. In one sense, the answer is no, for it was not a place where Jews, let alone Germans, were spoken of. Father Riquet had no more than a bit part in the memorial's construction, and this memorial, unlike the Deportation Chapel, was a public and not a religious space. At the same time, there was a deep desire to erect a monument that would communicate a big-tent interpretation of what the Deportation had signified, a monument that addressed deportees as such, whatever their political or religious affiliation. That universalizing aspiration no doubt flattened out the varieties of deportation experience, but it also endowed the monument with a forceful coherence. The universalism in question, moreover, was very much of a spiritual cast. The Crucifixion to be sure is not represented, nor are Christian symbols deployed, but the monument was consciously designed to provoke a movement of the spirit, and in this measure, it embodied in its own understated way the kind of Christian humanism that Father Riquet so fervently espoused.

Plans for construction of the memorial began to take shape in 1953 with the Réseau du souvenir taking the initiative. The president of its Commission artistique, Jean Cassou, had a site in mind on the eastern end of the Île de la Cité, and he won enthusiastic backing from Father Riquet. Riquet sermonized at Notre-Dame, and, as he saw it, a deportee monument, situated "in the shadow" of the cathedral, imparted to the memorial site a unique spiritual significance. Cassou solicited design proposals, and the commission went to Georges-Henri Pingusson and Raymond Veysset, the former an architect, the latter a sculptor.[35] They envisioned a monument below ground level, reached by descending stairs, the monument itself divided into two parts: an open space decorated with a sculptural element – a stele or a statue – and, facing it, a crypt.

Now, the Île de la Cité property that Cassou and Riquet had their eye on belonged to the city of Paris, and so Cassou needed the municipal council's accord before the Pingusson and Veysset project could move forward. In the event, there was resistance. Three kinds of objections were raised, the first touching on the site itself. Why a below-ground placement, some councilors wanted to know, rather than something more visible? Others worried about the monument's design, demanding that the memorial in no way disturb the harmony of the locale, no architectural or sculptural elements jutting up to compete with the towers and spire of Notre-Dame. Last of all, the councilors insisted that the monument symbolize "the deportation in a general manner," and that meant no racial or political references.[36]

This is where Paul Arrighi stepped in. Arrighi was a lawyer and onetime chief of the Paris bar. He was an accomplished man, and he had contacts: influential people like Edmond Michelet, whom Arrighi called on to lobby for the monument, even providing Michelet a list of councilors believed to be susceptible to persuasion. Arrighi also provided guarantees. The finished monument, he promised, would not disturb the sight lines of the Île de la Cité. On the question of racial and political references, Arrighi wrote a personal letter to the president of the municipal council's Commission des Beaux-Arts, assuring him in bluntest terms that the monument envisioned was not reserved for this group or that but for "all deportees, whoever they might be, men, women, bourgeois, workers or peasants, Israelites or free thinkers."[37]

The sources, however, do not disclose how the monument's partisans mollified the municipality's doubts about the below-ground site, but they do make clear why backers cared so much about the Île de la Cité setting. The Réseau du souvenir made every effort to drum up interest in the proposed monument. One text intended for public consumption vaunted the virtues of the chosen location in a language powerful in its religiosity: "Is this not the place where the Spirit dwells? Is it not the sacred Island, cradle of our Nation, the incarnation of the soul of France?" The crypt, it went on, was not intended as a site for noisy demonstrations but as a place of "pious pilgrimage."[38]

The Réseau du souvenir's lobbying, assurances, and counterarguments brought Paris' municipal authorities around. The Commission des Beaux-Arts at last okayed the project in March 1956, and the Commission du Vieux Paris followed suit the following June.

Pingusson in the meantime had refined the monument's design. But to understand better how he fleshed out the project, it is worth saying something first about the man himself. Pingusson was a modern architect who, with Robert Mallet-Stevens' backing, joined the Union des artistes modernes in 1933. Pingusson's version of modernity at this juncture tended more to the suave lines of art deco than to the exigent geometry of Le Corbusier. The reconstruction era after the war altered Pingusson's direction in two ways. He was drawn first of all into the orbit of Auguste Perret. This was a meaningful connection, because Perret was a pioneer of prefabrication and the use of reinforced concrete, commitments very much in evidence in Perret's own plans for the rebuilding of the bombed-out city of Le Havre. Just as important, the era of reconstruction afforded Pingusson a chance, indeed several, to act on his long-standing interest in religious architecture. He had always been a practicing Catholic, even something of a mystic, and wedded a woman of like-minded views in a ceremony at Notre-Dame Cathedral. In the 1930s, he had sketched unrealized plans for a number of churches, trying to imagine what a modern Christian architecture would look like. In the fifties, even as work on the construction of the Mémorial des Martyrs de la Déportation was getting underway, he was simultaneously involved in three church-building projects: the Église de la Nativité-de-la-Vierge at Fleury (1955–1962), the Église Saint-Maximin at Boust (1955–1963), and the Église Saint-Pierre at Borny (1956–1962).[39]

Pingusson's reimagining of church architecture was innovative in several respects. He wanted to tap into plainer, less embellished forms of spirituality and so went back to Christianity's beginnings, when primitive believers gathered before an altar situated at the center of the church sanctuary, not at the end of a long nave. This entailed eschewing the standard cruciform layout in favor of a rotundalike design topped by a dome. Pingusson had no liking for the mediocrity and commercialization of contemporary civilization and reflected on ways to enable congregants to leave behind the base cares of daily life when attending a place of worship. For the church at Boust, he conceived a parvis, a transitional

Figure 4.2 Stairs, parvis, and grill, Mémorial des Martyrs de la
Déportation, Paris, 1962

space of silence, which prepared believers exiting a profane world for
entry into a sacred one. This was an "experiential" architecture, which
transformed the spectator, and Pingusson made use of basic materials
(concrete and wood) and softened lighting (indirect or filtered through
stained glass) to heighten the overall spiritualizing impact of his design.[40]

Pingusson borrowed from this repertoire of forms and techniques in
the construction of the memorial. A visit was understood as a pilgrimage
that unfolded in phases, the first a phase of silence as the traveler
approached the monument across a garden. The monument proper
was entered via one of two narrow stone staircases that opened onto a
parvis below (see Figure 4.2). Thus, the pilgrim, like Dante himself,

Figure 4.3 Raymond Veysset, unbuilt stele, Mémorial des Martyrs de la Déportation, Paris, 1962. Reprinted with permission of the Cité de l'Architecture et du Patrimoine, Paris, and of Philippe Pingusson

departed the world of the living, making his way downward into a space of agony and hopelessness. Pingusson meant for the visitor to feel imprisoned, walled in without a view of the surrounding city, and to intensify the claustrophobia, he made use of "a powerful material," in this instance, concrete layered over with a mix of cement and crushed rock, the rock itself, in a symbolic gesture toward national unity, made up of samples culled from all of France's major mountain ranges. The initial plan envisaged a sculptural element in the middle of the parvis that bespoke the "Calvary" endured by the deportees, and the word was well chosen, given Veysset's projected design: the skeletal figure of a crucified man straining skyward carved out of a stele (see Figure 4.3).[41]

Pingusson, of course, understood that Dante was a chronicler not just of hell but also of paradise, of life triumphant over death, a belief, as he put it, "of which our religion is one of the indestructible forms." That part of the story was told in the crypt itself, accessed through a slitlike entrance between two giant blocks of concrete. Inside, visitors first found themselves in a rotunda, flanked on either side by "two funerary chapels." The chapels themselves were intended to house the ashes of deportees in triangular-shaped recesses and were illuminated by "a white shaft of light" piercing through "narrow windows high up." The

Figure 4.4 Crypt, Mémorial des Martyrs de la Déportation, Paris, 1962. Photo by Godong/Universal Images Group via Getty Images

"starkness" of the setting recalled nothing so much as "the cells through which the prisoners passed before death claimed them," and yet death never claimed them entirely, for in the middle of the rotunda flickered an eternal flame – in fact a small, electric bulb – that symbolized life never-ending, much as did the eternal flame under the Arc de Triomphe.[42]

Last of all, and this was supposed to be the final stop on the pilgrim's journey, a third gallery extended out from the rotunda, deeper into the crypt. At the front were interred the remains of an unknown deportee (the national cemetery at Struthof supplied the body), and at the back burned a light (see Figure 4.4). The gallery was lined on either side by rows of glowing crystals, 200,000 in all, each one supposed to represent the life of a deportee. The gallery was thus bathed in a penumbral light like a "*chapelle ardente.*" The phrase is Pingusson's own.[43]

The monument featured one last design element: inscriptions, nine in all, each a quotation. Pingusson himself is said to have designed the distinctive, cuneiformlike font. The range of sources is telling, expressive of a self-conscious political inclusiveness. Louis Aragon and Paul Éluard were cited, as was Father Augustin Maydieu. Maydieu was a Dominican priest and a complicated choice, for he had been associated, in the first years of the Occupation, with a Vichy-sponsored organization, the regime's leadership school at Uriage. On the other side of the ledger, Maydieu ended the war a résistant, spending time in a French prison for Resistance activities, and, in addition to that, he was a friend of Edmond Michelet's.[44] All the nation's mountain ranges had made a contribution to the memorial and so too the four corners of the Resistance.[45]

The monument was built almost as Pingusson wanted it, but not quite. The relevant municipal authorities had given the project a green light, but the central state administration still had a say in the matter. The monument's riverside locale impinged on the state's fluvial domain, and so Arrighi had to petition the relevant ministry, in this case the Ministère des Travaux publics, for authorization to proceed.[46] The minister made no fuss at all. The real trouble came from another quarter, the Ministère de l'Intérieur. The Commission centrale des Monuments commémoratifs, attached to the ministry, had a right to pass judgment, and there was much about Pingusson's project that the commissioners did not like, above all Veysset's stele, which was judged too "modern."[47]

The commission's opposition was finessed, thanks to a mix of pressure and concession. The Réseau du souvenir had an ally in the Seine prefecture, Richard Pouzet, himself a former concentration camp inmate who was, like Arrighi, a Mauthausen survivor. Pouzet did what he could to help out, providing insider advice and a backdoor conduit to the minister of the interior. Just as consequential was Edmond Michelet's intervention. De Gaulle returned to power in the spring of 1958 and named Michelet minister of veterans' affairs. Arrighi did not delay in soliciting Michelet's aid to break up the bureaucratic logjam, and Michelet, of course, obliged.[48]

The Réseau du souvenir made an effective end-run around the Commission centrale des Monuments commémoratifs, appealing to higher-ups, but it also made a key concession. Arrighi and Cassou agreed to shelve Veysset's sculpture, and Pingusson was prevailed on to go along. This was in 1958. There was talk of substituting a granite bloc with an inscription – Vercors' name was mentioned in this connection – but that proposal went nowhere. Pingusson worried that the parvis was now just too bare, "an incomprehensible void," but a solution was found. He had planned a narrow opening, a kind of peephole or judas window, at the eastern tip of the parvis, which allowed a glimpse of the passing Seine. This was covered over with a metal grill, a shrewd choice that enhanced the space's prisonlike effect.[49]

Once Pingusson had backed off on the Veysset stele, the commission's opposition, already softened by hard lobbying, melted away. It gave its go-ahead to the architect's plan in June 1958, removing the last administrative hurdle to the memorial's construction. All that remained was to get started and, more seriously, to settle the matter of funding.

It's at this point that the story takes a more overtly political turn. For the laying of the first stone, Arrighi went right to the top, writing a letter in July to the new head of state, asking de Gaulle himself to perform the honor. The General begged off with the plausible excuse that he was too busy. The Réseau du souvenir then turned to Geneviève de Gaulle Anthonioz, a fitting choice, not just because of the name she bore, but also because she was herself a onetime deportee and a woman of undisputed spiritual gravitas.[50] Ground was at last broken on the project in 1960. As for funding, the Réseau du souvenir made a valiant effort to solicit the needed money from former deportees and from deportee organizations, but the results proved inadequate. The ever-helpful Pouzet suggested that Réseau du souvenir representatives solicit the state's aid. Go knocking on Michelet's door, Pouzet advised, and Arrighi did just that, arranging a meeting in 1959 with the minister of veterans' affairs, though by then the minister in question was no longer Michelet but Michelet's successor, Raymond Triboulet. Triboulet, however, was no stranger, having belonged to the same Resistance network, Ceux de la Résistance, as Arrighi. The meeting was a success. All assembled agreed to launch a national subscription, which meant that the state was now prepared to bestow its official seal of approval on the Réseau du souvenir's fund-raising activities. A state decree of December 1960 announced the campaign, and the next month, a committee was constituted under the "high patronage" of General de Gaulle. Triboulet presided and Michelet and Arrighi were named vice-presidents.[51]

Now controversy began to swirl. The FINDIRP had not been invited to take part in the national fund-raising committee, nor, when the monument was inaugurated in April 1962, was it invited to take part in the ceremony, presided by General de Gaulle himself. Arrighi had a lame excuse. It was true, Arrighi conceded, that the FNDIRP as an organization had not been included, but members of affiliated amicales were, and so the FNDIRP was a virtual invitee. That wasn't much consolation, and *Le Patriote résistant* seized the occasion of the memorial's unveiling to vent. De Gaulle visited the monument, descending alone into the crypt; he made no speech, and the whole event took but a few minutes. The ceremony had a furtive character in the FNDIRP's judgment, as though it were an embarrassment. Maybe, the *Le Patriote résistant* insinuated, de Gaulle wanted to keep it all hush-hush so as not to offend his friends in Bonn. This monument spoke for a "certain Resistance," but not for the Resistance as a whole.[52]

The memorial, looked at from the moment of its completion, might appear much as the militants of the FNDIRP saw it, as a Gaullist edifice, enmeshed in the ongoing Cold War struggles of the day.[53] The story told here, however, begins at the beginning, in the early 1950s, when de Gaulle was not on the scene, and from this angle, it is the monument's religious dimension that is most compelling. The principals involved were almost all practicing Catholics, and when obstacles arose, it was to a network of comrades anchored in the Catholic Resistance – former deportees like Michelet – that the organizers turned for help. As for the monument itself, its major architectural elements – the crypt, the chapels, the parvis – were all of a religious character. Even the rotunda shape of the crypt's interior takes on a Christian significance in light of the architect Pingusson's predilection for Church-in-the-round design. For him, indeed, a visit to the memorial was intended to be a spiritual exercise. The spectator plumbed first the depths of the martyrs' torment, then to be uplifted by the promise of life everlasting as incarnated in the eternal flame. Last of all was the pilgrimage's terminus ad quem: the long corridor stretching back beyond the grave of the unknown deportee. The panels of light crystals on either side burned like so many thousands of memorial candles. Janet Flanner got it right. This was "holy architecture, like the small wayside chapels built in earlier times of still intense medieval belief."[54]

It was also modern architecture. Pingusson looked to a deep Christian past for inspiration, but a Christian past reinterpreted to suit modern needs: hence the materials used, concrete and cement, and hence the design, heavy on geometry and trimmed down to bare essentials. Indeed, this monument, unlike so many Great War memorials, was stripped of all human figuration. This was, to be sure, very much a last-minute decision. Veysset's stele remained a part of the plan until 1958, and even afterward Pingusson hoped to include a sculptural element. In 1961, he commissioned the sculptor Roger Desserprit to execute a bronze statue of a skeletal deportee, which was then placed atop the unknown martyr's tomb in time for the monument's 1962 inauguration. The result was unfortunate, and the statue soon vanished.[55] Thus, if more by happenstance than design, the starkness of the monument remained unrelieved by any human form, ratcheting up its weight and power. At the same time, with the scrapping of Veysset's stele, the monument was divested of its most Christian referent, the crucified deportee, and this in turn played to the advantage of its universalizing ambitions, for this was supposed to be above all a national memorial. The stone came from all over France, the quotations from all major currents of the Resistance. Little surprise then that the memorial, no sooner completed, was accorded an honored place in the ceremonials accompanying the annual Journée nationale de la Déportation. From 1963 on, the Saturday-night vigil around the torch of remembrance no longer took place at the Ministère des anciens

Combattants but at the crypt of the deportation monument on the Île de la Cité.[56] The memorial then carved out a national space and a sacred one that was almost but not quite Christian, where deportees of all persuasions might come together to mourn and to remember.

Of all persuasions? The FNDIRP didn't think so, and Jews might have felt the same. For reasons already adumbrated, they were passed over in silence at the Île de la Cité monument. Then again, Jews did have a monument of their own, the Tombeau du martyr Juif inconnu, completed in 1956 (discussed in the next chapter). Not just that; although absent from the Île de la Cité monument, they were, nonetheless, very much a part of the Catholic deportation narrative. They did not stand at the heart of the story, but they still had a meaningful role to play in it.

The Mystery of Israel

How could it be any different? Men like Father Riquet and Edmond Michelet, two of the Catholic Deportation's most prominent figures, were after all serious philo-Semites. Both had extended themselves to Jews in difficult times. Even before the war, Riquet had committed himself to fighting anti-Jewish prejudice, in the wake of Kristallnacht taking out membership in the Ligue internationale contre le racisme et l'antisémitisme. Then in 1941, the war itself now in full throttle, he preached an Easter sermon at the Église Saint-Séverin in the very heart of occupied Paris, in which he urged congregants to stand by their persecuted brethren, reminding them that Christ himself had been a Jew. Michelet's engagement was quieter but just as significant. Jews in flight from Hitler flooded into France in the 1930s, triggering a reflex of xenophobia. Yet, that wasn't Michelet's reaction. In June 1939, as the threat of hostilities loomed, he became involved in helping out Jewish refugee children, finding shelter for them in a convent nearby his home town of Brive.[57]

The two men's sympathies were sparked in part by sentiments of Christian charity, but there was more to it than that. Michelet devoted a chapter in Rue de la Liberté to a meditation on the Jews' fate in deportation. It was titled "… and on our children," a citation from the Gospel of Saint Matthew. The full passage, read every Palm Sunday as Michelet reminded his readers, tells of a critical moment. Pontius Pilate has given a lathered-up Jewish crowd a choice: to sacrifice Jesus or the troublemaker Barabbas. The rabble cries out for Jesus' death. Pilate washes his hands, and the Jews shout back: "His blood be on us and on our children." Michelet then goes on to recount the story of a convoy of Jewish children stopping at Dachau on the way to Auschwitz. The young faces, delicate and almond-eyed, make him think of the face of another Jewish child. To be sure, the Jews had faults, but that did not justify the vicious cruelty heaped on them. Indeed, in the camps, they had become sacrificial victims like the Savior himself, a sure sign that they occupied a special place in God's heart, that they were a "predestined race." And the Jews bore up under victimhood in a way that left Michelet awestruck. In 1966, Jean-François Steiner published *Treblinka*, a fictionalized account of a Sonderkommando uprising at the Treblinka extermination camp. Michelet reviewed the book for *Le Monde*. What had happened to the Jews in the camps, he remembered, had been so much more terrible than what had happened to nonracial deportees, and yet this people, scourged in body, had endured. There was "well and truly a mystery of Israel."[58]

Father Riquet thinking on the subject was not so different from Michelet's. In Riquet's Easter Week sermons of 1941, he drew an analogy between ancient Jerusalem and the Paris of the present day, both occupied cities, and then went on to praise the resistance of the Maccabees to the Hellenistic oppressor. Jesus, he continued, loved his people and his homeland. Christians were thus tied to Jews, a fraternity tempered in the fires of shared persecution at pagan hands. The common Abrahamic roots of the two religions was a theme Father Riquet reverted to in 1955 on the occasion of a tenth-anniversary celebration of the liberation of the camps. Jesus was a descendant of Abraham, he told those present, and so it behooved true-believing Christians to abjure anti-Semitism in all its forms, for to hate the Jews was to hate Jesus himself. Why God had conjoined the two religions in such an intimate bond was impossible to fathom. It was a mystery, "a mystery of mercy, salvation, and love."[59]

Michelet and Father Riquet did not gloss over Jewish suffering in the camps, but they thought it through using a repertoire of theological concepts that were of Christian invention. That theology was a relatively new one, fashioned in the 1930s and 1940s by a minority of churchmen who opposed the era's rising tide of racism and the Catholic Church's implication in it. These men, priests and theologians, were often onetime Jews called to the Cross, "border-crossers" as one historian has labeled them.[60] In France, the preeminent border-crosser was Jacques Maritain, a Protestant converted to Catholicism, who was married to yet another convert, Raïssa, a former Jew. Maritain, of course, was no stranger to Michelet. The two men were friends,[61] and Maritain's relationship with Father Riquet was closer still. The pair first met in 1916, when Maritain was teaching philosophy at a little seminary in Versailles and a teenaged Riquet was a student in the class. Maritain at the time was very much a man of the Right, as was Riquet, who had grown up in an anti-Semitic household. Master and acolyte then began to evolve, Maritain turning away from politics in favor of a more spiritual outlook, with Riquet following suit. In the 1930s, Jacques and Raïssa Maritain hosted get-togethers at their suburban home in Meudon, gathering around them a band of sympathetic spirits, Riquet, now a Jesuit priest, among them. The bond of confidence between the two ran deep, enough so that Maritain, invited to attend a mid-thirties Pax Romana conference in Austria but detained, turned to Riquet to go instead and to read the text that he had prepared. The subject: "impossible anti-Semitism."[62]

Anti-Semitism was deep-rooted among bien-pensant French Catholics, but there were some who had begun to think about a different approach to the "Jewish Question." The Catholic intellectual and writer Henri Daniel-Rops edited a collection of essays in 1937 titled *Les Juifs*, where the issue was hashed out. A couple of the essayists, Father Joseph Bonsirven and Paul Claudel, made gestures toward ecumenical under-standing, but they were still very much caught up in received ways of thinking. Judaism, as they saw it, was a dead religion, and the Jews themselves, in punishment for their stiff-necked denial of Christ's divin-ity, had been condemned to wander the earth, eternal nonconformists, stirring up trouble wherever they went. In the fullness of time, of course, as Saint Paul's Epistle to the Romans taught, the Jews would at last come to embrace the Cross, a conversion annunciatory of the end of days. Then, once more, the Jews would be welcomed back into the fold, embraced as older brothers who pioneered a monotheistic faith that Christianity had brought to completion and proselytized across the globe. The real question, on this understanding, was how Christians were to conduct themselves in the meantime. Father Bonsirven coun-seled the wise Christian not to turn Jews away with accusations and reproof but to reach out to them in a spirit of fraternity, hoping to draw them closer to the true faith and, in so doing, to advance, rather than to retard, God's salvific design.[63]

Maritain contributed an essay to the volume titled "L'impossible antisémitisme," and in it, he set aside Bonsirven and Claudel's half-hearted case against Christian Judeophobia, fashioning a position of his own, one more sympathetic to the plight of contemporary Jewry, although still riven with stereotypes and imbued with the assumptions of Catholic supersessionism.[64] God had made a covenant with the house of Israel, and, as Maritain saw it, the Almighty did not renege on promises made. The Jews remained a chosen people beloved of God, but chosen in what sense? The coming of the Messiah had divested them of the lead role in humankind's spiritual destiny. That had passed to Christianity, and insofar as Jews spurned the true Messiah, they were culpable of a deep unfaithfulness. At Easter services, congregations were called on to pray for the *"perfidis Judaeis."* The correct translation of the phrase, Maritain insisted, was not perfidious Jews but faithless Jews. That's why the Church branded them deicides, not because they had demanded Christ's crucifixion, but because, in the face of the Truth, they had refused to believe in Christ the Redeemer.

Israel's failings, however, were just half of the story on Maritain's accounting, for Jews nonetheless retained a part in the divine scheme, even if an earthbound and not a spiritual one. They were quick-witted and good at business, and they were also devotees of the absolute, ever prodding the world toward justice and, in that measure, advancing history down its predestined path. No wonder people hated them: the Jews reminded the run of humankind of their moral shortcomings, and humankind took its revenge with persecution and punishments. The Jews, all the same, were doing God's will. He loved them for it and extended to them protection from the worst, and thus a people so execrated and abused had endured. Such, as Maritain then comprehended it, was the mystery of Israel.[65]

Yet there was more. History had a telos, and as that end neared, the paths of justice and of salvation crossed, Jews and Christians coming together in the one, true Church, now made whole. The reconciliation Maritain foretold was in fact more one-sided than that. True, he did not speak of the conversion of the Jews, but he did of their "return." It was they who had to move off the mark, giving up the way of the world for that of the spirit, making possible the vision of plenitude that so exalted Maritain's imagination.

In the 1930s, the end of days might have seemed a remote prospect, and so Maritain was moved to pose the same question as had Father Bonsirven and Claudel: How was the wise Christian to behave himself while waiting? Maritain had a proposal at hand. Jews had a divine vocation, which commanded the respect of every right-believing Christian. They could be irritating, of course, but that was no excuse for anti-Semitism, an impossible position in light of Israel's special standing in God's heart and special role in God's scheme. In fact, given the house of Israel's very specialness, did it make any sense to advocate for Jewish assimilation, for the draining away of Jewish identity? What was needed, rather, was a new kind of pluralism, a faith-based society in which different communities – each distinct, each engaged in the fulfillment of its destiny – lived together. Herein lay the seed of a concept Maritain was to develop more fully once the war was underway, that of a "Judeo-Christian civilization" under threat from the blood lust of a new paganism.[66]

The onset of the war added a note of extreme urgency to Maritain's account of the Jewish predicament. He departed for the United States on a lecture tour in January 1940 and, in the wake of France's defeat that summer, elected to remain for the duration. He soon learned of the catastrophe ravaging European Jewry, and the more he learned, the more he cried out. Maritain, of course, did not have an exact knowledge of the genocide as it was happening, but he had an accurate enough grasp of its dimensions and modus operandi. In a talk to French exiles in New York in January 1943, he spoke of a million Jews already murdered with another four to five million in danger and of the existence of extermination facilities that made use of poison gas.[67]

To appreciate the intensity of Maritain's reaction, it's critical to understand how he thought about Christ as a man. He saw Jesus as a physical descendant of the house of Israel. Jesus, Mary, and all the apostles were Jews by birth. It followed, therefore, that Nazi hatred of the Jews was tantamount to a hatred of Christianity itself. Maritain had first encountered the idea that Judeophobia and Christophobia were twinned evils in the work of the Jewish intellectual Maurice Samuel, and he seized on it, citing approvingly from Samuel in a preface to "The Mystery of Israel," an English-language version published in 1941 of "L'impossible antisémitisme."[68]

The carnal identification of Jesus and the Jews mattered to Maritain in two ways. It added yet one more argument to the armamentarium against anti-Semitism. Anti-Semites and anti-Christians were secret sharers. Maritain knew full well that there were so-called Christians who reviled Jews, but the stress here is on "so-called." To the extent that a Christian reviled the Jews, he spat on the family that had brought Jesus into the world, on Mary most terribly. Indeed, he spat on the very faith he professed. Not just that: if Jesus and the Jews were of one flesh, then the genocide of the Jews amounted to a second Crucifixion. Maritain did not shy away from this conclusion or from making it public. In an April 1943 address to the 38th Council of the Union of American Hebrew Congregations, he spoke of the "Passion of Israel," which in these terrible times, he went on, had begun to take on "more and more distinctly the form of the Cross."[69]

The war, then, as Maritain understood it, opened a new era in human history, an "apocalyptic period."[70] The ravening anti-Semitism of the Nazi beast was a sign, and so too, in the war's aftermath, were the foundation of the State of Israel and the return of God's people to the land of their ancestors.[71] The divine design was inscrutable to mortal minds, but it was hard for a philosopher of Maritain's sensibilities not to see a providential hand at work in such epochal happenings. This is also a reminder that, deep as Maritain's sympathy for the fate of European Jewry ran, he still thought of the genocide within a wider eschatological frame that assigned an overarching Christian significance to Jewish suffering, the Jews cast as supporting players in a yet grander drama that had a Christian ending.[72]

Anne Frank and *The Deputy*

The "Christianization of the Shoah" is the phrase such reflections conjure up, but keep in mind that it is a complicated concept.[73] Christians – in the French context, Catholics – put the genocide to more than one use. They sometimes appropriated it for purposes of consolation or inspiration. This was in good measure Anne Frank's fate, the Jewish teenager turned into a Christlike figure herself or into an apostle of the brotherhood of humankind. Yet it was also possible to mobilize Jewish suffering as a goad to Christian self-examination. This is what happened in the "storm" stirred up by the performance of Rolf Hochhuth's *Der Stellvertreter*, which debuted in Paris in the winter of 1963.[74] Christian anti-Semites, as Maritain portrayed them, were not Christians according to the spirit. The Church, as an institution of the spirit, was thus preserved untainted, free from all "spot or wrinkle" in Maritain's words (citing from Saint Paul).[75] Hochhuth, by contrast, pointed the finger at real, existing Catholicism, indicting the pope himself, Pius XII, for a silence that amounted to complicity in Hitler's massacre of the Jews. *Der Stellvertreter* was a religious play that caused a religious uproar that set Catholic against Catholic. The Holocaust was the play's putative theme, but the real issue at stake was not the fate of the Jews, but the soul of the Church.[76]

Anne Frank's diary was first published in Dutch in 1947. A French edition came out three years later under the auspices of Calmann-Lévy, and it proved an extraordinary success. A deportee newspaper wrote of the book's "astonishing reverberations." Janet Flanner reported from Paris on how "widely and seriously read" the book was, identifying the author in a cringeworthy phrase as "a precocious, talented little Frankfurt Jewess." One avid reader of the French edition was Meyer Levin, who was so swept away that he moved heaven and earth to arrange and promote an English-language translation.[77]

A remarkable and inexplicable feature of the French version is its introduction, written by Henri Daniel-Rops. Daniel-Rops had an interest in Jewish affairs, but he was no philo-Semite. In 1945, he published a successful and popularizing volume, *Jésus en son temps*, which attempted to evoke the historical Palestine in which Jesus had grown up. The Jews played the part of foil in the story. They were a dry, hard people like the soil of Judea itself. They professed a ritualistic faith that was all law and no love. Worst of all, they hated Jesus, the grand priests persecuting him as Jeanne d'Arc had been persecuted by "theologians every bit as cunning." To be sure, it was Pontius Pilate who decreed Jesus' execution, but was he in fact responsible "morally"? Daniel-Rops raised the issue of deicide as a question, but it was clear where he stood, for consider, he continued, the fate that the Jews had suffered. In compensation for "the unbearable horror of the Crucifixion," they have been made to endure "the horror of the pogrom."[78]

This was too much for Jules Isaac, a well-known educator and a Jew who had spent much of the Occupation in hiding. Isaac dashed off a heated refutation, tearing into Daniel-Rops himself as a present-day Pilate. The Roman prefect had washed his hands of Jesus' death, and Daniel-Rops had done the same vis-à-vis the Jews. He shrugged off the unending violence perpetrated against them as an act of divine retribution and, in that way, sought to wash his hands "of the millions of Jewish martyrs murdered at Auschwitz." Isaac's cri de coeur was published in 1946. Daniel-Rops in response undertook to tone down the most contested passages in *Jésus en son temps*, but otherwise stood by the book's general, unsympathetic line on the Jews.[79]

This was the man selected to preface the *Journal de Anne Frank*, and the Anne he introduced to the French public was not very Jewish. To be sure, she had the kind of sparkling intelligence found in bright Jewish girls who so often outshone their "Aryan" counterparts (this is Daniel-Rops' language). At the same time, she was in possession of a "fresh little soul" and of a guileless faith in a God who watched over her. Daniel-Rops then went on to remind readers that it was not the God of Israel but God's son who had declared: "Suffer little children to come unto me" (Luke 18:16). The son had reached out to innocents (like Anne), and that's why innocents had from time immemorial so resonated to the appeal of the "Son of man." How indeed could God ever abandon Anne, who had etched in her heart such an "exact image" of him? Daniel-Rops is elliptical, never mentioning Jesus by name, but he makes plain that Anne's innocent soul is Christlike, that she has an idea of God, however inchoate, that is Christian at heart, and that she, though murdered in Bergen-Belsen, was still beloved of God (as God loved his only begotten son, crucified on the cross).[80] Daniel-Rops did not write to make Anne, a Jewish teenager, more accessible to a Christian readership but, rather, to Christianize her outright.

This was not Anne's fate in Father Riquet's hands. The Jesuit father, it happens, was a devotee of the Anne Frank story. He had a profound respect for Anne's Jewishness, but he also felt and deeply so that she had a universal message to deliver to the world. In 1957, Father Riquet gave a sermon at Notre-Dame in connection with that year's commemoration of the Journée nationale de la Déportation. In it, he quoted from the diary, citing a passage in which Anne expressed hope that the world, the "pitiless days" of the war once passed, would know again "order, repose, and peace." That same year, in the fall, the play version of the diary opened in Paris. The French theater journal, L'Avant-Scène, published the text, prefaced by three well-wishers: André Maurois, Claude Roy, and Father Riquet. Riquet's contribution spoke of Anne's dream of peace, recounting a youth excursion to Bergen-Belsen organized by a Jewish-Christian friendship association. The young people, Germans it seems in the majority, visited the camp in silence, the site of Anne Frank's final days. A few words were spoken and then prayers recited, the Kaddish alongside the Lord's Prayer.

At some point, it's not clear when, Father Riquet had an opportunity to meet Anne's father, Otto Frank. The two men spoke of the Great War, discovering that in 1918 they had both taken part in the battle of Saint-Quentin, albeit on opposite sides.[81]

Father Riquet's Anne was a figure of reconciliation, whose sacrifice raised hopes for a better future, one in which Christians and Jews, French and Germans would join hands in peace and brotherhood. Nor was he alone in such hopes. In the 1950s, a Belgian priest, Father Dominique Pire, oversaw construction of a series of "villages" to house persons displaced by the war. One of these was the village Anne Frank, dedicated in 1958 on a site just outside of Wuppertal, Germany. David Rousset served on the project's fund-raising committee. In 1961, the city of Frankfurt, hometown of the Frank family before it fled to Amsterdam, organized a memorial event in the Franks' honor. UNADIF sent two representatives to the ceremony, Father Riquet and Berthe Thiriart. In its account of the solemnities, the UNADIF newspaper, Le Déporté, quoted the by now celebrated passage in Anne's diary, expressing her unbroken faith in the innate goodness of men. To which the paper added a wish of its own for "the ultimate reconciliation of all Europe's peoples."[82]

Communists had mobilized Anne Frank in Cold War battles against racism. For non-communists as well, Anne wielded enormous symbolic power. They, with Catholics like Father Riquet in the forefront, cited Anne's sacrificial example. She had died so that ancient antagonisms, religious and national, might themselves be laid to rest. Where hatred had once reigned, there would now be a new order, a Europe united in peace, drawing spiritual sustenance from the enduring values of the Judeo-Christian tradition.

It's an inspiring vision (with Cold War applications of its own, of course), but there were Christians who did not share in it, who felt it failed to deal frankly enough with Christianity's own complicity in the Holocaust. Rolf Hochhuth was one such Christian, and he wrote a play about it, *Der Stellvertreter* (*Le Vicaire* in French and in English, *The Deputy*).

Hochhuth came to the subject through the story of Kurt Gerstein. Gerstein (1905–1945) was a historical figure, a Nazi-party member who was also a confessing Protestant. A troubled conscience turned him away from Nazism, and he was expelled from the party in 1936. Once the war began, however, Gerstein rejoined and, indeed, in 1941 volunteered for the SS, determined to learn about the inner workings of the regime in order to expose them. Such at any rate was the explanation he later gave. As an SS officer with technical skills (Gerstein was a trained engineer), he saw service in a variety of extermination camps, Auschwitz included, a shattering experience that prompted him to action. He contacted the papal nuncio in Germany to let him know of the catastrophe unfolding, but nothing came of such overtures. At the end of the war, Gerstein surrendered to French authorities, drafted a report about what he had witnessed, and then hanged himself.

Hochhuth had learned about Gerstein from the work of Léon Poliakov and built on it to construct the plot of *Der Stellvertreter*.[83] He added a fictional character, Father Riccardo Fontana, a young Jesuit priest on the rise who had an in at the Vatican. This made possible a double confrontation, first a local one in Germany between Gerstein and the papal nuncio with Riccardo as a witness and then a more epic one in Rome between Riccardo, spurred on by Gerstein's revelations, and the pope himself. The second confrontation is timed for maximum dramatic effect. It is October 1943, the very moment that the Nazis have begun to round up the Jews of Rome. On Hochhuth's telling, Riccardo is passionate and insubordinate, the pope cold and austere. Pius XII, ever the diplomat, is anxious to play a mediating role between Hitler and the Allies. He hopes to end the war with a Germany intact in order to block the advance of Soviet armies into the very heart of Christian Europe. This is why the Vatican geopolitician rebuffs the importuning Jesuit. The Jews of Rome will be deported, "under the Pope's windows," as Hochhuth phrases it, while the pope himself maintains a calculated silence.[84]

The indictment is a terrible one, and it is intensified by one last plot twist. Riccardo, in the face of the pope's obduracy, joins the convoy of Italian Jews en route to the camps, and thus the final scene of the play takes place at Auschwitz. This is a domain ruled over by the Doctor, a character modeled on Josef Mengele, who, as Hochhuth portrays him, is a figure of diabolical cruelty. The Doctor learns that a priest is in the camp, ferrets him out, and does all he can to break down the priest's faith. The play ends with Riccardo's defeat – he is shot down while making an attempt on the Doctor's life – and a voice-over then reads a dispatch from Germany's Vatican ambassador to Nazi authorities back home. The diplomat is reassuring: the pope's circumspection on "the Jewish problem" means that German-Vatican relations will remain, as they have been, on an even keel.[85]

The play, as written and as staged, was a modernist drama, one that critiqued the Church from a debunking, left perspective. Hochhuth wrote the text in free verse, in a cadenced, unrhyming poetry that highlighted the play's stylized, as opposed to realist, qualities. Hochhuth's stage directions for the Auschwitz scenes, indeed, discouraged any attempt at realism. It was Erwin Piscator, Brecht's long-time collaborator and a pioneer of modernist theater, who first staged the play at the Freie Volksbühne in Berlin in February 1963. *Le Vicaire* opened in Paris the following December at the Athénée, a theater made famous by the director and actor Louis Jouvet. It was co-directed by Peter Brook and François Darbon, working from a script prepared by Jorge Semprun, a man of many parts. In Semprun's estimation, it would have taken six hours to perform Hochhuth's play in its entirety, and so Semprun boiled it down to eight tableaux, inventing a new character altogether, the Narrator, to help speed the action along.[86]

These were experimentalists all, and that was the kind of theater Paris audiences, come to see *Le Vicaire*, were treated to. Spectators were greeted by a bare stage, save for a semicircle of chairs set against a dull, metallic backdrop. The actors, all dressed in gray cloth, then entered one by one and took their seats. As the first scene opened, décor was brought on stage, the actors involved rose and put on identifying insignia, and yet another one explained the setup to the audience. The sequence was repeated with every change of scene.

This was modernist theater then, and it was left-wing theater as well. Hochhuth chose a passage from Camus to preface the printed text. As for the play itself, it was replete with references to big business involvement, from Krupp on down, in the machinery of extermination. Brook and Darbon's set design for the Auschwitz episodes emphasized the camp's factory-like character. And Hochhuth's stage directions made yet one more point crystal clear: that the perpetrators of the crimes recreated on stage, a number of them real historical personalities, had not vanished from the face of the earth, but had gone on to successful careers in postwar West Germany. Fascism was not dead but lived on. As Semprun saw it, the play posed a fundamental dilemma that came in many variants. On the one side stood "an apparatus of power," on the other "a total human commitment to justice." The face-off between the pope and Riccardo was one instantiation of this opposition, but there had been others in other times and other places. Think, Semprun urged, of "the atomic bomb, Algeria, the cost of living, wages."[87]

There was much here to comfort the progressive-minded, but there should be no mistake that *Le Vicaire*, however much it lent itself to left-wing interpretation, was at base a religious drama, indeed, a Passion play. Hochhuth himself, after all, was a believing Protestant. Now, it is easy to spot the devil in Hochhuth's cast of characters. He is the Doctor, the personification, in Hochhuth's own words, "of Absolute Evil," "an uncanny visitant" of the sort encountered in "Christian mystery plays." The Christ figure is also not difficult to spot. Riccardo swaps identities with a Jew – Jacobson – whom he is trying to save, and he then passes himself off as a Jew to gain entry to the devil's kingdom, that is, to Auschwitz. There, Riccardo is mocked; what he witnesses makes him doubt God's grace; but he dies with a prayer on his lips, an entreaty to his savior: *In hora mortis meae voca me* (In the hour of my death call me). But who then is Pilate? There is a tense confrontation between Riccardo and the pope in the drama's penultimate act. Rome's Jewish population has been decimated by arrests, and Pius is about to sign a document, protesting in polite diplomatic terms, the deportation of "so many unfortunates." Father Riccardo interrupts the scene and pleads for a bolder statement that mentions the Jewish victims by name. The pontiff signs the original document anyway but, unsettled by the priest's badgering, accidentally spills ink on his fingers. He then turns the priest away and, as he does so, washes his hands to remove the ink spots.[88]

Yet this is a Passion play of a modern turn of mind. The Jews are not cast in the villain's part but are represented as brothers. God, Riccardo explains to a prelate of the Church, has "indissolubly linked us Christians to/the people to whom Jesus belonged."[89] Then, in the confrontation scene with the pope, he presses the argument even further, identifying himself overtly with the fate of the Jews by pinning a Star of David over his own heart (a star obtained from Jacobson). It is this gesture that so upsets the pope and that causes him to stain himself. The Jews are not complicit with evil but its victims, and as for evil itself, it is never defeated, at least not in the play. Riccardo is gunned down, and the evil Doctor, for the moment at least, gets away with murder. Hochhuth denies the spectator a redemptive finale.

The spectacle of evil triumphant poses troubling questions: Where is God in a creation that includes Auschwitz? And in the face of God's apparent silence, where do humankind's own responsibilities lie?

Hochhuth, as more than one observer remarked, was a Christian of a contemporary sort, a Kierkegaardian figure for whom faith was a leap and the human condition an anguish-filled trial without a God near at hand to make the choices easier.[90]

Le Vicaire was a Christian drama that pushed Christians to reflect on their faith, and "reflect" they did. When the play opened in Paris (to packed houses), the Action française turned out crowds to demonstrate in protest. Inside the theater, audience members interrupted performances, shouting out and throwing objects on stage. The Church of the Madeleine hosted an event in December to honor Pius XII's memory and make amends for the play's offenses against the Holy Father. The great and the good of Parisian society were in attendance, among them Maxime Weygand and Jean de Lattre de Tassigny.[91]

Yet, bien-pensants were not the only ones to have a say. The question of the pope's silence was not a new one among French Catholics. De Gaulle's provisional government appointed Maritain ambassador to the Holy See in 1945. That very same year, Claudel wrote him a letter and in it asked Maritain to petition the pope for a clear statement, "a solemn protestation" and not "feeble and vague laments," condemning the massacre of Jewish innocents. It's not clear how Maritain handled this matter, but the following year, he took an initiative of his own. Anti-Jewish pogroms in postwar Poland made clear that the "anti-Semitic psychosis" of the war years had not been rooted out. The Jewish people still trod "the road to Calvary," and it was the Church's duty to protest. Maritain asked Monsignor Montini, a senior member of the Vatican Secretariat of State, to persuade Pius to act, but the pope remained unmoved. Then it was François Mauriac's turn to step in. The future Nobel Prize winner prefaced Poliakov's Bréviaire de la haine (1951). He used the opportunity to honor what some members of France's Church had done to rescue Jews, but went on to express a deep regret that the pope, "the successor of the Galilean Simon Peter," had never taken an explicit stand against "the crucifixion of so many of the 'Lord's brothers.'"[92]

Hochhuth knew of Mauriac's questionings and indeed acknowledged the novelist as a precursor in an interview with Ramparts magazine. In that same interview, he disclosed that the character of Father Riccardo had been modeled on a real person, Provost Bernhard Lichtenberg. Lichtenberg was a German priest who had spoken out against Nazi anti-Semitism and against Hitler's euthanasia program, stands that had earned him arrest and deportation to Dachau. He died on the way. Le Vicaire was in fact dedicated to Lichtenberg and to a second priest, the anti-Nazi Father Maximilian Kolbe, who died a martyr at Auschwitz.[93]

All of which raises the question of Catholic deportees' reaction to the play. Father Riquet, for one, was unsympathetic. Hochhuth, he wrote, had not lived through the war and didn't understand the choices that had to be made. The rank-and-file clergy had done much to help out Jews; the Church was one body, and an offense to its head was an offense to all; and what would it have availed anyhow had the pope taken a more forthright position? Rémy Roure, a prewar Christian Democrat and Riquet's brother-in-arms in the anti-concentration camp movement, fired back that the play asked a legitimate question – *Why had the pope remained silent?* – one that deserved a more serious answer than a hail of stinkballs. Who knows for a certainty, he added, whether a papal declaration would have been as ineffective as Father Riquet implied?[94]

Such polemics suggest a Catholic community divided, and that was very much Léon Poliakov's own take on the situation. The Catholic mainstream, as he saw it, with *Le Figaro* acting as its spokesman, stood against Hochhuth, while *Le Monde* and "progressive Catholics" stood with him. There is something to be said for this assessment. *Le Monde*'s editor-in-chief, Hubert Beuve-Méry, was a forward-looking Catholic himself, and he assigned a like-minded correspondent, Jacques Nobécourt, to cover the controversy. Nobécourt went on to publish a book on the subject, and he did not hide his personal point of view, likening the Holocaust to a present-day Passion, "the Jewish Passion" reminding the world that Christ's sacrifice was never-ending and echoed down to the present day.[95] It's worth adding that Nobécourt's intervention was published by Le Seuil, whose own editor-in-chief, Paul Flamand, was likewise a Catholic of progressive views.

Le Vicaire then was not just a modernist play for the progressive-minded, it was also a Christian drama, addressed – in the French case – to Catholic audiences who did not react as one but fell out in controversy. On this reading, the Jews were little more than walk-ons. The dramatis personae of *Le Vicaire* included Jewish characters, Jacobson for example, but the main protagonists, the evil Doctor excepted, were all Christians. As for the tumult the play caused, the principals involved, as Nobécourt told it, were not Jews. Poliakov joined in but more as an interested spectator than as a star player. *Le Vicaire* was about the Holocaust, but the nub of the matter was what the Holocaust meant to Christians.

Catholic engagement with the deportation experience generated a narrative of extraordinary power. On the most fundamental level, the story of the Deportation was the story of spirit triumphant, of a Christian faith unbowed in the face of Nazi paganism. That triumph, exemplary in itself, held out the prospect of yet greater things to come – of a Europe reborn, at one with itself and steadied by the ballast of a new Christian humanism. That humanism, moreover, was of an inclusive sort. Its celebration of Christian values was a point of departure, but its ultimate destination was the affirmation of a Judeo-Christian civilization, itself a promise of yet greater things – of the ultimate "reintegration" that would announce Christ's second coming. From this perspective, even the Holocaust, a word that French Catholics used early and often, made sense. The Jews' martyrdom was a second Crucifixion and the creation of the State of Israel, resurrected from the ashes of the camps, a confirming sign that the divine plan had arrived at a critical watershed.[96]

Yet, as the stakes in the drama grew greater and greater, the place in it assigned to Jews took on a less human and more theological significance. They remained objects of fraternal solicitude (with Daniel-Rops an obvious and flagrant exception), brothers in the flesh who had endured an exceptional fate. But as that fate became ever more implicated in a grand, eschatological design, Jews themselves were reduced to simple instruments, second-rank actors in a millennial scheme whose lead roles, as in *Le Vicaire*, went to others.

So what happened, readers are bound to ask themselves, when Jews qua Jews talked about the Deportation? Did they even address the subject, and to the extent that they did, what stories did *they* have to tell?

5   The Six Million

It was once prevailing belief that French Jews in the immediate postwar years did not talk much about the Deportation and that, even when they did, it was to play down the specificities of Jewish experience. There was admittedly an initial outburst of memoir writing. A handful of Jews came back from the camps and, much as other deportees had done, set down on paper what had happened to them. Louise Alcan was a Jewish woman sent to Auschwitz. She was also a Communist, and the camp memoir she published in 1945 was told from the Party's point of view. It opened with a quote from Paul Éluard and included a scene of Christmas celebration, complete with tree and decorations, a fete for which Alcan composed a poem, dedicating a quatrain to each of her "comrades."[1] Suzanne Birnbaum's memoir, *Une Française juive est revenue*, came out the next year. As the title indicates, it was Birnbaum's identity as a Frenchwoman and not her Jewishness that was primordial, and the account concludes on a patriotic note, as she is trained back to "my old Paris" to be greeted at the station by the sounds of "La Marseillaise."[2] Jews then talked about the Deportation, but affirmations of Jewish identity were kept to a minimum, and soon enough the initial flood of memoir literature dried up. A "quasi-silence," it is said, then descended on France's Jews, now more engrossed in building new lives than in remembering lives lost.[3] In any event, no one in a nation recovering from war and Occupation wanted to listen to the grim stories of survivors.

This narrative of postwar memory making, or the absence of it, is less current today than it once was. It is now acknowledged that more was going on in the decades of postwar reconstruction. But what? In most accounts, the answer still remains a grudging one. The dead were never forgotten, it is conceded, but French Jews hesitated to make too demonstrative a show of remembering them. Rituals of commemoration there were, but they were confined to communal settings and drew a minimum of public attention to themselves.

The comportment of official Judaism is cited as a case in point. Since Napoleonic times, French Jewry has organized itself in a network of representative bodies or consistories, led in the main by the community's native-born leading lights. This was official Judaism. France's Consistoire central, seconded by its Paris branch, involved itself early on in remembering the victims of Nazi persecution. It followed the example set by the Amicale d'Auschwitz, repatriating ashes from Auschwitz-Birkenau, which were then distributed for commemorative purposes to communities across the nation. Since the Liberation in 1944, relatives of survivors had gathered every year at Drancy to recall deported loved ones.[4] In 1948, the Consistory moved the event indoors to the Grand Synagogue on the rue de la Victoire, and what had been an informal gathering became an annual memorial service. The year after that, a plaque was unveiled at the synagogue, dedicated to French Jewry's wartime dead and inscribed with the formula:

1939–1945. In memory of our brothers, soldiers and résistants, who died in the camps of the deportation, shot, tortured, burned, and of the numberless victims of Nazi barbarism.

Note, however, that such ceremonials were conducted inside, out of public view, and that, in the case of the plaque, the Jewish dead were not named as such but subsumed into more general categories of patriotic loss: soldiers, résistants, and victims of Nazi barbarism.[5]

The Consistory was not, of course, the sole body to take an interest in the fate of French Jewry under the Occupation. I have already made mention several times of the Centre de documentation juive contemporaine (CDJC), which was founded in 1943 and set about from the very outset assembling an archive of the Jewish experience in wartime. The CDJC in due course came to employ a cadre of historians who dedicated themselves with a single-minded devotion to revealing all the details of the Jewish catastrophe. It has been pointed out, however, that the men involved were not professionals credentialed by the university but self-educated amateurs, like Léon Poliakov, who was a lawyer by training. They were outliers who worked on the fringes of scholarship and enjoyed little recognition for all that they accomplished. The CDJC did not content itself just with archive collecting and the publication of historical treatises. It also oversaw the construction of a monument, dedicated in 1956, the Tombeau du Martyr juif inconnu. Yet, once again, the title is eloquent, calling to mind as it does the Tombeau du Soldat inconnu, the memorial to France's fallen in the Great War that is cradled in the shadows beneath the Arc de Triomphe. The Jewish tomb, moreover, like its Great War counterpart, featured an eternal flame, one more item evidencing how much Jewish commemoration in these years of "quasi-silence" cloaked itself in the mantle of French republican patriotism, a signal to anyone paying attention and, according to conventional wisdom, there were not many – that Jewish sacrifice was but one episode in a grander national epic.[6]

From this perspective, taking into account the memorial activities of the Consistory and CDJC does not change the overall story by much. Jewish memory was never more than a marginal phenomenon, and even when the community's losses were commemorated, it was sans expressions of Jewish particularity. The Consistory did not identify the Jewish dead as Jews, and the CDJC wrapped them in the colors of the national flag.

A closer look at the activities of the CDJC, however, will suggest that this picture stands in need of revision. There was a distinctive Jewish voice in the postwar remembrance of the Deportation, and it was not one crying in the wilderness. Jews were acknowledged members of the chorus, sometimes vocalizing in harmony with the others, but also sometimes singing a full-throated Jewish melody of their own. The CDJC had a Jewish story to tell, indeed, more than one, and the present chapter will undertake to identify what those stories were and how the CDJC went about their narration.

The CDJC Archive

The CDJC began as an archive, and it was Isaac Schneersohn who took the initiative. Schneersohn was Russian-born, the descendant of a distinguished line of Lubavitcher rabbis. He was ordained himself as a teenager but, down-to-earth man that he was, proved more adept at business than religious observance. He was known to sneak a smoke on the Sabbath and, by the 1950s, had strayed far enough to describe himself as "hardly practicing." Politics also mattered to Schneersohn, who in Russian days associated with Zionists and liberal-minded Kadets, frequentations that made life impossible for him once the Soviets took power. Schneersohn relocated to Paris and, in the wake of France's defeat in 1940, headed south, settling first in unoccupied Dordogne and then, when the Germans took over the southern zone in 1942, moving to Grenoble at that time under the comparatively lax authority of the Italians. There, in the spring of 1943, he met with officials from the French Jewish establishment, and they agreed to create an archive. The Wehrmacht's recent defeat at Stalingrad was fresh on everyone's minds, and the imagined archive was intended, not just to preserve the record of Jewish life under Nazi rule, but also to gather documentation that would aid Jews, once the Nazis were expelled, to recover stolen property and begin life anew.[7]

The Nazi occupation of Grenoble in September placed the project on hold, but it was relaunched a year later, this time in Paris. Schneersohn had come out of hiding and made a beeline to France's just liberated capital city. In October 1944, he set up the Centre de documentation des déportés et spoliés juifs, which underwent a name change the following summer, becoming the CDJC. The entrepreneurial Schneersohn lined up funding from the American Jewish Joint Distribution Committee, a US-based humanitarian organization, and began to assemble a staff. Léon Poliakov and Joseph Billig were among the first people hired.[8] Like Schneersohn himself, both were Russians who had decamped to the West in the aftermath of the Bolshevik Revolution. Poliakov, as already noted a trained lawyer, had moved to Paris, then to Berlin, and at last back again to Paris. Billig's background and itinerary were similar. He went first to Germany, earning a doctorate in philosophy from the University of Berlin in 1929, after which, consequent on Hitler's accession to power, he sought asylum in France. The two men were lettered polyglots, and they had one more trait in common. They had managed to survive the wreckage of the war years. Poliakov spent them in hiding in the south of France, while Billig, who had volunteered for French army service, ended up as a POW.[9]

Though neither had experience in archive collecting, they more than anyone else were responsible for laying the groundwork for the fledgling CDJC's documentarium. Poliakov, for a period Schneersohn's right-hand man, set the process in motion. He solicited a letter of introduction from Justin Godart, a Radical politician and associate of Schneersohn's, which he presented to the Sûreté, France's national police, along with an inquiry: Had the Sûreté come into possession of records relating to the Nazi occupation? It had, and the records in question were none other than the captured files of the SS's services in France. Poliakov, who knew German, also knew the value of the cache, which he persuaded the Sûreté to allow him to microfilm.[10] Some of this material was then made available to the French legal team, led by Edgar Faure, that participated in the prosecution of Nazi war criminals at Nuremberg. In 1946, Poliakov joined the team as an expert, while Billig attended the trials as CDJC representative. Poliakov and Billig, working together, cajoled Telford Taylor, the US prosecutor, into letting them photocopy reams of Nuremberg documents, a request Taylor acceded to, resulting in the shipment of three tons plus of material destined for the CDJC archive back home.[11]

The CDJC was not unique in its collecting efforts. Across Europe, from the very moment of liberation, survivors of the Nazi genocide had begun to amass evidence chronicling the cataclysm that had devastated

European Jewry. The center's trove, however, was among the largest, and the organization made a bid for leadership, convening in Paris in 1947 what one historian has called "the first European Jewish Holocaust conference." Thirty-two archivists from thirteen nations were in attendance, though it was the French who were most numerous, supplying just under half the delegates. The conference opened with renditions of "La Marseillaise" and "Hatikvah" (or "The Hope," soon to become the unofficial national anthem of the State of Israel), and Justin Godart provided the keynote address.[12]

The conference did not end, however, on a note of French-inspired unity as the CDJC had hoped. A number of participants felt that the future of world Jewry lay in Palestine, not in the Diaspora, let alone in France. There were differences as well on matters of language, the French advocating for French, while others favored Yiddish, and there were differences on matters of approach. Many delegates of Polish background – among them Philip Friedman, Joseph Wulf, and Michel Borwicz – had had experience in postwar Poland, collecting survivor testimony and disseminating questionnaires, taking a ground-up view with an aim to documenting Jewish losses and resistance. This was not the CDJC's angle of vision. Poliakov acknowledged that he was obsessed with what he called "*le secret des bourreaux*," the whys and wherefores of Nazi persecution, and it was just these matters that the CDJC archive, made up of perpetrator documents, was tailor-made to address. In light of such disagreements, the CDJC-sponsored conference – by its full name, the Conférence européenne des commissions historiques et des centres de documentation juifs – turned out to be a one-off event.[13]

The universe of Holocaust research was not a big one in the late 1940s, but the CDJC was already a leading player in it, even if it had aspired to a yet greater role. It was also a recognized source in France for anyone with an interest in the Deportation. As we have seen, a diverse cast of researchers – from Robert Merle to David Rousset to Olga Wormser-Migot to Henri Michel – at one point or another came knocking on its doors. The CDJC, however, was not content to be a mere resource. Schneersohn had ambitions, not only to collect documents, but also to publish.

History Writing

The CDJC research team was prolific, churning out scores of articles and books, and Schneersohn made sure that there were venues for such an outpouring, maintaining a journal, the *Bulletin du CDJC* or, as it was known from 1946, *Le Monde juif*, and a publishing house, the Éditions du

Centre. Serge Klarsfeld has characterized *Le Monde juif* as "the only publication in the world about the Shoah appearing without interruption since the end of the war."[14] As for the Éditions du Centre, Schneersohn was a jealous guardian of its interests, insisting that the scholars in his employ publish there and nowhere else, a rule that Poliakov was to break with regrettable consequences. Poliakov had completed work on *Bréviaire de la haine* and harbored hopes that it might reach a wide audience, a prospect he talked over with an old friend, yet another Russian émigré, Alexandre Kojève. Kojève steered Poliakov to Raymond Aron, who in turn steered him to the Calmann-Lévy publishing house, which undertook to print the book in 1951. It was the first ever document-based, synoptic study of the Nazi genocide of the Jews, an achievement that established Poliakov as a recognized pioneer. Raul Hilberg, a trailblazer in the field himself, hailed Poliakov as "the founder of this academic discipline that we now call 'the Holocaust.'" Schneersohn was not so admiring, however, and there followed a cooling of relations. Poliakov's salary was cut, and he separated from the CDJC altogether, not long thereafter.[15]

There was more than one "first" associated with the CDJC and its band of historians, but what about the history itself, the kind of history that they wrote? How did CDJC scholars tell the story of European Jewry's destruction, with what emphases and what lacunae?[16]

The bulk of the CDJC's research effort dealt with the mechanics of persecution. Poliakov had hoped to line up Jacques Maritain to write the introduction to *Bréviaire de la haine*. Maritain demurred but later authored a favorable review, and in it he wrote of Poliakov's handling of "the stages of the business of extermination." That was indeed Poliakov's general approach (though, as we'll see in a later chapter, the book was more multifaceted than that).[17] The Nazis were methodical, first stigmatizing Jewish communities and robbing them. Ghettoization followed and then deportation to the camps, where Jews were gassed and incinerated. This approach was step-by-step history of the sort Wormser-Migot and Michel had practiced, but with Jews situated not at the periphery but at the core of the narrative.

Georges Wellers wrote in a similar vein, though the story he developed was more concentrated on the French experience. Wellers was a Russian Jew who had migrated to France in the 1920s. In this respect, he was like many others in Schneersohn's circle, and, like them too, he was not an historian by training but something else, a biochemist. It was indeed Wellers' science background that in part enabled him to survive the war years. He was arrested in 1941 and interned at Drancy, where he assumed responsibility for the camp's hygienic services. The posting helped him to avoid deportation until 1944, when he was at last sent off to Auschwitz. Once more, he wound up in a "sheltered" position as a nurse in the Auschwitz infirmary. This spared him selection and death, though not extreme hardship. On return to France, Wellers set down on paper an account of his ordeal. The resulting text, *De Drancy à Auschwitz*, was published by the Éditions du Centre in 1946, with Schneersohn himself supplying a preface. For political internees, the itinerary of deportation was well known. Arrested résistants were first jailed before relocation to transit camps – Royallieu, for instance – and eventual deportation to the East. Weller's book mapped out a different geography, with Drancy, a locale specific to Jewish experience, at its center, and Wellers took pains to document how the camp's workings developed under a succession of Nazi overseers: Theodor Dannecker; Heinz Röthke; and the cruelest of them all, Alois Brunner.[18] *De Drancy à Auschwitz* earned Wellers a spot on the CDJC team and recognition not just as a man of science but also as an historian.

CDJC publications accented the particularities of the Jewish experience under Nazi rule and the particularities of Nazi motives vis-à-vis the Jews as well. For what had motivated Hitlerian policy? Capitalism? Racism born of capitalism? No, it was racism tout court. Hitler's minions meant to kill racial inferiors: Slavs, Roma, and Jews. Billig assembled a document collection on Nazi extermination policy in 1950 and titled it with lapidary simplicity *L'Allemagne et le génocide*. The true monument to Nazi bestiality was not, on Billig's accounting, the concentration camp but "the gas chamber, the crematorium, and the mass grave." The volume was prefaced by François de Menthon, a onetime Nuremberg prosecutor, who cited the work of Raphael Lemkin, inventor of the neologism "genocide." Billig then went on to boil down for readers the defining essence of the Nazis' genocidal policy: "They condemn a man not for what he does but for who he is."[19] The implication was clear enough. What had happened to European Jewry was distinct from what had happened to other groups of deportees, a catastrophe of a special kind that necessitated the coinage, as Lemkin had done, of an entirely new term.

It might be thought that the CDJC, unflinching as it was in its condemnation of German anti-Semitism, would be inclined to soft-pedal France's own complicity in the perpetration of Nazi crimes, but that's not quite right. After the July 1942 Vél d'hiv round-up, Drancy was swamped with a wave of new internees. Wellers' book contains an account of the event and reports how the newcomers remonstrated against the French police, without whose help "the Germans would not have been able to arrest a quarter of those rounded up."[20] A little later, a convoy of children was transferred to Drancy from Beaune-la-Rolande, and one little girl, as Wellers tells it, minced few words about the French role in the fate that had overtaken her family:

> It was the French who came to our place ... At Beaune-la-Rolande, it was French customs officials who detained my mother and my father and sent us, my sister and myself, away. And here, it is French gendarmes who stand guard.[21]

René Blum, director of the Ballet russe de Monte Carlo, younger brother of Léon (the former socialist premier of France), and himself a prisoner, was present on both occasions. Officials who behaved in such a way were not French, he protested. Wellers concludes the telling of these events with an account of Blum's own fate: he was deported to Auschwitz where he was murdered.

Wellers' *De Drancy à Auschwitz* was an early postwar text, and it may be that the kind of shots he took at Vichy complicity fell away in later CDJC publications. Yet, that's not so either. Jean Cassou was a friend of the CDJC. He was a former résistant who was married to a Jewish woman, Ida Jankélévitch, the sister of the philosopher Vladimir. However Cassou's CDJC connection originated, he figured among Schneersohn's stable of authors, publishing a brief volume with the Éditions du Centre in 1947 on the wartime pillage of Jewish artwork in France. In it, Cassou made clear that it was not just the Germans, Otto Abetz and the Einsatzstab Rosenberg, who were up to their elbows in the thieving, but Vichy too, a player of the second rank perhaps, but a player nonetheless.[22] The anti-Vichy drumbeat kept up with the release the following year of Poliakov's document collection on German racial policy in France titled *L'Étoile jaune*. The Germans were the principal target. It was they who had imposed the wearing of the yellow star on Occupied-Zone Jews in 1942, a measure the French public found revolting. Vichy, conscious of such opposition, balked at extending the policy to the unoccupied south, but, as Schneersohn underlined in the volume's introduction, what the regime did do was to require all Jews to have the word "*Juif*" stamped on their ration cards and identity papers. Justin Godart, who added a preface, did not hesitate to step up the indictment. He branded Pétain's conduct on the matter of stigmatizing Jews yet one more in a litany of "betrayals."[23] There was more in the same vein to come.

The CDJC's weightiest contribution on the question of Vichy anti-Semitism was Joseph Billig's three-volume work on Vichy's Commissariat général aux questions juives (1955, 1957, 1960). Billig acknowledged that relations between the Pétain government and the CGQJ had not always been harmonious, especially once Xavier Vallat, the commissariat's first chief, was replaced in May 1942 by the anti-Semitic ultra, Darquier de Pellepoix. That said, the CGQJ and its activities were very much, in Billig's phrasing, "in the logic of the Vichyite regime," for, there was no doubt about it, Pétain's was a racist government, which, without German prodding, had devised an anti-Semitic politics all its own. When the time came, moreover, Vichy took part in the implementation of Hitler's final solution, not always with enthusiasm, sometimes with foot-dragging, but for Billig the overall balance sheet was clear. The Germans would not have accomplished as much as they did without Vichy cooperation.[24]

CDJC researchers were determined to record the evil that the Germans had done – in France as elsewhere in Europe – but that did not mean they passed over in silence Vichy's compromising role when it came to racial persecution. What they had to say, moreover, was not uttered in hushed tones among themselves, but in publications backed by sheaves of incriminating evidence.

There were not just villains in the CDJC's story, but also heroes. The Italians were not the most important among them, but they were given their due. It was in the Italian-occupied zone after all that so many Jews and, indeed, so many future members of the CDJC had sheltered.[25] It was the French public, though, that received the most heartfelt kudos, a population, as CDJC researchers emphasized time and again, that in its great majority had repudiated instances of anti-Semitic cruelty from the roundups of Jews for deportation to the imposition of the yellow star in the Occupied Zone.[26]

Then there were the Jews themselves. The issue had its complexities. At Nazi command, French Jews had been made to organize a representative body, the Union générale des Israélites de France (UGIF), France's rough equivalent to the Jewish councils set up in the East. Hannah Arendt later excoriated such bodies as collaborationist organs that facilitated the Nazis' exterminationist agenda, but the CDJC's attitude was more mitigated. Wellers had had encounters with UGIF representatives during the war. He reacted to them with hostility at first but later developed second thoughts, as he learned over time how a number had acted "with courage and abnegation on behalf of people who were hunted down."[27] Schneersohn himself had worked hand in hand with UGIF officials in Grenoble during the war when he had first contemplated creating the CDJC. The *Judenräte* in the East may have deserved all the opprobrium heaped upon them, but, as the CDJC saw it, UGIF's record was more ambiguous.

On the matter of how the mass of European Jewry had comported themselves in the face of persecution, CDJC historians rendered a judgment that was no less nuanced, though on balance far more favorable. They posed the inevitable question, how it was that so many millions went to "the slaughter without pulling together and organizing a determined defense." The answer they formulated came in two parts, one that accepted the premise of passivity and one that did not. As to the first, had not centuries of experience taught Jews that the best way to deal with oppression was to bend the knee and wait for the whirlwind to pass? In any event, the Nazis had devised cruel and deceitful methods to disarm all opposition. In the camps, they set an aristocracy of criminals to lord it over the mass of inmates, a divide and conquer policy that had its ghetto equivalent. Power there was invested in Jewish councils and in the Jewish police who assisted them, creating an apparatus that set Jew against Jew.[28] By the time the Nazis began to empty the ghettos out, the Jews had few options left. Michel Mazor, the CDJC's chief archivist, was a Russian Jew who had taken up residence in Poland after the Bolshevik Revolution. He was interned in the Warsaw Ghetto and later herded into a boxcar destined for Treblinka. He escaped, but knew all too well the fate that awaited those who had not: to be stripped naked, shoved into a gas chamber, and murdered, and this, as he put it, while the world did nothing. The Jews were a people abandoned, and abandonment gave rise to despair and resignation.[29]

Yet despair and resignation were not the whole story, for Jews had in fact resisted, just as much if not more than other populations stalked by the Nazis. This was the second part of the CDJC response to the question of Jewish conduct in the face of the Nazis' exterminatory fanaticism. Poliakov's *Bréviaire de la haine* identified four camps – Belzec, Chelmno, Sobibor, and Treblinka – where Jews had been slated for immediate annihilation. In Auschwitz, new arrivals were subjected to selection, the old and the young, the weak and the infirm chosen for death, the rest for a life of forced labor until, weakened by work and malnutrition, they too in subsequent selections were dispatched to the gas chambers. In the *Vernichtungslager*, by contrast, there was no hope of survival, as new arrivals were marched straightaway to their deaths – all, that is, but a handful of the hale and hearty whom the SS tasked with disposing of the bodies of the murdered. In three of the death camps, and Poliakov listed them all, these so-called Sonderkommandos rose in desperate revolt: at Treblinka in August 1943, at Sobibor the following October, and at Chelmno in January 1944.[30]

Yet the most desperate and, at the same time, inspirational revolt was the rising of the Warsaw Ghetto in April-May 1943. Mazor had been deported from the ghetto some months before the rising's outbreak, but he had had enough personal experience of ghetto life that he believed he knew where the insurrection had come from, and he wrote about it in a CDJC publication, *La Cité engloutie* (1955). The ghetto in Mazor's accounting was a space unlike any other. Its inmates stood accused of no crime, except that of being Jewish, and the Nazis had little interest in whether the ghetto hummed with machinelike efficiency or not. In both respects, this was not the concentrationary universe as David Rousset depicted it. The ghetto's inhabitants, however, refused the humiliation and chaos that the Nazis exposed them to, organizing self-help groups and housing committees in a spontaneous upwelling of humanistic solidarity. These institutions operated outside the *Judenrat*'s purview, and the "great national movement" they represented fed straight into the Warsaw Ghetto uprising, "that Jewish Stalingrad" as it was characterized by David Knout, one of Mazor's colleagues at the CDJC.[31]

It is noteworthy how little Mazor credited the youth groups, Zionist or otherwise, which were in fact so central to the making of the revolt, but then again, he had left the ghetto at the end of 1942, many months before the revolt itself, and so was not witness to the final preparations for it. This did not mean, however, that the insurrection did not have a Zionist denouement. For Poliakov, events in Poland were a waystation on the Jewish people's transformation from an unarmed mass into a "warrior nation," a process begun in central Europe, the former heartland of world Jewry, and consummated in the land of Israel.[32]

CDJC historians had a story to tell, and it was different from the stories told by other groups of deportees. It was not about the concentrationary universe as a smooth-running capitalist enterprise, but about the machinery of anti-Semitism, which first stigmatized and quarantined. The geography of Jewish deportation differed as well from that of the politicals. For the Jews, there were transit camps like Drancy and walled-off ghettos, the Warsaw Ghetto the most notorious among them. From there, they were packed off not to work camps but to places of extermination: to Auschwitz, where there were selections that allowed a reprieve from instant extinction for a handful, and to Treblinka and its ilk, where the death sentence was executed without delay. The Germans were the masterminds behind the process, but they had accomplices, Vichy among them. The Italians and the French had refused such complicities, and in the end, the compromising conduct of the *Judenräte* notwithstanding, so too had the Jews themselves. Indeed, persecution fueled a national awakening that found its most powerful expression in the Warsaw Ghetto revolt and then in the founding of the State of Israel. In so many deportation narratives, the Jews played a subsidiary role as a suffering and, on some accounts, all too fissiparous mass that provided a backdrop to the real action, which centered on political agitation or spiritual sacrifice. For the CDJC, the Jews were at the center, and in the end they were the heroes of their own story.

It was not just that the CDJC team had a particular story to tell, but that they told it in a signature style. Mazor and Wellers wrote memoirs, enlivened by moving firsthand testimony. Mazor recalled the day his wife had escaped to freedom over the wall of the Warsaw Ghetto. Wellers remembered catching a glimpse of himself in the mirror after a recuperative stay in the infirmary at Buchenwald (where he had been relocated as the Red Army closed in on Auschwitz). Though not yet forty years of age, he understood at that moment why fellow inmates called him "the old man," for he had taken on the look of an octogenarian.[33] But Wellers' memoir, for all its personal detail, came encased in a heavy documentary carapace, and indeed, the document collection, most often assembled from the CDJC's own archive, was perhaps the preferred genre of the CDJC historian. Poliakov's *Bréviaire de la haine*, in comparison, was a work of history more conventional in design, the documents digested in order to construct a narrative in the author's own words. Yet, even so, Poliakov made an effort to fashion a voice that was focused on the unembroidered facts. "Avoid invective, and make the documents do the talking – they're sufficiently eloquent," that was how he summed up the way he worked.[34] The historian's task, as Mazor put it, was to let the documents "speak for themselves."[35] CDJC historians made a concerted effort to refuse effects and emotion. The cry of vengeance, the venting of hatred born of loss, such gestures had no place in texts that aspired to a scrupulous objectivity. In CDJC-style history, the document ruled, and the commentary that accompanied it was supposed to be framed in a prose sober and serene but also implacable.[36]

Such a modus operandi came at a cost. The documents deployed were almost always the perpetrator's documents, and so it was the Nazis who were heard speaking and not the Jews themselves, save sometimes at a remove. Overall, it was the killers and not their victims on whom the limelight fell. Why then pay such a steep price? It is tempting to place blame on the CDJC historians' amateur status. They were beginners, naïve in their faith in the document and in the scientific rigor of history writing itself, but such a dismissal is unjust. The CDJC historian was a Jew, writing about Jews, for a readership that was at least in part non-Jewish. It was no easy matter to make the story of European Jewry's destruction credible to such an audience. Wellers avowed how slow he was himself, even after several days at Auschwitz, to grasp the reality of the gas chambers, so monstrous and unthinkable was the fact.[37] So, why should readers, even of good faith, believe the testimony of survivors? It was necessary rather to allow the perpetrators to condemn themselves.

Even so, there was a problem, for the messenger bringing news of the perpetrator's deeds was a Jew, an interested party, maybe even a suspect one. Poliakov published document collections not just in France but also in the Bundesrepublik, partnering with Joseph Wulf who, himself a resident in Germany, knew all too well how blinkered the locals could be when it came to the subject of the Nazi genocide. There was no shortage of Germans who started with the assumption that Jews were biased and unreliable witnesses. To break through such resistance, Wulf counseled a "superhuman 'scientific' objectivity."[38] A Jew, speaking of the Jews' fate, had no choice but to take a moderate and restrained tone if he wanted to be believed, and it didn't hurt if he had some help into the bargain. The volumes that the Éditions du Centre issued were often prefaced, or followed by an afterword. This was also true of Poliakov's *Bréviaire de la haine*, which was published by Calmann-Lévy. In the event, the preface and afterword writers were almost always Gentiles, men like Justin Godart, François de Menthon, Father Michel Riquet, and in the case of Poliakov's volume, François Mauriac.[39] These were personalities of high repute, many of them former résistants, and an endorsement from such eminences imparted a veneer of trustworthiness to the texts that they introduced. Remember then the context in which the CDJC historians labored: a France that was ignorant and uncomprehending of what had happened to the Jews, in part because the facts themselves were so unbelievable, all the more so when the will to credit them was often lacking. That, more than inexperience or lack of sophistication, was why they practiced history the way they did.

The *Tombeau du Martyr Juif Inconnu*

Schneersohn was a man of boundless, demiurgic energy. An archive, a periodical, and a publishing house: these were a good start, but he wanted to add one more major element to the edifice he was constructing – a memorial. The Nazi genocide had swept away six million Jews, and they had died without sepulcher. Schneersohn meant to erect just such a gravesite, and he began soliciting funds and building permits in 1951. The first stone of the memorial was laid in 1953, and not three years later, the project in its entirety was completed. In its finished state, it was a remarkable achievement, for it featured not just a monument but also a multistory building that housed the CDJC archive, plus a library, a museum, and space for meetings. At that time, there was nothing else like it in the world, yet one more first to the CDJC's credit.

How did Schneersohn pull off such a feat, and what kind of monument was it that resulted from his exertions? This last question has given rise to more than one interpretation. The monument has gone by many names. From 1974 until 2005, it was known as the Mémorial du Martyr juif inconnu and thereafter as the Mémorial de la Shoah. Its name at its origins, however, was the Tombeau du Martyr juif inconnu, an obvious allusion, as already remarked, to the Tombeau du Soldat inconnu at the Arc de Triomphe, a connection highlighted by the eternal flame that was a common feature of both monuments. From this angle, Schneersohn's memorial appears an effort to model Jewish memory on the nation's own. It represented a bid to write the story of the Jews into that of the French Republic itself.

A more recent interpretation has homed in on the monument's globalizing aspirations. For a certainty, Schneersohn envisioned the building of the monument as a global effort. Among the first things he did was to found a Comité mondial or World Committee, which boasted the patronage of luminaries from Winston Churchill to Queen Elisabeth of Belgium to Vincent Auriol, president of the French Republic. To drum up financial backing, he traveled to the United States, meeting in New York with the likes of Eleanor Roosevelt, who not long before had been immersed in the crafting of the United Nations' Universal Declaration of Human Rights. In so doing, Schneersohn in effect undertook to underscore the universal element in Jewish suffering, casting Jewish experience not in particularistic terms but as a constitutive element of a nascent "discourse on human rights."[40]

Both ways of understanding the monument acknowledge its Jewish purpose, but that purpose is set in a wider frame, whether republicanizing or universalistic in aspiration. Each contains a critical kernel of truth, but, as I will argue, neither does full justice to the affirmative Jewishness of the tomb.[41] What such a claim means remains to be elucidated, which is not a straightforward task, as the notion of "Jewishness" itself admits of more than one meaning.

Let's start with the mechanics of the monument's construction. Schneersohn, as a worldly man, began with fund-raising. The lining up of well-known patrons was an exercise in publicity and an incentive to gift-giving, a show that serious people were willing to associate their names with what must therefore be a deserving enterprise. It also had a political dimension. Godart, a member of the Comité mondial, was dispatched to the Middle East in the summer of 1951 to explain the project to Israel's president Chaim Weizmann and prime minister David Ben-Gurion. They were brought on board, a coup, it was hoped, that would calm the opposition of those Zionists back home who felt that Israel, not France, was the most appropriate venue for a memorial to Europe's murdered Jews.[42]

That did not settle the matter, however. Schneersohn paid a visit to the United States in the fall of 1953 on a fund-raising tour that piqued Zionist sensibilities yet once again. He stopped first in New York City, receiving a welcome that exceeded all expectation. Jewish groups from across the spectrum rallied to Schneersohn's campaign, from the Yiddish-language press to labor organizations like the Workmen's Circle and ILGWU to mainstream organizations like the American Jewish Committee and B'nai B'rith. The New York City leg of the journey was capped off by a November meeting. Telford Taylor spoke, as did the French Consul General Jean de Lagarde and representatives of the American Labor Committee and AJC, but it was Eleanor Roosevelt's concluding remarks that left the most enduring impression. She urged all assembled to keep alive "the memory of the six million Jews massacred by the Nazis with an unheard-of ferocity."[43] Schneersohn then moved on to Cleveland, where he was hosted by Rabbi Abba Hillel Silver, a major figure in the Reform movement in the United States, who pledged $1,000 to jump-start a public subscription to fund Schneersohn's memorial project. It was at this juncture that Schneersohn received a telegram from Nahum Goldmann, a friend who was also president of the World Jewish Congress and a well-connected Zionist. The Israeli government desired to have a talk with him. [44] The preceding August, the Knesset had enacted legislation providing for creation of a genocide memorial in Israel, Yad Vashem, and Israeli officials worried that Schneersohn was poaching on fund-raising terrain they wanted for themselves.

Without delay, Schneersohn returned to Paris and then, in the company of Vidal Modiano, a member of Schneersohn's inner circle, made his way to Israel for a difficult negotiation. The CDJC team met with Minister of Education Ben-Zion Dinur, and an accord was hashed out and signed in the spring of 1954. Schneersohn made two concessions. The CDJC had intended its memorial to include a Yizkor or memory book inscribed with the names of the Jewish millions assassinated by the Nazis. It had in fact begun compiling a list of the dead, and Schneersohn promised to turn it over to Yad Vashem, which was henceforth awarded priority in the gathering of names. Schneersohn also pledged to scale back his fund-raising activities. For that sacrifice, however, he won a major concession in return. Nahum Goldmann was an original member of the Conference on Jewish Material Claims against Germany founded in 1951. German reparations payments were funneled through the Claims Conference, as it was called, which redistributed them as needed. Under the terms of the 1954 agreement, the Claims Conference was prevailed upon to supply Schneersohn the funding he required to

complete the Tombeau du Martyr juif inconnu. Yad Vashem had
asserted its precedence vis-à-vis Schneersohn's memorial, but at least
the project now had Israel's unreserved blessing – a sop to French
Zionists who still harbored second thoughts about the project – and,
most important of all, it appeared that Schneersohn's fund-raising head-
aches were over.[45]

Or almost. Elie Wiesel had attended the 1953 cornerstone laying and
was moved by the experience, but he balked at the deal with the Claims
Conference. It was not right, he felt, to use German money to construct a
monument to Jews the Germans themselves had murdered, and Wiesel's
reservations were shared by more official instances, the Consistory
among them. The CDJC devised a solution to appease its critics. Its
memorial project envisaged an underground crypt and the eventual
interment there of ashes from the camps. This was designed to be sacred
space, and Vidal Modiano tendered a solemn promise: not a cent of
Claims Conference funding would be used to build it, that money
coming instead from private sources.[46]

Schneersohn's fund-raising efforts are revelatory in two respects. The
CDJC had to work hard to clear a space in a French Jewish community
that was not always welcoming, and it succeeded, wedging itself in
between an official Judaism suspicious of newcomers and a Zionist
fraction that judged Schneersohn's approach too Diaspora-centered.
He succeeded, moreover, in a second sense. Jewish communities from
the United States to Israel were made to take note of Schneersohn's
ambitions. The monument he was planning was not meant to be a matter
of local interest alone, but one designed to speak to and for world Jewry
as a whole.[47]

How Schneersohn set about collecting funds says something about the
CDJC's place, real and hoped for, in Jewish life at home and abroad.
How he managed to pilot the project through the maze of France's
municipal and state bureaucracies is eloquent in its own way, providing
a clue to the network of friends and contacts Schneersohn was able to call
upon and, by extension, to the CDJC's place on the political checker-
board of France's Fourth Republic.

In July 1951, the Paris municipal council voted to set aside a plot of
land for the tomb and invited the prefect of the Seine to identify a suitable
lot "preferably" in Paris' IVe arrondissement.[48] Why the IVe? Because in
prewar days, it was here, in the Marais, that the city's Jewish community
had made its home. The prefect, Paul Haag, had just such a site available,
located on the rue Geoffroy-l'Asnier. It was not mere chance that
the French state found itself in a position to allocate property in the
neighborhood. This corner of Paris was run-down, and the rue

Geoffroy-l'Asnier area had been designated years before as one in need of refurbishment. During the war, Vichy authorities expropriated the land, profiting from the flight and dispossession of the local Jewish inhabitants, which were in good measure the result of the regime's own anti-Semitic policies.[49] In the event, the state did not redevelop the property but held onto it, until Haag awarded a portion to the CDJC, a decision formalized in the spring of 1952.

Schneersohn meanwhile set about assembling an executive committee to oversee the monument's progress, and Haag's contact on the committee was Georges Huisman, a Jew, a councilor of state, and a veteran arts administrator. In the run-up to the Second World War, Huisman had played a key role as director-general of fine arts in making arrangements for the removal of Paris' art masterpieces to safe storage outside the city. Vichy, however, did not value such service or Huisman's Jewishness, and he was sacked from his position in July 1940. Huisman then was a man with administrative connections who also knew the French art scene, and so it's little wonder that Schneersohn had wanted to recruit him to the memorial executive committee. In the event, the choice paid immediate dividends. When it came time to finding architects for the project, Huisman was prepared to take charge. He made a proposal to the executive committee: that it award the commission outright to the team of Georges Goldberg and Alexandre Persitz, forgoing the usual public competition. In June 1952, the committee assented to the recommendation, and it's not difficult to guess why.[50] Both men had direct knowledge of the catastrophe that they were appointed to commemorate. Goldberg had lost family members in the Nazi genocide, and Persitz had been deported to Auschwitz. Persitz's architectural credentials, moreover, were first-class. He had collaborated with Auguste Perret (like Georges-Henri Pingusson) in the postwar reconstruction of the bombed-out port of Le Havre, taking up a position after that as editor-in-chief of *Architecture d'aujourd'hui*, France's premier review of modernist design.

The site that Goldberg and Persitz had to work with imposed limitations on what they could do. The building at the rear of the lot was in a state of decrepitude, and it was desirable that the memorial back on to it in order to block it from view. Second of all, the rue Geoffroy-l'Asnier was a narrow street, and right nearby stood (and still stands) a school. In order not to block the sight lines of the school windows, the front portion of the tomb had to be low-lying, if not flush to the ground.[51] The architects found solutions to both problems, coming up with an original design scheme composed of three major elements: at the back, abutting the structure behind, a four-story building fronted by a large wall with a

Figure 5.1 Exterior view, Tombeau du Martyr Juif Inconnu, Paris, 1956

bronze Star of David affixed to its outward face; in front of that, a horizontal space; and beneath the surface, a pair of rooms – a room of remembrance and a crypt. A fourth element was added later, as the project was fine-tuned: a vasque or bronze cylinder, inscribed in relief with the names of concentration camps. It was sited a short distance in front of the memorial wall and featured a skylight through which natural light filtered, illuminating the crypt below (see Figure 5.1).

Goldberg and Huisman laid out the scheme to the memorial executive committee in January 1954. It is evident from the presentation that they anticipated push-back to the effect that this wasn't "Jewish architecture" of a conventional sort. Huisman acknowledged the objection, but countered that the decision to do something different was a conscious one. The idea was not to build a synagogue but a composition whose architectural elements were expressive in themselves. The committee, it appears, was persuaded and ratified the proposal without a dissenting vote.[52]

Haag was then brought into the loop, and, as he wrote to a colleague Pierre Couinaud (a Gaullist deputy who had also taken an interest in the project), he intended to involve himself "personally" in guiding it through the bureaucratic labyrinth that lay ahead.[53] The first hurdle was the Commission départementale des Sites, perspectives et paysages, and here there were no problems. The commission's chairman, Richard Pouzet, was very much in favor, and the commission followed Pouzet's lead, voting the project through unanimously. The Ministère de l'Intérieur's Commission centrale des Monuments commémoratifs, presided by the arts administrator Robert Rey, was almost as cooperative. The commission's chief architect judged the monument "of a great nobility and tact." He worried, though, that it was too austere, above all the monument wall, which was so bare and forbidding. In response, Louis Arretche, an associate of Goldberg and Persitz, sketched in changes to the scheme, which he submitted to the commission. It's not clear what alterations he proposed. In the end, the wall was covered with inscriptions, and this may have been on Arretche's recommendation. What is certain – and he said as much to the commissioners – is that he was determined to preserve the monument's "soberness" and "simplicity of line … avoiding the grandiloquence and allegories so full of pitfalls from the point of view of Art." Arretche's amendments, whatever they were, sufficed to bring the commission around.[54]

All that was needed now was a construction permit, and the man invested with the authority to issue it was the minister of the interior, François Mitterrand. The ministry stalled for reasons unknown. Schneersohn, however, was not one to be deterred, and a full-court press was mobilized. Couinaud lobbied Mitterrand and so too, it seems, did Jean Cassou and René Mayer, a well-connected Radical politician who was also a CDJC backer. Schneersohn himself went straight to the top, paying a visit to Mitterrand's superior, then Prime Minister Pierre Mendès France. All this worked to change the ministry's mind. Mitterrand signed off on the project in November 1954, construction powered forward, and the monument was ready for unveiling less than two years later.[55]

All things considered, the process had been an efficient and uncomplicated one. This was in part thanks to Schneersohn's personal dynamism and to the qualities of the project itself, its tact and sobriety. But it was also due to the cast of characters involved who hastened the project on its way: Huisman, Haag, Pouzet, Rey, Couinaud, Cassou, Mayer, and Mendès France. Who were these men? A number were Jewish: Huisman, who had spent much of the war in hiding in France; Mayer, who had served as a minister in de Gaulle's CFLN administration in

Algiers; and Mendès France, who had done the same (after a stint in the Free French Air Force). The others were not Jewish (although Cassou's wife was). What almost all of them did have in common was a connection to the Resistance. Cassou's and Pouzet's wartime credentials have already been cited in this and previous chapters. Couinaud and Rey both belonged to Resistance networks that came to the aid of downed aviators or Free French operatives on the run. The Gestapo in fact caught up with Couinaud, who ended the war as a concentration camp prisoner. As for Haag, he does not seem to have been a Resistance militant himself, but he was the father of one. Haag's son, also named Paul, was arrested for "acts of resistance" and died in deportation.[56]

Schneersohn's memorial scheme encountered not indifference but a well-intentioned welcome from the network of résistants who manned the institutions of the Fourth Republic. The fate that the Jews had suffered was not alien to them. Rather, they were moved to help out, extending patronage to the project that in the event proved indispensable to its speedy realization. Yet, what about the monument complex itself? Did it speak to the concerns of world Jewry, whose contributions had done so much to get the project off the ground? Or was it a monument of a different sort, affirmative of values, secular and republican, that might hold appeal for the cadre of well-wishers, résistants almost to a man, who had steered the project through to completion? In fact, do these two options even exhaust the full range of possibilities? The answer to such questions is not a simple one.

For a certainty, the project's backers knew how to frame it in the rhetoric of a soaring universalism. France, as Schneersohn explained, was the most fitting place for such a memorial, for France had proven itself time and again the most loyal friend of "the humanitarian and democratic ideal."[57] And in France, there was no more fitting site than the national capital. The memorial executive committee met in joint session with members of the Claims Conference in February 1955. The executive committee was represented by Daniel Mayer, another former résistant with a CDJC connection, who was designated to help make the memorial's case. He addressed the "why Paris" question head on, and the answer he formulated was a humanistic one: "Paris has played a front-rank role in the struggle for the liberation of man," words that carried a special weight coming from someone who was not just a former résistant but also a socialist deputy in the National Assembly representing a Parisian constituency.[58]

Such sentiments found an echo in the May 1953 ceremonials orchestrated in association with the laying of the monument's first stone. The scene was decorated with a giant Star of David draped in black crepe and a tricolor flag. A detachment of the Garde républicaine was on hand in full dress uniform, and there were musical selections, patriotic in theme. A trumpet blasted "Aux Champs" to open the proceedings, followed by "La Marseillaise." There were then speeches, after which "Aux Morts" was played. Like the American "Taps," this mournful melody, composed in 1932, is associated with the commemoration of fallen soldiers.[59] About the speeches, one merits singling out in the present connection, that of Pierre Couinaud, who talked about his own experience of deportation. He remembered "the human fraternity" that he had known in the camps and the "shared ideal" that had sustained the inmate population, himself included. Couinaud went on to cite the work of David Rousset and Georges Wellers, which had detailed "in such a faithful fashion" the truth about "the concentrationary universe," winding up the speech on a pacific note. Great as the suffering had been, Couinaud counseled all those assembled to turn a deaf ear to the siren calls of anger and vengeance.[60]

Some of the same ritual elements were replicated in October 1956, when the completed monument was inaugurated. The president of the National Assembly, André Le Troquer (also a former minister of Free France), attended. As he arrived, a detachment of the Garde républicaine presented arms, and "Aux Champs" was sounded. Pierre Ruais, the president of the Paris municipal council, was one orator among a half dozen, and he recalled the praiseworthy conduct of Paris' "non-Jewish inhabitants" under the Occupation, who had provided "aid and asylum to a pitiable prey of children, women, and the elderly."[61] The speeches once concluded, Le Troquer, hedged around by "orphans of the deportation," cut the monument ribbon, and, as in 1953, the Garde républicaine played "Aux morts." The minister descended into the crypt; an orphan lit the "flame"; and the ceremony drew to a close. The UNADIF newspaper, Le Déporté, reported on the event, and it did not hesitate to number the Jewish dead as brothers: "As for us, deportees like our Jewish comrades, we consider as our own all the unknown martyrs in whose memory this edifice was erected."[62]

This acknowledgment of comradeship, moreover, was no mere rhetorical flourish. In 1957, that year's observance of the Journée nationale de la Déportation featured a new element. Included on the scheduled program was a wreath-laying ceremony on Sunday morning, April 28, at the still new Tombeau du Martyr juif inconnu. Representatives from the Réseau du souvenir and associated deportee organizations took part. A visit to the crypt, followed by rendition of "Aux Morts" and a moment of silence, concluded the proceedings, and the participants then moved on to the next stop. The same ritual observance was performed the year following and the year after that and so on.[63] The CDJC was exultant that its memorial now ranked among the "high places of popular piety" alongside Mont-Valérien and the Arc de Triomphe.[64] Schneersohn had coveted such recognition, and it seems to have been Wellers who brought it about. Wellers was a member of UNADIF (he would serve at one point as the organization's vice-president) and, through UNADIF, made contact with the Réseau du souvenir, which proved amenable to Schneersohn's wish. There was one final gesture of inclusion. In October 1958, Schneersohn was inducted into the Légion d'honneur. René Cassin pinned on the medal in a ceremony attended by Cassou. Cassin, a luminary of French Jewish life, was a former résistant – yet one more – who had worked side by side with de Gaulle in London.[65]

This then is one way to read the monument: as an expression of the desire of French Jews to belong – to belong through ritual practices that mimicked the Republic's cult of the heroic dead and that inscribed the Jewish story of sacrifice into the nation's saga of Resistance. The CJDC extended its hand to the Fourth Republic and to the deportee community, and, no less remarkable, that gesture was reciprocated.

To leave the story there, however, is to miss much of the monument's complexity. I will start with a minor point. Deportation narratives, as I have observed, often came clothed in Christianizing garb, and the Tombeau du Martyr juif inconnu proved no exception, improbable as that might seem. Justin Godart was a man with a yearning for the universal, and to attain the heights he aspired to, he tended to a spiritualizing language that at times made him sound more like Jacques Maritain than the Lyonnais politician he was. Godart, of course, was invited to talk at the memorial's 1956 inauguration. He spoke, as he told the audience, not in hatred but in reverence for "those who suffered and died for the most serene spirituality ... for the inviolability and eminent dignity of the human person." These millions of Jewish martyrs, he went on, had not died in vain, because the lives taken from them had given new life "to the fatherland of their ancestors." In this instance the fatherland Godart had in mind was not France. From death, as he put it, had come resurrection, "the prodigious resurrection of Israel."[66]

These were not, it needs emphasizing, the passing sentiments of an orator carried away by the moment. Two sets of verse grace the front wall of the memorial, the topmost in Hebrew (about which more in a moment) and one underneath in French. It was Godart who supplied the latter. Here's the wording that he first proposed to the memorial executive committee:

> The forgetfulness of evil is evil's accomplice
> Remember the persecuted
> Blessed be they
> Remember the persecutors
> Cursed be they
> Before the unknown Jewish martyr
> Bow in respect and piety for the martyrs
> Follow in your thoughts the length of their dolorous path
> It will take you to the highest summit
> Of justice and truth

The committee opted to edit down the text. It was essential, Persitz insisted, to be "laconic." Others objected to the curse cast on the persecutors. The memorial was not an incitation to vengeance but a call to piety, and so the first five lines had to go, which they did.[67] Retained, however, was Godart's invitation to walk in thought down the martyrs' "dolorous path." The reference here is evident, calling to mind another martyr's path, the Via Dolorosa, which was the route Jesus himself had traced on the way to Golgotha.

Make no mistake, however. For all the referents of a republican, universalizing, or Christian nature, the Tombeau du Martyr juif inconnu was a Jewish monument, and it did not hide the fact. It's not just the monument's name and location that proclaimed its Jewishness, but also the Magen David motif, which was everywhere. On the outside, a great bronze Star of David ornamented the front wall, visible from afar. The latticework that decorated both sides of the building behind was patterned with Jewish stars. Inside, in the crypt, ashes from the camps were interred in an urn that was itself entombed in a large black marble slab sculpted in the shape of a Magen David. As for the skylight just overhead that illuminated the crypt, it too was in the shape of a Jewish star (see Figure 5.2).

To note the monument's pervasive Jewish symbolism, however, is just a starting point, for symbols can mean many things. Goldberg and Persitz, as noted, had no intention of building a synagogue-like edifice, which they did not, and to this degree, the memorial wasn't a religious monument of the usual kind. That said, biblical reference and religious observance were very much woven into the design of the structure and the way that it was used.

The major exterior design elements, the wall and the vasque in front of it, reminded Maurice Carr, a journalist for the *Jerusalem Post*, of "a giant grave and tombstone" with the vasque, on this reading, taking on the

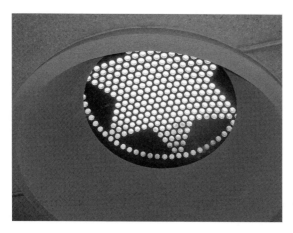

Figure 5.2 Crypt skylight, Tombeau du Martyr Juif Inconnu, Paris, 1956

aspect of a Yahrzeit or memorial candle.[68] On the wall itself were inscriptions, the uppermost in Hebrew characters adjuring passers-by to "Remember the evil that the Amalek of modern times has done to you. He has annihilated six million sons of Israel, men, women, children unarmed and defenseless." The author was Zalman Shneur, a Hebrew and Yiddish-language poet then resident in Israel. The relevance here is the invocation of Amalek, a figure from the Hebrew bible, the grandson of Esau and founder of the Amalekite people. The Amalekites were the first to war against the ancient Hebrews, and the two nations had remained adversaries ever since. Saul battled against the Amalekite king Agag, and in the Book of Esther, Haman, a descendant of Amalek's, schemed to destroy the Jewish people utterly. On Shneur's accounting, Hitler was just the most recent in a long line of mortal enemies, and in drawing that connection, he enrolled the genocide of the Jews into a millennial history that dated back to biblical times.[69]

A similar mix of Jewish religious forms and biblical referents was also in evidence inside the monument. From the very beginning, Goldberg and Persitz had imagined a downstairs made up of two spaces, an antechamber or memory room and the crypt proper. In the memory room was to be stored a library of Remembrance books, the volumes aligned in armoires built into the wall. It is a tradition in Jewish congregations to keep a list of the dead, and in the aftermath of the Second World War, that tradition was adapted by the decimated communities of Eastern Europe to preserve a record of all those who had been swept away, otherwise unmemorialized, in the Nazi genocide.[70] For

Figure 5.3 Crypt, Tombeau du Martyr Juif Inconnu, Paris, 1956.
Photo by Godong/Universal Images Group via Getty Images

Schneersohn, a rabbi and the son of rabbis, this was a sacred duty, for these dead had perished as martyrs, Kiddush HaShem, "in sanctification of the Holy Name."[71]

As for the crypt itself, this was the most sacred space of all, reached by a short downward flight of steps from the memory room (see Figure 5.3). At the crypt's center stands the Magen David–shaped black marble slab containing the ashes from the camps. Upon it burns a flame, an allusion to the eternal flame beneath the Arc de Triomphe but also to the Ner Tamid or eternal light located in every synagogue above the Torah Ark.[72] Three walls surround the star, and memorial planners debated whether to adorn them or not. At the outset, it was thought to decorate just the rear wall with an inscription in French to the "six million Jewish victims assassinated by Nazism," but the idea was scrapped.[73] A subsequent proposal provided for inscriptions on all three walls: a biblical text at the back, on the left verses from the "Chant des Partisans" of the Vilna Ghetto (known by the title "Zog nit keynmol" in the original Yiddish), and on the right a poem in French by Jean Cassou. This scheme too fell by the wayside. Cassou's poem celebrated the heroism and sacrifice of the Resistance, but it made no mention of Jews per se, an absence that the memorial executive committee deemed inappropriate for "a work essentially Jewish and ... international."[74] Along with Cassou's poem, out went the verses from the "Chant des partisans" of the Vilna Ghetto. There was to be just a single, biblical inscription on the back wall, with the two walls on either side left bare. The inscription that was in the end selected was composed of two verses and came from the most appropriate of sources, Lamentations (1:12 and 2:21). They were printed in the original Hebrew and translate as follows:

Behold, and see if there be any pain like unto my pain/My virgins and my young men are fallen by the sword.

At all the memorial's founding ceremonials, moreover, a rabbinic presence dignified the associated observances, which without fail included elements drawn from traditional Jewish religious practice. In 1953, at the cornerstone laying, a religious service followed on the speechmaking. Rabbi Jacob Kaplan presided. An orphan recited the Kaddish, the Jewish prayer for the dead, as the rue de la Victoire synagogue choir intoned the "Chant des partisans" of the Vilna Ghetto.[75] The inauguration event of 1956 was organized along similar lines – speeches followed by a religious ceremony – with one minor difference. Kaplan, now the Grand Rabbi of France, presided, and an orphan recited the Kaddish, but instead of the "Chant des partisans" of the Vilna Ghetto, a cantor, who was himself an Auschwitz survivor, chanted the El Malei Rachamim, a standard mourning prayer that beseeches a merciful God to gather in the souls of the departed.[76] Most solemn of all, however, was the February 24, 1957 inhumation of ashes from the camps. Camp survivors transported the ashes from the Montparnasse Cemetery to the memorial. They were then interred in the crypt and covered over with a layer of Jerusalem soil, those present sobbing all the while. For the occasion, the crypt was transformed into a cemetery, consecrated ground, which allowed for the performance of ritual burial services. Psalm 91 was read, a prayer for deliverance to the Lord, "my refuge and my fortress." Grand Rabbi Kaplan spoke, rendering homage "to our brothers and sisters who died in sanctification of God's name." The recitation of the Kaddish and the lighting of the Ner Tamid (that is how the sources referred to it) concluded the solemnities.[77]

The memorial, then, may not have been a synagogue-like space or a religious edifice in a conventional sense. But it did come steeped in the practices and symbolism of the Jewish faith and to that extent represented something more complicated than an assimilationist bid to smooth away the rough edges of Jewish experience, the better to fit it into the mold of a more universal story.

Recall also that this was a memorial to the murdered Jews of Europe. It did not, as did the Consistory plaque, refrain from naming the Jewish

Figure 5.4 Vasque, Tombeau du Martyr Juif Inconnu, Paris, 1956

dead as such, but singled them out for special remembrance. The monument's exterior wall was blazoned with Shneur's coded allusion to Hitler, the Amalek of modern times. There was also the vasque, sometimes described as a memorial candle but just as often interpreted as a concentration camp chimney, which makes sense in light of the names marked upon it: those of eleven camps from Auschwitz to Treblinka plus that of the Warsaw Ghetto (see Figure 5.4).[78] On the inside, the memory room is consecrated to the remembrance of the Jewish victims of Nazi barbarism, and the ashes interred in the crypt are the ashes of Jews murdered in the camps. I would cite just one final piece of evidence, having to do with the crypt's lighting scheme: it is illuminated by six floor lamps, each beam said to represent one million of the six million Jews who were Hitler's victims.[79]

For all these reasons, it is tempting to label the Tombeau du Martyr juif inconnu a Holocaust memorial, but the word needs to be used with caution in the present context. Godart uttered it at the cornerstone laying. He ventriloquized the dead as they called out from the tomb, imploring the living not to shed tears "for from our frightful ordeal has come forth our nation, for our holocaust has been the price of its resurrection on the land of our ancestors."[80] Godart, however, was alone in this regard. Schneersohn and the others balked at the word "Holocaust" with its sacrificial, Christianizing overtones, preferring instead to speak of the six million. These six million had died anonymous deaths, gassed and turned to ash, and the Tombeau de Martyr juif inconnu was designed to provide them the sepulcher that they had never had. Even more than that, however, it was designed to tell the world something about who they had been.

Now recall that Schneersohn and virtually all the men he worked with originated in Eastern Europe. This fact mattered a good deal, and it inflected the memorial's narrative of the Nazi genocide. On either side of the Magen David on the monument's front wall was etched an inscription, exhorting readers: "Never forget." One was written in Hebrew and the other in Yiddish. The Nazis did not just obliterate families and towns, they destroyed an entire civilization, and it was a Yiddish-speaking one. CDJC officials were committed to keeping the language alive, making an effort to see to it that a few words of Yiddish were pronounced on all ceremonial occasions.[81]

No less an effort was made, moreover, to preserve the memory of that community of Jews, Polish in the majority, for which Yiddish had been the mother tongue. This helps to explain why the Warsaw Ghetto, though not a camp, was singled out for mention on the vasque. This is also the moment to say something about the museum created in conjunction with the memorial. It had a permanent collection that laid out "the principal stages of Hitler's persecutions" with a special room set aside, a "chamber of horrors" as one journalist described it, for photographs of the most gruesome aspects of the Nazi genocide. The museum included a maquette of the Warsaw Ghetto, which was also the theme of more than one special exhibition.[82] Eight such special exhibitions in fact were mounted in the museum's first decade, two of them devoted to the camps, one to the machinery of destruction, one to Eichmann, but also two to the Warsaw Ghetto (more on the remaining two later). A catalogue was published in connection with the second of these shows, titled À la Glorieuse Mémoire des Juifs de Pologne (1961).[83] The Consistory plaque memorializing the wartime dead did not mention the Jews by name, but the CDJC knew no such hesitations. There had been six million killed: they were Jews, Yiddish-speakers, Poles, sons and daughters of a glorious civilization now extinguished.

That civilization had not died, however, without a fight. Resistance was yet another theme in the memorial's narrative arsenal, and it came with a Zionist overlay, the combativeness of Jews in the years of Nazi persecution prefiguring the combativeness of Israelis today. This story was not built into the monument the way the stories of Jewish remembrance and loss were, but it was very much a part of the commemorative practices associated with it. Think first of all of the synagogue choir singing the "Chant des partisans" of the Vilna Ghetto at the 1953 cornerstone ceremony. The event coincided almost to the day with the tenth anniversary of the crushing of the Warsaw Ghetto uprising. Couinaud spoke on the occasion and made a point of sending greetings to Israeli Prime Minister David Ben-Gurion. Shmuel Divon, the Israeli chargé d'affaires, was also on the roster of orators, and when it came his turn to speak, in a "spontaneous manifestation," the crowd present burst into "Hatikvah."[84]

The emotions ran yet higher in 1956, and well they might. The inauguration ceremony of that year coincided with the Suez crisis. The tribune was decorated with the flags of both France and Israel. The president of the Republic, René Coty, had been scheduled to attend but did not, detained by pressing matters of state (he paid a visit later in July 1957 to lay a wreath at the vasque and descend into the crypt).[85] For those who were present, the fighting overseas did not seem so far away. Nahum Goldmann invoked the ghetto revolts of Warsaw, Vilna, and Bialystok and then pivoted to the theme of Israel, the Jewish people's hope and answer to Nazi barbarism.[86] In 1956, as in 1953, the Israeli state was represented, although this time not by an embassy official but by the ambassador himself, Jacob Tsur. Tsur spoke first in French, saluting the Warsaw Ghetto heroes, "those last bands of men hunted down unarmed who knew how to put up a fight with what little strength remained, a fight without hope." He then switched to Hebrew, which was a breach of protocol. Diplomats were not supposed to speak in a language that might not be understood in the hosting country, but this did not stop Tsur, who had an urgent message to deliver. Israel was there, there to gather to its bosom the "surviving remnant" (Sh'erit HaPletah) of European Jewry and to build and defend a new Jewish reality, enabling thereby the spirit of those millions who had died "Kiddush HaShem" to live on. With that, Tsur concluded his remarks, quoting from the Book of Job (14:7–9):

> For there is hope of a tree,
> If it be cut down, that it will sprout again,
> And that the tender branch thereof will not cease.
> Though the root thereof wax old in the earth,
> And the stock thereof die in the ground;
> Yet through the scent of water it will bud,
> And put forth boughs like a plant.

The ambassador's message was a simple one. Israel had taken up the banner of revolt first raised by the ghetto fighters, and the tree of Jewish life, felled in Europe, was now blossoming anew in the Promised Land.[87]

The Warsaw Ghetto uprising and the founding of the State of Israel were indeed paired events in the CDJC imaginary. In April 1957, as already noted, the memorial was included in the commemoration of that year's Journée nationale de la Déportation. The official morning ceremony was brief, but Schneersohn organized a second, grander event in the afternoon, this one not national, but Jewish, honoring the Warsaw Ghetto revolt. A pattern of observance was thus established – an official morning event followed later in the day by a Jewish one – that was repeated every subsequent year. Then, in 1958, the memorial museum opened an exhibition devoted to Israel, titled "From Cataclysm to new life, twenty-five years of Jewish histories." The curators went all out, making use of documents, maps, films, maquettes, and lighting effects to create a multimedia experience that chronicled the renaissance of the Jewish people "on the land of its ancestors."[88] This then was the plot line of modern Jewish history as it unfurled across two continents: a people, unbowed even in martyrdom, was destroyed and then reborn. It bears a resemblance to the Christian story of death and resurrection, but with an important difference. The Jews were at one and the same time martyrs *and* fighters, and they had fought in old Europe as they did still in the Middle East.

The point was hammered home in the eighth exhibition in the memorial museum's inaugural cycle of shows. The theme this time was Jewish resistance in the fight against Hitler. The ghetto uprisings and Sonderkommando revolts were highlighted, but there was also an "Israeli section" designed to demonstrate the continuities in courage and heroism between Jewish resistance in Europe and present-day Israel's fight for survival. The theme, not a new one for the memorial museum, had added significance in January 1965, the date the exhibition opened. This was just three years after Eichmann's execution. The lead prosecutor at the Eichmann trial, Gideon Hausner, had raised time and again the question of Jewish passivity in the face of Nazi persecution. Europe's Jews had marched into the gas chambers like sheep to the slaughter – such was the image evoked. It was one that the memorial's creators never endorsed, and the 1965 exhibition was in this sense more than an informational exercise. It was also an argument.[89]

For so many reasons, then, the memorial complex was something remarkable. It was first of all resolute in its modernism. The architects used geometric forms and materials of an elemental, natural beauty. They kept decoration to a bare minimum, eschewing allegorical figures, indeed, any figures at all.[90] Sober, stripped down, these were the descriptors employed time and again to characterize Goldberg and Persitz's achievement. As for the archive and museum behind, they were functional in design, and the museum's curators strove to be as up-to-date and media savvy as possible. The idea was not to isolate objects but to frame them, to contextualize them as did "the most important historical and ethnographic museums."[91] Such modernist aspirations ought not to come as a surprise. Persitz's modernist bona fides have already been cited. From 1956, the president of the memorial's Museum Commission was Jean Cassou, a loyal CDJC associate who also happened to be director of Paris' Musée national d'art moderne.[92] The result of such combined efforts was a memorial ensemble unlike any other – a monument, museum, and archive all rolled into one – that established a template for future memorials, but in its time was without equivalent.[93]

All this creativity was applied in part to proclaim humanitarian ideals and to carve out a space for Jewish memory in France's national story of Deportation and Resistance. That's all true, but it's just the beginning of an interpretation. The memorial faced onto the street and proclaimed its Jewishness to all passersby, and what a complex Jewishness that was. The Jewish experience, the loss of six million, was sui generis; these hallowed dead were entitled to all the rites of mourning and remembrance that Jewish tradition afforded; and they deserved recognition, not just as martyrs, but as the fighters so many of them had been, résistants whose combative spirit lived on in the land of Israel. In unexpected measure, moreover, that recognition was forthcoming. Deportee organizations embraced the Jewish dead as comrades, and officials of the Republic from the president on down came to deliver speeches and pay respects.

Such a conclusion, however, raises yet further questions. Why first of all was France such a pioneer in memorializing the Jewish tragedy? And there's a second puzzle. It's long been thought, as noted, that the genocide was not talked about in the 1950s, the regnant silence preserved unbroken until the Eichmann trial in some accounts or the Six-Day War of 1967 in others. Yet, there's no doubt that the CDJC made a lot of noise in the fifties and that it was heard at least in certain quarters, all of which suggests that the notion of an ambient silence about the Nazi genocide deserves to be set aside. But does it?

The first question is the simpler of the two to deal with. France in the aftermath of the Second World War boasted a Jewish community of 200,000–250,000 persons, the largest such in Europe, apart from the Soviet Union.[94] Few French Jewish deportees returned from the camps, but many tens of thousands had survived the Occupation in hiding, among them men like Poliakov and Schneersohn. Like Poliakov and Schneersohn, many of the survivors were foreign-born, onetime refugees from an Eastern European world now vanished. These immigrants embraced France as a new homeland, subscribing to the tenets of a "Jewish republicanism" that recognized in the Republic's cult of liberty a secular variant of Jewish values. That did not mean, however, that they subscribed to the code of discretion practiced by French-born Jews, who were inclined to confine expressions of Jewish identity to the private sphere. These newcomers did not address the world with consistorial reticence, but were prepared to speak out.

France's Jewish community, moreover, was mutating in ways that made it more disposed to pay attention. The war years had pulverized Jewish life, but as the Occupation drew to a close and in its immediate aftermath, a rash of new Jewish organizations came into being to help knit the community back together: the Conseil représentatif des Israélites de France (CRIF), founded clandestinely during the war itself, and the Fonds social juif unifié (FSJU), which was launched in 1949. The former was an umbrella group that brought together representatives from diverse currents in Jewish life. It even included communist delegates in its first years, although they were frozen out in the early 1950s as Cold War differences hardened. As for the FSJU, it was a funding organism which, like the United Jewish Appeal in the United States, channeled monies to entities in need, the CDJC among them.[95] The Consistory was not excluded from this new institutional scaffolding. Indeed, by statute, it was authorized to name CRIF's president, but it was now one actor, however important, among many in a constellation of organizations that was engaged less in synagogue affairs than in the provision of youth and welfare services, the construction of community centers, and the like. This new apparatus, moreover, had ramifying connections to the wider world. There was an increasing receptivity to the Zionist project and an openness to American influence as well. Almost sixty percent of the FSJU's budget in 1960 derived from a single US source, the American Jewish Joint Distribution Committee. The CDJC's appearance on the scene was not an isolated event, but part of a process of communal reconstruction. The center's fit into this new world was not always an easy one, but fit it did. The FSJU's president from 1950 to 1982 was Guy de Rothschild, also one of the invited speakers at the memorial's corner-stone laying in 1953 and again at the 1956 inauguration ceremony. CRIF's president in the fifties and sixties was Vidal Modiano, the same man who accompanied Schneersohn to Israel in 1954 to negotiate the fund-raising deal with Yad Vashem.[96]

So why France? Because in the first place France had a Jewish community substantial in number and one that was edging out from under consistorial hegemony, even as it opened itself to new worlds, East and West. It was a community, moreover, composed in significant measure of immigrants who, though ardent French patriots, did not conceive of themselves the way the native-born did, as Israélites, bound as such to maintain a self-effacing façade when out in public.[97] This was the context that created an opening, one that Schneersohn and the CDJC seized upon.

There still remains the question of silence. One possibility is to acknowledge the CDJC's efforts yet query whether they had much resonance beyond a limited public. A portion of the Jewish community took an interest, as did deportee organizations like UNADIF and a gratin of officials, but that was it. I am uneasy with this solution. In 1947, the American war correspondent John Hersey published *The Wall*, a fictional account of life in the Warsaw Ghetto and of the ghetto's apocalyptic liquidation in 1943. In 1958, Leon Uris published *Exodus*, an epic novel of Israel's War of Independence that numbered among its characters an Auschwitz survivor, Dov Landau, who had been a Sonderkommando, then a displaced person in Cyprus, and, at last, a Zionist fighter in the paramilitary Irgun. Both books were smash hits in the United States, spending more weeks on the *New York Times* best-seller list than Anne Frank's diary. What matters for our purposes is that both were translated into French, Hersey's novel as *La Muraille* (1952) with a preface by the Free French hero Joseph Kessel, Uris' as *Exodus* (1959) tout court. Kessel hailed *La Muraille* as "one of the books of the century," and, indeed, it made a splash, running through edition after edition. As for *Exodus*, it notched up, in the estimation of one historian, "an enormous success," and Otto Preminger's film adaption, released in France in May 1961, did just as well, despite uneven reviews. It seems then that elements of the French public, readers and moviegoers alike, were willing to pay attention to the kinds of story the CDJC had to tell.[98]

The issue then might not be "silence" at all, but the nature of the stories told in those first postwar decades and, in addition to that, how they were told. The CDJC's historical scholarship was perpetrator-centered and archive-based, and the archives mined were in large part perpetrator archives. As for Nazism's Jewish victims, they did not so much speak for themselves as they were spoken for, and the narratives crafted most often had redemptive finales. The six million dead were martyrs who in the grand tradition of Jewish martyrology had died in sanctification of the Name, or they were résistants whose fighting spirit foreshadowed the birth of a new nation in the promised land of Israel. These stories were stories for Jews, but not just for them. They were told without rancor or vengeful intent, often prefaced by the legitimating remarks of reputable Gentiles, and this no doubt helped them to gain acceptance with non-Jewish audiences. These audiences, however, looked at Jewish experience not as self-contained and unique but as an episode, even a significant one, in a multichapter story whose contents they thought they already knew. That story was one of universalizing sound and fury. It came in many variants, all of them, though, focused on Nazi barbarism and the resistance of civilized humanity to it. From this perspective, the fate of European Jewry deserved acknowledgment, but it was not for all that the heart of the matter.

This is not silence, but it also is not the story of the Holocaust, as it has come be known. That event accented the victimization of Europe's Jews, and it was often narrated by survivors, camp survivors above all, called on to bear witness. What made the story so compelling was not so much the document as the survivors' own living testimony.[99] There may have been moments of redemption in the testimony they had to give, but there was also much in their experience that was unredeemable. And for a certainty, the Jewish catastrophe was no sidebar. It wasn't a piece of a larger puzzle, but the main event itself, a stand-alone catastrophe unique in awfulness that encapsulated the horrors of the world war, indeed, of the twentieth century in its entirety.

In this measure, the CDJC's narrative of what happened was not yet a Holocaust narrative. Even so, it's worth wondering why this version of events, whatever its virtues or limitations, didn't leave more of a memory trace. For later generations, it was effaced such that they, the children of the sixties and seventies, had the impression that they were discovering the wartime fate of France's Jews as though for the first time.

The explanation for why this should have been so lies in part in the recrudescence in the 1960s of Gaullist memory. The General returned to office in 1958. He had a clear and distinct idea of what the war years had been all about, and Jews qua Jews played next to no role in it. The fledgling Fifth Republic made the General's understanding its own and indeed trumpeted it far and wide. The CDJC's voice, the Jewish voice, was not silenced, but it was hard to pick out amidst the din of Gaullist mythmaking. That din was all the louder for the way it was broadcast, via monuments and ceremonials, of course, but more than that via the mass media, including not least of all television. It is to the Gaullist memorialization of the war years that I now turn.

The Gaullist epic has a birthdate: June 18, 1940. German armies had invaded France in May of that year, notching up victories at astounding speed. Defeat loomed, but France's prime minister, Paul Reynaud, wanted to carry on the fight. He was stymied by a bloc of ministers within his own cabinet, led by Maréchal Philippe Pétain, who favored petitioning for a cessation of hostilities. Reynaud recognized that he was losing control of the situation and on June 16 turned over the reins of power to Pétain. The very next day, the Maréchal issued a radio appeal, suing for an armistice. Charles de Gaulle, a two-star general then in London, did not intend to accept surrender. Winston Churchill's government made a BBC studio available to the General, and on June 18 he broadcast an appeal of his own. In its brevity and eloquence, de Gaulle's "appel du 18 juin" bears a resemblance to Lincoln's Gettysburg Address, and de Gaulle's speech, like Lincoln's, climaxed in a ringing plea. Lincoln had summoned Americans to "a new birth of freedom," and de Gaulle? He urged the French not to yield: "Whatever happens, the flame of French resistance must not and will not die."

So far as de Gaulle was concerned, that flame never did cease to burn. France – not the simulacrum of a nation represented by Pétain but true France – continued to battle Nazi barbarism in a single uninterrupted fight from 1939 straight through to 1945. That fight, in turn, was part of a yet grander struggle. It was an episode, albeit an epochal one, in what de Gaulle labeled in a speech of September 1941 "the thirty years' war for or against the universal domination of Germanism."[1]

The trope of a Thirty Years' War connected France's present conflict with an earlier one, the Great War, in which de Gaulle as a young officer had been wounded and taken prisoner. De Gaulle, in drawing a connection between the two wars, cast himself as a latter-day Clemenceau.[2] Clemenceau, as France's prime minister in the First World War, had saved the French Republic, and a grateful people had bestowed upon him the honorific title of "Father Victory." De Gaulle aspired to do the same in the Second World War and to earn in his turn the nation's unswerving devotion.

The idea of the Thirty Years' War, however, had a second coating of meaning, focused less on the Republic than on the nation and the nation conceived, not so much as the fruit of the French Revolution, but as a more enduring body that dated back centuries beyond the Revolution to medieval times. It is worth recalling in this connection that de Gaulle did not invent the Thirty Years' War idea. In January 1940, Henri Massis, a right-wing essayist with ties to the Action française, published a volume: *La Guerre de trente ans. Destin d'un âge, 1909–1939.*[3] This was the same Massis who in 1913 had copublished with Alfred de Tarde *Les Jeunes Gens d'aujourd'hui*, a key text in France's so-called National Revival. Massis and de Tarde, writing under the pseudonym Agathon, positioned themselves as spokesmen for a rising generation, one that preferred action to words, that rejected the newfangled theorizing of the modern university in the name of classical culture, and that staked all on the bedrock values of nation and religion, the better to steel itself for combat against France's enemies. History had gone on to prove who France's greatest enemy was – Germany – and Massis' two books taken together may thus be read as a gloss – one from the Right – on the experience of an age cohort scarred by two world wars and yet sustained throughout by the timeless ideals of faith and fatherland. Looked at this way, the Thirty Years' War trope is a value-laden one in several senses. In adopting it, de Gaulle was expressing first of all a generational identification. He was born in 1890, and the generational ordeal limned in Massis' oeuvre was very much de Gaulle's own. But the General was also aligning himself with a particular understanding of what it was that had made France strong and great across many lifetimes. He was expressing a commit-ment, not just to the Republic, but also to a set of values, traditionalist and conservative, that were rooted deep in the nation's past.

How de Gaulle conceived the war patterned how he commemorated it, both as a private citizen from the late 1940s into the 1950s and then again as head of state after 1958. There was always more than one France present on such occasions: the France of the Republic but also *la vieille France*.

What, it might be asked, has any of this to do with the Deportation? To the extent others were willing and he was able, de Gaulle absorbed the drama of the Deportation into the epic of Fighting France. Some variants of the deportation story lent themselves to such appropriation, but others did not. Not the communist story of anti-fascism, which Gaullists con-signed to second-class status when they acknowledged it at all, and not the CDJC's of racial persecution and Jewish resistance. Resistance mattered to de Gaulle, of course, but it was French resistance that counted most, with little margin for expressions of particularity.[4] Communists and Jews might well have felt relegated to the outer darkness in the Gaullist scheme of things. This might not have made much difference under the Fourth Republic, when the General lived in semi-retirement, but it came to weigh a great deal in the 1960s when he was back in power and in position to broadcast his version of events to the nation as a whole, all with the backing of state institutions and the state-controlled media.

In the Wilderness

At the Liberation, de Gaulle vied with the Communists over control of the memory of the war, a rivalry, as noted in earlier chapters, that ended in a draw. The fort at Mont-Valérien was the scene of the most intensive contestation. The PCF claimed the *clairière des fusillés* as consecrated ground, and de Gaulle fired back with a counterclaim of his own to the casemate where lay buried fifteen sons and daughters of France. Then in 1946, the General withdrew from public life. Why he did so need not detain us here. What counts for present purposes is that, despite the withdrawal, de Gaulle continued to observe the rites of remembrance at Mont-Valérien, refining a repertoire of symbols and practices that would become the stuff of national celebration when he returned to office just over a decade later.

Now is the moment to revisit in greater detail those early post-Liberation ceremonials. I evoked them in the chapter on communist memory, but this time I want to discuss them from the Gaullist point of view. Paris and its environs were liberated in August 1944. On November 1, All Saints' Day, a uniformed de Gaulle traveled out to Mont-Valérien in the near suburb of Suresnes to pay his respects. The following June 18, the first since the Liberation, he staged a victory parade on the Champs-Élysées. Mont-Valérien was not neglected, but the solemnities there were a quieter affair, de Gaulle lighting a flame in memory of France's fallen in the presence of two hundred Compagnons de la Libération. The Compagnons, it will be recalled, were members of an order the General had created during the war to honor the heroic sacrifice of soldiers and résistants who had rallied to the cause of Free France. These first two ceremonials, so far as Mont-Valérien was concerned, were modest affairs, grave and understated.[5]

Not so, however, the spectacle that unfolded across two days on November 10–11, 1945. This was the event that culminated in the inhumation at Mont-Valérien of the remains of fifteen dead Free

French men and women. It was in Paris that the proceedings began. On the evening of November 10, three funeral corteges, accompanied by units of the Garde républicaine and mounted colonial calvary converged on the Invalides. They conveyed the coffins of the fifteen, which were laid in state under the church dome. At midnight, in the Saint-Louis Chapel, Mass was said, and the next day – Armistice Day – horse-drawn caissons carried the coffins to the Arc de Triomphe, where they were set on a ring of catafalques encircling the Tombeau du Soldat inconnu. De Gaulle, in uniform once again, placed a wreath at the statue of Clemenceau on the Champs-Élysées and made a speech at the arch. In it, he called on the nation to unite as one to honor the fallen fifteen "gathered around him, known only to God, … who, beneath the sacred flame, represent the flower of our race cut down in the first battles of that thirty years' war." A military parade closed the ceremonies, and later that day, the coffins of the honored dead were transported to Mont-Valérien and laid to rest in a provisional crypt.[6]

This was a state funeral grandiose in scale, but de Gaulle would not preside over such a spectacular event again for many years. Effective in January 1946, he resigned as head of state, and out of office, he no longer had the power to orchestrate public commemorations. That didn't mean, however, that de Gaulle did not find a way to preside over unofficial events that enshrined, even if for a more select audience, the Gaullist understanding of what the Second World War had been all about.

In 1946, the General confided to Claude Mauriac (the novelist François Mauriac's eldest son) a heartfelt wish: that every year a commemorative ceremony take pace, linking the Arc de Triomphe and Mont-Valérien, such that the French public would come in time "to think of that Thirty Years' War as a whole."[7] De Gaulle, the man of action, took steps to realize that wish. He named a committee, the Comité du renouvellement de la Flamme au Mont-Valérien, and appointed the chancellor of the Ordre de la Libération to chair it, at that time Admiral Thierry d'Argenlieu. The committee itself was made up of representatives from fifteen recognized Resistance and deportee organizations, Léon Mazeaud's FNDIR and Irène de Lipkowski's ANFROM among them. D'Argenlieu's team went on to design a set of commemorative rites that would not vary except in detail for more than a decade to come.[8]

The timing of the event was never in question. Every June 18 from 1946 onward, loyalists of Free France were summoned to a commemoration of General de Gaulle's stirring call to arms. The celebration itself played out in two movements, the first centered on the Arc de Triomphe.[9] Members of the Ordre de la Libération (they were urged to turn out in uniform), joined by representatives of Resistance and deportee associations, gathered at the arch. A distinguished member of the order, Admiral Thierry d'Argenlieu, for example, or General Edgard de Larminat, lit a torch from the eternal flame. The torch once illuminated, a trumpet sounded "Aux morts"; the assembled observed a minute of silence; and then a cortege of vehicles – scout cars or half-tracks – conveyed the torch and various dignitaries to Mont-Valérien.[10]

The event now moved into its second phase, with de Gaulle himself as the star attraction. He arrived at the fort in an open car and was greeted by the chancellor. The crowd present was not large, composed in the main of Compagnons, Resistance veterans, and family members of the men and women buried in the crypt, their numbers rounded out by military units made available for the occasion. De Gaulle, after the chancellor's initial welcome, saluted the colors, reviewed the troops, and at last, joined by the chancellor, entered the burial vault to pay his respects. On leaving, the General positioned himself before a makeshift cenotaph, decorated with a large Cross of Lorraine, that was situated in front of the crypt. The still-burning torch was handed to him, and, with it, he illuminated a flame at the cenotaph's base. Once more, "Aux morts" was sounded and a moment of silence observed. "La Marseillaise" followed, and then de Gaulle circulated among the crowd, greeting old comrades-in-arms before departing.[11]

The event admitted of variations. It's not clear that military vehicles remained the preferred mode of transportation from the arch to Mont-Valérien. At Mont-Valérien itself, the troops on hand changed from year to year. In 1957, a detachment of cadets from the Saint-Cyr military academy took part, a development that delighted de Gaulle, who was a Saint-Cyr graduate himself. There were additions as well to the musical program that year, which alongside the usual selections included renditions of the "Chant des Partisans" and "Marche Lorraine."[12]

There were variations of a second kind as well, having to do not with the dramaturgy of the memorial event, but with the identity of the heroic dead. In 1952, a sixteenth coffin was interred in the crypt, that of Edmond Grethen, an official who had served in Indochina, where he was executed by the Japanese in 1945.[13] The timing – in the midst of France's current war in Indochina – was critical, the addition signaling the metropole's ongoing commitment to a region of the empire consecrated by the blood of the nation's finest. Two years later, a second addition was made, an urn of ashes from the camps, which was deposited in the crypt in April 1954 in connection with the observance of the first Journée nationale de la Déportation.[14]

So what did all the symbols and ceremonials signify? Every year, the chancellor of the order wrote to the prime minister to ask for help organizing the June 18 commemoration, for a modest financial subvention and the loan of troops. The ceremonials, the letter specified, involved no speechmaking. The objective was to create a "mystique of pious reflection," not to score political points, and so there was no reason for the government to withhold support, which in the event it did not.[15]

The wordlessness and solemnity of the event, however, ought not to obscure just how much it was invested with political meaning. That's most obvious in the Thirty Years' War theme, which emphasized the continuity of sacrifice from the First World War to the Second. A flame burned at the Arc de Triomphe in memory of the unknown soldier, as did a second one, lit from the first, in memory of the sixteen dead buried at Mont-Valérien. In the June 18 ceremonials, "Aux morts" was played at both sites and special honors accorded to old soldiers, like d'Argenlieu, Larminat, and de Gaulle himself, all three veterans of the twentieth century's two world wars. Homage was also paid to Georges Clemenceau, establishing a direct link between de Gaulle and his illustrious predecessor in wartime leadership. In all these ways, the June 18 ceremonials positioned the saga of Free France as an extension of the Republic's own unending battle against the German foe.

The notion of continuity was meaningful in a second sense. An armistice may have been signed in 1940, but it had not been legitimate. This was an article of faith in the Gaullist credo. True France never gave up the fight, and the dead at Mont-Valérien bore silent witness to the nation's refusal to yield. Who were they after all? Three (Hedhili ben Salem ben Hadj Mohamed Amar, Boutie Diasso Kal, and Pierre Ullmer) were soldiers killed in 1940; one (Antoine Mourgues) had died in 1942 in the Libyan desert, fighting with Free French forces; two (Berty Albrecht of Combat and Alfred Touny of the Organisation Civile et Militaire) were résistants executed by the Germans; six (Allal Ould M'Hamed ben Semers, Raymond Anne, Henri Arnaud, Georges Brière, Jean Charrier, and Maurice Duport) had fallen in 1944 in the battle to liberate France; and there were also three deportees (Raymond Bigosse, Maurice Debout, and Renée Lévy).[16] With the addition of Grethen in 1952, executed by the Japanese in Indochina, that makes sixteen. All phases of the fighting from the beginning of the war to the end were represented, as was every major theater of action from Africa to Indochina to France itself. The struggle had not ground to a halt with defeat in the Battle of France but had gone on, and it had been a global effort waged across continents.

This list will have prompted the sharp-eyed observer to some additional reflections. The Deportation had a part to play in the Gaullist story, but it was not the lead role. Just three of the sixteen at Mont-Valérien were deportees. To be sure, the crypt also included an urn of ashes from the camps. The deportee community, moreover, was involved in the flame-lighting ceremony at the Arc de Triomphe and, in the general organization of the June 18 ceremonials, as de jure members of the Comité du renouvellement de la Flamme. Still, a clear majority of the sixteen buried in the crypt were soldiers who had died arms in hand, and there can be no doubt that the June 18 event was above all else a martial affair. Just think of all the men in uniform, the military vehicles, the salute to the colors, the review of the troops, and more. The Deportation from this angle was but a moment, however important, however tragic, in the nation's battle to liberate itself.

It will also be noted that the list of sixteen includes names of the most varied sort. A program for the 1951 observance of the June 18 ceremony describes them as martyrs, hailing from "all races" and "all conditions."[17] A remarkable feature of the French Resistance was how unified it was. Free France fought shoulder to shoulder with maquis guerrillas, the exterior and interior Resistance fused under de Gaulle's tutelary command. As for Free France itself, it was made up of recruits from all over. Many were born in the hexagon, but Hedhili ben Salem ben Hadj Mohamed Amar was a Tunisian. Boutie Diasso Kal came from French West Africa. Allal Ould M'Hamed ben Semers had been born in Morocco. The martyred heroes at Mont-Valérien proclaimed France's unity: the unity of all French, of course, but the unity also of France and its empire. Little wonder then that colonial units were selected to accompany a cortege of coffins to the Invalides in November 1945. The war had made clear the importance of the empire to France, and that indissoluble bond between the hexagon and the peoples it governed worldwide was also part of the June 18 story.

It's worth asking, however, whether the idea of unity, important as it was, extended to all French in the same way, and the answer to that question is no. Not a single Communist figured among the dead commemorated at Mont-Valérien. The sixteen had been chosen by lot, of course, and so this absence could not have been deliberate. That said, it was still an erasure of significant proportion. Many, if not the majority, of victims executed by the Germans at Mont-Valérien had been members of the communist Resistance. During the war, the Germans had confined the condemned to a chapel before marching them down a pathway, a hundred yards or so in length, to the actual execution site, the *clairière des fusillés*. The walls of the chapel were covered with graffiti, including a prominent "Long Live the USSR," preserved to the present day. The June 18 ceremonial glossed over this aspect of the story, and the marginalization of the Communists extended as well to the organization of the event. The flame-lighting committee included a range of Resistance and deportee associations, but not a single one was communist. This oversight at least was not a consequence of chance.[18]

A second story was glossed over in Gaullist commemoration, that of the Jewish dead. The Germans executed hostages at Mont-Valérien, and more than a hundred of these had been Jews. The sixteen buried in the crypt did in fact include a Jewish woman, Renée Léa Lévy by her full name, who was the granddaughter of a well-known rabbi. She was there, however, not as a Jew but as a résistante (she had been a member of the Musée de l'homme network). De Gaulle had a story to tell, and it was emphatically not a communist story, nor a Jewish one. Perhaps too much should not be made of this. As a matter of principle, after all, the French Republic, Gaullist or otherwise, is not supposed to recognize distinctions among its citizens, whether of race, color, or creed.

That may be true in a general sense, but it was not altogether the case when it came to Mont Valérien–connected ceremonials, which featured religion in a variety of ways. In November 1945, after all, the nighttime vigil that preceded the main event was conducted in a church, and a Mass was said. Then there is Mont-Valérien itself, not the fort so much as the hill on which it is situated. In the centuries before the Revolution, this had been a site of pilgrimage. A long staircase ran from the bottom of the hill to the top, a string of chapels lining the route, each one representing a station of the Holy Cross. That's why the hill had a second name: Calvary. Such associations, of course, did not matter to the Germans, who converted Mont-Valérien into a killing ground not to reenact the Crucifixion, but to conduct the firing squad's noisy business behind high walls and a buffering distance from the listening ears of Parisians.[19]

For the French, though, the site did have religious resonance, and so too did the symbolism associated with it, the Cross of Lorraine first of all. This was the chosen emblem of Free France, and it enjoyed a place of prominence in all ceremonials linked to the Gaullist epic, the June 18 commemoration included. There is debate about how the cross achieved its paradigmatic status, but a consensus of opinion now assigns the initiative to Admiral Émile Muselier, in the early years of the war commander of the Free French Navy. The idea came to him in the summer of 1940 as he flew from Gibraltar to London on his way to de Gaulle's side. The Nazis had a symbol, the *croix gammée* or, as it is known in English, the swastika. Free France, Muselier reflected, needed a cross of its own, and what better choice than the Cross of Lorraine? The admiral's father, of course, originated from the region, but there was more to the admiral's thinking than that. The Lorraine was a frontier province, annexed by the Germans (along with Alsace) after France's defeat in the war of 1870–1871 and then reclaimed by France after the Great War. As such, it was a region of deep patriotic investment. During the Great War, Louis Ganne had tapped into that well of sentiment, composing one of France's favorite, Sousa-like marches, the "Marche Lorraine," a sometime selection, as we have seen, at June 18 observances. Muselier then was motivated by filial piety and a deep-seated patriotism, but there was yet one more impulse at work, a religious one. As he explained in a 1941 talk, Free France for him was not just a cause but "a true crusade," and it was just such a crusading spirit that the Cross of Lorraine was meant to summon up. How after all had the cross entered into France's symbolic repertoire? A thirteenth-century French knight, returning from the Crusades, had brought with him a relic, encased in a cross-shaped object. This cross, however, differed from the standard one of Latin Christianity in a critical respect. It did not have just a single transverse bar but two, a large one and above it one smaller. Jesus's arms had been nailed to the first, and to the second, according to tradition, an inscription had been affixed: *INRI* (the initials of a Latin phrase signifying "Jesus of Nazareth, King of the Jews"). This object found its way over time into the reliquary of the dukes of Lorraine, who adopted the device as their own, and this was the device that Muselier fixed on as the symbol of Free France. In July 1940, he ordered all ships in the Free French fleet to fly two flags, the tricolor and a blue ensign emblazoned with the Cross of Lorraine. The symbol caught on from there, one freighted with patriotic emotion to be sure, but also evocative of the Crusades and, indeed, of Christ's agony on the Cross.[20]

The crusading spirit was also part of the mystique of the wartime order that de Gaulle created, the Ordre de la Libération, which in the post-Liberation years was to occupy such a key place in the history of the June 18 celebrations. The idea for such an order came to de Gaulle in the fall of 1940 at a low point in the fortunes of Free France. An expedition to seize Dakar from Vichy forces had failed. The troops needed rallying, and de Gaulle thought up the order as a stratagem to stimulate martial devotion and emulation. An ordinance was drawn up in November that provided for the creation of a new honor in recognition of acts of exceptional valor in the service of "the liberation of France and its Empire." Recipients were awarded a medal, the Cross of the Liberation, and at the same time inducted into an order, presided by a chancellor. The first to serve in that capacity was Thierry d'Argenlieu who remained in the post from 1941 to 1958. The text of the 1940 ordinance characterized members of the order as *Compagnons*. A new rank was added in 1947, when de Gaulle was named grand master, a distinction that came, not with a medal, but with a livery chain, which he disported with especial pride. An official photograph was taken of de Gaulle as president in 1959, showing him bedecked in a lifetime's worth of medals and distinctions, and there he was with the livery chain of the order about his neck, wearing it where he might have worn (but did not) the ribbon of the Grand Cross of the Légion d'honneur, a preference indicative of which decoration he set greatest store by.

The Ordre de la Libération then was not of republican inspiration. Its origins were rather imperial and martial. De Gaulle conceived the idea in the midst of an imperial setback, and the 1940 ordinance instituting the order wasn't signed in London but in Brazzaville. In January 1946, de Gaulle proclaimed his intention to cease naming new members. There were a thousand or so Compagnons by that time. All but six were men, and three-quarters of the total were veterans of Free France, most of whom had joined up with de Gaulle in the first hour. The domestic Resistance and Deportation were not slighted, but together they accounted for less than a quarter of the inductees.[21]

Compagnons were soldiers, then, a band of brothers joined in struggle and sacrifice, but that wasn't all there was to it. De Gaulle was elevated to the grand mastership in 1947, and on that occasion, he delivered a speech lauding the order as a *"chevalerie exceptionnelle."* Compagnons were knights, the modern-day heirs of a chivalric tradition dating back to medieval times, one deeply anchored in the nation's history and literature. The Order of Saint-Louis, among the most prestigious of France's old regime military orders, was governed by a grand master. King Arthur's knights were sometimes known as Compagnons.[22] And de Gaulle's knights, like Arthur's, were embarked on a quest that had a spiritual dimension. The Cross of the Liberation was a medal suspended from a black-and-green ribbon, the colors representing mourning and hope (see Figure 6.1). The front side of the medal consisted of a gold rectangle, with a vertical sword, haft uppermost, superimposed upon it and a black Cross of Lorraine in turn superimposed on the sword. On the reverse, there was a Latin motto in relief, which read: *"Patriam servando, victoriam tulit"* (By serving the nation, victory is won). It's tempting to see a religious significance in an object of such design – a cross made up of a cross layered over an upright sword that might itself be taken for a cross. This may be an over-reading, but it is worth remembering that the initial text of the 1940 ordinance had referred to the order's members not as Compagnons but as *croisés* or "crusaders." The designation was changed

Figure 6.1 Cross of the Ordre de la Libération

on the urging of René Cassin (who was Jewish, it will be recalled). Remember also who the order's first chancellor was: Thierry d'Argenlieu, a member of the Discalced Carmelites, who had taken a monk's vows.[23] The Ordre de la Libération was not quite a crusading order, but almost, and it was led by a soldier-monk who would retire to the Carmelite monastery at Avon at the end of a long and varied career.

There is no reason to be surprised by such medievalizing and religious allusions. De Gaulle was after all the son of a nobleman and himself a practicing Catholic. In August 1944, he entered a just-liberated Paris, marching down the Champs-Élysées on his way to Notre-Dame Cathedral, where he took part in a Te Deum service and the recitation of the Magnificat. On his son's accounting, de Gaulle explained the choice to go to Notre-Dame this way: "When the king won a war, he went to render thanks to God. We go to Notre-Dame because He is the master of all things. And today, it is on us that He has bestowed victory."[24] This mixing of old regime and Catholic imagery was characteristic of de Gaulle, and it is very much in evidence once again in the celebrated first lines of the General's *Mémoires de guerre*. He had "a certain idea of France," he told readers. France, as he imagined her, was a woman, "such as the princess in a fairy tale or the Madonna on a frescoed wall."[25] It is not the gendered language that is at issue in the present context so much as the paired invocation of a princess in distress and the Virgin. For many, no doubt, these are images to stir the soul, but they do not form part of the republican imaginary.

De Gaulle's June 18 was a syncretic affair, mobilizing referents that were republican but also Catholic and old regime, and in this syncretism, the event captured something of de Gaulle's own mixed commitments. Let us now return briefly to that opening passage of the *Mémoires de guerre*. De Gaulle talked in sentimental terms about France – she was a woman in need of help, a Madonna deserving of reverence – but France, he went on, was also something more. Providence had singled it out for a special destiny. "France cannot be France without grandeur," and it's with these resounding words that the first paragraph of the war memoirs concludes.[26] In the 1950s, de Gaulle was the graying veteran of a wartime past fast receding into memory, and the June 18 commemoration an intimate rite observed among former comrades-in-arms. In 1958, however, de Gaulle was once again head of state, and the General's presence in the Élysée Palace had a transformational impact on the June 18 ceremonials. They now became a national event, and the organizers confronted a quandary: how to preserve the intimacy of old and at the same time to impart to the proceedings a note of grandeur, befitting a new regime and above all a new president, who placed such a high value on the notion of greatness.

The *Mémorial de la France Combattante*

The construction of a monument on the Mont-Valérien site, and an imposing one at that, made the challenge of preserving intimacy all the greater. There had long been talk in government circles of constructing just such a memorial, and in fact an interministerial committee charged with devising a plan had been formed in the late 1940s. Its brief was to locate an appropriate burial site at Mont-Valérien to accommodate the bodies of up to three thousand wartime dead, the victims of Nazi barbarism, and on that spot to build a necropolis. Committee members paid a visit to Mont-Valérien in 1949 and fixed on the fort's southwestern slope as the most suitable locale. A substantial plot was required, however, necessitating the annexation of a portion of the nearby Parc des Landes, property that was not yet under the central state's control. The relevant authorities – the mayor of Suresnes, where the fort was situated, and the prefect of the Seine – were petitioned for permission to appropriate the additional land, but negotiations proved fruitless. In 1954, the interministerial committee gave way to a new body, the Commission exécutive pour l'édification du mémorial du Mont-Valérien, presided over by Minister of Veterans' Affairs André Mutter; and yet still no agreement was reached. The memorial's partisans began to suspect that unnamed "hostile influences" were at work, blocking the project's progress.[27]

Then in 1958, all obstacles vanished at a stroke, and plans for the memorial jolted forward at high speed. It's not hard to explain the about-face. De Gaulle was back in power as of June, and within a matter of weeks he had sent a personal representative, Colonel Dominique Ponchardier, to attend the memorial commission's meetings. Ponchardier made it known in no uncertain terms that de Gaulle wanted the project completed within a year. The commission was joined by a second new member, de Gaulle's minister of veterans' affairs, Edmond Michelet, who proposed a simple yet radical solution to the commission's concerns about site dimensions: expropriate the needed parkland outright. The pressure was then turned up on the mayor of Suresnes, now under menace of an expropriation, and he at last folded, agreeing to concede the space demanded. Nonetheless, there remained anxieties about whether the location selected, even with a slice of parkland appended, was large enough. That problem solved itself, however, when it was learned that a necropolis was slated to be built at the Struthof Memorial site, then already under construction, obviating the need for one at Mont-Valérien. The memorial commission now had full authority to act, empowered as it was by a determined new head of state, and its mission was also much simplified.

The results were not long in coming. In November 1958, a decree was issued authorizing construction of the memorial, and shortly thereafter Colonel Félix Brunau, a government architect, was designated to draw up a blueprint.[28] Overall responsibility for the project was assigned to the Ministère des anciens Combattants. In an April 1959 meeting, de Gaulle made known to the minister, at that time Raymond Triboulet, just what kind of design he expected: "France never ceased to fight, that's what needs to expressed, etched in stone and bronze," and he had occasion to communicate the selfsame sentiments to the architect himself. The General did not want inscriptions on the monument's exterior, Brunau later reported, with a single exception: "He instructed me to figure there the dates 1939–1945."[29] Brunau also labored under a second set of constraints. There were three parts to the monument site, the monument

Figure 6.2 Mémorial de la France Combattante, Suresnes, 1960

proper and a short distance up the hill the *clairière des fusillés* and, a little further on, the chapel. It would be a challenge to find a way to fit these various pieces together.

Brunau gave priority to the first portion of his assignment, the monument, and the design he came up with included four major components: a giant wall, more than a football field and a half in length, bisected by a twelve-meter high Cross of Lorraine, itself flanked on either side by eight high reliefs for a total of sixteen; an elevated stage that ran along the base of the wall with an eternal flame situated in the middle at the foot of the cross; an esplanade in front of the monument, ten thousand meters square; and within, a crypt, accessed by two bronze doors, one on each side of the cross (see Figure 6.2). Ground was broken on the project in November 1959, and the work was done – or almost – in time for a June 1960 inauguration. De Gaulle had wanted a finished monument within a year, but instead it took two, still an expeditious achievement for an enterprise of such magnitude. The Fifth Republic was a regime of authority that got things done.

Progress on the layout of the *clairière*, however, was more uneven. In November 1959, at the request of an association of Resistance writers, a stone slab had been laid in the middle of the clearing, inscribed to the memory of the 4,500 résistants executed on the site (the actual figure was, in fact, closer to one thousand). Brunau took charge of this project, but once it was finished, he then devoted undivided attention to the execution of the monument below. Not until the monument's unveiling did he return to the design of the *clairière*, first constructing a staircase that led from the crypt to a path above – work on this was completed in 1961 – and later extending the path, such that it traced a circuit that wound northward to the chapel, looped back to the clearing, and from there reconnected to the crypt staircase. Construction on the duly named "*parcours du souvenir*" was concluded in 1962.[30]

De Gaulle found the memorial ensemble of an "imposing sobriety," and the themes it sounded might well have afforded him deep satisfaction.[31] As he had demanded, there were no inscriptions on the monument, save the two dates: 1939 to the left of the giant Cross of Lorraine and 1945 to the right. In 1974, the Ordre de la Libération arranged to have the base of the cross etched with a phrase adapted from de Gaulle's June 18 appeal – "whatever happens the flame of Resistance will not die" – but that was added some years after the General's death.[32] De Gaulle did not intend the monument as one to himself, but to the collective effort of Fighting France, and that effort, as he understood it, had unfolded in one uninterrupted flow. The inscribed dates made that plain, and the sixteen sculpted high reliefs punctuating the monument wall made just as plain that the effort involved had been a military one from first to last. They celebrated France's wartime exploits from the Narvik expedition of April–June 1940 to the liberation of Strasbourg and the crossing of the Rhine in March 1945, with stops along the way to commemorate victories in the North African desert (at the Fezzan and Bir Hakeim) and on the European continent (at Monte Cassino and Colmar). It has already been noted how many of the dead buried in the crypt were soldiers and how each represented an aspect of Free France's heroic combat. The message was clear: fighting France, *fighting* France, had remained steadfast, its ranks unbroken, in the face of the enemy. Which is just what de Gaulle saw when he first beheld the monument at the inauguration ceremony of 1960. That's it, he kept saying in repeated asides to General François Ingold, Thierry d'Argenlieu's successor as chancellor of the Ordre de la Libération, "The Resistance was a wall."[33]

And overtopping that wall was a massive Cross of Lorraine, the emblem par excellence of the Gaullist Resistance. The cross had patriotic resonance, no doubt, as an allusion to the lost provinces of Alsace-Lorraine, and Brunau underscored the connection, constructing it out of rose granite, the same material used in the construction of the region's perhaps most celebrated monument, the Strasbourg Cathedral.

The motif, moreover, was repeated in the design of the esplanade. The memorial was approachable from the esplanade via a long, straight pathway that ended in a short staircase leading up to the memorial's stage at the base of the Cross of Lorraine. The path was in turn traversed at two points: by a road some distance away and by the stage itself, all the elements together forming a second Cross of Lorraine, a horizontal shadow of the vertical one that loomed so large over the memorial as a whole.

A second Free France symbol also figured in the esplanade's layout, the *V* sign. Winston Churchill had first popularized it early in the war, raising two splayed fingers to form a *V* for Victory. The BBC urged occupied peoples across Europe to scrawl the letter on any and all surfaces as an expression of anti-German defiance. De Gaulle too adopted the gesture, flashing the *V* sign when he made speeches, and Free France propagandists followed the General's lead. The Cross of Lorraine was the Resistance's primordial emblem, but at times it was combined with the *V*, the cross inserted between the *V*'s two diverging arms. That indeed is just how the esplanade was laid out. A visitor, standing on the stage and facing to the south, looked out on a vast space that tapered in the distance, forming a *V* shape, the Cross of Lorraine pattern, already described, nested within it. The *V* appeared again in one of the sculpted cartouches, the one, in fact, representing the crossing of the Rhine (see Figure 6.3). This was the last in the suite of high reliefs on the monument's facade, and as such, it stood in affirmation that Free France's fight had ended in victory.

This victory had been won after a long and bitter struggle, one that encompassed the war of 1939–1945, but that was anchored deeper still in the nation's past, dating back to the Great War. The trope of the Thirty Years' War occupied a privileged place in the Gaullist narrative, and Brunau made sure to include referents to it in the memorial's design ensemble. Take the granite slab that he conceived for the *clairière des fusillés*. In choice of material and general design, it was modeled on the slab laid in the clearing at Rethondes where Maréchal Foch and representatives of the German high command had signed the armistice agreement that ended the Great War in November 1918.[34] A second point along the same lines: the Mémorial de la France combattante, like the Tombeau du Soldat inconnu at the Arc de Triomphe, came equipped with an eternal flame, an image close to de Gaulle's heart, symbolizing France's inextinguishable ardor in its decades-long combat against the hereditary enemy.

All this is patriotic and republican, very much so, with a heavy accent on the martial aspect of republican tradition ... and on its imperial

Figure 6.3 *Le Rhin*, Mémorial de la France Combattante, Suresnes, 1960

dimension too. So many of the dead buried in the crypt had connections to France's empire. Three were born there, and one had died on imperial soil, Edmond Grethen. A fifth, Antoine Mourgues, had been killed in action in Libya in the fight to liberate French North Africa. At the very last minute, these five were joined by one more, Corporal Maboulkede, a soldier from Chad who had died in combat in Provence. How he came to be included in this select group is instructive on several counts,[35] first of all, because he took the place of another person, Raymond Bigosse. Bigosse had died in deportation, but there were some in the deportee community who did not view him as a martyr, rather the contrary. They accused him of "selling out" comrades in the camps, and a jury of honor was convened in 1947, which investigated and confirmed the indictment. For the moment, Bigosse's body remained buried in the casemate at Mont-Valérien, but this would change in June 1960.

The new memorial was almost complete, and its unveiling was just days away. Triboulet, as minister of veterans' affairs, ordered Bigosse's remains relocated to a grave in Père-Lachaise Cemetery and at the same time sketched the kind of replacement he was looking for: "an African from the AEF [French Equatorial Africa], that first patch of Empire to rally to the Cause of Liberation."[36] The reasons behind Triboulet's selection are not difficult to divine. The war in Algeria was still in full spate in the summer of 1960, but – of even greater importance – France's onetime possessions in sub-Saharan Africa were at that very moment taking steps toward independent statehood. Triboulet's determination to honor an African soldier, it may be ventured, was intended to send a signal to these new states in the making: that France valued their past service and sacrifice and that the ties, military and sentimental, binding France to its peoples overseas remained ongoing.[37] In the event, the chancellor of the Ordre de Libération found a candidate suitable to Triboulet's agenda, Corporal Maboulkede, although the choice does not appear to have been made until the fall, well after the memorial's June unveiling. This means that one of the coffins of the honored dead would have been empty at the moment of its transfer from casemate to crypt.

I have made the claim that de Gaulle's imagining of France was as much medieval and Catholic as it was republican in inspiration. The Mont-Valérien memorial is not often thought of in this light, yet these values too found expression in its design. The Cross of Lorraine, of course, was the memorial's dominating element, and it was as much a crusading as a patriotic motif. There was also a Cross of Lorraine inside the crypt, chased on the bronze door of a compartment containing the visitor's book de Gaulle himself had signed when he first entered on June 18, 1960. On the wall above the compartment was stamped in gold lettering the Latin motto of the Ordre de la Libération. The order, chivalric in conception, was indeed a presiding spirit in the crypt. To be sure, just two of the sixteen interred there in flag-draped coffins were Compagnons, Berty Albrecht and Alfred Touny, but an additional space was set aside for the eventual burial of a seventeenth person, the Ordre de la Libération's last surviving member. When it came time to organize the ceremonials associated with the monument's inauguration, the Ministère des anciens Combattants tried to assert its precedence, but de Gaulle, after a tussle among the interested parties, awarded that honor instead to the Ordre de la Libération. The order was a brotherhood-in-arms, its members knights of the *patrie*, and this memorial belonged to them in a special way.

On the matter of religion, is it necessary to insist again on the Christian meaning of the repeated cross motif? Now take one more look at the high relief representing the crossing of the Rhine, that body ascending with its arms outstretched and its naked torso wrapped in a loincloth: it's hard not to think of the risen Christ.

A government monuments commission debated and approved Brunau's memorial design, and in discussion members time and again had recourse to Christian imagery to describe the project. The monument as a whole was characterized as a "Golgotha of the Resistance." The sixteen high reliefs recounted chapter-by-chapter a story of redemptive sacrifice, the sequence of images constituting what was said to be a veritable *"chemin de croix."*[38] The archives of the Ordre de la Libération contain an item that speaks of the reliefs in similar language. The men and women of the Resistance, their exploits on the battlefield and in clandestinity evoked by eloquent "allegories," were not just heroes but, in the document's phrasing, "Artisans of the Resurrection."[39] There is one last piece of clinching evidence. Henri Lagriffoul composed the bronze cartouche representing the Deportation (see Figure 6.4). He opted for a heart tangled in barbed wire, two gaunt hands tearing at the barbs to free the heart from its bonds. Once more, the image conjures Christian associations, this time to the Sacred Heart of Jesus wreathed in a crown of thorns. The archives provide confirmation of the association, describing "the tortured heart" as emblematic of the "calvary" that the victims of deportation had been made to endure.[40]

The Deportation, then, although not the dominant element in the memorial's narrative, which accented feats of arms more than redemptive suffering, was still very much a venerated presence, and not just on the memorial wall but in the crypt as well. The coffins of the fallen heroes were arranged in a semicircle. The urn of ashes collected from the camps, topped by a metal sculpture of a rising flame, was cradled in the center. A plaque attached to the urn described its contents: "martyrs' ashes from the camps of the deportation."

Brunau's commemorative ensemble had a complex narrative to tell, at once patriotic and religious, republican and old regime. It recounted that narrative in an expansive way, incorporating all major phases of the nation's wartime effort: Free France, the Resistance proper, and the Deportation. As for the communist side of the story, it received short shrift in this telling. The *clairière des fusillés*, so central to communist remembrance, was indeed included in Brunau's overall scheme, but it was assigned a second-rank status.

It was rather the Mémorial de la France combattante that occupied center stage, a grandiose affair that acknowledged the pain of martyrdom but placed yet greater stress on France and its empire's will to fight. This was a modern monument, its component parts – a cross, a wall,

Figure 6.4 *La Déportation*, Mémorial de la France Combattante, Suresnes, 1960

a crypt – abstracted and laid out with a geometrical simplicity. It did not, however, eschew the image, as did the Jewish memorial in the Marais or the Deportation Memorial on the Île de la Cité, and it made ample use of allegory, that old standby of commemorative practice and tradition. There were theatrical elements built in as well. Stone bleachers embraced the esplanade on either side, and the monument's grand wall was in fact fronted by a stage. So this was a modern monument but not a modernist one. It was sober and imposing, much as de Gaulle himself remarked, but it was imposing in a way that bordered on the spectacular.

The June 18 Ceremonials Redux

There is no doubt how much the new memorial meant to de Gaulle. He had applied pressure to rush its completion and for a simple reason. De Gaulle wanted to stage a ceremonial at the site that would speak to the nation about what the new Gaullist regime, the Fifth Republic, stood for. That event took place over a two-day period, June 17–18, 1960, even though the monument was not in fact completed. Three of the sculpted cartouches hadn't yet been cast, and in their place were substituted plaster reproductions painted over to look like bronze.[41] No matter: de Gaulle was determined to plow ahead.

The memorial inauguration of June 1960 was a one-of-a-kind happening, but unique as it was, it built on a tradition of ritual observance already a decade and a half in the making. De Gaulle after all had commemorated June 18 since the end of the war, and, prior to the monument's unveiling, he had had two opportunities – in 1958 and again in 1959 – to mark the day as head of state. General de Gaulle, it is known, liked events that were simple and short.[42] Yet, on these first two occasions of de Gaulle's presidency, the Mont-Valérien ceremonials took a ritual turn that ran counter to his preferences.

In 1958–1959, there were two major changes in how the proceedings were conducted. General de Gaulle now presided not just at the Mont-Valérien portion of the observances but also at the torch ceremony at the Arc de Triomphe. The General's presence at the torch lighting in 1958 had an electrifying effect on the throngs of people in attendance. Keep in mind just how much the war in North Africa was a matter of public concern at the time. Contemporary newsreels picked up the rhythmic chants of *"Algérie française"* emanating from the crowd. In fact, there was a parallel celebration that day in Algiers itself, this one presided by Jacques Massu, a member of the Ordre de la Libération, who read out loud two documents: de Gaulle's June 18 appeal and the May 15, 1958 communiqué he had issued, declaring his readiness to assume power in face of the Fourth Republic's flailing management of the Algerian crisis. De Gaulle was ever more central to a celebration that was at the very same time ever more dogged by the war in Algeria.[43]

The mention of newsreels gives a clue as to the second way in which the 1958-1959 observances differed from what had come before. The media played a much more important role. In 1958, there was an eight-minute spot about the event on the television news, and that evening's programming also included a documentary, *Sur les traces de Jean Moulin*. The next year was no different. Evening TV aired a "retrospective" on June 1940 by the documentary filmmaker Frédéric Rossif, followed by a filmed retransmission of de Gaulle leading ceremonials at Mont-Valérien.[44]

The event was now a very public affair, which disrupted the intimacy of old, and the extravaganza mounted in connection with the June 17–18 inaugural just exacerbated the problem. Organizers wanted the event to have an "exceptional éclat," and that's part of why an extra day was added.[45] The proceedings began on the evening of the 17th at Mont-Valérien. The sixteen coffins and urn of ashes were moved by torchlight from the casemate to the new memorial. As a drum roll played, each coffin was laid out in front of one of the sculpted high reliefs while the urn of ashes was placed at the foot of the cross. Clergy from all of France's major religions – Catholicism, Protestantism, Judaism, Islam – then recited prayers for the dead, after which, the coffins and urn were transferred to their final resting place inside the crypt. Music accompanied the ceremonials. The "Chant des Partisans" was played as the coffins were removed from the casemate, and "La Marseillaise" as they were conveyed into the crypt. There was also cannon fire at the very end, a salvo sounding at midnight to close the ceremonies. De Gaulle did not attend, but Michel Debré, the prime minister, did, as did de Gaulle's minister of veterans' affairs, Triboulet, who was very moved, describing the ceremony as "the most impressive I've ever experienced in my life."[46] It might well be asked whether the French public had a chance to be similarly moved. The event after all was conducted in a suburb, far from the city center, and in nighttime at that. The answer is still yes, for the ceremony was televised live with commentary from a distinguished writer and journalist, Michel Droit, who was also himself a onetime résistant.[47]

As for June 18 proper, the ceremony that day played out in two parts, according to custom. De Gaulle was not in attendance at the Arc de Triomphe torch lighting as he had been in 1958 and 1959, leaving conduct of that ceremony in the hands of Resistance and deportee associations. At Mont-Valérien, however, he was very much present, and so were the crowds and media. The Ministère des anciens Combattants issued twenty thousand invitations, and many of the invitees brought additional family members along. Organizers, hoping to shape press commentary, drafted and disseminated a model text that described the monument and the ceremony's component parts.[48] De Gaulle himself arrived on the scene in an open car, wearing the uniform of a brigadier general, the rank he had held in 1940. He was greeted by the chancellor of the Ordre de la Libération, General Ingold, and the two men entered the crypt together. On exiting, de Gaulle relit the eternal flame and observed a moment of silence. He then turned to shake hands with members of the crowd, after which he left.[49]

This was all in the classic Gaullist style. The event was choreographed with care. It was short and to the point, and there were no speeches, indeed no public words at all. De Gaulle appeared in simple attire, not as some bemedaled brass hat, but as the leader of Free France, and throughout he remained silent and most of the time alone, a man at once austere and towering, who stood above and apart from the rest.[50] The media amplified the image, which was the desired effect, but the crush of people was just too much. Attendees didn't sit where they were supposed to, and the General had a hard time working his way through the crowd the way he liked.

The balance between publicness and intimacy was not right. General Ingold was aware of the problem and determined that 1961 would be different, the start of what he hoped would be "a new tradition."[51] In years subsequent to the grand inauguration, organizers did indeed reduce the number of invitations, and more attention was paid to monitoring the seating arrangements. From 1962, the Comité du renouvellement de la Flamme handed over responsibility for managing the Arc de Triomphe torch ceremony to the Ordre de la Libération, which was now in charge of the day's proceedings from beginning to end. The attention paid to the media, however, did not diminish. State-run outlets, of course, required no encouragement, but organizers felt that private radio needed a little prodding. In 1963, the Ordre de la Libération circulated materials about the June 18 ceremony, its history and protocols, to all the major radio stations operating on France's periphery: Radio Monte-Carlo, Radio Luxembourg, and Europe no. 1 (which broadcast from the Saarland).[52] France and its near neighbors deserved to know about the event.

Such refinements made, the June 18 solemnities now settled into a routine. The event was grand and solemn at the same time. The Arc de Triomphe leg of the day's proceedings occupied a less central place, attenuating the link between the sacrifices of the Great War and those of Fighting France without ever breaking it.[53] At Mont-Valérien itself, a sense of sober meditation had been restored. De Gaulle remained the cynosure of the proceedings there, silent and aloof, an imposing figure. The day's events and the monument where they were staged told a story of patriotic service across thirty years. France and its empire had rallied to defend the cause of liberty, taking up arms as one under the undisputed leadership of General de Gaulle and his band of first-hour comrades. That cause had also been a crusade, a struggle not just to liberate France, but to effect its resurrection, and that had indeed been the final outcome, the nation rising once again, bringing home victory under the sign of the Cross of Lorraine. The Deportation was recognized as a valued part of this story but not its most important element. The Communists had no role in it at all, and the Jews but a small and unarticulated one, concentrated in the lone figure of Renée Lévy. This was the message, powerful and compelling but at the same time partial, that was conveyed to the happy few who happened to be in physical attendance. But not just to them: for it was also broadcast, via radio and TV, to the nation as a whole and beyond.[54]

Rallying the Deportee Community

What's interesting to remark is how strong the magnetic attraction of the Gaullist message was on the community of deportees, most of whom were drawn into its force field, with some notable exceptions, as will be seen. FNDIR and ANFROM, of course, were committed from the very start. They had long been core participants in the June 18 torch-lighting ceremonials at the Arc de Triomphe and would remain so.

Individual survivors too rallied around de Gaulle. Among that number, unsurprisingly, was Edmond Michelet, a founding father of the Amicale de Dachau. He was a longtime Gaullist stalwart. Michelet's memoir of concentration camp life, *Rue de la Liberté*, included a letter from de Gaulle to the author, addressed "My dear friend."[55] De Gaulle also had friends in the seniormost ranks of ADIR: Geneviève de Gaulle Anthonioz and Germaine Tillion. De Gaulle Anthonioz's Gaullist allegiances require no explanation. They ran so deep they even impacted how she ran ADIR, which, when she was president, refrained from critiquing France's use of torture on Algerian detainees until the last possible moment, a cautious *prise de position* that prompted Anise Postel-Vinay's resignation as ADIR's secretary-general in 1962.[56] As for Germaine Tillion, she had been a Gaullist of the first hour since 1940. Reared in "French traditions of patriotism," it was a choice, as she put it, that "was self-evident." In May 1958, on the eve of the General's return to power, she signed an open appeal, petitioning the president of the Republic to invite de Gaulle to form a "government of public safety." She was still voting for de Gaulle in the presidential elections of 1965, but then again who was the alternative? De Gaulle's opponent was François Mitterrand, who, as minister of justice in the mid-fifties, had sanctioned the first executions of FLN militants, a repressive measure that Tillion was never able to forgive.[57] To the names of Michelet, de Gaulle Anthonioz, and Tillion should be added a fourth, that of David Rousset, who in 1967 ran on the Gaullist ticket in that year's legislative elections, advertising himself to voters as a "left Gaullist."

The deportee mainstream then rallied to de Gaulle's side: FNDIR, ANFROM, leading lights of the Amicale de Dachau and ADIR, and not least of all the dean of deportee anti-totalitarians, David Rousset. It ought not to be thought, moreover, that de Gaulle was content to bask passively in such spontaneous expressions of loyalty. In fact, he made every effort to cultivate the deportee community, maneuvering to situate himself at the fulcrum of a unified deportation memory. The General made appearances at deportee events and extended patronage to deportee organizations, by such means enlisting the deportation narrative into the service of his own, the Gaullist story of national concord.[58]

The Struthof Memorial was unveiled in July 1960, not much more than a month after the inauguration of the Mémorial de la France combattante, and the two ceremonies bore a striking resemblance to one another. The Struthof observances unfolded over two days, a nighttime ceremony of prayers amidst torchlight, followed by the unveiling proper. De Gaulle did not attend the first portion of the ceremony but was there at the second, silent and uniformed, his movements mapped out with scrupulous attention to detail. The Struthof event was a more modest affair than the one the month preceding, but the choreography was the same.

Just under two years later, in April 1962, the Mémorial des Martyrs de la Déportation was itself ready for unveiling. As he so often did on such occasions, de Gaulle showed up in uniform and descended into the crypt. He reemerged and, flanked by his ministers, Michel Debré and Raymond Triboulet (the same two who had presided at the nighttime ceremony at Mont-Valérien in June 1960), shook hands with members of the small crowd in attendance.

Then in April 1965, de Gaulle was on hand once more, taking part in that year's Journée nationale de la Déportation. He was this time a minor player and not the main attraction. The Journée, its name notwithstanding, was a multiday affair, made up of visits to a variety of sites, both sacred and profane. So how then did de Gaulle manage to insert himself into the proceedings? Accompanied by his wife, he went to Sunday morning Mass at Notre-Dame Cathedral, where he listened to a sermon by the Deportation's most celebrated clerical spokesman, Father Michel Riquet.[59]

It was impossible to be in two places at once, and so de Gaulle could not attend the ceremony at the Mémorial du Martyr juif inconnu, also scheduled for Sunday morning. That responsibility was not ignored, however, but assigned to de Gaulle's prime minister at the time, Georges Pompidou. The General, in any event, had already made a nod toward Jewish memory. In 1959, he was invited to head the Comité mondial of the Tombeau du Martyr juif inconnu, an honor, it seems, that he was pleased to accept.[60] These were small gestures no doubt, but ones that the Jewish community found gratifying.

Not so gratified, however, were the Communists, who chafed at the backseat status that the Gaullist narrative had relegated them to. They had nothing but mocking words for the inauguration ceremony that de

Gaulle presided at the Île de la Cité Deportation Memorial in April 1962. By the FNDIRP's accounting, the General had whisked in and out again, as though trying to downplay the event, lest it offend German sensibilities at a time when de Gaulle was negotiating a rapprochement with the Federal Republic. Chancellor Adenauer himself paid a visit to Paris in July, and the FNDIRP exploited the occasion to make its anti-Gaullist and anti-German animus known. Marcel Paul, one of the FNDIRP's senior officers, attended a demonstration organized by MRAP at the Tombeau du Martyr juif inconnu. A cortege then marched the short distance from there to the Mémorial des Martyrs de la Déportation on the Île de la Cité for a second rally. This one was led by the FNDIRP itself under the slogan "No alliance with German militarism."[61] There was also bitter complaint about the difficulty of access to the *clairière des fusillés*. This was space sacred to communist memory, but since its refurbishment in 1962, the Ministère des anciens Combattants would not permit the laying of wreaths at the memorial slab, obstructionism that the FNDIRP understood as a deliberate affront.[62]

It was time for the PCF to reassert itself in the memory wars, and Paris area militants thought they knew just what was needed: a museum that would stand in refutation of de Gaulle's martial narrative, celebrating instead what workers and Communists on the ground had done to liberate France.[63] Georges Marrane, the communist mayor of Ivry-sur-Seine, called a press conference in December 1964 to announce plans to build just such an edifice, and he had a site in mind, Ivry itself, an appropriate choice in so many ways. Ivry, located south of Paris, was a working-class suburb and party strong-hold, for decades represented in parliament by the PCF's longtime leader, Maurice Thorez. In addition, the town was, in Marrane's wording, "a high place of the Resistance" because here, in the local cemetery, were buried a host of Resistance heroes, a number of them executed by the Germans at Mont-Valérien.[64] A symbolic cornerstone laying was arranged in 1969, and three years later, a fund-raising association, headed up by Marrane, was launched.[65]

It didn't take long, however, for impediments to crop up, and the most important one was financing. Sufficient funds to construct an altogether new building were lacking, and so the project moldered along year after year until 1980 when the municipality of Champigny-sur-Marne stepped in. Champigny was yet another PCF bastion, represented by the Party's then general secretary, Georges Marchais. What Champigny had that Ivry did not was a structure ready-made that it was willing to make available to house the Party's long dreamed-of Resistance museum, and thus Champigny it was, "*faute de mieux*."[66]

The museum, dubbed the Musée de la Résistance nationale, at long last opened its doors in 1985, but what a poor relation it was among all the monuments and memorials to wartime memory. It was situated in a remote township, an hour and a half from Paris.[67] The building was an aging multistory affair that had been repurposed to create exhibition space. As for the permanent exhibition, it included objects and paraphernalia from the war years, but its main feature was a suite of seventy-one panels, which told the story of the Resistance and Deportation as the Party understood them. The panels themselves were made up of documents and images – tracts, newspaper clippings, and the like – almost all facsimiles.

After decades of effort, this was a meager result.[68] The Gaullist Fifth Republic wrapped itself in the colors of wartime sacrifice, and deportee organizations of all stripes proved willing to enroll in the Gaullist lists. The Communists were not so willing, of course, but they found themselves reduced to also-rans. In the memory wars of the immediate postwar years, they had been able to fight de Gaulle toe to toe, but by the mid-sixties, that was no longer the case, a sign of just how commanding the Gaullist version of events had become.

Enchantment

It was not just among former deportees that Gaullist memory won out. The General's new regime bent every effort to make sure that its message was relayed to the nation as a whole and did so with an unsurpassed media flair. One historian has characterized mid-sixties France as a nation under "enchantment," under Gaullist enchantment to be precise, and the phrase is a well-chosen one.[69]

France's youth were a prime target of such efforts, and what better way to stimulate its interest than an essay contest, or so ex-deportees imagined. In May of 1961, building on a private-sector initiative, the Ministère de l'Éducation nationale created the Concours national de la Résistance et de la Déportation, a competition aimed at France's student population who were invited to submit reflections on the subject; the winning essayist was awarded a book prize. The Réseau du souvenir had urged the ministry to take the initiative, and the first awarding of the prize, in the spring of 1962, was timed to coincide with the inauguration of the Deportation Memorial on the Île de la Cité, which the Réseau du souvenir had done so much to realize. In light of the competition's origins, it's not surprising to discover that the prize jury was comprised in the majority of representatives from the Resistance and deportee communities, including two from the Réseau du souvenir and two from

UNADIF. Not invited to take part was the FNDIRP, which had to wait until 1982 before the ministry asked it to send a delegate to sit on the national jury.[70] The deportee community's investment in the project helps to account for the competition's subject matter, of course, but also for the book award selection. In 1962, a copy of de Gaulle's *Mémoires de guerre* was bestowed on the competition laureate. In 1974, it seems, de Gaulle's memoirs had given way to a deportee classic, Olga Wormser-Migot and Henri Michel's *Tragédie de la Déportation*.[71] It should not be thought, moreover, that the Concours was a minor affair of interest to just a handful. In 1990, an estimated fifty thousand students competed for the top honor in that year's contest.[72]

The audience was yet bigger for the pantheonization of Jean Moulin in 1964, and the reason for that is simple: the ceremony was televised live. Moulin was de Gaulle's emissary to the Resistance on the Continent. He had labored tirelessly to build Resistance unity, efforts cut short when he was betrayed to the Germans in June 1943. Moulin did not speak under torture and died while in enemy custody. The idea to honor him had welled up from below, originating with the Union des résistants, déportés, internés et familles de morts de l'Hérault, the department where Moulin was born. André Malraux, the minister of cultural affairs, and Georges Pompidou, the prime minister, talked the matter over in May 1963 and decided to run with it. The twentieth anniversary of the Liberation was approaching, and it seemed fitting to mark the occasion with a grand ceremonial, focused on the transfer of Moulin's remains to the Pantheon. Time, however, was in short supply, and it proved necessary to schedule the solemnities toward the very end of December 1964, almost the last possible minute for a twentieth-anniversary celebration.

As for the event itself, it bore more than a passing resemblance to the ceremonials mounted in connection with the unveiling of the Mémorial de la France combattante. Moulin's pantheonization, like the unveiling, took place over a two-day period, December 18–19.[73] On the first day, a coffin containing Moulin's remains was conveyed to the Mémorial des Martyrs de la Déportation on the Île de la Cité, where it lay in state. A rotating honor guard, made up of 194 Compagnons of the Ordre de la Libération, supplemented by a sampling of Resistance personalities, stood watch as the public paid its last respects, the great bell of Notre-Dame tolling all the while. At ten in the evening, a torchlight cortege, led by a detachment of the Garde républicaine, transferred the coffin to the Pantheon, where it was placed on a catafalque just in front. The next day, a frigid one, the great and mighty of the Republic gathered on that spot, General de Gaulle presiding, clad in the uniform of the two-star general he had once been.

De Gaulle, as was his custom, did not speak, but Malraux did, delivering himself of an oration that was brief – about twenty minutes in length – and noteworthy for its concentrated emotion.[74] Malraux opened with a pious wish, that the day's ceremony make Moulin's name known to the millions of French children born since he had died. Malraux then went on to express a second hope in a contorted and meaning-packed phrase: "May the commemorations of two world wars end with the resurrection of the people of shadows that this man animated, whom he symbolizes, and whom he causes to enter here as a humble and solemn honor guard gathered round his mortal remains." In a single stroke, the minister invoked the Thirty Years' War motif, equated Moulin and the Resistance (which Moulin had at once breathed life into and incarnated), and proposed that Moulin's pantheonization tokened not just a death but also a resurrection of the man and of the movement he stood for. That movement, furthermore, was made up, not just of résistants, but also of deportees, a point Malraux underlined in the speech's next-to-last paragraph. He apostrophized Moulin, addressing him with the familiarity of a comrade and entreating him to "enter here with your terrible cortege":

With all those who died in the cellars, like you, without breaking; and what is perhaps more atrocious still who did break; with all those wearing the striped uniforms and shaven heads of the concentration camps, with the last swaying body in the hideous rows of Night and Fog, felled by the blows of the rifle butt, with the eight thousand French women who never returned from the labor camps, with the last woman who died at Ravensbrück sacrificing her life to protect one of our own.

The playing of the "Chant des partisans" followed Malraux's oration. There was a parade of troops, and then a party of soldiers carried Moulin's coffin into the Pantheon, laying it to rest under the cupola. De Gaulle, joined by four of his ministers and the chancellor of the Ordre de la Libération, entered to pay their last respects and observe a moment of silence.

The evening proceedings of December 18, it appears, were not televised, but those of the following day were, and it is clear what message viewers, above all the young people among them, were meant to take away. Moulin's interment drew the curtain on that thirty-year cycle of conflict bracketed by the two world wars. Moulin himself was a glorious martyr, a Frenchman who had died that the nation might live. It was he as no other who had built Resistance unity, a unity under de Gaulle's leadership that signified France's unyielding will to fight. The martyrs in that fight included, of course, the résistant who died arms in hand but also the starved and battered deportee with shaven head.

It was a moving and majestic epic. At the same time, as others have remarked, much was left out of it. For all the talk of deportees and concentration camps, Jews didn't merit a mention, nor did Vichy for that matter. The subject of empire, an important leitmotiv in earlier Gaullist ceremonials, was absent from this one. Factor in that earlier in the month, on December 17, parliament had enacted a bill amnestying perpetrators of crimes committed in prosecution of the Algerian War, and it begins to look like the pantheonization ceremony signaled a symbolic pivot, Gaullist memory turning away from empire, which was now treated as a chapter at last closed. Finally, there is the place of Communists in the event. They were not obliterated. Marcel Paul was on hand to watch over Moulin's coffin at the Mémorial des Martyrs de la Déportation, and Malraux's speech made a brief reference to the "Communist Party," whose troops, he reminded listeners, had, like those of "the army of Africa," consented to fight under de Gaulle's unified command. That's not a lot, however, and many militants had expected as much, one grouping, the communist-oriented Association nationale des anciens combattants de la Résistance, opting to absent itself from the proceedings, citing as an excuse that it had not been invited.

The state's publicity machinery cranked into high gear once more in 1966 on the occasion of the debut of a major hit movie, *Paris, brûle-t-il?*[75] The movie recounts the saga of the Liberation of Paris in August 1944. It is not a deportation story, although it does include a deportation scene. It deserves at least a cursory examination if just for that, but even more so for what it has to say about the media-fueled muscularity of Gaullist memory in mid-sixties France. The film was based on a best-selling book of the same title, co-authored by Larry Collins and Dominique Lapierre, which was published in 1965. Two American producers competed for the film production rights: Darryl Zanuck and the Austrian-born Paul Graetz.

They had once been collaborators, working together for a period on *The Longest Day* (1962), which in many respects provided a template for the later *Paris brûle-t-il? The Longest Day* dealt with the D-Day invasion and did so with the same reverence that *Paris brûle-t-il?* accorded the Liberation of Paris. *The Longest Day* was History with a capital H, sometimes sententious and stilted in tone, but told with an epic sweep, boosted by performances from a huge, star-studded, and almost all-male cast (which included Henry Fonda, Robert Mitchum, and John Wayne). Zanuck and Graetz, however, had had a falling out during the making of *The Longest Day*, prompting Graetz's departure from the film, which is why the two men were competitors rather than partners in the effort to bring *Paris brûle-t-il?* to the silver screen. In this instance, it was Graetz who won out.

There was a second competition involved in the making of the film, this one having to do with the screenwriters. A French team – Jean Aurenche, Pierre Bost, and Claude Brûlé – were edged out by an American duo, Francis Ford Coppola and Gore Vidal, whippersnappers compared to Aurenche and Bost, longtime veterans of France's quality cinema. On the matter of the movie's director, however, there was no dispute. Graetz wanted René Clément, an established figure and maker of the Resistance film classic, *La Bataille du rail* (1945), and so Clément it was.

Politics shadowed the movie at every turn, no surprise given the hot-button subject. The PCF had its version of events, one that insisted on the centrality of armed insurrection to Paris's liberation. The Gaullists had another, which accented the moderating role of Gaullist résistants and the last-minute arrival of Lerclerc's armored column, which together combined to speed the Germans' exit without exposing the city to the kind of wholesale destruction the Nazis had inflicted on Warsaw. The Party had hopes that Clément's film might reflect its line. Clément after all had directed *La Bataille du rail*, a documentary-like dramatization of the role of rail workers in sabotaging German efforts to mount a counter-offensive in response to the D-Day landings. The PCF, moreover, was a powerhouse in the world of cinema trade unionism and thus in a position to complicate the making of any movie it did not like. Clément was well aware of this and invited a party representative, in the event Henri Rol-Tanguy (a battle-tested Communist who had been commander of Free French Forces in the Paris region at the time of the Liberation) to serve as a historical advisor. The Gaullists, however, had assets of their own. Clément filmed in Paris and its environs, dramatizing the fighting in the streets and the approach and arrival of French (and American) army units. For this, he needed and obtained permissions from Minister of the Interior Roger Frey and from Minister of Cultural Affairs André Malraux, both hard-core Gaullists. It helped that Collins and Lapierre's text was already weighted in favor of the Gaullist side. The screenwriters felt the push and pull of influences, which Vidal summed up with characteristic wit: "Parts of the book, even though based on real events, couldn't be used; if we offended de Gaulle, we couldn't work in the streets, if we offended the Communists, we would lose the electricians and machinists."[76]

In the end, it was the Gaullist line that won top billing. Rol-Tanguy, a central figure in the actual fighting, had his day on screen, but the film never identified him as a Communist, and a second-rank actor, Bruno Cremer, was assigned the part. Communists, once again never named as such, were portrayed throughout as full of fight, but they were also hotheaded. The Gaullists by contrast manifested a greater pragmatism, none more so than de Gaulle's military delegate on the spot, Jacques Chaban-Delmas (Alain Delon), who counseled patience. "Think," he entreated a fellow résistante, Françoise Labé (Leslie Caron), "what happened to Warsaw." The picture makes plain that this was just the fate Hitler intended for the City of Light. He had given orders to destroy Paris rather than surrender it to the Allies, and near the movie's conclusion, the German commanding officer in Paris, General Dietrich von Choltitz, receives an urgent call from the Führer who demands to know: "Is Paris burning?" But the city does not burn. Leclerc's armored column charges in at the last moment, the Germans depart, and the movie winds up with two scenes in quick succession: actual newsreel footage of General de Gaulle marching down the Champs-Élysées as the city's church bells peal, followed by a shot of Paris, the first color shot in an otherwise black-and-white movie, accompanied by the sound of accordion music. In the end, it was de Gaulle who liberated Paris and put color back into the city's cheeks.

In overall interpretation, the movie was faithful to the book, but there were spots, as Vidal's remarks remind us, where it deviated. One personality was erased outright. Georges Bidault was the most senior civilian résistant on the scene in August 1944, and yet he didn't figure in the film for one obvious reason. Bidault had been a vigorous opponent of Algerian independence and fallen out with de Gaulle over the issue. The General was determined to turn the page so far as *Algérie française* was concerned, and the representation of an outspoken critic on screen, in a heroic context at that, just wouldn't do. There were some additions to the story as well and one in particular that is pertinent to this discussion. The Labé couple, Bernard and Françoise, do not exist in the book. He is a Resistance fighter imprisoned at Fresnes, and she is his wife, determined to rescue him. The rescue attempt takes place at a train station, as the Germans funnel prisoners into freight cars en route to deportation. It fails, and Bernard is killed. The scene is an incidental one, but an indication of how inevitable the deportation motif had become.

Gaullist officialdom recognized the blockbuster potential of *Paris brûle-t-il?* and lent its hand to turning the film's Parisian release into a citywide spectacular. The movie premiered in an evening screening at the Palais de Chaillot on October 24, 1966. An audience of twenty-five hundred was invited to attend, and they entered the theater, passing between hedgerows of torch-bearing Gardes républicaines. At the same time, all of Paris' major monuments were illuminated, even as a column of tanks, itself illuminated by spotlight, retraced the path followed by Leclerc's armored column in August 1944. At the end of the screening, as the theatergoers exited, they were greeted by song, Mireille Mathieu perched on the first floor of the Eiffel Tower belting out the "Chant des partisans" and by a fireworks display (dampened by uncooperative weather). All the hoopla made manifest that this wasn't just any movie, but one that enjoyed official backing, and the movie proved to be the hit that officialdom had anticipated. Its Paris run alone drew in a million viewers.[77]

"Like a wall": that was how de Gaulle thought of the Resistance, and in its way, Gaullist memory of the war years was also like a wall. French men and women, looking back in time from the late 1960s, had a difficult time seeing over it. The landscape of commemoration they saw around them was a Gaullist one, and all that had gone before lay obscured in the wall's shadow. Or else it had been incorporated, brick by brick, into the structure of the wall itself. Communist memory was another matter. It lived on, albeit in much reduced circumstances, a little brother muscled aside by an all-too-brawny older sibling. It was Gaullist memory's stirring message of national unity that accounted in part for its power, but there is no gainsaying how much the backing of the state and of public media worked to amplify its voice and to drown out those of others. One voice, however, was not silenced. The Gaullist din notwithstanding, Jews managed to make themselves heard, and they did so not by soliloquizing but by entering into conversation, often painful and full of misunderstanding, with others and with their Catholic brethren in particular. It is to an account of that Jewish-Christian dialogue that we now turn.

Part II

Shoah

7   Holocaust

Catholics like Jacques Maritain tried to make sense of the Holocaust within a Christian framework. This involved an appropriation and one that Jews did not always welcome. Jews also addressed Christians on the subject, at times in tones of entreaty. In the run-up to the war and during the war itself, the painter Marc Chagall returned over and again to the theme of the crucified Christ. Chagall's Christ, however, was very much a Jew, clad in a loincloth that was itself painted to resemble a Jewish prayer shawl or tallit. The message was unambiguous. The persecution of the Jews was a modern-day Crucifixion, and Christians of good conscience, like Chagall's own friends Jacques and Raïssa Maritain, were adjured to come to the aid of their Jewish brethren in agony. The tone of address, however, just as often took an accusatory turn, as it did in the writings of Jules Isaac (1877–1963), an historian and educator who had lost a wife and daughter in the genocide. From time immemorial, he wrote, Christians had spoken evil of the Jews, reproving them for not acknowledging Christ's divinity, a stubborn refusal, Christians believed, that had earned the Jews God's wrath and, in punishment, centuries of homelessness and suffering. Even worse, Christians had branded Jews as deicides, citing Scripture in evidence. The Gospel of Saint Matthew recounted how the Jewish high priest Caiaphas had conspired to effect Jesus's crucifixion as a false messiah and then how the Jews of Jerusalem, offered the possibility of sacrificing the criminal Barabbas, cried out instead for Jesus's death, shouting even as they did: "His blood be on us, and on our children" (Matthew, 27:25). For Isaac, such teachings, "the teaching of contempt" as he labeled them, incited anti-Semitic hatred, which in turn stoked the homicidal fury that had eventually led to Auschwitz.[1] Christianity itself on this accounting bore a burden of responsibility for the Holocaust, and when Isaac made such accusations, he was not talking to fellow Jews alone but to Christians as well, to Catholics and Protestants of good will like his colleagues in the Amitié Judéo-Chrétienne, an interfaith association born of the postwar that he himself had helped to found.

It should not be thought that Chagall and Isaac were exceptional figures, for there were many others – historians like Léon Poliakov and Saul Friedländer, writers like Elie Wiesel and André Schwarz-Bart – who addressed Christians in similar terms, inviting them to reflect on the murder of the Jews by the light of the Cross but also in the burning glare of the concentration camp chimney. What is striking is how many interlocutors they found, from the Maritains to the Nobel-winning novelist François Mauriac to the publisher-in-chief at Le Seuil, Paul Flamand.

Did such dialogue come at too great a cost? And did it make any difference? Jewish speakers framed what they had to say in language and images meaningful to Christians. Elie Wiesel published a concentration camp text in Yiddish in 1956 titled *Un di velt hot geshvign* (*And the World Remained Silent*). The narrative concluded with an angry peroration, excoriating world opinion, which had kept silent during the Holocaust, for keeping silent once again as the perpetrator of the crime, Germany, rearmed itself. A French version came out two years later with a title change. *Un di velt hot geshvign* had become *La Nuit*, and along the way the concluding outburst was excised. In the original, Wiesel told of the marauding conduct of camp prisoners once released. In the French, it was food first and foremost, not vengeance, that the survivors craved. In the passage from Yiddish to French, it seems, much of Wiesel's anger had been drained away.[2] It is well worth asking, as some have done, whether such self-censorship was the price Wiesel had to pay to gain access to a Gentile readership. André Schwarz-Bart's *Le Dernier des Justes* (1959) has been reproached on related grounds. Schwarz-Bart published in French, so there was nothing to be lost in translation. What he did do was to present the narrative's Jewish protagonist, Ernie Levy, in Christlike terms. Levy is a righteous man who volunteers to go to Drancy to remain by the side of the woman he loves, Golda. When a trainload of Jewish children is shipped from Drancy to Auschwitz, Ernie steps forward once more to join them, providing consolation to the children on the train ride and all the way into the gas chamber itself. Throughout, Levy is described as a sacrificial lamb, a man of sorrows who takes upon himself the sins of the world. From this angle, Schwarz-Bart's understanding of the Holocaust appears centered on willing sacrifice, just as Wiesel's narrative spoke in the accents of restraint, both approaches calibrated to touch the hearts of Christian readers.

A different angle of interpretation will be adopted here. The writers and artists under discussion made use of elements in Jewish tradition with a remarkable creativity to speak in terms that Christians understood: to grab them by the collar and provoke them to think in critical ways about their own religious inheritance. The result was meaningful in two respects. Christians who entered into the exchange made it possible for the Jewish voice to be heard, and in addition to that, Christians themselves began to change, to revise and in the long run to jettison the teaching of contempt.[3] Let there be no misunderstanding, however. The path to such rethinking was not a smooth one, but strewn with recriminations and foot-dragging. Yet both sides pushed on, arriving with the passage of time at a space of greater mutual understanding.

Marc Chagall and the Maritains

Chagall and the Maritains first met in 1928, and the acquaintance blossomed into a friendship in the decade that followed. The artist, accompanied by his wife, Bella, became regulars at the Maritains' social gatherings at Meudon. During the war, the Chagalls followed the path of exile, settling in New York City, as did the Maritains, and the two couples remained in friendly contact.[4] It seems an unlikely partnership, Chagall, the painter of Hasidic background, and Maritain, the Catholic philosopher, but there were people and interests that brought them together, first of all Maritain's wife, Raïssa. She was a Jewish woman converted to Christianity, who had been born in Russia. Chagall and Raïssa came from a similar Hasidic milieu and were known to communicate in Russian together.[5] She was, moreover, an *exaltée* and a mystic and recognized in Chagall a kindred spirit. It made a difference, moreover, that both the Maritains were taken with the painter's art, above all when he turned to religious subjects.

Chagall made a trip to Palestine in 1931 in the company of Edmond Fleg, then at work on a book about Jewish understandings of Jesus. The art dealer Ambroise Vollard had commissioned Chagall the year proceeding to prepare a suite of Hebrew Bible illustrations, which no doubt accounts for the artist's own interest in a visit to the Holy Land. Jacques Maritain admired what he saw of the work, and in fact the Maritain home at Meudon featured a Chagall on the wall alongside portraits of Saint Thomas and the philo-Semitic Catholic writer Léon Bloy.[6]

Chagall's turn to New Testament imagery in the late 1930s and on into the war deepened the connection. In 1938, shaken by the intensification of anti-Semitic persecution, the artist painted *The White Crucifixion* (see Figure 7.1). At the center of the canvas hovers a crucified Jesus. He is a Jew and is identified as such in many ways, most obviously by the tallit that covers the lower portion of his body. At Jesus' feet burns a menorah and above the figure is imprinted a double inscription: the Latin initials *INRI* and just beneath, written out in Aramaic, the translation: Jesus of Nazareth, King of the Jews. The world that Jesus hovers over is one of

Figure 7.1 Marc Chagall, *The White Crucifixion*, 1938. The Art Institute of Chicago/Art Resource, NY

pogroms and flight. Persecutors have set a synagogue ablaze in the painting's top right corner; a Torah scroll burns in the quadrant beneath; and everywhere Jews dressed in shtetl garb are fleeing to save themselves. The theme became an obsession of Chagall's in the years ahead. He painted and repainted the subject, adding and subtracting elements. In *La Crucifixion en jaune* (1942–1943), the crucified Christ is still a Jew, but now he wears, in addition to the tallit, tefillin or phylacteries, a ritual article worn by Jewish men at prayer. Beside him, floating in space, is an unscrolled Torah, and beneath him a woman and child, walking alongside a donkey, headed into exile, an allusion to the flight of Mary and the infant Jesus into Egypt. A variant of that image – of Mary and the baby Jesus in flight, this time with an angel above showing the way – made it onto the cover of the Christmas 1943 issue of *Vogue* magazine.[7]

Chagall himself provided a clue as to what he was about in an exchange the next year with a curator at the Museum of Modern Art in New York, James Johnson Sweeney: "For me Christ was a great poet, the teaching of whose poetry has been forgotten by the modern world."[8] There is an indictment implicit in such words: that Christians today no longer harken to Christ's teachings, and it's a charge hammered home in the artist's work. Christians reverence the Gospels, but the gospel accounts of flight and crucifixion, Chagall's art tells us, are not just stories pre-served in pious memory, but living ones now reenacted in an anguished present as Jewish sacred objects are put to the torch and the Jews themselves nailed to the Cross or driven into exile. Chagall addressed Christians, as a leading scholar of the subject has put it, "in their own symbolic language," as a way of awakening them from a heedless and unfeeling indifference.[9]

The Maritains, however, *were* paying attention. In 1939, Raïssa wrote a poem about Chagall that made reference to *The White Crucifixion* and its Christ "Spread across a lost world/In a vast ivory space."[10] While in New York during the war, on the urging of fellow Catholic-in-exile Father Marie-Alain Couturier, she dedicated a whole book to the artist whom she embraced as "a primitive of the race of Christ." Chagall the man, as Raïssa saw him, stood at the very intersection of the Old and New Testaments, a personification of the bond between the two, and that bond was no less evident in the artist's work, which united "the Passion of Christ to that of the Chosen People." Raïssa Maritain's Chagall may not have been a believing Christian, but he was a Jew, a brother by the flesh, with a profound grasp of "the symbols" of the Christian faith.[11]

For Jacques Maritain, that understanding was a wake-up call. He resonated to *The White Crucifixion*, as did Raïssa. In a 1944 radio address, Maritain spoke about "the passion of Israel," which had "more and more distinctly taken on the form of the cross." The remark, it bears adding, was preceded by an evocation of Chagall's 1938 painting. Maritain read the swirling images that spun around Christ – "spread across a fallen world" – as a "great tempest" that threatened to sweep away "the unfor-tunate Jews" caught up in its powerful winds.[12] The Passion of Israel, the crucifixion of a people, demanded that Christians of good faith take action, and that's what Maritain did. De Gaulle named him ambassador to the Vatican in 1945. The next year, scores of Jews were murdered in the Kielce pogroms in Poland. Maritain fired off a letter to Monsignor

Montini of the Vatican Secretariat of State, imploring the Holy See to take a stand against "the antisemitic psychosis." "The people of Israel," he wrote, had been "thrown onto the road of Calvary and formed into the sufferings of its Messiah," torments that demanded from the pontiff a counter-act of "justice and reparation."[13]

Pius XII did not act, but there was movement on another front. Good Friday services featured a cycle of prayers, including one "*pro perfidis Judaeis*," "for the perfidious Jews" as it was most often translated. A genuflection accompanied each prayer in the cycle, but not the prayer for the Jews, who were deemed unworthy of such a gesture of respect. The practice, as might be imagined, was troubling to Jews, and Maritain sympathized. In 1948, just as he was about to depart his ambassadorial post, he paid a final visit to Montini and took advantage of the moment to urge the Holy See to alter the wording of the prayer. On this point, he received a reassurance that a change was in the offing, which in fact it was. The Church in mid-June 1948 made known that it had no objection to translating "*perfidis*" as "unfaithful." The Jews remained as ever an obstinate people, who refused to believe, but at least their refusal was no longer presented as a sign of deceit or treachery.[14]

Léon Poliakov and François Mauriac

Léon Poliakov, like Chagall, had a Christian interlocutor: François Mauriac. Mauriac prefaced Poliakov's pioneering masterwork on the genocide of the Jews, *Bréviaire de la haine* (1951), praising its objective approach. Others might write in a spirit of revenge or hate but not Poliakov, who wrote in the objective tones of the archival historian.[15] It's true that Poliakov worked very much in the document-based vein favored by the CDJC, but that didn't mean he was a mere clinician. Indeed, he elaborated a religious interpretation of Nazism, derived in equal parts from the work of David Rousset and Jacques Maritain, which posed a pointed challenge to thinking Christians. Mauriac was just such a person, and Poliakov's analysis prompted him to some serious soul-searching.

Nazism, as Poliakov understood it, was a faith, much as Rousset had claimed. The Nazi creed worshipped at the altar of racial purity, and that altar cried out for blood. For Rousset, it was camp inmates who were the designated sacrificial victims, but in Poliakov's rendering, it was the Jews. They, in the Nazi vulgate, were the embodiment of evil, and, as such, the act of extirpating them – and Poliakov used the word *holocaust* in this connection – resembled a religious rite, which explains why it was infused with a kind of "sacred horror." Maritain had spoken of the mystery of Israel. For Poliakov, there existed a second mystery no less imponderable, "the mystery of anti-Semitism."[16]

Poliakov followed Maritain in writing of Nazism as a species of neo-paganism. The Nazis singled out the Jews for special torment and did so because the Jews symbolized a moral tradition they execrated, a tradition that was not, however, the sole possession of the Jews. Christians too shared in it, and in this measure the martyrdom of the Jews was at the same time an attack on Christianity. Poliakov made an explicit reference to Maritain on just this point. The Nazis, he wrote, were anti-Semites and for that very reason enemies of the Judeo-Christian tradition. Poliakov then added one more to the list of charges, indicting them as the "Antichrist." From this perspective, the Nazi extermination of the Jews took on the aspect of a veritable "Calvary," once again Poliakov's own word.[17]

Yet, Poliakov's analysis did not stop here. Nazi hatred of the Jews was anti-Christian in essence, but at the same time it drew energy from elements within the Christian tradition itself. Poliakov had the tact to frame the allegation in the form of a question: "A catechism inculcated across the centuries to all Christian children, does it not teach them that the Jews, Jesus' murderers, are damnable?" Didn't Good Friday prayers, he went on, remind congregants in all too vivid terms that the Jews were a people of perfidy? Poliakov's implication is evident: such characterizations primed Christians to accept that Jews merited the punishments heaped upon them, genocide included. Recall now the title of Poliakov's book, *Breviary of Hate*, which is the literal translation of *Brévaire de la haine*. The liturgy of anti-Semitism was not an invention of the Nazis alone, but had its roots in Christian teachings. Poliakov leveled this accusation in the context of discussing the pope's wartime silence even as "factories of death" reduced millions of Jews to ash. No doubt, he acknowledged, many clergy had taken enormous risks to rescue Jews, motivated by "the élan of the first Christian martyrs," and to this extent they had remained true to the fraternal message of the Gospels. Yet at the same time, too many Christians, following the pope's own example, had turned away, blinded by prejudices that they had learned in church but which were not Christian in spirit.[18] This was a line of analysis Maritain, for one, could not follow. He was prepared to concede that there was a true Christianity and a perverted, earthbound variant, but he could not swallow such a pointed critique of the pope's conduct, and that's more or less what he said in the otherwise laudatory review he wrote of Poliakov's book.[19]

Mauriac, by contrast, knew no such hesitations. What a coup it was for Poliakov's publisher, Calmann-Lévy, to have secured a preface from the novelist. He was a long-sitting member of the Académie française and on the cusp of becoming the Nobel laureate in literature (1952). He was also a Catholic of independent views who had long anguished about the fate of the Jews in wartime France. During the Occupation, as we have seen, he published a clandestine text that talked about witnessing the awful spectacle of Jewish children packed into freight cars at the gare d'Austerlitz. He reprised the episode in the preface he wrote to *Brévaire de la haine*, and the context was a meditation on the responsibility of the bystander in the face of evil. The issue gnawed at him as a Frenchman. After all, as he wrote in the preface, it was men in French uniform who had stood guard over the children at the fateful railroad station. It gnawed at him as a Catholic as well. Pius XII had made "diplomatic allusions" to the persecution of the Jews but had never spoken out to condemn it in words that were clear and forthright. Then again, such evasions and silences were all too comprehensible, for was not Christianity itself heir to an age-old "tradition of hatred against the 'deicide race'?" The time had come to begin anew, Mauriac wrote, to reconnect with Christianity's origins when the first church, the Church of Jerusalem, had been populated by Jews.[20]

Mauriac's effort at comprehension was profound. This didn't mean he avoided all stereotyping. The writer came from a conservative background, and so it's not surprising to learn that his brother, Pierre, whom he much admired, had been a Pétainist and lifelong "disciple of Maurras."[21] In the 1930s, Mauriac himself had sniped against Jewish "clannishness" and intrusiveness and the Jews' predilection for financial finagling. A note of such bias even found its way into Mauriac's preface. He observed that "a certain form of Jewish behavior" had contributed to the ferment of anti-Semitic hatred. It's a vague allusion, to be sure, but less so in light of the lines that followed. Mauriac went on to explain that Israel, the new Jewish state, had done a good deal to deliver Jews from the errors of past ways, thus drawing an implicit contrast between the deficient Diaspora Jew and the Zionist pioneer, whose heroic qualities helped to make up for the flaws of his European coreligionists. This may be too harsh a reading, but don't forget that in the mid-fifties, Mauriac was not above making invidious distinctions among different kinds of Jews in French public life, juxtaposing "the great French Israelite René Mayer" with "the little Jew, Mendès France."[22]

Mauriac also manifested a tendency, as did many well-meaning Catholics, to speak about the Jewish genocide in Christianizing terms. The preface referred to Jews as the Savior's "brothers" and to the Jewish children he had seen at the gare d'Austerlitz as so many "lambs." And just as Jesus, the lamb of God, had been crucified, so too had European

Jewry undergone a *"mise en croix."*[23] At the same time, it should be kept in mind that Poliakov had also addressed Christian readers in language keyed to a Christian world view, and so it is not altogether fair to reproach a Christian reader, like Mauriac, for responding in kind.

The Poliakov-Mauriac dialogue was textually mediated, Poliakov's book raising and framing issues that Mauriac's preface then reflected upon. Mauriac took more than one step in Poliakov's direction, but a distance remained. It was challenging for the writer to abandon old stereotypes and even harder to think about Jewish experience as such, without looking at it through the filtering lens of Christian belief.

Elie Wiesel and François Mauriac

Some of the same problems would reemerge in Mauriac's dealings with Elie Wiesel. The encounter between the two men played out on multiple levels. Mauriac wrote a preface to Wiesel's *La Nuit* as he had to Poliakov's book and once again found himself confronted with a text that tested his beliefs, obliging him to fashion a response, which he did in his usual Christianizing idiom. The relationship between the two men, however, was not just mediated through texts but also face-to-face. In 1944, a teenaged Wiesel had been deported from the Hungarian town of Sighet to Auschwitz. He survived the camp and survived too the death march from Auschwitz to Buchenwald, where he was liberated by American troops in the spring of 1945. Wiesel relocated to France and was educated there, finding employment in 1950 as Paris correspondent for the Israeli newspaper *Yedioth Ahronoth*. In that capacity, he unsuccessfully sought out an interview with Mendès France. Wiesel bumped into Mauriac at a reception at the Israeli embassy and arranged an interview with the writer in the hope of getting to Mendès France through him. The meeting took place in May 1955.[24] It did not go well at first but ended in an emotional rapprochement, with Mauriac pressing Wiesel to write about his wartime ordeal. In due course, Wiesel delivered a manuscript to Mauriac, who arranged its publication in 1958 with Éditions de Minuit under the title, *La Nuit*.[25] In the meantime, the personal bond between the two men deepened and would endure right up to Mauriac's death in 1970.

So Wiesel's entry onto the French stage was facilitated by a Christian, but did that make a difference? On one line of interpretation, it did, and a major one. Wiesel first composed his manuscript in Yiddish. He embarked on the project on return from the camps and then completed it in a frenetic burst in 1954. The finished text was published in a Yiddish-language book series in Argentina two years later. It was not then titled *La Nuit* but rather, as noted, *Un di velt hot geshvign*. Prompted by Mauriac's admonition to speak out, Wiesel returned to what he had written and reworked it: cutting down the text from several hundred pages to a lean one hundred and seventy-eight, rendering it into a "terse, telegraphic" French prose, and altering the manuscript's tone in the process.[26] The Yiddish version seethed with fury – how so will be discussed in more detail below – but in the French, that anger had been muted, and what took its place was the hauntedness of a Jewish martyr, shaken by God's silence in the face of the most unspeakable horrors. The transformation was Wiesel's own handiwork, but it was undertaken under Mauriac's tutelary supervision, resulting in a book that was in form and substance accessible to a Christian readership that might otherwise have been put off by what one informed critic has called "the scandal of Jewish rage."[27]

Yet there is another way of looking at the question. Wiesel was and remained a religious man, a Hasid by birth and education, and it is possible to read *La Nuit* in that light. The text was a "historical document" about life and death in the camps, but it was also, as one interpreter has put it, a dialogue, "permanent and continuous," between "Elie Wiesel and the [Hebrew] Bible."[28] Wiesel bore witness to what he had seen, but he at the same time made use of biblical referents – the stories of Job and Isaac – to pattern the narrative he constructed. From this perspective, any role Mauriac might have played in the shaping of the book was of secondary importance.

The view that will be staked out here cleaves closer to the second interpretation than to the first. Wiesel did indeed adjust the original text to reach a non-Yiddish audience, and in more ways than one. His decision to write in French was in itself an acculturating gesture. He cast *La Nuit* in a narrative prose and made use of literary devices that were attuned to speak to a French-language readership, one, indeed, immersed in the Existentialist trends and preoccupations of the era. It is true, in addition, that the very real anger of *Un di velt hot geshvign* was attenuated. The outcome, however, was not a watered-down compromise, half-Jewish and half-Christian, but a powerful statement about the camp experience from a Jewish perspective that was at its core religious in nature.

Let's start with Mauriac's preface. The novelist, of course, was a man of faith, a Christian who couldn't help but present Wiesel and Wiesel's narrative in Christianizing terms. The initial meeting between the two men, as I said, got off to a rocky start. In Wiesel's version, that was because Mauriac kept talking about "the life – and more so, the death – of a young Jew from Nazareth" – until Wiesel lost patience, blurting out that he had known children, Jewish children, "each of whom had suffered a thousand, six million times more than Christ on the cross." An indignant Wiesel then stormed out, followed to the landing by Mauriac who, now in tears, entreated the reporter to come back. It was a breakthrough moment.[29] Mauriac's account does not include the scene on the landing. As he told it in the preface to *La Nuit*, the pivotal moment in the interview came when Mauriac brought up the oft-repeated story of seeing Jewish children crammed into freight cars at the gare d'Austerlitz (although in this telling it was Mauriac's wife, not he himself, who had done the witnessing). Wiesel interrupted the writer, saying, "I am one of them," and in so saying he appeared to Mauriac in a new guise. Wiesel himself was one of those "lambs" and so began Mauriac's reinvention of Wiesel as a figure from Bible times.[30] The preface characterized him as a "young Israeli" (which he was not), a "chosen of God" with the look of a "Lazarus brought back to life," a brother who, for all Mauriac knew, resembled that other "Israeli … whose cross conquered the world."[31]

These were themes that Mauriac would revert to time and again in later writing. Mauriac's Wiesel was a man who straddled the two Testaments, a true descendent of the "race of John the Baptist." He was an innocent, Mauriac wrote, who had escaped Herod's massacre, and on occasion the writer was prepared to take the analogizing a dramatic step further. He published a meditation on Christ's message in 1958, *Le Fils de l'homme*, and forwarded a copy to Wiesel with a dedication: "to Elie Wiesel, who is a crucified Jewish child, who is the incarnation of so many more." Wiesel, as Mauriac envisioned the man, resembled Christ himself.[32]

The murder of the Jews then was a human tragedy, but it also had greater significance, and Mauriac's preface hinted at what that significance was. Modern-day pagans, he wrote had martyred Israel on the altar of "Race, the most voracious of all the idols." Yet, from the ashes of this "holocaust," from the "crematoria" and "charnel houses" of the camps, Zion had been reborn. The hand of Providence, it was implied, was at work in this story of sacrifice and resurrection, and Mauriac wondered whether he should have made an effort to communicate that comforting thought to Wiesel on their first meeting. He doubted, though, that the young man who then stood before him would have found solace in such a message, a young man who just years before had experienced such terrible loss and, perhaps the worst loss of all, the shattering of an innocent's faith in God's grace. Maybe, Mauriac reflected, he ought to have made the attempt, but instead he wrapped Wiesel in a tearful embrace.[33]

La Nuit was Wiesel's first book in French, and the reader coming upon it entered the narrative through the portals of Mauriac's preface. The tone was loving, Mauriac reaching out as best he could to a brother in pain and inviting the reader to do the same. Mauriac contemplated the Holocaust by the merciful light of Christian redemption, but he understood that this was not possible for Wiesel himself, still at grips with that most appalling of questions: How could a loving God allow such a terrible fate to befall his chosen people?

Yet did the book itself conform to the expectations that Mauriac's introduction, wittingly or not, contributed to formulating? It is no doubt the case that the narrative, as it migrated from Yiddish to French, lost elements of its Jewishness. In the original Yiddish, the text makes reference to an encounter in Buchenwald with hometown friends, Erwin Farkash and Anshy Meisner. They and their Yiddish-sounding names fall by the wayside in the French edition. *La Nuit*'s protagonist, Eliezer, is deported along with his father, and the relationship between the two and how camp life deforms it is one of the narrative's emotional epicenters. In the original account, the father dies, and a precise date – a rarity in the text, which accentuates the weight of the event – is provided: the Eighteenth of Shevat, 1945. Eliezer rues that there is no minyan or quorum of adult men to recite the Kaddish, no one to light a candle for the deceased, and no grave to bury him in. In French, the father's death is dated, not according to the Hebrew calendar, but the Gregorian one; the Kaddish becomes "a prayer"; and the minyan reference is dropped altogether. These are all minor retouchings, so many adjustments to make the text comprehensible to readers not versed in Jewish religious life. Yet they do add up, making the French edition that much more abstracted from the specifics of the Jewish milieu.[34]

Of greater moment, however, is the change in the book's emotional valence as it made its way from Yiddish into French. In *Un di velt hot geshvign*, the camp's male inmates celebrate the High Holy Days of Rosh Hashanah and Yom Kippur. The intense communion of the worshipers creates an atmosphere almost hallucinatory, firing a spark that attests to the intensity of the men's faith and prompting an angry Eliezer in response to rail against God's unworthy silence. There is more railing at the end of the book. In the final pages, Buchenwald is liberated. The Jewish survivors do not think of those who have died. They want to eat. They descend on nearby Weimar to pillage ... "And to rape German women [*shikses*]." As for Eliezer, he falls ill, suspended between life and death. By chance, he espies himself in a mirror (shades of George Wellers), the first time he has seen himself since deportation, and what he sees is a cadaver. The sight causes him, propelled by a reinvigorated will to live, to make a fist and smash the glass. The Yiddish text then apostrophizes the reader. It is but a decade later, and Germany is a sovereign state once more and rearmed. The world remained silent while the Germans murdered the Jews of Europe, and it remains silent still, moving the author to pose a concluding question: Was it worth smashing the mirror after all? Eliezer is driven by a rage to live in the Yiddish text, and he is at the same time an angry man, angry at God, the Germans, and the world.[35]

The anger does not subside altogether in the French text, but almost. The camp inmates' pious observance of the High Holy Days still provokes an outburst from Eliezer. The congregants manifest a strength and grandeur that is greater than God's. The Almighty is undeserving of the praise bestowed upon him, and to protest his silence, Eliezer refuses to fast on Yom Kippur. On the matter of the book's final passages, the reference to pillage and rape is cut out completely. The freed inmates feel no impulse to vengeance at all. They just want food, clothes, and to chase after girls. The book's anti-German finale is also expunged. The French-language edition then concludes with the dramatic mirror scene, but now rewritten. There is no violent gesture. Eliezer does not break the glass but looks at himself, a haggard, corpselike figure, and that image, as he lets the reader know, has stayed with him ever since.[36] The book's protagonist is in revolt against God. Yet he is not a vindictive man, but rather one haunted by death. The voice of the author is not that of an accuser (except when it comes to God) but that of a revenant or, as Mauriac saw it, a Lazarus.

The change in emotional tone is a matter of some significance. It may have come at Mauriac's behest, or it may not. Jews, after all, were capable of censoring themselves. CDJC historians, it will be remembered, worked hard to fashion a scientific prose, one purged of anger and emotional pleading. Remember too how the CDJC, deliberating on what inscriptions to etch on the front wall of the Tombeau du Martyr juif inconnu, deleted portions of one text deemed too unforgiving. Jews who wanted to talk to Gentile audiences about the genocide were conscious that expressions of anger and vengeance might prove self-defeating, alienating readers who might better be spoken to in less astringent words.

Wiesel in this respect was a case in point, but it is not adequate to characterize the language of address he sought to craft as Christianizing. It was a huge step for Wiesel to reinvent himself as a writer, and a writer of French at that. He came from a religious background that did not take a positive view of writers of books. This was an activity, in Wiesel's own words, for "someone with nothing else to do."[37] Wiesel the survivor, however, had an urgent story to tell, religious inhibitions or no. He told it first in Yiddish and then in a totally new language. Wiesel first studied French with a private tutor assigned to him by the Jewish agency that had taken him in after the war. That tutor was not just anyone, but François Wahl, an Existentialist philosopher and man of letters, who converted the young Wiesel into an admirer of France's great classical authors, Corneille and Racine.[38] Wiesel went on to take courses at the Sorbonne and there, among fellow students, was exposed to the modern literature of the day, to Sartre and Camus above all, then very much in vogue. The French language provided Wiesel a new home. Its strangeness, as well as its clarity and precision, enabled him to think at a remove about a subject – what he had experienced in the camps – that was otherwise too close and upsetting to talk about. What appealed to Wiesel about Existentialism was not so much its philosophical stance as its literary methods. That's why he liked Camus better than Sartre, and in the spareness of Wiesel's own prose, it's possible to detect the influence of Camus, that master of "short, direct sentences."[39]

Yet, Sartre was not altogether without influence – the Sartre, that is, who wrote about people making hard choices *en situation*. Think of Wiesel's second novel, *L'Aube* (1960), dedicated by the way to Mauriac. In it, the protagonist, a camp survivor who has emigrated to Mandate Palestine and joined a Zionist paramilitary organization, spends a night guarding a British military hostage whom he is assigned to execute at dawn. Will the survivor, who was once a victim, become a killer himself? Or think of Wiesel's fourth novel, *La Ville de la Chance* (1964). The central figure once again is a survivor, Michael. After the war, he wants to return to the village where he was born, located now behind the Iron Curtain, and is assisted by a *passeur* (smuggler), Pedro. The communist authorities capture Michael and subject him to a harsh interrogation to make him betray the smuggler's identity. Will he hold out long enough to allow Pedro time to escape the country?

Here is the point to raise the matter of Wiesel's French-language title *La Nuit*. It came from Wiesel's publisher, Jérôme Lindon, and it has been argued that, in suggesting it, Lindon was inviting readers to make a connection between Wiesel's text and Resnais and Cayrol's *Nuit et Brouillard*.[40] The evidence for such a claim is plausible, even if circumstantial. Lindon was a man of the independent Left and a fierce opponent of the Algerian War. The same year that he published *La Nuit*, he also published Henri Alleg's, *La Question*. Lindon's Third World sympathies led him to sign the "Manifeste des 121" in 1960, and Resnais, as we know, did the same. Lindon and the filmmaker traveled in the same political circles, making credible the claim that the publisher had an allusion to Resnais' work in mind when he proposed a new title for

Wiesel's book, one bound to reverberate with French-language readers in a way that a direct translation of *Un di velt hot geshvign* would not.

What's to be concluded from all this? Wiesel's adoption of French as a language of expression was de facto a turning away from Yiddish, a move that entailed stepping back from his Jewish past. But Wiesel did not take that step to ingratiate himself with a Christian readership so much as to write himself into a new literary tradition, a French one. [41] As he did so, he worked out a style, an Existentialist-inflected idiom, that made the urgent message he had to convey accessible, as it would not have been in Yiddish, to a wide, contemporary audience. And he raised themes – like the revolt against God – that were familiar to present-day readers, articulating them in a recognizable prose style and setting the whole in the context of an ongoing public debate about the Deportation and its meanings.

Yet, this line of interpretation tells just a portion of the story. It scants religion, and religion in the end stands at the very core of Wiesel's vision. Not Christian religion, by the way. Wiesel never liked the "Christological nuances" of Mauriac's preface and had the opportunity to say as much to the Nobel Prize winner. There are Christians, Wiesel told him, who sympathize with the sorrowing Jew but have trouble with Jews who are proud and happy: "Certain Christians only like the Jew when he's on the cross."[42] As for Christianity itself, it bore a heavy burden of responsibility for Auschwitz, its anti-Semitic teachings having paved the way for mass murder. Christians indeed had done more to betray Christ's teachings than the Jews ever had, and Auschwitz stood in awful testimony to the failure of Christian civilization. As Wiesel told a well-disposed Catholic interviewer in 1971: "The sincere Christian knows that what died in Auschwitz was not the Jewish people but Christianity."[43] The claim is hyperbolic, but it makes painfully clear that Wiesel did not hesitate to be challenging when in dialogue with Christian interlocutors, Mauriac included. In fact, Mauriac's willingness to acknowledge Christian responsibility was just what made a sympathetic relationship between the two men possible in the first place.

A suggestion of Wiesel's confrontational stance finds its way into *La Nuit*. A Dutch kapo at Auschwitz is aided by a beautiful young boy of twelve, a *pipel*, with the features of a "sad-eyed angel." The SS discover that they have been stockpiling arms. The Dutchman vanishes. The *pipel* is tortured, refuses to talk, and is then dispatched to the gallows. Along with him, two more plotters are hanged. They die crying out "Long live liberty," but the boy does not expire right away. He weighs too little for his neck to break, and so he strangles breath by breath as the assembled prisoners are made to watch in horror. The scene, with its trio of victims, among them an innocent "servant" who agonizes as he dies, is a Passion scene, but on this occasion, the innocent does not rise again. That evening's soup, Eliezer tells the reader, tasted like death. Mauriac for one got the message. He made a reference to the scene in his preface, hearing in it an echo of Nietzsche's aphorism: "God is dead."[44]

La Nuit was a challenge to Christianity, and it was a challenge to Judaism as well, although one formulated very much in Jewish terms. The narrative opens in a small town, Sighet. The protagonist, Eliezer, comes from a Hasidic family. Father, never named, is a cultivated man who maintains a business. Eliezer, however, is not so practical-minded but yearns for God and plunges into the Kabbalah and Zohar to draw closer to him. History, however, interrupts such mystical pursuits. The Germans arrive. The Jews are ghettoized and then deported. Eliezer describes the brutalities of the train ride and then the separation of the family on the ramp at Auschwitz. This is the last time Eliezer will see his mother and his sister Tzipora. Mauriac's preface associated Wiesel's book with the story of Anne Frank,[45] but the world Wiesel conjured up was not Frank's. It wasn't the world of assimilated Jews but of orthodox believers, and the setting is different as well, a little Jewish town in the East, not a big, cosmopolitan center like Amsterdam. And of course, Anne Frank's diary terminates when she is captured. Wiesel's narrative will introduce the reader into the precincts of Auschwitz itself.

What the narrator will discover there is unbelievable, but Wiesel has been careful to prepare the reader to give credence to Eliezer's testimony. The book opens with the story of Moishe the Beadle, a meaningful decision because it enables Wiesel to take on the issue of believability right from the start. Moishe is among the first group of Jews deported from Sighet. The Germans take them to a forest and execute every single one, babies included. Moishe is wounded and left for dead. He extracts himself from the mound of corpses and finds his way back home, but no one in Sighet believes the tale he has to tell. At last, Eliezer's family is itself deported, and the train trip to Auschwitz is harrowing and hallucinatory. Customary restraints break down, and a young couple makes love in the car (a scene Lindon appreciated for its taboo-breaking frankness).[46] One of the deportees, Madame Schächter, goes mad and shouts over and over again: "A fire! I see a fire!" The others attribute such expostulations to insanity, but Madame Schächter's words are prophetic. The first sight that greets the deportees on arrival at Auschwitz is the camp's crematoria chimneys, spouting fire amidst the stench of burned flesh. There follows the selection, and Eliezer is chosen to live. A veteran detainee, however, spewing abusive epithets, makes sure that he and the rest of the newcomers don't harbor any false hopes. In the end, he tells them, they are all destined to end up as ash and smoke. Then Eliezer approaches a ditch in flames. A truck dumps babies into it, and Eliezer is aghast: "Babies! Yes, I saw it, with my own eyes!" It is a shocking scene, an epitome of the incredible reality of Auschwitz. Eliezer, who has resisted the truth of the camps, is now made to look it full in the face, and readers too, who have accompanied Eliezer down the path of disillusionment, are compelled to believe the unbelievable along with him.[47]

It's at this moment that Eliezer first entertains thoughts of a revolt against God. The notion was a modish one in the Existentialist 1950s, but for Wiesel, the theological questions that Auschwitz raised were not just modish conceits but matters of urgent importance that were to preoccupy him for decades to come. In La Nuit, the trials and cruelties of camp life cause Eliezer to lose faith in God's goodness, but not in God himself. He refuses to fast on Yom Kippur; he no longer prays; but he still believes. "How I sided with Job!" the narrator exclaims. "I did not deny His existence but I doubted His absolute justice."[48] At times, Wiesel was prepared to press the case against God even further. As he told an interviewer in the late 1970s, it's not just that God had shown himself wanting, but that he had broken his Covenant with the Jewish people, failing to protect them as he had promised he would. Looked at this way, Auschwitz was not just one more ordeal, however terrible, in the Jews' sempiternal history of suffering, but a moment of epochal rupture, on a par with the revelation at Sinai.[49]

It is well known that Wiesel did as much as anyone to popularize the idea of the Holocaust in the United States, and he explained why the term appealed to him in a 1964 article in the New York Times. It had Biblical referents, which imparted to "the event some obscure mystical magnitude."[50] Wiesel interpreted Auschwitz using the vocabulary and stories supplied by the Hebrew Bible, and the relationship he staked out in relation to the Catastrophe was not so much that of Lazarus, but of the long-suffering man from the Land of Uz.

Nor was the story of Job the sole Biblical referent that structured the book's narrative. La Nuit is the story of a father and son. Eliezer's father is a man of intelligence and accomplishment, but the camp experience will step by step break him down. He doesn't know how to march in step, and he doesn't know how to defend himself. Kapos beat him, fellow inmates steal his food, and then he falls ill, his gut ravaged by a terrible, thirst-inducing dysentery. Eliezer admires and loves his father and does all he can to remain by his side. Yet, as the father fails, he becomes a humiliation and an encumbrance to his son. Eliezer looks on in ashamed silence as a Roma kapo strikes the old man. A starving Eliezer begins to crave his father's ration of bread. The camp more and more reduces the boy to a creature of appetite, a stomach ravenous for food and ready to betray the obligations of filial piety to obtain it. Thus, the dilemma is set up: Will Eliezer stand by his father or abandon him?

The narrative throws out clues along the way as to how the drama will turn out. Early on, the narrator tells the story of Bela Katz, a Sonderkommando who loads his own father's corpse into a crematorium oven. On the death march from Auschwitz to Buchenwald, Rab Eliahu, a righteous man renowned for his purity of heart, is left behind by a son, who pushes to the head of the column, hoping to rid himself of the paternal burden. The last leg of the journey is accomplished by train, and on the way Eliezer witnesses a son who beats his father to death to rob him of a morsel of bread.

Eliezer proves no stronger than the rest. He too will abandon his father and does so in a scene that is wrenching to read. Father and son have made it to Buchenwald. The father, in a state of terrible dehydration, begs for something to drink. The cries enrage a passing SS officer who beats the ailing man into silence. The last word he utters before losing consciousness is "Eliezer." He dies during the night and is carted away to be incinerated. The narrator supplies the exact date, January 28, 1945. Eliezer reflects on the scenes he has just witnessed. Through it all, he had done nothing. Is he ashamed of himself? Does he have tears to shed? In truth, what he feels deep down is relief. "Free at last!" It is with these burning and self-accusatory words that the chapter ends.[51]

Scholars have interpreted this story as a reenactment of the Akedah or binding of Isaac.[52] In Genesis 22, God tests Abraham's faith, commanding him to offer up his only son, Isaac, as a burnt sacrifice. Abraham does as ordered, taking the boy to a sacrificial site and tying him up, but at the last moment an angel intervenes to stay Abraham's hand, and a ram is sacrificed instead. In Wiesel's retelling, the roles are switched around: the son sacrifices the father, and this time, there is no last-minute reprieve. Wiesel himself encouraged such a reading, describing *La Nuit* in a later interview as "the binding of Isaac in reverse."[53] He was even willing to personalize this line of analysis, to compare, that is, his own parents to Abraham and Sarah, a comparison, of course, that cast Wiesel himself in the role of a latter-day Isaac. And just as Wiesel saw himself as a Holocaust survivor, in much the same way did he see Isaac, whom he once characterized as "the first survivor of the Holocaust."[54]

Wiesel worked out of a Jewish context, but one in dialogue with a wider world that was French and Christian. He wrote in a terse, pithy prose that echoed of Camus. The Yiddish version of the narrative scolded readers, reminding them of their complicity then and now in the genocide of the Jews. The French text eliminated references to the present-day and was more parsimonious in its references to Jewish spe-cificity. The result is a chronicle that almost stands outside of historical time, fablelike in its narrative unfolding.[55] The fable, however, still remains a Jewish one, embedded in the stories of the Hebrew Bible.

Yet, as the informed reader well knows, those stories also have a charged meaning for Christians, the binding of Isaac not least of all, which in Christian theology figures as a foretelling of Jesus' Crucifixion.[56] Wiesel and Wiesel's narrator Eliezer might speak of Job and Isaac, but to a reader like Mauriac what came to mind was Lazarus, not to say Christ himself. Then there was the very word *Holocaust*, which both men embraced for its mystical meanings, though Wiesel's mobiliza-tion of the term had more to do with the Covenant and its fate in the flames of Auschwitz than with the Christian mystery of sacrifice and resurrection.

The two men approached each other through religion, arriving from different directions and narrowing their differences along the way. The meeting of minds, of course, was never complete. How could it be, given the gap between Jewish and Christian world views? The occasion of Mauriac's death in 1970 attests to the distance that still separated the two men, as close as they became. Funeral services were held at Notre-Dame, and the cathedral was full, so much so that Wiesel, who had come to attend, opted to remain outside.[57]

André Schwarz-Bart and Le Seuil

Wiesel's *La Nuit* was well received by critics but did not meet with resounding public enthusiasm, retailing an impressive but not earth-shattering 100,000 copies in its first twenty years.[58] In contrast, André Schwarz-Bart's *Le Dernier des Justes*, published in September 1959, was a runaway best-seller. In a little over a year, it had racked up sales of almost one million, and it was a critical hit as well.[59] The prize committees of the Prix Goncourt and of the Prix Femina, two of the most prestigious literary awards in France, competed with each other to see which would be first to recognize Schwarz-Bart's achievement (the Prix Goncourt won out).

There is no simple explanation for Schwarz-Bart's success. He was a first-time author, an unknown quantity, from an immigrant Jewish back-ground. His book, unlike Wiesel's, did not boast a preface from a renowned Gentile author.[60] Schwarz-Bart's publisher, Le Seuil, had a reputation for turning out high-quality books, sometimes challenging, sometimes avant-garde, but never before had one of its authors garnered a major literary prize like the Prix Goncourt. Then there is the book itself, which was long at roughly four hundred pages and which in form mixed genres with freewheeling abandon. It moved in and out, from legend to chronicle to novel, as Le Seuil's back cover blurb to the 1980 edition put it, and the characterization is a fair one.[61]

The story opens in York in 1185 in a besieged tower where Jews, led by Rabbi Yom Tov Levy, have taken refuge from an enraged Christian mob that demands they convert or die. The Jews choose death, and the rabbi kills his flock before killing himself. The Christians recover Levy's body and burn it. "The holocaust of the tower," as the narrator informs us, is a minor episode in the long history of Jewish martyrdom, but it bears recounting because it is the source of a legend.[62] In every generation, according to Talmudic sources, there arose among the Jews righteous men, Lamed-Vavniks. A Lamed-Vavnik took upon himself the sorrows of his brothers and sisters and laid them at God's feet. God in turn was moved to pardon the sins of his people, allowing the world to go on. At any one time, there were said to be thirty-six Lamed-Vavniks, hence the name, which means "thirty-sixer" in Hebrew-Yiddish. In Schwarz-Bart's telling, Rabbi Levy was one of these, a calling, and a burden, that he passes on as a legacy to his descendants. It is the story of that line that Schwarz-Bart chronicles, tarrying over the destinies of two in particular: Mordechai Levy who, until the upheavals of the Great War, lived in Zemyock, a shtetl in the Polish-speaking East, and his grandson Ernie Levy, who assumes the Lamed-Vav's sacrificial mantle and goes on to die in a gas chamber at Auschwitz. Ernie will leave behind no issue, and so it is he who is the last of the Just.

It may be that the French public was primed for such a story. Wiesel had published *La Nuit* the year before. The movie version of Anne Frank's diary was playing to receptive audiences at the very moment Schwarz-Bart's novel appeared.[63] There's no doubt that the book made for compelling reading. Paul-André Lesort, an editor at Le Seuil, read a late-version manuscript, which left him in a state of emotional upheaval, somewhere between astonishment and terror.[64] Claude Lanzmann brought the text to Simone de Beauvoir's attention. She doubted that a work of fiction would have much to add on a subject already treated in depth by historians like Léon Poliakov. But then she read the novel, a "written cry," as she called it (borrowing a phrase from Jean Cocteau), and was unable to put it down.[65] The genre mixing was a risk, but it worked, creating a story that was at once epic and personal, combining sweep and intense emotion.

The novel, moreover, generated controversy as much as acclaim, which was wounding for Schwarz-Bart but may well have been a boost to sales. Critics indicted Schwarz-Bart on charges of plagiarism and sloppy research. He had distorted the story of the Lamed-Vavniks, it was pointed out, making of them the descendants of a family line when in fact – that is, according to the actual legend – they had been random figures, unrelated to one another. There was also the criticism that Schwarz-Bart was a Christianizer, the author of a novel that accented Jewish passivity in the face of victimization, and what may have made this accusation most hurtful was that it came from Jewish sources. Arnold Mandel, a well-known contributor to *L'Arche*, dismissed *Le Dernier des Justes* as "so much Christology." It turned Jews into a "people-Christ" who accepted suffering, when in fact the suffering, unwanted and undeserved, was imposed upon them. Indeed, Poliakov chimed in, that's just how it pleased Christians to think about Jews, as so many sacrificial lambs, and Schwarz-Bart's novel had played right into that impulse.[66]

That's not, however, how I see the matter. The argument here will be similar in thrust to that developed in relation to Wiesel's *La Nuit*. *Le Dernier des Justes* was double-edged. It was not a sop to Christian conscience, but a provocation that addressed Christians in forms and tropes they understood in order to prompt them to reflect on Christianity's role in the Holocaust. But over and above that, the novel was a heartfelt paean to a Jewish way of being, even as that way was wiped off the face of the earth.

What needs to be acknowledged right from the start was how compelling French Catholics found *Le Dernier des Justes*. Schwarz-Bart had trouble placing his manuscript, which was baggy and overlong. Le Seuil, however, proved receptive. Schwarz-Bart had published an excerpt in *L'Arche* in late 1956, and Serge Montigny, a member of Le Seuil's editorial board, spotted it and approached Schwarz-Bart, who was not yet ready to commit. When in time he was, he reactivated the Le Seuil connection, reaching out to Montigny, but getting through instead to Paul-André Lesort.

Lesort was in charge of the publishing house's religion list, a responsibility appropriate to a man said to be of "flamboyant" Catholic convictions. He was swept away by the Schwarz-Bart manuscript, as we have seen, which he read as a Passion story.[67] The text did need a beginning-to-end rewrite, however, and Lesort sat Schwarz-Bart down in an abbey in provincial France to do the necessary work. *Le Dernier des Justes* was the result, and for such efforts, Jean Lacouture, Flamand's biographer and a Le Seuil veteran himself, dubbed Lesort the book's "midwife."[68]

This raises the question of Flamand's own interest in *Le Dernier des Justes*, and he was very much a partisan. His fascination with the concentration camp experience supplies a partial explanation for his engagement in the project. Jean Cayrol was a member of the Le Seuil editorial board. Flamand and he were on good terms and had occasion to talk about Cayrol's deportation ordeal. Flamand's daughter recalls a traumatizing anecdote about camp life, which her father recounted to her as Cayrol had recounted it to him. One day, as if by miracle, Cayrol had come upon a potato which he proceeded to cook in the embers of still-burning ash just removed from the concentration camp crematorium.[69] Le Seuil published Grete Buber-Neumann's camp memoir in 1949, Wiesel's fiction after *La Nuit* (Lindon was no longer interested), and from 1974, the translation of Alexander Solzhenitsyn's oeuvre, starting with *The Gulag Archipelago* and moving on from there.[70] Yet it wasn't just the camp experience that drew Flamand to Schwarz-Bart's text. Flamand was himself a believing Christian with an ecumenical turn of mind. Wiesel described him this way: "A devout but enlightened Catholic, he [Flamand] was interested in Jewish tradition and culture as a means of gaining greater insight into his own."[71] What Flamand thought he heard in Schwarz-Bart's text was Jewish tradition, indeed, the Jewish people itself, speaking in an unmediated way about its joys and sufferings.[72] There is some condescension in this formulation, which treats Schwarz-Bart more as a mouthpiece than as an author, but the point remains that Flamand embraced *Le Dernier des Justes* because, as a Catholic, he found its very Jewishness illuminating.

Flamand's reaction, moreover, was far from unique among Catholic thinkers and critics. *Le Dernier des Justes* reminded Father Lucien Guissard of Camus' oeuvre, with Schwarz-Bart addressing the same kinds of question as did the Existentialist writer – "What is a Just man?" for example – but from a religious angle. And Jean-Marie Domenach read *Le Dernier des Justes* as a "novel of compassion" that elevated the Jewish experience, "the holocaust of the Jewish people" as he referred to it, into a form of universal sacrifice.[73] Domenach was at the time editor-in-chief of *Esprit* and Father Guissard was chief literary critic at *La Croix*. These men were the gratin of France's postwar Catholic intelligentsia. No organization better represented the way of thinking of such men than the Centre catholique des intellectuels français (CCIF), founded at the Liberation.[74] In 1960, the CCIF devoted an entire session to a debate of Schwarz-Bart's novel, inviting Jewish interlocutors to join in, testimony to the novel's singular impact on the Catholic imagination. On this very point, it has been reported that copies of the book were spotted on the congress-goers' table at Vatican II.[75]

French Catholic intellectuals felt that Schwarz-Bart's novel was aimed at them, and they were not altogether wrong. Ernie Levy is time and again described as a Christlike figure. The Levy family settles in Zemyock in 1792, where it will remain for well over a century. That's where

Mordechai is born, as well as his son Benjamin. The Great War, however, unleashes the furies of anti-Semitism, and a pogrom drives the
family westward to the fictional German town of Stillenstadt. It's not
long afterward that Ernie is born, a gentle boy doted on by Grandmother
Judith, who calls him "my lamb of sorrow."[76] Ernie succeeds at school
and befriends a pretty blonde German girl, Ilse. Ilse also spends time
with a band of Gentile boys, and the group, Ernie included, decides for
its own amusement to reenact the trial of Jesus. Ilse plays Christ, and an
unwilling Ernie is assigned the role of the Jews. In fact, when the time
comes for him to call out for Ilse's blood, he refuses to do so, and the
Gentile boys grow angry. One strikes Ernie "for Jesus," and Ernie hits
the ground unconscious, "arms in a cross." Schwarz-Bart winds up the
scene, making sure the reader knows that the action coincided with the
Nazis' accession to power: "It was the year 1933 after the coming of
Jesus, the fair messenger of impossible love."[77]

The years following bring to the Jews of Stillenstadt an escalating
sequence of humiliations. Ernie is at first a match for them. A pogrom
is under way, and Brown Shirts threaten to attack the synagogue that the
Levys attend. The congregants are present, Ernie among them, and as
the confrontation grows tense, he steps forward, a mere child, and lets
out a bleat. The gesture doesn't enrage the Nazis but amuses them, and
they desist. All the while, Grandfather Mordechai looks on in amaze-
ment, recognizing in little Ernie, the lamb of sorrow, "our expiatory
beast." It's at this juncture that he tells the boy of the legend of the
Lamed-Vav, and Ernie without delay begins to ready himself for the
martyrdom that he believes lies ahead. He burns the palm of one hand
over a candle, a training exercise for the fire that will one day consume
him whole, *en holocauste*, in the text's words, waking up the next morning
with "a splendid stigmata." But it is further humiliation, not martyrdom,
that awaits Ernie in the near term, and he goes mad. Germany treats him
like a dog, and he begins to act like one, a bout of insanity that leads to a
suicide attempt. Ernie throws himself from a height. He does not die but
is marked again, this time by a "white barbed-wire line" etched across his
forehead. Kristallnacht soon follows, and the Levy family at last takes
flight to Paris, Ernie in tow, that lamb of sorrow with one hand scarred as
though by a nail and a forehead scratched as though by a crown of
thorns.[78]

France affords a respite, but a temporary one. Ernie, sane again and
now maturing, meets a Jewish woman, Golda, and falls in love. It is the
spring of 1943. She will be arrested and sent to Drancy. He follows her
there and demands to be let in, so that he might remain by Golda's side.
A convoy of children arrives at Drancy; Schwarz-Bart had read Wellers'

memoir and borrowed from it to recreate the scene. Golda and Ernie take the children in hand, and when they are deported to Auschwitz, stripped first of all valuables by French police and the SS, Golda and Ernie volunteer to join them. They calm the young ones with words of reassurance, and as the convoy arrives at the camp, Ernie sheds tears of blood. They all enter the gas chamber together, Ernie in the lead: "This way, my little lambs."[79]

It's not hard to understand why Lesort, Schwarz-Bart's editor, interpreted *Le Dernier des Justes* as a Passion story or why Schwarz-Bart's coreligionists Mandel and Poliakov reproached him for Christianizing the Holocaust. These readings, however, don't do justice to the subtlety of Schwarz-Bart's characterization of Ernie Levy. Golda and Ernie spend an idyllic late summer day together not long before she is taken away to Drancy. She wonders why the Christians hate the Jews so, and Ernie replies with thoughts about who the real Jesus was: "a simple Jew like your father," he tells Golda, "a sort of Hasid." She then strokes the scar on Ernie's forehead, and he continues to speak, referring now to Jesus by his Hebrew name: "Poor Yehoshua," Ernie laments. "He was a little Jew from our parts, a real Just man, you know." Golda then takes out her harmonica, plays a tune, "Hatikvah," and the scene concludes.[80]

The Jesus Ernie resembles is Jesus understood as a righteous Jew. He is more like the righteous servant limned in the verses of Isaiah 53 than the Christ of the Gospels. Isaiah, to be sure, is understood by Christian theologians in typological terms. The prophet describes the servant as a "man of sorrows," who "hath borne our griefs" and is "brought as a lamb to the slaughter," and in all these respects, he may be and has been interpreted as a prefiguration of Christ.[81] Schwarz-Bart's Just Man then occupies a theological space at the very intersection of Jewish and Christian belief, but I think it is clear in the end on which side of the border the Lamed-Vav stands. As Mordechai had explained to his wife back in Zemyock days, a Just Man is not a miracle worker, but a miracle in himself. And it is as a Jewish Just Man that Ernie will die. The words he utters in the gas chamber are not Jesus' on the Cross – "Father, forgive them; for they know not what they do" (Luke 23:34) or the more plaintive, "My God, my God, why hast thou forsaken me?" (Matthew 27:46). Rather, he, with the others, recite the Shema, the Jewish declaration of faith and the Jewish martyr's prayer. Ernie then says farewell to Golda and thinks of Rabbi Hanina ben Teradion, who in Roman times was burned alive, wrapped in a Torah scroll, for teaching the Law. The Rabbi's disciples were made to watch (as Eliezer was made to watch the *pipel*'s torment in *La Nuit*), and they call out: What do you see? To which the rabbi responds, "I see a parchment that is burning, but the words take flight," leaving the reader to ponder just what he meant. That men might die, but God's word is eternal? It's a reassuring thought, but Schwarz-Bart's conclusion steers in a less consolatory direction. Ernie's death was died six million times, the narrator tells us, a people of *Luftmenschen* turned to *Luft*, their ashes blown to the four winds. There is no memorial for a mourner to visit, but the narrator invites the "estimable reader," ourselves, to think of them from time to time with melancholy on a stormy day.[82]

Schwarz-Bart paints Ernie Levy in Christological hues, but Ernie dies the death of a Jewish martyr, not a Christian one. Ernie's fate, moreover, was not just individual but emblematic. A whole world was destroyed at Auschwitz, an East European world of Jewish piety and gentleness.[83] Schwarz-Bart's portrayal of the Jews of Zemyock is a loving one. The narrator of *Le Dernier des Justes* describes the town as a "boutique of dreams" and its inhabitants as "gentle souls."[84] They live outside historical time, their lives unfolding to the rhythms of the liturgical calendar. This is the world and these the people whom the Holocaust will wipe away. Schwarz-Bart mourned their passing, and for him the loss was very much a personal one. His father came from a small town in Poland, perhaps not unlike Zemyock. Schwarz-Bart's family – he, his parents, and two siblings – spoke Yiddish at home. And all, save Schwarz-Bart himself, were deported to the East, where they were murdered. *Le Dernier des Justes* is a story of Jewish martyrdom, and it is also a moving expression of filial devotion.

Why then bother with all the Christian imagery? To attract the attention of a Christian readership, no doubt, but also to provoke Christians to serious self-reflection. Unsurprisingly, Chagall liked Schwarz-Bart's novel and offered to illustrate it, a proposition, it seems, that Le Seuil entertained.[85] Just as Chagall had meant to prick the Christian conscience, so too did Schwarz-Bart. Zemyock is a place out of time … but not altogether. As a young man, Mordechai is provoked into a fight by anti-Semitic taunts, an experience, we are told, that yanks him into "the Christian universe of violence." Then comes the Great War, and Jews, like everyone else, are drafted into service "in order to fight among themselves like those cruel beasts of Christians." Timeless Zemyock will be swallowed up in the violence of Christian time, and that will also be the fate of the Jews of Stillenstadt. During the Kristallnacht pogrom of November 1938, the Nazis destroy a Jewish temple in the city, but the congregants retrieve the Torah scrolls and confide them to the Levys for safekeeping. A mob surrounds the Levy home, intent on desecrating the sacred texts, and Mordechai arms himself with an iron bar to protect them. Wearing phylacteries and a prayer shawl, he confronts the angry crowd and bellows at them: "For a thousand years, hah, the Christians have been trying to kill us," but the Jews have survived, he goes on, because they have never yielded up their books.[86] The very structure of Schwarz-Bart's narrative is designed to bear out that accusation of millennial persecution, beginning as it does with "the holocaust of the tower" at York and ending a thousand years later with the Nazi genocide of the Jews. Hundreds of years of burning pyres have ended in the crematorium, and the novel's narrator says as much. This is the very thesis of Jules Isaac's scholarship, and Schwarz-Bart did not hesitate to acknowledge the debt he owed to the older historian. Asked about the matter by an interviewer, he replied: *Le Dernier des Justes* "is a continuation of Jules Isaac; without him, it wouldn't be."[87]

Like Wiesel, Schwarz-Bart wanted Christians to listen and to think, which is not to say that the two men approached the Holocaust from the same perspective. Some of the differences are apparent. Wiesel's narrative revolved around camp life. It was anchored in personal experience and written in a clipped, compressed prose. Schwarz-Bart's novel was just that – a novel, fiction – and what interested him was all that led up to the camps, the evocation of an extinguished world in an emotion-charged language that at times spilled into the lyrical. And Wiesel was, of course, a believer. The challenge to faith that the Holocaust posed never ceased to trouble him. Schwarz-Bart, by contrast, had neither Wiesel's Hasidic background, nor his religious training and passion, although he did want to pay tribute to a universe of faith that now lay in ruins.

Yet the most important distinction between the two turned on how each understood the meaning of Auschwitz. They agreed that it represented a rent in history. Wiesel, however, wrote from within the Jewish religious tradition. Auschwitz was a turning point in the story of God's Covenant with the Jewish people, but that Covenant still remained valid. For Schwarz-Bart, who asked the questions that the faithful asked but was not one himself, the Holocaust demolished the possibility of belief along with the human community where that belief had once found its home. Auschwitz marked what he called "the end of the theological age."[88] This helps makes sense of the lacerating prayer with which *Le Dernier des Justes* ends. The words "And praised be the Eternal One" are intoned over and again, but interspersed among them are the names of all the camps: Auschwitz, Majdanek, Treblinka. Schwarz-Bart revolts against God, not by doubting the Eternal's justice, but by turning his back in anger.[89]

What path then remained open for a man like Schwarz-Bart once *Le Dernier des Justes* lay behind him? The answer is twofold. As a young man, Schwarz-Bart had been a Communist and a résistant, and that combative spirit never left him. He departed for Martinique not long after publication of *Le Dernier des Justes* and took up the cause of Third World revolt. He returned to sign the "Manifeste des 121" and, as Simone de Beauvoir tells it, the time spent in the Caribbean had converted him to "a belief in revolution by violence," a position Schwarz-Bart's fleshed out in his third novel, *La Mulâtresse Solitude* (Le Seuil 1972).[90] The book, set in the Napoleonic era, is similar in design to *Le Dernier des Justes*, opening in a tranquil, Zemyock-like West African village. Slavers, "white seigneurs," seize a woman.[91] She is made to endure the horrors of the Middle Passage, of deportation, and on the way to the New World is raped. Guadeloupe is her ultimate destination, and once arrived, she gives birth to a daughter, Rosalie, who will later take the name Solitude. Solitude is raised amidst the humiliations of human bondage. Treated like a dog, she will for a period, as did Ernie Levy, act like one. *La Mulâtresse Solitude*, however, does not end in sacrifice but in armed insurrection. Maroons in the island's mountainous interior have risen in revolt, and Solitude will join them, killing a French soldier as she makes her way to the maroon encampment. The French army sets out on a mission to search and destroy, and the insurrectionaries make a last stand at the Habitation Danglemont. They are besieged, and rather than surrender, blow themselves up. Solitude does not die, but is captured and executed, and with her execution, she enters into legend.

Identification with Third World revolt afforded Schwarz-Bart one way forward. Identification with a Jewish will to fight provided a second. Recall now how *La Mulâtresse Solitude* concludes. The Habitation Danglemont is described as a "place of holocaust."[92] In the novel's epilogue, the site has become a tourist destination. Just as the narrator of *Le Dernier des Justes* invites the reader to think of the six million dead on a windswept day, so the narrator of *La Mûlatresse Solitude* invites the visiting tourist to remember those immolated at the Habitation Danglemont. With an effort of imagination, we are told, the shadows of the dead will rise again, roaming among us much like "the phantoms that are said to roam among the humiliated ruins of the Warsaw Ghetto."[93] Schwarz-Bart pairs Caribbean slavery and the Holocaust, maroon insurrection and ghetto revolt. He had mobilized the pairing once before at the very beginning of his second book, *Un Plat de porc aux bananes vertes* (Le Seuil, 1967), coauthored with his wife, Simone. The novel's dedication page is eloquent in its brevity: "To Aimé Césaire and to Elie Wiesel."[94] Schwarz-Bart and Wiesel used to run into each in the corridors of Le Seuil, but they also, from time to time, met in other climes and latitudes. Wiesel tells of one such encounter on an Israeli bus in 1973 on the way to the northern front at the time of the Yom Kippur War. As Schwarz-Bart saw it, Jews under siege, like the slaves of the Caribbean, had the right to take up arms and make a stand.[95]

Saul Friedländer and Le Seuil

Le Seuil launched the career of Schwarz-Bart. It also had a hand in launching the career of a second Holocaust writer who likewise went on to great public acclaim, the historian Saul Friedländer. Much like Schwarz-Bart's *Le Dernier des Justes*, Friedländer's early work addressed the theme of Catholic-Jewish relations, not so much his first publication, *Hitler et les États-Unis* (1963), as the two that followed: *Pie XII et le IIIe Reich* (1964) and *Kurt Gerstein ou l'ambiguité du bien* (1967). In the former, he examined the motives that underlay the Vatican's silence in the face of the Nazi persecution of the Jews, a subject Rolf Hochhuth had already treated (see Chapter 4), although not with the documentary rigor that Friedländer, a professional historian, brought to it. The second book is an examination of Kurt Gerstein's exertions to inform the world of the extermination of the Jews, efforts that fell on the deaf ears of "the Christian West" (in Friedländer's phrasing), which for prudential reasons preferred inaction to intervention.[96]

These are now well-worn topics in Holocaust historiography, albeit still controversial ones, but they were not when Friedländer first took them head on. He had been reluctant at first to pursue this path. He was Jewish, born in Prague in 1932 to a German-speaking family. The Friedländers fled from Czechoslovakia to France in 1939, and then later, as the persecution of Jews in France accelerated, the parents placed the boy in a Catholic boarding school in Montluçon. He survived the war (Friedländer's parents did not), and he felt indebted to the Church, which is why he hesitated to plunge into an exposé of its wartime complicities. Yet, he did so in the end, along the way coming to terms with his own personal past, a process that culminated in the publication of *Quand vient le souvenir...* (1978), a spellbinding memoir of Friedländer's loss and rediscovery of Jewish identity as a young man. At the same time, Friedländer's scholarship worked as a goad to Christians, to men of restless conscience like Flamand, who were moved to press the Vatican for an explanation of the ambiguities of its Holocaust-era record. As in the cases of Wiesel and Schwarz-Bart before him, Friedländer told a story that was Jewish and personal but that was also framed as an incitation to Christian civilization to think about itself.

It all began with the discovery of a document. Friedländer was a doctoral student, researching US-German relations, the subject of his dissertation and first book. He came upon a misplaced item, a cable from the Reich's embassy in the Vatican to the Foreign Office back home. The wire explained that the Vatican had been in touch with the director of the Berlin Opera, who was planning to be in Rome, inviting him to perform extracts from Wagner's *Parsifal* in the papal apartments. It was the document's date that caught Friedländer's eye and disturbed him, December 1941, the very moment Hitler's Wehrmacht was sweeping across the Soviet Union, massacring Jews in its wake. How could Pius XII remain in amicable communication with German higher-ups at such a time?[97] Friedländer was cognizant of all that the Church had done for him and, "in memory of my Christian years," as he later told Flamand, opted not to look more deeply into the matter. The situation changed, however, when the storm over Hochhuth's *Le Vicaire* broke in late 1963. During the hiatus between semesters (Friedländer then held a university teaching post in Geneva), he returned to the German archives, focusing now on the Reich's relations with the Vatican. He discovered a trove of information as well as a significant lacuna. The dossier dealing with the critical months between September 1943 and February 1944 had gone missing, never to be found. The Nazi roundup of Rome's Jews had taken place during this very period.[98]

Friedländer knew that he had the makings of a powerful book. The problem was to find a publisher, and he first turned to Jérôme Lindon, who expressed an immediate interest. On sober reflection, however, Friedländer had second thoughts about whether Éditions de Minuit was the wisest choice. He himself was a Jew, writing about a subject of vital interest, not just to Jews, but also and above all to Catholics. Lindon was also a Jew and a leftist into the bargain who had just published Henri Alleg's incendiary *La Question*. Would the public trust in a text published with such a pedigree? Friedländer backed out of the deal with Lindon, leaving the publisher in a fury and Friedländer himself in a state of agitation. That's how Elie Wiesel came upon him, fretting over publishers while popping a Valium in a boulevard Saint-Germain café. Wiesel proposed a solution: Let's go to Le Seuil and talk to Paul Flamand, which they did the next day.[99]

Flamand's response, like Lindon's, was favorable, but Le Seuil was also worried about establishing the text's credibility. It brought in Jacques Nobécourt to comb through the book and turn down the rhetorical volume where needed. Nobécourt, of course, was a perfect choice for the job from Le Seuil's point of view. He was a journalist at *Le Monde*, who had published a volume on the *Le Vicaire* controversy under Le Seuil's own imprimatur. As for Friedländer, he had from the beginning envisioned a text that was as "objective" as possible and so welcomed Nobécourt's interventions.[100] The result was a boiled-down manuscript, not much over two hundred pages, which was constructed out of documents accompanied by a bare minimum of explanatory commentary.

Lean as the text was, there was no doubt as to its message. Pius XII had stood silent as the Jews of Europe were murdered. Why he had done so admitted of many explanations. Pius XII had been a diplomat before becoming pope, spending the 1920s in Germany as the Vatican's nuncio to Bavaria. There he had developed an abiding attachment to German culture, a sympathy that made him reluctant as pope to take sides against the Nazi regime. For sure, he worried how such a course of action might affect the interests of the German Church and, indeed, of the Church as an institution overall. But Pius XII's overarching concern – and on this point the documents were clear – was a fear of Bolshevism. Nazi Germany, whatever its sins, was Christian Europe's last rampart against Stalin, and for that reason, if for no other, it did not serve the Church to entangle itself in a dangerous public face-off with the Nazi dictatorship. The fate of the Jews was just not worth the candle.

This was explosive material, above all coming from a Jew, however neutral the voice he assumed. Le Seuil was aware of the risks and took steps to shore up Friedländer's bona fides and to protect its own flanks. It invited Alfred Grosser first of all to provide an afterword. Grosser was a professor of international relations at Sciences Po, a leading specialist in Franco-German relations, and a Jewish convert to Catholicism into the bargain.[101] What he had to say provided readers a thoughtful and reassuring interpretive grid for thinking about the material they had just read. The Church during the war, as Grosser laid it out, had faced a daunting dilemma, having to choose between looking after its own and its moral mission to all of humankind. Creon-like, it had chosen to protect its institutional interests. Was it right to do so? It didn't seem so, but Grosser hesitated to pronounce a definitive judgment until the Vatican had had chance to present its own version of events. In the meantime, Grosser proffered, the Church had begun to change its ways, and he cited in proof the conduct of Archbishop Duval of Algiers, who had taken a stand against atrocities during the Algerian War (Grosser was not more specific than that) and of American bishops in the US South, who had spoken out for civil rights.[102]

On the matter of the Church's version of events, Le Seuil did its level best to persuade the Vatican to yield up its own archival holdings. This was a matter of simple fairness, made all the more urgent by the high stakes involved. Jean Lacouture, then a member of Le Seuil's editorial board, took an active hand in the negotiations. He sent a copy of Friedländer's as yet unpublished manuscript to Father Daniel Pezeril (a well-known figure in the Latin Quarter and future auxiliary bishop of

Paris), who in turn contacted the Papal Secretariat in Rome. The response was not discouraging: the Vatican had no plans to open its archives, but it also had no deep objection to Friedländer's book, so long as it did not call into question "the rectitude of Pius XII." Pezeril decided to pursue the matter further and sent Friedländer's text to the papal secretary himself, Dom Pasquale Macchi. It seems, moreover, that Flamand also got involved, making a trip to Rome to press Le Seuil's case in person.[103]

All to no avail, but Le Seuil had made a good-faith effort, and that was the point. The publishing house had held back the publication of Friedländer's book while negotiations with the Vatican played out. Once these reached a dead end, Le Seuil felt free at last to release the text, which it did. The publishers spelled out on the dust jacket just what lay in store for the reader: an objective, documents-based account that pursued the truth as far as possible in the regrettable absence of material from the Vatican archives.[104]

Le Seuil went to considerable lengths to make sure that *Pie XII et le IIIe Reich* would pass muster with its target audience, Catholic readers. Friedländer made a contribution of his own, submitting his prepublication manuscript to the critical scrutiny not just of Nobécourt but of "numerous people," as he himself put it, "especially Catholic priests." Such scrupulous preparations ultimately paid off. *Pie XII et le IIIe Reich* did not prove the runaway success that Schwarz-Bart's novel had been, but it sold well, over fifty thousand copies in France alone. [105] As for the book's critique of the Vatican's comportment during the war, this remains a subject of debate to the present day.

Friedländer's own reckoning with the subject was also far from over. He attacked it again in his next book, this one about Gerstein. The volume would never have come into being without Léon Poliakov's mediation. Friedländer first arrived at the topic after reading an article on Gerstein that Poliakov had written. It was Poliakov who then introduced the young historian to the Gerstein archive in Westphalia and Poliakov again who agreed to supply an afterword to the book that was the fruit of Friedländer's labors.[106] This book was not a document collection, but written in the author's own voice, and that voice was accusatory. Friedländer tracked Gerstein's efforts to alert the German Church, the Allies, and the Holy See to the realities of the Holocaust. The information got through, but the responsible parties all opted to do nothing. This is what made the Jewish tragedy such a unique one, Friedländer concluded, "the complete passivity of the others," and a little further on in the text he makes clear just who those "others" were: "the Christian West in its entirety."[107] The compassionate actions of individual Christians had saved Friedländer during the war, but the Church as an institution and Christianity as a civilization had stood aside while the Jews were murdered, and in that measure, they were parties to the crime.

Friedländer's reckoning with Christianity was not just a professional matter but also one that was intensely personal. He had undergone four years of Freudian psychoanalysis while in Geneva and, in the wake of the Gerstein book, went on to explore the terrain of psychohistory.[108] Then, in the 1970s, Friedländer became a part-time resident in Israel. He continued to teach at Geneva but took up a joint appointment, first at the Hebrew University, then at Tel Aviv. Friedländer knew Israel well. He had immigrated there in 1948 with the intention of taking part in the War of Independence, and had stayed on. A diplomatic posting brought him back to France in the early fifties, where he ended up enrolling as a student at Sciences Po. It was the scholar's life that led Friedländer to Geneva, but then in the mid-1970s, now at mid-life and still prone to bouts of anxiety, he found himself again in Israel for part of the year. The past, so long tamped down, surged up once more, and he felt the impulse to write of his childhood.

The problem was how to proceed. Friedländer sketched a first effort and shared it with Flamand, who found it lifeless. He then contacted a good friend, Claude Lanzmann, and made a proposal. Lanzmann was invited to interview Friedländer and, via conversation, to draw him out, but this scheme didn't work either. In the meantime, Friedländer had entered into correspondence with a friend from Catholic school days, now a Trappist monk. He composed an unsent letter to the man, recalling the time they had spent together in Montluçon, and that technique at last unlocked the past. Friedländer was able to find a way forward in imaginary dialogue with a onetime Christian schoolmate.[109]

In important respects, the memoir that resulted, *Quand vient le souvenir...* (published by Le Seuil), was just that: a dialogue with Christianity. Friedländer was born Pavel and assumed the name Paul when the Friedländer family moved to France. It was as Paul, or to be more exact, Paul-Henri Ferland, that he was known at Catholic boarding school. The memoir ends, however, with Friedländer on a boat on the way to Israel and to a new name as well, that of the memoir's author, Saul.[110] The book then is a Paul-to-Saul story, and like the story of the Apostle Paul who made the same journey but in reverse, there is a road-to-Damascus moment. Friedländer's father consented to Paul's baptism when he entered the boarding school, a rigorist, antimodernist establishment loyal to the Vichy regime. At the Occupation's end, Friedländer's surviving relatives come looking for him and need to call in the public authorities to arm-twist school officials into the boy's release. Before they let him go, however, they take steps to buttress his budding Catholic faith. Friedländer was administered First Communion early and sent in January or February 1946 to nearby Saint-Etienne for a heart-to-heart with a Jesuit father, who had once taught at the school and already knew Friedländer. The youth had expressed an interest in becoming a priest, and that was the subject the two were to talk over. The conversation, however, took a life-changing turn. The priest and the boy entered a church together, and as they stood contemplating an image of Christ on the Cross, the Jesuit Father asked: "Didn't your parents die at Auschwitz?" He went on to explain to a stunned Friedländer what Auschwitz was and what had happened to Jews there. On return to the Jesuit's rooms, they read a text together about anti-Semitism in France, and Friedländer grasped for the first time in a long while that he was a Jew.[111]

It was an imagined conversation with a Trappist monk that opened the floodgates of wartime memory, and it was a Jesuit father, as a crucified Christ looked on, who helped bring Friedländer, whether the priest intended it or not, back to Judaism. It was a Catholic editor, Paul Flamand, who enabled the historian's first foray into Holocaust history, and the very subject of those first efforts was the Church's own passivity in the face of the Holocaust.

Catholics and Jews entered into dialogue about the Holocaust in the first postwar decades, a conversation already well under way in the 1950s. What is remarkable about the give-and-take is how powerful the Jewish voice was, and that was thanks in part to Christian efforts. It was Christians who enabled Jews to speak and who acted to magnify what they had to say. The Maritains touted Chagall; Mauriac prefaced the works of Poliakov and Wiesel; Le Seuil published Wiesel, Schwarz-Bart, and Friedländer. The two sides settled on a common word – Holocaust – to describe the catastrophe that had decimated European Jewry, and they both worried about how to present the subject to a public bound to be skeptical. To that end, Christians and Jews alike espoused an ethic of restraint that forswore finger-pointing and calls for revenge.

It should not be thought, however, that all was harmony and concord in such exchanges. Christians interpreted the Holocaust as a reenactment of Christ's Passion, a providential understanding that Jewish artists and authors were willing to play off of but not to endorse. Jews for their part made use of Christianizing imagery, not to Christianize the Holocaust, but to persuade their Gentile interlocutors to think about Christian complicity in the massacre of the six million. Jews did not speak in anger, but they accused all the same. The message did not always come through loud and clear. Wiesel and Schwarz-Bart were oftentimes interpreted as Christianizers when in fact they were not. At the same time, there were men like Mauriac who did get it and proved willing to acknowledge that Church-sanctioned anti-Semitism had played a part in the Jewish tragedy.

The Jewish voice, however, was addressed not just to Christians but to readers of all kinds, fellow Jews not least of all. And what an inventive voice it was, from Chagall's eclectic mix of Surrealist and Cubist technique to Schwarz-Bart's genre-bending fiction. It's not clear at all how Wiesel's *La Nuit* is to be categorized. It was an act of witnessing, but Wiesel's attention to style and form, the fable-making art in it, makes the narrative something more complicated. The book is not a novel, yet it is more than testimony. Then there is the subject matter addressed in all such works: the Jews themselves, who were not just one actor among many, but stood at the heart of the story. There are other victims, to be sure, but the Holocaust was first and foremost a catastrophe that had happened to the Jews, and not just any catastrophe. It entailed the destruction of an entire Yiddish-speaking civilization, centered on the small towns and shtetls – the Sighets and Zemyocks – of Eastern Europe. Even more momentous, it constituted a rent in the fabric of Jewish time. In Wiesel's accounting, the Holocaust marked a turning point in God's Covenant with the Jewish people, in Schwarz-Bart's the end of "the theological age." As for what the future held in store for the Jews, who could foresee? But it was clear that the land of Zion lay on the horizon, just as it did in the concluding sentence of Friedländer's memoir: "Out of the darkness there loomed up before us the land of Israel."[112]

The dialogue between Christians and Jews was fruitful many times over. Jewish writers and artists reached a wider audience than ever before, and that audience was made aware of the destructive force of the Holocaust. No doubt such results came at a price. Jews tempered their words, the better to be listened to. Yet they still got the point across: Christian civilization was implicated in the Holocaust, and just as Jews had had to come to terms with the catastrophe, so too did Christians.

But did they? It's evident that Maritain, Mauriac, and Flamand took the matter to heart. It may be that they had individual motives for doing so, born of family sympathies or personal remorse. Maritain was married to a converted Jew. Mauriac's brother was a die-hard Pétainist. Flamand too had a Vichy connection, having served for a period as a senior official in a Vichy-sponsored arts association, Jeune France. All true, but the Catholic response involved more than a handful of individuals, however distinguished. In the 1950s, Father Couturier invited Chagall to design stained-glass windows for the Church of Notre-Dame de Toute Grâce at

Assy, the first of many Church commissions. Catholic intellectuals debated Schwarz-Bart's novel. Priests read Friedländer's work on Pius XII. The Church itself, moreover, took steps to mitigate the anti-Jewish elements in the Good Friday liturgy. And there was more: while the Vatican held the line on opening its wartime archive, it did, as will be seen, undertake a major rethinking of its teachings on the Jews. Interfaith dialogue, once again, had a part to play in the transformation, but this is a subject deserving of its own chapter, and in this one, Jules Isaac, who has hovered so far on the margins of the story, will move into the spotlight.

The interfaith dialogue of the postwar years was not just a matter of publishers and authors, of writers and their publics. It also played itself out in the agonistic realm of polemic and clashing institutions. On the Jewish side, the chief polemicist was Jules Isaac, a man of prickly and argumentative temperament, and well he might be, having spent the war in hiding even as his wife and daughter were deported to their deaths. Isaac launched a slashing attack on the Catholic Church's teachings about the Jews, and he found sympathetic interlocutors on the Christian side in men of good will like Jacques Maritain and Jacques Madaule. An international conference of Christians and Jews met in the Swiss town of Seelisberg in 1947 to discuss the future of ecumenicalism in the wake of the Holocaust. Isaac profited from the occasion to press the Roman Catholic Church to amend its teachings on the Jews and, in consultation with Maritain, among others, sketched out a program of reform, summed up in a set of theses, eighteen in all, later boiled down to ten. The Seelisberg meeting also had an institutional spin-off, the Amitié Judéo-Chrétienne de France (AJ-C), which was, just as its name indicated, an interfaith friendship association. Isaac and Madaule were among its guiding lights, and Isaac used the AJ-C as a platform to preach the Seelisberg gospel.

Such preachings were not without effect. Isaac was invited twice to the Vatican, in 1949 and again in 1960, and both times, he communicated the Seelisberg theses to the pope. Pius XII was polite and noncommittal, but John XXIII was more than that. He had announced plans in 1959 to convene a major Church conclave to update Catholic doctrine, what has come to be known as Vatican II, and, prompted by the exchange with Isaac, he added a new item to the agenda, Catholic doctrine on the Jews. The result of the conclave's deliberations on the subject was a papal declaration, Nostra Aetate or In Our Times, which amounted to "a decisive point of no-return" in Jewish-Christian relations, as one eminent Church historian has put it.[1]

This is a compelling and uplifting narrative, but it does not tell the whole story. At every step, there was resistance. Catholics were reluctant to give up on long-held beliefs about the Jews. Some of these were no doubt anchored in prejudice, but others had deeper, theological roots. The Jews were deicides who had refused and continued to refuse Jesus as the Messiah. Judaism was for that reason a religion dried up and outworn, which had spurned new life. God's Covenant with the Jewish people had lost validity as a result, superseded by a new Testament, which announced to the world Christ's saving grace. The Jews, however, were destined to repent, to convert person-by-person and at the end of time as a people, to the new faith, and with every conversion, the moment of the Messiah's Second Coming came that much closer. Such views percolated to the surface at Seelisberg, among the AJ-C membership, and at Vatican II as well, complicating efforts at reconciliation. The argument at times turned fierce, and in 1953 exploded into an event of national – even international – proportions, the Finaly Affair.

Jewish-Christian relations in France are pockmarked by affairs. In 1858, authorities in the Papal States seized a Jewish child, Edgardo Mortara, from his family. This amounted to a state-sanctioned kidnapping, but Church officials felt justified in acting as they had done. The boy had fallen ill, and his Catholic nurse, fearing for his soul, had had him baptized. Once afforded the sacrament of baptism, official reasoning went, the child belonged to the Church and no longer to the family he had been born in. French Jews campaigned for Mortara's release – the Alliance israélite universelle (AIU) grew out of such efforts – but to no effect. The Church held on to the boy, who grew up to become a priest. A second affair erupted at the end of the century, this one yet more wounding. In 1894, Captain Alfred Dreyfus, an Alsatian Jew, was found guilty of spying for the Germans and was packed off to Devil's Island. Dreyfus was an innocent man, but innocent or not, he rotted away in prison for five years. All the while, the Dreyfus family lobbied for a new trial, and they found allies in Georges Clemenceau, the novelist Émile Zola, and members of the Ligue des droits de l'homme, a human rights organization founded in 1898 in the very midst of the affair. Dreyfus won a second trial, but was found guilty once again, this time by a military court less interested in truth than in protecting the army's prestige. And the army found support of its own among anti-Semitic elements within the Catholic Church, an alliance that transformed the Dreyfus Affair, once about obtaining justice for an innocent man, into an epic battle between secularists and institutionalized religion. Dreyfus was at last exonerated in 1906, but the passions the affair had aroused – anticlerical on one side and anti-Semitic on the other – festered.

They came into play once more in the Finaly Affair. The Finalys – a father, mother, and two small boys, Robert and Gérald – were a Jewish family who had fled to France from Austria in 1938 after the Anschluss. The boys were both circumcised, and Robert had French citizenship. During the war, the parents were deported and murdered at Auschwitz, but they had taken steps to save their sons, who were confided to a friend, who in turn confided them to a Catholic religious order (the Sisters of Notre-Dame de Sion), who in turn farmed them out to a crèche run by Mlle Antoinette Brun. At the Liberation, Robert and Gérald's aunts, one from New Zealand, the other from Israel, came looking for them. Brun expressed an intention to return the boys but then changed her mind, and, in 1948, in a surprise move, she arranged for them to be baptized, which rallied some Church authorities to her side. The matter then went to trial, and when the court, after years of wrangling, at last decided against Brun in 1952, the Grenoble branch of the Sisters of Notre-Dame de Sion spirited the boys away to the Basque country in Spain, in effect kidnapping them, as Edgardo Mortara had been kidnapped almost a century before, and with this, the fate of Robert and Gérald became an affair, a source of bitter polemic that made headlines across the nation, with Jews and Catholics squaring off in angry confrontation.

Yet, despite all the resistance and despite the Finaly Affair itself, Jews and Catholics found a way toward ecumenical entente. It was the memory of deportation that made the difference. Jews, fueled by such memories, did not back down, and Christians, who were beginning to grasp the enormity of the Holocaust, proved willing over time to let go of age-old prejudice and belief.

Seelisberg and the Amitié Judéo-Chrétienne de France

The postwar moment was a propitious one for Jewish-Christian rapprochement. On the Catholic side, the well-meaning were conscience-stricken by what had happened to the Jews. The religious Order of Notre-Dame de Sion had been founded in 1843 by Théodore Ratisbonne, a Jew who had abandoned Judaism to become a Catholic priest. As noted, many Christians believed that the conversion of Jews to the true faith would hasten the Messiah's Second Coming, and the new order dedicated itself to proselytizing with that end in mind. Notre-Dame de Sion maintained a review, which had ceased publication during the Second World War. When it started up again in 1947, the review featured a new name, *Cahiers sioniens*, and a new director, Father Marcel Leroux, both signals that the order was contemplating a change of direction. In this vein, the renamed journal's first issue made clear that the proselytizing practices of old no longer enjoyed the same high priority. It evoked the memory of "six million Jews ... annihilated" and announced in plainest language the journal's editorial position: "In these pages, we never wish to forget the appalling holocaust of an entire people."[2] Leroux died of a heart attack not long thereafter, but was succeeded by a man no less committed, Father Paul Démann, who was himself a converted Jew. Démann let it be known from the outset that he considered anti-Semitism a sin, a crime against Christianity, and in this respect, he was following in the footsteps of Jacques Maritain.

Both men, Démann and Maritain, had a role to play in the 1947 Seelisberg conference, if at a distance. The former, working with Jesuit Father Jean Daniélou, the historian Henri-Irénée Marrou, and Jules Isaac, helped to prepare the French delegation to the congress.[3] Maritain, occupied with his duties as ambassador to the Vatican, was unable to be present, but he sent an open letter that laid out in brief his thinking on Jewish-Christian relations. The bond between the two religions was familial in Maritain's telling, with the Jews cast in the role of older brothers, and it was historical as well. Six million Jews had died in the gas chambers of Hitler's death camps, a veritable Calvary, and why? Because of a raging racial hatred, aimed at Jews – that much was obvious – but also at Christ (and by extension all Christians), who was himself Jewish "in his race." Maritain repudiated all expressions of contempt for his Jewish brothers. They were not perfidious (just unbelieving), nor were they a "deicide race." Saint Paul (Romans 9–11) had prophesied the Jews' ultimate embrace of the true Messiah, and Maritain shared in such hopes, but he interpreted this "future reintegration," as he called it, not as a conversion, mass or individual, but as a "plenitude."[4]

As for the Seelisberg conference itself, it convened under the auspices of the International Council of Christians and Jews, which also decided on the conference theme: how to combat anti-Semitism. Roughly seventy persons took part, Christians and Jews from a dozen nations. Isaac was one of them, as was France's Rabbi Jacob Kaplan. They spoke in vigorous and, when necessary, contentious tones about the issue at hand. The two were named to serve on the conference's Commission des Églises, and Isaac submitted a list of eighteen points for the commission members' consideration, all critical of traditional Christian teachings on the Jews. A Vatican representative chaired the group, Father Calliste Lopinot, and he proved a source of exasperation. Lopinot was willing to acknowledge errors on the Church's part, but insisted that the Jews do the same, which prompted an outburst from Rabbi Kaplan: "The Synagogue's wrongs! ... What wrongs did we commit?"[5] What, in a word, had the Jews done to deserve the fate reserved for them? No, Rabbi Kaplan implied, this was a moment for Christian self-reflection, not for Jewish mea culpas. In the face of such remonstrations, Father Lopinot stepped aside and was replaced by the more sympathetic Father Jean de Menasce (another converted Jew), who pledged to move the discussions forward in a spirit of "mutual respect."[6] When the time came to write up a report, the Jewish members of the commission absented themselves. Christian doctrine was at stake, and Christians had the right to decide such matters among themselves, which they did, whittling down Isaac's propositions to ten. The gist of the declaration that resulted was this: Jesus had been a Jew, as had been his apostles and first disciples. It was incumbent on the Church not to denigrate biblical Judaism or to blame all Jews for the Crucifixion. Christ died for our sins, for the sins of *all* humankind, and so Jews didn't deserve to be singled out and reviled as accursed. Indeed, they remained special to God; and by way of conclusion, the document cited from Saint Paul's Epistle to the Romans (11:28–29): "They are beloved for the fathers' sakes/For the gifts and calling of God are without repentance."[7]

Isaac for one had hoped for more – most important, for a franker condemnation of the accusation of deicide – but this was a good start. For the French delegation, there was an added bonus. The Seelisberg meeting set the stage for the creation back home of a permanent body, L'Amitié Judéo-Chrétienne de France, which dedicated itself, among other tasks, to the propagation of the Seelisberg theses. The AJ-C got off to a sputtering start in November 1947 in Edmond Fleg's Paris apartment, sputtering because the turnout was small. A second meeting the next February, once more in Fleg's apartment, was more successful, followed by a third in July, which marked the moment of the AJ-C's official founding. Isaac had in the meantime begun to assert himself. It was he who drafted the association's statutes, and it was he again who insisted that a Christian, in the event Henri-Irénée Marrou, occupy the AJ-C presidency.

Isaac's dynamism expressed itself in print as well. He published *Jésus et Israël* in April 1948, an epic critique of Church doctrine on the Jews at almost six hundred pages. The book, coupled with Isaac's role at Seelisberg and investment in the AJ-C, established him as a figure to contend with in the world of Jewish-Christian relations and, indeed, earned him an audience with Pius XII. This took place in October of the following year, to mixed results. Isaac submitted the Seelisberg declaration to the Holy Father who, it is reported, regarded the text with some suspicion. Isaac also urged the pope to revise further the Easter liturgy, and on this score, there was progress, not right away, but in time.

The translation of *"pro perfidis Judaeis"* had already undergone a revision, as noted earlier, and then in 1955, it was decided to include a genuflection when the Easter prayer for the Jews was recited, as a sign of consideration. Isaac's audience with the pope lasted just a half-dozen minutes. Pius bestowed a medal on him, pronounced a triple blessing, and that was that.[8]

Still, how much had been accomplished in the span of just a few years. Christians, in a spirit of repentance, had entered into interfaith dialogue and showed themselves willing, despite some reserves, to amend their thinking about the Jews. The dialogue took place, moreover, on multiple levels. It was local and French, but it was also international, reaching even into the sacred precincts of the Vatican, which was guarded in its reaction but not altogether unresponsive.

What this narrative understates, however, is how much bad feeling was involved along the way, how much hurt, misunderstanding, and disputation. On the Jewish end, the principal protagonist was Isaac himself, who proved a skilled debater, ever ready to take on a fight when he felt Jewish honor at stake.

Jules Isaac

Isaac was not the likeliest choice for the role of Jewish paladin.[9] He was a humanist by training who knew Greek but not Hebrew. In the interwar decades, he had made a name for himself as the author of the Malet and Isaac handbook series. The series, a compendium of teaching manuals for high-school history teachers, was started prior to the Great War by Albert Malet. Malet, however, was killed in combat in 1915, and Isaac, until then Malet's second-in-command, took over the collection from there. The endeavor was an exercise in civic republicanism if ever there was one, but Isaac, a passionate Dreyfusard in younger days, was more than a match for the job. On the matter of belief, he considered himself an agnostic, a pagan at heart, though late in life he developed a measure of sympathy for what he called "Jewish spirituality." This didn't mean, though, that Judaism as a religion mattered to him. In AJ-C debates, Isaac was known to question tenets of Jewish belief, Jewish Election for instance, causing embarrassment to more pious Jews present, like Rabbi Kaplan.[10]

The Second World War shattered Isaac's family and career, and he emerged from it a man transformed. In addition to writing high school teaching manuals, Isaac held a government position as inspector of public instruction. The Vichy regime fired him from the post because he was a Jew. Isaac headed southward to the relative safety of the

Unoccupied Zone, joined by his family (he had a wife, two sons, and a daughter). He set to work on a book about Jewish-Christian relations, which induced him to seek out a location with good library facilities near at hand – Riom, as it turned out – where the Isaacs took up residence in the fall of 1943. By then, the Germans had occupied all of France, and the hunt for Jews was on. Isaac's daughter and one son were arrested and deported; the son would return, but not the daughter. A second son volunteered to fight for Free France. Then Isaac's wife was taken in dramatic circumstances. Isaac himself was out of the house when the police came for her. He returned to an empty apartment and, realizing what had happened, scooped up the still uncompleted manuscript of what was to become *Jésus et Israël* and fled to the depths of Berry. A well-disposed local priest opened the stacks of a nearby convent library to Isaac, allowing him to continue work on the book, which was finished not long after the Liberation. Isaac had trouble finding a publisher, but thanks to the intervention of a Protestant minister, Pastor Charles Westphal (also a future member of the AJ-C), Albin Michel agreed to accept the manuscript. *Jésus et Israël* appeared in the spring of 1948, and within a month, it had sold 11,000 copies.[11] A revised version came out in 1959, followed three years later by the publication of *L'Enseignement du mépris* (in English, *The Teaching of Contempt*), a succinct summing up of Isaac's critique of Church doctrine on the Jews.

The war then marked a caesura in Isaac's life. He entered it as a respected and accomplished republican educator; he exited as a student of Jewish-Christian relations and of the Christian origins of modern anti-Semitism, a man not just esteemed but renowned, not to say notorious. Christians themselves enabled the transformation, the Berry priest and Pastor Westphal, and it's hard in this connection not to be reminded of the circumstances that surrounded the publication of André Schwarz-Bart's *Le Dernier des Justes*, which likewise owed so much to Gentile intercessors. Yet it was the loss of family that made the most profound difference in the redirection of Isaac's life. *Jésus et Israël* was dedicated "To my wife, to my daughter/martyrs," and the book's final sentences concluded with a mournful plea: "The glow of Auschwitz's crematorium oven is the beacon that lights, that orients all my thoughts. O my Jewish brothers, and you too my Christian brothers, do you not see how that light blends with another, the light of the Cross?"[12] This was a book, from beginning to end, haunted by the Holocaust.[13]

At a first glance, however, that's not the way the book reads. The author presents himself more as a didact than a man in sorrow. He's an exegete who has toiled his way through the New Testament with a single objective: to dismantle the whole range of arguments drawn from the text to disparage Jews and their religion. Indeed, for much of *Jésus et Israël* that's how Isaac proceeds, buttressing his refutations as he goes with citations from contemporary historical scholarship about biblical Palestine that allow him to contextualize and, in so doing, to undercut the New Testament's most accusatory passages. The volume boasted all the trappings of positivist scholarship, and at moments it calls to mind a lawyer's brief that ticks off points, one after another, subjecting each to logical scrutiny.

In fact, in its point-by-point approach, the book also has at times the look of a fleshed-out version of the Seelisberg declaration. Jesus was a Jew from a modest artisan background. The Jewish religion was a vital faith, not a ritualistic one. The synagogue was a democratic space, where Jesus himself had taught. And so forth. In the first two parts (there were four), the text is punctuated with the occasional provocation. Jesus set himself up against elements in official Judaism that were too enmeshed, as Isaac saw it, in worldly matters. Isaac didn't deny that there were Jews lacking in genuine spirituality, but what religion, he asked, didn't have its share of Tartuffes?[14] Most of the time, though, Isaac tried to keep up positivist appearances. That effort collapsed, however, at the end of *Jésus et Israël*. In part three, Isaac's anger breaks through, and it's not hard to guess why, for as he drafted it, he was himself on the run and dealing with the loss of a wife and children. The book's final portion was completed after the war, too soon for the still-raw wounds of loss to have scarred over.

What's at issue in the book's concluding passages is the trial of Jesus as recounted in the Gospels, a moment of supreme drama that contributed so much to poisoning Christian attitudes toward the Jews. In the New Testament's account, it is the Jewish high priest, Caiaphas, who plays the villain's part. He is dead set on eliminating Jesus, reviled as a blasphemous upstart and false Messiah. Caiaphas and a panel of like-minded judges interrogate the man from Nazareth and then turn him over to Pontius Pilate for trial and eventual execution. The Roman governor questions Jesus in turn, but finds no evidence against him. Pilate is under pressure to act, however, and maneuvers to unburden himself of responsibility, arranging for the Jewish crowd to decide instead. There will be a death sentence, as Caiaphas had desired, but it will be up to the Jews themselves to choose who is to die, whether Jesus (an innocent) or the reprobate Barabbas, and the crowd calls out for Jesus' blood. The Jews by that choice condemned themselves as deicides, and God punished them, casting them to the four winds and dooming their descendants to lives of misery. Jewish pain stood in proof of Jewish wrongdoing and in confirmation of Jesus' Messianic title.

Isaac mobilized the historical record to argue against this account. It was Roman authorities, he argued, who were in charge in Palestine, and so it was they and not the Jews who were ultimately to blame for the Crucifixion. Jewish dispersion, moreover, was well under way before Jesus ever appeared on the scene. Most Jews already resided outside of Palestine, so most Jews bore no responsibility at all for Jesus' death. And to the extent the dispersion was already a *fait accompli* in Jesus' lifetime, it made no sense to interpret it as punishment for the crime of deicide. As for the community of Palestinian Jews, it no doubt fell on hard times in the Christian era, but that decline was extended over centuries, a gradual process, and not the result of some sudden and severe divine decree.

Isaac, however, was not content to marshal arguments, but also pressed his case by other means, elaborating a set of historical analogies meant to sting the conscience of Catholic and French readers. Catholic France, he proposed, boasted a Caiaphas of its own. Think, Isaac went on, of the trial of Jeanne d'Arc. English armies were stationed on French soil at the time, and elements of the French Catholic hierarchy sided with the foreign occupier. The bishop of Beauvais, Pierre Cauchon, engineered Jeanne's trial to discredit the maid and thereby advance the English cause. Who played the high priest's role in this story? Isaac did not hesitate to name names: "the Lord Bishop Pierre Cauchon, he is Caiaphas."[15]

Nor was Bishop Cauchon the last of his ilk. The Gospel of Saint John presented Caiaphas as a Machiavellian figure who had schemed not just to suppress blasphemy but also to preserve Jewish interests. Biblical Palestine was then in ferment, with the Romans intent on exacting retribution. Why not, Saint John's Caiaphas calculated, deflect attention from the Jews? Why not make a scapegoat of Jesus, sacrificing one man, even an innocent one, to protect the nation as a whole? Isaac had seen this sort of logic at work before in French history. Not fifty years ago, he wrote (remember that *Jésus et Israël* was published in 1948), "France's Catholic world, arrayed to a man behind its clergy," had ganged up on "an innocent Jew" in the nation's name.[16] The allusion, of course, was to the Dreyfus Affair, with Dreyfus in this instance assigned Jesus' role and the Catholic Church that of the Jewish high priest.

But the decisive analogy for Isaac was a more contemporary one. Ancient Palestine was a land under occupation, as France had been under the Nazis. Looked at through this lens, Pilate was not a mere governor but a "Roman Gauleiter," an anti-Semite bent on the persecution of the Jews. In which case, Caiaphas was not just a schemer but a collaborator, the spokesman for a "despotic and servile … oligarchy." He was, as Isaac put it with polemical acerbity, "*Vichy à Jérusalem,*" in effect a latter-day Pétain. Isaac then invited readers to imagine a crowd gathered in front of German headquarters in Paris in 1942. Gabriel Péri (a Communist and résistant, though that's not specified) is dragged before the assembled. Isaac then lets the reader know what he expects the people to shout out: "Up against the wall."[17]

Isaac's allusions are not always spelled out. He doesn't identify Dreyfus by name or Pétain, and he doesn't explain who Gabriel Péri was. Yet the attentive reader gets the message and the injunction to self-examination that it contains. Because a senior churchman conspired in Jeanne d'Arc's death, are French Catholics forever guilty of the crime? Because the Church was complicit in railroading Dreyfus, is it guilty of the same calculated cruelty as Caiaphas when he railroaded Jesus? Because a crowd of French men and women in an era of Occupation howled for the head of a countryman, does that mean that all French men and women were collaborators?

Isaac launched one final salvo against the charge of deicide, and it was the most explosive one of all. The deicide libel, he wrote, was a "murderous tradition, I've said it once and will say it again, that led to Auschwitz."[18] Nazism's genocidal racism was a monstrous parasite that fed off of millennia of hate-filled Christian teachings. In the fourth century, John Chrysostom, deacon of Antioch, had scorned Judaism as a disease that needed rooting out, and the imperial authorities took heed, putting synagogues to the torch, "illustrious precedents," as Isaac called them, "for Hitler, Darnand, the SS, and their brothers in the French Milice." A few pages on, Isaac made sure to include Protestantism in the general indictment, assigning to Luther "the place he is due in the first rank of (Auschwitz's) Christian precursors."[19] Isaac kept pounding away at the theme, moreover, in *L'Enseignement du mépris*. When the Crusaders captured Jerusalem in the eleventh century, he wrote, Jews sheltered in their synagogues, where the Crusaders burned them alive, yet another "sad precedent," this one for the German incineration of French villagers at Oradour in June 1944. Isaac then went on to remind readers of how many Nazi hierarchs – Himmler, Eichmann, Höss – had come from Catholic backgrounds.[20] These are fierce words. *Jésus et Israël*, its positivist façade notwithstanding, packed an in-your-face, argumentative punch, and Christianity was in the cross hairs.

Jésus et Israël was a work of scholarship, a synoptic critique of Christian anti-Semitism that veiled its polemical edge. Isaac's flair for polemic, however, was not always so camouflaged. Before and after the publication of *Jésus et Israël*, he embroiled himself in a series of one-on-one affrays. These were not erudite affairs but jousts, and along the way Isaac locked horns with a widening cast of adversaries, from usual suspects like Daniel-Rops to Father Daniélou and Marrou, who were supposed to be friends.

Jésus et Israël was peppered with digs at Daniel-Rops,[21] which was little wonder, as Isaac had a grievance against the man, one already aired in print. This episode was discussed in Chapter 4, and so there's no need to rehearse it again in detail. In 1945, Daniel-Rops had published a popularizing history of biblical Palestine and, in it, parroted conventional Christian wisdom on the Jews: they were an obstinate and proud people who professed a loveless religion; the Jewish high priest Caiaphas had conspired against Jesus; and the Jews, past and present, who refused to acknowledge Jesus as the Messiah, were in effect taking the side of Christ's killer. They thus stood guilty of deicide, and the pogroms visited on them over the course of history were in just recompense for such perfidy.

Isaac was outraged when he read this and wrote an open letter, dated April 1946, to Daniel-Rops, a "letter of rupture" as he called it. Isaac was categorical. There was no justification, divine or otherwise, for the assassination of six million Jews. The kind of punitive logic Daniel-Rops engaged in had led straight to the horrors of Auschwitz. This was Phariseeism, but of a Christian variety, and it was odious. Instead of blaming the Jews for Christ's death, Isaac proposed that humankind in its entirety bore the burden of guilt, for all us, he reminded Daniel-Rops, are sinners. This was how Charles Péguy had understood Christ's sacrifice, and Isaac's invocation of Péguy's name was heartfelt.[22] To an entire generation, Péguy had been a shining example, a Dreyfusard turned believing Catholic who died a hero's death on the field of honor in the Great War. Isaac identified himself with that generation, but the bond between the two men ran even deeper than that, for they had been friends since Dreyfusard days, when as young men they had militated side by side.

Isaac's missive was written before the Seelisberg conference and before the publication of *Jésus et Israël*. The arguments he sketched in the letter were undeveloped and the tone scorching, which may explain why he had trouble finding a venue willing to print it. Isaac approached *Esprit* first, which was edited by Emmanuel Mounier who, though himself a progressive Catholic, refused to publish the text. It was Jean Cassou and the Resistance author Vercors who came to Isaac's rescue. Cassou was editor-in-chief at *Europe* and Vercors a member of its editorial board, sitting alongside Louis Aragon, Paul Éluard, and Louis Martin-Chauffier. It was in the pages of *Europe* then, a journal of the militant, fellow-traveling Left, that Isaac's letter appeared in July 1946.[23]

The subsequent publication of *Jésus et Israël* elevated Isaac into a figure of note, but notoriety did not bring an end to polemics, and indeed, the next time that Isaac found himself in a public dispute, it was with an AJ-C colleague, Father Jean Daniélou. The two appeared together in a June 1948 radio debate, and the subject was Isaac's book. Daniélou took the opportunity to contest its main theses. Isaac, he argued, had exaggerated Christ's rootedness in Jewish life, which he rose above. Jesus *was* the Messiah, and so Jesus' death was indeed a deicide. And Christians still had a mission vis-à-vis the Jews: to convert them.[24] There were Christians who took Isaac's criticism of Church teachings to heart – François Mauriac, for example – but Daniélou was only willing to go so far.

The same was true of Henri-Irénée Marrou, yet another AJ-C comrade. Marrou, a professor at the Sorbonne, published a stinging review of *Jésus et Israël* in June 1949. The two men had major theological differences. Marrou felt that the Hitlerian regime was a blasphemous one and that Nazi anti-Semitism, in striking at the Jewish people, struck also, via the Jews, at Christianity itself. For that reason, he avowed a kinship with Jews as brothers in persecution. But it was not Christianity, he believed, that had propagated anti-Semitism, and to the extent it had, the fault lay with the Jews themselves who were obdurate in refusing to acknowledge Jesus as the Messiah. They had in effect taken Caiaphas' part. They were in error – "the Jew is wrong" is how Marrou put it – and error had its costs. Judaism had lost God's favor and Christianity taken its place as the new Israel. This is the nub of supersessionist thinking, and it is why Christians do not refer to the Hebrew Bible as such but rather as the Old Testament. This was painful enough for Isaac to hear, but Marrou added insult to injury, dismissing Isaac's scholarship as dry-as-dust positivism that was out of touch with current historiographical trends. The role played by *Esprit* in the controversy that ensued did not help to calm the waters. The journal had earlier rejected Isaac's open letter to Daniel-Rops. It did publish his reply to Marrou, but it edited the text down, printed it in small type, and banished it to the journal's back pages.[25]

Isaac would not stand for such condescension and made a commotion, so much so that Marrou, who regretted the upset he had caused, felt obliged to step down as AJ-C president. He was succeeded by Jacques Madaule, who also professed fraternal feelings toward the Jews but of a more intimate nature. They were, he believed, Christianity's older brothers and not just coequals in persecution. As Madaule saw it, the persistence of the Jews across the centuries, despite all manner of persecution, was a sure sign that they occupied a special place, however hard to decipher, in God's providential design. He also saw God's hand at work in the creation of the State of Israel, which he understood in Christian terms as a saga of sacrifice and resurrection. The new state, he wrote, owed its existence to the exertions of a generation of men and women, onetime "victims of Nazi crematoria" who had been transfigured into soldiers and pioneers, redeemers of the land. Madaule cared enough about the land, indeed, that he paid a first visit to Palestine/Israel in 1937 and a second one in 1951.[26]

The Finaly Affair

Isaac's polemical sparring brought to the surface unresolved differences between Catholics and Jews, but such flare-ups were as nothing compared to the rancor stoked by the Finaly Affair. Each side in the confrontation came face-to-face with a difficult choice, and to grasp just how difficult, it is worth recapitulating in brief how the Finaly Affair became just that, a cause célèbre that, if but for a moment, stirred the national conscience.[27]

During the war, Jews in desperation had placed their children with Catholic institutions for safekeeping. Sometimes – Saul Friedländer's case is an example – the families consented to baptism; sometimes, they did not, but a baptism took place nonetheless; and sometimes yet again, and this was the most frequent circumstance, there was no baptism at all. At the Liberation, the Church had to make up its mind what to do with such hidden children when parents, relatives, or Jewish institutions came looking for them. The decision was easiest when it came to the unbaptized. The Church felt it had no special claims on such children, and they were returned. In the case of baptized children, however, the choice was not so clear. The salvation of souls was at stake, and the Vatican ended up sending mixed signals. When the claimants were Jewish institutions, the Holy See advised against restitution.[28] When they were parents, the Church had no choice but to yield the children up. But what about that category in between? What was to be done with baptized Jewish children orphaned in the Holocaust, but not bereft of extended family willing to care for them? This was Friedländer's situation and, as we have seen, it required the full force of the law to oblige the Montluçon boarding school that had cared for him during the war to yield him up.

This was also the case of the Finaly boys after 1948, once Mlle Brun had seen to it that they were baptized. It looked like the law was going to settle this matter as well. In June 1952, the Grenoble Court of Appeals ordered Mlle Brun to release the children to Moïse Keller, the lawyer for the boys' Israeli aunt, Hedwig Rosner. Brun, however, refused, and in the meantime, the Grenoble branch of Notre-Dame de Sion whisked Robert and Gérald off under assumed names first to Marseille, then to Bayonne, and eventually out of France altogether to the Basque country in Franco's Spain. It wasn't long before the Finaly case became a full-blown affair. The Jewish publicist and jurist Wladimir Rabinovitch (Rabi for short) launched a campaign for the children's release in the Zionist journal *La Terre retrouvée*. After that came the court-ordered arrest in January of 1953 of Mlle Brun, and the month following of Mother Antonine, mother superior of the Grenoble house of the Sisters of Notre-Dame de Sion. The latter in particular, publicized in the press with an accompanying photo, caused an outcry. A mother superior in jail? This was scandalous news, and there were plenty of people inside the Church and out ready to take the part of a nun persecuted by the law and Zionist zealots like Rabi.

This then was the Church's dilemma. Did it side with Mother Antonine, do what lay in its power to hold on to the Finaly boys, and brave the anticlerical onslaught bound to follow? Or did it look for a way out of the impasse, infuriating its own hard-liners in the process?

The Jewish community also faced a dilemma. It had a hard-line option of its own, which was to press kidnapping charges against Mlle Brun and her accomplices, all the while drumming up public – indeed, world – support through a press campaign. This course of action had its partisans, Rabi and Keller among them. In April, they joined forces with an array of interested organizations – from stalwarts of the anticlerical Left like the Ligue des droits de l'homme to global bodies like the World Jewish Congress – to form the Comité national Finaly. Mme Rosner's backers lashed into the Church, drawing parallels between the abduction of the Finaly brothers and the kidnapping of Edgardo Mortara, between the Finaly Affair and the Dreyfus Affair. Worse, the Church was accused of aligning itself with the ultra-Right. It was carrying forward the destruction of Jewish life that the Nazis had begun, and, critics charged, it had found an eager partner in that endeavor in fascist Spain.[29]

There was an alternative to confrontation, however, which was the path of negotiation, and this was the line pursued by the Consistory and the Alliance israélite universelle. The former deputed Rabbi Kaplan to enter into contact with Church officials to discuss the boys' return, which he did in the first weeks of February 1953, with promising initial results. He contacted the office of the archbishop of Paris, Cardinal Feltin, which in turn put him in touch with the superior general of the Order of the Sisters of Notre-Dame de Sion. She was not at first sympathetic but came around in the end. The Church's interest, the superior general concluded, dictated that the Finaly boys be handed over. As for the AIU, its president, René Cassin, fired off a telegram in February, calling on the Vatican to intervene, and a second one along the same lines in March to France's foreign minister, the Christian Democrat Georges Bidault.

The champions of negotiation had a committee of their own, the Commission mixte Finaly, which grouped together under Rabbi Kaplan's leadership representatives from mainstream Jewish associations: the Consistory, AIU, CRIF, and FSJU. Rabbi Kaplan, moreover, had his own technique for keeping up the pressure, not a press campaign, but a Passover appeal to Jewish families to set two empty places for the Finaly brothers at the Seder dinner table. What better way, the Rabbi explained, to express the Jewish community's abiding solidarity with two young boys "snatched from their family and turned away ... from the Jewish religion for which their parents had died as martyrs in deportation."[30]

In June 1953, Church authorities arranged the return of the Finaly brothers to France, an apparent triumph for Kaplan and the partisans of conciliation on both sides. Yet it should not be thought that the route toward this outcome was a direct one. It was marked rather by twists and double-dealing, and at every turn, it seems, wartime memory bore down on the actors, causing them to act in ways that both hindered and in the end aided in finding an exit.

Mother Antonine's conduct throughout the affair provides an example of a twist. She wanted the Church to hold on to the Finaly brothers, and in September 1952 in light of the law's disposition to judge otherwise, she consulted Cardinal Gerlier, Archbishop of Lyon, about how to proceed. Gerlier's advice: do what's necessary so that the boys might be raised "in the Christian faith," and that's what she did, hiding Robert and Gérald away in one safe house after another. Mother Antonine, as it turns out, knew something about clandestine networks and the concealment of persons wanted by the authorities. During the war, she had been active in a Resistance organization, L'Amitié chrétienne, which was in fact headquartered in the offices of the Lyon branch of Notre-Dame de Sion. L'Amitié chrétienne provided Jews in flight false papers and found them hiding places. These were the networks Mother Antonine activated to come to the "rescue" of the Finaly brothers, and that's indeed how she understood what she was doing. Yesterday's enemies were the Nazis, today's the minions of the French state. In both instances, moreover, Mother Antonine understood herself as standing up for the oppressed against their persecutors. She lived the Finaly Affair, as she talked about it some years later, in "the ambiance of the Resistance."[31]

Cardinal Gerlier's role in the affair was, by contrast, more ambiguous,[32] not to say duplicitous. On the surface, it appeared that he was all in favor of a negotiated settlement. He called in Father Pierre Chaillet, a Jesuit priest, for assistance. Chaillet was instructed to get in touch with Rabbi Kaplan, which he did by working through the intermediary of a common acquaintance, André Weil, a member of the Consistory. The idea was to strike a bargain with the Rosner family: the return of the Finaly brothers in exchange for a waiver of all criminal charges against Mlle Brun. A secret accord to that effect was signed by Father Chaillet and Mme Rosner on March 6, 1953. Word of the agreement, though not its precise terms, leaked out, but that didn't change the situation. Rabbi Kaplan's hopes for an amicable resolution appeared on the way to realization, and yet the boys were still not produced as promised.

Church officials took steps to allay the rabbi's growing concern. They succeeded in tracking Robert and Gérald's general whereabouts to Spain and then called in a woman respected on all sides to assist in the hunt for them there. She was Germaine Ribière, a Catholic who had distinguished herself during the war in the ranks of L'Amitié chrétienne, engaging in selfless risk-taking in order to save Jews, acts that the State of Israel later recognized, naming her a Righteous among Nations.[33]

In fact, the entire team working on finding the boys was so composed as to persuade Rabbi Kaplan of Cardinal Gerlier's bona fides. Ribière was not the sole grande résistante in the group. Father Chaillet was another. He had spoken out early on during the Occupation against Vichy's racial policies; he was active, like Ribiére, in the rescue work of L'Amitié chrétienne, which landed him for a period in a Gestapo cell; and like Ribière once again, he was later designated a Righteous among Nations by the State of Israel. After the war, Father Chaillet remained involved in Resistance-linked charitable activities, serving as president of the Comité des oeuvres sociales des organisations de Résistance. It so happened that the committee's treasurer was himself a former Amitié chrétienne activist, none other than André Weil.

Then there was Cardinal Gerlier himself, for many Jews a reassuring figure. Though a staunch Pétainist, he had written a public letter of protest to the Maréchal in the aftermath of the August 1942 round-up of Jews in the southern zone. Such a gesture was not just meaningful in an abstract sense to Rabbi Kaplan. The rabbi had two sons of his own who had taken refuge in Lyon during the war, and it was the men and women of L'Amitié chrétienne, under Cardinal Gerlier's patronage, who had furnished them with new identities.[34]

So, to all appearances, it looked like the brotherhood of Christians and Jews, born of wartime rescue efforts, was about to yield welcome fruit in the postwar, all parties working together toward an amicable resolution of the Finaly Affair. Cardinal Gerlier's motives, however, were not so upfront, as we have seen. He desired that the Finaly boys remain in the faith. Having counseled Mother Antonine to resist, he went looking for counsel himself, addressing a discreet inquiry to the Vatican, which responded in a letter of January 23, 1953. The Vatican's advice had more than one moving part. The boys had been baptized, which conferred on the Church rightful moral custody over them until such time as they were in a position to make up their own minds what they believed. In the meantime, the letter instructed the Cardinal to prolong the affair and abet Mlle Brun in her obstructionism, but with a hard-to-apply caveat: that such foot-dragging not cause "grave damage" to the Church.[35] This was the line Gerlier opted to pursue. He acted as though he wanted a deal, but behind the scenes, in accord with the Vatican's recommendations, he was stalling and encouraging Mother Antonine to do the same.

This state of affairs would not last, however, because all the delay did finally prove detrimental to the Church's reputation and institutional peace of mind. Rabbi Kaplan eventually lost patience, renouncing the March bargain at a June 5 press conference. The Cour de cassation, France's court of final appeal, was scheduled to decide the case's ultimate disposition later in the month, and it was clear that the Church was going to come out a loser.

Just as bad, the Church was taking a thrashing in the public uproar that the affair had stirred. When the affair began to heat up, Catholic opinion was more or less united in support of the Church's position. Not the AJ-C, of course which, now under Madaule's leadership, proved a reliable friend to Jews in difficult times, advocating for the boys' speedy return to France.[36] Francois Mauriac, by contrast, was not so sure, adopting an initial line close to the Vatican's. Neither the relatives in Tel Aviv nor Brun, he argued, had a claim on the souls of Robert and Gérald, who had a right to decide for themselves once they reached maturity. In any event, it wouldn't be necessary to wait that long, Mauriac added with a bigoted flourish, as it was well known how precocious Jewish children were. And while waiting for maturity to arrive, Marrou chimed in, it made most sense to place the boys in a "neutral establishment."[37] That was also the course of action favored by Father Michel Riquet. He acknowledged that Mlle Brun had committed an error, however understandable, when she orchestrated Robert and Gérald's baptism. It was not right to impose Church membership on the boys who after all had been circumcised, a clear sign that the family intended them to be raised as Jews. Yet it was important to remember at the same time, Father Riquet added, that the father had made sure to arrange French citizenship for the older brother, another kind of sign, this one demonstrating that he intended Robert at least to be raised as French. So, the most equitable solution was to keep the brothers in France for the time being, educating them in a setting agreed upon by all parties – a Resistance-run children's home, for example – until such

time as they were in a position to choose "freely." Father Riquet persuaded UNADIF to endorse this course of action and then presented
himself to Gerlier as a good-faith intermediary, a proposal the cardinal
politely swatted down.[38]

The Church's near-united front, however, did not long endure. It was
not just the other side's vituperations that caused it to bend, but also the
way some of its own proponents conducted themselves, dredging up
ghosts from a reactionary past that many progressive-minded Catholics
had hoped would remain buried once and for all now that the war was
over. A number of Catholics found it all too tempting to smear the Jews
as ungrateful. Christians had braved every danger to save the Finaly boys;
Mlle Brun had been a model of maternal care; and now the Jews coveted
souls that no longer belonged to them. Mlle Brun's lawyer proposed a
reason why, invoking the specter of "Judeo-Masonry," ever ready to
conspire against the nation's interests.[39] *La Croix* pointed the finger at
Zionism. Mme Rosner wanted to haul the boys off to Israel, a foreign
land they knew nothing of, and the Rosner family lawyer, Moïse Keller,
was all too willing to connive in the plot. He was a well-known Zionist
after all and a Communist (he was in fact an ex-party member).[40]

Mlle Brun's most vociferous partisans spewed up intolerance of a kind
that brought back for many unwelcome memories of Vichy-era anti-
Semitism. This was more than Mauriac, for one, was prepared to stomach. He published a retraction of his earlier views in *Le Figaro* in early
June, acknowledging that the Finaly brothers had in fact been kidnapped,
not rescued. The affair had brought to the surface two mirroring passions, anti-Semitism and anticlericalism, and it was high time to lay
them, and the affair as well, to rest. Finally, Cardinal Gerlier too began
to experience a change of heart. He had been told to hold on to the boys,
but not at the peril of the Church's reputation. The Church's reputation
was taking heavy fire, and so at last Gerlier abandoned the path of
double-dealing. The French Church, he explained in a public declaration, no longer endorsed the view that it had a claim on children
baptized without the knowledge or consent of their parents, and the
cardinal pressed the Basque priests holding the boys to return them,
pressure redoubled when the Vatican itself decided to intervene.[41] The
affair was causing the Church irreparable harm, and so the Holy See in its
turn came around to supporting a negotiated way out.

Now the Finaly Affair speeded toward resolution. Robert and Gérald
were back in France on June 26, where they were placed in the care of
André Weil. The Cour de cassation, as anticipated, decided against Mlle
Brun, but she was let off when the Rosner family withdrew all complaints
against her. They had agreed to drop charges in exchange for passports

for the boys, and when the passports were delivered, the brothers in late July boarded a plane for Israel accompanied by Mme Rosner and her husband.

The affair was over, but it had lasting consequences for both France's Jewish community and the Catholic Church. The Consistory, which had thrown its weight behind Rabbi Kaplan, emerged with its hand strengthened. By statute, it had the right to name the president of the CRIF, and its man at the head of the organization was, as we have seen, Vidal Modiano. In the aftermath of the affair, Modiano felt empowered to undertake a housecleaning. He oversaw a rewriting of the CRIF's statutes, which henceforth required member groups to "labor in the service of the Jewish people," an innocuous-sounding phrase but one, when applied in practice, that resulted in the marginalization of communist-linked bodies like the Union des Juifs pour la résistance et l'entraide. As for Rabbi Kaplan, the affair's lead protagonist on the Jewish side, he was rewarded with a promotion, becoming Grand Rabbi of France in 1955. The Finaly Affair rallied France's Jews around mainstream organizations. Anticlericals, left-wing Zionists and left-wingers tout court were dealt a setback, while partisans of conciliation with the Catholic Church received a boost.[42] This affair had not ended as the Mortara Affair had, an outcome, as Grand Rabbi Kaplan wrote to Weil, of "great importance for the relations between Church and Synagogue."[43]

The Finaly Affair was no less consequential for the Church. The Sisters of Notre-Dame de Sion experienced the affair as an "electro-shock" that moved them to reconceive the order's mission.[44] They abandoned proselytizing among the Jews altogether. In October 1955, the Mother House in Paris opened a Centre d'études et d'information pour Israël. It was better, the sisters felt, to get to know and to understand what Judaism was about than to pursue individual conversions. The Vatican was also on the verge of a sea change. It reexamined the issue of the Easter prayer for the conversion of the Jews once more in 1955, instructing congregants to kneel during the prayer's recitation and then in 1959, with John XXIII now in charge, suppressing the contested word "*perfidis*" entirely.[45] Jules Isaac did not play a major role in the Finaly Affair. The AJ-C branch in Aix, over which he presided, urged the brothers' return, and that seems to have been the extent of his engagement. Post-Finaly, however, the Church, wanting to repair interfaith relations, came looking for interlocutors in France, and it addressed itself to Isaac first. Father Augustin Bea, the pope's confessor, paid several visits to the hexagon in the late 1950s, cultivating relations with the author of *Jésus et Israël* and, through him, also making the acquaintance of Grand Rabbi Kaplan.[46] In the wake of the Finaly Affair, the Vatican seemed disposed to listen to and respond to Jews and Jewish concerns in a way it had not been previously, and in this measure the Finaly Affair paved the way for Nostra Aetate, Vatican II's ground-breaking declaration on Jewish-Christian relations.

Nostra Aetate

The story of Nostra Aetate's genesis has been told before and told well. A cadre of Jewish converts to Catholicism, many of them German, had been laboring since the interwar decades to reorient Church doctrine on the Jews, and they, with the backing of yet another German, Cardinal Bea (he was elevated to the College of Cardinals by John XXIII in 1959), helped to work out a set of proposals that informed the crafting of Nostra Aetate, passed by the Vatican Council in the fall of 1965 by a crushing majority. The declaration itself repudiated anti-Semitism. It acknowledged what the Church owed to Judaism, and it further acknowledged that the Jews remained "most dear" to God, who had made a promise to them that he still meant to keep. The Jews were, of course, expected to convert someday, but that moment of conversion was postponed to an unspecified future. In the meantime, it was incumbent on the two faiths to enter into fraternal dialogue.[47] On the matter of the "decide" accusation, however, the Church hedged. Nostra Aetate instructed Christians not to hold all Jews responsible, the living and the dead, but it didn't reject the word "deicide" outright, nor did it foreclose the possibility that the Jews of Christ's time, or some portion of them, might be judged as accomplices in the Savior's Crucifixion.

It is still worth revisiting the story in the present context for two reasons. First, it was Jules Isaac who persuaded the Church to address the question of Jewish-Christian relations at all, which had not originally figured on the Vatican II agenda. The conclave encountered meaningful resistance when it took the issue up, which helps to explain its unwillingness to reject the deicide accusation plain and simple. Yet, it acted nonetheless to revise Church teachings on the Jews, with Nostra Aetate as the end product. Propelling it to act were Church Fathers like Bea himself, determined to confront the legacy of the Holocaust directly. Nostra Aetate was in the first instance the result of Isaac's prodding, but in the end, it was elements within the Church itself, conscience-stricken by the Jewish tragedy, who drove the process of doctrinal revision forward to its momentous conclusion.

Daniel and Cletta Mayer, it seems, were the first to float the idea that Isaac seek out an audience with Pope John. They were a remarkable couple, both ex-résistants and senior figures in France's socialist party, who also happened to be Jews. They enlisted the help of another socialist, Vincent Auriol, a former president of the Republic, who undertook to iron out the details of the visit with Vatican authorities. An aging Isaac (he was born in 1877) then traveled to Rome in the company of André Weil, where he met with Pope John XXIII on June 13, 1960.[48]

The meeting lasted twenty minutes, but Isaac made the most of his time. He came prepared with a dossier under his arm containing among other things the Seelisberg points, which he handed over to the pope. Isaac spoke of prejudice against the Jews: of pagan anti-Semitism, of "racist, Hitlerian anti-Semitism," and of the Church's own "teaching of contempt." Last of all, he proposed to the pope that the Vatican Council form a subcommission to study the problem. The atmosphere was cordial. Isaac bowed his head when the two men first met, and they then shook hands. At the end, an expectant Isaac inquired if there was any reason to hope, and the pope replied with words of encouragement, now celebrated: "You have a right to more than hope."[49]

The pope was a good as his word. Two days later, Bea and Isaac talked over the subcommission project at some length, and the cardinal then proceeded to assemble the body, stocking it with theologians favorable to interfaith reconciliation, among them the Jewish convert Johannes Oesterreicher (who was also close to Jacques Maritain).[50] The group understood its brief in broad terms, and that meant tackling the full gamut of issues dividing Christians and Jews, the charge of deicide included. [51]

None of this would have happened had not Isaac, with backing from elements of France's political and Jewish elite, petitioned the papacy to act and had not the Roman Catholic Church, in the aftermath of the Finaly Affair, been prepared to respond. A rocky road, however, still lay ahead.

Traditionalists in Catholic ranks opposed any change, and they cited the Gospels chapter and verse to demonstrate that received Church wisdom on the Jews had got it right from the start. They found allies, moreover, in the Eastern Churches, which had fraught relations with the new state of Israel and weren't at all disposed to make life easier for Jews. The same goes a fortiori for the governments of Syria and Jordan, which threatened retribution in the event the deicide accusation was dropped. It took all of Cardinal Bea's diplomatic and rhetorical skills to keep the issue on the council docket. In the wake of the "appalling crimes of National Socialism against six million Jews," he wrote to the pope in December 1962, the Church was duty-bound to undertake a "purification of spirit and conscience."[52] John XXIII was sensitive to such arguments and stood by Bea.

His successor, however, was less committed. John died in June 1963, just as the council debates were about to begin, and was succeeded by Paul VI. The new pontiff had worked closely with Pius XII during the war and was concerned to protect Pius' reputation. He was also closer to the traditionalists, delivering an Easter Sunday sermon in the spring of 1965 that endorsed the Gospel of Saint John's account of the Crucifixion story and of the Jews' nefarious role in it.[53]

Yet, as draft succeeded draft, the proposal to rethink the deicide question kept resurfacing. The Eichmann trial was not long in the past. Copies of Schwarz-Bart's *Le Dernier des Justes* were spotted on the council table during the debates. Then in February 1963 came the Berlin opening of Rolf Hochhuth's bombshell play, *Der Stellvertreter*.[54] The Holocaust pressed in from all sides, and under the circumstances it proved impossible for the assembled Council Fathers to evade the subject.[55]

Pope Paul VI's visit to the Holy Land in January 1964 provides a clue as to how the matter was to be resolved. The trip was historic – it was the first pontifical expedition outside of Italy in well over a hundred years – and it was brief, lasting just a couple of days. The pope traveled to holy sites and met with prelates of the Eastern Churches. He also met with the president of Israel, though he never publicly mentioned Israel by name, a state the Vatican did not then recognize. As the same time, the pope dispatched the dean of the College of Cardinals, Eugène Tisserant, to Yad Vashem, where Tisserant lit six candles in memory of the six million Jewish dead.[56]

The Eastern Churches and the pope himself were not keen to absolve the Jews of the deicide accusation, yet it was imperative, nonetheless, that the Church deal with the issue, that it acknowledge in some way the catastrophe that had afflicted European Jewry in the Holocaust. Cardinal Bea, it seems, understood that a compromise was unavoidable, whatever his own feelings, and so he turned his efforts to formulating its terms. In the final version of Nostra Aetate, promulgated in 1965, the text made no explicit reference to "deicide," but it did state in plainest terms: "what happened in His passion cannot be charged against all the Jews, without distinction, then alive, nor against the Jews of today."

Jules Isaac died in 1963 and so was not alive to witness the end result of the process he had helped to initiate. But his AJ-C comrades were and so was Grand Rabbi Kaplan. They experienced a mix of emotions in the wake of Vatican II: gratification that the Church had decided to take action but also disappointment and in some cases bitterness that it had refrained from condemning the notion of "deicide" full-throatedly. So, there still remained work to be done, but it was now to be done in a new climate of ecumenicalism. Father Daniélou had crossed oratorical swords with Isaac. The Finaly Affair had placed Father Riquet in a defensive crouch. But there they were in 1966, sharing the podium with Grand Rabbi Kaplan at public events to explicate the changes that Nostra Aetate entailed. In 1969, Daniélou was made a cardinal, and that very same year, the French episcopacy constituted a committee "on relations with Judaism." In 1974, the Vatican set up just such a committee of its own, which a year later issued a set of guidelines detailing how best to disseminate and apply the Church's revised teachings on the Jews.[57]

None of this is to say that the era of controversies was over, far from it, but a Rubicon had been crossed. The Church turned its back on a set of age-old teachings; it revised its liturgy; and it reached out to Jews in a way it had never done before. These decisions were undertaken in the shadow of the Holocaust, and they were undertaken in response to pressures both from within the Church and without. Catholic clergy conducted a dialogue about the catastrophe amongst themselves, but they also entered into dialogue with their Jewish brothers, and it was from both sets of conversations, often testy and full of recrimination, that the Church's change of course came about.

From the Jewish point of view, this was an aggiornamento of epochal significance. There were those who doubted whether interfaith engagement was worth all the effort, but the affirmative resolution of the Finaly Affair, Nostra Aetate, and the rapprochement between Jews and Christians that followed pointed toward a more positive assessment. What resulted from such engagement, moreover, was not just an improvement in interfaith relations, but a greater awareness of the Holocaust itself, in France and beyond, as a Jewish tragedy. It had not been easy to achieve such results, but Jules Isaac and Grand Rabbi Kaplan had persevered, finding Catholic interlocutors, ever more numerous, who were willing to persevere with them.

9 Witnesses

The CDJC had spoken of European Jewry's destruction and lobbied hard to win the Jewish story a recognized place in the narrative of the Deportation. The genocide of the Jews in time acquired a name in its own right, the Holocaust. It came freighted with weighty religious connotations, which is not surprising in light of how much interfaith dialogue had contributed to the diffusion of the notion in the first place. What happened, however, when Jews talked about themselves, not in concert with others, but unaccompanied?

The literature on the Holocaust is punctuated with turning points, and 1961, the year Israel placed Adolf Eichmann on trial, is said to be one of them.[1] Yet, it's worth reflecting for a moment whether the trial made that much of a difference in the French case. France was present at the event in more ways than one. The proceedings opened in April. Georges Wellers testified in May, one of the hundred-plus witnesses called to the bar by Gideon Hausner, the prosecutor. Clips from Resnais and Cayrol's *Nuit et Brouillard* were shown in closed session in June, with the public (but not journalists) excluded. On the matter of press coverage, *Le Monde* dispatched correspondents – first Jean-Marc Théolleyre and then André Scemama – who provided reportage into the summer months. The trial adjourned in August, reconvening briefly in December when the verdict, a death sentence, was handed down. *Le Monde* also covered the sentencing. So the trial was reported on, although as a rule the stories didn't make the front page, and little wonder. The Algerian War was in full throttle, and in April, just as the hearings were getting underway, a military putsch in Algiers threatened to topple France's constitutional order.[2]

The Eichmann trial was not just a journalistic event, but also an electronic one. Radio reporting on the proceedings gripped the Israeli public's imagination. The Israeli government, moreover, made a supreme effort to provide television coverage to the world, contracting with an American production company for that purpose, which in turn hired the documentarist Leo Hurwitz to direct. The trial was filmed and

287

the reels sent abroad for retransmission. Hurwitz's innovative camera placement enabled viewers to take in the celebrated courtroom mise-en-scène, the man in the glass booth and all, and the visuals were riveting.[3] The drama of the event engrossed television audiences in the United States and Germany, but it is not clear that the same happened in France. Wellers' testimony was broadcast, that much is certain.[4] Overall, however, historians have yet to pin down just how much television time was devoted to the proceedings, and with what impact.[5] The French public, it may be ventured, was aware of the Eichmann trial, but less so than publics elsewhere, in part because it had other matters on its mind and in part because the TV coverage appears not to have been as thorough.

France's Jewish community, however, was paying attention. In March 1961, at the moment the Eichmann trial was beginning in Jerusalem, *L'Arche* interviewed eight authors, a mix of Jews and non-Jews, putting the identical question to them all: Was it possible to write a fictional treatment of "the concentrationary tragedy"?[6] The framing of the question attests to the enduring hold of the concentrationary paradigm, even among Jews. It wasn't just Eichmann's impending prosecution that occasioned the inquiry. Schwarz-Bart's *Le Dernier des Justes* won the Prix Goncourt in 1959. The next year, *Le Sel et le soufre*, a novel by a newcomer to France's literary scene, Anna Langfus, took home the Prix Charles Veillon. Neither Schwarz-Bart's book, nor Langfus' was in fact a concentrationary text. Schwarz-Bart's narrative ends in the camps, but it is not set there. Langfus' unfolds in Nazi-occupied Poland. The protagonist, Maria, is never deported, but lives through a nightmarish odyssey that takes her from a bourgeois Jewish home in an unnamed Polish city through a series of ordeals: ghettoization, flight, capture, torture, imprisonment, and flight once more. Her journey ends where it began, with a return "home," now no longer a middle-class sanctuary but an empty shell, its former inhabitants all murdered except for Maria herself.

What *L'Arche* did get right was that the first years of the 1960s constituted a representational crossroads. Authors like Schwarz-Bart had created an opening for narratives about the Jewish tragedy, one that was seized on and exploited by others. Langfus was one of these, and *Le Sel et le soufre* was just the beginning. She wrote two more novels: *Les Bagages de sable* (1962), a Prix Goncourt winner in its own right, and *Saute, Barbara* (1965). Langfus, moreover, was not alone. Piotr Rawicz published *Le Sang du ciel* in 1961, a riotous, antinomian rewriting of *Le Sel et le soufre* (more on that presently), which was also a prizewinner, garnering the Prix Rivarol for best French-language novel written by a foreign author. The very same year, 1961, the television director Frédéric Rossif released *Le Temps du ghetto*, a documentary study of life in the

Warsaw Ghetto. The movie was a first in many ways. It was the first French documentary ever to treat the Jewish tragedy as an event unto itself.[7] It was the first to make ample use of survivor testimony and was, in fact, distributed in the United States under the title, *The Witnesses*.[8] It was also the first of its kind to air on French TV, this in 1964, thanks to Rossif's connections in the television world.[9] Langfus for one was shaken up by *Le Temps du ghetto* and said as much in a review published in *L'Arche*: "I lived these images. They are my past, my agony, my fear."[10]

Langfus' reaction is revelatory as to why the early 1960s were such a watershed. All these works were executed by Jews – and Jews who had direct knowledge of the Holocaust. Langfus' own life experience was not so different from that of Maria. Rawicz was deported to Auschwitz. Rossif, born to a family of Yugoslavian Jews, lost both parents and a sister to the genocide. And the art that Langfus, Rawicz, and Rossif created attracted genuine public interest. It was not overlooked but won recognition and accolades. Perhaps most important of all, all three artists spoke about the Holocaust in a new key. Langfus' *Le Sel et le soufre* concluded in loss and desolation. Rawicz's text was transgressive and ironic. Rossif's movie called up memories of anguish and fear. This was a Holocaust without heroes, an event dark and devastating, a catastrophe unredeemed.

But note how the Eichmann trial has begun to recede from the focus of attention. It helped to augment the Jewish voice, but did not create it. That was the work of writers and filmmakers who pried wider the representational window that pioneers like Wiesel and Schwarz-Bart had cracked open. Out of interfaith dialogue, a solo voice took flight, one that articulated the story of the Jewish catastrophe in the most somber tones. From this angle, the emergence of Holocaust conscious-ness has less to do with turning points – though these still matter as accelerators – than with the changing character of the story told, and by that is meant not just what was said but the way it was said, a line of analysis that will highlight just how pathbreaking the early 1960s work of Langfus, Rawicz, and Rossif really was.

The Jew as Hero

L'Arche's 1961 inquiry laid bare deep differences among the writers consulted. One of the participants was Manès Sperber, author of ... *qu'une larme dans l'océan*, published in 1952. The book is a fictionalized account of a Jewish partisan revolt in the Nazi-occupied East, and so it's only natural that Sperber spoke up for the virtues of fictionalization. There is, however, a narrowness to the position he defended. A novel,

Sperber argued, above all one that dealt with the fate of the Jews, needed a hero, an active agent prepared to take up the fight: "For the novelist, as for the philosopher, the meaning of this catastrophe becomes clear only at the moment when, in the forests of Poland and in the Warsaw Ghetto, the living dead [*les morts en sursis*] transform themselves into uncompromising combatants."[11]

Such views help explain Sperber's deep distaste for André Schwarz-Bart's *Le Dernier des Justes*. Ernie Levy was too much the suffering martyr. It didn't help that Schwarz-Bart's book was such a breakthrough success, which grated on Sperber, vexed that a novelist just starting out and still so young had achieved a level of recognition that eluded a veteran like himself (Sperber was born in 1905). According to rumor, the older writer found a chance to take his revenge, helping to compile a damning dossier on *Le Dernier des Justes*, which a hostile reviewer used to write a slashing critique.[12]

It bears considering whether Sperber's novelistic practices lived up to the heroic standard he set, and they did ... or almost. His book ... *qu'une larme dans l'océan* tells of the fate of the Jews of Wolyna, a town in eastern Poland. They are rounded up by the Germans, a remnant taking refuge in a nearby forest. Rubin, an atheist city Jew and man of action, endeavors to mobilize the Jews to defend themselves, first against the Nazis and then against anti-Semitic Polish partisans, but to little effect. The Jewish community of Wolyna is decimated, and as the story ends, Rubin departs for Palestine, ever the fighter. The novel included a preface by André Malraux, a fitting choice for a narrative with an action hero at its center.[13]

In fact, however, ... *qu'une larme dans l'océan* was more complicated than that, for Rubin has a foil, indeed, two. The first is Wolyna's Tsaddik, a venerable religious man who urges the town Jews to accept the martyr's fate that awaits them. The second is Bynie, the Tsaddik's son, who joins Rubin in the forest but is not himself much of a combatant, opting at a critical moment to observe the Sabbath rather than to build barricades against marauding Polish partisans. Yet, Bynie is also a man of childlike innocence. Wounded by the Polish partisans, he hides out in a convent and there begins to work miracles, or so the credulous locals believe. They imagine Bynie, so young and yet so wise, to have curative powers, and for whatever reason, the sick children brought to him by the local peasants do heal. He will die of his own injuries, nonetheless: his is not the path to the future. But what Bynie represents – an intense and centered faith – holds an unmistakable appeal, complicating the novel's dominant theme of a call to arms.

Political militancy leavened by a lingering regard for the religious sensibilities of old: that amalgam was very much Sperber's own. He was born before the Great War into an observant Polish-Jewish family but turned to activism as a young man, enlisting first in the Hashomer Hatzair and then, after moving to Berlin, in the German Communist Party. He parted ways with the Party in the late 1930s, yet remained a man of the Left. He also retained, as a recent evocation has reminded us, an enduring attachment to "the Jewish identity of his childhood years."[14]

Anna Langfus

Such complexities, however, were not manifest in Sperber's *prise de position* in *L'Arche*. There, he presented himself as an unalloyed advocate of the good fight, and on that score, Anna Langfus, for one, had a different position to stake out. People were flawed, she believed, and to convey the tragedy of their circumstances, there was no need to idealize them. Victimization did not make a saint of the sufferer; he remained, as she put it, "a man who suffers, that's all."[15]

A second bone of contention divided the writers, and on this one as well Langfus had something original to say. A couple of the authors – Louis Martin-Chauffier and Elie Wiesel – wrote of the necessity of bearing witness. It was the author's duty to recount what he had seen and endured in the camps, a responsibility that disallowed fictionalization. Langfus by contrast thought it was critical for writers to maintain "distance." It's not that "raw documents" were incapable of conveying the truth of human pain. In Langfus' view, Anne Frank's diary was a case in point, because there was no denying how touched readers were by its simplicity and candor. Yet oftentimes, she reflected, it was more effective to come at the subject by indirection through "litotes," "reticence," and "ellipsis."[16] There were moments when mere description proved inadequate to communicate the pain of profound loss. Distance, reticence, and a refusal of idealization – these would be the hallmarks of Langfus' own fiction. Her protagonists are not heroes, but imperfect beings ground down by cruelty. They toil to reconnect to a life scarred by the death of loved ones, and they fail at the task.

Langfus knew of what she wrote, though she had more success than her characters in navigating a way out of the despondency brought on by wartime loss. She was born Anna Szternfinkiel in Lublin into a well-off family. Anna married young to Jakub Rajs, and the newlyweds spent a year in prewar Belgium, where Jakub studied engineering. The outbreak of hostilities brought an end to happy days. Anna and Jakub were confined to the Lublin Ghetto, as were the Szternfinkiel parents, who did not survive the war. Anna and her husband, however, were more fortunate, at least for a while, contriving to escape the ghetto and join the Polish Resistance. They were pursued by the Germans, hid out in a forest, and then were captured. Jakub Rajs was executed, but Anna succeeded in persuading the Germans that she was Catholic, not Jewish, and wound up in prison instead. At the end of the war, Anna Rajs, now alone in the world, emigrated to Paris and started anew. She married a hometown boy, Aron Langfus, who had also emigrated to France, and they had a daughter, Maria, named after Anna's dead mother. "Whether you want it or not," she said of the decision, "they live on in you."[17] Langfus involved herself in Jewish intellectual life, doing interviews and reviews for *L'Arche*. She also molded herself into a writer, first of plays and then of novels. Langfus took to the French language, developing a special admiration for the *mesure* of the classics. To write about the life that was taken from her, she craved distance. The foreignness of French and the restraint of the classical style afforded Langfus the detachment she was looking for.[18]

A fatal heart attack cut short Langfus' career in 1966, but not before she had completed a trio of novels. A protagonist stands at the heart of each, and all three of them are shattered beings. There is not a Job, a saint, or a ghetto fighter among the group. They have fought just to survive. Survival amidst crushing loss is their sole reward, and they have the psychic scars to show for it.

The first of Langfus' protagonists was Maria, the main character in *Le Sel et le soufre*. As the novel opens, she enjoys the self-centered satisfactions of a young woman raised in middle-class comfort, but that world is blown apart in the book's very first pages. The war has begun, and Maria's hometown (never identified) is under bombardment, one bomb splintering into shards the glass chandelier that hangs in the family dining room. With home destroyed in symbol as in fact, Maria's wanderings begin. She is not alone at first, but accompanied by family members and by the man she loves, Jacques. The parents are soon left behind, destined to be swallowed up in the Nazi killing machine. Jacques and Maria flee here and there, at one point posing as Christian Poles. They encounter German soldiers in a forest, and at first the masquerade succeeds. The pair are invited to join a genteel Nazi soirée, which gathers, the narrator tells us, in a "baroque room, amid Germans who are killing Jews, and not so far away Poles who have a gift for recognizing Jews and an appetite for denouncing them."[19] The atmosphere is disturbing and hallucinatory. A ghetto is burning not far off, the assembled revelers learn, while Maria herself is swept up in the dizzying whirl of a waltz with a German officer.

Then Jacques is found out to be a Jew, and Maria, as his partner, also falls under suspicion. They are tortured. He is beaten in front of her to make her talk, and, under the pressure, she begins to unravel, hearing a voice shout out, one that she suspects is in fact her own. Jacques dies, and Maria is now all by herself. She is no longer the self-regarding girl she was at the novel's beginning, but a hardened and resourceful survivor. She has survived torture; she has survived the death of the people she loved most; and she will survive prison too, where the Germans, persuaded at last she is the Catholic she pretends to be, confine her.

At the war's end, Maria will make her way back to the family home through a lawless and war-devastated landscape. The place is now occupied by others, but she enters still and finds her way to the basement, where she discovers her nursemaid's trunk. It is empty when she looks inside. The life she had known in childhood has vanished. Maria embraces the object. It is part cradle, part coffin, all that remains of the shipwreck of a former life. (It is hard for an American reader not to think of Ishmael clinging to Queequeg's coffin in the final scene of Melville's *Moby Dick*.) She hears herself crying as she hugs the trunk and then falls asleep. When Maria next awakens, it is still dark, but she knows a new day is beginning, the first "of those numberless days that remain for me to live up top."[20] She has been condemned to life, and with that the novel concludes.[21]

Le Sel et le soufre has the look of a Bildungsroman. Its protagonist matures over the course of the action, discovering unsuspected inner resources along the way. Critics then and since have said as much, recognizing at the same time that Maria's apprenticeship is not a story of growth but of psychic dislocation.[22] She soldiers on but becomes more and more estranged from herself and more and more unmoored from life. The protagonist's transformation unfolds in an atmosphere more dreamlike than real. Langfus provides neither dates nor place names, with the result that the narrative reads less like a transcription of events than an exploration of Maria's fragmenting inner life. The novel's circular construction, ending in the same location as it started, underlines just how much she has lost as a consequence of what she's had to go through. Maria is marooned in the world, robbed of loved ones. The future lies before her, a desolate, burned-over landscape. In Deuteronomy (29:23), the Lord threatens Israelites who fail to keep the Covenant with a blast of salt and brimstone, like the leveling blaze that he had rained down on Sodom and Gomorrah. For Maria, the Lord's curse has come to pass. Langfus' biblical citation is not to be understood as an injunction to remain faithful in order to forestall God's wrath. There is no transcendent backdrop to the novel. What Langfus is evoking is the epic proportion of the survivor's loss. She is alone and disoriented in the world, and all that lies before her is a joyless future.

Many contemporaries read Langfus' novel as a testimony, but it is more than that. It is a hard-nosed investigation of the fractured psychology of a survivor, and Langfus would deepen that line of investigation in her next two novels.[23] Both are set in the aftermath of the war and both framed as first-person narratives. The narrator in *Les Bagages de sable* is Maria, the same character as in *Le Sel et le soufre*, now grown older. Lest there be any doubt, *Les Bagages de sable* opens with a scene – a hallucination – that draws a direct connection to the earlier text. Maria returns to her Paris apartment and there finds waiting for her the specters of her parents and of her lover, Jacques, with whom she converses.

The protagonist of *Saute, Barbara* is someone new, a Polish Jew named Michael. He has fought as a partisan and finds himself in postwar Berlin, now a soldier of occupation decked out in a Russian uniform. Michael is an embittered man, haunted by the loss of a wife and of a daughter, Barbara. In partisan days, the Nazis had come to the family apartment in Lublin, hunting for him. He escaped through a window, while they were taken away and murdered.

In certain respects, the two novels call to mind Charlotte Delbo's later work. There is the same effort to plumb the challenges of life "afterwards" and to write from a different perspective, from that of a Jew as Delbo had done in *Mesure de nos jours*, from that of a man as Langfus did in *Saute, Barbara*. But Delbo is always buoyed by a sense of the collectivity and its power to provide emotional sustenance, even if meager, to the exposed individual. For Langfus, there are no such consolations. Her protagonists are solitary when the stories begin, and they are solitary at the end, weighed down by leaden memories that numb the soul, as in Maria's case, or that poison it, as in Michael's.

The Maria of *Les Bagages de sable* makes an attempt to rebuild a life in spite all she has lost, but she fails. At the novel's outset, she is an isolate who keeps company with ghosts. Maria playacts at living, all the while contemplating suicide. Things seem to take a turn for the better when she meets an older gentleman, Caron. He pursues her, and they strike up a relationship and head south for a beach holiday. At the shore, Maria falls in with a band of young people, including a fourteen-year-old girl, Anny, who reminds Maria of herself, as she had been before the war. Between Maria, Caron, and Anny, it's as though a new family has risen from the ashes of the old one.[24] But then Anny drowns in ambiguous circumstances. She may have died by accident, or it might have been a suicide. It next turns out that Caron has a wife, who shows up to put a stop to the affair. The vacation idyll thus comes to an abrupt end. Maria packs her bags to return home. She departs for Paris, not a light-hearted ex-vacationer, but an isolate once more, who has taken a stab at living but missed the mark. The burden she has to carry, now with the addition of a suitcase full of sand, is all the greater.

The novel was short, clocking in at just over two hundred pages, and the prose was sober and uncluttered. Langfus did not break the narrative into sections or chapters, but laid it out in a single, uninterrupted jet. The reader was invited to enter into the flow of Maria's consciousness and to experience alongside her the dull throb of melancholia. The public, it seems, responded to the invitation, because the novel sold well, an estimated 150,000 copies in its first months. Critics liked it as well. *Les Bagages de sable* won the 1962 Prix Goncourt. Claude Roy, writing in *Libération*, ranked Langfus in the same class as Cayrol, Duras, and Camus.[25]

The Camus comparison was raised again when Langfus' final novel was published, and for obvious reasons.[26] The central character in *Saute, Barbara* bears a passing resemblance to Meursault, the protagonist of Camus' *L'Étranger* (1942). Both men are detached beings, drifting through life, and both commit a murder. That, however, is as far as the parallels go, for Michael is no Existentialist antihero, but a survivor crushed beneath a survivor's guilt.

Michael is also, in many ways, a despicable figure. When the story opens, he is wandering through a bombed-out Berlin, "that enemy city," as he calls it later in the novel.[27] Michael is in a cold fury, and his anger focuses first on a stray cat, which he kills with his bare hands. He then comes upon a little girl, Minna, skipping rope. She is terrified at Michael's approach, which pleases him. He has come to Berlin for just that reason, to strike terror in the German city's children. Michael kidnaps the frightened child and flees to Paris. There, he poses as a concentration camp survivor, passing off Minna, now renamed Barbara, as his daughter. The refugee authorities take pity on him with an unctuous condescension that Michael secretly disdains. They find him a job with a Jewish furrier, Mr. Roth, a fatuous man who takes a liking to his new employee. Roth is also the doting father of Leah and encourages a romance between the young woman and Michael. Michael plays along, even though he has no deep feelings for her, and, for a moment, he imagines that a new life is about to begin, that he will recover the family he lost back in Poland. He also knows that he's just playing a part, and that the whole courtship, indeed, everything that he is pretending to be, is a sham. Such then are our hero's distinguishing traits: he's a cat-killer, a kidnapper, and an impostor.

It is just as clear that Michael is a man in deep pain, and the reader is told at the outset why. When the Nazis came for him in Lublin, he fled through the window. He was frightened, but his wife urged him to go, calling out "Jump, jump."[28] He jumped, he abandoned his family, and they, not he, were killed. Michael survived, but he is now a hollowed-out being, anguished by loss and self-accusation. It is an awful fate, which deforms his personality and turns him cruel. When first arrived in Paris, while still looking for a place to live, Michael comes upon a vagrant. He tells Minna/Barbara to skip rope for the man (she has brought her jump rope from Berlin), and when the child balks, he commands over and over again, "Jump," until she is reduced to tears.[29] If only Michael's wife and daughter had jumped as he had done, they too might have survived, but they did not, and so the pretend Barbara, whether she likes it or not, is made to jump in their stead.

In the end, Michael does not go through with the cruel farce he has enmeshed himself in. He does not marry Leah but takes Minna/Barbara back to Berlin. The child, still with jump rope in hand, is restored to her family. As for Michael, he has reached a dead end. The final scene finds him seated, still in Berlin. A stranger approaches, asking the time. The man has a crisp hair part and a military bearing. He's a real German. Michael pulls out a gun, a service revolver from Russian army days, and shoots the man.

Saute, Barbara is a grim and depressing novel. Like *Le Sel et le soufre*, it is circular in construction. The survivor does not progress in life but, quite the contrary, learns that what has been lost – home, family – cannot be recovered, a pitiless lesson that is not a source of strength but of despair. As a character, Michael is more like the Maria of *Les Bagages de sable* than the adaptive Maria of *Le Sel et le soufre*. He, like she, pretends to live; both are doubled selves who act out parts, even as they watch themselves play at normality. Michael, however, is no melancholic. He is angry, guilt-ridden, and violent. Langfus was uncompromising in her explorations of the survivor sensibility. She was not interested in heroic, redemptive action, but in the genocide's ravaging impact on those who outlived it. This is realism of a sort, a tough-minded, psychological realism that refuses pathos and the comforts of sentiment and solidarity.

Piotr Rawicz

Anna Langfus and Piotr Rawicz had occasion to meet. Langfus' publisher, Gallimard, also published *Le Sang du ciel*, which came out in 1961. It stirred an immediate scandal. The editors at *L'Arche* took note, writing of the novel's "black humor" and "sacrilege," and the journal dispatched Langfus to talk with the author. The interview did not go well.

Langfus might well have gone into the encounter with suspicions about Rawicz. In plot design, Rawicz's novel pastiches in obvious ways Langfus' *Le Sel et le soufre*. *Le Sang du ciel* recounts the wartime tribulations of a Ukrainian Jew, Boris, in a three-part narrative. In the first, Boris is locked up in an unnamed ghetto. In the second, he takes flight under an assumed name, Yuri Goletz, in the company of his partner Naomi, the two posing as a married Christian couple. They encounter a cultivated German officer; they find work in a convalescent home for wounded German soldiers; and then, fearing discovery, they take flight once more. The novel's final part opens with the arrest of Boris/Yuri (Naomi escapes). The Germans believe him to be a Polish Jew masquerading as a Christian and torture him to wring out a confession. Boris/Yuri holds out and is at last released.

It is easy to imagine that Langfus might have felt some ambivalence about a novel that was in rough outline a replica of her own. As for the interview itself, Rawicz seemed to revel in the perverse. He had interpolated poetry into *Le Sang du ciel*, and, as he told a nonplussed Langfus, those poetic interludes were what mattered most to him in the text. Eichmann was no doubt a "scumbag [*crapule*]," but he, Rawicz, didn't wish to see the man executed. There was no such thing as a good person, the interviewee remonstrated, and humans, Eichmann included, had more in common than not. Not least of all, Rawicz spoke about the war years as a welcome revelation of the universe's true nature. The era, he said, had allowed him to enter into "the Garden": "this war is for me one of the proofs of God's existence." What was Edenic about the war? Langfus was bound to wonder, and what for that matter did the catastrophe that landed on the Jews have to do with demonstrating God's existence?

Rawicz presented himself in the interview as a norm-busting artist who repudiated conventions, whether literary or moral. Yet he also presented himself as a believing Jew who felt, as he put it, a deep and abiding "love for Jews and Judaism." Langfus seemed glad to have the interview over, and Rawicz was too. He expressed relief at the end that Langfus hadn't asked him, as so many previous interviewers had, about the parallels between *Le Sang du ciel* and the New Novel. As to how the disparate pieces of Rawicz's life and oeuvre fit together and what, if anything, he owed to writers like Langfus herself, all that was left up to the reader to sort out.[30]

For, in truth, Rawicz and Langfus had much in common. He was an East European Jew (from Lvov, not Lublin) who had been hunted down by the Nazi behemoth. He survived thanks to a quick wit and an exceptional mastery of the region's languages – that and an "Aryan" appearance, which allowed him to pass as a Christian Ukrainian. The war once over, he wedded Anka, a longtime partner and fellow survivor, and the two made their way to Paris. What sustained him there were many of the same things that had sustained Langfus: marriage, the sociability of fellow Jews, and literature. When he himself sat down to write, the language he chose to write in – and Rawicz, like Langfus had more than one option – was French.

That, however, is where the similarities ended. Rawicz's war included an extended stay in a concentration camp. In 1942, he was detained in a German roundup. Even under interrogation, he stuck to the story that he was a Christian, and the ploy worked, up to a point. The Germans dispatched him to Auschwitz, but as a Christian, not a Jew, which boosted Rawicz's chances of making it through, and he did. Relocated to Paris after the war, Rawicz's constructed a new life that was more bohemian than conventional. Langfus took up residence in a housing block in the modern Paris suburb of Sarcelles. Rawicz, by contrast, made a beeline for the Latin Quarter and fell in with a brilliant but also sometimes troubled crowd. His wife, who went by an adopted name, Anne Dastrée, was a filmmaker, who helped to promote the career of a still very young Roman Polanski.[31] Rawicz himself befriended Elie Wiesel, with whom he was known to attend Yom Kippur services. He also befriended Jerzy Kosinski, a fellow writer and celebrated poseur.[32] All of them led lives raked over by the Holocaust. All were creative spirits. As for troubles, Polanski remains to this day sought after by American law enforcement for crimes committed against an underage teenager. Kosinski ended a suicide and so, for that matter, did Rawicz who took his own life in 1982.

Rawicz' literary tastes befitted the life that he lived. Not for him the French classics: he preferred the absurd and the cruel – Alfred Jarry, Raymond Queneau, Eugène Ionesco, Jean Genet.[33] When it came time to writing in French, he rejected the restraint and understatement that Langfus valued so much for a prose that caromed between the monstrous and the lyrical. Rawicz's novel was not a probing, serious-minded exploration of the survivor's mental disorientation and breakdown. It was rather a deranging evocation of one man's journey through a world perverse in its construction and effects. The hero of the narrative, Boris, was in fact not much of a hero, and Boris' narrative, full of scenes of sex, horror, and a crazed hilarity, was designed not to convince the reader of its truth but rather to rattle the reader's very grasp of what the truth was.

Rawicz detested Leon Uris' *Exodus*. He didn't like its "stylistic conformism," the way it spoke of criminals, torturers, and victims, deploying an impoverished vocabulary that imparted an easy dramatic clarity to the action. The action itself, as he saw it, was the standard stuff of best-sellers, a hodgepodge of bargain basement theatricality and manipulation that cheapened the event it was supposed to describe.[34]

Rawicz was determined to proceed otherwise. In *Le Sang du ciel*, the ghetto is not named as such. It is the "forbidden place." The Nazis are "the invader" or "the hunters" and the Jews, "my people" or "the prey." The allusive character of the language pares back the text's specificity, transforming the narrative itself in the process into something more abstract, more surreal. And what of that narrative? The story opens at a café on the boulevard Montparnasse. A manuscript is turned over to the "author." It's said to have been written by Boris/Yuri, who sometimes composes in the first person, sometimes in the third. Boris/Yuri has incorporated into it poetry and passages from the diary of a fellow ghetto-dweller named David G., a young psychopath with whom Boris/Yuri once worked in the ghetto hospital. Then the "author" tells us that he has corrected and amended the text in various unidentified places. At the very end, we are returned once more to the boulevard Montparnasse, but now the "author" is no longer so authorial. He is more like a street vendor who has laid out his wares or a beggar who cadges small change or a cigarette in compensation for a story well told. How true is this story, we have to ask ourselves, given its source and construction?

Then there is our "hero," Boris/Yuri, a complex character to say the least. He frequents the ghetto chief, Leon L., a skilled word-spinner who does the Germans' bidding, selecting and rounding up fellow Jews for deportation. Still in ghetto days, Boris finds a sheltered job for himself in a hospital, and there becomes friendly with David G., a disturbed young man who likes to masturbate and tells of killing the family cat to exasperate a mother whom he hates. Boris himself is a man of robust sexual appetites. Not ten pages into the novel, as the town Jews on Nazi command gather in a central square, Boris eyes a band of young girls "whose hips and breasts were beginning to round out." He knows they are all doomed, and the feeling that the scene arouses in him is at once horrible and repellant. It is jealousy, "jealousy ... of the flame that in my stead will lick these breasts and hips to death."[35] A little further on, the Germans come upon an improvised ghetto kindergarten hidden away in a factory, and Boris happens to be present. One of the children sticks a tongue out at the Nazis, and they slice it off. The Germans then run amok. Boris tries to shield a little girl, and a Nazi gouges out her eyes, placing the bloody orbs, once sparkling diamonds, into Boris' hands.

"It's only the Creator," Boris thinks in a flash, "who in His wealth and His prodigality would allow such a waste!" This is followed by a scene of unspeakable horror, as the Germans do their worst: "The belly of the Universe, the belly of Being split open, its filthy guts spilling into the room." The Nazis massacre all the children, forty of them, and rape and murder their teachers. Boris is invited by a German corporal to join in the appalling bacchanal, issuing a veiled threat in the event he does not. "Boris," the author tells us, "doesn't say whether he declined the invitation."[36]

Yet Boris, implicated as he is in the horrors of the ghetto, is also capable of more tender feelings. He loves the people of his town, "my people," with all their bizarreries and flaws. What he feels for Naomi is carnal, but it is also something more caring than that. Finally, as the novel careers toward its conclusion, Yuri is captured and assigned to a prison cell filled with fellow Jews. Among them are a young couple, both partisans, and the man has been wounded. Yuri describes the injury this way: "What status it bestowed on the young man among people like ourselves who have never touched a weapon. It shines resplendently like the burning candles at the feast of Hanukkah."[37]

Rawicz himself, however irreverent he tried to be, still reverenced what he called "*Netzach Yisrael*," a mystical term from the Hebrew, signifying the eternity or enduring personality of the Jewish people.[38] In *Le Sang du ciel*, he found an image to convey that everlastingness, one borrowed from Jewish tradition (and also from André Schwarz-Bart). The Nazis have set a ghetto work team to breaking up Jewish tombstones. Boris sees the Hebrew inscriptions smashed to dust and asks what will become of them as they are scattered under the sledgehammer's blows and take flight. Will the sacred letters explode like avenging cannon fire when they come into contact with the profane world? Will they reconstitute themselves to create a new community in parts as yet unknown?[39] Whatever happens, they will not disappear without a trace. In one form or another, they, like the Jewish people, will go on.

Rawicz's narrative is an unstable one. Its central character is a mixed figure, capable of depth of feeling, but also implicated in the monstrousness he's witnessing. Those monstrous scenes, moreover, begin to multiply in the novel's middle passages, compounding the reader's disquiet. The most monstrous of them all takes place in the second part when Boris, now Yuri, and Naomi are in flight. They take up with a German lieutenant, a cultivated man, who invites them to the officer's mess and talks to them of theosophy. Yuri looks out the window and sees a cabbage patch. A cook is emptying garbage; there are pigs gobbling it up and chewing on the cabbage heads; a German soldier pisses on one of them.

Then the scene, so normal at first glance, comes into ghastly focus. These are not cabbages at all but human heads, the bodies buried up to the neck. The horror of the spectacle causes Yuri to step out of character for a moment and smash the window. The visual horror then becomes an aural one. Yuri hears "a dampened sound, half-rasped, half-sung which came from as far away as the stars." It is the words of the Shema.[40]

This scene unfolds just over halfway through the novel, marking a nadir. It's not that the tone then turns toward the upbeat, but other registers are explored. *Le Sang du ciel* sparked scandal for its frankness in dealing with matters of the body. Some of this has to do with Boris' self-proclaimed lustfulness, but most of all it has to do with his penis, which is called on to perform a star turn in the novel's final part. It opens with Yuri's capture. The Germans make him drop his pants, exposing what the text calls Yuri's "bluish shaft" with the sign of the Covenant inscribed upon it.[41] Yuri has an explanation: he is not circumcised because he is the Polish Jew the Germans believe him to be but because he'd had a venereal disease that required the operation by way of a cure. The Germans beat him to make him confess that he's lying; he's imprisoned; and Yuri plumbs the depths of abjection, at one point attempting suicide. All the while, officials come and go, inspecting Yuri's pathetic member. Rawicz at first proposed titling the novel, *Histoire de la queue*, "*queue*" in this instance meaning rod, tool, or dick in French slang.[42] Gallimard vetoed the idea, but he did succeed in naming the book's first part "The Rod or the art of comparing" and its third "The Rod and the failure of comparisons."

Abjection will mutate into comedy in the novel's closing portion. The hinge moment is a scene taken straight out of Wiesel. Yuri's German tormentors put him in front of a mirror. He hasn't seen himself in over two months, and in the face he gazes on, swollen from beatings, he recognizes qualities in himself he has not recognized before. It is the face of a man of dubious character, the kind who might cuckold another. It is the face of a sly dog, and that vision is, as the narrator characterizes it, "a liberation."[43] Yuri will apply his wits to the matter of survival. He spills to the Germans all right. He doesn't tell them that he's a Jew, however, or even a Pole. Rather, he claims to be a Ukrainian and a fanatic nationalist at that. Yuri's captors still keep an eye on his penis but now bring in a learned Ukrainian to put Yuri's new identity to the test. Yuri speaks the language, reveals an insider's knowledge of Ukrainian literary culture, and outsmarts his examiner at every turn, even reproaching the gentleman for working with the Germans, which a true patriot like Yuri himself would never do. The scheme works. Yuri's wits and language skills rescue him, and the novel concludes with what the narrator calls, using the English, a "happy end."[44]

The notion, of course, is drenched in irony. The attentive reader will have followed Yuri/Boris downward into an abyss of horror, and part of what makes the novel so disturbing is that the horror Rawicz lays out before us is not just man-made but has a cosmic dimension. There is a Creator, a Being, behind it all, and that Being is wasteful of the beauties of creation. After Yuri is captured by the "invader," he is imprisoned, first with Jews, then with Poles, who mock and humiliate him. Out of these depths, a realization wells up: God is mad. What other way, Yuri reflects, is there to conceive of him in a world so hard-hearted: "... a NORMAL God, a God who wasn't mad, would that be endurable?"[45] Where then does that leave an insignificant creature like himself, "an exhausted insect," as the text characterizes him? Yuri then proposes a commandment of his own: "Let each and every one fall crazy in love with each and every one, with him, with her. Let each and every one rise to a height worthy of MY God: to a crime of passion, to a suicide of passion! May the Universe consume itself in a perpetual orgasm, in the ultimate crime passionnel!"[46]

The ravings of a man at the end of his rope? Maybe not, for in more ways than one they approximate Rawicz's own way of thinking about existence. God, as he saw it, was mad as a hatter, "fit to be tied," and he was cruel. "In the beginning, God created suffering": such was Rawicz's rewriting of the Bible's opening verse.[47]

Rawicz never wrote another novel, but he did follow up *Le Sang du ciel* some years later with *Bloc-notes d'un contre-révolutionnaire* (1969), a curious mélange made up of Rawicz's own ruminations about Latin Quarter life and the events of May 1968 (which he detested), interspersed with the sayings of local friends and acquaintances. In it, Rawicz continues to reflect on the human condition in a universe ruled over by an unhinged divinity. One of the characters he crosses paths with, S.N., has this to say on the subject: "Men are congenital idiots. Otherwise ... they would have committed suicide right at the start, on the doorstep of creation. They would have refused the guinea pig's role that a celestial kapo, some assistant god has assigned them to."[48]

In this light, it becomes clearer why Rawicz referred to his Auschwitz years with flippant gratitude. It was in that pit that the true nature of Creation in all its cruelty was revealed to him.

Yet the revelation did not drive Rawicz to utter despair, because human beings had contrived to find supports even in a world so designed. There was sex first of all. As Serge D., one of Rawicz's Latin Quarter companions put it: "Orgasm is God's only true ambassador in this base world."[49] Then there was writing itself, an act, like sex, that fended off the solitude that he felt was the lot of all humans, none more than himself. Rawicz did indeed feel borne down on by loneliness, not just as a human being, but also as a Jew on whom the world had turned its back.[50]

Which raises the question of the Jews' place in Rawicz' ontology, and it was, as might be imagined, an exceptional one. The Jews, he told a 1974 conference, were like everyone else, just a little more so. They were an "ontological concentrate," an essence of humanity, and God took advantage of their all-too-humanness to conduct an experiment.[51] Rawicz explained its purpose this way: "to determine how far He could go in the treatment of the human species. The Jewish condition was thus the human condition pushed to its farthest extreme—an exploration, forced or voluntary, of limits."[52]

There is no heroism and little even of consolation in such a vision. Not just the individual Jew, but the Jews as a people, stand alone in a universe that has singled them out for an exemplary fate. Yet, blaspheming as Rawicz was, he remained in his idiosyncratic way a believing Jew, one who believed in the everlastingness of Israel and in the existence of a God, however demented and pitiless. His tastes in literature ran to the absurd and the cruel, but he was also a Bible reader, and it will come as no surprise which books he liked best: Ecclesiastes, with its hard-earned, fatalist wisdom, and, of course, The Song of Songs, which clad holiness in the language of eroticism.[53]

Frédéric Rossif

Frédéric Rossif was as resolute as Langfus and Rawicz in his refusal of heroism. Rossif's documentary on the Warsaw Ghetto includes an account of the ghetto revolt, and in the making of the film, he in fact consulted with a genuine hero of the uprising, Antek (Yitzhak Zuckerman). Yet, the movie begins and ends with documentary footage of the ghetto in ruins. In addition to such footage, Rossif included the testimony of thirty-two witnesses, and Antek himself is not one of them. The director had made a conscious choice to find ordinary men and women to testify. As he told an interviewer: "I refused to retell the story of martyrdom. I was determined to present witnesses who were men and not heroes."[54] The result was a film that was nightmarish. Roman Polanski, who had survived the Cracow Ghetto, was chilled when he saw the documentary many decades later in 1988, and commented, "It affected me more than when I lived it."[55]

It's not clear how Rossif came to make the movie. He was a television director and producer, well-known for wildlife documentaries. In 1959, he collaborated in the production of France's pioneering television news magazine, *Cinq colonnes à la une*, and, *pace* Rossif himself, it was he who had come up with the name.[56] Rossif's family had been wiped out in the Nazi genocide. For a certainty, he read Léon Poliakov's French translation of Emanuel Ringelblum's Warsaw Ghetto diary, published in 1959, which he used in structuring his own narrative of life in the ghetto. Erwin Leiser's documentary on the Third Reich, *Mein Kampf*, which included an eight-minute Nazi-filmed sequence on ghetto life, was released in Paris in November 1960. In just a few weeks' time, it attracted a viewership in excess of 100,000, and Rossif may well have been among that number.[57] Whatever Rossif's inspiration, he threw himself into the making of *Le Temps du ghetto* with an intense, personal commitment.

In narrative design, the film was a beginning-to-end story. Rossif touched on the major episodes of the ghetto's history (many of them now iconic) one by one. In July 1942, the Jewish Council chief Adam Czerniakow, at long last recognizing the futility of cooperating with the Nazis, committed suicide. The next month, the Germans deported almost two hundred orphans to Treblinka, and the orphanage director, Janusz Korczak, refusing to abandon the children, marched with them in ordered rows as they made their way to the Umschlagplatz, the holding area near the train station, from which they were all shipped to their deaths. And as repeated selections and deportations thinned out the ghetto's population, a desperate remnant rose in revolt in April 1943. These events had been chronicled in print – in John Hersey's *La Muraille*, in Michel Mazor's *La Cité engloutie* – but they had never before been screened in French movie houses, let alone accompanied by documentary footage, much of it altogether new to postwar audiences. The film ran at just under an hour and twenty minutes, almost three-quarters of it devoted to archival clips culled from German sources by Rossif himself, who proved an adept and indefatigable researcher.

The film's narrative structure was not innovative, but its content was, and so too the way it employed testimony. Rossif made use of eyewitnesses, recruiting them, forty-four in all and every one a survivor of the Warsaw Ghetto, by advertising in both the Yiddish and mainstream press. He brought his subjects into the studio and shared with them elements of the documentation he planned to use. The people were then invited to talk in front of the camera, their memories jogged by what they had just seen. Rossif urged them to speak, not in the neutral tones of an observer of events, but with unedited spontaneity.[58] "Don't tell us what happened at that moment," he instructed one witness, "but what you said to yourself in your heart, in secret."[59] The interviews that resulted were long, lasting up to two hours, as the survivors opened up on a subject many had not spoken about before. The footage was then edited down to snippets, sometimes a few seconds in length, sometimes just over a minute. In total, Rossif included testimony from thirty-two witnesses, adding up to a rough twenty minutes of running time.[60]

Rossif was attentive not just to the interview process, but also to how the witnesses looked and sounded on screen. Each was clad in a black turtleneck sweater. The subjects were then filmed in closeup, either from the front or in profile, their heads haloed in darkness. These were faces that welled up out of the black, their features visible in detail as they flickered with emotion.[61] Rossif wanted to make the past live again in the witnesses' words and expressions. Claude Lanzmann was dismissive of *Le Temps du ghetto*. He reproached Rossif for making use of archival material tainted by its Nazi source.[62] But when it came to the handling of faces – faces worked over by memory – Rossif was mining a vein that Lanzmann, whether he acknowledged it or not, would later exploit himself. On the matter of voice, Rossif's witnesses spoke in an accented French, reciting in the present tense as though the experiences they limned were happening even as they talked. None of them was named, and Rossif adjusted the soundtrack to make sure the volume level was the same for all. The overall effect was to iron out the speakers' individuality and the original spontaneity of their testimony. As one critic noted at the time, Rossif's subjects seemed to speak in a "concerted," almost scripted manner, just the opposite of the kind of extemporaneous expression that characterized Jean Rouch's *cinéma vérité*. Rossif concurred with the critic's observation. The film's witnesses, as he meant to present them, were not so much individuals as members of an ensemble, like "the choir in an ancient tragedy." They did not testify as at a trial, but incanted, conjuring from the depths of memory an atrocious past.[63]

Nor is the viewer left in doubt as to how atrocious that past was. This was communicated in part by the film's visual elements, of course, but also by the words of the witnesses and by the accompanying voice-over commentary, which was written by the journalist Madeleine Chapsal (see the discussion of her that follows). The speakers are hard on Czerniakow, the *Judenrat*, and the ghetto police in the Jewish Council's employ. They are branded as collaborators, "functionaries of fear," who in the name of saving Jews brought torment to them. The ghetto uprising is remembered with pride, but also terror. Indeed, terror, fear, and "eternal anxiety" come across as the ghetto-dwellers' most constant companions. And a sense of abandonment. One interviewee spoke of the "void" overhead, while "crime" went about its cruel business unchecked. How hard it was, we are told, "to believe in God," as children were dying in the streets. All the while, even as the ghetto cried out, there came no reply, whether from God or from the world beyond. No one stood up for the Jews. The ghetto's story, as told in *Le Temps du ghetto*, is one of fear, isolation, and ever-present death – by disease and starvation in the ghetto, by extermination in the murder camps of Treblinka and Majdanek. It is a harrowing vision and a bleak one.

The documentary is not well-remembered today, though it made a mark in its time. This was thanks in some measure to the quality of Rossif's team and to its connections in the media world. The film's technical consultant, Michel Borwicz, was an expert on the genocide, both as a survivor who knew about the Jewish tragedy from personal experience and as a pioneering archivist and independent scholar. Pierre Braunberger was the producer, a cinema veteran who had proved himself willing on more than one occasion to take a risk. He had backed the documentary investigations of Jean Rouch as well as the cinematic experimentalism of the New Wave, at that moment just starting out.

Now's the moment to say something more about Madeleine Chapsal, who composed the commentary of *Le Temps du ghetto*. She was a writer on the staff of *L'Express*, a news magazine among the first of its kind in France (she was also married – until 1960 – to one of the magazine's cofounders, Jean-Jacques Servan-Schreiber). The journal styled itself as modern, progressive, and youthful, and indeed, it made the study of the young a house specialty. It was in the context of one such study that *L'Express*'s other cofounder, Françoise Giroud, in fact coined the term "New Wave" to characterize the baby-boom generation then coming of age.[64]

Chapsal contributed to *Le Temps du ghetto* first and foremost as author of the film's narration, but she also found a way to render additional service in her capacity as a media person. In May 1961, as the documentary went through production, she published an article about it in *L'Express* under the title "The interior trial." The title implied a connection to the Eichmann trial, which was about to enter its second month, an allusion Chapsal then made explicit in the text that followed. A few months later, in November, she published a multipart series in *France-Soir*, France's largest circulation news daily. Each article was devoted to an eyewitness account of Warsaw Ghetto life. There were six in total, all harvested from the testimonies taken in the filming of *Le Temps du ghetto*.[65] The documentary did not lack for publicity. It had some success at the box office. Finally, a rare achievement, it was accorded a screening on French television in 1964.

None of this – Langfus' and Rawicz's novels, Rossif's documentary –
broke open the hardening carapace of the Gaullist narrative of wartime
experience. It would also be hard to make the case that the early 1960s
moment marked the breakthrough of a full-fledged Holocaust consciousness. The word *Holocaust* did not much figure, if at all, in the vocabulary
of the artists in question, not at that time. It wasn't the Jewish tragedy
that *L'Arche* invited a number of them to reflect on, but the concentrationary tragedy. Yet a new kind of voice, speaking through the interstices
of the concentrationary paradigm, was beginning to make itself heard. It
was a Jewish one, talking about what happened to the Jews as a subject in
its own right. That voice did not talk of martyrs and heroes, nor did it
seek out an honored niche for Jews in the deportation pantheon. It spoke
rather of isolation, fear, irretrievable loss, and the lure of suicide, and did
so in tones of melancholy and anger. There was no happy ending to this
story. Rawicz of course had toyed with the idea, but he did so in order to
subvert it. The problem these artists confronted – and as we have seen,
they were not the first in this respect – was how to find a form adequate to
convey an experience at once so awful and so exceptional.

Langfus and Rawicz worked in a variety of modes – the realist, but also
the ironic and comedic. They built narratives circular in design; they
included poetry and hallucination in their texts; they cast about for
means to pry open the mind of the survivor and lay it bare. This was
Rossif's objective as well, although he worked, not from his own experience, but from that of others. He staged his subjects' testimonials in such
a way that memories long dormant were reawakened and articulated with
an immediacy that made them all the more unsettling. Such proceedings
prompted critics to think of Camus or the New Novel or *cinema vérité*,
but none of these associations quite fit.

The Jewish voice was in this measure sui generis. But note also that
none of the artists tackled the subject of the camps head on. The names
of Treblinka and Majdanek were mentioned. It was clear these were
camps of a special kind, death camps, but the machinery of death itself
was not explored. None of the artists, moreover, talked about France –
about how France's wartime government, Vichy, had collaborated with
the Nazis in the genocide of the Jews. And the Jewish voice, while
audible, was not loud. The Eichmann trial helped it in all its singularity
to win an attentive and sympathetic hearing, but not more. All this would
change, however, in the years ahead, as the decade of the 1960s drew to a
close and the decade of the 1970s began.

10   Generation

The Arab–Israeli War of June 1967 caused a shudder of fear to run through France's Jewish community. It appeared that Israel's very existence hung in the balance, while the world stood by and watched, abandoning the Jews to their fate, as it had done a quarter century before. Worse still, France arrayed itself among the bystanders. It had made clear in the run-up to the war that it condemned whichever side attacked first, and it was Israel, in a preemptive strike, that had done just that, earning France's censure. France owed Israel a consignment of Mirage jets, bought and paid for, but it refused to deliver them. The war ended in a crushing Israeli victory, but this did not quiet emotions in France. In November, many months after the conclusion of hostilities, de Gaulle spelled out the rationale for France's Mideast policy at a news conference. Even as he urged the triumphant Israelis to moderation, he expressed concern that such advice would go unheeded. For the Jews, the General explained, remained what they had been "from time immemorial, an elite people sure of itself and domineering."[1] The fatal words had been pronounced. De Gaulle, in a New Year's conversation with Grand Rabbi Kaplan, tried to explain them away, saying he had intended them as "an encomium," not a slur, but it was too late.[2]

France's Jews reacted in dismay. The Fifth Republic stood aside when the Jewish state faced mortal danger, and its president justified the decision in words that, as the literary scholar Richard Marienstras characterized them, amounted to "a veiled appeal to anti-Semitism."[3] Raymond Aron, for one, was whipped up by the events of 1967. He was not a man to advertise his Jewishness, but the Arab–Israeli War awakened in him "an irresistible sentiment of solidarity." Aron said so out loud in the pages of *Le Figaro*, and he was not alone in the feeling.[4]

Historians have identified the very real shock caused by the Arab–Israeli War as a turning point in French Holocaust consciousness.[5] The event, it is said, left French Jews feeling forsaken and beleaguered, which led them to look on themselves in a new light. They were a group apart with an identity all their own, and at the core of that identity lay the trauma of the Holocaust, a tragedy specific to the Jews that marked them in a way it had marked no one else.

The view elaborated in these pages will take a different tack, emphasizing generation more than the shock of the Arab-Israeli War. The very mention of the word *generation* in this context is bound to provoke thoughts of 1968, and that's not a mistaken association, but it's important to be clear on two points. The first has to do with what is meant by generation. Baby boomers, the children of the postwar era, did indeed play a part in raising public awareness of the Jewish tragedy. The banner carriers of the new Holocaust consciousness, however, also included figures a few years older, men like Pierre Vidal-Naquet (b. 1930) and Serge Klarsfeld (b. 1935), who had been youths or children during the war. A generational memory motivated them, a memory of parents persecuted, deported, and murdered, a mother and father in Vidal-Naquet's case, a father in Klarsfeld's. They had an intimate familiarity with loss and knew, moreover, of France's implication in the disappearance of family members who had been tracked down not in some distant land like Poland or Ukraine but in France itself. Each experienced, moreover, a moment of awakening that spurred them to action. Klarsfeld dates his to a visit he paid to Auschwitz in February 1965, a journey undertaken out of devotion to the father who had died there. On the Auschwitz-Birkenau ramp, as Klarsfeld tells the story, he heard an "imperious call to shoulder my responsibilities as a Jew."[6] Vidal-Naquet also heard a call, but his came a year later, prompted by the Steiner Affair.

Jean-François Steiner was a French-born journalist who had lost a parent to the Holocaust. In 1966, he published a novel about the 1943 Sonderkommando revolt at Treblinka, which, even as it heroicized the rebels, highlighted just how passive the mass of the camp's Jewish inmates had been, marching to their deaths in the by now familiar phrase "like lambs to the slaughter." The accusation of passivity ignited a controversy that swept up a generation of young Jews, Vidal-Naquet included, then at the beginning of a distinguished academic career as a classicist.[7] The idea of generation, as it will be used here, is a capacious one. It is made up of more than one element: baby boomers, of course, but also a cohort a little older, the so-called "1.5 generation."[8]

What has any of this to do with 1968? This issue too calls out for a clarification. It was a set of events, to be sure, but 1968 also connotes something bigger: an era when the received truths of the postwar order were called into question and cut down to size. The era of 1968, so defined, was consequential for Holocaust consciousness in more ways than one. It witnessed the eclipse of the epic stories, Gaullist and communist, that had once enjoyed pride of place in postwar public consciousness, constraining and patterning how the French thought about the Deportation. It was self-styled sixty-eighters, mirror-breakers that they were, in Henry Rousso's famous characterization, who took the gleeful lead in detonating these grand narratives.[9] They were aided in the task by that past master of iconoclasm, the documentarist Marcel Ophuls (b. 1927), who released two classics of cinematic debunking in these years dealing with the legacy of the war: *Le Chagrin et la pitié* (1969) and the lesser known but no less compelling *Memory of Justice* (1976).

As old stories were ushered out, a new, Jewish one entered in, and with unprecedented fanfare thanks to savvy use of the media. Sixty-eighters were adept at staging events that concentrated the public's attention, a tactic that militants of Jewish memory made a conscious and successful bid to imitate, none more so than the husband-and-wife team of Serge and Beate Klarsfeld. The 1968 era mattered in one more way, having less to do with the May events proper than with their aftermath, that is, with the fading of Marxist enthusiasms once the Revolution so much bally-hooed by sixty-eighters failed to materialize. On this score, it was not just the miscarriage of revolution in France that stoked disillusionment, but also the ever harder to deny breakdown of Third World revolutions, as exemplified by red Cambodia's collapse into authoritarianism and mass murder.[10] From left-wing disillusionment was born a turn to identity politics, a phenomenon that was general in its expression, affecting many groups, baby-boomer Jews included. For these young Jews, moreover, coming to terms with what Jewishness meant in France entailed willy-nilly a coming to terms with France's own role in the Final Solution.

The 1968 era was a long one, extending from the mid-1960s deep into the decade that followed and even a little beyond. So far as Holocaust consciousness is concerned, this was a momentous time that saw a massive clearing of the narrative decks, the deployment of novel forms of protest that enabled a new story to be heard, and the maturation of an audience ready to listen and take action. The question still remains as to what that "new story" looked like, an issue that will be addressed along the way as the present chapter unfolds.

The Right to Difference

What is said to have made the 1967 war such a turning point is the sudden and dramatic realization of Jewish isolation that it provoked. Yet, there's another way to track the genealogy of such feelings of apartness, this one less zeroed in on events abroad than on happenings at home, the Steiner controversy first of all. It reminded Jews how the world had abandoned them at a time of the most urgent need. How then were Jews, aware of the world's indifference, to make a way for themselves, to strike out on a path of their own? It was this question that preoccupied the members of the Cercle Gaston Crémieux, an association of Jewish intellectuals created in the wake of the Steiner Affair, and they found an answer in an affirmation of what they called the right to difference.

There is more than one way to read Jean-François Steiner's *Treblinka: la révolte d'un camp d'extermination* (1966). It was on one level a dramatic – at moments, exciting – account of a camp revolt, couched in a language full of Sartrean allusion. The inmates stockpile arms and plan an attack, all the while debating the necessity and meaning of action. Steiner identified himself as a man of the Left. He was born Jean-François Cohen, but the war led to a name change. His father died in deportation; his mother remarried to Ozias Steiner, a Jewish physician; and Jean-François Cohen then became Jean-François Steiner. Steiner's adoptive father was a Spanish Civil War veteran and a Communist, and this was the milieu the young man grew up in. As an aspiring writer, he felt the powerful tug of Existentialism. He published in Sartre's *Les Temps modernes*, and Simone de Beauvoir herself supplied Steiner's *Treblinka* with a praise-filled preface.[11] Well she might have, for the book's plot line enacted in narrative form the analysis of the master–slave relationship that was so central to Sartre's philosophical magnum opus, *L'Être et le néant* (1943). The Nazis are the masters, described in clinical terms as "the technicians." They degrade the Jewish inmates who, in the depths of despair, experience the chilling "breath of nothingnesss [*souffle du néant*]." The void welling up before them, the Jews cease to fear death, a liberation in itself, and they then rise in revolt, shucking off "their slave condition" and embarking on what Steiner calls "the reconquest of their humanity."[12] The book's mix of action and philosophy captured the reading public's imagination, and the novel ended up selling an impressive 100,000 copies in its first year.[13]

A second reading of the book is also possible, one focused not so much on the revolt as on the passivity of the millions who died without revolting. Treblinka was an Aktion Reinhard camp, one of three, along with Belzec and Sobibor. The camps were so named after SS commander Reinhard Heydrich, who had been assassinated by a Czech resistance commando in June 1942. These camps had a single purpose: the extermination of Jews. The victims were trained in and, once arrived, dispatched straight to the gas chambers, with the result that the actual camp populations were relatively small, consisting of the SS, their Ukrainian helpers, and a crew of Sonderkommandos, who were themselves slated for eventual extinction. The Aktion Reinhard killing centers were operational for just a brief period in 1942–1943, and yet in that short span they swallowed up the lives of an estimated 1.5 million Jews.

Steiner had nothing but admiration for the Treblinka insurgents. At the same time, he was rueful of how many Jews had had to die before a remnant took action, and that spectacle – the spectacle of so many Jews dying without a fight – stirred in him feelings of shame. As Steiner expressed it in a magazine interview not long after his novel's publication: "I felt ashamed to be one of this people's sons, six million of whose members allowed themselves to be led to the slaughter like sheep."[14] Remember now how Gideon Hausner had badgered camp survivors at the Eichmann trial to explain why they had not resisted. Steiner was picking up on that line of inquiry, and the questioning would grow all the louder before 1966 was out, because it was later in that year that the French translation of Hannah Arendt's *Eichmann in Jerusalem* appeared.[15] The Arendt text, serialized first in the *New Yorker* and then published as a book in 1963, added to the charge of passivity an accusation yet more inflammatory. The *Judenräte* that had managed ghetto life under German rule, she argued, had abetted the implementation of the Final Solution. They helped the Nazis kill more Jews than otherwise possible, and so, to this this extent, the Jews were not just passive victims but collaborators in their own murder.

Such charges, as might be supposed, incited the fury of France's Jewish intelligentsia. Anti-Semites had long bandied about the stereotype of the spineless Jew, and now Steiner was doing just the same. Such was Léon Poliakov's protest, and, seconded by Henry Bulawko and Vladimir Jankélévitch, he organized a vigilance committee to defend the honor of murdered deportees and résistants. For others, what was most painful in Steiner's position was its apparent lack of empathy. How were unarmed and disoriented Jews supposed to behave, shipped to a distant forest in Poland, where in a matter of hours they were liquidated? The Jewish philosopher, Emmanuel Levinas, wrote about the "forsakenness" of the Jews, abandoned by erstwhile friends, chased out of France, indeed, hounded everywhere.[16] Pierre Vidal-Naquet felt much the same way. He took part in a debate about Steiner's book in June 1966. David Rousset, it happens, was also a participant, and he spoke out against the novel because, as he saw it, it fractured the fraternity of deportees, separating out what had happened to the Jews from the common fate of all. Vidal-Naquet challenged Rousset on this very point. What solidarity was Rousset talking about?, Vidal-Naquet wanted to know. The Jews had been the targets of an exterminatory fury in a way other groups of deportees had not, and no one stood up for them. They were not included in the general camaraderie, but were made to endure a special kind of aloneness, what Vidal-Naquet called, "a Jewish solitude."[17] The release of Arendt's *Eichmann in Jerusalem* toward the end of the year just added fuel to the polemics. *Le Nouvel Observateur* published a series of articles about the book. The final one – with the provocative title, "Hannah Arendt, is she a Nazi?" – was made up of letters of protest, one of them signed by Marienstras (among others).[18] Manès Sperber piled on a few months later with a piece in *Le Monde*. The note he struck was one now gaining currency: the world, Sperber reminded readers, had turned its back on six million helpless Jews who had neither friends nor allies to succor them. That, and not Jewish passivity, was the real scandal of the Nazi genocide.[19]

For all Steiner's emphasis on passivity, that story – the story of Jews having to go it alone – was one he had sympathy for, which points to a third way to read *Treblinka*. The novel, after all, is about Jews and no one else. The camp it describes is not Buchenwald, a concentration camp reserved until the Reich's final days for political deportees; it's not even about Auschwitz, a mixed-use camp designed both to exploit and to exterminate. It's about, as the book's subtitle explained, a unique camp form, one dedicated to mass murder pure and simple, and the victims were all Jews.[20] The rebels as well were all Jews, and Steiner made clear what he thought had spurred them to act. It was not anti-fascist commitment as at Buchenwald, but a more complicated amalgam of emotions: existential angst in the face of the void but also a deep-seated sentiment of collective belonging reawakened by the miseries of camp life. The world had left the Jews to their own devices, and they found within themselves the resources to fight back, rediscovering in the process a sense of group identity, indeed, a sense of nationhood. "The Jew more than anyone else," the novel's narrator tells us at the very moment the spirit of revolt begins to percolate, "fulfills himself through his national community."[21] It's not difficult to imagine how such a budding sense of national community might spill over into Zionism, and, indeed, Zionists of the *marxisant* Hashomer Hatzair variety figured prominently among Steiner's cast of Treblinka rebels.

At the same time, the desire to belong might just as well lead to a different kind of commitment, centered not on Zion but on the cultural or ethnic dimensions of Jewish peoplehood, and that's the path a number of the Steiner controversy veterans took. Marienstras and Vidal-Naquet both crossed paths once more in the ranks of the Cercle Gaston Crémieux, an organization dedicated to a renewal of Jewish life in the Diaspora. The circle announced its existence in a manifesto that *L'Arche* published in January 1968, but its beginnings dated back to the year preceding. As the circle's name proclaimed, its orientation was left-wing.

Gaston Crémieux was a nineteenth-century figure, a Jewish lawyer from the Midi and radical republican who played a leadership role in the Marseille Commune of 1871 and was executed for it. This is not to say that all members of the Cercle Crémieux were on the Left, but Vidal-Naquet for a certainty was. He had made known loud and clear his opposition to France's war in Algeria, signing his name to the "Manifeste des 121," a risky gesture for an academic just starting out. The circle, as noted, was Diaspora-oriented, and this translated into a sympathetic embrace of one of the Diaspora's most emblematic languages, Yiddish. It's not surprising then to encounter Rachel Ertel among the circle's members. She was one of France's leading specialists in Yiddish literature and a key interpreter of Elie Wiesel's oeuvre. For the same reason, it's not surprising to hear voices critical of Israel emanating from the organization's ranks, none more forceful than Marienstras' own. He was no anti-Zionist – Israel's existence for him was non-negotiable – but, as he saw it, that didn't oblige Diaspora Jews to remain silent when Israel's policies wandered from the path of justice. Last of all, circle militants cared deeply about the particular fate of Jews in the Holocaust. Ertel's connection to Wiesel has just been mentioned. Vidal-Naquet was destined to play a lead role in the 1980s in France's fight against Holocaust denial. Along these lines, one more Cercle Gaston Crémieux participant merits mention: Claude Lanzmann, the future creator of *Shoah*, by some lights the most powerful movie about the Nazi genocide ever made. The circle was among the first to claim a "right to difference," the right of minorities – in this instance, Jews – to refuse absorption into the universality of Frenchness. And for circle members that idea of difference came wrapped up in the Jews' unique and terrible fate in the Holocaust.[22]

Marcel Ophuls, Mirror-Breaker

Jewish intellectuals and writers had begun to articulate a sense of apartness prior to the 1967 Arab–Israeli War. The war itself intensified such sentiments, helping to diffuse them among widening swaths of France's Jewish community. May 1968 – or, to be more precise – the fallout from the May events propelled the process a huge step forward. Now it was no longer just French Jews who found themselves face-to-face with the Holocaust and the world's implication in it, but ever more the French nation itself, made to confront its own complicity in the implementation of the Final Solution in a way it had not before. What made such a sea change even imaginable in the first place was a weakening of the grip of Gaullist memory. It made a vast difference, of course, that the General was no longer on the scene. He retired from public office in 1969 and died the following year. Even as de Gaulle departed the public stage, the Resistance epic he had worked so hard to incarnate came under intensifying critical scrutiny.

In the world of print, the foremost exemplar of that new spirit of criticism was Robert Paxton's *Vichy France: Old Guard and New Order*, published first in the United States in 1972 and then in French translation a year later. Paxton mobilized German as well as French archives to demonstrate that Pétain's regime had not been the work of a mere "handful of *misérables*," as de Gaulle had once dismissively declared in a wartime address. It had recruited its cadres from the ranks of France's best and brightest; it had ideological roots that ran deep into the national past; and for longer than many might want to concede, it had enjoyed the backing of all too many French men and women.[23] Paxton (b. 1932) was not of an age to be a student demonstrator, but he shared with sixty-eighters a revulsion against the United States' war in Viet Nam, and the back dustjacket of *Vichy France* made that plain enough to the perspicacious reader:

Indeed, it may be the German occupiers rather than the Vichy majority whom Americans, as residents of the most powerful state on earth, should scrutinize most unblinkingly. The deeds of occupier and occupied alike suggest that there come cruel times when to save a nation's deepest values one must disobey the state.

When it came to film, it was Marcel Ophuls who led the anti-Gaullist charge. Ophuls was, like Paxton, of foreign origin (he was born in Germany). Though no youngster in 1968, he had more than a brush with the turbulent politics of the times. He was director, moreover, of a work, *Le Chagrin et la pitié*, that took a fresh look at France under the Occupation, one that subverted the Gaullist story from beginning to end.

Ophuls had a firsthand connection to France's May events, although admittedly a small one. His father, Max, the celebrated film director, was a German Jew who fled to France in 1933, bringing his family with him. The defeat of 1940 motivated a second relocation, this time to Hollywood, where the young Ophuls grew up, later serving in the American armed forces. He returned to France after that, worked for a period in film, and then settled into a job at French state television, which is where the May events found him. Television personnel voted to go on strike, and Ophuls was keen to join in, to make common cause, as he put it, "with students and the working class," evincing more enthusiasm for militant action than did fellow employee, Frédéric Rossif, who favored a speedy return to work.[24]

In 1968's aftermath, Ophuls, now a controversial figure, headed across the Rhine to take up a position at German TV. He persuaded superiors to let him make a documentary film about France under the Occupation; they agreed; and within a year, he had assembled and edited *Le Chagrin et la pitié*. The film was first released on German television, but its French counterpart refused to follow suit. The movie, it is true, was long, running at over four hours. The real problem, however, lay elsewhere. Simone Veil, who sat on state television's board of directors, threatened to resign if it greenlighted the showing of Ophuls' movie, and she did not mince words as to why. Because the documentary, as she saw it, presented the Occupation-era French as so many "bastards [*salauds*]," ever ready to denounce, ever reluctant to resist ("with the exception of the Communists"). That was a vision all too pleasing to the young, who were thrilled to think ill of their parents, but, in Veil's estimation, all this was nothing more than a "pseudo-truth." Veil, who was Jewish and an Auschwitz survivor, claimed that Germaine Tillion, another former deportee, felt much the same as she did about the film.[25] The board's director, *pace* Ophuls, was moved to take the matter up with de Gaulle himself (though Ophuls provides no evidence for this). The General, on Ophul's telling, sided with Veil, opining with an Olympian flourish: "France does not need truths; France needs hope."[26]

So, the film was not aired on French television in 1969, and a prolonged scramble ensued to find another venue for its release. François Truffaut took charge and prevailed upon fellow film director Louis Malle, who ran a Latin Quarter movie house, the Saint-Séverin, to screen it there. Ophuls attended the April 1971 opening and was astounded by the crush of young people, guitar-wielding "hippies" and all, waiting in line to buy tickets.[27] The film, now in increasing demand, moved to a more capacious theater on the Champs-Élysées, and in its 87-week run, it sold an estimated 600,000 seats. That was surpassed by the viewership it garnered when it was at last broadcast on French television in 1981. The socialists were then in power, and they did not share in Veil and Tillion's reservations about the movie. Fifteen million viewers tuned in to watch, testimony to the remarkable progress of the documentary's reputation.[28]

What was the fuss all about? The film purports to chronicle the life of Clermont-Ferrand, a provincial town in the Auvergne, under German Occupation. Ophuls made use of newsreel footage for the purpose, but the bulk of the running time is given over to interviews with thirty-five subjects, twenty-five of them French, the rest British and German. There is some voice-over scene setting, but otherwise no accompanying commentary to articulate an explicit point of view. Ophuls, however, found other ways to make perfectly clear just where he stood.

There is first of all Ophuls' selection of witnesses. Most of them are ordinary people: farmers, school teachers, small businessmen. The roster is rounded out with a handful of résistants, some lesser known figures, others more celebrated, like Emmanuel d'Astier de la Vigerie, a senior personality in Libération-Sud. Ophuls also included a sampling of marquee names: Anthony Eden, who had been in charge of Britain's wartime relations with the Free French, and former Prime Minister Pierre Mendès France, who effected a daring escape from a Vichy-run jail in Clermont-Ferrand, which he talked about in the documentary with humor and Gallic charm.

What no doubt upset many viewers partial to stories of Resistance heroism and sacrifice was the inclusion of a whole cast of unsavory types, René de Chambrun not least among them. He was married to the daughter of Vice-Premier Pierre Laval, an *auvergnat* himself and the Maréchal's second-in-command, and it is infuriating to watch Chambrun as he trims and weasels in defense of his father-in-law's record of collaboration. Christian de la Mazière, also interviewed, is not so much repellant as fascinating in a repellant way. He's an aristocrat who absorbed the family's visceral anti-Semitism with his mother's milk. De la Mazière talks about what he did during the Occupation with an unruffled frankness: how he went all in for collaboration, joining the Waffen SS and fighting with Hitler's armies on the Eastern Front. But in many ways, the sleaziest of all Ophuls' dubious characters is Marius Klein, a Clermont-Ferrand haberdasher. Ophuls' prefilm research revealed that a number of town merchants had taken out ads in a local newspaper, *Le Moniteur,* to alert potential clients not to mistake them for Jews. A certain Marius Klein was one of these. Late one afternoon, just as Ophuls was winding up that day's shoot, he spotted the man's shop and, accompanied by his crew, trooped in for an impromptu interview. M. Klein proved a willing subject at first, but turned ever more evasive and self-justifying as the documentarist confronted him with the facts. Along the way, a damning picture of what Vichy really was comes into focus. It was an anti-Semitic regime, a fact that did not trouble many Frenchmen who, like Klein, happily went about their business, keeping an eye on their own interests all the while. Yes, the witnesses do present an ugly portrait of France under the Occupation, a land populated by *collabos*, anti-Semites, and opportunists all too willing to go along to get along.

It's unfair, however, to aver, as did Veil, that Ophuls was neglectful of the Resistance. No doubt, he minimized de Gaulle's contribution. The General makes a cameo appearance in the documentary's newsreel footage, and that's all. Ophuls is not much more generous to the

Communists, contra Veil. Party bigwig Jacques Duclos is interviewed, but it's not clear why, as he played no role in the Auvergne Resistance. The PCF gets short shrift otherwise, and that's not because there was a dearth of Communists active in the regional underground. Clermont-Ferrand was a working-class town, headquarters of the Michelin tire works, and as such home to working-class militants of every political hue, Communists included.[29] Yet, while Ophuls slighted Gaullists and Communists, he accorded other résistants ample screen time: Colonel Raymond du Jonchay, for example, who commanded the underground army in the region; or the legendary local maquisard, Émile Coulaudon, aka Colonel Gaspard; or d'Astier de la Vigerie. Du Jonchay, however, turns out to be an ambiguous character, a monarchist with blinkered views about leftist résistants. Colonel Gaspard is a true hero, no question, but a Resistance comrade also lets on that he had an outsized appetite for glory. Then there's d'Astier, so full of aristocratic suavity, who delivers himself of a judgment on the Resistance that the film almost appears to endorse. They were, he lets on, a band of misfits, looked at askance by France's conformist bourgeoisie.

Yet, is this really film's final word on the Resistance? Not quite, for the film does feature résistants, more unalloyed in their heroism, like Alexis and Louis Grave and, of course, Mendès France himself. The Grave brothers are peasants, modest people, who do not boast or brag, and they take a forgiving view of human affairs. One was denounced by a neighbor and deported to Buchenwald. He knows who it was, and the neighbor still lives nearby, but what's the point, the brothers muse, in trying to settle accounts? They did what they had to do, and there's an end of it. Mendès France is every bit as sympathetic. He had been a deputy when the war began, enlisting in the Air Force to take part in the fight. When the Germans routed France's armies in 1940, he, in the company a score of fellow deputies, departed to North Africa, determined not to concede defeat. For this, the Vichy authorities arrested Mendès France and charged him with desertion. In the movie interview, Mendès France speaks of his trial and of the courtroom spectators, right-thinking Vichyites sweating with hatred. He tells too of how he escaped prison, climbing over a wall, an escape delayed, as he relates it with a twinkle in his eye, by two lovers on a bench below, the man courting the woman until she acquiesces. Here is a remarkable man, indeed, a loyalist of the Republic, who knows about hate and love and who retains his humanity throughout. Ophuls in a later interview allowed that Mendès France was the public figure he admired most.[30]

It is worth underlining, moreover, just what it signified to record a flattering portrait of Mendès France in 1969. The year before, the ex-premier had attended a huge student-sponsored rally in Charléty Stadium in the heat of the May 1968 events. Mendès France did not speak, but his presence imparted a sheen of legitimacy to the occasion. In lionizing Mendès France, as Ophuls did in *Le Chagrin et la pitié*, he was celebrating someone who was a Resistance hero of unimpeachable integrity, but also a public figure who at the time of the filming was a notorious thorn in the side of the Gaullist Republic.

The focus on Mendès France was nervy, but then again, nerviness was a key feature of Ophuls' modus operandi, a way to make subjects betray truths they might otherwise prefer to conceal. Now's the moment to say something about Ophuls' interviewing technique, for it was not just via the selection of interviewees that Ophuls conveyed a point of view, but also in the way he went about questioning them. Take the exchange he conducted with the haberdasher Klein. At the outset, the man is all too pleased that Ophuls takes an interest in him. Ophuls notes the multiple ribbons on Klein's lapel, so many tokens of valorous service in the Great War. Ophuls praises the man's courage, evoking protestations of modesty. The filmmaker then enquires about Jewish store owners, who had once been numerous in the neighborhood. Yes, comes the reply, there had been a number, but they went into exile during the war. "Exile?," queries Ophuls. And then he hits the off-balance Klein with a question about the advertisement in *Le Moniteur*. The shopkeeper, taken aback, comments on how well-informed Ophuls seems to be, and then begins to stumble from one equivocation to the next, laying bare in the process the moral squalor of Vichy and the implication of average Frenchmen like Klein himself in what Vichy was.

Here then is Ophuls, the interviewer, at work. He has a point of departure, an idea, but not a preconceived plan of attack. He does not express in so many words what he thinks, but the interview process, with Ophuls laying on confrontational questions to steer the exchange in the desired direction, leads toward the revelation of a truth and leads the viewer toward moral clarity. Ophuls did not worship at the altar of objectivity. He had strong views, but he communicated them, not in bold declarations, but through the give-and-take of open-ended dialogue.[31]

And through juxtaposition. Ophuls is hard on Maurice Chevalier in *Le Chagrin et la pitié*. He includes a clip of the singer, speaking in English, in which Chevalier explains that he had never toured wartime Germany as some had accused him of doing. He performed once for the French inmates of a German POW camp, he continues, but that was it, not much of an offense, if offense at all. But elsewhere, Ophuls shows newsreel footage of Pétain on a tour, greeted by local dignitaries and enthusiastic crowds. He intercuts shots of men flashing the fascist salute. All this is accompanied by a song, "Ça sent si bon la France," a lilting tribute to the charms of French life. The song was released during the Occupation, and the chanteur is Maurice Chevalier. Thus, the viewer is guided to a conclusion, whether a fair one or not. Even if Chevalier was not a *collabo*, he did supply a jaunty soundtrack to a regime that was. Once again, Ophuls does not make a bald statement, but leaves the juxtaposed images and musical accompaniment to do the expressive work.

Of course, none of this had much to do with the Deportation. Ophuls on more than one occasion conceded that he never addressed the Holocaust head on,[32] a fair enough self-assessment, which is not to the say that he avoided the subject completely. The Klein interview, for one, spotlights the ambient anti-Semitism of the Vichy era. More specifics are supplied by Claude Lévy, yet another former résistant, who is heard in voice-over, explaining images of the July 1942 roundup of Jews conducted at German behest by Parisian police. The victims, we are informed, were incarcerated at the Vél d'hiv, which Ophuls treats as a stand-in for the general fate of French Jews under the Occupation.[33] That said, the Jewish story is not Ophuls' main preoccupation. He wants to know, not so much about the Occupation's victims, as about what the common run of French men and women did (or failed to do) during the war, and in working out an answer, he spurned the received wisdom of Resistance elders, substituting a story of his own at once more ambiguous and accusatory. In this – and here Simone Veil is not far off the mark – he was doing generational work, helping the young to gain critical distance from the stories of Resistance derring-do they had been reared on. That reckoning, moreover, comes wrapped in a politics that is unabashedly left-wing.

Lest there be any doubt on this score, it's worth tarrying for a moment over Ophuls' documentary, *Memory of Justice*, released in 1976. Ophuls described it as his most personal movie. He featured family members in it, including his wife Régine who regrets Ophuls' predilection for grim subject matter. He also included a scene filmed when he was a teacher at Princeton University, showing himself and a classful of eager students reflecting on the documentary's themes. On the matter of theme, *Memory of Justice* is divided into two parts, the first an examination of the Nuremberg trials. The second, titled "Nuremberg and Other Places," explores crimes committed by the French in Algeria and by the Americans in Viet Nam, a juxtaposition (one of Ophuls' preferred techniques, as we have seen) that compels the viewer to pose a series of troubling questions. The French and Americans tried German war criminals at Nuremberg. Was this an example, we are led to ask, of victor's justice? Didn't the United States also commit crimes during the Second World War? It firebombed Dresden and dropped a nuclear device on Hiroshima, both subjects addressed by interviewees in the film, the former by Telford Taylor, who has already made several appearances in this book, the latter by Daniel Ellsberg, who requires no introduction. Yet the most pressing and disturbing question we're invited to think about is whether the French in Algeria and the Americans in Viet Nam were as culpable as the Nazis condemned at Nuremberg. Ophuls' Princeton students have little doubt that the answer is in the affirmative. Just to ask such a question (and to implicate Ellsberg in the posing of it) is a political provocation, one with obvious sixties overtones.

Indeed, Ophuls' implication in the politics of the American sixties seems to have run even deeper than his engagement with France's May events. During the filming of *Memory of Justice*, he attended a commemorative ceremony at Kent State University in honor of four students shot and killed there by national guardsmen during a 1970 antiwar demonstration. Ellsberg, with a copy of *The Pentagon Papers* in hand, was among the speakers, while a camouflage-clad Jane Fonda ("our very own Jane," as Ophuls described her affectionately) circulated among the crowd.

As the film entered the editing phase, Ophuls came under pressure from producers, unhappy with its antiwar tenor, who pressed him to include material critical of the Soviet Union. He dug in his heels, declaring himself ready to abandon the project, and the producers placed the rough-cut film under sequester in London. It was later liberated by subterfuge and spirited away to New York, where Ophuls set up shop in an editing studio paid for thanks to the largesse of a sympathetic benefactor, Hamilton Fish. That was the very place Mike Nichols viewed the finished product, and he was so staggered by what he saw that he undertook to line up Paramount to handle the film's American distribution. Nichols, German-born like Ophuls, was the director of a sixties classic of his own, *The Graduate* (1967), complete with a folk-rock soundtrack by Simon and Garfunkel. As for Fish, he was a man of parts in progressive circles, who went on to acquire *The Nation*, and, in partnership with Victor Navasky, to turn the magazine into a beacon of left-wing opinion.[34]

The making of *Memory of Justice* drew Ophuls into the orbit of the American New Left. It also enabled him to treat the question of generation with a directness not possible in *Le Chagrin et la pitié*, which was constrained by its tight focus on wartime events. In *Memory of Justice*, Ophuls orchestrates a series of confrontations between young and old. Among the most arresting is that between the German-born Beate

Klarsfeld and her mother, Helen Künzel. Klarsfeld was a celebrated, indeed, notorious figure when *Memory of Justice* was made. In November 1968, she had slapped the German chancellor, Kurt Kiesinger, in the face, while photographers snapped away. Kiesinger was an ex-Nazi who had reinvented himself after the war as a Christian Democrat, and Klarsfeld wanted to cast a bright light on the man's Nazi-era record. In *Memory of Justice*, she explains to Ophuls how she had come to France in 1960, wanting to escape from a suffocating petit-bourgeois milieu, which had learned nothing from the war and forgotten everything. She met Serge Klarsfeld, who introduced her into the Klarsfeld family circle, and from them she learned about the Nazi genocide of the Jews. As she went on to explain: "I met Serge in the metro, he is the son of a Jew who died in deportation, while my father fought in the Wehrmacht, his was killed by German men the same age as my father." Frau Künzel in the meantime lets on that she is mortified by what her daughter had done to the German chancellor, blaming Beate's misconduct on Serge (the Jew), who must have put her up to it. It's an ugly scene that dramatizes generational difference, all to the advantage of the young.[35]

It's not always the young, however, who have the last word, and that's part of what makes *Memory of Justice* such gripping viewing. Like *Le Chagrin et la pitié*, *Memory of Justice* has a moral anchor, and he is Taylor, a retired general and career lawyer who is also a prominent critic of the US war in Viet Nam. Unlike the Princeton students who conflate German and American atrocities, Taylor does not. He condemns them both – it is necessary to resist political crime whatever form it takes – but he does not believe the United States to be a modern-day avatar of Nazi Germany. Ophuls' memoir includes a story revelatory of Ophuls' own investment in Taylor's point of view. It takes place at a 1976 screening of *Memory of Justice*, and the setting is that year's New York Film Festival. A debate follows the event, and, according to Ophuls, Ellsberg, who was in the audience, stood up to make an avowal. He, Ellsberg, had spent hours in filmed conversation with the director, but all that talk had ended up edited down to a mere ten minutes of screen time. No, Ellsberg acknowledged, it was not he, "the integral pacifist," who was the real hero of the movie, Ophuls's hero. It was, rather, "General Taylor."[36]

Militants of Memory

Ophuls laid into the Gaullist narrative of Resistance and Deportation with a will, and he found an audience receptive to such iconoclasm in a left-leaning sixties generation well-disposed to looking at France's wartime past anew. Paxton's book stoked that fervor to a white heat, and the Vichy regime, once the poor relative of historical studies, became a topic of furious public debate in the 1970s. But not just Vichy. That mirror-breaking "sixties" moment created an opening for other stories to make themselves heard, the Jewish story first and foremost. Paxton himself would have a hand in this. He was recruited by Roger Errera, a Jewish lawyer and human rights advocate, to write a book about Vichy and the Jews, a task he undertook in partnership with a Canadian colleague, Michael Marrus. The result was *Vichy et les Juifs* (1981), also published in English that same year.

In Ophuls' oeuvre, the Jews' fate never became the main plot line, though it always remained a theme. Others in France, however, militated to move the Jewish tragedy to the fore, and no one did more in this connection than the Klarsfelds, who brought a canny mix of techniques to their campaigning. They were Nazi-hunters who dug up the buried and compromising pasts of public figures like Kurt Kiesinger. There was a spectacular dimension to such efforts, but they were always undergirded by archival sleuthing that supplied documentary backup for the accusations made, and the archive the Klarsfeld exploited most often was that of the Centre de documentation juive contemporaine. When it came to evidence, the Klarsfelds were old school. When it came to tactics, however, they borrowed a page, more than one, from the sixty-eighter playbook.

The Kiesinger imbroglio, already mentioned, provides a vivid illustration of the way the Klarsfelds went about their business.[37] In March 1968, Beate Klarsfeld (b. 1939) traveled to West Berlin and paid a visit to the Dutschke family: Rudi, the student revolutionary, his wife Gretel, and their son "Che." Klarsfeld remembers how impressed she was by the militancy of the student band Dutschke had gathered around himself. In May, once back in Paris, she plunged into the militant scene there, rushing down to the Sorbonne to set up a Comité d'action franco-allemand and organizing a sit-in at a youth services office of the German Embassy. Yet, all the while, Beate kept an eye on what was happening in the Federal Republic. Kiesinger had been named chancellor in 1966, and she found it intolerable that a man with a Nazi past – he had joined the Party in 1933 – was managing unperturbed West Germany's affairs of state. With Serge's help, she began to compile a dossier on Kiesinger's record of Nazi service.

Serge knew where to turn for information, the CDJC, an institution he had had dealings with before. Serge Klarsfeld was raised in a cosmopolitan milieu, knowing little about Jewish religious practice or history. As a teenager, he became friends with two classmates, Jean-Jacques Weiss and

Georges Perec (the future novelist). All three had lost immediate family in the Holocaust, but it was sport that they palavered about. Yet, in 1953, there Klarsfeld was, for some unarticulated reason, present at the cornerstone laying of the Tombeau du Martyr juif inconnu. In 1965, soon to become a father himself, he was set to wondering what had happened to his own, and he turned to the CDJC archive for assistance. It led him to the ramp at Auschwitz-Birkenau and the revelation on that spot of a personal vocation.[38] So, it is little wonder that Klarsfeld went knocking at the CDJC's door once more for help tracking down information on Kiesinger. One of the CDJC's house historians, Joseph Billig, was there to lend a hand, working shoulder to shoulder with the Klarsfelds on assembling the Kiesinger file. In later years, Klarsfeld, by then an accomplished research historian in his own right, paid homage to Billig's example and mentorship: "It was working with him that shaped me."[39]

It was one thing to have the lowdown on Kiesinger, but it was another to catch the public's eye. Beate found a way, having learned a lesson from Berlin's student revolutionaries. "My dossiers would have no impact," she intuited, "unless accompanied by spectacular gestures that the press, avid for the sensational, would hasten to report on."[40] In the early spring of 1968, Beate attended a session of the Bundestag and heckled Kiesinger from the galleries. She shouted at him "Kiesinger, Nazi, resign!" and was ejected by guards for her pains. Beate had arranged for a photographer to be present, so all this was caught on camera, with the snapshots appearing in the next day's newspapers. She was just getting started. Beate found a way to acquire a fake journalist's pass, recruited yet another photographer, and then infiltrated the November 1968 party congress of the Christian Democratic Union. When Kiesinger took the podium to speak, she leapt on stage, crying out "Nazi, Nazi," and delivered him a smack in the face. This too stirred a scandal in the press with photos and all. It also occasioned a trial, followed by appeals, the kind of public proceedings typical of the era, where testimony and theater competed for the public's attention. The theatrics were supplied by Klarsfeld's lawyer, Horst Mahler, who scorned the standard jurist's robe in favor of a jacket and turtleneck, a calculated sartorial snub to the dignity of the court,[41] and by Beate Klarsfeld herself who likened the court to a Nazi tribunal. On the matter of testimony, Serge recruited Billig to take the stand as an expert witness at Beate's first appeals hearing. It was not long thereafter that the trio, the two Klarsfelds and Billig, published their findings on Kiesinger's disreputable past in book form, complete with a preface by the novelist Heinrich Böll.

All this happened far from France, but the Klarsfelds' next set of targets – Kurt Lischka and Herbert Martin Hagen – brought the agitation a step closer to the hexagon. Lischka and Hagen had been SS officers and senior police officials in Paris during the war, major players in the implementation of the Final Solution in France. In 1971, in conversation with Yaron London, an Israeli television official, Beate Klarsfeld mentioned that she knew of Lischka's German whereabouts. London proposed that Beate make a documentary about the man for Israeli television. The Klarsfelds assembled a crew and a dossier (once again compiled from the CDJC archive), and headed to Cologne, where Lischka lived, to confront him on film. A similar operation, once again with dossier in hand, was mounted against Hagen. It doesn't appear that the documentary was ever made, but the Klarsfelds now had a cause: to bring these two criminals to justice, and they pursued it with relentless ingenuity. A kidnapping was their first gambit, which, though botched, did succeed in making headlines. They then recruited Ralph Feigelson, an ex-deportee, to hand-deliver the Lischka and Hagen files to German judicial authorities, which Feigelson did, dressed in the striped uniform of a former camp inmate and wearing medals he had earned during the war for Resistance heroism. The uniforms were donned once again in 1973, this time by Henri Pudeleau and Julien Aubart, the former an Auschwitz survivor, the latter a onetime political deportee. The occasion was a commando action led by Beate Klarsfeld at Lischka's place of work, which caused a ruckus, broken windows, and a rough confrontation with the police. Pudeleau and Aubart were arrested and released after paying a fine.

Beate, however, was not taken into custody. She was now a wanted woman, and she stage-managed the circumstances of her arrest once again in spectacular fashion. In April 1974, she sneaked into Germany, surfacing at the Dachau concentration camp in the company of Pudeleau and a second ex-deportee, Henri Wolff, both dressed in camp garb. The police and press had been tipped off, and what resulted was an arrest, to be sure, but also a media frenzy that was followed by yet another trial, which just raised the stakes.[42]

It was an obvious scandal that Beate Klarsfeld might spend time in jail while Nazis like Lischka and Hagen roamed free, and the German authorities felt compelled to take action at last. In 1979, Lischka and Hagen were brought to justice in Cologne, alongside a third accused, Ernst Heinrichsohn. All were convicted and sentenced, but the hearing was as meaningful for what happened outside the courtroom as for what transpired within.

The Klarsfelds' exploits had earned them not just public notoriety but also a loyal following, men like Pudeleau, and he was far from alone. Henri Golub had lost both parents to the Holocaust as a toddler, and for him and his wife Françoise, the Klarsfelds' Nazi-hunting campaign was a "revelation" that provided a sense of purpose. Golub joined ranks with the Klarsfelds in 1975 and later introduced them to another couple, similar in profile, Gilbert and Charlotte Ermann. Serge Klarsfeld delivered a eulogy at Gilbert Ermann's funeral in 1983, recalling his service in France's armed Resistance and the Ermann couple's devotion later in life to the Nazi-hunting mission. They had been let down in the past by a "political ideal," Klarsfeld explained, without specifying which one, but among us, he went on, they had found a spirit of camaraderie that proved steadfast and rewarding.[43] The bereft and the disillusioned rallied to the Klarsfelds, who set them to work, and the work in question involved the usual Klarsfeld mix of archival digging and militant action.

On the matter of digging, Serge Klarsfeld went to great lengths to raise public awareness of the Holocaust as the Lischka–Hagen–Heinrichsohn trial loomed. He covered the publication costs of a Billig text on the genocide of the Jews, as well as a document collection detailing the crimes of the three accused.[44] He also oversaw the compilation of an exhaustive list of every Jew in France swept away in the tidal wave of the Final Solution. The endeavor cost money and man-hours, but the Klarsfelds' growing band pitched in to help, the Golubs with fund-raising, the Ermanns with the statistics.[45] The end product, *Le Mémorial de la Déportation des juifs de France*, was published in 1978. It was not a handsome volume, but a rough-and-ready assemblage of typescript numbers and names. Yet, how many names there were! – almost 80,000 – and Klarsfeld detailed as best he could who they were, where they had been born, and the fate meted out to each of them: death by execution, death in an internment camp on French soil, death in deportation. When it came to the deportees, Klarsfeld listed them trainload by trainload, with the names in each convoy arranged in alphabetical order. For Jews wanting to know what had happened to murdered loved ones, it was not a difficult exercise to track down the names of the lost. That's what Georges Perec did, searching out – and finding – his mother's name (she was deported to Auschwitz) when he stumbled on a copy of Klarsfeld's volume on a colleague's bookshelf.[46] As did Annette Zaidman, who lost a father and a brother in the Holocaust. She looked them up in *Le Mémorial* and within a week's time, as she tells it, hastened to enlist in "Klarsfeld's band," becoming one of the group's mainstays.[47] In time, the group gelled into a formal organization, Les Fils et les Filles des Déportés juifs de France (FFDJF). At its founding in January 1979, the association numbered five hundred members, and it did not take long before it made its presence felt.[48]

As so often where the Klarsfelds were involved, archival work was a preface to militancy. A demonstration was planned for the opening of the Lischka–Hagen–Heinrichsohn trial in October, the FFDJF coordinating the event in partnership with the FSJU, CRIF, and Consistory. A special train, booked for the purpose, conveyed six hundred Jewish youth from the gare du Nord to Cologne, and, once arrived, they marched, banners unfurled and chanting slogans, with Golub (FFDJF president) and Zaidman (its secretary-general) at the head of the column. The route home was not direct but included a stopover at Drancy, where the rabbi of the rue Copernic Synagogue, Daniel Farhi, recited the Kaddish.[49] A second, larger march, this one involving fifteen hundred participants, took place in January 1980, just before the trial verdict was rendered.[50] The Klarsfelds now had troops to command, which made them that much more formidable, and the word "troops" is a fitting one. The FFDJF marched beneath a flag of its own devising, a blue Jewish star set against a white field, and its militants sported badges that identified them as "militants of memory."[51]

The Holocaust in France

The confrontational tactics of the Klarsfelds and the FFDJF elevated the Holocaust into a matter of headline-grabbing urgency. The public, like it or not, was made to take notice. It's worth asking, though, whether the contours of the Jewish story changed as it moved from the sidelines to center stage, and the answer is yes.

Most important of all, its French dimension became ever more inescapable. The pursuit of Lischka and Hagen highlighted how the implementation of the Final Solution had played out in France, but that still left unaddressed the question of France's own implication in the genocide. Klarsfeld was well aware of the lacuna and resolved to do something about it.[52]

There had been a scandal over President Georges Pompidou's 1971 decision to pardon Paul Touvier. Touvier had been a senior member of the Milice, Vichy's political police, and in that capacity overseen the despoliation, torture, and execution of Jews. He also knew how to play the choir boy, and there were unreconstructed elements in the Catholic Church ready to speak up for him, which may account in part for Pompidou's clemency. Once discovered, however, it caused an uproar, leading to Touvier's indictment in 1973. He then disappeared underground, shielded by sympathetic Catholic clerics, and for the moment the public climate calmed.

The question of Vichy's complicity in the Final Solution erupted to the surface once more in October 1978. This time, it was an interview that ignited the outcry. Louis Darquier de Pellepoix, a fanatic anti-Semite, had for a period directed Vichy's Commissariat général aux questions juives, taking refuge after the war in Franco's Spain, where he lived in comparative anonymity. In 1978, however, a journalist from *L'Express* tracked him down. The always cynical Darquier made the most of the moment. He'd had nothing to do with the Vél d'hiv roundup, he expatiated. That was the work of René Bousquet, Vichy's chief of police. Darquier's finger-pointing was also a wily dig at postwar French justice. Bousquet, culpable as he was, had managed to escape retribution at the war's end and then gone on to a successful postwar career in public affairs. What hypocrisy, Darquier insinuated, that he, an "innocent" man, had to stew in exile, while the guilty Bousquet prospered. Then Darquier delivered himself of the ultimate provocation: the Holocaust was a Jewish invention. Lice, not Jews, he scoffed, had been gassed at Auschwitz, and that was all there was to it. It was an appalling performance.

Klarsfeld swung into action. Touvier was in hiding. Bousquet, so well-connected, was for the moment out of reach. Not so, however, Bousquet's right-hand man at Vichy police, Jean Leguay. Leguay too had dodged punishment at the Liberation, fleeing to the United States and maintaining a low profile until it was safe to slip back into a France turned forgetful. Klarsfeld knew of him, though, and assembled a dossier on the man. In November 1978, just one month after the Darquier interview, the Nazi-hunter filed a complaint against Leguay, accusing the former police official of crimes against humanity. The French courts took up the case that next March, the first of its kind to head to trial, and the FFDJF mobilized to keep up the pressure.[53]

Leguay died in 1989 before the trial even began, but that didn't change the situation. There was now, thanks to the Klarsfelds' activism, building momentum to settle accounts with Vichy's anti-Semitic past through the courts, and a spate of indictments soon followed. Touvier was run to ground in 1989, tried, and five years later condemned to life imprisonment. Then it was the turn of Bousquet, once seemingly unassailable. He was brought up on charges in 1991 (but assassinated before the case went to trial). The last in the line was Maurice Papon, once a senior Vichy official in the Gironde, who had made a career-saving switch late in the Occupation, rendering service to elements in the Gaullist Resistance. As the man in charge of Jewish affairs in wartime Bordeaux, he had overseen the roundup and deportation of Jews, crimes for which he evaded punishment until 1998 when, after years of legal wrangling, he was convicted and sentenced to ten years in prison. The Leguay case then inaugurated two decades of litigation that kept the French perpetrators of the Final Solution constantly in the public eye.

It was not just the identities of the perpetrators that became known in these years but also the identities of the victims. Klarsfeld's *Mémorial* is, of course, a case in point, supplying a name and all the personhood attached to a name to every Jewish deportee, but that wasn't all. Part of what made the genocide unique was its targeting of entire families, not just the adult members. What more powerful way to hammer home the Holocaust's uniqueness than to publicize the fate of its most vulnerable victims, the mothers and children? This was a natural, almost inevitable move for militants of memory who were themselves sons and daughters of the Holocaust, and it was a strategy bound to touch the public's sympathies in a way few others could.

Klaus Barbie, Gestapo chief in Lyon during the Occupation, committed many crimes, not least among them the torture of Jean Moulin. In April 1944, he dispatched a telex to headquarters in Paris, announcing that he had liquidated a Jewish home for children in the commune of Izieu, located a little over an hour's drive northeast of Lyon. Fifty-one children and teachers had been netted in the roundup, he reported, and sent to Drancy. This was the first stop on a longer voyage that just one of them returned from, Léa Feldblum, a teacher.

At the Liberation, Barbie avoided having to pay for his offenses. He was an intelligence officer skilled at ferreting out Communists, and US intelligence found in him a useful recruit. Barbie, however, remained a wanted man – he was known as the "butcher of Lyon" after all – and French authorities were on the hunt for him. The United States, with the assistance of Catholic clergy, maneuvered to protect its asset and arranged Barbie's escape by way of a so-called ratline to Latin America, where he settled in Bolivia.

In July 1971, the CDJC's Michel Mazor informed Beate Klarsfeld that the Munich prosecutor's office was about to close the books on the Barbie case, an eventuality she was determined to forestall.[54] Research in the center's archives turned up a photocopy of Barbie's fateful telex. It also helped identify who the Izieu children had been, all forty-four of them. The Klarsfelds, as per custom, assembled a dossier on the victims and set to work. They tracked down Fortunée Benguigui, a mother who in wartime had confided three sons, aged five to twelve, to the Izieu home for safekeeping while she remained in Marseille. Beate Klarsfeld prevailed on Mme Benguigui, the "martyr mother" (in Beate's words), to travel to Munich, where the two sat themselves on the steps of the city courthouse, Mme Benguigui holding aloft a photograph of her murdered boys.[55] The two women proclaimed a hunger strike until the prosecutor took action. He consented to do so after reviewing the CDJC evidence, reopening the judicial proceedings, and furnishing Beate with leads as to Barbie's whereabouts in Bolivia.

The scene of action then shifted to La Paz, but the modus operandi remained much the same. The Klarsfelds located a second Izieu mother, Ita Halaunbrenner, who had lost two daughters to Barbie's cruelty, Claudine and Mina, ages five and eight. She traveled with Beate to La Paz. Once arrived, Beate deposited the CDJC dossier with local authorities, and then, despite the admonitions of Bolivian officials, called a press conference. She spoke first, followed by Mme Halaunbrenner whose "Calvary as a woman and Jewish mother" (Beate's words once again) moved the journalists present.[56] This was a perilous act. Bolivia at the time was under the thumb of a hardened military dictator, Colonel Hugo Banzer, and Barbie had worked for the Banzer regime as an intelligence advisor. Beate's last coup was a sit-in in front of Barbie's place of work. This took place in March 1972, with Mme Halaunbrenner, wrapped in chains and brandishing an accusatory sign, itemizing Barbie's crimes. Despite the flurry of negative publicity, Banzer did not budge. The Klarsfelds, in cahoots with Régis Debray (who knew something about Bolivia), contemplated kidnapping Barbie and hauling him away through Chile.[57] That option was foreclosed, however, in September 1973 when Chile's Allende government, which might have been willing to grant the plotters safe passage, was overthrown by General Augusto Pinochet in a right-wing coup. Progress on the Barbie case now appeared stalled, until 1982, when democracy was restored in Bolivia. In a flash, Barbie was extradited to France, placed on trial, and five years later condemned to a life term.

The Topography of Grief

The Klarsfelds' unrelenting agitations unmasked the perpetrators; they riveted attention on the pathos of the victims' loss and at the same time mapped a geography of grief, centered on locales like the Vél d'hiv, Drancy, and Izieu, which were now more and more tightly linked in the public imagination with the execution of the Final Solution in France. This was a geography already well known to French Jews, but that knowledge, galvanized by an emergent consciousness of the Holocaust's uniqueness, propelled changes in how these sites were memorialized, underscoring with a new insistence that these places had been places of Jewish suffering.

The Cité de la Muette was a modernist housing complex, located in Paris' northeastern suburb of Drancy just a short distance from a major rail line. During the Occupation, the Germans converted it into a transit camp, a place to gather Jews destined for eventual deportation to the East. In the immediate postwar era, the Consistory had organized annual memorial services there for the Jewish martyrs of Nazi barbarism, a practice terminated when residents moved back into the buildings and the site returned to what it had once been, a housing project. In 1973, however, the sculptor Shelomo Selinger was commissioned to build a monument at the site, which was unveiled three years later. Selinger was a Polish Jew who had an intimate knowledge of Holocaust tragedy. He lost both parents and a sibling to the Nazis and had spent time in nine different camps himself. He survived at all thanks to a Soviet soldier who discovered him half-dead atop a pile of corpses. Selinger was restored to life, but remembered little of what had happened to him and was still in a state of amnesia when he emigrated to Israel after the war. Memory subsequently returned. He took up sculpting. And in pursuit of his art, he relocated to Paris in the 1950s.

Selinger's Drancy monument is noteworthy for its representation of the Deportation as a Jewish trauma. It consists of three rose granite blocks, accessed by four seven-step stairways, two in the front and two in the back (see Figure 10.1). The pylons on the left and right form doors, "gates of death" as Selinger called them in an interview. Between the two stood a third block, larger in scale, carved to depict a swirling mass of interlaced bodies perched on a bed of flames. Most of these are fluid, abstract forms, but on the block's reverse side, it is possible to make out a mother and child pairing. These are the condemned, of all ages, of all genders, departing from Drancy, the antechamber of death, en route to the inferno of the camps.

The condemned twist and turn, but they also pray. One, a man, is wearing phylacteries, the prayer box on his forehead clearly visible. Selinger made sure to include ten figures, the prescribed number for a minyan, the minimum required, as he put it, to recite prayers for the dead. Indeed, the very shape of the monument has a religious significance. Its three stones recalled the w-shaped Hebrew letter shin, the letter inscribed on the mezuzah affixed to the doorpost of every Jewish home. The mezuzah in turn contains a slip of parchment with passages from Deuteronomy inscribed upon it, Deuteronomy 6:4 the first of them, from which the words of the Shema are taken.

In case the forms were too abstract for the uninformed to make sense of, there is text on the left pylon, which explains what Drancy was, how many "Jewish martyrs of France" passed through the camp, and the

Figure 10.1 Drancy Memorial, Drancy, 1976

ultimate fate that awaited them. The right pylon has text as well, a polyglot mix of French, Hebrew, and Yiddish. The French is taken from Lamentations 1:12: "Behold, and see if there be any pain like unto my pain." Beneath it, the Hebrew original is provided. And at the bottom, a Yiddish text invites the passerby to remember the "holy ones" murdered by the Nazis. The citation from Lamentations is also to be found on the back wall of the crypt at the Tombeau du Martyr juif inconnu.[58]

There was no mistaking that this was a monument to the Jewish dead, to a Yiddish-speaking world extinguished, all framed in an imagery that was powerfully Jewish in ways religious and biblical. There it was, facing onto the avenue Jean-Jaurès in Drancy, a town with a communist mayor. How did such a monument – so Jewish, so religious – come to be built in what was then a red suburb?

Jews in deportee organizations began to grow more assertive about their Jewishness in the 1970s. At its origins, the Amicale d'Auschwitz, even though it counted a numerous Jewish rank-and-file, was run at the top by PCF notables like Marie-Claude Vaillant-Couturier. The leading personality in the Yiddishophone AADJF was Henry Bulawko, a man of the *marxisant* Left who, though not a Communist himself, enjoyed warm and ongoing relations with party comrades. These organizations leaned Left, but the nature of their leftism began to change in the 1970s. It may have been the Arab–Israeli War that initiated the process, awakening once inchoate feelings of solidarity with the Jewish state. Many deportees, whatever reserves they may have harbored about Israeli policy, did not want to see Israel itself erased from the map. Yet more consequential was the wave of anti-Zionism that emanated from the Eastern bloc post-1968. For the Eastern bloc too had known unrest that year, and communist authorities deployed anti-Zionist rhetoric against Eastern bloc sixty-eighters to rouse public prejudice against them. The Yom Kippur War of 1973 just turned the volume up on the anti-Zionist sloganeering, and then came the Soviet-backed United Nations resolution of 1975 equating Zionism with racism. This was too much: Jewish members of the Amicale d'Auschwitz stepped forward to protest, and at the same time non-Jewish members began to step back, in many cases leaving the organization altogether. Bulawko himself also experienced a change of heart. He had militated shoulder to shoulder with Communists during the war, and it was Soviet troops who saved him, the survivor of an Auschwitz death march, at the war's end. That didn't stop him, however, from recognizing in Eastern bloc anti-Zionism a recrudescence of a form of bigotry he knew all too well, anti-Semitism.[59]

The proposal to build a Drancy monument originated with the Amicale des anciens déportés juifs de France, over which Bulawko then presided. The site had a personal meaning for him, as he had transited through Drancy himself on the way to Auschwitz. It was Bulawko who partnered with the communist mayor of the township, Maurice Nilès, a fellow résistant, to make Shelomo Selinger's memorial a reality.[60] Bulawko rejected Soviet anti-Zionism, yet remained a man of the Left, with a record of comradeship that enabled him to partner with people like Nilès with whom he shared a militant past.

As for the remaking of the Vél d'hiv site, it played out in two parts, both of them marked by contention on the Left. Since the war's end, small crowds had assembled every July 16 to commemorate the Vél d'hiv roundup in ceremonials officiated by the AADJF with the communist-aligned FNDIRP playing a backup role. The Vél d'hiv cycling arena itself was torn down in the 1950s, to be replaced by a bland office block, but that didn't alter the pattern of memorial activity. Then, a pair of 1970s movies brought renewed pubic attention to the Vél d'hiv story, Michel Mitrani's *Les Guichets du Louvre* (1974), in which a non-Jewish teenager makes futile efforts to alert Jews to the coming roundup, and Joseph Losey's *Monsieur Klein* (1976), in which a non-Jew with a Jewish-sounding name mistakenly winds up a Vél d'hiv detainee. At the same time, as we have seen, the AADJF had begun to back away from its communist associations, with the result that as the decade of the eighties opened, the Vél d'hiv had become at once a more high-profile site and one less tethered to the communist narrative of the Deportation. These developments found formal expression in 1982, when the AADJF ceded management of the July 16 commemoration to the Conseil représentatif des Israélites de France. Bulawko stayed on as master of ceremonies, but it was now no longer the Left that ran the event. FNDIRP felt the slight, which it did not leave unanswered, deciding to arrange a second set of ceremonials all its own.[61] The mainstreaming of the Vél d'hiv was made official in 1986, when the CRIF invited the mayor of Paris, Jacques Chirac, to address that year's July 16 event. The CRIF had acted on Klarsfeld's suggestion, and Chirac returned the favor, making a speech that cited information from Klarsfeld's scholarship. On the same occasion, the mayor unveiled a plaque on a small plot (situated just across the street from the Bir Hakeim metro station) where the defunct cycling arena had once stood. It identified in no uncertain terms who the perpetrators and victims of the Vél d'hiv roundup had been: the perpetrators, "the Vichy police" working on German orders; the victims, 13,152 Jews, children, women, and men, the figures for each category listed in that order.[62] Chirac performed one last action that day, yet another unveiling, this one of a street sign, renaming a nearby plaza on the quai de Grenelle as the "Place des Martyrs juifs du Vélodrome d'hiver."

In round one of the Vél d'hiv memorial battles, the Communists lost control of the site. The arena had once been a gathering place to remember the fallen in the struggle against Nazi barbarism; it was now dedicated to the memory of murdered Jews. In round two, the consecration of Jewish memory was elevated from a local event that engaged Parisian officialdom into one of national proportions.

It was the Touvier trial that set off the chain reaction. In April 1992, a Paris court threw out the case against Touvier, arguing that the acts he was accused of did not constitute crimes against humanity.[63] The charges were reinstated on appeal before the year was out, but the damage had been done. Elements of France's judiciary, it seemed, nursed second thoughts about facing squarely Vichy complicity in the murder of French Jewry. It also seemed that the president of the Republic, François Mitterrand, shared in that reluctance. The Paris press revealed in early July that Mitterrand had made arrangements over a period of years to lay a wreath every Armistice Day at Pétain's grave on the Île d'Yeu. This might be passed off as a patriotic gesture in recognition of the "victor of Verdun," but Mitterrand had once worked at Vichy and, in the postwar, remained on close terms with former Vichyites like René Bousquet. It might well be wondered whether the president harbored lingering sympathies for the old Maréchal. It was to dissipate such suspicions that Mitterrand consented to make a nonspeaking appearance at the fiftieth anniversary commemoration of the Vél d'hiv roundup later that month.

The event turned out to be an explosive one. On the initiative of Anna Senik (b. 1938), who had spent the war in hiding in rural France, a petition circulated some weeks preceding that called on the president of the Republic to acknowledge the French state's compromising participation in the persecution of Jews. Hundreds signed their names, and *Le Monde* agreed to publish the document, which it did on June 17. The petition was sponsored by an ad hoc committee, the Comité Vél d'hiv' 42, made up of eleven members, most of them unknown to the newspaper's readership. Yet, the concatenation of circumstances – the Touvier Affair, the resurrection of Mitterrand's Vichy past, and the petition itself – put pressure on the president to react. He refused to do so, however, arguing that the French Republic had no obligation to assume responsibility for acts committed by an illegitimate regime like Vichy. Thus, when Mitterrand showed up that July 16 at the Vél d'hiv, he was greeted by many of the young people in the crowd with jeers and taunts, "*Mitterrand à Vichy*," a shocking breach of decorum on such a solemn occasion. That very same day, the Comité Vél d'hiv published a second appeal to the president in *Le Monde*, demanding that he make a gesture of contrition that engaged the nation as a whole, as Willy Brandt had done in 1970 when, as German chancellor, he knelt before the Ghetto Fighters monument in Warsaw. Mitterrand did not take up the challenge, and the committee then turned its attention to parliament, lobbying deputies to enact legislation designating July 16 as a national day of remembrance.

Mitterrand meanwhile went ahead with the usual plans to lay a wreath at Pétain's tomb the next November 11, which the local prefect in fact did on the president's behalf. Klarsfeld and a delegation of Jewish students were on hand to protest, and then on the 12th, Klarsfeld arranged for the laying of a wreath at the Vél d'hiv, this one in the shape of a Francisque – an axe-shaped badge awarded by the Vichy state for outstanding service to the regime – with a dedication attached: "To François Mitterrand with all my gratitude, signed Philippe Pétain." Pétain, of course, had awarded Mitterrand a Francisque back in Vichy days, which is what made Klarsfeld's act, as Klarsfeld himself characterized it, so "insolent."[64]

Now, at last, Mitterrand buckled. He made the proposal to designate July 16 as a Vél d'hiv day of remembrance his own. He acted by executive order, rather than pursuing the legislative path, and so was decreed into

Figure 10.2 Vél d'Hiv Memorial, Quai de Grenelle, Paris, 1994

existence in February 1993 the Journée nationale commémorative des persécutions racistes et antisémites commises sous l'autorité de fait dite 'gouvernement de l'État français.'[65] This was a first of its kind, as no European state had ever before set aside a day devoted to the memorialization of Holocaust victims per se.[66] The Journée nationale de la Déportation was still observed, but henceforth, it had a twin, signaling the formal hiving off of Jewish deportation memory from that of deportees in general.

Now that the Vél d'hiv had become a site of national remembrance, officials deemed the cramped quarters across from the Bir Hakeim metro station no longer adequate to accommodate the associated ceremonials. Plans were made to beautify the more spacious quai de Grenelle nearby, and these included commissioning a commemorative sculptural ensemble. The winning design (see Figure 10.2) was that of Walter Spitzer, depicting seven bronze figures seated on a stone base. The figures – two men, two women (one of them pregnant), and three children – were deportees, recognizable as such not just by their disheveled and downcast appearance but also by a telltale suitcase. The stone base, curved in shape, recalled the banked surface of a cycling arena. A plaque attached to the ensemble identified the figures as victims of racist and anti-Semitic crimes committed on the authority of the Vichy state. The inaugural ceremony took place on July 17, 1994 with Mitterrand himself in attendance.

The children of Izieu were not forgotten amidst this proliferating whirl of official ceremonials. Their turn to be recognized came in the spring of 1994. It's not as though the children's fate had never before been acknowledged. In 1946, at a crossroads downhill from the site of the Izieu home, a commemorative obelisk was erected, carved with explanatory and memorial inscriptions. One of these identified the perpetrators – they were Germans – but not the victims, except to say that they were children and educators (although a hint of who in fact they had been was provided by a high relief on the obelisk's pedestal, which represented the heads of a girl and boy set against a Magen David). This would all change in the wake of the Barbie trial. In 1989, one of the monument's inscriptions was rewritten, and now the language was explicit. Barbie was mentioned by name. As for Barbie's victims, they were described as innocents, shot, deported and exterminated "because they were Jews." Then the following year, a plaque was added to the actual Izieu home, which spelled out, as had not been spelled out before, that the children who once sheltered there were not just any children but Jewish children. These emendations were a prelude to a yet more official recognition. The home was made into a memorial museum, dedicated to the history, the Jewish history, of what had happened on that spot. The president of the Republic, François Mitterrand himself, presided at the inaugural ceremony in April 1994.[67]

So, the Holocaust now had a topography and a day all its own, and it was the Comité Vél d'hiv that had set the final phase of the memorialization process in motion.[68] Who were these people? A number, perhaps the majority, had entered into politics in the early 1960s via membership in the PCF-affiliated Union des étudiants communistes (UEC; Debray had also belonged). This was true of Senik's brother, André, and of the Comité Vél d'hiv's most storied adherent, Jean-Pierre Le Dantec. The UEC's aggressive opposition to France's war in Algeria landed it in difficulties with cautious party leaders, and young militants, in pursuit of a more revolutionary line, moved on to redder pastures: to the Union des Jeunesses Communistes Marxistes-Léninistes (the path followed by Le Dantec) or the Maoist Gauche prolétarienne. In a word, the Comité Vél d'hiv was made up in large part of onetime student revolutionaries.[69]

They were also bound by a second commonality: mothers and fathers who had lived the Second World War as adults. The parents, of course, had not all lived the war in the same way. Anna Senik's father was a Communist, but other parents had been other things, Gaullists or Jews on the run. Yet, whatever the family background, the elders had retailed stories about the war, and come the 1980s and 1990s, the next generation no longer believed them. Or, as Senik phrased it, the children no longer swallowed "the Gaullist and Communist fabrication that all France had been résistante."[70] It was not just the older generation's "official lie" that the young rejected but also its "official silence," fifty years' worth, on the matter of France's own role in the genocide of the Jews.[71] It was not as student revolutionaries, however, that the sons and daughters assumed the task of breaking that silence. The Marxism of more youthful days had lost its militant edge. But when it came to attitude and tactics – demonstrations, confrontations, and so on – , they did indeed react as sixty-eighters. To quote Senik one last time: "we had the necessary insolence: that's what May '68 was all about."[72]

The sons and daughters of deportees battered at the walls of the Gaullist memory palace with pickaxes and, even as they did so, they began to lay stone by stone the foundations of a new understanding of the Deportation. The world had turned its back on the Jews as they were destroyed, and the Jews did not die as deported résistants had. They were herded into extermination camps like Treblinka and gassed en masse, with no exceptions made for mothers and children. It was a gross injustice to blame such unfortunates, who were victims after all, for passivity in the face of Nazi duplicity and violence. Unarmed and without experience of arms, beaten upon and abandoned, they faced the most desperate and hopeless of situations. Vichy had been complicit in this grisly endeavor, rounding up Jews and deporting them. France's vanished Jews deserved memorialization, and the sons and daughters made sure that they got it, changing the nation's memorial landscape in the process. The high places of memory – Mont-Valérien, Struthof, and the like – were joined by a new set of sites: the Vél d'hiv, Drancy, and Izieu. All this was accomplished with an attention-grabbing fanfare. The political militancy of '68 may have begun to fade, but not the sixty-eighters' militant flair, and in the klieg lights of media publicity, the Holocaust's contours sharpened and came into view as never before. Yet, for these militants of memory, a question still nagged: Why hadn't this happened sooner? Why was it that they, the children, had had to do the memory work their parents would not or could not do?

11 "The Return of the Repressed"

Histories of Holocaust memory sometimes begin with a chapter on forgetting, which reads more or less like this. Deportees returned from the camps. Memoirs were published or begun and put aside, and then a long silence settled in. There were new lives to build in an era of reconstruction, and no one wanted to listen to painful stories about the Jews. Primo Levi had difficulties finding a publisher for *Se questo è un uomo* (1947). When Simone Veil tried to tell people about Auschwitz, she was met with distracted looks. And so, the tragic memory of what had happened was hushed, this while Gaullist and communist narratives about the war, so full of heroics, flourished. On the matter of Jewish loss, an older generation had failed to transmit, tamping down excruciating memories or neutralizing them with pacifying myths. The young suffered for these silences, but then in the 1960s and 1970s, they found a voice.[1]

This book has argued that the silence so central to this narrative was no silence at all. Jews and Jewish losses were talked about by Jews themselves but also by others, and it wasn't all talk. Political deportees embraced Jews as comrades-in-arms. Representatives of the French state turned out to take part in Jewish remembrance events. A conscience-stricken Catholic Church, prodded both from within and without, undertook an epochal rethinking of its teaching on the Jews. So, the problem is not to explain the silence of the war generation but to account for why successive generations, even as they awakened to the scope and magnitude of the Jewish tragedy, came to the misplaced conviction that they were discoverers of a continent previously unexplored.

Some elements of a possible answer are already in place. A first piece has to do with the kinds of story that the war generation told, stories about martyrdom and heroism, in which the Jewish dead were often (though not always) mixed in with all the rest. Such narratives, moreover, sometimes came couched in a religious idiom that didn't resonate with young people more intent on movies, sports, and not least of all the politics of the Left. Christian-Jewish dialogue had begun to cast a light on the specificities of the Jewish experience, bringing the singularity of its contours into sharper relief, but secular-minded baby boomers weren't paying close attention. In any event, bright as that light was, it was outshone by the dazzle of the Gaullist epic, resplendent in the glare of mass media coverage. It would take all the resourcefulness of Marcel Ophuls, the Klarsfelds, and others like them to break the Gaullist spell and rouse the public to an awareness of what wartime France had really been like. The now disenchanted looked about with blinking eyes, angry that no one had told them about all this before, that they had been soothed with bogus stories of consolation and derring-do. To them, the most pressing problem was not the one raised here, why so much of the memory work of the war generation remained invisible to those who came after. It was, rather, a different one: how to make sense of the apparent delay, decades long, between the Holocaust and its remembering, between loss and the mourning of loss.

The young discovered an answer ready to hand in contemporary psychiatric thinking about trauma. From the psychiatric point of view, the experience of trauma is too overpowering for victims to confront head on. They recoil instead, repressing psychic blows rather than dealing with them. The repressed, however, will out, and trauma in time makes its return, resurfacing in the form of symptoms – flashbacks, nightmares, suicidal thoughts, and the like. Now, there is a "cure" for such ills, if cure is the right word, and, for psychiatrists, it lies in a working through of the originary blow via talk and analysis. The recovery of memory on this accounting is a therapeutic exercise that allows victims to give narrative form to their lives and to manage in the process the ruptures born of profound emotional shocks.

It's not hard to understand the power and attraction of such an interpretive framework to young people in search of reasons for the supposed silence of their elders. It accounted first of all for why parents traumatized by the Holocaust were so buttoned up. The children of survivors, moreover, had had to live with that reticence, a painful burden in its own right. They were heirs to a trauma, which left unnamed, had made for a difficult growing up. The "return of the repressed" narrative offered a diagnosis, and, it also pointed a way forward. There were techniques for dealing with an unmastered past, therapy, of course, but literature as well. Writing and talking afforded the sons and daughters the means to sort out what gnawed at them, and such working through proved a veritable release. Once damned up energies poured into a militant project that aimed at bringing repressed experience to light – the better to help out survivors who had labored too long under the weight of unbearable memory, the better to effect a long-postponed settling of accounts with inconvenient historical truths. The "return of the repressed" template appealed in large measure because at the level of individual and familial experience it did indeed make a lot of sense.

But does it make as much sense when applied to understanding the behavior of larger groups, of collectivities like nations or generations? Not really, as will be argued here, which is why I have chosen to place this chapter's title in quotation marks. The template is problematic in two respects. First of all, it effaces the very real memory work that the war generation engaged in, making that work hard to see, if not whiting it out entirely. In so doing, it has facilitated the erasure of a complex memorial past and in the process helped to fashion what a number of scholars are now calling "the myth of silence."[2]

The template, moreover, makes the crystallization of Holocaust consciousness appear to be a natural, almost inevitable development, when in point of fact it was one propelled by intense political emotion. From the psychiatric perspective, as already noted, repressed trauma is bound to make its return, an initial period of latency giving way to symptomatic behavior, and such a schema provides a tempting way to think about how awareness of the Holocaust progressed, an initial period of silence giving way in the 1960s and 1970s to voice, to the voluble eruption of a hitherto unarticulated Holocaust consciousness. This reading of events has the ring of plausibility, coming as it does framed in the language of psychiatric science. As regards Holocaust consciousness, however, the psychiatric template did not gain currency at just any moment but at one politically charged, and that moment was the '68 era when generational revolt, stoked by antiwar and anti-imperialist fervor, injected into public affairs disruptive notes of insolence and iconoclasm. This was the climate in which Holocaust consciousness took flight, one stamped by politics as much as by therapeutic intent. Indeed, the "return of the repressed" story itself, while it might now have a scientific, above politics look to it, was very much inflected by the era's politics when it first made its appearance in the mid-sixties as a way of thinking about the traumas of the Second World War.

The Work of Mourning

It is easy enough to claim that the silence-to-voice narrative was born of the '68 moment (and shaped by it), but tracking the narrative's progress and development through the era is another matter. That very word, *narrative*, however, points to a place where to begin, with literature. The era's fiction is packed with stories of eruptive memory, and it is precisely Holocaust memory that bursts time and again into the plotlines. There are numerous examples of such work, and a trio of them will be examined here: Romain Gary's, *La Danse de Gengis Cohn* (1967), Patrick Modiano's *Le Place de l'étoile* (1968), and Georges Perec's *W ou le souvenir d'enfance* (1975). The accents of the era are easy to pick out in all three novels, ludic and anti-conventional as they are in form and tone, but such irreverence served a cathartic purpose, dredging up a past that refused to let go so that it, at last, might be faced down.

Romain Gary's was once a name to conjure with. He was a genuine war hero who had flown planes for Free France, a record of service that earned him induction into that "exceptional knighthood" (de Gaulle's term), the Ordre de la Libération. Once the war had ended, Gary continued to serve, now as a member of France's diplomatic corps. At the same time, he pursued a parallel career as a writer, churning out action novels full of sound and fury. Partisan combat in the forests of Eastern Europe is the subject of *Éducation européenne* (1945). In *Les Racines du ciel* (1956), it is the exploits of an ecologist on the run in French Equatorial Africa. "Ecologist" is something of an anachronism, of course, as the word, though it existed, was not yet in wide usage, but Gary, when he talked about the book in retrospect, liked to refer to it as "the first ecological novel."[3] Its hero after all is a man named Morel, an ex-résistant and deportee, who has moved to Africa and taken up the cause of the elephant. Morel mounts a campaign to save the animals from bloodthirsty game-hunters. He breaks the law, and the authorities pursue him, suspecting that Morel's "idealism" is just a front for anticolonial subversion. The novel won a Prix Goncourt, and in the US, it was made into a movie, starring Trevor Howard as Morel.

Gary's connection to the American film industry was in fact more than a passing one. In 1956, France's diplomatic service named him consul general in Los Angeles, a posting that brought him into contact with Hollywood royalty. Gary stepped down from the position after a few years but continued to be involved in Hollywood affairs. He worked on the screenplay of *The Longest Day*; he tried his hand at directing; and he ended up marrying a real star, Jean Seberg, in 1962. Of all the Hollywood personalities he had dealings with, however, the one he was most drawn to was Groucho Marx. "[H]e influenced me as a writer," Gary later said of Groucho, and why? Because Groucho practiced "an aggressive humor."[4] It was a brand of wit, as Gary saw it, that had originated in the ghetto. The ghetto laugh – half comic, half belligerent – was the weapon the unarmed had forged to fight back against anti-Semitism, and it was that laugh, which was also Groucho's, that so fascinated Gary.

All this seems a far remove from '68, but it's not. Gary's marriage to Seberg was a rocky one and ended in divorce in 1970. It didn't help that she was so involved with the Black Panther Party, which earned her the harassing attentions of the FBI. However much Gary detested racism, and he did, the Panthers' militancy was more than he bargained for. That said, he did have a sixties moment of his own. In 1964, Gary published *Ski Bum*, a minor novel written in English about a draft-dodging American, Lenny, who heads to Switzerland to live the catch-as-catch can life of a ski instructor. Lenny wants to live above the squalor and pettiness of the "shit level down there," but he's also something of a lost soul, until he meets Jess.[5] She's the daughter of a US diplomat based in Geneva, an idealistic young woman who believes in progressive causes. In fact, she works for one of them, the SPCA (animal protection again). They will fall in love, a joining of souls that allows the disenchanted Lenny to reconnect. Gary understood the novel as in part a valedictory to a once confident, pre-Viet Nam War America, now no longer so sure of itself, which is why he titled the French version *Adieu Gary Cooper*. The story's main protagonists, however, were baby boomers on the look-out for something to believe in, and the novel, it seems, appealed to young readers, enough so that Hollywood calculated there might be a market for a movie version of it. Gary liked to think the novel's themes and characters were annunciatory of "May'68."[6] One last detail: among Lenny's band of young knockabouts is a poet, Genghis Cohn.

The punning name must have tickled Gary's fancy, for he used it again in *La Danse de Gengis Cohn*, this time not just for a walk-on character but for the title role. The novel has topical referents. Kurt Kiesinger makes an appearance, mentioned in a sarcastic aside as a Nazi who had served the party for a *mere* twelve years, and so too does Jean-François Steiner, chided for blaming European Jewry's wartime fate on the victims themselves. There is no mistaking then that this is a sixties text, and it also happens to be one of the first that evokes the Holocaust in psychiatric terms as a trauma long repressed that refuses to remain bottled up, time and again spilling into people's lives, sometimes to antic effect.

The novel's star performer is Moishe Cohn, a Jewish comic with kinky hair like Harpo Marx's. He had worked the German cabaret circuit before the war with an act that mixed hilarity and aggression. He entered dancing with violin in hand and then proceeded to skewer his audience with a cruelty that earned him a nickname, Genghis. Genghis Cohn was shot during the war by a German SS, Hauptjudenfresser Schatz as the novel names him in punning Yiddish (the term means Head Jew-eater). But Cohn did not depart this world without one last gesture of insolence. As Schatz prepares to fire, Cohn drops his trousers and moons the Nazi, inviting him to "*Kish mir in tuchas*."[7] Cohn dies, but he does not stay dead and returns like a dybbuk, a malicious spirit, to haunt Schatz. That's how the novel opens, in 1966, with Schatz now a police official in the town of Licht, a respected man but also one possessed. Cohn is always by the ex-Nazi's side, cajoling him into learning Yiddish, urging him to cook Jewish delicacies, in general, maneuvering Schatz to act like a Jew, sometimes in ways that embarrass him in front of fellow police officers.

A series of sex murders in the nearby forest of Geist – the victims are men who seem to have died in ecstasy – attract Schatz's attentions. The murderers are a couple, Lily and Florian, she luring the men, seeking a satisfaction from them that they are unable to supply, he executing them at the critical moment. The allegory is transparent and not very compelling, Lily standing in for Art (men seek to serve her but never measure up) and Florian for Death, but this section of the novel does provide one scene of comic excess. Death, it turns out, knows Yiddish, and Cohn asks him where he learned it. Berlitz perhaps? "No, Treblinka," comes the reply.[8] Cohn also begins to wonder whether the story he finds himself in is not the one he thought it to be. He had believed himself a character inhabiting "the subconscious" of a German.[9] Yet, maybe, he wonders, all of the story's characters are figments – himself as well as Schatz and the others –the imagined creations of some sex-obsessed maniac. And maybe, the speculation goes on, that maniac is a "writer," inventing this very story to exorcise himself of his own demons. Thus, the reader is invited to think of the book in hand as itself a kind of therapeutic enterprise, a way for the author to purge his own unconscious of the darknesses that possess it.[10]

The novel's final section opens with Cohn reflecting on the future that lies before him. The pope has pardoned the Jews (an allusion to Vatican II), and the world in general seems to be opening its arms to the people it once cursed. Does Cohn, however, want to enter into that fraternal embrace, to become a part of *their* "historical tapestry," *their* "knighthood" (just one among numerous Gaullist references in the novel's concluding passages)?[11] Then Cohn steps aside, ceding center-stage to the "writer," or Romain as he's identified on the novel's next-to-last page. Romain has traveled to Poland with his wife to pay a visit to the monument to the Warsaw Ghetto uprising. He faints, hallucinates, and babbles in Polish. A witness to the scene wonders how it happens that a foreigner is fluent in "the tongue of Mickiewicz," and a conversation ensues between the witness and the wife with the wife speaking first:

– He studied his humanities here, in the ghetto…
– Ah! We didn't know he was Jewish…
– He didn't either.[12]

As Gary's biographer David Bellos notes, such a finale situates the novel in a "well-established genre: the novel of the rediscovery of roots."[13]

Which raises the question of what those roots were, not an easy one to untangle, for Gary was born under a different name, Roman Kacew. The date was 1914 and the place Vilnius, then in Russia, today in Lithuania.[14] His mother, Mina, was a Jew and a zealous Francophile who spirited her son away to Nice in 1928, intent on exposing him to better things. Her devotion to France never dimmed, although she lived long enough to experience the first years of Vichy rule and to suffer from the regime's anti-Semitic persecutions.[15] Gary then knew something about the costs of anti-Semitism, and the subject was never far from the novelist's thoughts. His fiction abounds in Jewish characters, many of them with a Holocaust connection like the photographer Abe Fields in *Les Racines du ciel*. Fields is on the scene in Africa to cover Morel's jungle hegira but ends up befriending the man, in part because he himself, as the son of parents "gassed at Auschwitz," has an instinctive sympathy for the oppressed.[16] What makes *La Danse de Gengis Cohn* special, however, is that it's now the novel's main character and not a sidekick who is marked by the Holocaust. And what makes it pertinent in the present context is not just its sixties topicality but Gary's casting of Holocaust memory at a mid-sixties moment as a return of the repressed.

The novel also happens to be, in Bellos' words, "indescribably funny and outrageously tasteless,"[17] and it was not the last of its kind. Another, just as outrageous in its own way, followed on the comic heels of *La Danse de Gengis Cohn*, Patrick Modiano's debut novel, *La Place de l'étoile*. It's not a challenge to put a finger on why critics and historians have singled out this book as such a mirror-breaking text, the '68er novel par excellence.[18] There is first of all its date of publication, 1968. Then there is its playful quality.[19] The novel's very title is a pun. The book opens with a vignette about Occupation-era Paris. It is 1942, and a German soldier asks a Frenchman on the street where to find the Place de l'Étoile. The Frenchman by way of reply does not provide directions but points to the left side of his chest, the spot where Jews were made to wear the yellow Star of David. Finally, there's the name of the novel's hero, Raphaël Schlemilovitch, a play on the Yiddish word, schlemiel, meaning loser or patsy.

The novel that follows proves relentless in its comic iconoclasm. The dating of the action is never specified, but it's sometime after the war. The narration is in the first-person, Schlemilovitch recounting to us his travails as a Jew, and the first of these is a contretemps with an anti-Semitic polemicist, Doctor Louis-Ferdinand Bardamu. This is yet one more instance of Modiano's wordplay, for Bardamu happens to be the fictional protagonist of another novel, *Voyage au bout de la nuit*, authored by the notorious anti-Semitic writer Louis-Ferdinand Céline. Schlemilovitch has inherited a fortune, and Bardamu slams into him as just one more well-heeled Jew who likes to flash his money around. What then follows is a sequence of episodes, more or less droll, with Schlemilovitch in each trying to pin down what it means to be a Jew. He adapts various personae, all of them variations on one or another anti-Semitic stereotype. He also encounters on his picaresque way every imaginable species of anti-Semite, and France, it seems, is teeming with them, racists, Jew-baiters, and unrepentant Vichyites.

Schlemilovitch, for all his efforts, can't figure out who he is, and the novel ends in a delirious hallucination and Schlemilovitch's breakdown. He has sought safe haven in Israel, where he's sent to a "disciplinary kibbutz."[20] The Israelis mean to purge him of his European complexes and remake him into a tough Jew. Schlemilovitch, however, is incorrigible, and the more he remains set in his Diasporic ways, the more the Israelis become German-like and the kibbutz itself a simulacrum of a concentration camp. Schlemilovitch contrives to escape, disguised in an SS uniform. An Israeli commandant catches up with him in Paris, and the clock seems to turn back to Occupation days with all identities now turned topsy-turvy. Schlemilovitch, a Jew dressed as a Nazi, is about to be executed by an Israeli who acts like an SS man. Schlemilovitch's head threatens to burst, and that's when he wakes up in a psychiatric clinic. Doctor Sigmund Freud sits at Schlemilovitch's bedside and promises to make a normal man of him, "healthy, optimistic, and sporting." The cure starts with some reading, and Freud hands Schlemilovitch a tract titled *Réflexions sur la question juive* by Jean-Paul Schweitzer de la Sarthe, yet another pun. Schweitzer is, of course, Jean-Paul Sartre's mother's maiden name. The book Freud urges on Schlemilovitch, however, is a very real one. Sartre published an extended essay by that title in 1946, an analysis of the Jewish condition in the postwar era. The stereotypical "Jew," on Sartre's accounting, was a phantasm of the anti-Semite's imagining, a bad-faith invention that enabled bigots to avoid dealing with the world's real problems. It was up to the Jew to refuse such stereotyping and assert an authentic selfhood, whatever that might be (more on Sartre's text in the next chapter). This is the book Freud commands Schlemilovitch to read, promising that it will help him to heal. He'll learn from it first of all that "THE JEW DOES NOT EXIST," that he is an illusion, and that once the illusion is shed, all the anxieties born of an outworn "Yiddish paranoia" will disappear along with. "We live today in a pacified world," Freud declares: "Himmler is dead..."[21] Such reassuring nostrums don't reassure, and the conundrum of what it means to be a

Jew remains unresolved. The novel concludes with Schlemilovitch sinking into exhaustion.

The war years did indeed haunt Modiano, even though, as someone born in July 1945, he had no first-hand experience of them. For Modiano's parents, however, it was another matter.[22] His non-Jewish mother was an indifferent, temperamental parent, more interested in her theatrical career and cultivating actor friends well connected in collaborationist circles than in looking after her children (Modiano had a brother). His father was a Sephardic Jew and a man of dubious character, who slithered through the Occupation, keeping his head down and eking out a living off of dodgy dealings. Writing enabled Modiano to break free from an unhappy family life but not from the Occupation's disruptive and disturbing fallout. It was like a bad dream he couldn't wake from, and he returned to the subject time and again in his fiction. In *La Place de l'étoile*, he treated it with a sixty-eighter's barbed humor but after that with an ever-darkening palette.[23]

Freud was a figure of fun in *La Place de l'étoile*. For Geroges Perec, however, analysis was a more serious business. He completed a round of therapy in mid-1975 just as the first reviews of *W ou le souvenir d'enfance* were coming in.[24] That coincidence points the way toward a reading of the book, as a parallel effort, this one literary and not therapeutic, to confront and work through a past scarred by loss.

Both Perec's parents were Jewish. His father was killed in action as a soldier in 1940. Perec himself (b. 1936) spent the first years of the Occupation with his mother in Paris, but in 1942, as their situation became more precarious, she put the boy on a train headed south, even as she herself opted to remain behind. Perec boarded at a Catholic school (and was baptized), but he also had family nearby, an aunt, Esther, and an uncle, whom he visited on week-ends. Perec never saw his mother again. She was arrested in 1943, interned at Drancy, and then deported to Auschwitz.

Perec's teen companion, Serge Klarsfeld, remembers him as a youth full of talk about cycling. Yet, Perec also read Robert Antelme's concentration camp memoir, *L'Espèce humaine*. He saw and loved Alain Resnais' *Hiroshina mon amour*.[25] Perec was drawn to authors and cineastes for whom the war and the memory of its costs were consuming preoccupations, and such themes reverberated in Perec's own work.

He is known as a man with an enthusiasm and aptitude for puzzles, and there's no doubt that he brought that puzzler's temperament to bear when he set out to become a writer. In the 1960s, Perec fell in with a loose-knit band of literary experimentalists. They had a name, the Ouvroir de littérature potentielle or OuLiPo, and they had an agenda: to explore what happens when writers renounce accepted literary conventions, choosing to work instead under alternative constraints that were self-invented and self-imposed. The idea was to discover what truths and what liberations such formalist play might reveal. Perec wrote *La Disparition* (1969) under this dispensation, and the constraint he opted for was a formidable one: to write an entire novel absent the letter "e". It's not just that Perec, a fabulous wordsmith, pulled off the feat with extraordinary verbal flair but that he turned absence itself into a powerful and unsettling theme. The novel opens with a mysterious disappearance, that of Anton Voyl (another punning name). Friends and family go looking for him, but they too disappear one by one. Even as the characters vanish, images of a blank whiteness accumulate, from Moby Dick on down. Perec succeeds in making palpable what's not there. What's not there, of course is a letter, but it's also worth noting that "e" when pronounced in French sounds like "*eux*" or, in English, "they." A letter lacks, but "they" have also vanished. Perec's parents? Is that possibility too much of a stretch?

"[W]riting 1968 as it happened" is how Bellos characterizes *La Disparition*, so heterodox was it in design and theme,[26] and *W* picked up where *La Disparition* left off. Perec published excerpts from the work in 1969–1970 in Maurice Nadeau's *La Quinzaine littéraire*, set it aside to work on other things, and then returned to the manuscript, which he finished in 1974. *W* was published the next year.

The book is made up of two stories told in parallel. The first is that of a man, an army deserter, hiding out under a name borrowed from another, Gaspard Winckler. The pseudo-Winckler learns that the real one has sailed to an encampment in faraway Tierra del Fuego and been lost there, the victim of a shipwreck experience. What was the actual Winckler's fate? This is what the pseudo-Winckler sets out to learn, voyaging to Tierra del Fuego himself and returning, Ishmael-like, with a tale to tell. The second story is autobiographical, that of Perec's own life, though it's important to keep in mind that the narrator is unreliable, retailing facts that are not always so. The gamesmanship begins right from the start when the narrator intimates that he hasn't any memories of childhood, leaving the reader to wonder just what to make of the outpouring of memory that follows. He also lets on that the book's first plotline, Garspard Winckler's, is a rewriting of a story he had made up as a thirteen-year old.[27] Perec proceeds to toggle back and forth between the two stories, using different typefaces, italics for Winckler's and roman for Perec's, to help the reader keep them straight.

Then, right smack in the middle, there's a break in the text, a blank page, followed by a page with an ellipsis in parentheses (…), followed by another blank page. What has happened? Right before the ellipsis opens, the pseudo-Winckler is just getting ready to set out for Tierra del Fuego, and the narrator bids farewell to his mother at the gare de Lyon. It is 1942.

After the ellipsis closes, the two stories start up again and begin to converge. The first, still in italics, recounts what was discovered when the pseudo-Winckler arrives at the island of W in Tierra del Fuego. He finds there a cluster of Olympic-style villages for athletes in training. It soon becomes clear, however, that the island's inhabitants are not athletes at all. They're inmates, made to wear striped uniforms with a white triangle sewn on them. They're also made to compete. The events, however, turn out to be so many struggles for survival with the losers condemned to death by hanging or stoning. As for the island's overseers, they're guards, not trainers, who bark out *"Schnell! Schnell!"* as they crowd the inmates into W's stadium.[28] Perec's autobiographical recollections also take a concentrationary turn. He remembers the provincial school that he attended during the war; he remembers the Liberation; he remembers shaking hands at a huge demonstration with an idolized visiting dignitary, François Billoux (who was a communist official, though Perec doesn't says so); and he remembers traveling to Paris to visit an exhibition on concentration camps, singling out one set of images for special mention: photos of ovens clawed by the fingers of gassing victims [sic].

Winckler's last entry talks about the mounds of eyeglasses, wedding rings, and gold teeth recuperated from the dead athletes. Perec's is a long citation from David Rousset's *L'Univers concentrationnaire*, followed by one final reflection. Perec doesn't recall why as a twelve-year old (he's twelve now, not thirteen) he set Winckler's tale in Chile, but the choice was an adventitious one: "Pinochet's fascists took it upon themselves to make my phantasm resonate."[29]

The reader of the preceding chapters will know how to unpack Perec's pile-on of allusions: from the camp exposition that Edgar Morin had a hand in organizing just after the war to Alain Resnais' movies, *Nuit et Brouillard* and *Hiroshima mon amour*. Such images encapsulate a particular understanding of the camps, not as extermination factories as in Jean-François Steiner's work, but as sites of murderous exploitation as in Rousset's. It's an old way of thinking about the camps with an unmistakable left-wing pedigree. In case there's any doubt, Perec's concluding invocation of the fascist Pinochet's "camps of deportation" clinches the case. These are also the book's final words.[30]

It won't do, however, to stop the analysis there. *W* is about the camps, but it is also and above all about what the camps did to Jewish families like Perec's. That ellipsis midway through the book arrives at just the moment the narrator is separated from his mother, and the reader is bound to reflect on what happened to her. The passages that follow are an imagining, personal but oblique, of the inferno in which she will be consumed. The Winckler story changes venue, relocating from Europe to Tierra del Fuego, the land of fire, and the narrator's story winds up in the ovens. This was Perec's mother's fate, and Perec musters all the art he can to imagine and to face it. He dedicates the volume "for E." That "E" might be Aunt Esther who did so much to look after him when he was bereft as a boy. It might also be "*Eux*" once again, "They," or the mother and father he lost to the war. There is a moment in *W* when the narrator ruminates on why he's writing, why he's so invested in recovering memories of his parents: "writing," he says, "is the memory of their death and the affirmation of my life."[31] *W* is the result of that effort. It is an act of grieving, a gesture of devotion to the dead that enables Perec himself to move forward...and in certain ways to put the past behind him. Perec's masterpiece, *La Vie mode d'emploi* (1978), includes a black-bordered document dated 1973, announcing the death of the celebrated puzzle-maker, Gaspard Winckler.[32] Writing was indeed a way to confront the past: to exorcise it and to lay it to rest.

Working through the Past

Psychiatry had a name to describe such exorcistic labors: *le travail de deuil* or, in English, the work of mourning. The concept was part of a larger theoretical framework, conceived to deal with repressed childhood trauma and its disruptive consequences in adult life. What is striking for our purposes is how adaptable this framework proved to be to an understanding of Holocaust trauma and the silences that enshrouded it. No less striking is the framework's easy migration from the realm of psychiatric analysis, attuned to the treatment of individual neuroses, to that of historical explanation, which operated at the level of larger groups, national or sociological. As the return-of-the-repressed narrative moved out of the literary realm into that of psychiatry, it shed more than a little of its zestful iconoclasm, taking on a soberer, more scientific aspect. And as it migrated from the personal to the historical, its explanatory ambitions expanded. Now at stake were no longer silences within the family, which were real enough, but an imagined national silence, which was much less so. These developments played themselves out amidst the turbulent politics of the 1960s and 1970s, and once again, as with literary treatments of the subject, it is not difficult to detect the era's influence at work.

Marcel Ophuls' *Memory of Justice* (1976) featured cameo appearances by two well-known psychiatric couples: Robert Jay and Betty Jean Lifton, who were American, and Alexander and Margerete Mitscherlich, who were German. The Liftons had worked with Hiroshima survivors and returning Viet Nam War veterans, developing an expertise in dealing with the scars that trauma left. The scars were not always evident, not right away. Victims tried to leave a hurtful past behind, to return to a normal life or at least the appearance of one. Yet the past kept breaking to the surface, and it surged up in patterns of behavior that caused pain to the victims and also to those who lived with them. Robert Lifton, it will come as no surprise, played a key role in winning recognition for a new category of psychiatric diagnosis, Post-Traumatic Stress Syndrome, and he understood almost immediately that the category had application to Holocaust survivors as well as to veterans shattered by the shock of combat. Like the Liftons, the Mitscherlichs had an interest in trauma, though of a different sort, one that affected the mental well-being, less of individuals, than of nations, and the national psyche that most preoccupied them was Germany's. The German people, as they saw it, had never owned up to the love the Führer once awakened in them. The trauma of Hitler's death, this was the trauma they refused to confront or to work through. It was a past, because unmastered, that continued to roil the present. Such was the line of analysis elaborated in the Mitscherlichs' most celebrated work, *Die Unfähigkeit zu trauern* (1967) or, in French, *Le Deuil impossible* (1972). [33] Here then was a package of concepts – trauma, repression, syndrome, the unmastered past – that promised to help in accounting for the Holocaust generation's silences and for the doleful effects that resulted from them. [34]

The effects had indeed been doleful, for the children of the Holocaust not least of all. *Children of the Holocaust*: that's the title of a book by an American journalist, Helen Epstein, published in 1979. In it, Epstein meditated on what it was like to grow up in a household shadowed by the experience of the Holocaust – both her parents had survived the camps – and globetrotting journalist that she was, she complemented such personal recollections with interview material culled from encounters on multiple continents with others, like herself, the children of survivors. A group portrait emerges from this mix of memory and conversation. A thick cloud of things unsaid hung over such families. The children knew something terrible had happened without ever quite knowing the details. They also knew they were meant to be happy in a way denied to their parents. They had to make good, to succeed, to change the world for the better, and such pressures, gentle and burdensome at the same time because born of parental love, bore down on them. Facts and feelings that did not fit, disturbing how life was supposed to be, were locked away, "in my strong box" as Epstein put it, there to fester. Thus, the Holocaust generation's repressions and silences left their mark on the next generation down. When Epstein's volume was published in French a quarter of a century later, the title was translated as *Le Traumatisme en héritage* (2005).[35]

The idea of a fortified space within was not Epstein's own invention. Bruno Bettelheim, an Austrian-born psychiatrist who fled to the US in 1939, had published *The Empty Fortress* in 1967, which appeared in French translation two years later under the title *La Forteresse vide*. The book examined the cases of two autistic girls and one autistic boy, supplemented by a brief discussion of so-called feral children (one of them, Anna, a Holocaust survivor). It diagnoses autism as a reaction formation to early life trauma, with withholding, "refrigerator" mothers identified as the principal agents of their children's emotional pain. The world is a cold, hostile place, and the child, in self-defense, cuts off from it, retreating inward. It's not necessary here to rehearse all that's tendentious in Bettelheim's theorizing (the refusal of genetic etiology, the blaming of mothers, etc.). What does bear noting is that Bettelheim was looking at autism through the prism of his own experience of trauma, a period of months spent in Dachau and Buchenwald before he made his escape to the US. In the camps, he had observed at close hand how Nazi brutality damaged adults. It broke them down and caused them to regress. The cruelty of the camps was designed to make prisoners lose self-respect, to think of themselves as the camp guards thought of them, or, in the language of psychiatry, to identify with the aggressor. These were subjects Bettelheim developed in a series of essays, collected in a stand-alone volume, *The Informed Heart: Autonomy in a Mass* Age, published in English in 1960 and in French in 1972. The collection's last essay but one treated a well-worn theme: why didn't the Jews resist? The French public, of course, had already confronted the issue, and it was one in any event that didn't seem to have the same purchase in France as it did in places like the United States and Israel, which had never known Nazi occupation first hand. The volume also included a take-down of *The Diary of Anne Frank*, not so much the book itself, as the play, which culminated in Anne's declaration of faith in humankind's ultimate goodness. For Bettelheim, this was an act of denial, a refusal to look the reality of human aggression square in the face. When it came to confronting the gas chambers, people preferred to turn away or to make up reassuring stories.[36] This was all too typical of the group-think characteristic of mass civilization, and in making this move, Bettelheim shifted the unit of analysis from the individual plane to that of the collectivity.

Bettelheim, the man, and the concepts he developed, were known in French psychiatric circles, enough so that he was enlisted to supply an admiring postface to Claudine Vegh's *Je ne lui ai pas dit au revoir. Des enfants de déportés parlent* (1979). In many respects, this book resembled Epstein's. It collected testimony from children, now grown to adulthood, who had lost a parent or both to deportation. Vegh's personal story was also included. She spent the war in the care of a loving Gentile family in provincial France. Her father was deported to Auschwitz never to return; her mother survived. But the differences between the two books are no less important. Vegh was a child psychologist, not a journalist, and the testimonies she reports are less conversational and more structured than in Epstein's volume. Vegh's subjects, moreover, were not the children of survivors, born after the war, so much as "hidden children" who had lived lives in concealment under the Occupation. Their families had been torn apart, never again to be made whole. It is difficult for Vegh to persuade her subjects to open up. She encounters an initial "wall of silence" as Bettelheim's postface puts it.[37] When in the end they do speak, the emotions are raw, anguish, and melancholy, of course, but also shame and anger. For these hurting souls, the working through of loss remains a work in progress.

Psychiatry developed an interpretive template to conceptualize the Holocaust and its effects, one that spilled well beyond psychiatry's own disciplinary bounds. It was borrowed from widely by others, with historians in the forefront, and in this they were encouraged by psychiatric practitioners like the Mitscherlichs and Bettelheim who spoke with conviction about the impact of wartime trauma on the state of the national psyche or on the characterological dilemmas facing mass man.[38]

A cost was incurred, however, as the template migrated from the domain of the private and familial to that of history and politics. The language of psychiatry is a scientific one that does not make explicit its rootedness in historical moment or context. Yet, in France, that language caught on at a particular conjuncture, the 1960s and 1970s, and the temper and politics of the era – the sixty-eighter's ludic insolence, the trauma of the Viet Nam vet, the fury of the young at the wartime lies and complicities of their elders – played a crucial part in shaping the purposes to which it was put. Note also how the psychiatric template in its turn shapes our understanding of what the Holocaust was, the trauma of traumas. This is an understanding hard to contest, but it is also one that cancels out older narratives focused on heroic or redemptive action. Indeed, because it defines all that came before under the sign of silence, falsification, or repression, it makes it difficult to see, let alone appreciate, the varied efforts already made to come to grips with the genocide.

The Gaullist narrative erected a barrier that blocked the view of such efforts. When that wall came down under sixty-eight hammer blows, the memory landscape that came into view, illuminated by the light of psychiatric science, was not an empty one but populated by survivors laboring under a pall of choking silence. This was not a mistaken finding. But the psychiatric model further posited that a traumatized silence was all there was to observe, that indeed to look for more was in all probability a futile exercise. *That* assumption, as we have seen, was mistaken.

On this reading of events, the demolition of the Gaullist memory palace was not the consequence of some vague "return of the repressed" but of the political fury of sixty-eighters who went about their destructive business with a mix of righteous fury and impertinent laughter. And as the Gaullist citadel tumbled, the Holocaust at last came into plain view, rising on the horizon like some "black sun" in Claude Lanzmann's striking turn of phrase.[39] What a black sun it was, a traumatic event that reverberated across the generations, bringing anguish to those who had lived it as to their children. This was not some abstract tragedy but one with a human face, and those faces still lived and live among us, if not as survivors, then as reflections in the faces of the victims' children. It was a dark and haunting vision, and it would get darker still.

12 Shoah

In 1997, Prime Minister Alain Juppé appointed a former deportee, Jean Mattéoli, to preside a commission charged with investigating the spoliation of Jewish property during the war. Wealth recovered was returned to its rightful owners or their heirs. Unclaimed funds, however, were set aside to finance the creation of a new organism, the Fondation pour la mémoire de la Shoah, which began operations in 2001 under the direction of Simone Veil.[1] Four years later, the long-established Mémorial du Martyr juif inconnu metamorphosed into the Mémorial de la Shoah. A wall of names was added to the monument's design that enumerated every Jew in France murdered in the genocide. What these changes owed to Serge Klarsfeld does not require detailing at length. Veil had belonged to Klarsfeld's FFDJF since 1979, and Klarsfeld in turn was nominated to the fledgling foundation's board of directors.[2] It was Klarsfeld's own memorial, moreover, *Le Mémorial de la Déportation des juifs de France*, that generated the roster of names that then made its way onto the Mémorial de la Shoah's wall of remembrance.

Thus, in a burst, the word Shoah seemed to sweep away all other words before it, Holocaust included, and it is well worth wondering how this came about. The answer is on one level a simple one. Simple in that the word, *Shoah*, had acquired wide currency in the wake of the release of Claude Lanzmann's film by that title in 1985. The movie, although more than nine hours long, had been a *succès d'estime* at the box office, enough so that TF1, a privatized television station anxious to demonstrate its cultural seriousness, decided it was worth airing, commercial free, on four consecutive nights in the summer of 1987. Critics hailed the film as a monument in its own right, the movie and its reception combining to consecrate the name, *Shoah*, making also-rans of competitors.[3]

The new word, however, was a strange one, a foreign import from the Hebrew meaning calamity or disaster. Lanzmann in fact had chosen it for its very strangeness, the better to capture a sense of the uniqueness of the phenomenon it denoted. It was in the course of making *Shoah*, that he had come to a clear understanding of wherein that uniqueness resided. Lanzmann's vision was a dark one. He likened the Shoah, after all, to a black sun. For him, it was an event above all else about death and not anyone's death but that of the Jews, "my people" as he called them. They died in the gas chambers of the Aktion Reinhard camps and at Chelmno, murdered by the Nazis, traduced by their neighbors, and abandoned by the world. What made Lanzmann's film so devastating was not just the vision that informed it, but also how that vision was actualized. For this movie was a "documentary" that wasn't one: it rejected the use of archival footage, and it made next to no use of actual documents. What Lanzmann did instead was to interview on camera, often at actual camp sites, revenants from the land of the dead, men and women who had seen the machinery of death at work and lived to tell about it. As they spoke, the past came alive once again in all its appalling detail, and we the viewers are made to see the Shoah, not as a tragedy that happened long ago, but as a catastrophe unfolding before our very eyes. How was it that Lanzmann came to make such a film, one destined to change how the French (and not just the French) spoke and thought about the genocide?

Claude Lanzmann

Lanzmann was not an obvious candidate for the job. As a young man, he was more interested in writing than in film, in the politics of the Left than in Judaism. Yet by mid-life, he had altered course, and it was Sartre's influence and a series of visits to Israel that made the difference.

Lanzmann the leftist firebrand has already made more than one appearance in these pages. He was a fighter from early on. Lanzmann (b. 1925) began high-school in Paris in the late thirties. He moved to Clermont-Ferrand in the Unoccupied Zone after the defeat, safer terrain for a Jew, transferring to the Lycée Blaise-Pascal. There, he organized a Resistance cell and in the summer of 1943 joined the Jeunesses communistes. He didn't stick with the Party but still remembers the pang of emotion that swept over him at the news of Stalin's death in 1953.[4] It didn't take long, however, for Lanzmann, the ex-Communist, to find a new political home. He fell in with Sartre's band at *Les Temps modernes*. This was a change of direction but not by much. Sartre was in fellow-traveling mode in the postwar years, and Lanzmann himself remained a man of powerful revolutionary convictions. Simone de Beauvoir recalls him as someone for whom politics came first, who said "the most extreme things" in an off-hand way, and who embraced the truths of Marxism as self-evident.[5]

These truths helped to fuel Lanzmann's ardent anticolonialism. In 1956, French military authorities hijacked a plane transporting FLN leaders, among them Mohamed Boudiaf and Ahmed Ben Bella, both of whom were jailed. Lanzmann visited Boudiaf in prison, and he was on yet better terms with Ben Bella, who spoke of the young Frenchman as "my brother." Sartre supplied an introduction to Frantz Fanon's *Les Damnés de la terre* (1961), a text noteworthy for its exaltation of the emancipatory possibilities of anticolonial violence. It was Lanzmann who acted as intermediary between the two men.[6] So, it comes as no surprise to encounter Lanzmann's name among the signatories of the "Manifeste des 121," a militant gesture that landed him in trouble with the law for inciting insubordination.

Such revolutionary enthusiasms abated, however, as the 1960s wore on, and the reason for that was Lanzmann's deepening attachment to Israel. Ben Bella, as first president of an independent Algeria, pledged a hundred thousand troops for the liberation of Palestine. Lanzmann experienced the declaration as a blow. "For me," he said in later years, "it was all over, I believed it possible at one and the same time to advocate for the independence of Algeria and for the existence of the State of Israel. I was mistaken." Nor was this the last blow of its kind. Lanzmann, though no longer the Third Worldist he had once been, still dreamed of Israeli/Palestinian reconciliation and to that end invited members of both camps to contribute to a forum on the Middle East in the pages of *Les Temps modernes*. The issue, a mammoth one, was published in 1967, but Maxime Rodinson's lead essay ruined the occasion for Lanzmann. Rodinson's contribution treated Israel as a colonial state, deserving of the fate experienced by other colonial states, and this Lanzmann was unable to abide.[7]

Why Israel mattered so much to Lanzmann requires some explanation. He was a combative man, no doubt, but he also recalled a moment from childhood when the will to fight failed him. It was in the run-up to the war when he was still a high-school student in Paris. Anti-Semitism was rampant among the students, and the teachers turned a blind eye. A fellow Jew was pummeled on a regular basis at recess, but Lanzmann hid out rather than standing up for his tormented classmate. In class, there was a discussion of Shakespeare's *The Merchant of Venice*, and a Gentile student took the occasion to make a sneering aside to Lanzmann: "But you too, you're a little Jew." Lanzmann thinking back as an adult knew what he wished he had done: smack the boy in the face, but instead, he denied who he was.[8]

For Lanzmann, Sartre's *Réflexions sur la question juive* (1946) came as a bracing restorative. Wartime events had made Lanzmann an untrusting man. As he looked about himself at the Liberation, what he saw was a France "infested with anti-Semites," a place intolerable to live in.[9] Sartre's tract, however, changed that.[10] The philosopher recognized the Jews' situation, the humiliation and fear that weighed on them, and he proposed a way out. The shamefaced Jew played into the anti-Semite's hands. The more he hid himself, the more he confirmed and reinforced the oppressor's stereotypes. The way to fight back, Sartre counseled, was to cast fear aside, to assume and not to evade Jewishness. The self-affirming Jew, one who defined himself instead of being defined by others, was on the path to a liberating authenticity. Sartre, the *marxisant* revolutionary, however was not content to stop the analysis there. He didn't see racism and prejudice as things in themselves but as weapons that capitalism made use of to divide and rule. To defeat bigots and the stereotypes they wielded to such damaging effect, it was therefore necessary to defeat capitalism first. Readers might well wonder what was to become of Jews in a post-capitalist world, one that no longer broke humanity down along identitarian lines. Did Sartre's scheme leave any room for affirmations of particularity, once the socialist revolution had done its work? The answer is very little, for after the revolution there would be Christian and Jew no more, neither black nor white, but one identity common to all, that of human being. It's a beautiful vision, but note that in the end all those particularities once so dear to people, Jewishness included, were slated to wither away.[11] Down this path, Lanzmann was not prepared to follow, which of course didn't stop him from taking the Sartrean counsel to pursue an authentic Jewishness very much to heart.

That pursuit started with a name. As Lanzmann later put it: "I would be the Negro, I would be the Jew," but the act of self-naming was just a beginning.[12] For what did the word *Jew* mean after all? Lanzmann had no religious training and was never to receive any. He didn't attend synagogue or know the basic prayers of the Jewish liturgy. Jewish history? He didn't feel much connection to it. Israel? Lanzmann knew nothing of it either.[13]

Yet, when it came to Israel, Lanzmann was curious. He had a ready pen, a talent for prose that enabled him to earn a living as a re-write man for the commercial press. It was also an asset recognized by the editors at *Les Temps modernes*, where Lanzmann had begun to publish. The idea came to him: he should make a trip to Israel and report back, which he did in 1952, and the visit proved transformative. In Israel, Lanzmann discovered what he called "Jewish positivity," not traits and characteristic as anti-Semites imagined them, but as flesh-and-blood Jews lived them out without worrying what the Gentile might think.[14] Lanzmann recollected one moment vividly. It was the day after Simchat Torah, a joyous holiday celebrating the completion of that year's cycle of Torah readings. The setting was a Yeshiva, a Jewish school, where the Master presided at a festive meal, tossing out morsels of pickled herring to his disciples amidst generalizing chaos. The scene staggered Lanzmann. These people, so different from himself, were nonetheless "my people, the Jewish people stronger than a thousand deaths..."[15] He related his enthusiasm to Sartre who urged him to write it all up, but able a writer as Lanzmann was, the subject exceeded him. In 1968, he found himself back in Israel once more. He had come as a journalist, assigned to report on what Israeli life was like in the aftermath of the 1967 war. Lanzmann put together a television broadcast but didn't care for how the producers edited it. Then another transformative moment ensued. A "wealthy patron" (never identified) encouraged Lanzmann to try expressing himself in a new medium, to make a documentary of his own, that is, and one that got right, without distorting edits, what Israel was all about. Lanzmann was willing to make the attempt. The writer now turned novice filmmaker threw himself into the project.[16]

The result was *Pourquoi Israël*, an interesting movie that was in many respects a forerunner to *Shoah*, above all in filmmaking technique. The documentary is long for the genre, over three hours, and is made up of interviews conducted by Lanzmann himself who from time to time enters the frame. The subjects are Israelis – what they think about their country, how they understand what it means to be Jewish – and there are no archives or voice-over to correct, substantiate, or subvert what the witnesses have to say. Not least of all, the movie is circular in design. It opens with a scene of Gert Granach singing a Spartakist *Freiheit* song to the accompaniment of the accordion. The setting then shifts to Yad Vashem, with a shot of the Hall of Remembrance, followed by one of the Hall of Names. In the first, the names of killing sites and the most important concentration and extermination camps can be seen, laid out across a vast, half-lit floor. The second shows a room where the records of all the Jewish murdered are kept. These are, we are told, the "archives of death." The Hall of Names is then returned to in the documentary's penultimate sequence with Lanzmann himself shown poring over the list of the many Lanzmanns killed in the genocide, and we are also returned to Gert Granach, who is once again singing songs of revolutionary aspiration. All these techniques, Lanzmann would use again in *Shoah*.

The paired scenes that frame the movie – of Granach and Yad Vashem – say a good deal about Lanzmann's preoccupations at the time: that he was and remained a man of the Left but also that he was an awakening Jew. At various points in the documentary, Lanzmann interviews a Jewish policeman, visits a prison run by Jews and populated by Jewish prisoners, and attends a torchlight ceremony at the Wailing Wall where paratroopers are sworn in. The cop, the prison guard, the beret-wearing paratrooper, Lanzmann has met such figures before back in France, but there they were "other," the agents of class oppression, and not, as in Israel, fellow Jews. Lanzmann also talks to dockworkers and to prosperous-looking kibbutzniks, asking them about class divisions. These are real enough comes the reply, but the differences are not so sharp as to generate a deep enmity, a genuine "class struggle." Israel after all is a fraternal society, "because we are all Jews," as the policeman at one point tells Lanzmann, and the filmmaker comes around to subscribing to that view himself. He follows the travails of a Russian immigrant who has a difficult time integrating. The man ends up contemplating a move to America, and Lanzmann lets on that life won't be any easier in the United States, a capitalist society that lacks in fraternal feeling. Yet, there is little of fraternity, the skeptical viewer is bound to observe, in Israel's occupation of the territories seized in the war of 1967. Lanzmann the erstwhile anti-imperialist does not evade the issue altogether. He visits Hebron; he visits the Gaza strip. The documentarist does not interview Palestinian locals, but he does interact with settlers and soldiers, and it's evident that an argument is under way. The settlers make clear that they don't intend to budge. Israel, as they see it, has ancient and biblical ties to Hebron and Gaza that no one can break. There is a moderate, counter-voice in Lanzmann's film, however, urging some kind of compromise with the Palestinians, lest Israel itself turn into an imperial power like all the others. As to how Lanzmann situates himself in the debate, he never takes a position outright. He does, however, let the soldiers have the final word: the work of occupation, they report, is dirty work.

So, Israel has all the attributes of a "normal" society: an army, a police force, a prison system, a class structure, but it is not one. In Lanzmann's portrait, the Israelis feel a singular kinship with one another that causes him, the one-time Marxist, to marvel, and he reflects on where that sentiment comes from. The army looms large in Israeli life; the nation's citizens live under a permanent state of siege; the memories of a mass murder committed but a quarter-century ago remain raw. All these influences have converged to mute differences, but the most powerful common bond of all is Jewishness (Lanzmann interviews an Arab-Israeli construction worker, but otherwise Israel's Arab population does not get a chance to speak). Yet Jewishness is perhaps the film's biggest puzzle, for how many different kinds of Jews there are. Lanzmann encounters sabras, Germans, Russians, North Africans, socialist kibbutzniks, and

Orthodox Yeshiva bochurs. He, of course, does not pronounce on who's found the right path. It's the variety that he takes delight in.

Even more than delight, *Pourquoi Israël* communicates Lanzmann's visceral attachment to Jewishness in all its profusion. In one scene, he accompanies a Russian immigrant to the Wailing Wall. The man is shaken by the experience: "it's been two thousand years since I was here," he says, and a current of "tenderness," almost "palpable," travels between the two men. Later on, Lanzmann makes a trip to the Negev desert and meets an aging pioneer who recalls the hardscrabble life of the first settlers on the scene. Things were very difficult, the man explains, but they won't be for his grand-daughter, the first native-born Israeli in the family. The thought of a better life for the child causes the speaker to choke up, and Lanzmann too is moved, entering the picture to give the man an embrace.[17] Last of all, there is the movie's second to last scene in the Hall of Names at Yad Vashem, with Lanzmann looking up all the Lanzmanns who died in the genocide. Asked later whether they were relatives, he replied: "No, but they're people of my people, which amounts to the same thing."[18]

Pourquoi Israël premiered in 1973 just as the Yom Kippur War was beginning. An official at the Israeli Ministry of Foreign Affairs, Alouf Hareven, happened to see it and contacted Lanzmann with a proposal. "There's no movie about the Shoah...which shows it from our perspective, from the point of view of the Jews." He invited Lanzmann to make such a film, and the documentarist took up the challenge, spending a year devouring literature on the subject, from Gerald Reitlinger and Raoul Hilberg on down. He was now embarked on a voyage that would not arrive in port until 1985.[19]

Negationism[20]

It's not as though Lanzmann knew from the beginning precisely what kind of movie he wanted to make. He worked that out along the way, and the learning process was inflected by contemporary events, two in particular, that helped to refine his thinking and filmmaking practice.

The first touched on a matter of fact. A band of self-styled revisionists called into question whether the Germans had indeed made use of gas chambers to murder Jews or anyone else. The most extreme negationists, as proponents of such views came to known, went even further, denying that there had ever been a genocide in the first place, and of all the negationists, the most notorious was Robert Faurisson, a professor of French literature at the University of Lyon.

Faurisson had begun to research the existence (or non-existence, as he saw it) of gas chambers in the 1970s. It didn't take long for Faurisson's disingenuous inquiries to make him persona non grata at the CDJC archives. He also made himself an unwelcome presence at an academic conference in Lyon in January 1978. The subject was the wartime role and complicities of the French Catholic Church, and Faurisson caused an uproar when he made a declaration from the floor: the gas chambers, the extermination, the genocide, none of this had ever happened. He wrote up such views in tract form with an inflammatory claim appended – that Zionists had invented the whole thing. A right-wing periodical, *Défense de l'"Occident,* edited by the die-hard fascist Maurice Bardèche, was thrilled to publish such provocations. Then in October, Darquier de Pellepoix surfaced in an interview, ever the unrepentant anti-Semite. No Jews had been gassed at Auschwitz, he declared, just lice.

It was in such a charged atmosphere that Faurisson's university decided the next month to suspend him, which turned him into a victim. University colleagues, even as they distanced themselves from Faurisson's views, published a protest in *Le Monde* in the name of academic freedom. The paper felt it owed its readers an account of the negationist's position, which it duly published in December. Georges Wellers and Olga Wormser-Migot also weighed in, contributing reasoned refutations of Faurisson's claims. Faurisson, now under direct fire, demanded the right to reply, which was granted. Such media maneuverings thrust the Holocaust-denier, once a figure on the margins, into the hot center of what was becoming a national scandal.

An unlikely ally rallied to Faurisson's side in the person of Pierre Guillaume, a former sixty-eighter, who on and off over the years had run a publishing house, La Vieille Taupe. Old Mole, that's what Marx called the Revolution in *The Eighteenth Brumaire of Louis Bonaparte.* Bonaparte's 1851 coup d'état had driven the Revolution underground, but it still burrowed away, readying itself for the final confrontation with capitalism, and so Guillaume might have thought of himself, churning up the dirt in the aftermath of 1968. It is possible to venture a guess as to why such a man was drawn to the likes of Faurisson. The two shared one and the same conviction that the Holocaust was a lie cooked up by Zionists to keep Palestinians and Germans ground down. In 1980, La Vieille Taupe published a text by Faurisson in which he defended himself against charges of falsifying history, complete with introductory remarks by Noam Chomsky touting the virtues of free speech.[21]

Faurisson's carryings-on, of course, did not go unanswered. Historians launched the first salvo. Léon Poliakov and Pierre Vidal-Naquet circulated a petition, signed by thirty-four colleagues, attesting to the factuality of the camps and the gas chambers, which *Le Monde* printed in February 1979. This intervention was soon followed by a pair of withering anti-negationist critiques, the first appearing in *Les Temps modernes* in June 1980, the second in *Esprit* three months later. The piece in *Les Temps modernes* was penned by Nadine Fresco, that in *Esprit* by Vidal-Naquet who scorned Faurisson as "a paper Eichmann." As historians will do, moreover, they published books. Georges Wellers's *Les Chambres à gaz ont existé* came out in 1981, Vidal-Naquet's, *Les Assassins de la mémoire* in 1987. Deportee organizations also joined in the fray, nine of them banding together to accuse Faurisson of "racial defamation." A court found him guilty as charged in 1981 and sentenced him to pay a symbolic one franc fine. This is how academics and informed citizens conduct themselves, signing petitions, publishing books and articles, and taking the matter to court.[22]

Serge Klarsfeld, however, adopted a different strategy, focused less on the printed word than on images. Research in preparation for the 1979 Cologne trial of Hagen, Lischka, and Heinrichsohn had uncovered a cache of photos in the Jewish State Museum in Prague, chronicling the arrival of a convoy of Hungarian Jews at Auschwitz in the spring of 1944. On further inquiry, it was discovered that the pictures were copies of originals that had belonged to Lili (sometimes spelled Lilly) Zelmanovic, herself a Hungarian Jew and former deportee. She submitted seventy of them in evidence when she testified at the 1964 Frankfurt trial of German Auschwitz personnel. SS officers had taken the images and made them into an album (the album included 193 photos, a good deal more than the 70 submitted at trial). The collection fell into Lili Zelmanovic's hands by chance when she was liberated from the Dora-Nordhausen camp, and she held onto it because she recognized in the photos the likenesses of people she had known from back home. Klarsfeld tracked Zelmanovic, now Lili Jacob, to Miami where he paid her a visit in July 1980. He persuaded her to donate the album to Yad Vashem and to authorize him to publish a facsimile for free distribution to interested parties, a task he accomplished before the year was out. Klarsfeld made clear in the introduction what the stakes were. These were photos taken inside Auschwitz; they had an established provenance; and no one, not even the defendants' lawyers at the Frankfurt trial, had contested the album's veracity.[23] Auschwitz was not some Zionist phantasmagoria but a real camp where real Jews had been deported en masse.

The album was made available in a French edition in 1983 and it inspired the director, Alain Jaubert, to make a short film on the subject (under forty-five minutes) released a year later. *Auschwitz, l'album de la mémoire* (1984) is a thoughtful work, a reflection as much on all that the photos don't tell as on what they do. Jaubert showed the album photos to four former deportees, all women, all Jews, and then filmed what they had to say in reaction. The images summoned up memories that brought to life the story the album narrated, and Jaubert included as well readings from concentration camp classics – Cayrol, Delbo, Wiesel – to develop the picture further. The album is thus treated as a portal, a narrow window that opened onto something much bigger, what Jaubert in a later interview called "the immensity of the deportation." In that same interview, he acknowledged that it was the negationist controversy that had motivated him, as it had Klarsfeld, to take counter-measures, which is to say, to make the film.[24] What the movie did not show, as the album did not show, was the ultimate fate that awaited the new arrivals on the Auschwitz-Birkenau ramp.

How in fact was it possible to convince people, beset by negationist insinuations, that the gas chambers had indeed existed? Klarsfeld made the effort with an assist from the art of David Olère. Olère was a Polish-born Jew and graphic artist who had emigrated to Paris in the 1920s, where he found a job designing publicity posters for Paramount Pictures. He was arrested by French police in 1943 and deported to Auschwitz. At the camp, he worked as a Sonderkommando, emptying gas chambers and helping to burn cadavers. Through it all, Olère survived, and once liberated he began to draw and paint what he had seen and taken part in. When the artist died in 1985, his widow and son, Alexandre Oler, confided these images to Klarsfeld who arranged for the publication of a *catalogue raisonné* in 1989 and then nine years later of something more complex, an album. The album, which appeared in both English and French editions, featured reproductions of Olère's artwork with poems interspersed among them. Alexandre Oler supplied the verse, which explains why he was accorded equal billing as the book's co-author. Klarsfeld himself furnished a forward. In the French edition, he explained how he had selected the images from a group Olère had executed just after the war when the artist's memories of Auschwitz were still fresh and urgent.[25] Also included in the album were a few examples of later work, this image dating from 1960 or somewhat later among the most disturbing (see Figure 12.1). Klarsfeld underlined its particular importance, reminding readers that no photo, no sketch, no image of any kind apart from this one existed, documenting the gassing of the one million Jews who had perished at Auschwitz. The album included in addition a timeline of Olère's life. The artist had died in 1985, the timeline indicated, and accompanying text noted that it was not illness that had killed him but, as the English edition put it, "despair at hearing university 'intellectuals' say that the

Figure 12.1 David Olère, *Gassing*, 1960–1980. Reprinted with permission of The Auschwitz-Birkenau State Museum, Oswiecim (Poland) and of Marc Oler

genocide which he personally witnessed did not exist and was mere Zionist propaganda."[26]

How to enter into the gas chambers, how to accompany those about to die on the last stage of a terrible journey: these were questions that ate at Lanzmann as well. In *Shoah*, he devised a means to enable the living to imagine the unimaginable (more on that in a moment). In the meantime, fighter that he was, Lanzmann wasn't about to let the negationists escape without hitting back. In 1980, Filip Müller published a memoir titled in French, *Trois Ans dans une chambre à gaz d'Auschwitz*. Müller, a Czechoslovakian Jew, had been a Sonderkommando at Auschwitz, and his memoir related what he had seen and done in that capacity. Lanzmann had already interviewed the man in preparation for *Shoah*, a remarkable and moving encounter. The filmmaker, as someone who knew Müller and knew about the genocide, was an ideal choice to write a preface to the former Sonderkommando's book. There is a well-known Auschwitz story about a woman dancer from Warsaw made to undress before entering the gas chamber. She did a strip-tease as she sidled up to a mesmerized SS guard before seizing his gun and shooting him. Müller's account confirms the story, and Lanzmann's preface makes a point of mentioning this. Jews, even at the most vulnerable moment of all, did not go without a fight. And go where? Into the gas chambers, and for Lanzmann, herein lay the paramount importance of Müller's testimony. He had seen the inside of the gas chambers, and as an eyewitness, what he had to report stood in refutation, as Lanzmann's preface phrased it, of "all those who, elevating their ignorance, their refusal to inform themselves, their bad faith and their anti-Semitism masked behind a façade of 'revisionist' skepticism, today pose snickering and smart-alecky questions about the 'how' and 'why' of it, with the aim of sewing doubt about the technical possibility of massacre on such a scale."[27]

Holocaust in America

In France, the scandal of negationism unfolded in parallel to a second set of controversies, this one having to do, not with the facts of the genocide, but with how to tell the story. On four consecutive nights in April 1978, NBC broadcast a blockbuster television series, *Holocaust*, written by Gerald Green and directed by Marvin Chomsky (cousin to Noam). It was an event, one that attracted an estimated one hundred million viewers.[28] This was not the first historical miniseries of its kind to attract a mass audience in the United States. It had an antecedent in *Roots*, which aired the year preceding and on which Chomsky had also worked. *Roots* dramatized the epic saga of an African-American family across the generations from its subjugation into slavery in colonial times to its entry into freedom in the wake of the Civil War. *Holocaust* had similar epic ambitions. It too used the fate of a family to structure its story line. Only now, it was the genocide of the Jews, not slavery, that was the center of attention. The public tuned in to watch *Holocaust* in large numbers, but not everyone shared in the general enthusiasm. Elie Wiesel dismissed the miniseries in the *New York Times* as a trivializing soap-opera inadequate to the gravity of its subject.[29] The same debate would also play out in France when Antenne 2 televised *Holocaust* there in February-March 1979. This event, like its American counterpart, caught the general public's imagination, and there were likewise French critics who objected to the miniseries' melodramatic approach. In France, as in the US, *Holocaust* fired up an argument about the ethics of representation. Lanzmann took a side in the fight and along the way situated the "American approach" as a contrast to his own.[30]

Holocaust was melodramatic, no doubt.[31] It tells a sweeping story, that of the Weisses, an assimilated middle-class German-Jewish family. The father, Josef, a respected Berlin physician, is married to Berta, a cultured, piano-playing housewife. They have three children – Karl, Rudi, and Anna – and Dr. Weiss has a brother Moses who lives in Warsaw. The Weiss family saga is recounted in parallel to a second one, that of Erik and Marta Dorf, an "Aryan" couple. She is a Lady Macbeth figure, he a smooth-faced young man who rises in the ranks of the SS, egged on by his ambitious wife. The miniseries traces what happens to this cast of characters in the era of the Holocaust, and it is nothing good. The Weiss parents will be gassed at Auschwitz. Anna, the youngest child, is raped by Nazis early in the story. She goes mad and is confined to a psychiatric hospital at Hadamar where she is euthanized. Karl, an artist, spends a period in the Theresienstadt concentration camp, where he continues to create, but in the end, he too is dispatched to Auschwitz to be murdered. Uncle Moses Weiss will die in the Warsaw Ghetto uprising. Rudi alone survives, having fled eastward to join a band of Jewish partisans in Ukraine. As for Erik Dorf, he is there at every turn as the Nazis conceive the Final Solution and set its machinery in motion. He's present at Babi Yar in 1941, when German killing units massacre over thirty thousand Jews in the early months of the Russian campaign. He attends the Wannsee Conference in 1942 where the modalities of the Final Solution are worked out. Along the way, he will cross paths with all the great and powerful in the SS: from Himmler to Heydrich to Eichmann. At the war's end, rather than face prosecution, Dorf commits suicide.

The destinies of a varied and numerous cast allow Green and Chomsky to explore the Holocaust in all its dimensions, to provide a picture of what it entailed from beginning to end. The series has at times the quality of a history lesson, and that may be why it's been called a "docudrama," a pigeon-holing label that its producer did not like.[32] The didacticism, however, is leavened by fine acting. Sam Wanamaker, a veteran of stage and screen, was nominated for an Emmy in the role of Moses Weiss. Two younger cast members, Michael Moriarty as Erik

Dorf and Meryl Streep as Inga Helms Weiss, were not just nominated but won the award.

The Streep role bears further commentary. Inga Helms is a Christian woman who marries Karl Weiss, and in fact, the series opens with their marriage ceremony. She is a good soul, who attends the church of a priest opposed to the Nazi regime, a man destined for deportation himself. Christian viewers had a way into the series via Inga, a reassuring figure to identify with. And there was nothing too Jewish about the Weiss family either, nothing that might make them strange or unappealing to Gentile audiences. These are characters, the movie seems to say, much like ourselves, people we might have been had we lived at another time and place, and so we are called upon to think about the choices we might have made in their stead.

A second observation about Inga Weiss: she is a loyal wife who stands by her artist husband. Indeed, when the series ends, something of Karl will live on, for Inga has given birth to a son named Josef after her late father-in-law. Nor is Karl's line the only one that will survive. Rudi too is a survivor. The very final shot of *Holocaust* shows him playing soccer with a group of Jewish boys who have outlived the ordeals of the war. Rudi is now working for a Zionist emigration agency, and it is to be imagined that these children, and maybe Rudi himself, will soon be on their way to Palestine. It would not be right to say that the series has a happy ending – so many have died in the years gone before – but there are consolations. The Weiss parents, even in death, salvage an element of dignity. The elders are shown going to the gas chambers in a state of a quiet self-possession. Moses, the resistance fighter, dies a hero's death, executed by the Germans. There is still a future, moreover, for the Weiss family's surviving members, who have new lives to construct.

Holocaust is epic, moving, and instructive, but it is also not over-demanding of its audience. Viewers are allowed to find solace in the Weiss family's stoic, sometimes heroic qualities and are spared the full, shocking horror of the genocide. The camera pans over mounds of dead, and there is blood. But it is impossible to show the vomit, shit, and melting human fat which bodies in extremis, gassed and burned, emit, and the series does not try to. On top of that, the series concludes on a hopeful note that a better future may lay in store for the handful who have made it through. Part Four, the series' final part, is titled after all "The Saving Remnant."

There is an unpretentious straightforwardness to *Holocaust*. Here's the genocide in all its phases, the miniseries tells us, here's what the perpetrators look like, and here's a family, not so different from our own, which lived these terrible events.

French TV at first hesitated to purchase the rights to the miniseries, but then one station, Antenne 2, seized the opportunity. The Darquier de Pellepoix interview had just made headlines, and with the Holocaust now a subject of national furor, the timeliness of the miniseries argued in its favor.[33] The station arranged to make the most of the occasion. It opted to run the program over a four-week period – one episode per week from February 13 through March 6, 1979 – with the last installment followed by an edition of the TV news magazine, *Les Dossiers de l'écran*, which was given over to a discussion of the issues raised by the series. The producer of the show assembled a panel of talking heads with some familiar faces among them: Marie-Claude Vaillant-Couturier, Simone Veil, and Georges Wellers. In addition, an effort was made to involve viewers who were urged to call in questions, and a youth panel was also put together and invited to pose questions of its own. One of the adult participants, a former deportee, declared the series "true enough" to what he had lived through. All agreed that the Germans had reserved a special fate for the Jews who, as Vaillant-Couturier acknowledged, suffered "a hundred times worse" in the camps than other categories of prisoner. There was argument about Jewish passivity and allusions to Vichy's role in the Final Solution (a subject not addressed in *Holocaust*). Overall, the response was positive, although a few downbeat notes were sounded. One youth panelist, who had visited a concentration camp site, found that experience a good deal more instructive than the miniseries. Veil judged the program, so full of good sentiments, "too optimistic." Wellers, in a similar vein, spoke of the incommunicability of the events represented. In the meantime, queries poured in from the public, which two station employees sifted through as best they could.[34] Viewers were riveted and the debate high-minded and constrained.

It grew less so as it spilled out of the confines of the TV studio into the public square. *Holocaust* had its defenders, Joseph Rovan for one, himself a former deportee. He applauded the way the miniseries helped viewers to enter into the events through identification with the characters. This was "a television of popular instruction," and how many, he noted, stood in need of just such edification. The Germans did, of course, and Rovan was pleased to report the miniseries' profound impact on audiences across the Rhine. But the French too stood in need of enlightenment, and in this connection, Rovan regretted that Ophuls' *Le Chagrin et la pitié* had yet to be aired on national television.[35] Ophuls himself did not condemn the series. It was flawed no doubt, but at least it made no pretensions to philosophic or artistic profundity. *Holocaust*, as he put it with faint praise, was "not ignoble."[36] Others were less generous.

Charlotte Delbo dismissed *Holocaust* as a "bad feuilleton," and Vidal-Naquet lamented the series' commercialism. He had another movie to recommend, Ophuls' *Memory of Justice*, which, he maintained, obliged the viewer, not just to feel, but to think and think hard. And the editor-in-chief of *Esprit*, Paul Thibaud, deplored the easy sentimentalism that identification with the Weiss family – so proper, so upstanding – enabled. All such critiques implied that there was another, more satisfactory way to deal with the challenge of depicting the Holocaust without specifying how that might be done.[37]

Lanzmann's own critique of *Holocaust* articulated what such an alternative approach might look like, one that refused facile theatrics, commercialism, and any trace of sentimentality. The critique appeared in article form in the pages of *Les Temps modernes* in June 1979. Lanzmann attacked first the miniseries' disposition to universalize. The Weiss family was presented as a family much like any other, and what was it that the viewer was supposed to think they were up against: fascism, man's cruelty to man, evil? No, Lanzmann shot back, the genocide's real target was not humanity in general but the Jews, a people forsaken by the world and then murdered "in the most poignant of solitudes." They experienced a unique fate, and it was the radical uniqueness of the genocide that *Holocaust*, so anxious to generalize its appeal, so keen on fostering audience identification, had failed to transmit. That failure was compounded by the way the miniseries dealt with the violence of the camps. The death that awaited the Jews – humiliated, starved, beaten with whips and clubs as they were driven into gas chambers – was not a genteel and decorous death but one whose full horror it was impossible to communicate. The very attempt to do so, however realistic the means, was bound to fall short and, in falling short, to trivialize. The radical uniqueness of the genocide and the impossibility of plumbing the depths of its violence ringed the Holocaust in what Lanzmann called a "circle of flame." It was a monstrosity altogether outside the normal, an event out of time. The historical imagination, so wrapped up in chronology and sequences of cause and effect, was no help at all when it came to capturing the "hallucinatory intemporality" of the Holocaust. For that, "another logic" was required, one that did not treat death as the end-point of a step-by-step process but that took death as its point of departure, one that did not treat the Holocaust as a past over and done with but as a presence embedded in the here-and-now just waiting to make itself manifest before our bewildered eyes. Lanzmann let the reader know that he was working on just such a film.[38]

Shoah

The making of *Pourquoi Israël* had taught Lanzmann something about
documentary filmmaking: how to use interviews, without archival backup or detailed commentary, to sketch a picture of polyphonic complexity.
He would continue along the same lines in *Shoah*, relying on image and
dialogue to convey what he had to say. Lanzmann, as we have seen,
envisioned the Holocaust as a unique and bounded phenomenon, a
citadel of horror girdled round by a moat of fire. This may be why he
chose to map out its frontiers with a film circular in design like *Pourquoi
Israël*. *Shoah* opens with the return of Simon Srebnik, a survivor, to the
extermination camp of Chelmno. It ends with a shot of rolling trains. For
Jews destined to die in the genocide, there was a point of no return, that
moment when they stepped into the cattle cars. *Shoah* then begins in a
camp and winds up looping back to the train ride where the extermination process began.[39]

Lanzmann conceived the Shoah, not just as a space unto itself, but also
as a phenomenon out of time, and this too is communicated in the film's
framing. *Shoah* is divided into two parts, or eras as the film labels them,
and each concludes with a brief coda. The first coda deals with the
German company, Saurer, that manufactured the gas vans used to
exterminate Jews at Chelmno. It winds up with a shot of a Saurer truck
driving down a German highway in the present day. The company, it's
clear, is still very much in business. The second coda, as already noted,
ends with the image of a train in motion, which is also the film's final
shot. The train appears destined to rumble on "interminably" as
Lanzmann later put it: "Which is as much to say that the Holocaust has
no end."[40] The Shoah is still on the road, still on the rails. It's an event
"of our day" as we are told at the movie's very beginning when Srebnik is
first introduced and one that continues to unfold into the future.

How then to come to grips with an event so walled off, so intemporal?
Lanzmann was determined to find a way to enter in, a way to accompany
the victims to the end and to make viewers come along with. He wanted
no truck with the historian's chronological reconstructions, but flesh-
and-blood historians, two in particular, provided him critical assistance,
material and conceptual, in sorting this problem through.

When Lanzmann set to work on the making *Shoah*, one of the first
things he did was to consult with Yehuda Bauer, a professor of Holocaust
studies at the Hebrew University in Jerusalem. Bauer grasped
Lanzmann's objective and how essential it was that he speak to onetime Sonderkommandos, the men, who in fact and as no other, knew the

gas chambers from the inside. It was the Israeli historian, indeed, who first put Lanzmann on to Filip Müller.[41]

Lanzmann's dealings with Raoul Hilberg were just as meaningful. The filmmaker read Hilberg's three-volume magnum opus, *The Destruction of the European Jews*, more than once, and he included an interview with Hilberg in *Shoah*, the sole historian so honored.[42] The choice was not just an honorific one, however. Hilberg had an unparalleled grasp of the transportation apparatus that had made it possible for the Nazis to deport Jews from the four corners of occupied Europe to killing centers in the East. Better than any man alive, he understood that decisive step in the extermination process, the point of no-return when Jews climbed onto the trains. Lanzmann also owed a major conceptual debt to Hilberg. For the historian, the Holocaust was not just about victims and perpetrators. Yet another group was involved, third parties who witnessed what was happening, sympathizing with the Jews or jeering at them.

Who were these bystanders? Lanzmann had not initially wanted to travel to Poland, but he came in time to realize the necessity of such a visit, which he made for the first time in 1978.[43] It proved a pivotal moment because in Poland Lanzmann was obliged to engage face-to-face with Poles of the wartime generation, for him the quintessential bystanders. There was also a second reason why the trip mattered. Lanzmann journeyed to the sites where the extermination had taken place. It was not the architecture of the camps that gripped him, little of which remained in any event.[44] Rather, it was the landscape, the space of mass murder, and it came to him to interview survivors on-site, a stratagem that might trigger them into reliving for the camera what they had seen there. *Le Lieu et la parole*, place and word: for a while, until *Shoah* replaced it, that was the working title of Lanzmann's movie.[45]

So, now at last, Lanzmann had a way into the Shoah's exterminating circle of fire: witnesses, with the heaviest emphasis placed on the testimony of Sonderkommandos. The bulk of Lanzmann's movie is given over to interviews with people who had run the camps, survived them, or lived nearby in their shadow. There are thirty-two principal subjects in all, and these individual interviews are rounded out by group interviews with anonymous Polish peasants in the towns of Grabów and Chelmno and with equally anonymous workers in the Treblinka railyards. The voices speak in multiple tongues – German, Polish, Hebrew, Yiddish, English – but they soon begin to add up.

In significant ways, Lanzmann's handling of witnesses built on the example set by Marcel Ophuls. This was a sensitive point for Ophuls who felt Lanzmann's work owed an unacknowledged debt to his own, and there's some truth to this claim when it comes to Lanzmann's encounters with witnesses, German and Polish, he had reason to dislike.[46] Lanzmann on these occasions made use of Ophuls-style juxtapositions. Take, for example, the interview with Franz Grassler, a deputy to the SS officer in command of the Warsaw Ghetto. Grassler, in answer to Lanzmann's questioning, claims he remembers little about his activities in Warsaw days. There were problems with population management, he recalls, and some difficulties with provisioning. All the while, Lanzmann intercuts Grassler's evasive answers with shots of Hilberg, who reads excerpts from the diary of Adam Czerniakow, the head of the ghetto's Jewish Council. Czerniakow does not hem and haw but details the miseries of ghetto life, miseries that were not incidental problems but the calculated consequence of German policy. Lanzmann subjects a second German witness to the same treatment, Walter Stier, employing Hilberg once again as a corrective. Stier was the Reich's traffic manager in charge of shipping Jews to the East. He avers that he knew next to nothing about the human cargo – it might have been made up of Jews or maybe it was criminals – and that he knew even less, just rumors, about where the people were headed. Hilberg is then brought on to give the lie to such evasions. Reich traffic managers, he demonstrates, kept meticulous itineraries of the human "merchandise" they were tasked with transporting, from the first stop to the last as well as all points in between. It cost money, of course, to move bodies on such a scale, and Hilberg then goes on to spell out how the fares were defrayed out of the proceeds from confiscated Jewish property.

Ophuls' influence on Lanzmann's modus operandi is evident not just in the way he used juxtapositions to make a point but also in the way he conducted the actual interviews themselves. Like Ophuls, Lanzmann, the interviewer, could be insinuating. The opening sequence of the second era features an exchange, captured on a hidden camera, with Franz Suchomel, an SS guard who oversaw the extermination process at Treblinka. With Suchomel, Lanzmann assumes a cool, professional demeanor, soliciting information just to set the historical record straight, even as he cajoles the Nazi into spilling self-incriminating details of the most horrific kind. Lanzmann does the same with the citizens of Grabów, who at his informed prodding, reveal themselves brimming with anti-Semitic bigotry. And like Ophuls once again, Lanzmann could be confrontational. In *Shoah*, he interviews a Polish farmer who imitates what "Jewish," i.e. Yiddish, sounds like, and the filmmaker calls him out on the point. Ophuls relished the scene, seeing in Lanzmann's "passionate anger" a feeling like his own when he squared off with the shopkeeper Marius Klein in *Le Chagrin et la pitié*.[47] But for squaring off, there's no sequence more unnerving than the one between Lanzmann and the SS officer, Josef Oberhauser, a veteran of the Belzec extermination camp. Lanzmann had tracked the man down to Munich where he was working in a bar. Oberhauser stonewalls the filmmaker, and the more importuning Lanzmann's questions become, the more murderous turns Oberhauser's glare.

Lanzmann made effective use of ruse and aggression to catch out bigots and criminals, and in this he was indeed following in Ophuls' footsteps. Yet, in the end, such was not Lanzmann's overriding concern. What mattered to him a good deal more was pinning down the factuality of what happened, and to that end he didn't so much juxtapose testimonies as sequence them such that one account confirmed the next. In the Suchomel interview, the SS remembers a song that Jewish Sonderkommandos were made to sing as they set about their awful work. Lanzmann also interviews one of these Jewish Sonderkommandos, Richard Glazar. In the event, what the Nazi Suchomel remembers of Treblinka does not differ in substance from Glazar's recollections. Glazar also recalls how a trainload of Jews arriving from Theresienstadt was greeted by Polish onlookers with a gesture, a finger slashing the throat. Polish interviewees corroborate the fact, as does the Polish train engineer, Henrik Gawkowski, who was in charge of driving convoys the last leg of their journey from the Treblinka station into the camp proper. What better rebuttal to negationist "skepticism" was there than the mutually reinforcing testimony from sources so disparate.

Yet, even more than the facts, Lanzmann was after the emotional truth of the Shoah. He was determined to summon up visions of the terrible things that had transpired, powerful visions with a raw, felt immediacy that would take possession of interviewee and audience alike. Lanzmann's editor, Ziva Postec, evaluated the interviews he had filmed on a three-star scale, awarding three stars for the most dramatic. Included in the top category was Lanzmann's exchange with Jan Karski, and it's not hard to see why.[48] Karski was a Polish Catholic, commissioned by the national underground to investigate the circumstances of the Jews under Nazi rule. He made two visits to the Warsaw Ghetto and a third one, in disguise, to a site he believed to be the Belzec extermination camp. In the ghetto, he was led around by two men, one a Zionist, one a Bundist, and what Karski saw, the wretchedness and desperation, stunned him. His guides enjoin him to convey the news to the Allies, an awesome responsibility that Karski took with the utmost seriousness and in the end to little avail. It's clear in the interview that Karski had set aside these recollections for many years, but as he begins to talk, with Lanzmann's camera close upon him, it all comes back with a crushing vividness. Karski is a forceful, intelligent man, and yet he breaks down sobbing under the weight of the memories he has conjured.

The same kind of emotional outburst erupts in the interview with Müller, a former Sonderkommando, another man who has seen too much. He speaks in German, telling Lanzmann what it's like when the doors of the gas chamber are opened after use. The evaporating Zyklon B crystals, dropped on the chamber floor, have emitted a lethal gas that rises. There is evidence, amidst the vomit and excrement, of struggle. The bodies are heaped in a pile with the strongest, who have fought to gasp one last breath of unpoisoned air, piled at the top. Müller is a person of strong character, and he is a practiced witness who has testified before. Finally, however, he too will break down. He is a Czechoslovak, and a convoy of countrymen arrives. The Nazis tell them to undress. The people guess what's in store for them, balk, and break into song instead. They sing the Czechoslovak national anthem, then "Hatikvah," and Müller, overwhelmed, wants to enter the gas chamber with them. They command him to live, so that he might bear witness, and he obeys. The scene was unbearable for Müller then, and it is unbearable for him (and for the viewer) now. He begins to cry.

Lanzmann's exchanges with Karski and Müller are filmed indoors, the subjects seated in conventional postures. With Simon Srebnik, however, the filmmaker attempts something different. The two men travel together to Chelmno, and, as they pace the fields where once the campsite stood, Srebnik is moved to relive the horror of back then. He speaks in German: "it was here. They burned people here... *Ja, das ist das Platz.*" Srebnik tries to provide details but acknowledges the impossibility of accurate description. The scene, however, is imprinted on the man's face. It's in his eyes, and the viewer, looking at him, tries to imagine what Srebnik is seeing. The mise-en-scène helps to make the past live once more, expression, place, and word calling up a picture that the viewer struggles to read and flesh out through an effort of imagination.

On the matter of staging, however, the nec plus ultra in Lanzmann's *Shoah* is the barber shop interview with Abraham Bomba. Bomba was a Treblinka Sonderkommando, a barber by trade who cut the hair of deportees, sometimes in the gas chambers themselves. After the war, he emigrated to New York City, and Lanzmann had a first, preliminary conversation with him there in the mid-seventies. When Lanzmann was ready to film, however, the barber had departed for parts unknown, and it took time and effort to track him down at long last in Israel. Bomba didn't feel up to talking in front of the camera, but Lanzmann devised a means to enable him to do so. The filmmaker rented a barber shop in Tel Aviv and populated it with faux customers. Bomba was set to work clipping the hair of a supposed client, in fact a friend of Bomba's choosing. He begins to snip away, the setting and the gestures putting him at ease, allowing him to enter into himself and reconnect to the past.[49] He remembers a women's transport arriving from his home town in Poland. A team of barbers, including himself and a friend, are assigned to cut their hair. A number of the women know Bomba and ask him what lies in store. Then there's the barber friend whose wife and daughter enter the gas chamber. Bomba can't continue: it's too painful. "Go on, Abe. You must go on," urges Lanzmann, and Bomba does, relating how the man cut the hair of the women dearest to him, spinning out the minutes to prolong what time they had left together. It's an excruciating moment, one of intense and deep emotion, but also one that required careful staging to make it happen. One informed commentator has written of Lanzmann's "psychodramatic" approach, and in this instance, the characterization could not be more apt.[50]

Indeed, to achieve the desired effect, Lanzmann was prepared to go the extra step, not just to stage interviews, but even to reenact events. Toward the end of the first era, he films a scene at the town church in Chelmno. It is the Virgin's Feast Day, and a crowd of Polish celebrants gathers in front, Srebnik standing among them. They explain how in wartime the Germans had detained a convoy of Jews in the church and the next day transported them to a burial site in a nearby forest, gassing them along the way. It took fifty van loads to complete the job. The church is then filmed from the back-end of a vehicle as it drives away (wisps of the vehicle's exhaust are visible), and this is followed by a sequence of shots: of a paved road; of Pan Falborski, a Polish local, who explains that this was the very route the gas vans had taken to the mass grave; and of the road again as it grows muddy. Srebnik is now heard in voice over, talking about what will happen when the van arrives at its destination, and at last the camera comes to a stop at a plot of green, forested land. The audience has made the same journey in real time as the Jews who were murdered did back then. The whole sequence has taken just a few minutes. Was that how long it took for the victims to asphyxiate?[51]

The most celebrated reenactment in the movie, is of course, that of Henrik Gawkowski driving a train as it chugs into the Treblinka station. Lanzmann rented an engine for the shot, not a simple proposition as it necessitated the cooperation of Polish rail authorities. In the scene, Gawkowski, a weathered-looking man, is shown leaning out of the engine cab, craning backward as if to see the (non-existent) transport of Jews behind. A sign comes into focus as the locomotive grinds to a halt: it is Treblinka. Then, unbidden, Gawkowski makes the throat-slitting gesture

Figure 12.2 Claude Lanzmann and poster, Paris, 1986. Photo by
Raphael Gaillarde/Gamma-Rapho via Getty Images

and repeats it more than once. The entire sequence is wordless. The
reenactment has triggered a physical memory, propelling Gawkowski and
the viewer back in time to the moment the gesture was first made,
collapsing the distance between past and present. It's that scene – of
Gawkowski's face and the Treblinka sign – that has been used time and
again to advertise the movie (see Figure 12.2). It serves as a reminder that
Shoah is not a documentary of the conventional sort, made up of archival
footage and talking heads, but a film that derives a portion of its power
from stagings and reenactments. It is, as Lanzmann himself called it, a
"fiction of the real."[52]

It is not difficult to point out the many lacunae in Lanzmann's movie.
France is nowhere to be seen. Apart from Karski's testimony and a nod

to the Warsaw Ghetto uprising at the film's end, ghetto life and all the controversy associated with it are passed over.[53] There are women's voices, seven among the principals plus a number of unidentified female Polish locals, but over all they do not command the same attention as do their male counterparts. In *Shoah*'s defense, it is a movie about the last leg – about the killing camps – and so it's little wonder that France and the ghetto are relegated to the wings. In a movie about the machinery of death, it's little wonder again that the Sonderkommando, always a man, stands front and center.

There are yet weightier absences, however. Nazi killing commandos, Einsatzgruppen, massacred over a million Jews behind German lines on the Eastern front. No member is interviewed, making the movie that much less comprehensive. This was a gap Lanzmann was aware of and regretted.[54] It's clear from a number of the witnesses that the Nazi extermination apparatus was manned, not just by Germans, but also by Ukrainian auxiliaries, but no Ukrainian figures among the interviewees. The SS, moreover, targeted Roma as well as Jews for extermination. The *Dossiers de l'écran* panel convened after the broadcast of *Holocaust* included a Roma survivor, but Lanzmann does not.[55] Such exclusions simplify the landscape he has to deal with, pruning a complicated topography down to three main groups – Poles, Germans, and Jews. About each, Lanzmann has an interpretive point or points to make.

The Polish government made angry representations to French officials when *Shoah* was released, and the reason is not hard to find.[56] The small towns in Poland where Lanzmann filmed, Grabów and Chelmno, are populated by peasants still living in the nineteenth century. That's at least how Lanzmann presents them, the women in headscarves, the men driving horse-drawn carts.[57] Without self-consciousness, these people retail the hoariest of anti-Semitic stereotypes: the Jews are rich and grasping; they're deicides. In front of the Chelmno church, with Srebnik present, one parishioner cites a rabbi alleged to have said the Holocaust was a punishment visited on the Jews for the wrongs they had committed. Not that the parishioner says so himself; he's just reporting. It's an ecce homo moment, for there's Srebnik, the real Christ, standing amidst a crowd that mocks him. Lanzmann casts these Poles, and they abet him in the casting, as purveyors of a millennial Christian anti-Semitism, and in this, he replicates the interpretive schema of André Schwarz-Bart's *Le Dernier des Justes* and of Hilberg's own *The Destruction of the European Jews*.[58]

Lanzmann's portrait, however, is not altogether one-sided. Pan Falborski isn't a villain. In one scene, a Polish railway man is filmed as he recalls witnessing the murder of a Jewish woman, a mother, who was shot through the heart by Nazi guards. The memory causes the man to choke up, and Lanzmann reaches out in sympathy. Gawkowski, of course, is the very face of the movie, at least for publicity purposes. And Lanzmann's feelings for Karski are admiring and powerful. He filmed Karski over a two-day period, in the end opting to cut much of the footage. He later edited the unused material to make another film, this one – *The Karski Report* (2010) – devoted entirely to Karski's testimony. Here was a figure then, an extraordinary and courageous one, who mattered to Lanzmann, and the filmmaker does not obfuscate who Karski was: a practicing Catholic and a deep Polish patriot outraged by the crimes committed by the Nazi Occupier against the Polish nation. Karski is also aware – and he says so himself in the *Shoah* interview – that the Jews were made to suffer a fate even worse, an "unprecedented" fate, and that too is part of why Lanzmann is drawn to the man.[59]

Most of the Germans Lanzmann interviews equivocate and evade, and that's part of the point. The cases of Franz Grassler and Walter Stier have already been discussed. The Nazis won't take responsibility for their crimes with one exception, that of Suchomel, who withholds very little. Lanzmann's camera was hidden, of course (which was also true of the unforthcoming Stier). There is some staging involved – Lanzmann sets Suchomel up with a camp plan and a pointer – which may have helped to loosen the man's tongue. What's clear, from Suchomel's testimony, is the calculated cruelty of Nazi policy. It may have had an abstract, bureaucratic quality back in Berlin, but on the ground, at Treblinka, the story was altogether different. The SS separated the men and women and murdered the men first, as it was feared they, more than the women, might put up a fight. The path from the ramp to the gas chambers, the "*Himmelweg*" or "road to heaven" as it was called, was camouflaged in pine branches to conceal from the prisoners where they were headed. When at last the realization of impending death dawned, there were auxiliaries on hand with whips to beat the condemned into submission. The clean-up was horrible, and Suchomel explains the operation in detail. From beginning to end, he estimates, it took about two hours to murder an entire convoy of Jews. Lanzmann's German witnesses paint a portrait of Nazi evil, and it is not a banal one. The perpetrators may pretend they're simple cogs, bureaucratic problem solvers, but the bureaucrat's pose is a lie, one more in a regime that fetishized deceit in furtherance of sadistic and murderous intent.

Yet, it's not really the Nazi mind that Lanzmann is intent on fathoming. No German indeed makes an appearance in *Shoah* until the movie is hours old. What's more important is a rounded picture of the Jews' situation, of what it was they were up against. The enemy was efficient, deceitful, and cruel. The Polish countryside – populated by peasants marinated in an age-old anti-Semitism – offered small hope of sanctuary. As Lanzmann's Jewish witnesses repeat over and again: we were alone and abandoned. There was no one there to help us.

It's hard to overestimate how important this theme was to Lanzmann. Srebnik opens the first era, and he also concludes it, explaining to his interlocutor in the era's final scenes how the gas vans at Chelmno worked. He then tells Lanzmann what he thought to himself at the time: "I'll be the only one left, if I get out of here." The second era winds up sounding the exact same note. Lanzmann shows a sequence filmed at the Ghetto Fighters' Kibbutz in Israel, and the subject is Simha Rottem shot in close-up. He took part in the Warsaw uprising and remembers emerging from the ghetto's ruins at the end, a solitary figure. "I am the last Jew," Rottem recalls having said to himself.

Now, I've said more than once that Lanzmann was a battler, and so the informed viewer might well be tempted to look for traces of that fighting spirit in *Shoah*. Israel is present in the film. It was Israeli seed funds after all that financed Lanzmann's first explorations of the subject in the seventies (the funding dried up before the decade was out). Many of Lanzmann's interview subjects, of course, live in Israel, and he filmed them where they lived. Then there is the way he chose to end the movie (or just about), at the Ghetto Fighters' Kibbutz. A Jewish underground had existed, and it did take up arms. Indeed, the movie Lanzmann made after *Shoah* was *Tsahal* (1995), a paean to Israel's defense forces which included a long sequence on the fighting prowess of the Merkava attack tank. That appears to settle the matter: Lanzmann's *Shoah* comes with what one critic has called a "Zionist closure" that, in the words of another, "set the stage" for a subsequent film, *Tsahal*, more Zionist still.[60]

There are reasons, however, not to endorse such a conclusion. While filming *Shoah*, Lanzmann interviewed Yehuda Lerner, a Polish Jew who ended up at Sobibor. The Jews there, a number of them Soviet army veterans, put to use the skills they had learned in the service to organize a revolt. Lerner took part, burying a hatchet in the head of an SS man, an episode he rehearses at length for Lanzmann, speaking in Hebrew all the while. None of this footage made it into *Shoah* but was set aside for a later movie, *Sobibór, October 14, 1943, 4 p.m.* (2001). The Filip Müller interview in *Shoah* does include talk about plans for a prisoner revolt at Auschwitz. The point Müller wants to make, however, is that Jewish inmates did not receive unreserved cooperation from non-Jewish prisoners who were in less of a hurry to act. On the matter of Rottem's testimony, it's the final image that abides, that of a Jew who feels himself alone in the world. Remember too that there's a second person present at the kibbutz interview, a genuine hero of the ghetto uprising, Itzhak Zuckerman. His face is ravaged by drink, and he says little. In response to Lanzmann's probing, he does make one devastating revelation: "if you could lick my heart, you would be poisoned." The accent is not on heroics – these are saved for another film – or even on Israel as the ghetto uprising's heir but on a sense of abandonment and of lives undone.

That intuition shapes how Lanzmann himself relates to his Jewish interviewees. He does not treat them as comrades-in-arms, people with whom to swap tales of the good fight or of survival against all odds. They are not there to tell us how they cheated death and afterward went about building new lives. They are there as eyewitnesses to the genocide of European Jewry. No one still alive ever came closer to the scene of the crime, and that closeness is burned in their memories and on their faces and burns again when they find the words to speak. It's critical to grasp just how firm Lanzmann's conviction on this point was. When Israeli funding petered out, Lanzmann traveled to the United States to find backers. American investors wanted a story of uplift, and the filmmaker sensed it. "If I had said," he later wrote, "My message is: 'Never again' or 'Love one another,' the wallets would no doubt have opened," but he refused to make promises of consolation, and the refusal cost him.[61] Not a single US dollar was invested in the project.

It's just as critical to grasp that Lanzmann's vision, hard-nosed as it was and as he was in sticking to it, was leavened by a deep compassion for his Jewish subjects. Early on in the film, Lanzmann interviews Michaël Podchlebnik, a Chelmno Sonderkommando. There is a smile frozen on the man's face. He's seen too much and is reluctant to talk. Lanzmann keeps at it and presses Podchlebnik about the smile. The man's reply is direct: it's that or tears, "and if you're going to live, it's better to smile." Podchlebnik is now almost in tears himself, and Lanzmann's hand enters the frame to rub Podchlebnik's arm. The same dynamic is at work in the interview with Bomba. Bomba at some point wants to stop, but the filmmaker won't let him. Is it heartlessness? No, Lanzmann has genuine feeling for the man he calls Abe, someone he took to right away when they first met back in New York. But they have a task to discharge, a necessary task…and a painful one, and it's clear that Lanzmann empathizes with that pain.[62] In a sequence toward the movie's end, which deals with the Jews of Corfu, such sympathies rise to the surface once more. The sequence is a curious one on first viewing. Of all Europe's decimated communities, why zoom in on this one? Lanzmann was good friends with Albert Cohen, a Greek Jew, who had left home to make a career as an international civil servant in Switzerland. In the 1950s and

1960s, Lanzmann used to make monthly visits to Geneva to visit with the man. Cohen, it happens, was also a novelist who wrote wonderful stories, full of humor and tenderness, about the Jews of Corfu, stories that evoked a world that was as good-hearted as it was comic. It's in Cohen's spirit, with a true tenderness of feeling that is at the same time a tribute to the novelist, that Lanzmann engages with the remnants of Jewish Corfu, recapturing a glimpse of what the community once was and how it came to be a shadow of its former self.[63]

This then was the movie Lanzmann released in 1985, a long day's journey into the realm of the dead. Lanzmann is a compassionate man; Israel and the fighting spirit it incarnates hover on the film's edges; there are people in the film, extraordinary people, who have been to hell and back. The overall tone, however, neither consoles nor reassures. The deaths spoken of were horrible and violent, and the people who bear witness to what happened still bear wounds that remain unhealed.

In the immediate postwar years, Buchenwald had been the emblematic camp. Later, it was Auschwitz. Lanzmann reconfigured the geography once more, reorienting the focus of attention to the Aktion Reinhard camps and to Chelmno. These were extermination centers, and the men, women, and children slated for extermination were Jews, not soldiers skilled at arms, but gentle souls like the Jews of Corfu. These people were made to suffer a fate unlike any other, gassed and incinerated by the millions. A mere handful of revenants remained to tell the world, the once uncaring world, what had happened, and the testimonies of these men and women make up the backbone of Lanzmann's movie.

It's hard to imagine such a film catching the public's imagination, and yet it did. *Shoah* had friends in high places, which no doubt helped. When Lanzmann's fund-raising efforts in the US reached an impasse, he turned next to Jewish sources in France, and there he met with greater success. André Wormser was a figure to reckon with: the son of Clemenceau's chef de cabinet, Georges Wormser; a mover in France's Jewish community; and a well-to-do banker. He had also attended high school with Lanzmann in Clermont-Ferrand, and that connection provided the filmmaker entry into a world of French donors, large and small, who kept the *Shoah* project afloat. In the film's final stages, one more source materialized: France's socialist government. François Mitterrand became president in 1981. Jacques Lang took over as minister of culture that same year. Both men, as it happened, took an interest in the completion of Lanzmann's movie.[64] Mitterrand paid a visit to Israel in 1982, an event that enthused Lanzmann who called it an *acte libérateur* on a par with Sartre's *Réflexions sur la question juive*. Sartre had acknowledged the Jews as self-fashioners with the power to define who they were, and now

Mitterrand was doing the same, extending recognition to Israel as the collective, national expression of Jewish agency.[65] *Shoah* opened three years later at a theater on the avenue Wagram, not far from the Place de l'Étoile, and who was in attendance but the president of the Republic in the flesh.[66]

Patronage in high places may have given *Shoah* a needed boost, but that was not what made its fortunes. Lanzmann tallied the movie's theater viewership in the tens of thousands, a respectable but not crushing box-office performance. What made the real difference was the film's appearance on the airwaves, and the moment of its broadcast turned out to be one propitious to a sympathetic reception. When TF1 showed *Shoah* in 1987, the Klaus Barbie trial was just getting underway, and the negationist wave had not yet receded. Partisans acclaimed the movie as a rebuttal to unrepentant Nazis and Holocaust deniers. That explains in part Vidal-Naquet's vehement embrace of the movie which he hailed as "a great historical work." Ophuls' assessment – "The greatest documentary about contemporary history ever made" – was not far different. Lanzmann had not conceived the film as a documentary, a Procrustean category for a genre-busting film such as *Shoah*. In the context of the moment, however, it was the movie's documentary aspects that grabbed the public's attention and contributed to consolidating its reputation.[67]

Yet, such a category error didn't really matter. The movie had caught fire, and in a short span, the French began to speak less of the Holocaust, still the preferred word in English, and more of the Shoah, a singular term for a singular event.

Epilogue and Conclusion

For moment, it looked like the Holocaust variant of the deportation story might eclipse all the others. Visit the 97th division of Père-Lachaise Cemetery today and take a look at the Auschwitz memorial. A plaque is fastened onto the pedestal that speaks of the "victims of anti-Semitic persecution," seventy-six thousand of them, and stones have been placed on the base in accordance with Jewish funerary practice. This is a Holocaust monument, isn't it? The passerby may puzzle as to why so many communist greats are buried in the vicinity and about the curious proximity of the Mur des Fédérés. The puzzle, of course, is not hard to resolve. The plaque was added in 1995, a small adjustment, but one that altered the monument's general aspect.[1] It had been erected under PCF auspices in days gone by, but that past was now a faded memory, replaced by a new one centered on Jewish victimization.

Indeed, the entire memorial neighborhood has undergone a change and not just because this monument or that has been retouched and assigned a new meaning in the process. People who visit Père-Lachaise now come equipped with a different set of expectations. When they think about the camps, they think first of the Holocaust. What then did the nearby memorials to Buchenwald, Dachau, and Mauthausen signify? Not the tens of thousands of résistants swallowed up by the Nazi Moloch but the singular and unprecedented fate of the Jews. Present-day sightseers who stroll the quarter's hushed allées can't help but see the Holocaust all about them, not the "communist pantheon" the division had once been.[2] This is how powerful Holocaust consciousness has become, enough so to obscure forms of memory that preceded it.

History, of course, didn't come to an end when the twentieth century ended, and neither did argument about the memory of the Deportation. On July 16, 1995, President of the Republic Jacques Chirac delivered an address at the Vél d'hiv memorial site on the quai de Grenelle. He acknowledged, as had never been acknowledged before by the nation's highest public official, the French state's complicity in the deportation of Jews. Yet, that wasn't all the president said. France, he went on, was not "an anti-Semitic country" but the homeland of liberty. Negationism and ethnic cleansing, these were the very antithesis of what the nation stood for, the opposite of "a certain idea of France." During the war, General de Gaulle had incarnated that "idea" in London, and at home, in the hexagon, de Gaulle's example found a ready echo in those French families, so numerous, whose "fraternal and heroic action" had saved "three quarters of the Jewish community." Chirac saluted these families, these "Righteous among nations" (*Justes parmi les nations*) in his words, as France's true representatives, not Vichy.[3]

In Chirac's remarks can be detected the accents of a new understanding of the Holocaust, one with ramifications for Europe and beyond as well as for France. For Europe and beyond, the message was clear: Never again. Genocide was an evil, and where it loomed, heroic and fraternal action was justified, even "humanitarian intervention" of the sort NATO forces, France's included, would soon engage in to stymie Serb ethnic cleansing in Kosovo. The European Union was also moved to take action in the Holocaust's name, albeit of a less military kind. Every May 9, the EU celebrates Europe Day. It was on that date in 1950 that Robert Schuman announced the creation of the European Coal and Steel Community, a curtain-raiser to the EU's own founding seven years later. A second commemorative day was added to the union's calendar in 2002, January 27, the anniversary of the liberation of Auschwitz. This one was dubbed Holocaust Remembrance Day, a name changed to International Holocaust Remembrance Day when the United Nations voted in 2005 to elevate the commemoration into a world event. Thus, the Holocaust was impressed into service once again: as a counter-image or negative memory against which, in Henry Rousso's words, "a new European, indeed, world humanism" defined itself.[4] It's not clear that anyone asked Jews how they felt about this, whether or not they wanted their losses mobilized in the name of someone else's cause, however grand and noble.

Chirac's address also had implications for the Holocaust's place in France's own regime of memory. That phrase, the "Righteous among nations," was of Israeli and not French invention. In 1962, Yad Vashem set aside a plot for an Avenue of the Righteous, planting eleven trees to honor eleven non-Jews who had risked all to save Jewish lives during the Holocaust. These were exceptional people – exceptional in their generosity of spirit amidst a sea of cruelty – and they deserved singling out. The number grew over the years, although it never counted more than a few hundred French people. Until the 1980s, that is, when French Jews organized a committee tasked with identifying French rescuers and compiling dossiers on them for Yad Vashem's vetting. France's quotient of *Justes* shot up in consequence, climbing to an estimated 3,760 by 2014, a rough fifteen percent of the total.[5]

The CDJC also took up the cause of the righteous Gentile, creating its own Allée des Justes in 2000, which ran alongside the northern face of the Mémorial du Martyr juif inconnu. Six years later, it inaugurated a wall of the righteous on that very spot, which acknowledged France's many rescuers each by name. It was Simone Veil's turn to act next. In her capacity as president of the Fondation pour la mémoire de la Shoah, she proposed to President Chirac that the Republic itself pay homage to France's righteous at the Pantheon, one of the nation's most hallowed sites.

An Israeli term was thus appropriated for French purposes to express gratitude and at the same time to elevate the profile of men and women who had done so much to save the nation's honor in the dark days of the Occupation. It was not just so-called memory entrepreneurs who came to embrace this way of thinking but representatives of the state itself. President Chirac's salute to France's righteous in 1995 was a first gesture in this direction, and it was just such sentiments that motivated him a dozen years later to respond in the affirmative to Veil's proposal. In January 2007, with Veil at his side, he presided at the unveiling of a brass inscription in the Pantheon's crypt, which was dedicated to the memory of the "*Justes de France*," so many bright lights who had refused "to die out" (*de s'éteindre*) in the face of intolerance and inhumanity. But note how the meaning of a *Juste* has evolved as the state itself became involved. The righteous Gentile was no longer that rare exception but the emblem of a larger body, the French nation, which, a handful apart, had remained true in the hardest of times to the principles of liberty, equality, and fraternity.[6] It's not hard to detect the Gaullist allusions in all this. Hadn't Chirac after all characterized the righteous as embodiments of "a certain idea of France," a phrase borrowed from de Gaulle's war memoirs? As for the Pantheon inscription, its evocation of the righteous as undying lights echoed the ringing call to arms that concluded de Gaulle's June 18 appeal: "...the flame of French Resistance must not and will not die" ("...*la flamme de la Résistance française ne doit pas s'éteindre et ne s'éteindra pas*). The Holocaust was a catastrophic event, no doubt, and Vichy was implicated in it, but not the French people who had stood with de Gaulle and taken risks to save Jews, making the moral choice when it was dangerous to do so.

Now think for a moment of the most recent additions to the Pantheon's roster of national heroes. Pierre Brossolette, Geneviève de Gaulle Anthonioz, Germaine Tillion, and Jean Zay were interred there as a foursome in 2015. Simone Veil joined them in 2018. The newcomers opened up the Gaullist epic to make it more inclusive, but the overall plotline remained the same. Brossolette and Zay were socialists, the former a résistant who died in Gestapo custody, the latter a one-time minister in Léon Blum's Popular Front government murdered in 1944 by miliciens. As for de Gaulle Anthonioz, Tillion, and Veil, they were all ex-deportees, not to mention women. The first two had been sent to Ravensbrück for acts of resistance, the third to Auschwitz because she was a Jew. Deportees, both Jewish and non-Jewish, now lie side by side in a monument ever more intertwined with the memory of the Resistance. Jean Moulin, de Gaulle's emissary in France, had lain there since 1964. Today, he finds himself in the company of a widening cast of Second World War heroes. What had sustained them all in the final analysis was the basic decency of ordinary French people, the righteous of France. It's a unifying vision that harks back to the highpoint of Gaullist memory in the mid-sixties with a trio of significant revisions: de Gaulle, important a figure as he was and remains, is no longer the alpha and omega of the story; it's not as though the Holocaust has become so, but the Jewish tragedy, which the Gaullist epic once glossed over, is now assigned a weighty chapter of its own; and the Communists don't even merit a mention. In the present moment, yet once again, the story of the Deportation is coming in for a rewrite, and there will be other rewrites to come no doubt, a reminder that, like history tout court, the history of deportation memory has no telos.

Narratives of the Deportation

Now it is time to reflect, not on where deportation memory stands today, but on the journey that has brought us to this point. The concentration-ary paradigm dominated France's memory battles in the first postwar decades, but it's important to recognize at the same time just how fragmented the paradigm was.[7] The Communists propagated a version that discerned in the camps avatars of capitalism itself, the precipitate of an exploitative system with all its mystifications stripped away. From this perspective, conjuring the memory of the camps was not just a memorial exercise, meaningful as that was, but a maneuver in the ongoing fight against fascism and fascism's heirs in the postwar world, West Germany and its superpower patron, the United States.

In the deportee community, the Communists enjoyed a hegemonic moment post Liberation, but it was a fleeting one. The onset of the Cold War incited breakaways, the first led by David Rousset, the inventor of the term "concentrationary universe." What the camps represented, as Rousset saw it, was not fascism alone but authoritarianism in all its guises, and in a Cold War context, that perspective placed the Soviet Union in the dock as Nazism's totalitarian twin. For Catholics, like Jacques Maritain and Father Riquet, it was not the authoritarianism of such regimes, Nazi and Soviet, that made them so menacing as their paganism and idolatrous worship of the state instead of the one, true God. Jews, Isaac Schneersohn's CDJC in the forefront, sought to find a place for themselves in this scheme of things. They too had resisted, rising in revolt in the camps and in the Warsaw Ghetto; they had remained loyal to the Republic and all it represented; and they were friends of Israel, which had stood fast with France during the 1956 invasion of Suez. In laying out such claims, the CDJC did not hide its Jewishness but asserted it in rhetoric and ritual, and more than that, it won the place it sought, thanks to friends in the deportee community and in the Fourth Republic's corridors of power.

The Cold War splintered deportee memory, a fracture that was compounded yet again by Algeria's fight for independence from French colonial rule. Deportees and résistants on the non-communist Left recognized the Algerians' struggle as akin to the one they had waged against the Nazis. The tactics were the same, guerrilla warfare, and so was the enemy, an occupier who did not scruple to employ torture or to round up and intern enemy combatants in camps. Indeed, it is remarkable how many of the actors in this story, the story of deportation memory, turn up as signatories of the "Manifeste des 121." For such men and women, the concentration camp was not an apanage of any one kind of regime but an every-present potentiality of modern life itself, a monster with one eye open as Jean Cayrol called it, primed to reawaken when the fires of racism and xenophobia were stoked once more.

Yet another development reconfigured the landscape of deportee memory, de Gaulle's return to power in 1958, which proved a veritable earthquake. It's sometimes thought that Gaullist memory dominated from the moment of the Liberation itself, but that wasn't the case. True, the General went toe to toe with the Communists in the memory battles of 1944–1946, but then he retreated. He took part in the annual June 18 commemorations of Free France's exploits, but the ceremonials were intimate affairs that engaged the Gaullist faithful but not the public at large. This changed in 1958. The Gaullist Fifth Republic took memory management very much to heart, staging a sequence of grand events – the unveiling of the Mont-Valérien memorial, the transfer of Moulin's remains to the Pantheon, the release of *Paris brûle-t-il?* – that dramatized de Gaulle's version of wartime events. The motif of the Thirty Years' War loomed large in the Gaullist schema. Its importance diminished with the passage of time, but otherwise, the major elements of the

Gaullist story remained intact. France had stood united against the Occupier; it had never ceased to fight; and it had done so under the leadership of a maverick general, a larger than life figure, Charles de Gaulle. The General rallied wide swaths of the deportee community to his way of thinking, and the mainstream media, much of it under state control, blared the message to a public willing enough to be caught up in it. Thus, to young people coming of age in the mid-sixties, it might well have looked as though Gaullist memory had always monopolized the limelight (with a cameo part reserved for the Communists), but understandable as such an assumption might be, it was not accurate.

One consequence, not to say objective, of Gaullist memorial practice was to rally the nation around the image of a united Resistance, which also happened to be a way to pacify the domestic divisions born of the Algerian War and move beyond them. That war had torn apart not just the nation but the deportee community as well, many former deportees (but by no means all) recognizing in France's ruthless conduct in Algeria a facsimile of the Nazi ruthlessness they had known in the concentration camps. In this way, the memory wall that de Gaulle erected obscured more than one calamitous past, what had happened to the Jews in the Second World War but also and at the same time what France had done in North Africa. In the 1970s, the young woke from the spell de Gaulle had woven about the Second World War, but it is worth asking whether they did the same when it came to Algeria. I believe the answer is no, which is as much to say that the Gaullist era succeeded at least in this: it interrupted the multidirectional pairing, once so powerful, of the camps of deportation and the camps of colonial counter-insurgency.[8]

The memory of the Deportation then did indeed haunt France in the immediate postwar decades, and it was a memory centered on the camp experience. In this measure, it is right to speak, as scholars have done, of a prevailing concentrationary paradigm. So long, that is, as a number of qualifications are kept in mind. The memory of the camps, first of all, was never a unitary phenomenon but one that admitted of multiple, often contesting variants, patterned by political commitment and religious affiliation. Just as critical to note is the way events – the Cold War, the Algerian War, and de Gaulle's return to power, to name the most important – impacted the ebb and flow of public memory. Yet one more proviso: even at its mid-sixties apogee, the concentrationary paradigm never silenced Jewish voices. De Gaulle himself understood that something terrible had happened to the Jews, although that "something" was not key to the story he wanted to tell. Yet, just because de Gaulle was not preoccupied with the Jewish tragedy didn't mean that others weren't, Jews themselves first of all, as evidenced by the unflagging memory campaigning of the CDJC. Deportee associations, communist and non-communist alike, also made a space for Jewish expression, even if a circumscribed one that wrapped Jewish suffering, significant as it was, into a grand, national epic of resistance and deportee martyrdom. No doubt, there was a price to be paid for such inclusion. Jews trod with care when talking out loud about the genocide. The CDJC's genocide historians, as we have seen, wrote in tones of restraint, accenting what the perpetrators had done more than Jewish suffering. And to the degree the Jewish story was in fact folded into that of the Resistance, the singularity of what had happened to the Jews was ironed out.

With time, however, this would change. The Jewish voice grew more distinct and more voluble, and as it did so, the concentrationary paradigm ceded ground, without ever fading away, to a new regime of memory, this one indeed highlighting the special fate of the Jews. The process began earlier than sometimes supposed, before the 1967 war, even before the Eichmann trial. It wasn't happenings in faraway Israel that jump-started the change but, at least as argued here, interfaith dialogue. Exchanges between Catholics and Jews, at first so full of stammering and incomprehension, soon gathered momentum, compelling the Church and in due course the French public itself to take a sympathetic interest in what had happened to the Jews. Chagall's paintings, the Finaly Affair, Jules Isaac's untiring exertions, all prompted painful soul-searching about Christian Europe's complicity in the Nazi genocide. Christianity's centuries-long perpetuation of anti-Semitic prejudice had greased the rails that transported six million Jews to their deaths: such was Isaac's terrible accusation. The Church answered back, rethinking its teachings on the Jews, an epochal aggiornamento that culminated in the Vatican's promulgation of Nostra Aetate in 1965. It wasn't just the Hierarchy that opened itself to the Jewish experience but elements of the laity too, literary figures like François Mauriac and publishers like Paul Flamand. Such men were not just good listeners but conducted themselves as patrons, prefacing and editing Jewish authors – Elie Wiesel, André Schwarz-Bart, Saul Friedländer – who treated the murder of Europe's Jews not just as a piece of the deportation story but as the heart of the matter. This publishing renaissance just picked up steam as the decade of the sixties wore on. The number of prize-winning novelists who dealt with Holocaust themes accumulated, Anna Langfus garnering the Prix Goncourt in 1962, Piotr Rawicz the Prix Rivarol that same year, and Patrick Modiano a host of honors in 1968 on publication of *La Place de l'étoile*. Figure in the best-sellers like Jean-François Steiner's *Treblinka* (1966), and it's clear that the French public, the reading public in any event, had developed a powerful appetite for Holocaust-related books.

So, even at the very moment the Gaullist narrative of Resistance and Deportation contrived to outshine all others, another story, a Jewish one, was stirring, taking form and catching the public eye as it did. It did not take long before such rumbles of memory turned into an eruption, and a generational shift is what set off the explosion.

The notion of generation has a complex meaning in this context. It is a phenomenon of age cohorts and two in particular: the so-called 1.5 generation made up of Jewish children who had spent the war in hiding, even as they lost one parent or both to the Nazi genocide, and the sons and daughters of Holocaust survivors who were born after the war.[9] But the notion also has a second dimension, having to do less with parentage and the Occupation than with the historical conjuncture that formed the young as they reached maturity or just beyond. It's tempting to sum up that conjuncture in a single date, 1968, but that's too narrow a perspective if '68 is taken to signify the turbulent events of May and nothing more. It will serve, though, if a wider view is adopted, one that treats '68 as exemplary of an extended period of public contestation running from the mid-sixties through the dawn of the Mitterrand era. These years witnessed a questioning of the postwar order in all its aspects, the era's memory politics included.

That questioning targeted first and foremost the Gaullist narrative of the war, then so overpowering. The idea was not to supplant the General's account with the communist alternative but to sweep both away and start anew, and no work better incarnated that housecleaning impulse than Marcel Ophuls' *Le Chagrin et la pitié* (1969). Such clearing of the memory decks created an opening for the Jewish story to push through, and that story gained in urgency with the passage of time. It was fueled by events in the Middle East, the wars of 1967 and 1973, which impressed on the young the precariousness of the Jewish presence in that region, at the same time invigorating a sense of Jewish selfhood. This sense, moreover, grew all the stronger as the "sixties" faded, taking with them expectations of a revolution that never came to pass. So many young people, washed up on shore by the great Marxist wave, now found themselves marooned as it receded, turning to identity politics as an alternative path forward, a development that affected young Jews as it affected many others. Beate and Serge Klarsfeld tapped into these energies, using sixty-eighter tactics to mobilize and concentrate them. The media coverage and the court cases that followed ramped up the volume, commanding the public's attention in a way it had never been commanded before. The Holocaust was everywhere, in the news, at the cinema, and above all on television.

The state too began to take an interest. It's not as though it had never paid attention before. The public authorities had patronized CDJC events in Fourth Republic days. What was new, as the decade of the 1980s began, was that it was now the Fifth Republic, very much in a post-Gaullist frame of mind, that started to engage itself. Claude Lanzmann's *Shoah* is a landmark in the history of Holocaust representation, so much so that it gave the phenomenon a new name. The movie's 1985 release was an event in its own right, indeed, a national one with François Mitterrand, the president of the Republic himself in attendance. Mitterrand, of course, had a fraught relationship with France's wartime past. He maintained ongoing attachments to Vichy-era friends and to the memory of Maréchal Pétain, but Jacques Chirac knew no such equivocations. As the Republic's head of state, he bestowed the nation's blessing on Holocaust memory, even as he adapted that memory in subtle and not so subtle ways to draft it into the service of "a certain idea of France."

On this accounting, Holocaust consciousness did not break upon the French scene like some belated thunderclap, bringing to a sudden end decades of postwar silence. Rather, it was molded in a long-term process that got started early, even before the Occupation had ended, with the founding of the CDJC. Events mattered in powering the process forward – the Eichmann trial, the 1967 Arab-Israeli war – but they did not constitute decisive turning points. Of greater moment were developments of a less pin-point character: the interfaith confrontations of the 1950s and early sixties and the generational changing of the guard that followed not long thereafter. These initiated widening sectors of French opinion into the Holocaust story, the reading public first of all and then movie-going and television audiences after that. The electronic media, as well as print, played a key role in all this, amplifying what Jews had to say and extending its reach, a fact that doesn't always receive the attention it deserves.

As the Jewish voice swelled, the Holocaust story itself began to change and this in more than one respect. It's obvious that very few people, if anyone, grasped the full extent of the Jewish tragedy from the very first. That story had to be fleshed out, which happened over time, and, as it did, it became ever clearer that the fate that the Jews had suffered was distinct from that inflicted on political deportees.

This was not how things looked at the beginning, of course. Then, it was the resemblances that most struck commentators. Jews, like résistants, had been arrested, detained in transit facilities, and then trained off in cattle cars to camps in the East, none more notorious than Auschwitz, which in time attained synechdochic status for the Deportation as whole. As Auschwitz became better known as a camp, moreover, it soon sufficed to cite one or the other of its component parts – the barbed wire or the crematorium chimney – to summon up the full horror of what its inmates, résistants but also Jews, had been made to endure. Such an understanding did not erase Jews from the picture, but it cast them not as lead players but as second-order figures, however deserving in sympathy.

That changed with the representational burst of the late fifties and early sixties. Read Wiesel or Schwarz-Bart, Langfus or Rawicz, look at Rossif's documentary: it's Jews who are speaking, and they talk of a lost world in the East, sometimes in the accents of the region. That world might have been bourgeois and aspirational as it was in Langfus' novel of shipwreck, *Le Sel et le soufre*, or it might have been small-town and Yiddish-speaking as it was in Wiesel's and Schwarz-Bart's work. In all its variety and vitality, however, that world was now razed, its inhabitants stigmatized, ghettoized, and murdered in a paroxysm of cruelty that dealt lethal blows not just to a people but to a civilization and a language. This was a set of experiences sui generis. There had not been ghettoes in France. France, however hard hit, had not been destroyed the way Poland was. And French survivors of Deportation – a narrow majority in the case of non-Jews – did not find themselves stranded in a universe still steeped in anti-Semitism but in general had homes and families to return to.

The Steiner controversy hammered home the exterminatory efficiency of the Nazi killing machine. It also stirred fierce debate about Jewish passivity in the face of Nazi persecution. This was a tender subject, for implicit in the allegation of Jewish passivity was the insinuation that Jews had failed to do enough to save themselves. Steiner was shouted down on this point, however, because French Jews knew from direct experience, unlike Israelis or Americans, what it was like to live under Nazi occupation – to be hounded by a cruel persecutor amidst dogging anxieties about where to turn for help. They also knew that Jews had resisted, a point that the CDJC insisted on whenever and wherever it could.

The Steiner controversy, furthermore, made eminently clear, contra the concentrationary paradigm, that not all camps were the same.[10] Rousset had been imprisoned in Buchenwald, Father Riquet in Dachau, Jorge Semprun in Mauthausen, and Charlotte Delbo in Auschwitz. They had all borne up under a harsh regimen of punitive work and extreme physical deprivation. Delbo understood, however, that the Auschwitz she knew, Auschwitz the work camp, was not the whole story, that for the camp's Jewish inmates there was but a single exit, up the chimney. Steiner's book relocated the center of the camp story even further to the East, to Treblinka. Here, next to no one survived because the camp's objective was not a punishing exploitation but *Vernichtung* plain and simple. It was not necessary to build barracks to house the camp's population because almost no one lived there. It was not necessary to organize work commandos or satellite work camps because labor was not what the camp was about. With one exception...there was work for Sonderkommandos, those unfortunates burdened with the task of disposing of the bodies of the murdered.

In Steiner's work, the Sonderkommando is a combative figure who first plumbs the depths of abjection, so that he might later rise in revolt. In Claude Lanzmann's *Shoah*, he is a revenant, returned from the land of the dead, that rare being who has looked on the face of the Gorgon and not turned to stone. In the concentrationary story, there is scant place for Treblinka or for Chelmno, Majdanek, Sobibor, and Belzec. Yet, for Lanzmann, these are the sites that count most, the places where the Shoah happened. There is no one left to tell of them but the Sonderkommando who has entered the gas chamber and come out again, more dead than alive, a figure with no equivalent in the concentrationary regime of memory.[11]

To the French public, these revelations were riveting. Steiner's novel sold well; Lanzmann's movie was heralded as a masterpiece. Yet, how far away the events they related, situated deep in the forests of Eastern Europe, must have seemed. In the 1970s and 1980s, however, the Holocaust came home. It's not that the Vél d'hiv was a secret. There was a plaque on the site, and every year mourners gathered on the spot to observe memorial services. Nor was Drancy a site unknown. As early as 1946, Georges Wellers had published a book on life in the camp and cited Drancy by name in the volume's title: *De Drancy à Auschwitz*. What had changed in the decades since was the arrival on the scene of a clamorous, youthful cohort, self-styled militants of memory eager to unmask the lies of their elders: to expose Vichy's complicity and, indeed, the complicity of so many ordinary French men and women in the implementation of the Final Solution. Vichy officials were called to account in court, and the Vél d'hiv and Drancy became spaces of activism. In time, brand-new monuments were erected on the sites that left no doubt it was Jews who been made to suffer there, not just on the Occupier's orders, but on the authority of the *État français* itself.

Thus, an alternative memorial landscape was articulated that mapped out the distinct pathway that France's Jews had followed to extinction, from the Vél d'hiv to Drancy on to the death camps in the East. This was not the circuit of monuments visited every April on the occasion of the Journée nationale de la Déportation. That sequence ran from the Deportation Chapel at the Église Saint-Roch to the Tomb of the Unknown Soldier, with stops along the way at the Mémorial des Martyrs de la Déportation and the Tombeau du Martyr juif inconnu.

As the names of *these* monuments attest, it was martyrs and fighters who were the objects of veneration. That was not the tone set by the new generation of monuments, whose inscriptions talked, rather, of persecution and victimization. This shift too was part of the changing Holocaust story. The first "Holocaust" monument, the Tombeau du Martyr juif inconnu, was erected in 1956 in memory of the six million who had perished "without sepulcher." The memorial, designed to resemble a grave-marker, was intended as a substitute tomb where the anonymous dead might at last be mourned as they deserved. And so they were, as martyrs who had died Kiddush HaShem, in sanctification of the Name. Speakers at memorial events reminded a grieving community that Jews had resisted the fate that Nazi barbarism had condemned them to. They had risen in revolt in the Warsaw Ghetto, and though the ghetto was leveled, its fighting spirit lived on, the torch of resistance finding a new home in the fledgling State of Israel. Contrast this mode of understanding, so full of redemptive accents, with the story Lanzmann tells in *Shoah*, a story that ends in the gas chambers of the Aktion Reinhard camps. The Warsaw Ghetto uprising hovers on the movie's margins, as does Israel, but Lanzmann refuses the viewer any easy consolations or catharsis. The world abandoned the Jews to a monstrous fate. Few survived, and the handful who did felt a terrible solitude, as though they were the last Jew alive stranded amidst smoking ruins.

The Holocaust story did not stand on its own at first but existed within the folds of a larger entity, the concentrationary paradigm. It grew apart in time, however, and altered its valence as it did. Yet always, even from the beginning, it was a presence. There was never a silence to break, as asserted by so many latter-day militants of memory. It's important, nonetheless, to grasp why the claim was lodged in the first place and what made it seem so believable.

First of all, there were real silences. The Allied powers did indeed stand aside while European Jewry was massacred, opting not to act on news of the genocide conveyed by "messengers of disaster" like Jan Karski.[12] Within survivors' families, subjects were not discussed. Who wanted to confront the pain and the loss, and who even had the words to do so? Anyhow, it was better for the children not to know about such things. Why dwell on death when there were new lives to live?

Jews nonetheless gathered amongst themselves to mourn their losses. It's worth considering, though, how much the children absorbed what was happening around them. The parents belonged to a Yiddish-speaking past, but for the young other horizons beckoned, a world of French hopes and aspirations. Georges Perec and Serge Klarsfeld talked about sport. Lanzmann plunged headlong into the class struggle. For all kinds of reasons, children don't hear what their elders have to teach them. They choose to leave the old neighborhood and its stock of memories in pursuit of something new that will be their own. A past that fails to transmit, that too is a kind of silence.

All was not in fact silence, of course, but even so, how commanding was the Jewish voice in those early postwar years? It was just one among many and far from the most assertive. CDJC historians piped up, but they did so with moderation and decorum, taking pains not to alienate an incredulous public. It took not just pains but time, moreover, to build up a rounded picture of the genocide: how the Nazi apparatus of destruction worked, the travails of Jews caught up in it, which varied from Anne Frank's end of the continent to Elie Wiesel's, and the indifference or complicity of third parties (the French included). In the meantime, it was all too easy to lose the Holocaust story in the crowd of others about the Deportation. The Holocaust loomed in the 1950s, but it did not loom large, for a certainty not as large as it would in later years.

Still, how unmindful a person must have been, looking back from the vantage point of the seventies or eighties, to a see nothing but a landscape flattened out by repression, to hear nothing but the muffle of bottled-up memory. What of all the prize-winning books? What of all the best-sellers? Is it really necessary to rehearse once more the many Holocaust-related confrontations that punctuated French public life in the first postwar decades: from the Finaly Affair to the storm over *Le Vicaire* to the Steiner controversy?

It may be that people were preoccupied with other concerns, not paying attention so to speak, and for that reason they missed out on what was happening all around them. It may also be that Holocaust stories of the kind tendered by the CDJC were set in a key many – the young in particular – were not attuned to. There was too much talk about religion, about martyrs and heroes. On top of that, there was the blinding sun of Gaullist memory. De Gaulle's star reached its zenith in the mid-sixties, radiating a light that cast so much else into shadow. Stare upon it too long, which is what the state-managed media invited citizens to do, and things that might otherwise have appeared plain as day ceased to be visible.[13]

That sun set, however, and, the blindfold now removed, a new generation looked upon the Holocaust as though for the first time. As for explaining the silence preceding (which was not one), an account lay ready to hand. The war generation had many reasons to want to forget. For the victims, the memories were painful. For the perpetrators, oblivion was all too convenient. For the mass of ordinary French people, Gaullist mythmaking salved a national conscience wounded by defeat and the demeaning compromises of the Occupation. Yet, as psychiatrists knew from clinical experience, the repressed will out, returning with a vengeance in the form of symptoms, often debilitating ones. With time and analysis, of course, there was reason to hope that the traumas of the past might yet be mastered, and it was that task of "working through" that the rising generation set for itself. As that working through proceeded, the "myth of silence," which was its premise, hardened into the concrete of received wisdom.

Representation in the Aftermath of Catastrophe

The concentrationary paradigm did not make it easy for the uniqueness of the Jewish story to find expression.[14] It is a paradox of the new, Holocaust-centered regime of memory that other Deportation stories, the tables now turned, have come to be subsumed within *it*. This conclusion opened with an instance of such transformation – the metamorphosis of the communist corner of Père-Lachaise into a site of Holocaust memory. Such conflations elide the specifics of experience and to this degree obscure more than they reveal. But what about representational practice? It is common usage today to treat Antelme and Delbo as Holocaust writers and Resnais as a Holocaust filmmaker. Yet, does that make any sense? The answer, in my view, is more in the negative than in the positive.

The "no" portion of the answer ought to be obvious by now. The Holocaust has an iconography all its own. Flash a yellow Star of David, and today's viewer will know in an instant that it's the fate of Jews that's at stake. The ghetto child, with frightened face and arms upraised, has become the very emblem of anti-Semitic persecution. And of course, the way Lanzmann tells it, the Shoah was an event unlike any other, a story without a moral of any kind. In Antelme, Delbo, and Semprun, camp inmates have resources to fall back on: comradeship, literature, resistance. They find ways to survive, but for Lanzmann, the Shoah is not about life or the triumph of the human spirit. It is about death, and the gas chamber is its final stop. Now, this is a radical understanding, one that insists not just on uniqueness but also on incomparability, and the filmmaker has been accused for that reason of sacralizing the event.[15] In this respect, Lanzmann's vision has apparent affinities with trauma narratives that treat survivors as exceptional beings, hallowed messengers returned from an alternate universe of horror with lessons to teach. But the affinities in my view do not run deep, for Lanzmann's survivors are like Langfus'. They are not saints but people who have suffered, "that's all" as Langfus herself put it. They don't have lessons to teach, whether about tolerance ("Never again") or about fraternity ("Love one another"). But they do tell us that the Shoah was unparalleled in its monstrousness. It is an event that stands apart, and in this sense, Lanzmann does indeed ring the Holocaust about with flame, like an island of fire cut off from the flow of history. For an historian wedded to explanation and to comparison, this is a step too far. Yet, at the heart of Lanzmann's understanding is a claim that is compelling: the Holocaust was first and foremost a Jewish catastrophe. It was about the extermination of European Jewry, every man, woman, and child, and the destruction along with of an East European, Yiddish-speaking civilization that has never come back to life. This was not what Delbo and Resnais were talking about, however wondrous the works they created.

There is a good case to be made, notwithstanding, for discussing the likes of a Semprun or a Wiesel side by side, however distinct the stories they had to relate. For at various moments, they went through experiences that overlapped. Each was a deportee after all and, as such, braved the harrowing train ride to an SS-run camp. The Liberation indeed found them both prisoners at Buchenwald, gaunt survivors with the cadaverous look of a man brought back from the dead.[16] Such intersections help make sense of the iconographic overlap between the Holocaust story and deportation stories of other kinds. Résistants, like Jews, were deported in boxcars; they wore striped uniforms with identifying triangles sewn on; they lived in barracks encircled by barbed wire; and, once dead, they were incinerated in the camp crematorium. Such was the common fate of deportees, and that common fate generated a vocabulary, a set of symbols, that might be used to aid readers and viewers in understanding what the Deportation had been like for one and all.

There is more to the making of stories, of course, than imagery, however evocative. There are also questions of form and narrative technique, and when it comes to these, the intersections between the Holocaust story and the rest become yet more insistent.

One reason why has to do with the utter unbelievability of what deportees, whoever they were, had had to live through. During the Great War, France's home front had been fed stories of the Hun's barbarism, leaving many in the war's aftermath in a skeptical frame of mind about accusations of atrocity. Jews, according to stereotype, were known whiners, always full of complaint. So, no doubt the Nazis were a bad lot, people might have reassured themselves, but was it possible that they had created a camp universe as cruel and murderous as it was said to have been? How to break through such disbelief, this was the first obstacle that confronted anyone, résistant or Jew, historian or artist, who wanted to tell an uncomprehending world about the Deportation.

Photographers had a solution: shoot photos of the camps, with the victims' corpses in piles and witnesses in the frame to situate the pictures in time and space.[17] CDJC historians had a solution of their own: let the documents speak for themselves, an approach that they stuck to across decades of research and that was adopted in later years by worthy successors like Serge Klarsfeld. For would-be authors who had known the camps first hand – Antelme, Delbo, Wiesel – relating what they had lived through was full of pitfalls. Write with too much style, and the result was "literature," a self-indulgent display of the artist's talents that drew attention away from the subject matter, amounting to a betrayal of the dead to whom a debt of piety was owed. The task was to craft a style that was not a style, to compose a trimmed down prose that was frank and unsparing in its confrontation with the horrors of camp life and bodies in pain.[18] Literary critics have tried to give a name to the genre born of such efforts with "concentrationary realism," "documentary realism," and "traumatic realism" among the leading contenders.[19]

Important as the "realist" strain was, however, it didn't exhaust all the possibilities. How after all was it conceivable to evoke the true insanity of the Nazis' murderous enterprise with a mere recitation of the facts or to capture something of the victims' disorientation and despair? These were challenges that invited experimentation in narrative modes and techniques that exceeded the bounds of realist convention.[20]

Wiesel's *La Nuit* is often read as an act of witness, which it is, but it is more than that. The book engages with the Akedah story but turns it inside out. It traces what seems a linear path through the horrors of Auschwitz, but, fable-like, it is rhythmed by premonitions and prefigurations. Schwarz-Bart, as we have seen, mixed genres with abandon, setting the story of Ernie Levy's life and death in a millennial frame that was itself a blend of legend and epic. Anna Langfus' *Le Sel et le soufre* is a Bildungsroman but in reverse, the protagonist's education in life winding down into bereaved aloneness. Indeed, bereavement shadows all her work, which is blotched with eruptions of whirling madness and hallucination. As for Piotr Rawicz, he delineates a world, appetitive and cruel, ruled over by a crazed deity. And in the novels of Romain Gary and Patrick Modiano, the craziness takes a comic turn, the humor as dark as it is, sometimes, hilarious. In such fictions, the world spirals from the real into the surreal, and as it does, the "heroes" trapped in its toils prove themselves all too human. They cling to life, they play fast and loose with the reader's sympathies, and they even commit wrongs themselves, kidnapping and murder in the case of Michael in Langfus' *Saute, Barbara*.

It wasn't just Jewish authors, of course, who set aside convention. In Delbo's work, experience breaks down into fragments. The world of the concentration camp is a place out of time and those who live in it doubled beings, at once bodies under duress and observers who seem to watch it all from a great distance. That doubleness persists, moreover, even post-Liberation, as normal lives are reconstructed, "normal" lives, that is, ravaged by physical ailments, flashbacks, and a nagging sadness. This is very much the story related in Cayrol's work on "concentrationary dreams." For camp inmates, dreams are an avenue of escape, an exit into color and imagination or into God's embrace. For the survivor, however, they are a source of danger that drag the dreamer back into a nightmarish past that won't let go. The haunted survivor was a figure common to non-Jews and Jews alike, to Delbo and Cayrol as to Wiesel, and all of them resorted to literary devices, sometimes realist but often not, to conjure a sense of that haunted quality.

And for those elements of the camp experience that eluded the prose-writer's narrative gifts or that were judged unsuited to prose expression, yet other means were invented. Rolf Hochhuth wrote *Le Vicaire* in free verse. Cayrol turned to poetry, and Delbo inserted short poems into her mosaic of prose vignettes. There were even ways to communicate without saying a word. The huge white margins in Delbo's printed texts hinted at how much was left unsaid, inviting the reader the fill in the void. Blankness, of course, was a persistent motif in Perec's oeuvre. In *W ou le souvenir d'enfance*, he had recourse to a well-placed ellipsis, a simple three dots to signify what had happened to a mother vanished into the flames of Auschwitz.

Documentary as the realism of a Delbo or Wiesel might have been, they did far more than just recite the facts. Genre busting and narratological innovation were the order of the day in the literature of the Deportation, which on reflection, makes obvious sense.[21] Here was an event to beggar the imagination, one that transgressed every norm. Conventional forms were bound to be inadequate to conveying what it had been like, so how else to proceed but by experimental means?

This is just as true, even more so, when it comes to "documentary" film-making. I have used quotation marks because one of the films I've discussed, *Shoah*, is not a documentary at all. It makes no use of archival footage. There are documents, just a few: Lanzmann at one point reads a despairing letter written by the rabbi of Grabòw in 1942; Raul Hilberg explicates on camera a traffic manager's dispatch, detailing plans for training Jews to the camps; and that's it. Now, Resnais and Cayrol's *Nuit et Brouillard*, Rouch and Morin's *Chronique d'un été*, Rossif's *Le Temps du ghetto*, and Ophuls' *Le Chagrin et la pitié* are indeed documentaries, but observe how original they are in form and technique. Resnais switches back and forth between black-and-white and color footage, a stratagem that inspired numerous imitators, among them Steven Spielberg who made liberal use of it in *Schindler's List* (1994). Then there's Cayrol's commentary, which, even as it chronicles the Deportation, sounds a note of poetic alert. Rouch and Morin's documentary approached its subject from a social science perspective, equal parts anthropology and sociology. The movie dug for the truth but at the same time questioned the possibility of finding it. This was a new kind of filmmaking, and a neologism was invented to characterize it, *cinéma vérité*. Rossif's movie was in many respects more conventional but not in all, not for sure in the way it elicited and staged eyewitness testimony, turning talking heads into a Greek chorus that summoned up an anguished past out of the darkness. Last of all, there is Ophuls' film, a mirror-breaking exercise which explodes lies and equivocations. Eyewitnesses are themselves under accusation, not relating the truth, but yielding it up as they wriggle in the interviewer's gun sights.

Even when it came to commemoration, the impulse to create new forms was powerful. I say "even" because tradition exercises a deep and abiding attraction where the care of the dead is concerned, one near impossible to forgo. Nor was it forgone in the case of deportees, but it was modified, and that's the point. The Deportation was such a violation of norms that observance of the customary rites, as important as that remained, was judged insufficient unto itself. Something more needed to be done, something new acknowledging that the nature of this loss was unlike any other that had gone before.

So, let us begin the discussion of commemorative practice by first giving tradition its due. The Great War left a deep imprint on how France's fallen were mourned, a legacy that proved inescapable when it came to mourning the deportee dead. In the case of Gaullist memory, how could it be otherwise? For the General, the First World War and the Second were conjoined events, the terminal nodes of a single, thirty-year arc. All who had sacrificed in that struggle, deportees included, deserved the same rites of remembrance and respect. An eternal flame burned at the Arc de Triomphe? Then Mont-Valérien too would have a flame, and every year a torch was carried from one to the next in solemn recognition of the bond, sealed in blood, that connected the two.[22] For Jews too, the

Great War set commemorative precedents worthy of emulation. The Tombeau du Martyr juif inconnu also had its eternal flame, and, in fact, the monument's very name was modeled on a Great War prototype, The Tomb of the Unknown Soldier. When it came to actual ceremonials, moreover, just about everyone borrowed from the Great War's stock of rites and observances. It was the practice when honoring fallen *poilus* to conclude events with prayers for the dead, the playing of taps, and a moment of silence.[23] The identical repertoire was drawn on for occasions commemorating deportees.

The mention of prayer is a reminder of religion's pervasiveness in the framing of the Deportation story, whatever the variant.[24] Deportees after all were so often cast as martyrs: Jewish martyrs who died with the Shema on their lips or Christian martyrs agonizing as Christ had on the Cross. Deportee narratives brimmed with scriptural allusion and citation from Lamentations and Job to the New Testament Gospels. And religious elements adorned the monuments raised in the deportees' memory. Think of the cylinder at the Jewish memorial in the Marais, which called to mind a Yahrzeit candle; or of the emaciated figure wafting upward at the Struthof memorial as though resurrected from the dead; or of the giant Cross of Lorraine that towers over Mont-Valérien. It's not hard to understand why religion mattered so much in the memorialization of deportees. Faith gave meaning to the sacrifices made and the losses endured. It afforded consolation. It's important to keep in mind at the same time just how religious 1950s France was (and not just France), the war and the Cold War working like bellows to fan the sparks of spiritual commitment.

Yet, just as striking were the efforts made to envelop traditional practice in a commemorative frame that was pathbreaking in conception.[25] Didn't the unprecedented character of the catastrophe demand memorial forms no less unprecedented? The PCF called on the talents of Picasso and Léger to supply imagery. The CDJC turned to a modernist architect, Alexandre Persitz, to design the Tombeau du Martyr juif inconnu. Georges-Henri Pingusson, who drew up the blueprint for the deportee monument on the Île de la Cité, was a member in good standing of the Union des artistes modernes. The structures they conceived were indeed modern, abstract and minimalist, composed of elemental shapes and shorn of decorative detail. The architects made a point, moreover, of doing without figurative representation. How different from Great War memorials which afforded statuary such a singular prominence.

To be sure, there were deportee memorials, as at Struthof, where the human body did indeed feature, but it was not modeled in the same way that Great War memorials modeled the body. Great War statuary favored realist or allegorical modes or a mix of the two.[26] Think of the broken body of a fallen *poilu* cradled by a winged victory. At Struthof, by contrast, the deportee body was stylized, emaciated and stick-like, and this was done by design to signify a break with World War One antecedents. As for allegory, even when sculptors of the Deportation resorted to it, they did so by giving the form a fresh twist. Now think of the Deportation cartouche at Mont-Valérien. Here was the Sacred Heart of Jesus transformed into a mid-twentieth-century icon, a shredded heart trussed in the barbed wire of the concentration camp. Urns of ashes and the flames of the crematorium, these too were adopted as design elements, constituting a new iconographic repertoire that symbolized a kind of experience that had no forebears: the hell, not of the trenches, but of Buchenwald and Auschwitz. Even the rituals associated with deportation monuments, laden with tradition as they were, received an update, as the musical accompaniment made manifest. The "Marseillaise" was played on almost every occasion, of course, but Jews added "Hatikvah" and the "Chant des partisans" of the Vilna Ghetto to the ceremonial songbook and résistants the "Chant des partisans" and the "Chant des marais."

The hell of the camps was more punishing for Jews than it was for résistants, but when it came to limning its contours, similar techniques were applied. The French came in time to understand the two experiences as distinct. Yet, the resemblance they bore to one other, as siblings born into the same family of misery, induced artists, writers, filmmakers, and architects to deal with the two in a common formal vocabulary, one that often blurred the very real boundaries between them. So, Delbo was not a Holocaust writer as Wiesel was, nor Resnais a Holocaust filmmaker like Lanzmann, but it is easy to understand why critics of today treat them so. They all were at grips with a catastrophe unprecedented in nature. They all wanted to communicate the enormity of that terrible shipwreck and what it had cost in human terms. And to that end, they all experimented with forms of a radical newness. For these many reasons, it makes sense to consider them as a group. Provided, of course, it is remembered that what binds them together is not the trauma of the Holocaust but memories of Deportation.

Readers may or may not find such arguments persuasive, but I hope at a minimum they will feel drawn to revisit or visit for the first time the art, books, monuments, and movies that have been encountered in the preceding pages. The French-language body of work on the Deportation is astounding for its breadth and invention, which calls for an explanation in its own right. There remains then yet one more question to address, which, I promise, will be the last.

The Deportation assumed such outsized proportions in France in part because of demography. A rough fifty thousand French deportees made it back home at the Liberation. A mere handful of these were Jews, of course, but France nonetheless possessed the second-largest Jewish community in Europe. Three-quarters of its Jewish inhabitants had survived the war in exile or in hiding, and their ranks swelled in the war's aftermath as remnants of East European Jewry, made to feel unwanted at home by their Christian neighbors, migrated westward. France had a unique mix of populations with an investment in the memory of the Deportation: résistants of many hues, plus a varied array of Jewish actors, both native-born and immigrant. The United States and Israel welcomed large numbers of Holocaust survivors after the war, but neither had known German Occupation, and neither boasted the record of Resistance that France did. The Holocaust came in time to weigh on the German conscience, but there were not many Jews on hand to speak up on their own behalf about the crimes the Nazis had perpetrated.

The Deportation also mattered deeply to the French for reasons that were numerous and varied. The memory of it was and remained a balm to a nation smarting from the sting of defeat and enemy occupation. The war years, thanks to deportee sacrifice, were not just a story of humiliation but also of redemptive martyrdom. The figure of the martyred deportee was thus freighted with an incontestable moral authority, and currents in French public life, political and religious, coveted that authority for themselves. How the competition played out among them was shaped by the vagaries of events, some unique to France (like the Algerian War and de Gaulle's return to power), others less so (like '68, the wars in the Middle East, and the negationist crisis). But always, the memory of the Deportation remained in the public eye at once a moral beacon and a bone of contention.

Deportation memory drew energy from the nation's political conflicts, and in equal, if not greater measure, it drew energy from the creative currents that galvanized France's cultural scene in the postwar decades. It's not just that Rousset wanted to borrow a page from Jarry, or Semprun a page from Proust, or Wiesel (as so many others) a page from Camus. The framers of Deportation memory did not just content themselves with looking for models. They were active participants, sometimes leading ones, in the era's creative movements: from Surrealism and Existentialism to modernist architecture, from the New Wave and New Novel to OuLiPo. In some instances – documentary filmmaking is an example – deportation-themed work stood at the genre's very cutting edge.[27]

The tragedy of the Deportation hung over French public life in the aftermath of the war and indeed remains a spectral presence to the present day. It shaped public consciousness; it generated debate; and it was memorialized with an unmatched creative genius, bequeathing a body of work not just to France but to the entire world that is by turns poignant and disturbing, humane and challenging. What the Deportation has to tell us about ourselves has lost none of its grim urgency.

Notes

Introduction

1 Olivier Lalieu, "Le statut juridique du déporté et les enjeux de mémoire de 1948 à nos jours," in Tal Brutmann, Laurent Joly, and Annette Wieviorka, eds., *Qu'est ce qu'un déporté? Histoire et mémoires des déportations de la Second Guerre mondiale* (Paris, 2009), 333–334. For the figure of 41,000 deported résistants, see François Cochet, *Les Exclus de la victoire. Histoire des prisonniers de guerre, déportés et S.T.O. (1945–1985)* (Paris, 1992), 20. Other sources propose different sets of figures, but these do not change the general picture, the orders of magnitude remaining more or less the same. See Jean-Marc Dreyfus, *Ami, si tu tombes … Les déportés résistants des camps au souvenir 1945–2005* (Paris, 2005), 14; Thomas Fontaine, *Déportations & genocide, l'impossible oubli* (Paris, 2009), 118.

2 Sylvie Lindeperg and Annette Wieviorka, *Univers concentrationnaire et génocide. Voir, savoir, comprendre* (Paris, 2008), 7.

3 Also published in 1946 was Eugen Kogon's *Der SS-Staat*. Kogon's title, like Rousset's, conjured the image of the camps as a world apart – in this instance, of a state within a state.

4 Lemkin is the subject of a recent book: Annette Becker, *Messagers du désastre. Raphael Lemkin, Jan Karski et les génocides* (Paris, 2018).

5 Bettina Stangneth, *Eichmann before Jerusalem: The Unexamined Life of a Mass Murderer*, tr. Ruth Martin (New York, 2014), 60.

6 Cited in Paule Berger Marx, *Les Relations entre les juifs et les catholiques dans la France de l'après-guerre 1945–1965* (Paris, 2009), 58.

7 Léon Poliakov, *Bréviaire de la haine. Le IIIe Reich et les Juifs* (Paris, 1951), 176.

8 The coinage "Yiddish public sphere" is David Cesarini's. Cesarini, "Introduction," in idem. and Eric J. Lundquist, eds., *After the Holocaust: Challenging the Myth of Silence* (New York, 2012), 6.

9 Georges Bensoussan, *Auschwitz en héritage? D'un bon usage de la mémoire* (Paris, 1998); Barbie Zelizer, *Remembering to Forget: Holocaust Memory through the Camera's Eye* (Chicago, 1998), 163–165; Lindeperg and Wieviorka, *Univers concentrationnaire et génocide*, 23–25.

10 For the "sacralization" of the deportee, see Pieter Lagrou, *Mémoires patriotiques et Occupation nazie. Résistants, requis et déportés en Europe occidentale, 1945–1965* (Brussels, 2003), 224, 284.

11 For "regime of memory" as an idea, see Samuel Moyn, *A Holocaust Controversy: The Treblinka Affair in Postwar France* (Waltham, MA, 2005), 11.

12 The expression "reversal of memories" is Lagrou's. See idem, "Victims of Genocide and National Memory: Belgium, France and the Netherlands 1945–1965," *Past & Present*, no. 154 (February, 1997), 185.

13 Simon Perego, 'Pleurons-les, bénissons leurs noms.' *Les Commémorations de la Shoah et de la Seconde Guerre mondiale dans le monde juif parisien entre 1944 et 1967: rituels, mémoires et identités* (Doctoral thesis, Institut d'Études Politiques de Paris, 2016), 435.

14 Laura Jockusch, "Breaking the Silence: The Centre de Documentation Juive Contemporaine in Paris and the Writing of Holocaust History in Liberated France," in Cesarini and Sundquist, eds., *After the Holocaust*, 67–81. In the same volume, see also: Mark L. Smith, "No Silence in Yiddish: Popular and Scholarly Writing about the Holocaust in the Early Postwar Years," 55–66; and David G. Roskies, "Dividing the Ruins: Communal Memory in Yiddish and Hebrew," 82–101.

15 The most forceful exponent of this way of thinking is François Azouvi. Idem, *Le Mythe du grand silence. Auschwitz, les Français, la mémoire* (Paris, 2012).

16 Henry Rousso, *Face au Passé. Essais sur la mémoire contemporaine* (Paris, 2016), 47–48, 235; Charles S. Maier, "A Surfeit of Memory? Reflections on History, Melancholy, and Denial," *History and Memory*, 5 (Fall–Winter 1993), 136–152.

17 Annette Wieviorka, *L'Ère du témoin* (Paris, 1998); Joan B. Wolf, *Harnessing the Holocaust: The Politics of Memory in France* (Stanford, CA, 2004).

18 Azouvi, *Le Mythe du grand silence*, passim.

19 Wolf, *Harnessing the Holocaust*, 19; Cesarini, "Introduction," in Cesarini and Lundquist, eds., *After the Holocaust*, 10.

20 Moyn, *A Holocaust Controversy*, is a major exception.

21 Annette Insdorf, *Indelible Shadows: Film and the Holocaust*, Third Edition (New York, 2003); Sidra DeKoven Ezrahi, *By Words Alone: The Holocaust in Literature* (Chicago, 1980).

22 Suzanne Liandrat-Guigues and Jean-Louis Leutrat, *Alain Resnais. Liaisons secrètes et accords vagabonds* (Paris, 2006), 215–217.

23 Jorge Semprun and Elie Wiesel, *Se taire est impossible* (Paris, 1995).

1 Le Parti des Déportés

1 Olivier Lalieu, *La Résistance française à Buchenwald* (Paris, 2012), 312.

2 Stéphane Courtois, "Luttes politiques et élaboration d'une histoire: le PCF historien du PCF dans la Deuxième Guerre mondiale," *Communisme*, no. 4 (1983), 18–19.

3 Gérard Namer, *La Commémoration en France, 1944–1982. Batailles pour la mémoire* (Paris, 1983), 8; Nicole Racine-Furlaud, "18 juin 1940 ou 10 juillet 1940, batailles de mémoire," in Stéphane Courtois and Marc Lazar, eds., *50 Ans d'une passion française. De Gaulle et les communistes* (Paris, 1991), 197–215.

4 Namer, *La Commémoration*, 20–21; Claire Cameron, ed., *Le Mont-Valérien. Résistance, Répression et Mémoire* (Montreuil, 2008), 28; Frédéric Turpin, *Le Mont-Valérien: de l'histoire à la mémoire* (Paris, 2003), 28.

5 Namer, *La Commémoration*, 74; Jean-Marc Dreyfus, *Ami, si tu tombes … Les déportés résistants des camps au souvenir, 1945–2005* (Paris, 2005), 48; Danielle Tartakowsky, *Le Pouvoir est dans la rue: Crises politiques et manifestations en France* (Paris, 1998), 131. It will come as no surprise to Americans that Paul Robeson, Pete Seeger, and Joan Baez all performed versions of the song. The "Chant des marais" has been scored more than once, but the best-known adaptation is Hanns Eisler's of 1935. Eisler was a German composer at home in party circles.

6 Olivier Wieviorka, *La Mémoire désunie: Le souvenir politique des années sombres, de la Libération à nos jours* (Paris, 2010), 106; Serge Barcellini, "Les cérémonies du 11 novembre 1945. Une apothéose commémorative gaulliste," in Christiane Franck, ed., *La France de 1945. Résistances, retours, renaissances* (Caen, 1996), 96; Danielle Tartakowsky, *Nous irons chanter sur vos tombes: Le Père-Lachaise, XIXe-XXe siècle* (Paris, 1999), 169–170 and 250n19.

7 Henri Frenay, *La Nuit finira: Mémoires de résistance, 1940–1945* (Paris, 2006), 791–793, 801–803; Barcellini, "Les cérémonies du 11 novembre 1945," 85–87, 92–93, 99.

8 Danielle Tartakowsky, "Des 18 juin 'de souveraineté quand même' (1946–1957)," in Philippe Oulmont, ed., *Les 18 juin: Combats et commémorations* (Paris, 2011), 158–160.

9 Barcellini, "Les cérémonies du 11 novembre 1945," 98–100; "La F.N.D.I.R.P. a célébré la mémoire de ses héros," *Le Patriote résistant*, 15 November 1946; "Pèlerinage au Mont-Valérien," *Le Patriote résistant*, 21 November 1947; "Du Mont-Valérien au Théresin," *La Patriote résistant*, 22 November 1950.

10 Leclerc died an untimely death in 1947, the victim of an airplane accident. His remains were interred in the Invalides, a singular honor.

11 Musée de la Résistance nationale (MRN), Fonds Tollet (bis), carton 35, dossier Fabien, letter from Beyer to Vigne, 29 July 1946.

12 Monique Georges, *Le Colonel Fabien était mon père* (Paris, 2009), 255, 265, 270.

13 MRN, Fonds Tollet (bis), carton 35, dossier Fabien, flier, C. Lucibello, Comité Fabien, 20 June 1946; press release, C. Lucibello, 13 July 1946.

14 MRN, Fonds Tollet (bis), carton 35, dossier Fabien, letter from C. Lucibello to Mme Lebon, Mme Katz, 26 July [194]6.

15 Tartakowsky, *Nous irons chanter*, 167.

16 Annette Wieviorka, *Déportation et génocide: Entre la mémoire et l'oubli* (Paris, 1992), 124–128.

17 Serge Wolikow, *Les Combats de la mémoire. La FNDIRP de 1945 à nos jours* (Paris, 2006), 70.

18 This is certainly how deportee memoirs represented the relationship between green and red triangles. It has been argued, however, that the rivalry between the two groups was not always so destructive. See Nikolaus Wachsmann, *KL: A History of the Nazi Concentration Camps* (New York, 2016), 146–147.

19 On the CIF and Buchenwald revolt, see Lalieu, *La Résistance française à Buchenwald*, passim.

20 Claude Lévy, "Une association de déportés en son temps: L'Amicale des déportés d'Auschwitz et des camps de Haute Silésie," in Alfred Wahl, ed., *Mémoire de la Seconde Guerre mondiale: Actes du colloque de Metz, 6–8 octobre 1983* (Metz, 1984), 151–153.

21 Gérard Huber, *Une Vie après la vie. Biographie d'Henry Bulawko (1918–2011)* (Paris 2012), 57, 79, 99, 149. Bulawko's party connection would attenuate over time. In 1989, he accompanied then President François Mitterrand on a trip to Auschwitz. He did the same with President Jacques Chirac in 2005.

22 Dreyfus, *Ami, si tu tombes…*, 79–82; Lalieu, "Le statut juridique du déporté et les enjeux de mémoire, de 1948 à nos jours," in Tal Bruttmann, Laurent Joly, and Annette Wieviorka, eds., *Qu'est-ce qu'un déporté? Histoire et mémoires des déportations de la Seconde Guerre mondiale* (Paris, 2009), 340–341, 344.

23 Wolikow, *Combats de la mémoire*, 79; MRN, papiers Marie-Claude Vaillant-Couturier, ARCH HP 216, carton IF 1086, dossier Déportés du travail. The circular is undated but makes reference to a recent statement by Mathilde Péri for which a date is given: May 1949.

24 Serge Barcellini and Annette Wieviorka, *Passant, souviens-toi! Les Lieux du souvenir de la Second Guerre mondiale en France* (Paris, 1995), 437, 443.

25 MRN, papiers Marie-Claude Vaillant-Couturier, ARCH HP 221, carton IK 1086, dossier "À régler avec Marie-Claude Vaillant-Couturier," subdossier "Déportés du travail," letter from M. Lancelle, Association départementale de la Seine des Déportés du travail, to Mme le Député, 8 October 1956.

26 And to a second pairing as well, Guy Môquet and Gilbert Dru, the former a Communist, the latter a Catholic.

27 RP Riquet, "Compiègne, témoignage de résistance," *Le Patriote résistant*, 1 August 1946; François Cochet, *Les Exclus de la victoire. Histoire des prisonniers de guerre, déportés et S.T.0. (1945–1985)* (Paris, 1992), 163.

28 Philippe Buton, *Les Lendemains qui déchantent. Le Parti communiste français à la Libération* (Paris, 1993), 266–268.

29 "Ohé! les vaillants," *Le Vaillant*, 31 0ctober 1946; "Guy Moquet, Martyr de la France," *Tarzan*, 3 October 1946; article on Colonel Fabien by Ginette Cros and Pierre Kast, *Filles de France*, 15 July 1945, 12. Môquet's name was sometimes written without the circumflex.

30 MRN, Fonds Moquet (Serge et Guy), mémoire 1944–1946 (Correspondance, tractes), en cours de classement, newspaper clipping, *La Voix du XVIIème*, August 1945.

31 Pierre Olivier, "Guy Moquet," *Le Vaillant*, 12 December 1946.

32 MRN, Fonds Moquet, en cours de classement, Max Rainat, typescript, *Mort pour la Vie*, 44; and ibid., *Le Benjamin de Châteaubriant* (Paris, n.d. [1947?]), 30.

33 See Annette Wieviorka, "La mémoire communiste d'Auschwitz," in Stéphane Courtois, Marc Lazar, and Shmuel Trigano, eds., *Rigueur et passion: Mélanges offerts en hommage à Annie Kriegel* (Paris, 1994), 225–226; and Violaine Gelly and Paul Gradvohl, *Charlotte Delbo* (Paris, 2013), 160–161.

34 Pierrette Flotte, "Marie-Claude est revenue," *Filles de France*, 1 August 1945, 13; "Légion d'Honneur," *Filles de France*, 9 January 1946, 12; "Tâche sacrée," *Filles de France*, 20 February 1946, 3.

35 Marie-Claude Vaillant-Couturier, "3 Noëls," *Filles de France, numéro spécial de Noël, 1945,* 4.

36 "Légion d'Honneur," *Filles de France,* 9 January 1946, 12.

37 MRN, papiers Marie-Claude Vaillant-Couturier, ARCH HP 222, carton IL 1086, letter from Union des jeunes filles de France to Vaillant-Couturier, 1 July 1949.

38 Simone Téry, *Du Soleil plein le coeur. La merveilleuse histoire de Danielle Casanova* (Paris, 1949), 230, 260, 269, 272.

39 Barcellini and Wieviorka, *Passant, souviens-toi!* 291.

40 This was Salmon's first major work since returning from the camps. It was not the last time, however, that she would treat the subject. In 1965, Salmon sculpted a bronze statue of a dying prisoner – *Le Déporté* in French, *Der sterbende Häftling* in German – as part of a larger memorial ensemble at the Neuengamme concentration camp. The figure, all bones, writhes and twists, creating a shape more abstract than human.

41 Barcellini and Wieviorka, *Passant, souviens-toi!* 374–376.

42 Jay Winter, *Sites of Memory, Sites of Mourning: The Great War in European Cultural History* (Cambridge, 1995), 228; Barcellini and Wieviorka, *Passant, souviens-toi!* 373.

43 Barcellini and Wieviorka, *Passant, souviens-toi!* 418; "Courrier des amicales," *Le Patriote résistant,* January 1963. The Buchenwald-Dora monument was inaugurated in 1964, but a version was completed and put on display earlier.

44 Wolikow, *Les Combats de la mémoire,* 247–248; "Auschwitz," *Le Patriote résistant,* 1 July 1953; "L'inauguration du monument de Buchenwald-Dora," *Le Patriote résistant,* May 1964.

45 Gertje R. Utley, *Picasso: The Communist Years* (New Haven, 2000), 106–107, 117. Picasso named a daughter after the dove, Paloma.

46 Utley, *Picasso,* 166.

47 See the exposition catalogue, *Picasso et la guerre* (Paris, 2019), 286–287. The exposition was mounted at the Musée de l'Armée at the Invalides. See also the discussion in Utley, *Picasso,* 152ff.

48 Dreyfus, *Ami, si tu tombes...,* 76; C. Lévy, "Une association de déportés," 154.

49 F.N.D.I.R.P., *La Déportation* (Paris, 1967).

50 AN AJ 2157, Dossier, Exposition "Résistance-Déportation," Rennes, May 1957; Dossier, "Exposition d'Auxerre," July 1959.

51 William Rubin, *Picasso in the Collection of the Museum of Modern Art* (New York, 1972), 166; Pierre Daix, *Picasso créateur: la vie intime et l'oeuvre* (Paris, 1987), 293–294.

52 Sarah Wilson, "Paris Post War: In Search of the Absolute," in Frances Morris, ed., *Paris Post War: Art and Existentialism, 1944–55,* exhibition catalogue, Tate Gallery (London, 1993), 28; William Rubin, ed., *Picasso, a Retrospective* (New York, 1980), 380.

53 Utley, *Picasso,* 107, 184–192.

54 Martin Crowley, *Robert Antelme. L'humanité irréductible* (Paris, 2004), 92–106; idem, *Robert Antelme: Humanity, Community, Testimony* (Oxford, 2003), 44–47; Utley, *Picasso,* 142.

55 Cited in Crowley, *Robert Antelme. L'humanité irréductible*, 175.
56 Robert Antelme, *L'Espèce humaine* (Paris, 1957), 204–205.
57 Cited in Crowley, *Robert Antelme. L'humanité irréductible*, 88.
58 For these passages, see Antelme, *L'Espèce humaine*, 61–62, 80, 84, 321.
59 Antelme, *L'Espèce humaine*, 15, 106–107; Crowley, *Robert Antelme. L'humanité irréductible*, 25–26, 72–73; idem, *Robert Antelme: Humanity, Community, Testimony*, 2, 11.
60 Utley, *Picasso*, 107.
61 Cited in Wieviorka, *Déportation et génocide*, 312.
62 Edgar Morin, "L'Espèce humaine," *Le Patriote résistant*, 1 July 1949.
63 Lalieu, *Buchenwald*, 271, 275–276.
64 MRN, papiers Marcel Paul, NE 2528 qua, Don de Lévy Bardavid, dossier Buchenwald (Lutte contre l'oubli. Un héros nommé: Marcel Paul), 3 cahiers.
65 Wieviorka, *Déportation et génocide*, 307; Ilan Avisar, *Screening the Holocaust: Cinema's Images of the Unimaginable* (Bloomington, IN, 1988), 35–38; Sylvie Lindeperg and Annette Wieviorka, *L'Univers concentrationnaire et génocide. Voir, savoir, comprendre* (Paris, 2008), 52, 55.
66 Marcel Paul's remarks were made at the FNDIRP national congress in January 1950. See "Non! Le Comité National n'a pas suivi les scissionnistes," *Le Patriote résistant*, 27 February 1950; and also Louise Alcan, "Gloire à nos libérateurs," *Le Patriote résistant*, 27 February 1950.
67 Lalieu, *La Déportation fragmentée: Les anciens déportés parlent de politique, 1945–1980* (Paris, 1994), 128–129; "Contre la bombe atomique," *Le Patriote résistant*, 28 April 1950.
68 "Un appel du conseil de la Fédération internationale des anciens prisonniers politiques," *Le Patriote résistant*, 15 August 1947; MRN, papiers Marie–Claude Vaillant-Couturier, ARCH HP214, carton ID, dossier "Lettres contre les accords de Bonn," undated flier (calling for a demonstration on 31 January 1954); ARCH HP218 carton IH, unmarked dossier, letter from Louise Alcan to M. le Député, 27 August 1954.
69 Höss himself would be tried in Poland and executed there in 1947.
70 Robert Merle, *La Mort est mon métier* (Paris, 1972), preface to the 1972 edition, 1; interview with Merle published in *L'Express*, 25 September 2003, accessed on line at: www.lexpress.fr/informations/j-ai-toujours-cru-en-mon-succès (12 November 2013); Huber, *Bulawko*, 149; Emmanuelle Cordenod-Roiron, "Aragon derrière l'emblème politique: où en est-on?" in Guillaume Bridet and Christian Petr, eds., *Écrivains communistes français: Enjeux et perspectives* (Paris, 2011), 80. Merle was a member of MRAP's committee of honor.
71 Merle, *La Mort est mon métier*, 298.
72 Ibid., 363–364.
73 Henri Bulawko, "Amicale des déportés Juifs," *Le Patriote résistant*, 1 December 1952; "C'est le nazisme qui a tué les Rosenberg," *Le Patriote résistant*, 1 July 1953.
74 For the preceding, see Nicole Racine-Furlaud, "18 juin 1940 ou 10 juillet 1940," passim.
75 Cited in Jean-Michel Chaumont, *La Concurrence des victimes. Génocide, identité, reconnaissance* (Paris, 1997), 38.

76 F.N.D.I.R.P., *La Déportation*, 209–212.

77 "En même temps au Père-Lachaise a été inauguré le monument aux morts d'Auschwitz," *Le Patriote résistant*, 1 July 1949; "Le monument à la mémoire des Martyrs de Mauthausen a été inauguré au Père-Lachaise," *Le Patriote résistant*, June 1958; "Là où jadis se dressait le Vél d'hiv," *Le Patriote résistant*, August 1963; Rebecca Clifford, *Commemorating the Holocaust: The Dilemmas of Remembrance in France and Italy* (Oxford, 2013), 46–47.

78 "Où en sommes-nous," *Le Patriote résistant*, 23 March 1948; Lalieu, *La Déportation fragmentée*, 62.

79 The French-language text of the play was published in *L'Avant-Scène-fémina-théâtre*, no. 192 (nd).

80 Marcel Verfeuil, "La Pièce," *Le Patriote résistant*, October 1957; M.V., "Le journal de Anne Frank et son public," *Le Patriote résistant*, November 1957.

81 Raph Feigelson, "Retour de Jérusalem, Madeleine Jacob nous dit 'Eichmann est le monstre à l'état pur,'" *Le Patriote résistant*, June 1961.

82 Pieter Lagrou, *Mémoires patriotiques et Occupation nazie: Résistants, requis et déportés en Europe occidentale, 1945–1965* (Brussels, 2003), 224; Cochet, *Les Exclus*, 75.

83 Annette Wieviorka, *Déportation et génocide*, 136; idem, "La mémoire communiste d'Auschwitz," passim.

2 The Concentrationary Universe

1 Germaine Tillion, *À la Recherche du vrai et du juste. À propos rompus avec le siècle. Textes réunis et présentés par Tzvetan Todorov* (Paris, 2001), 37.

2 Tillion's sister, Hélène Parmelin, was a journalist for *L'Humanité*, a partner of the communist painter Édouard Pignon, and a good friend of Picasso's.

3 Michel Borwicz, *Écrits des condamnés à mort sous l'occupation allemande (1939–1945), étude sociologique* (Paris, 1954).

4 For a full treatment of the subject, see Emma Kuby, *Political Survivors: The Resistance, the Cold War, and the Fight against Concentration Camps after 1945* (Ithaca, NY, 2019).

5 Émile Copfermann, *David Rousset. Une vie dans le siècle* (Paris, 1991), 78.

6 Kuby discusses Rousset's CIA connections in detail. See idem *Political Survivors*, 88–93.

7 For the preceding see, Copfermann, *David Rousset*, 28–31, 78, 102–103, 106–11; Thomas Wieder, "L'affaire David Rousset et la figure du déporté: les rescapés des camps nazis contre les camps soviétiques," in Tal Bruttmann, Laurent Joly, and Annette Wieviorka, eds., *Qu'est-ce qu'un déporté? Histoire et mémoires des déportations de la Seconde Guerre mondiale* (Paris, 2009), 314–315; and Annie Cohen-Solal, *Sartre: A Life*, tr. Anna Cancogni (New York, 1987), 308.

8 Copfermann, *David Rousset*, 53, 64.

9 Ibid., 17–18.

10 Léon Poliakov, *L'Envers du destin. Entretiens avec Georges Elia Sarfati* (Paris, 1989), 62–63; Kuby, *Political Survivors*, 102.

11 Samuel Moyn, "From *L'univers concentrationnaire* to the Jewish Genocide: Pierre Vidal-Naquet and the Treblinka Controversy," in Julian Bourg, ed., *After the Deluge: New Perspectives on the Intellectual and Cultural History of Postwar France* (Lanham, MD, 2004), 282.

12 David Rousset, *L'Univers concentrationnaire* (Paris, 1965 [orig. 1946]), 114–116; idem, *Les Jours de notre mort* (Paris, 1947), 126.

13 David Rousset, *Le Pitre ne rit pas* (Paris, 1948), 245.

14 Rousset, *L'Univers concentrationnaire*, 109.

15 Ibid., 9, 13, 107.

16 Rousset, *Le Pitre ne rit pas*, 126.

17 Rousset, *L'Univers concentrationnaire*, 108–111; idem, *Les Jours de notre mort*, 125

18 Rousset, *L'Univers concentrationnaire*, 76, 81, 185.

19 Rousset, *Les Jours de notre mort*, 170, 356.

20 Ibid., 120–121, 172, 325, 676.

21 Ibid., 361, 384.

22 Ibid., 760.

23 Copfermann, *David Rousset*, 115–117, 197–209; David Rousset, Gérard Rosenthal, Théo Bernard, *Pour la Vérité sur les camps concentrationnaires (un procès antistalinien à Paris)* (Paris, 1990), 9–10.

24 "Les anciens déportés qui ont quitté F.I.N.D.I.R.P.," *Le Monde*, 1 February 1950. The *Le Monde* article is reprinted at the back of Rousset, Rosenthal, Bernard, *Pour la Vérité sur les camps concentrationnaires*, np.

25 Jean-Marc Dreyfus, *Ami, si tu tombes... Les déportés résistants des camps au souvenir, 1945–2005* (Paris, 2005), 190; Rousset, Rosenthal, Bernard, *Pour la Vérité sur les camps concentrationnaires*, 253; Tillion, *À la Recherche du vrai et du juste*, 197.

26 F.-H. Manhès, "Qui veut empoisonner l'opinion?" *Le Patriote résistant*, 27 February 1950.

27 Wieder, "L'affaire David Rousset," 321.

28 Dreyfus, *Ami, si tu tombes...* 69–70; Tillion, *À la Recherche du vrai et du juste*, 204.

29 Anise Girard Postel-Vinet [sic], "Notre enquête," *Voix et visages*, no. 13 (April 1948); "Notre enquête," *Voix et visages*, no. 14 (May 1948).

30 "Un appel de David Rousset," *Voix et visages*, no. 23 (December 1949–January 1950).

31 Olivier Lalieu, *La Déportation fragmentée: les anciens déportés parlent de politique, 1945–1980* (Paris, 1994), 91, 140.

32 Serge Wolikow, *Les Combats de la mémoire. La FNDIRP de 1945 à nos jours* (Paris, 2006), 97; Olivier Lalieu, "Le statut juridique du déporté et les enjeux de mémoire, de 1948 à nos jours," in Bruttmann Joly, and Wieviorka, eds., *Qu'est-ce qu'un déporté?* 337; Dreyfus, *Ami, si tu tombes...* 63, 65.

33 Robert Steegman, *Le Struthof KL-Natzweiler. Histoire d'un camp de concentration en Alsace annexée, 1941–1945* (Strasbourg, 2005), 25.

34 SHD (Service historique de la Défense, Division des archives des victimes des conflits contemporains, Caen) AC 27 P 864, Struthof, dossier Nécropole du Struthof, Travaux, Monument Historique, letter from Henri Queuille to the

Minister of Veterans' Affairs, 7 October 1949 and document authored by [Alexandre] Mattei, directeur du contententieux, 11 January 1950.

35 SHD 27 P 864, Struthof, dossier Nécropole du Struthof, Travaux, Monument Historique, "Delavallade, chef de service, note pour Monsieur le Directeur," 14 November 1949; AC 27 P 857, Struthof, dossier Historique Aide-mémoire, "Note sur l'ancien camp du Struthof-Natzwiller, 23/9/53"; AC 27 P 861, Struthof, dossier Cérémonie 1960, "Cérémonie d'inauguration," 1 July 1960.

36 SHD AC 27 P 857, Struthof, dossier Membres du Comité national, "Extrait du Journal Officiel du Lundi 14 et Mardi 15 Décembre 1953"; "Liste des membres du Comité national du Struthof," n.d.; and dossier Réunions du Comité national, 1953–1954, "Compte-rendu de la séance du 10 novembre 1953." The dating of this last document suggests that the Comité national began to meet even before its membership was announced in the *Journal officiel*.

37 SHD AC 27 P 857, Struthof, dossier Nécropole du Struthof, Textes 1949–1961, "Arrêté du 31 décembre 1954."

38 SHD AC 27 P 857, Struthof, dossier Comptes-rendus de la Commission exécutive 1954–1956, "22 février 1955."

39 Monnet cited in Serge Barcellini and Annette Wieviorka, *Passant, souviens-toi! Les lieux du souvenir de la Second Guerre mondiale en France* (Paris, 1995), 415–416.

40 SHD AC 27 P 857, Struthof, dossier Comptes-rendus de la Commission exécutive 1954–1956, "22 février 1955."

41 SHD AC 27 P 857, Struthof, dossier Comptes-rendus de la Commission exécutive 1954–1956, "Comité national, 24 mars 1955." The commission had debated another possibility, decorating all the graves with a stele identical in shape, with particularizing details etched on the stones. This was rejected in favor of the military option, and the decision had a Christianizing consequence. Of the thousand plus graves at the Struthof cemetery, all but two (one of a nonbeliever, a second of a Jew) were marked with crosses. See Serge Barcellini, "Le gazage de 87 juifs au camp de Natzweiler-Struthof: les malaises de la mémoire," in Annette Wieviorka and Claude Mouchard, eds., *La Shoah: témoignages, savoir, oeuvres* (Saint-Denis, 1999), 335.

42 SHD AC P 857, Struthof, dossier Comptes-rendus de la Commission exécutive 1954–1956, "20 janvier 1955" and "22 février 1955."

43 "Struthof, le cheminement du souvenir," *Le Déporté*, nos. 204–205 (June–July 1965); SHD AC 27 P 870, dossier Nécropole du Struthof, Musée, "Programme du Musée de la Déportation au Struthof," 3 March 1965.

44 Barcellini, "Le gazage de 87 juifs au camp de Natzweiler-Struthof," passim.; and Mechtild Gilzmer, *Mémoires de pierre. Les monuments commémoratifs en France après 1944* (Paris, 2009), 153.

45 SHD AC 27 P 857, Struthof, dossier Comptes-rendus de la Commission exécutive, 1957–1966, "Comité national, 25 mars 1958"; dossier Réunions du Comité national, 1953–1954, "5 mars [1954]."

46 AN 72 AJ 2159, Réseau du souvenir, dossier Veillée, flier and poster; letter from Paul Arrighi to Jean Vilar, 25 March 1955;

47 SHD AC 27 P 857, Struthof, dossier Comptes-rendus de la Commission exécutive 1957–1966, "3 avril 1957" and "17 octobre 1960"; "Au Struthof," *Le Patriote résistant* (July 1962).

48 SHD AC 27 P 864, Struthof, dossier Nécropole du Struthof, Travaux, Monument Historique, "5/8/57, Note pour Monsieur le Directeur du Cabinet"; AC 27 P 857, Struthof, dossier Comptes-rendus de la Commission exécutive 1957–1966, "14 mai 1959" and "1 juin 1959."

49 "Le général de Gaulle inaugurera samedi le mémorial national de la déportation de Struthof," *Le Monde*, 23 July 1960; J.-F. Simon, "Le corps du déporté inconnu a été transféré au mémorial de Struthof qu'a inauguré le général de Gaulle," *Le Monde*, 24–25 July 1960; SHD AC 27 P 861, Struthof, dossier Cérémonie 1960, "Rapport (Camp du Struthof)."

50 SHD AC 27 P 861, Struthof, dossier Cérémonie 1960, "Cérémonie d'inauguration du mémorial de Struthof par Monsieur le Général de Gaulle Président de la République, 23 juillet 1960"; J. F. Simon, "Le corps du déporté inconnu a été transféré au mémorial de Struthof qu'a inauguré le général de Gaulle," *Le Monde*, 24–25 July 1960.

51 A Cross of Lorraine was in fact erected at the foot of the camp, but this did not take place until the 1970s. See SHD AC 27 P 865, Struthof, dossier Nécropole du Struthof, Travaux stèle au lieu dit "La Sablière," "3 janvier 1979."

52 AN 72 AJ 2141, Réseau du souvenir, dossier Projets et démarches, "Membres de la Commission UNADIF du Souvenir," nd; "Commission du Souvenir, Visite à Monsieur Michel," 12 December 1950; "Réunion constitutive du Réseau du Souvenir du 20 mai 1952"; flier, "le Réseau du souvenir, Historia testis," nd. See also the discussion in Olivier Lalieu, "Les résistants et l'invention du 'devoir de mémoire,'" *Les Associations d'anciens résistants et la fabrique de la mémoire de la Seconde Guerre Mondiale. Sous la direction de Gilles Vergnon et Michèle Battesti. Journée d'études du 19 octobre 2005, Vincennes, Cahiers du centre d'études d'histoire de la défense*, no. 28 (2006), 91–95.

53 Lalieu, "Les résistants et l'invention du 'devoir de mémoire,'" 96; Michel Riquet, *Le Rebelle discipliné. Entretiens avec Alain-Gilles Minella* (Paris, 1993), 118, 131.

54 AN 72 AJ 2160, Réseau du souvenir, dossier Loi du 14 avril.

55 Sylvie Lindeperg and Annette Wieviorka, *Univers concentrationnaire et génocide. Voir, savoir, comprendre* (Paris, 2008), 13–16, 29–30; Lindeperg, "L'atelier d'Olga Wormser. De l'accueil des déportés à l'écriture de l'histoire (1945–1979)," in Bruttmann, Joly, and Wieviorka, *Qu'est-ce qu'un déporté?* 299, 301, 305.

56 Lindeperg and Wieviorka, *Univers concentrationnaire*, 44–45; G. Ferrières, "Exposition de la Résistance, de la Libération et de la Déportation," *Voix et visages*, no. 44 (December 1954).

57 Olga Wormser and Henri Michel, *Tragédie de la Déportation, 1940–1945. Témoignages de survivants des camps de concentration allemands* (Paris, 1954), 10.

58 Ibid., 293–294, 508–509.

59 The text in question is Mauriac's *Le Livre noir* (1943), which he published clandestinely under the pseudonym Forez. Cited in Wormser and Michel, *Tragédie de la Déportation*, 30.

60 Wormser and Michel, *Tragédie de la Déportation*, 28 n1.

61 Ibid., 507. See also Lindeperg, "L'atelier d'Olga Wormser," 305. The tally of six million Jewish dead jibes with estimates then and now, though not all six million were burned in crematoria.

62 AN 72 AJ 2141, Réseau du souvenir, dossier Projets et démarches, "Compte-rendu de la visite du 22 janvier 1951 de Mm. Schneersohn, Poliakov…"

63 AN AJ 2158, Réseau du souvenir, dossier Commission historique, undated document.

64 AN AJ 2159, Réseau du souvenir, dossier *Tragédie de la Déportation*, sous-d Correspondance de Mme Lazard, letter from Mme Lazard to Edmond Fleg, 30 July 1954; sous-d Correspondance et pièces diverses, letter from Dan Avny, Israeli embassy, to Arrighi, 16 July 1954; sous-d Correspondance et pièces diverses, letter from Arrighi, to S.E Monseigneur Montini, 28 December 1954.

65 Michael Rothberg, *Multidirectional Memory: Remembering the Holocaust in the Age of Decolonization* (Stanford, 2009).

66 Germaine Tillion, "Ravensbrück," *Les Cahiers du Rhône*, 20 (December 1946), 60–62.

67 Tillion, "Ravensbrück," 46–48, 50.

68 Tillion, "Ravensbrück," 14, 24–25, 45; idem, *La Traversée du mal. Entretien avec Jean Lacouture* (Paris, 1997), 73. For a good discussion of this, see Donald Reid, *Germaine Tillion, Lucie Aubrac, and the Politics of Memories of the French Resistance* (Newcastle, 2008), 19–20.

69 Tillion, *Ravensbrück* (Paris, 1973), 26, 63–64; idem, *Ravensbrück* (Paris, 1988), 33, 212–213.

70 Tillion, "Ravensbrück," 19, 29; idem, *Ravensbrück* (1988), 161; Reid, *Germaine Tillion*, 100–105.

71 Tillion, "Ravensbrück," 28, 38; idem, *Ravensbrück* (1988), 187, 205, 209, 478.

72 Tillion, "Ravensbrück," 37.

73 Tillion, *À la Recherche du vrai et du juste*, 36, 52; idem, *Ravensbrück* (1988), 64.

74 Emma Kuby, "In the Shadow of the Concentration Camp: David Rousset and the Limits of Apoliticism in Postwar French Thought," *Modern Intellectual History*, 11 (April 2014), 171; idem, *Political Survivors*, 117.

75 Maurice Thiriart, "La polémique s'achève," *Le Déporté*, no. 174 (January 1963). *Le Déporté* was the joint press organ of FNDIR-UNADIF. See also Catherine Goetschel, "À propos de l'appel de David Rousset," *Voix et visages*, no. 87 (January–February 1963).

76 Germaine Tillion, "L'Algérie en 1956," *Voix et visages*, no. 53 (September–October 1956); idem, "L'Algérie en 1957," *Voix et visages*, no. 55 (January–February 1957); Anne Fernier, introduction to Tillion, *L'Algérie en 1957* (Paris, 1957), 8–9.

77 Tillion, *L'Algérie en 1957*, passim.

78 Germaine Tillion, "L'Algérie française," *Voix et visages*, no. 55 (January–February 1957); the discussion in Reid, *Germaine Tillion*, 46–47, 83n; and Tillion, *L'Algérie en 1957*, 41.

79 Kuby, *Political Survivors*, 209.

80 Tillion, *La Traversée du mal*, 111–118.

81 Kuby, *Political Survivors*, 210–212; Tillion, *Les Ennemis complémentaires* (Paris, 1960), 31–33; idem, *À la Recherche du vrai et du juste*, 20–21, 40.

82 Simone de Beauvoir, *La Force des choses* (Paris, 1963), 460–462. See also Reid, *Germaine Tillion*, 83n.

83 Tillion, *À la Recherche du vrai et du juste*, 58.

84 Olga Wormser-Migot, *Le Système concentrationnaire nazi (1933–1945)* (Paris, 1968), 401–402.

85 Wormser-Migot, *Le Système concentrationnaire*, 11–13.

86 Ibid., 588–589, 595–597.

87 Ibid., 588.

88 Ibid., 583.

89 Reid, *Germaine Tillion*, 26, 28, 30; Lindeperg and Wieviorka, *Univers concentrationnaire*, 36, 38. But see also Bertrand Hamelin and Thomas Fontaine, "L'erreur d'Olga Wormser-Migot sur les chambres à gaz de Ravensbrück et de Mauthausen," *En Jeu. Histoires et mémoires vivantes*, no. 2 (December 2013), 54, 58.

90 For the camp as synecdoche, see Samuel Moyn, "In the Aftermath of Camps," in Frank Biess and Robert G. Moeller, eds., *Histories of the Aftermath: The Legacies of the Second World War in Europe* (New York, 2010), 49.

3 Monster with One Eye Open

1 Cited in Thomas Wieder, "L'affaire David Rousset et la figure du déporté: les rescapés des camps nazis contre les camps soviétiques," in Tal Bruttmann, Laurent Joly, and Annette Wieviorka, eds., *Qu'est-ce qu'un déporté? Histoire et mémoires des déportations de la Seconde Guerre mondiale* (Paris, 2009), 316.

2 Debarati Sanyal, "Auschwitz as Allegory in *Night and Fog*," in Griselda Pollock and Max Silverman, eds., *Concentrationary Cinema: Aesthetics as Political Resistance in Alain Resnais' "Night and Fog" (1955)* (New York, 2011), 165–170.

3 My special thanks to Emma Kuby for helping me to think this point through.

4 Michael Rothberg, *Multidirectional Memory: Remembering the Holocaust in the Age of Decolonization* (Stanford, 2009), 7, 22.

5 Sylvie Lindeperg, *"Nuit et Brouillard": un film dans l'histoire* (Paris, 2007), 44, 47; Suzanne Liandrat-Guigues and Jean-Louis Leutrat, *Alain Resnais. Liaisons secrètes, accords vagabonds* (Paris, 2006), 14, 199, 215.

6 www.theguardian.com/artanddesign/2014/feb/26/susan-philipsz-berlin-turner-prize-hanns-eisler, accessed 21 February 2015.

7 Lindeperg, *"Nuit et Brouillard,"* 245; idem, *"Night and Fog*: Inventing a Perspective," in Jean-Michel Frodon, ed., *Cinema and the Shoah: An Art Confronts the Tragedy of the Twentieth Century* (Albany, NY, 2010), 75; Richard Raskin, *Nuit et Brouillard by Alain Resnais: On the Making, Reception and Functions of a Major Documentary Film* (Aarhus, 1987), 29.

8 Rémo Forlani, as cited in Robert Benayoun, *Alain Resnais, arpenteur de l'imaginaire: de Hiroshima à Mélo* (Paris, 1980), 275. On Resnais' background, see Benayoun, *Alain Resnais*, 45–46; Liandrat-Guigues and Leutrat, *Alain Resnais*, 28–29; on Travail et Culture, see Nord, *France's New Deal: From the Thirties to the Postwar Era* (Princeton, 2010), 311, 316.

9 Liandrat-Guigues and Leutrat, *Alain Resnais*, 211, 256 n16; Jean Cayrol, *Il était une fois Jean Cayrol* (Paris, 1982), 107–108.

10 Resnais, from a 1961 interview, cited in André Pierre Colombat, *The Holocaust in French Film* (Metuchen, NJ, 1993), 153.

11 Cayrol, *Il était une fois*, 100–101, 199. The priest in Louis Malle's *Au revoir, les enfants* was modeled on Père Jacques.

12 Cayrol, *Il était une fois*, 106, 200–201.

13 Cayrol, "Chant funèbre à la mémoire du Révérend Père Jacques," *Poèmes de la nuit et du brouillard, suivis de Larmes publiques* (Paris, 1946), 86, 94. For "the Beast," see "Février 1944," in *Alerte aux ombres 1944–1945* (Paris, 1997), 24.

14 Cayrol, *Alerte aux ombres 1944–1945*, 106.

15 Cayrol, "Les rêves lazaréens," in *Oeuvre lazaréenne* (Paris, 2007), 789.

16 Sidra DeKoven Ezrahi, *By Words Alone: The Holocaust in Literature* (Chicago, 1980), 91; Cayrol, "Pour un romanesque lazaréen," in *Oeuvre lazaréenne*, 813, 817.

17 Cayrol, "Pour un romanesque lazaréen," 803, 805.

18 Raskin, *Nuit et Brouillard*, 29.

19 Cayrol's title in turn refers to a category of camp prisoner, deportees who had been "disappeared," vanishing into *Nacht und Nebel*, night and fog, their fate and whereabouts kept secret from friends and relatives back home.

20 The story is told in Raskin, *Nuit et Brouillard*, 57.

21 Interview with Charles K. Krantz in Krantz, "Teaching *Night and Fog*: History and Historiography," *Film & History*, 15 (February 1985), 7.

22 René Prédal, *Alain Resnais* (Paris, 1968), 130; Resnais interview, 18 February 1986, cited in Raskin, *Nuit et Brouillard*, 51.

23 Cayrol, "Nuit et Brouillard (commentaire)," in *Oeuvre lazaréenne*, 1001.

24 Krantz, "Teaching *Night and Fog*: History and Historiography," 7.

25 Annette Insdorf, *Indelible Shadows: Film and the Holocaust*, Third Edition (New York, 2003), 37.

26 André Bazin, "Nuit et Brouillard," *Radio-Cinéma-Télévision*, 9 February 1956, cited in Raskin, *Nuit et Brouillard*, 139.

27 François Truffaut, "Petit journal du cinema," *Cahiers du cinéma*, February 1956, cited in idem, 138.

28 Reprinted in *Le Patriote résistant*, May 1956, under the title "Jean Cayrol." See also: Archives Nationales, Paris (AN) 72 AJ 2160, Réseau du souvenir, dossier Radio, Films, sous-d *Nuit et Brouillard* letter from Arrighi to Rémy Roure, 25 May 1956, and undated and handwritten press communiqué; and letter from Sacha Vierny to Richard Raskin, 24 November 1986 in Raskin, *Nuit et Brouillard*, 3. Vierny was the cinematographer on *Nuit et Brouillard*.

29 Cayrol, "Nuit et Brouillard (commentaire)," *Oeuvre lazaréenne*, 992.

30 Jean Cayrol, "Nous avons conçu 'Nuit et brouillard' comme un dispositif d'alerte," *Les Lettres françaises*, 9 February 1956, cited in Raskin, *Nuit et*

Brouillard, 137. Sylvie Lindeperg has sharp observations to make on these various points. See Lindeperg, *"Nuit et Brouillard,"* 108; and idem, "Conversations at the Mill," in Frodon, ed., *Cinema and the Shoah*, 130.

31 Prédal writes that the film is about "the extermination of the Jews": idem, *Alain Resnais*, 147. For Klarsfeld, see Christian Delage, "Nuit et Brouillard, un tournant dans la mémoire de la Shoah," *Politix*, no. 61 (2003), 81–94.

32 Once again, I am following Lindeperg's lead: Lindeperg and Wieviorka, *Univers concentrationnaire et génocide. Voir, savoir, comprendre* (Paris, 2008), 60, 62; "Conversations at the Mill," 130. See also Arnaud Desplechin's remarks in "Conversations at the Mill," 127.

33 Liandrat-Guigues and Leutrat, *Alain Resnais*, 215. Lanzmann went even further, discouraging anyone from showing *Nuit et Brouillard* and *Shoah* on the same bill. The subject matter, he felt, was not the same, and no one should be misled into thinking so. Resnais did not disagree. Ibid., 217.

34 AN 72 AJ 2160, Réseau du souvenir, dossier Radio, films, sous-d *Nuit et Brouillard*, letter from Ch. Joineau, secrétaire-général FINDIRP to Chers amis, 9 April 1956; letter from Louis Faucon, writing on behalf of Prime Minister Guy Mollet, to Paul Arrighi, 6 June 1956; Raskin, *Nuit et Brouillard*, 41, 44.

35 AN 72 AJ 2160, Réseau du souvenir, dossier Radio, films, sous-d *Nuit et Brouillard*, letter from Paul Arrighi to Jean Cayrol, 4 January 1956; B. Thiriart to [Henri] Michel, 3 May 1956; letter from Paul Arrighi to Société Argos-Films, 21 May 1957; "Article pour le Bulletin no. 6," nd.

36 Prédal, *Alain Resnais*, 145.

37 Daniel Anselme, *On Leave*, tr. David Bellos (New York, 2014 [orig. 1957]), 72, 116–117.

38 Benayoun, *Alain Resnais*, 62.

39 See Resnais' interview with Claude-Jean Philippe, July 27, 1980. The interview is a bonus feature, included on the Criterion Collection DVD of *Hiroshima mon amour*.

40 Rémi Fournier Lanzoni, *French Cinema: From Its Beginnings to the Present* (New York, 2002), 229.

41 James Monaco, *Alain Resnais* (New York, 1979), 34. For a critique of the movie's Eurocentrism, see Sandrine Sanos, "'My Body Was Aflame with His Memory': War, Gender, and Colonial Ghosts, in Hiroshima mon amour," *Gender & History*, 28 (November 2016), np. Consulted online, 9 October 2018.

42 Prédal, *Alain Resnais*, 104, 166.

43 All this is recounted in Semprun's memoir: *L'Écriture ou la vie* (Paris, 2012 [orig. 1994]), 201, 261, 286, 293–295, 306–306, 421.

44 For these two incidents, see Semprun, *Le Grand Voyage* (Paris, 2013 [orig. 1963]), 55–56, 242.

45 Ibid., 116, 118, 196, 210.

46 Ibid., 202.

47 Ibid., 86, 228; Cynthia Haft, *The Theme of Nazi Concentration Camps in French Literature* (The Hague and Paris, 1973), 42–43.

48 Monaco, *Alain Resnais*, 97. Resnais did eventually get to work on a Vietnam picture, contributing a segment to the collaborative, antiwar *Loin du Vietnam* (1967), and Semprun would similarily work on a film about Greece, writing the screenplay for Costa-Gavras' *Z* (1969).

49 See the discussion in Prédal, *Alain Resnais*, 127, 156–157.

50 Semprun, *L'Écriture ou la vie*, 261.

51 Paul Henley, *The Adventure of the Real: Jean Rouch and the Craft of Ethnographic Cinema* (Chicago, 2009), 136.

52 Bernard Cazes and Edgar Morin, "La question du bien-être," *Arguments*, no. 22 (1961), 1–3; Morin, "Nouvelle âge: crise du bonheur et problématique de la vie privée," book preface, 1968, reprinted in idem, *Sociologie* (Paris, 1984), 380–384.

53 Emmanuel Lemieux, *Edgar Morin, l'indiscipliné* (Paris, 2009), 157, 178, 188, 249, 302.

54 Edgar Morin, *Autocritique* (Paris, 1970), 71; Lemieux, *Edgar Morin*, 210–211; Alain Navarro, *1945: le retour des absents* (Paris, 2015), 206–210. Many thanks to Emma Kuby for this last reference.

55 Morin, *Autocritique*, 118; 154–155.

56 Ibid., 165–173; Lemieux, *Edgar Morin*, 280, 292, 384.

57 Morin, *Autocritique*, 191–193, 195; Lemieux, *Edgar Morin*, 77, 342, 347–348, 350, 356–357.

58 Paul Stoller, *The Cinematic Griot: The Ethnography of Jean Rouch* (Chicago, 1992), 31–32.

59 Rouch interview with Lucien Taylor, 1990, reprinted in Steven Feld, ed. and trans., *Ciné-Ethnography: Jean Rouch* (Minneapolis, 2003), 132. See also in ibid., pp. 130–131, 134.

60 Stoller, *Cinematic Griot*, 133, 147, 151; Henley, *The Adventure of the Real*, 82.

61 Henley, *The Adventure of the Real*, 80.

62 Ibid., 27; Steven Ungar, "Whose Voice? Whose Film?: Jean Rouch, Oumarou Ganda, and *Moi, un noir*," in Joram ten Brink, *Building Bridges: The Cinema of Jean Rouch* (London, 2007), 120–121; Rouch, interview with Lucien Taylor, 1990, reprinted in Feld, ed. and trans., *Ciné-Ethnography*, 139.

63 Ungar, "Whose Voice? Whose Film?" 119.

64 Henley, *The Adventure of the Real*, xv, 91.

65 Ibid., 100.

66 Morin, "Chronicle of a Film," in Feld, ed. and trans., *Ciné-Ethnography*, 249.

67 Ibid., 235; Henley, *The Adventure of the Real*, 154–155.

68 Marceline Loridan-Ivens, *Ma Vie balagan* (Paris, 2008), 180.

69 For a fine discussion of these scenes, see Ungar, "In the Thick of Things: Rouch and Morin's Chronique d'un été Reconsidered," *French Cultural Studies*, 14 (2003), 12–13.

70 Joshua Hirsch, *Afterimage: Film, Trauma, and the Holocaust* (Philadelphia, 2004), 67. See also Rouch, "The Cinema of the Future?" in Feld, ed. and trans., *Ciné-Ethnography*, 271–272; and Henley, *The Adventure of the Real*, 160–162.

71 Marceline, "The Point of View of the 'Characters,'" in Feld, ed. and trans., *Ciné-Ethnography*, 341.

72 Loridan-Ivens, *Ma Vie balagan*, 185. For Loridan-Ivens, there was a Viet Nam connection as well. She married the radical documentarist, Joris Ivens, and the two traveled to Hanoi in 1967 to make a movie about the war. They wanted to film in a restricted military zone and were having difficulty obtaining permission. A meeting with Ho Chi Minh resolved the problem. He spotted the number on her arm and remarked: "You, you were at Auschwitz?" and, with that, granted her the access Ivens and she had been seeking. Ibid., 189–190.

73 Marceline, "The Point of View of the 'Characters'," 342. It is worth mentioning in this connection that Marceline's opposition to the Algerian War was not just verbal. She too, like her onetime boyfriend Jean-Pierre Sergent, did clandestine work for the FLN. Loridan-Ivens, *Ma Vie balagan*, 175-176

74 Violaine Gelly and Paul Gradvohl, *Charlotte Delbo* (Paris, 2013), 241.

75 Ghislaine Dunant, *Charlotte Delbo: la vie retrouvée* (Paris, 2016), 77, 279, 324–325.

76 Gelly and Gradvohl, *Charlotte Delbo*, 175, 204.

77 Delbo, *Le Convoi du 24 janvier* (Paris, 1965), 8.

78 Delbo, *Aucun de nous ne reviendra* (Paris, 1970), 26–27.

79 Nicole Thatcher, *Charlotte Delbo: une voix singulière. Mémoire, témoignage et littérature* (Paris, 2003), 15–16, 172.

80 Both incidents are recounted in the second volume of Delbo's Auschwitz trilogy, *Une Connaissance inutile* (Paris, 1970), 88–96, 123–124.

81 For these two vignettes, see *Aucun de nous ne reviendra*, 105–107; 167–168.

82 See the vignette entitled "Thirst" in *Aucun de nous ne reviendra*, 114–123.

83 Delbo, *Une Connaissance inutile*, 63. See also idem, *Aucun de nous ne reviendra*, 23, 174; and Thatcher, *Charlotte Delbo*, 238–239.

84 Delbo's suite of portraits in *Le Convoi du 24 janvier* includes accounts of what happened to each woman after the war. The final volume of her deportation trilogy, *Mesure de nos jours*, narrates the experience of reentry, of life after Auschwitz.

85 Delbo, *Une Connaissance inutile*, 38–41.

86 Thatcher, *Charlotte Delbo*, 34; Delbo, *Mesure de nos jours* (Paris, 1971), 100–123.

87 Delbo, *Une Connaissance inutile*, 79–87.

88 Thatcher, *Charlotte Delbo*, 48.

89 Delbo, *Le Convoi du 24 janvier*, 63, 282–283.

90 Delbo, *Mesure de nos jours*, 151–166. In 1981, Delbo wrote to a friend: "I haven't had anything to do with the PC since 1945. Seeing the cadres in deportation left me cold immediately." Letter from Delbo to Philippe Robrieux, April 1981, cited in Gelly and Gradvohl, *Charlotte Delbo*, 164-165.

91 Letter from Madame F.B. to *France-Observateur*, 20 October 1960, in Delbo, *Les Belles Lettres* (Paris, 1961), 107–108.

92 Delbo, *La Mémoire et les jours* (Paris, 1995 [orig. 1985]), 137. See also Gelly and Gradvohl, *Charlotte Delbo*, 240.

93 Letter from Georges Arnaud to *France-Observateur*, 23 June 1960, and Delbo's own remarks in Delbo, *Les Belles Lettres*, 66, 47. Arnaud was the author of *Le Salaire de la peur*, which was made into a movie starring Yves

Montand. See also the letter from Francis Jeanson to Jean-Paul Sartre, first printed in *Les Temps modernes* (April–May 1960) and reprinted in ibid., 27.

94 For these incidents, see Delbo, *Une Connaissance inutile*, 31–32, 97–111.
95 See also Thatcher, *Charlotte Delbo*, 15.

4 The Triumph of the Spirit

1 Shelley Hornstein, "Invisible Topographies: Looking for the *Mémorial de la Déportation* in Paris," in Hornstein and Florence Jacobowitz, eds., *Image and Remembrance. Representation and the Holocaust* (Bloomington, 2003), 318.
2 Geneviève de Gaulle, "Prier," *Les Cahiers du Rhône*, 20 (December 1946), 187; "Témoignage Henri Boussel," in Christian Bernadac, *Les Sorciers du ciel* (Paris, 1969), 73; APFCJ Fonds Riquet, La Déportation, 8, dossier Conférences, sous-d 2 Conférences 1945, document dated 16 June 1945, 10.
3 APFCJ Fonds Riquet, La Déportation, 10, dossier M. Riquet et la déportation, articles 1945–1991, typed ms. "Lourdes 1946–1966."
4 Geneviève de Gaulle Anthonioz, *La Traversée de la nuit* (Paris, 1998), 25. The war was drawing to a close, and the SS didn't want a prisoner named de Gaulle to die in the camps. That's why she was isolated.
5 Paul Arrighi, "Notes sur le système concentrationnaire," *Revue d'Histoire de la deuxième Guerre Mondiale*, no. 8 (October 1952), 35.
6 Letter from Michelet to his wife, 12 May [1943], cited in Claude Michelet, *Mon Père Edmond Michelet* (Paris, 1981) 84.
7 De Gaulle Anthonioz, *La Traversée de la nuit*, 13.
8 Edmond Michelet, *Rue de la Liberté. Dachau 1943–1945* (Paris, 1955), 222; Claude Michelet, *Mon Père*, 102.
9 See, for example, "Témoignage inédit Pierre Traversat," and "Témoignage polonaise. M. Wadseck" in Bernadac, *Les Sorciers*, 25, 76–77; Louis Martin-Chauffier, *L'Homme et la bête* (Paris, 1947), 203–204; Michelet, *Rue de la Liberté*, 112, 115.
10 Michelet, *Rue de la Liberté*, 112; R. P. Humbert, cited in Bernadac, *Les Sorciers*, 344–346.
11 De Gaulle Anthonioz, *La Traversée de la nuit*, 29–30.
12 "Témoignage polonais. M. Wadseck," in Bernadac, *Les Sorciers*, 77.
13 APFCJ Fonds Riquet, La Déportation, 8, dossier Allocutions, homélies 1945–1988, Saint-Sévérin (13 mai 1945)"; Michelet, *Rue de la Liberté*, 115.
14 Claude Michelet, *Mon Père*, 106; "Manuscrit inédit du R.P. Humbert," in Bernadac, *Les Sorciers*, 368.
15 "Témoignage Jean Cayrol," in Bernadac, *Les Sorciers*, 77–78. See also "Témoignages recueillis par le père Philippe de la Trinité," "Témoignage Henri Boussel," and "Témoignage Roger Heim," in idem, 62, 73, 74–75.
16 Martin-Chauffier, *L'Homme et la bête*, 89, 119; Geneviève de Gaulle, "Prier," 188; Edmond Michelet, *Rue de la Liberté*, 246.
17 APFCJ Fonds Riquet, La Déportation, 10, dossier M. Riquet et la déportation, articles 1945–1991, typed ms., "La souffrance dans le régime concentrationnaire," nd.

18 Author's testimony, "Témoignages sur Auschwitz du père Garecki," and "Manuscrit inédit du R.P. Humbert," in Bernadac, *Les Sorciers*, 121, 228–229, 244–245, 252.

19 "Témoignage Mgr Jules Jost," in Bernadac, *Les Sorciers*, 296; APFCJ Fonds Riquet, La Déportation, 8, dossier (rose), ms. of speech delivered at the Centre Jean Moulin on the occasion of the twenty-fifth anniversary of France's liberation.

20 Martin-Chauffier, *L'Examen des consciences* (Paris, 1961), 112–113; Claude Michelet, *Mon Père*, 188.

21 APFCJ Fonds Riquet La Déportation, 10, dossier M. Riquet et la déportation, articles s.d., typed ms. "La vraie question," for *Le Figaro littéraire*, 12 November, no year given.

22 APFCJ Fonds Riquet, La Déportation, 10, dossier M. Riquet et la déportation, articles s.d., untitled ms., a remembrance of Paul Arrighi who died in 1975.

23 "Témoignage Henri Boussel," in Bernadac, *Les Sorciers*, 73–74; Michelet, *Rue de la Liberté*, 203 (the chapter in which Michelet recounts this story is entitled "A Samaritan"); and Martin-Chauffier, *L'Homme et la bête*, 195.

24 Frédérique Neau-Dufour, *Geneviève de Gaulle Anthonioz* (Paris, 2015), 223–248; de Gaulle, "Prier," 189.

25 APFCJ Fonds Riquet, La Déportation, 10, dossier M. Riquet et la déportation, articles 1945–1991, typed ms., 28 April 1991.

26 Michel Riquet, *Le Rebelle discipliné. Entretiens avec Alain-Gilles Minella* (Paris, 1993), 65–69; APFCJ Fonds Riquet, Riquet-Maritain Correspondance, 42, dossier Lettres de Jacques Maritain, 1917–1970, letter from Riquet to "Bien Cher Jacques," 4 August 1945; Riquet, "'L'Europe à Mauthausen, souvenir de la maison des morts," *Études: Revue catholique d'intérêt général* (June 1945): 291, 303.

27 APFCJ Fonds Riquet, La Déportation, 8, dossier Allocutions, homélies 1945–1988, two documents: "Palais de Chaillot, 7 juillet 1945" and an aide-mémoire describing the event, dated 12 July 1945.

28 Riquet, *Le Rebelle discipliné*, 135–139, 155.

29 Patrick Amsellem, *Remembering the Past, Constructing the Future: The Memorial to the Deportation in Paris and Experimental Commemoration after the Second World War* (New York University, Ph.D. dissertation, 2007), 63.

30 Serge Barcellini and Annette Wieviorka, *Passant, souviens-toi! Les lieux du souvenir de la Seconde Guerre mondiale en France* (Paris, 1995), 412.

31 AN 72 AJ 2160, Réseau du souvenir, dossier Commission spirituelle, "Lettre de Paul Claudel au Grand Rabbin de Paris," 4 May 1952; "Visite à M. Paul Claudel," 6 May 1952.

32 Serge Barcellini, "Sur deux journées nationales commémorant la déportation et les persécutions des 'années noires'," *Vingtième Siècle*, no. 45 (January–March 1995), 83–84.

33 "Journée nationale de la Déportation," *Voix et Visages*, no. 56 (March–April 1957); "Journée nationale de la Déportation," *Voix et Visages*, no. 57 (May–June 1957); "Cérémonie du 26 avril 1959, " *Voix et visages*, 67 (March–April

1959); Journée nationale de la Déportation," *Voix et visages*, 79 (May–June 1961).

34 Anise Postel-Vinay, "24 avril 1960, Journée nationale de la Déportation," *Voix et Visages*, no. 74 (May–June 1960).

35 AN 72 AJ 2161, Réseau du souvenir, dossier Cassou, Assemblée générale du 19 décembre 1953, extrait du rapport fait par M. Jean Cassou; dossier Réseau du souvenir, "Cheminement chronologique du projet de crypte," n.d.; Dossier Pouzet, "Commission du Vieux Paris, 7 juin 1956," 10; APFCJ Fonds Riquet, La Déportation, 10, dossier M. Riquet et la déportation, articles s.d., typed ms., "Crypte du déporté", n.d.

36 AN 72 AJ 2161, Réseau du souvenir, dossier Pouzet, Commission du Vieux Paris, 7 juin 1956, 13–14; dossier Listes, letter from Frédéric Dupont to M. Legaret, 21 April 1954.

37 AN 72 AJ 2161, Réseau du souvenir, dossier Listes, letter from Arrighi to M. Fruh, 20 January 1954; letter from Arrighi to Edmond Michelet, 16 January 1956; letter from Arrighi to Henri Michel, 17 January 1956.

38 AN 72 AJ 2161, Réseau du souvenir, dossier Réseau du souvenir, untitled and undated typescript, 1, 3; brochure cited in Hornstein, "Invisible Topographies," 312.

39 Simon Texier, *Georges-Henri Pingusson. Architecte, 1894–1978. La Poétique pour doctrine* (Paris, 2006), 38, 118, 120–122, 194–195, 256, 263, 271–272

40 For the notion of an experiential architecture, see Amsellem, *Remembering the Past*, 94; for the rest, see Texier, *Pingusson*, 116, 162, 260, 262.

41 AN 72 AJ 2161, Réseau du souvenir, dossier Réseau du souvenir, untitled and undated typescript, 2; AN 72 AJ 2165, Réseau du souvenir, dossier Pingusson, G.-H. Pingusson, "Monument aux Déportés, disposition générale du monument, mars 1954"; G. H. Pingusson, "Monument description sur les matériaux employés," nd. (but side by side with preceding document); untitled and undated typescript signed by Pingusson.

42 AN 72 AJ 2165, Réseau du souvenir, dossier Pingusson, G.-H. Pingusson, "Monument aux Déportés, disposition générale du monument, mars 1954"; handwritten document from Pingusson to Mme Christian Lazard, with typed text attached, 11 January 1960; AN 72 AJ 2167, Réseau du souvenir, dossier Édition d'une plaquette sur le monument, undated brochure in English, "Memorial to Martyrs of Deportation."

43 AN 72 AJ 2165, Réseau du souvenir, dossier Pingusson, untitled and undated typescript signed by Pingusson.

44 Claude Michelet, *Mon Père*, 50.

45 Amsellem, *Remembering the Past*, 128–129. The other six sources were: the Chant des Marais, Robert Desnos (twice), Antoine de Saint-Exupéry, Jean-Paul Sartre, and Vercors. No Jewish voice, however, was represented, a significant absence in a chorus that otherwise represented the full range of Resistance voices.

46 AN 72 AJ 2161, Réseau du souvenir, dossier Réseau du souvenir, note on phone call from the ministry to the Réseau du souvenir, 21 April 1959.

47 AN 72 AJ 2161, Réseau du souvenir, dossier Cassou, letter from Arrighi to Cassou, 12 September 1957.

48 For Pouzet, see AN 72 AJ 2161, Réseau du souvenir, dossier Pouzet, passim; for Michelet, see dossier Réseau du souvenir, letters from Arrighi to Michelet, 11 June 1958 and 12 July 1958.

49 AN 72 AJ 2161, Réseau du souvenir, dossier Cassou, letter from Cassou to Arrighi, 13 September 1957; dossier Réseau, "Rendez-vous du 10 juillet chez Monsieur Pouzet"; G-H Pingusson, "Note à l'attention de Monsieur le Président de la Commission centrale des Monuments commémoratifs," attached to letter from Arrighi to Préfet de la Seine Pelletier, 28 March 1958; AN 72 AJ 2165, Réseau du souvenir, dossier Pingusson, handwritten note from G-H Pingusson to Mme Christian Lazard, 24 July 1958.

50 AN 72 AJ 2161, Réseau du souvenir, dossier Réseau du souvenir, letter from Charles de Gaulle to Arrighi, 31 July 1958 and from de Gaulle Anthonioz to Arrighi, 29 July 1958.

51 AN 72 AJ 2161, Réseau du souvenir, dossier Pouzet, document dated 14 October 1958, recounting Arrighi's meeting with Pouzet; AN 72 AJ 2162, Réseau du souvenir, dossier Crypte souscription nationale, sous-d Démarches auprès du Ministère des Anciens Combattants, 1958–1961, "Compte-rendu de la Réunion tenue le 22 avril 1959"; Marie Granet, *Ceux de la Résistance (1940–1944)* (Paris, 1964), 266; AN 72 AJ 2141, Réseau du souvenir, dossier Projets, "Souscription nationale," text of 13 December 1960 decree and 10 January 1961 arrêté.

52 AN 72 AJ 2166, Réseau du souvenir, dossier Crypte Inauguration, letter from Arrighi to Octave Rabaté, 18 April 1962; Cécile Lesieur, "Le vrai Mémorial de la Résistance et de la Déportation reste à faire," *Le Patriote résistant*, May 1962.

53 Caroline Wiedmer, *The Claims of Memory: Representations of the Holocaust in Contemporary Germany and France* (Ithaca, NY, 1999), 33–36.

54 AN 72 AJ 2167, Réseau du souvenir, dossier Entretien et exploitation du Mémorial, 1961–1992, Genêt (Janet Flanner), letter from Paris, *The New Yorker*, 12 May 1962, 149.

55 AN 72 AJ 2166, Réseau du souvenir, dossier Relations, letter from G.-H. Pingusson to M. Desserprit, 10 October 1961; dossier Crypte Inauguration, newspaper clipping, "Le Général de Gaulle inaugurera le monument souterrain du déporté inconnu," *Le Monde*, 12 April 1962; newspaper clipping, *Arts*, 18 April 1962.

56 "Journée de la Déportation," *Voix et Visages*, no. 89 (July–October 1963).

57 Sylvie Bernay, *L'Église de France face à la persécution des Juifs, 1940–1944* (Paris, 2012), 109. Bernay insists that the object of the effort was rescue, not conversion. See also Riquet, *Le Rebelle discipliné*, 98, 184

58 Michelet, *Rue de la Liberté*, 106–108; idem, "Treblinka," *Le Monde*, 2 April 1966.

59 Sylvie Bernay, "Le Père Michel Riquet. Du philosémitisme d'action lors des années sombres au dialogue interreligieux," *Archives Juives*, no. 40 (2007), 107; Paule Berger Marx, *Les Relations entre les juifs et les catholiques dans la France de l'après-guerre, 1945–1965* (Paris, 2009), 337–339.

60 John Connelly, *From Enemy to Brother: The Revolution in Catholic Teaching on the Jews, 1933–1965* (Cambridge, MA, 2012), 3, 5, 63.

61 Riquet, *Le Rebelle discipliné*, 127.

62 Ibid., 26–27; Michel Fourcade, "Jacques Maritain et le Père Riquet: fécondité d'une 'grande amitié'," *Bulletin de la Fraternité d'Abraham*, no. 110 (April 2001), 5, 7; Riquet, *Un Chrétien face à Israël* (Paris, 1975), 20.

63 Paul Claudel, "Trois lettres sur Israël,"and Joseph Bonsirven, "La conversion d'Israël," in Henri Daniel-Rops, ed., *Les Juifs* (Paris, 1937), vi–ix, 301–303, 315–316. See also Joseph Bonsirven, *Les Juifs et Jésus. Attitudes nouvelles* (Paris, 1937), 187–188.

64 For what follows, see "L'impossible antisémitisme," in Daniel-Rops, ed., *Les Juifs*, 44–71.

65 "L'impossible antisémitisme" was translated into English as "The Mystery of Israel," in *Ransoming the Time* (New York, 1941): 141–179.

66 See Maritain, Address to the Latin-American Seminar on Social Studies, Washington, 23 August 1942, "The Crisis of Civilization," and Maritain, "Anti-Semitism as a Problem for the Jew," *The Commonweal* (25 September 1942), both reprinted in idem, *Pour la Justice. Articles et discours (1940–1945)* (New York, 1945), 154, 163.

67 The text is reproduced in Jacques Maritain, *Le Mystère d'Israël et autres essais* (Paris, 1965), 163–179.

68 Maritain, "The Mystery of Israel," 144–145; see also Maritain's radio message of 5 January 1944, titled "La Passion d'Israël," reproduced in idem, *Le Mystère d'Israël et autres essais*, 202–203.

69 Cited in Richard Francis Crane, *Passion of Israel: Jacques Maritain, Catholic Conscience, and the Holocaust* (Scranton, PA, 2010), 91.

70 Cited from *A Christian Looks at the Jewish Question* (1939) in Crane, *Passion of Israel*, 49.

71 See ibid., 124–127.

72 Rabbi Leon Klenicki, "Jacques Maritain's Vision of Judaism and Anti-Semitism," in Robert Royal, ed., *Jacques Maritain and the Jews* (Mishawaka, IN, 1994), 73–74.

73 Georges Bensoussan, "Éditorial," *Revue d'histoire de la Shoah*, 192 (January–June 2010), 13.

74 Eric Bentley, ed., *The Storm over The Deputy* (New York, 1964).

75 Maritain, citing from Saint Paul's Epistle to the Ephesians (5:27), in his review of Léon Poliakov's *Bréviaire de la haine*: "Breviary of Hate," *Social Research*, 20 (Summer 1953), 227.

76 This is not how François Azouvi understands the play. See Azouvi, *Le Mythe du grand silence. Auschwitz, les Français, la mémoire* (Paris, 2012), 195–210. The view presented here is closer to Alvin H. Rosenfeld's. See Rosenfeld, *A Double Dying: Reflections on Holocaust Literature* (Bloomington and Indianapolis, 1980), 139–152.

77 Tony Kushner, "'I Want to Go on Living after My Death': The Memory of Anne Frank," in Martin Evans and Kenneth Lunn, eds., *War and Memory in the Twentieth Century* (Oxford, 1997), 5, 12; Anne Fernier, "Le journal d'Anne Frank," *Voix et Visages*, n. 57 (May–June 1957); Genêt (Janet Flanner), "Letter from Paris," *The New Yorker* (11 November 1950), 142.

78 Henri Daniel-Rops, *Jésus en son temps* (Paris, 1945), 196, 239–240; Daniel-Rops, cited in Berger Marx, *Les Relations entre les juifs et les catholiques*, 125.

79 Carol Iancu, "Les réactions des milieux chrétiens face à Jules Isaac," *Revue de l'histoire de la Shoah*, no. 192 (January–June 2010), 165–167.

80 Henri Daniel-Rops, "Préface," *Journal de Anne Frank* (Paris, 1950), ix, xiii–xiv.

81 Riquet cited in Anne Fernier, "Le Journal d'Anne Frank," *Voix et Visages*, no. 57 (May–June 1957); Riquet, "Du souvenir à l'amour," in special issue of *L'Avant-Scène-fémina-théâtre* dedicated to *Le Journal de Anne Frank*, no. 192 (nd), 9; Riquet, *Le Rebelle discipliné*, 179.

82 "Une nouvelle pierre pour le village 'Anne Frank'," *Le Déporté*, no. 141 (April 1960); "Cérémonie à la mémoire d'Anne Frank à Francfort," *Le Déporté*, no. 155–156 (June–July 1961).

83 Jacques Nobécourt, *"Le Vicaire" et l'histoire* (Paris, 1964), 254; Patricia Marx, interview with Hochhuth in *Partisan Review* (summer 1964), reprinted in Bentley, ed., *The Storm over The Deputy*, 54.

84 Rolf Hochhuth, *The Deputy*, tr. Richard and Clara Winston (Baltimore, MD, 1997), 125. For a scholarly discussion of the pope's conduct, see Michael Phayer, *The Catholic Church and the Holocaust, 1930–1965* (Bloomington, IN, 2000), xv, 30, 221–222.

85 Hochhuth, *The Deputy*, 284–285.

86 Interview with Semprun, Claude Olivier, "Et nous, témoins, juges, accusés…" *Les Lettres françaises* (26 December 1963).

87 Ibid., and Semprun cited in Nobécourt, *"Le Vicaire,"* 301. All the same, Semprun may have had more understanding of the play's religious implications than he let on. Semprun's father was a member of the Spanish Republic's diplomatic corps. He was also a progressive Catholic who visited Maritain at Meudon and was a member of Emmanuel Mounier's *Esprit* collective. The Civil War obliged the Semprun family to relocate to Paris, and there the young Jorge was taken up by a Mounier acolyte, Jean-Marie Soutou. Semprun talks about the *Esprit* connection in *Adieu, vive clarté…* (Paris, 1998), dedication to Soutou and 166, 267. For Maritain, see Jean-Luc Barré, *Jacques et Raïssa Maritain. Les mendiants du ciel* (Paris, 2009), 426.

88 Hochhuth, *The Deputy*, 31–32, 216–219, 283.

89 Ibid., 117.

90 Roger Paret, writing in *France-Observateur*, as cited in Nobécourt, *"Le Vicaire,"* 304; Semprun in Olivier, "Et nous, témoins, juges, accusés…"; Hochhuth himself invoked Kierkegaard to describe Gerstein. See his interview with Judy Stone in *Ramparts* (Spring 1964), reprinted in Bentley, ed., *The Storm over The Deputy*, 49.

91 Nobécourt, *"Le Vicaire,"* 64, 311; Jacqueline Rameil, "Le Vicaire," *Voix et Visages*, no. 92 (January–February 1964).

92 Claudel cited in Crane, *Passion of Israel*, 165–166 n108. For Maritain, see ibid., 107–108. And for Mauriac, see his introduction to Léon Poliakov, *Bréviaire de la haine* (Paris, 1951), 8.

93 Hochhuth to Judy Stone, *Ramparts* (Spring 1964), in Bentley, ed., *The Storm over The Deputy*, 50; Hochhuth, *The Deputy*, 3.

94 Nobécourt, *"Le Vicaire,"* discusses the exchange, 91–92. See also APFCJ
Fonds Riquet, 10, dossier M. Riquet et la déportation, articles, s.d., undated
and unsourced news clipping, Jacques Villard, "À propos du 'Vicaire'. Une
interview exclusive du R.P. Riquet."

95 Poliakov, "L'Opinion française devant le Vicaire," *L'Arche* (January 1964),
15; Berger Marx, *Les Relations entre les juifs et les catholiques*, 342; Nobécourt,
"Le Vicaire," 285, 292.

96 Maritain as cited in Crane, *Passion of Israel*, 125–127.

5 The Six Million

1 Louise Alcan, *Sans Armes et sans bagages* (Limoges, 1945), 7, 77; see also
Annette Wieviorka, "Indicible ou inaudible? La déportation: premiers récits,"
Pardès, nos. 9–10 (1989), 47.

2 Suzanne Birnbaum, *Une Française juive est revenue* (Paris, 1946), 146.

3 Georges Bensoussan, *Auschwitz en heritage? D'un bon usage de la mémoire*
(Paris, 1998), 36–37, 41; Maud S. Mandel, *In the Aftermath of Genocide:
Armenians and Jews in Twentieth-Century France* (Durham, NC, 2003), 52;
Pierre Nora, "Mémoire et identité juives dans la France contemporaine," *Le
Débat*, no.131 (September–October 2004), 23.

4 In 1944, 1947, and 1948 but not in 1945. See Simon Perego, 'Pleurons-les,
bénissons leurs noms'. *Les commémorations de la Shoah et de la Seconde Guerre
mondiale dans le monde juif parisien entre 1944 et 1967: rituels, mémoires, identités*
(Doctoral thesis, Institute d'Études Politiques de Paris, 2016), I:196.

5 Annette Wieviorka, *Déportation et génocide. Entre la mémoire et l'oubli* (Paris,
1992), 391–393, 402–404; Simon Perego, "Histoire, justice, mémoire: le
Centre de documentation juive contemporaine et le Mémorial du Martyr juif
inconnu, 1956–1969" (Master's thesis, Institut d'Études Politiques de Paris,
2007), 259–263.

6 Bensoussan, *Auschwitz en héritage?* 43; Sylvie Lindeperg and Annette
Wieviorka, *Univers concentrationnaire et génocide. Voir, savoir, comprendre*
(Paris, 2008), 23–24; Laura Jockusch, *Collect and Record! Jewish Holocaust
Documentation in Early Postwar Europe* (New York, 2012), 82.

7 Léon Poliakov, *L'Auberge des musiciens. Mémoires* (Paris, 1981), 164; Perego,
"Histoire, justice, mémoire," 46–47; Poznanski, "La Création du Centre de
documentation juive contemporaine en France (avril 1943)," *Vingtième Siècle*,
no. 63 (July–September 1999), 51–63.

8 Simon Perego and Renée Poznanski, *Le Centre de documentation juive contemporaine. 1943–2013: documenter la Shoah* (Paris, 2013), 17, 19; Perego,
"Histoire, justice, mémoire," 37, 40; Annette Wieviorka, *Il y a 50 ans. Aux
origines du Mémorial de la Shoah* (Paris, 2006), 5.

9 Poliakov, *L'Auberge*, 28, 30, 36, 103ff.; Perego and Poznanski, *Le Centre de
documentation juive contemporaine*, 45.

10 Poliakov, *L'Auberge*, 165–166; Wieviorka, *Il y a cinquante ans*, 6; Perego and
Poznanski, *Le Centre de documentation juive contemporaine*, 20.

11 Perego and Poznanski, *Le Centre de documentation juive contemporaine*, 20; Jockusch, *Collect and Record!* 63–64; Laura Jockusch, "Breaking the Silence: the Centre de Documentation Juive Contemporaine in Paris and the Writing of Holocaust History in Liberated France," in David Cesarini and Eric J. Sundquist, eds., *After the Holocaust: Challenging the Myth of Silence* (New York, 2012), 71.

12 Jockusch, *Collect and Record!* 3; idem, "Breaking the Silence: the Centre de Documentation Juive Contemporaine in Paris and the Writing of Holocaust History in Liberated France," 74–75.

13 See the pioneering account, in Jockusch, *Collect and Record!* Ch. 5 see also Poliakov, *L'Auberge*, 165.

14 Serge Klarsfeld, "Georges Wellers est mort," *Le Monde juif*, no. 143 (July–September 1991), 130.

15 Raul Hilberg, "The Development of Holocaust Research—A Personal Overview," in David Bankier and Dan Michman, eds., *Holocaust Historiography in Context: Emergence, Challenges, Polemics and Achievements* (Jerusalem, 2008), 27; Georges Bensoussan, "The Jewish Contemporary Documentation Center (CDJC) and Holocaust Research in France, 1945–1970," in Bankier and Michman, eds., *Holocaust Historiography*, 248; Poliakov, *L'Auberge*, 178–180.

16 On this point, see Diane Afoumado's discussion of the contents of *Le Monde juif*: Afoumado, "1946–2016: 60 ans dans l'histoire d'une revue," *Revue d'histoire de la Shoah*, no. 185 (July–December 2006), 485–509.

17 Jacques Maritain, "Breviary of Hate," *Social Research*, 20 (Summer 1953), 220–222.

18 Georges Wellers, *De Drancy à Auschwitz* (Paris, 1946), part I.

19 Joesph Billig, *L'Allemagne et le génocide, plans et réalisations* (Paris, 1950), 26, 106.

20 Wellers, *De Drancy à Auschwitz*, 141–142.

21 Ibid., 144–145.

22 Jean Cassou, *Le Pillage par les Allemands des oeuvres d'art et des bibliothèques appartenant à des Juifs de France* (Paris, 1947), 11.

23 Léon Poliakov, *L'Étoile jaune* (Paris, 1949), Schneersohn intro., 7, Godart preface, 9.

24 Joseph Billig, *Le Commissariat général aux Questions juives (1941–1944)* (Paris, 1955), I:15, 344; idem, *Le Commissariat général* (Paris, 1957), II:346–347; idem, *Le Commissariat général* (Paris, 1960), III:9, 11, 321.

25 Poliakov, *La Condition des juifs en France sous l'Occupation italienne* (Paris, 1946), Schneersohn's introduction, 7–8 and Poliakov's text, 18–19.

26 Poliakov, *L'Étoile jaune* (Paris, 1949), 83, 93 and Schneersohn's introduction, 6–7; Wellers, *L'Étoile jaune à l'heure de Vichy* (Paris, 1973), 262, 268.

27 Wellers, *De Drancy à Auschwitz*, 171–172.

28 Poliakov, *Bréviaire de la haine. Le IIIe Reich et les Juifs* (Paris, 1951), 336–340.

29 Michel Mazor, *La Cité engloutie (Souvenirs du ghetto de Varsovie)* (Paris, 1955), 135.

30 There were also Sonderkommando units at Auschwitz, and in the fall of 1944, they too rose in revolt. Léon Poliakov, *Bréviaire de la haine*, 296–298, 310–311.

31 Michel Mazor, *La Cité engloutie*, 28, 34, 99, 176–177; David Knout, *La Bataille du ghetto de Varsovie, vue et racontée par les Allemands* (Paris, 1946), 7.

32 Léon Poliakov, *Bréviaire de la haine*, 444–446, 451. See also Wellers, *L'Étoile jaune*, 326.

33 Wellers, *De Drancy à Auschwitz*, 230; Mazor, *La Cité engloutie*, ch. 15.

34 Poliakov, *L'Envers du destin. Entretiens avec Georges Elia Sarfati* (Paris, 1989), 67.

35 CDJC MMJI, 255, Pose 1ère pierre, brochures, M.M. [Michel Mazor], "Documents speak...The 'Monde Juif', voice of the C.D.J.C.," in *Ten Years of the Jewish Contemporary Documentation Center* (in English).

36 See François Mauriac's introduction to Poliakov's *Bréviaire de la haine*, 8; Poliakov, *L'Auberge*, 178 Godart's introduction to Poliakov's *Étoile jaune*, 10; Father Riquet's afterward to Wellers' *L'Étoile jaune*, 355; and Jockusch, *Collect and Record!* 66.

37 Georges Wellers, *L'Étoile jaune*, 7, 12.

38 Cited by Nicolas Berg, "Joseph Wulf: A Forgotten Outsider among Holocaust Scholars," in Bankier and Michman, eds., *Holocaust Historiography*, 191.

39 On the matter of prefaces, see Francine Kauffmann, "Les enjeux de la polémique autour du premier best-seller français de la littérature de la Shoah," *Revue d'histoire de la Shoah*, no. 176 (September–December 2002), 69n.

40 Johannes Heuman, "Promoting Global Holocaust Memory in the Era of the Cold War: The Tomb of the Unknown Jewish Martyr in Paris," *History & Memory*, 27 (Spring/Summer 2015), 145,

41 On this point, see Perego, "Les commémorations de la destruction des juifs d'Europe au Mémorial du Martyr juif inconnu du milieu des années 1950 à la fin des années 1960," *Revue d'histoire de la Shoah*, no. 193 (July–December 2010), 505.

42 CDJC (MMJI), 171, Procès-verbaux Réunions (Mémorial) 1955–1958, brochure, "Rapports et Bilan...présentés à l'Assemblée générale en date du 15 décembre 1957," 4; CDJC MMJI, 177, Réunions du Comité mondial, dossier 1952–1954, "5-3-52 Note pour la Commission des finances," 2 and "Réunion du Comité mondial et du comité exécutif, 23 juin 1952," 3.

43 "La campagne en faveur du tombeau du Martyr juif inconnu bat son plein: M. I. Schneersohn aux États-Unis," *Le Monde juif*, no. 66 (December 1953), 13. See also CDJC MMJI, 177, Réunions du Comité mondial, dossier 1952–1954, "Memorandum 22-9-53," 1–2, and "20 janvier 1954, Réunion du Comité mondial et du comité exécutif," 2–4.

44 "La campagne en faveur du tombeau du Martyr juif inconnu bat son plein: M. I. Schneersohn aux États-Unis," 14–15.

45 CDJC (MMJI), 171, Procès-verbaux Réunions (Mémorial) 1955–1958, brochure, "Rapports et Bilan...présentés à l'Assemblée générale en date du 15 décembre 1957," 7; CDJC MMJI, 177, Réunions du Comité mondial, dossier 1952–1954, "20 janvier 1954, Réunion du Comité mondial et du comité exécutif," 4–6; Annette Wieviorka, *Il y a 50 ans*, 21–22.

46 CDJC MMJI, 244, Travaux, 1955, 1956, dossier Permis de construction, "Traduction de l'article d'Elie Wiesel," nd (1955), 2; CDJC MMJI, 241,

Construction, projets architecturaux, dessins, plans, dossier Projets architectes, letter from Ph. Hosiasson to Huisman, 10 June 1954; and CDJC (MMJI), 171, Procès-verbaux, Réunions (Mémorial) 1955–1958, dossier Mémorial, "7 décembre 1955," 4.

47 Annette Wieviorka, "Un lieu de mémoire: le Mémorial du Martyr juif inconnu," *Pardès*, no. 2 (1985), 91; Simon Perego, "Histoire, justice, mémoire," 58.

48 CDJC MMJI, 241, Construction, projets architecturaux, dessins, plans, dossier Bail, Renouvelement [sic], "23 avril 1952, Conseil municipal, séance du 10 avril 1952," 227.

49 Isabelle Backouche and Sarah Gensburger, "Anti-Semitism and Urban Development in France in the Second World War: The Case of Îlot 16 in Paris," *Contemporary European History*, 23 (August 2014), 381–403.

50 CDJC MMJI, 177, Réunions du Comité mondial, dossier 1952–1954, "Procès-verbal de la réunion du Comité exécutif du Mémorial, 5 juin 1952."

51 CDJC MMJI, 250, Mémorial, Construction, dossier 1953, 1954, "November 6, 1953, Project for the Tomb of the Unknown Martyred Jew [in English]."

52 CDJC MMJI, 177, Réunions du Comité mondial, dossier 1952–1954, "20 janvier 1954," 14–16.

53 CDJC MMJI, 241, Construction, projets architecturaux, dessins, plans, dossier Projets, architectes, "Note concernant l'examen du projet du Mémorial du Martyr juif inconnu," 10 May 1954, and letter from Paul Haag to Pierre Couinaud, 25 May 1954.

54 CDJC MMJI, 241, Construction, projets architecturaux, dessins, plans, dossier Projets, architectes, letter from Richard Pouzet to Georges Huisman, 26 May 1954, and Rapport concernant le monument à la mémoire du Martyr juif inconnu, 24 juillet 1954, signé A. Laprade"; CDJC MMJI, 250, Mémorial, Construction, dossier 1953–1954, letter from L. Arretche to Président (Robert Rey), 9 August 1954.

55 CDJC MMJI, 241, Construction, projets architecturaux, dessins, plans, dossier Projets, architectes, note from Ph. Hosiasson to M. Schneersohn, 6 June 1954; CDJC (MMJI), 171, Procès-verbaux, Réunions (Mémorial) 1955–1958, dossier Mémorial, "Compte-rendu de la réunion du Comité exécutif, 8 juin 1955," 1–3.

56 CDJC (MMJI), 171, Procès-verbaux, Réunions (Mémorial) 1955–1958, brochure, "Rapports et Bilan," 5; www.ajpn.org/personne-Paul-Haag-3559.html, accessed 15 July 2016.

57 Cited in Wieviorka, *Il y cinquante ans*, 17.

58 CDJC MMJI, 244, Travaux, 1955, 1956, dossier Permis de construction, "Déclarations importantes faites au cours de la réunion commune du comité du mémorial et de la Claims Conference, le 7 février 1955," 4.

59 Annette Wieviorka has written on this aspect of the ceremony. See Wieviorka, *Il y cinquante ans*, 20; idem, "Un lieu de Mémoire et d'Histoire: Le Mémorial du Martyr juif inconnu," *Revue de l'Université de Bruxelles*, nos. 1/2 (1987), 122.

60 CDJC MMJI, 253, Mémorial, Cérémonie pose de la 1ère pierre 1953, dossier Cérémonie du 17 mai 1953, "Discours de M. le Docteur Couinaud," 5–6.

61 CDJC MMJI, 260, Mémorial, inauguration, discours, dossier Discours, "Discours de M. Pierre Ruais, Président du Conseil Municipal de Paris."

62 CDJC MMJI, 259, Mémorial, inauguration, untitled dossier, clipping from *Le Déporté*, L.D., "Le Mémorial du Martyr juif inconnu," November 1956. See also in the same dossier clippings from *France-Soir*, "Le Mémorial du Martyr juif inconnu a été inauguré," 31 October 1956, and from *Le Déporté*, Michel Wellers, "Inauguration du Mémorial du Martyr juif inconnu à Paris," November 1956.

63 Perego, "Histoire, justice, mémoire," 272; Serge Barcellini, "Sur deux journées nationales commémorant la déportation et les persécutions des 'années noires,'" *Vingtième Siècle*, no. 45 (January–March 1995), 84.

64 CDJC MMJI, 256, Mémorial, inauguration, dossier Programmes des architectes, "Programme des activités du Mémorial du Martyr juif inconnu," nd [1957–1958], 1.

65 For these last two items, see: Perego, "Histoire, justice, mémoire," 67, 271; Olivier Lalieu, *Histoire de la mémoire de la Shoah* (Paris, 2015), 56.

66 CDJC MMJI, 260, Mémorial, inauguration, discours, dossier Discours, "Discours de M. Justin Godart."

67 CDJC MMJI, 244, Travaux, 1955, 1956, dossier Permis de construction, letter from Godart to Schneersohn, 22 May [1955]; CDJC [MMJI], 171, Procès-verbaux Réunions (Mémorial) 1955–1958, dossier Mémorial, "Compte-rendu de la réunion conjointe du Comité exécutif et des membres du Comité mondial, 7 décembre 1955," 3; Perego, "Histoire, justice, mémoire," 253–254. On Godart, see Annette Wieviorka, "Le combat de Justin Godart pour l'érection du 'tombeau du martyr juif inconnu'," in idem, ed., *Justin Godart. Un homme dans son siècle (1871–1956)* (Paris, 2004), 133–134.

68 CDJC MMJI, 258, Inauguration presse, dossier Inauguration presse, clipping from the *Jerusalem Post*, Maurice Carr, "6 Million Dead Not Forgotten," 30 September 1956.

69 See Francine Kaufmann's discussion of Amalek in Kaufmann, *Pour Relire "Le Dernier des Justes";* (Paris, 1986), 84.

70 CDJC MMJI, 255, Pose 1ère Pierre, Brochures, "Six millions de juifs morts sans sépulture…ont enfin trouvé leur tombeau symbolique." For a full discussion of this, see Annette Wieviorka and Itzhok Niborski, *Les Livres du souvenir. Mémoriaux juifs de Pologne* (Paris, 1983), 9–11, 15.

71 CDJC MMJI, 242, Construction, plans, dossier Inauguration préparation, "Le mémorial du Martyr juif inconnu," 2. See also Perego, "Histoire, justice, mémoire," 242.

72 Lindeperg and Wieviorka, *Univers concentrationnaire et génocide*, 75.

73 CDJC MMJI, 244, Travaux 1955, 1956, dossier Permis de construction, photo.

74 CDJC MMJI, 241, Construction, projets architecturaux, dessins, plans, dossier Projets de constructions, drawing of the crypt; CDJC MMJI, 250, Mémorial construction, dossier Crypte, untitled document listing proposed wall texts; CDJC (MMJI), 171, Procès-verbaux Réunions (Mémorial) 1955–1958, dossier Comptes-rendus des réunions diverses 1956,

"Compte-rendu de la séance du Comité exécutif et des membres du Comité mondial, 6 juin 1956," 3.

75 CDJC MMJI, 253, Mémorial, cérémonie pose de la 1ère pierre 1953, dossier Cérémonie du 17 mai 1953, "Nouvelles Juives Mondiales," 19 May 1953"; Wieviorka, *Il y a cinquante ans*, 20.

76 CDJC MMJI, 258, Inauguration presse, dossier Inauguration presse, clipping from *La Voix*, "L'inauguration du Mémorial du Martyr juif inconnu," 6 November 1956; CDJC MMJI, 256, Mémorial inauguration, dossier Inauguration, "Cérémonie Inauguration du Mémorial du Martyr juif inconnu."

77 CDJC MMJI, 258, Inauguration presse, dossier Inauguration presse, undated document [1957], "L'inhumation des cendres au Mémorial du Martyr juif," 2. See also François Azouvi, *Le Mythe du grand silence. Auschwitz, les Français, la mémoire* (Paris, 2012), 238, and Perego, 'Pleurons-les, bénissons leurs noms,' II:1046–1047.

78 The camp names are: Auschwitz, Belzec, Bergen-Belsen, Buchenwald, Chelmno, Dachau, Majdanek, Mauthausen, Sobibor, Struthof, and Treblinka. See also Perego, "Histoire, justice, mémoire," 248.

79 CDJC MMJI, 244, Travaux, 1955, 1956, dossier Permis de construction, "Déclarations importantes faites au cours de la réunion commune du Comité du memorial et de la Claims Conference, le 7 février 1955," 3.

80 CDJC MMJI, 253, Mémorial, cérémonie pose de la 1ère pierre 1953, dossier Cérémonie du 17 mai 1953, "Nouvelles Juives Mondiales," 19 May 1953.

81 CDJC MMJI, 253, Mémorial, cérémonie pose de la 1ère pierre 1953, dossier Cérémonie du 17 mai 1953, "Compte-rendu de la réunion du 1er février 1953 de la Commission d'organisation de la pose de la première pierre," 2; Perego, "Histoire, justice, mémoire," 293.

82 CDJC MMJI, 242, Construction, plans, dossier Inauguration, préparation, "Le Mémorial du Martyr juif inconnu à Paris, 2 juin 1956," 4; CDJC MMJI, 258, Inauguration presse, dossier Inauguration presse, clipping from the *Jerusalem Post*, Maurice Carr, "6 Million Dead Not Forgotten," 30 September 1956.

83 Perego, "Histoire, justice, mémoire," 126–127; MMJI CDJC, 339, Cahiers sur le CDJC, catalogue, "À la Glorieuse Mémoire des Juifs de Pologne" (Paris, 1961).

84 CDJC MMJI, 253, Mémorial, cérémonie pose de la 1ère pierre 1953, dossier Cérémonie du 17 mai 1953, "Nouvelles Juives Mondiales," 19 May 1953, 2; Jockusch, *Collect and Record!* 79.

85 Schneersohn reminded Coty on the occasion that the president's visit coincided almost to the day with the fifteenth anniversary of the Vél d'hiv roundup. CDJC MMJI, 252, Brochures 1ère pierre, brochure "supplement au no. 10 de 'La Revue du CDJC'," 20–21; Perego, "Histoire, justice, mémoire," 66.

86 CDJC MMJI, 260, Mémorial, inauguration, discours, dossier Discours, Nahum Goldmann, 2–4.

87 CDJC MMJI, 260, Mémorial, inauguration, discours, dossier Discours, Jacob Tsur, np. My special thanks to Ronny Regev for her help with

translating from the Hebrew. See also CDJC MMJI, 259, Mémorial, inauguration, untitled dossier, clipping from *Le Déporté*, L.D., "Le Mémorial du
Martyr juif inconnu," November 1956.

88 CDJC MMJI, 252, Brochures 1ère pierre, brochure "Exposition internationale.
Du Cataclysme à la Vie nouvelle, ving-cinq années d'histoires juives," 1–4.

89 CDJC MMJI, 663, Exposition "La Lutte des Juifs contre l'Hitlérisme,"
dossier Exposition, "Note d'information sur les préparatifs de l'Exposition
'Les Juifs dans la lutte contre l'hitlérisme, 7 décembre 1964,'" 4; Georges
Wellers, "L'Exposition 'Les Juifs dans la lutte contre l'hitlérisme,'" *Le
Déporté*, no. 200 (March 1965).

90 Seven figurative bas-reliefs, representing various aspects of the Nazi genocide, are now affixed on the right wall of the memorial courtyard. They
are the creation of Arbit Blatas, a Lithuanian sculptor who had come to
Paris as a young man to work alongside École de Paris artists Chaim
Soutine and Ossip Zadkine. A first edition of the reliefs was unveiled at
the Campo del Ghetto Nuovo in Venice in 1980. The second edition, the
one that hangs on the memorial wall in Paris, was unveiled the year after.
CDJC MMJI, 241, Construction, projets architecturaux, dessins, plans,
dossier Projets architecture, clipping from an unnamed periodical, Henry
Tanner, "Blatas Monument to Holocaust Unveiled in Venice," 28 April
1980; and letter from Alain de Rothschild to Giorgio Voghera, 15
April 1981.

91 CDJC MMJI, 241, Construction, projets architecturaux, dessins, plans, dossier Projets, architectes, "Note sur l'organisation du Musée du Mémorial du
Martyr juif inconnu, 24 juin 1954."

92 CDJC [MMJI], 171, Procès-verbaux Réunions (Mémorial) 1955–1958, dossier Comptes-rendus des réunions diverses 1956, "Compte-rendu de la
séance de la Commission du Musée, 7 mars 1956." Olga Wormser-Migot
and André Michel were present at the meeting.

93 Annette Wieviorka, "Le combat de Justin Godart pour l'érection du 'tombeau du martyr juif inconnu,'" 135.

94 Annette Wieviorka, *Déportation et génocide*, 338.

95 Laura Hobson Faure, *Un 'plan Marshall juif'. La Présence juive américaine après
la Shoah* (Paris, 2018), 180.

96 See Doris Bensimon, *Les Juifs de France et leurs relations avec Israël, 1945–1988*
(Paris, 1989), 64–73; Maud S. Mandel, *In the Aftermath of Genocide*, 148, 170,
175; and idem, "Philanthropy or Cultural Imperialism? The Impact of
American Jewish Aid in Post-Holocaust France," *Jewish Social Studies*, 9
(Fall 2002), 76–79, 85; Daniella Doron, *Jewish Youth and Identity in
Postwar France: Rebuilding Family and Nation* (Bloomington, IN, 2015),
208; Faure, *Un 'plan Marshall juif'*, 204.

97 For a similar line of argument, see Perego, "Histoire, justice, mémoire," 310.

98 Cesarini, "Challenging the 'Myth of Silence': Postwar Responses to the
Destruction of European Jewry," in idem and Sundquist, eds. ed., *After the
Holocaust*, 30; Joseph Kessel, preface to John Hersey, *La Muraille*, 15th
edition (Paris, 1952), 13; Azouvi, *Le Mythe du grand silence*, 141–145,
170–172.

99 See Annette Wieviorka, *L'Ère du témoin* (Paris, 1998), passim. In Wieviorka's view, it was the Eichmann trial of 1961 that brought the Holocaust to public attention in France, and what made the trial so transformative, she proposes, was the vivid testimony of the hundred-plus witnesses called on to tell their stories.

6 The Thirty Years' War

1 Charles de Gaulle, radio speech of 18 September 1941, http://fresques.ina.fr/de-gaulle/fiche-media/Gaulle00403/le-pere-la-defaite.html, accessed 7 December 2017.

2 Odile Rudelle, "Politique de la mémoire: politique de la postérité," in *De Gaulle en son siècle* (Paris, 1991), I: 157. See also Sudhir Hazareesingh, *Le Mythe gaullien* (Paris, 2010), 50.

3 Matthias Waechter, "De Gaulles 30jähriger Krieg. Die Résistance und die Erinnerung an 1918," in Jost Dülffer and Gerd Krumeich, eds., *Die verlorene Frieden. Politik und Kriegskultur nach 1918* (Essen, 2002), 52–56.

4 Olivier Wieviorka, *La Mémoire désunie. Le souvenir politique des années sombres de la Libération à nos jours* (Paris, 2010), 61.

5 See the photo of the wreath-laying in Claire Cameron, ed., *Le Mont-Valérien. Résistance, Répression et Mémoire* (Montreuil, 2008), 28. For 18 June 1945, see Nicole Racine-Furlaud, "Mémoire du 18 juin 1940," in *De Gaulle en son siècle* (Paris, 1991), I: 551; and Frédéric Turpin, *Le Mont-Valérien: de l'histoire à la mémoire* (Paris, 2003), 26.

6 Serge Barcellini, "Les cérémonies du 11 novembre 1945: une apothéose commémorative gaulliste," in Christiane Franck, ed., *La France de 1945. Résistances, retours, renaissances* (Caen, 1996), 85–86, 89; see also the photos in Cameron, ed., *Le Mont-Valérien*, 29–35.

7 Cited in Hazareesingh, *Le Mythe gaullien*, 91.

8 Vladimir Trouplin, "Les organisateurs et le Mont Valérien," in Philippe Oulmont, ed., *Les 18 Juin. Combats et commémorations* (Brussels, 2011), 238–239; ACOL, Fonds 18 juin, 1950–1955, dossier 18 juin 1950, "Notes de service," nd; 1954–1955, dossier 18 juin 1954, "Associations qui raniment la Flamme le 18 juin 1954," nd.

9 Danielle Tartakowsky, "Des 18 Juin 'de souveraineté quand même' 1946–1957," in Oulmont, ed., *Les 18 Juin*, 159.

10 ACOL, Fonds 18 juin, 1945–1949, dossier 18 juin 1947, "18 juin 1947," nd; 1945–1949, dossier 18 juin 1949, sous-d Lettres officielles, letter from Lieutenant-Colonel Jonas to Compagnons de la Libération, 2 June 1949; 1950–1955, dossier 18 June 1951,"Programme des manifestations," nd.

11 ACOL, Fonds 18 juin, 1945–1949, dossier 18 juin 1947, "18 juin 1947," nd; 1945–1949, dossier 18 juin 1948, "Mont-Valérien," nd; and photos, Cameron, ed., *Le Mont-Valérien*, 40, 42 (the second photo is from 1959).

12 ACOL, Fonds 18 juin, 1955–1959, dossier 18 juin 1957, untitled document, nd.

13 ACOL, Fonds 18 juin, 1950–1955, dossier 18 juin 1952, "Programme de la cérémonie," nd.

14 Claire Cameron and Franck Segrétain, "Le Mont-Valérien, lieu d'histoire, lieu de mémoire," in Cameron, ed., *Le Mont-Valérien*, 20 and 26n16.

15 ACOL, Fonds 18 juin, 1945–1949, dossier 18 juin 1949, sous-d Lettres officielles, letter from Thierry d'Argenlieu to Monsieur le Président [Henri Queuille], 2 May 1949; 1950–1955, dossier 18 juin 1951, sous-d Notes de service, letter from Henri Queuille to Thierry d'Argenlieu, 31 May 1951; 1960–1961, dossier 18 juin 1960, sous-d Correspondance avec l'Élysée, "Cérémonie du 18 juin," 28 March 1960.

16 Anne and Debout were armed résistants, soldiers of the Forces Françaises de l'Intérieur. The former died in combat, the latter in deportation.

17 ACOL, Fonds 18 juin, 1950–1955, dossier 18 juin 1951, "Programme des manifestations," nd.

18 Trouplin, "Les organisateurs et le Mont Valérien," in Oulmont, ed., *Les 18 Juin*, 239–240; Hazareesingh, *Le Mythe gaullien*, 113.

19 Julien Joly, "Intervenir dans un lieu de mémoire: architecture et temporalité," in Cameron, ed., *Le Mont-Valérien*, 260.

20 For the history of the Cross of Lorraine, see: Pascal Sigoda, "Symbolique et historique de la Croix de Lorraine," *Études gaulliennes*, 4 (January–March 1976), 33–35; François Broche, "Croix de Lorraine," in Broche, Georges Caïtucoli, and Jean-François Muracciole, eds., *Dictionnaire de la France Libre* (Paris, 2010), 386–387; and Serge Barcellini and Annette Wieviorka, *Passant, souviens-toi! Les lieux du souvenir de la Seconde Guerre mondiale en France* (Paris, 1995), 19.

21 For the two preceding paragraphs, see Guillaume Piketty, "Économie morale de la reconnaissance. L'Ordre de la Libération au péril de la sortie de la Seconde Guerre mondiale, *Histoire@Polique*, 3 (2007), 5–5.

22 Piketty, "Économie morale de la reconnaissance," 5–5. And a special thanks to William Jordan, who provided information on the nature of medieval and early modern military orders.

23 Eric T. Jennings, *Free French Africa in World War II: The African Resistance* (New York, 2015), 263–264; Thomas Vaisset, "Thierry d'Argenlieu," in Broche, Caïtucoli, and Muracciole, eds. *Dictionnaire de la France Libre*, 1399–1400.

24 Cited in Hazareesingh, *Le Mythe gaullien*, 201.

25 Charles de Gaulle, *Mémoires de guerre* (Paris, 1989 [orig. 1954]), 9.

26 Ibid.

27 SHD AC 27 P 875, Mont-Valérien, dossier Procès-verbaux des réunions de la Commission interministérielle 1949, "Procès-verbal, 25 May 1949"; dossier Réunions relatives à la creation de la Nécropole 1948–1959, "Note pour Monsieur le Ministre," 6 April 1955, "Note pour Monsieur Quinson sous-secrétaire d'Etat," 29 August 1957, and "Note pour Monsieur le Directeur adjoint," 12 November 1957; and dossier Textes 1945–1969, *Journal officiel*, 12 May 1954, announcing the creation of the Commission exécutive.

28 SHD AC 27 P 875, Mont-Valérien, dossier Réunions relatives à la création de la Nécropole 1948–1959, "Procès-verbal de la Réunion tenue le samedi

21 juin 1958"; dossier 1953–1965 Réunions, "Procès-verbal de la Conférence tenue le 10 juillet 1958" and "Procès-verbal de la Réunion tenue le vendredi 11 juillet 1958"; dossier Procès-verbaux des Réunions de chantier 1959–1960, "Procès-verbal de la Réunion de chantier, 11 May 1959"; dossier Textes, "Textes relatifs au Mont-Valérien," nd.

29 Raymond Triboulet, *Un Ministre du Général* (Paris, 1985), 41; MOL, K Mémoire, 3K Mont-Valérien, dossier Mont-Valérien, letter from Félix Brunau to Mon Général [de Boissieu], 6 June 1974.

30 Cameron and Segrétain, "Le Mont-Valérien, lieu d'histoire, lieu de mémoire," in Cameron, *Le Mont-Valérien*, 21; Barcellini and Wieviorka, *Passant, souviens-toi!* 167 SHD AC 27 P 877, Mont-Valérien, dossier Travaux Crypte, sous-d Escalier de la Crypte; AC 27 P 879, Mont-Valérien, dossier Clairière des fusillés, "Delavallade, rapport de présentation," 19 June 1958.

31 ACOL, Fonds 18 juin, 1960-1961, 18 juin 1961, dossier Correspondance Colonel Brunau, letter from Général Ingold to Colonel Brunau, 23 June 1960.

32 MOL, K Mémoire, 3K Mont-Valérien, dossier Mont-Valérien, letter from C. Hettier de Boislambert to M. Koumskoff, 21 June 1974. Brunau was displeased with the addition: same dossier, letter from Félix Brunau to Mon Général [de Boissieu], 6 June 1974. Note that the inscription is a shortened version of what de Gaulle actually said.

33 ACOL, Fonds 18 juin, 1960–1961, dossier 18 juin 1961, sous-d Correspondance Colonel Brunau, letter from Général Ingold to Colonel Brunau, 23 June 1960.

34 Turpin, *Le Mont-Valérien*, 54.

35 For what follows, see MOL, K Mémoire, 3K Mont-Valérien, dossier Affaire Bigosse.

36 MOL, K Mémoire, 3K Mont-Valérien, dossier Affaire Bigosse, note from Triboulet, dated 10 June 1960.

37 For a similar line of interpretation, see Mechtild Gilzmer, *Mémoires de pierre. Les monuments commémoratifs en France après 1944* (Paris, 2009), 118.

38 Cited in Gilzmer, *Mémoires de pierre*, 121–123.

39 ACOL, Fonds 18 juin, 1960–1961, dossier 18 juin 1961, sous-d Mémorial de la France combattante, "Haut-Lieu du Mont-Valérien," nd, 4.

40 MOL, K Mémoire, 3K Mont-Valérien, dossier Mont-Valérien, "Haut-Lieu du Mont-Valérien," nd, 6.

41 SHD AC 27 P 879, Mont-Valérien, dossier Travaux d'art, Hauts-reliefs, "Delavallade. Note pour Mademoiselle Mirande," 17 March 1960, and letter from René Juteau to Messieurs, 18 January 1961.

42 Hazareesingh, "Les 18 juin sous la Ve République. Les années de Gaulle (1958-1969)," in Oulmont, ed., *Les 18 juin*, 201.

43 ACOL, Fonds 18 juin, 1955–1959, dossier 18 juin 1958 et 1959 (compléments), sous-d Notes de service, "Note de service, 14 juin 1958" and "Note de service, 13 juin 1959."

44 Racine-Furlaud, "Mémoire du 18 juin," I:558; Évelyne Cohen, "La mémoire du 18 juin à travers les actualités cinématographiques et les émissions de la

télévision française (1945–2006), in Oulmont, ed., *Les 18 Juin*, 335; Sylvie Lindeperg, *Les Écrans de l'ombre. La Seconde Guerre mondiale dans le cinéma français (1944–1969)* (Paris, 1997), 342–343.

45 ACOL, Fonds 18 juin, 1960–1961, dossier 18 juin 1960, sous-d Correspondance avec l'Élysée, letter from Général Ingold to Mon Général, 3 May 1960.

46 Triboulet, *Un Ministre*, 41. See also SHD AC 27 AP 875, Mont-Valérien, dossier Cérémonies, requêtes, clipping from *Le Figaro*, 18–19 June 1960; and Hazareesingh, *Le Mythe gaullien*, 243 n121.

47 Cohen, "La mémoire du 18 juin," 338.

48 ACOL, Fonds 18 juin, 1960–1961, dossier 18 juin 1961, loose document, "Rapport du Colonel Saint-Pérouse sur la cérémonie du 18 juin 1960 au Mont-Valérien," 24 June 1960; dossier Correspondance avec l'Élysée, undated and untitled document for journalists outlining how they might speak about the monument and the ceremony.

49 ACOL, Fonds 18 juin, 1960–1961, dossier 18 juin 1960, sous-d Correspondance avec l'Élysée, "Cérémonie de la flamme au monument de la France combattante," 20 (?) May 1960 and "Inauguration du monument par MM Triboulet et Bruneau [sic]," nd.

50 The best source on the Gaullist style is Hazareesingh, *Le Mythe gaullien*, 66, 81, 115; and idem, "Les 18 juin sous la Ve République. Les années de Gaulle (1958–1969)," 201, 207.

51 ACOL, Fonds 18 juin, 1960–1961, dossier 18 juin 1961, sous-d Cérémonie du 18 juin au Mont-Valérien, "1ère Réunion du travail, 25 avril 1961," 1–3.

52 ACOL, Fonds 18 juin, 1963–1964, dossier 18 juin 1963, sous-d Lettres (Reportages, Radios), letters to Radio Monte-Carlo, Radio Luxembourg, Europe no. 1.

53 Trouplin, "Les organisateurs et le Mont Valérien," 240.

54 De Gaulle, earlier than many politicians, understood the communicative power of television. See Julian Jackson, *De Gaulle* (Cambridge, MA, 2018), 622.

55 Edmond Michelet, *Rue de la Liberté. Dachau 1943–1945* (Paris, 1955). The letter is printed just after the copyright page.

56 Olivier Lalieu, *La Déportation fragmentée: les anciens déportés parlent de politique, 1945-1980* (Paris, 1994), 151, 153–154.

57 Germaine Tillion, *La Traversée du mal. Entretien avec Jean Lacouture* (Paris, 1997), 41, 49; idem, *Les Ennemis complémentaires. Guerre d'Algérie* (Paris, 2005), 301–302; idem, *À la Recherche du vrai et du juste. À propos rompus avec le siècle* (Paris, 2001), 388.

58 Gilzmer, *Mémoires de pierre*, 7; Wieviorka, *La Mémoire désunie*, 164–165.

59 "Le XXe anniversaire de la Libération des camps," *Voix et Visages*, no. 99 (May–June 1965).

60 Johannes Heuman, *The Holocaust and French Historical Culture, 1945–65* (London, 2015), 134.

61 AN 72 AJ 2166, Réseau du souvenir, dossier Inauguration, "Paris anti-raciste se souvient," clipping from *Droit et Liberté*, July 1962; clipping from *L'Humanité*, 4 July 1962; and "Les manifestations contre la nazisme," clipping from *Liberté de l'Est*, 6 July 1962.

62 "Le Courrier des Amicales," *Le Patriote résistant*, May 1963.

63 For what follows, see Lindsay Montaillier, *Le Musée de la Résistance nationale de Champigny-sur-Marne (de 1965 à nos jours): une histoire complexe et évolutive*, (Mémoire de maîtrise, Université de Paris-I, 2003), 2 vols.

64 Ibid., I: 19.

65 Ibid., I: 20, 40.

66 Ibid., I: 48.

67 See the 2002 interview with historian Germaine Willard in Montaillier, *Le Musée de la Résistance nationale*, II: 23.

68 The Museum is now in the process of refurbishment. The MRN, it is worth adding, possesses a sizeable collection of Boris Taslitzky's wartime oeuvre. Indeed, its central stairwell features a massive Taslitzky mural, representing the weighing in at a Vichy prison of three naked male résistants, the men's pendulous scrotums outsized in relation to their emaciated bodies. The Museum also boasts significant archival holdings, housed in a separate building, the Centre Jean Cassou, which opened in 2000.

69 Lindeperg, *Les Écrans de l'ombre*, 323.

70 There is some difference of opinion about the details of the competition organization. I have followed Denis Mazzucchetti, "Le concours national de la Résistance: une pédagogie de 'l'esprit de la Résistance'," in Gilles Vergnon and Michèle Battesti, eds., *Les Associations d'anciens résistants et la fabrique de la mémoire de la seconde guerre mondiale, Cahiers du Centre d'études d'histoire de la Défense*, no. 28 (Vincennes, 2006), 73–86. See also Olivier Lalieu, "L'invention du 'devoir de mémoire,'" *Vingtième Siècle*, no. 69 (January–March 2001), 88 and 88n10; Wieviorka, *La Mémoire désunie*, 160; and AN 72 AJ 2158, Réseau du souvenir, dossier Concours national de la Résistance et de la Déportation, letter from J. Auban, Ministère de l'Éducation nationale to Réseau du souvenir, 19 April 1961.

71 AN 72 AJ 2158, Réseau du souvenir, dossier Prix d'histoire au concours général, letter from R. Hammond, Ministère de l'Éducation nationale, to Réseau du souvenir, 14 June 1962; and letter from P. Daste, Ministère de l'Éducation nationale to Réseau du souvenir, 29 May 1974.

72 Lalieu, "L'invention du 'devoir de mémoire,'" 88n9.

73 Henry Rousso, *Le Syndrome de Vichy. 1944–198...* (Paris, 1987), 95–100.

74 For the speech, see www.ina.fr/video/I00013168, accessed 17 August 2019.

75 For what follows, see Lindeperg, *Les Écrans de l'ombre*, 344–355.

76 Cited in Lindeperg, *Les Écrans de l'ombre*, 347.

77 Lindeperg, *Les Écrans de l'ombre*, 356–361; Wieviorka, *La Mémoire désunie*, 156.

7 Holocaust

1 Jules Isaac, *Jésus et Israël* (Paris, 1959 [orig. 1948]); ibid., *L'Enseignement du mépris* (Paris, 1962).

2 Naomi Seidman, "Elie Wiesel and the Scandal of Jewish Rage," *Jewish Social Studies*, 3 (Fall 1996), 1–19.

3 Pierre Nora, "Mémoire et identité juives dans la France contemporaine. Les grands déterminants," *Le Débat*, no. 131 (September–October 2004), 24; Samuel Moyn, *A Holocaust Controversy: The Treblinka Affair in Postwar France* (Waltham, MA, 2005) 12, 73, 25; François Azouvi, *Le Mythe du grand silence. Auschwitz, les Français, la mémoire* (Paris, 2012), 53.

4 Jackie Wullschlager, *Chagall* (New York, 2008), 345–346, 399.

5 Brenna Moore, *Sacred Dread: Raïssa Maritain, the Allure of Suffering, and the French Catholic Revival* (Notre Dame, IN, 2012), 138.

6 Ziva Amishai-Maisels, *Depiction and Interpretation: The Influence of the Holocaust on the Visual Arts* (Oxford, 1993), 182; Wullschlager, *Chagall*, 341, 346, 353; Jean-Luc Barré, *Jacques et Raïssa Maritain. Les mendiants du ciel* (Paris, 2009), 276.

7 Amishai-Maisels, *Depiction and Interpretation*, 24.

8 Cited in Amishai-Maisels, "Chagall's 'White Crucifixion,'" *Art Institute of Chicago Museum Studies*, 17 (1991), 152.

9 Ibid., 151. My indebtedness to Amishai-Maisels' treatment of the subject is evident. See also Jeremy Cohen, *Christ Killers: The Jews and the Passion from the Bible to the Big Screen* (New York, 2007), 166.

10 Cited in Moore, *Sacred Dread*, 137.

11 For the preceding, see: Judith D. Suther, "Images of Indestructible Israël: Raïssa Maritain on Marc Chagall," in Robert Royal, ed., *Jacques Maritain and the Jews* (Notre Dame, IN, 1994), 157; and Raïssa Maritain, "Chagall," *L'Art sacré*, nos. 11–12 (July–August 1950), 26–30.

12 Maritain, "La passion d'Israël," (1944), reprinted in idem, *Le Mystère d'Israël et autres essais* (Paris, 1965), 202–203.

13 Richard Francis Crane, *Passion of Israel: Jacques Maritain, Catholic Conscience, and the Holocaust* (Scranton, PA, 2010), 107–108.

14 Paule Berger Marx, *Les Relations entre les juifs et les catholiques dans la France de l'après-guerre 1945–1965* (Paris, 2009), 405–406.

15 François Mauriac, preface to Léon Poliakov, *Bréviaire de la haine. Le IIIe Reich et les Juifs* (Paris, 1974 [orig. 1951]), 8.

16 Poliakov was borrowing from Jacques Madaule on this point. See Poliakov, *Bréviaire de la haine*, 21–24 and 442n1. Jonathan Judaken has explored this line of analysis. See idem, "Léon Poliakov, the Origins of Holocaust Studies, and Theories of Anti-Semitism: Rereading *Bréviaire de la haine*," in Seán Hand and Steven T. Katz, eds., *Post-Holocaust France and the Jews, 1945–1955* (New York, 2015), 177–185.

17 Poliakov, *Bréviaire de la haine*, 22n1, 442–443.

18 Ibid., 436–437, 440–443.

19 See Crane, *Passion of Israel*, 116–117.

20 Mauriac preface to Poliakov, *Bréviaire de la haine*, 8–10.

21 Mauriac, *Bloc-notes* (Paris, 1993), entry of 23 April 1963, III: 346.

22 Mauriac, preface to Poliakov, *Bréviaire de la haine*, 9. For Mauriac in the 1930s and on Mendès France, see Saul Friedländer, *Nazi Germany and the Jews, 1939–1945: The Years of Extermination* (New York, 2007), 113; and idem, *Où mène le souvenir. Ma vie* (Paris, 2016), 42.

23 Mauriac, preface to Poliakov, *Bréviaire de la haine*, 8, 10.

24 Wiesel dates the meeting to 1954 in *Un Juif aujourd'hui: récits, essais, dialogues* (Paris, 1977), 28–29. Elsewhere, he writes about the rendezvous taking place in the spring of 1955: *All Rivers Run to the Sea. Memoirs* (New York, 1995), 258. Mauriac himself wrote of a May 1955 encounter: *Bloc-notes* (Paris, 1993), entry of 14 May 1955, I: 271.

25 Mauriac tried first to place the text with his own publisher, Grasset, but was refused. In the meantime, he was contacted by Lindon, who was fishing for a preface to yet another survivor memoir, Micheline Maurel's *Un Camp très ordinaire* (Paris, 1957). Mauriac agreed on condition that Lindon take a look at Wiesel's manuscript. See Michaël de Saint-Cheron, *Entretiens avec Élie Wiesel, 1984–2000* (Paris, 2008), 96.

26 See Wiesel, *All Rivers Run to the Sea*, 239, 241; Colin Davis, *Elie Wiesel's Secretive Texts* (Gainesville, FL, 1994), 55. The first draft of Wiesel's Yiddish manuscript ran to eight hundred pages. It was whittled down to under two hundred and fifty for the Yiddish-language publication and to under two hundred pages for the French edition. In a 1992 interview, Wiesel claimed that he prepared the French text from the Yiddish original, condensing it from "some eight hundred pages" to "a hundred and sixty." See Harry James Cargas, *Conversations with Elie Wiesel* (South Bend, IN, 1992 [orig. 1976, under the title *Harry James Cargas in Conversation with Elie Wiesel*]), 89. In his memoirs, however, Wiesel credits Lindon with making the final cut that dropped the text to "178" pages. See idem, *All Rivers Run to the Sea*, 319.

27 The phrase is taken from the title of Naomi Seidman's article cited above, "Elie Wiesel and the Scandal of Jewish Rage." See also David G. Roskies, *Against the Apocalypse. Reponses to Catastrophe in Modern Jewish Culture* (Cambridge, MA, 1984), 301–302.

28 Davis, *Elie Wiesel's Secretive Texts*, 53; André Neher, *L'Exil de la parole. Du silence biblique au silence d'Auschwitz* (Paris, 1970), 233.

29 Wiesel, *All Rivers Run to the Sea*, 266; idem, *Un Juif aujourd'hui*, 30.

30 Mauriac's preface to Wiesel, *La Nuit* (Paris, 2007 [orig. 1958]), 25–26.

31 Ibid., *La Nuit*, 27–28, 30.

32 Mauriac, *Bloc-notes*, entry of 29 May 1963, III: 361–362; Saint-Cheron, *Élie Wiesel. Pèlerin de la mémoire* (Paris, 1994), 154; and Roskies, *Against the Apocalypse*, 262.

33 Mauriac, preface to Wiesel, *La Nuit*, 29–30.

34 I owe David Bellos special thanks for making available to me a copy of Wiesel's Yiddish-language *Un di velt hot geshvign*. I am indebted to Simon Backer who provided me a translation of portions of the text and to Rafi Lehmann who also provided help. For the discussion earlier, see Wiesel, *Un di velt hot geshvign* (Buenos Aires, 1956), 237–239; idem, *La Nuit*, 194–195.

35 Rachel Ertel, "Écrits en yiddish," in Michaël de Saint-Cheron, ed., *Une Parole pour l'avenir: autour d'Élie Wiesel. Colloque de Cerisy* (Paris, 1996), 37–38. Wiesel, *Un di velt hot geshvign*, 244–245.

36 Wiesel, *La Nuit*, 199–200.

37 Cargas, *Conversations with Elie Wiesel*, 33.

38 Saint-Cheron, *Élie Wiesel*, 115–116.

39 Cargas, *Conversations with Elie Wiesel*, 65–66, 138; interview with Ira Nadel, 29 September 1979, reprinted in Irving Abrahamson, ed., *Against Silence: The Voice and Vision of Elie Wiesel* (New York, 1985), II: 111–112. See also Francine Kaufmann, "La naissance d'un discours littéraire juif autour de la Shoa [sic] en France et en Israël: parallélismes et dissemblances," *Pardès*, nos. 9–10 (1989), 69; Omer Bartov, *Mirrors of Destruction: War, Genocide, and Modern Identity* (New York, 2000), 196–197; Anny Dayan Rosenman, *Les Alphabets de la Shoah: survivre, témoigner, écrire* (Paris, 2013), 44; and Alan Mintz, "Du silence à l'évidence: interprétation de la Shoa dans la culture américaine," in Françoise S. Ouzan and Dan Michman, *De la Mémoire de la Shoa dans le monde juif* (Paris, 2008), 267. On Camus, see Alice Kaplan, *Looking for The Stranger: Albert Camus and the Life of a Literary Classic* (Chicago, 2016), 159.

40 David Bellos has written a suggestive six-page fragment, *How* Night *was Made*, which addresses the literary qualities of Wiesel's narrative. I am grateful to him once again for sharing it with me and for allowing me to cite from it. For the allusion to Resnais' documentary in Wiesel's title, see p. 4.

41 Bellos, passim.

42 Wiesel, *Un Juif aujourd'hui*, 28; see also Saint-Cheron, *Élie Wiesel*, 153.

43 Interview between H. J. Cargas and Wiesel, September 1971, reprinted in Abrahamson, ed., *Against Silence*, I: 272. In the same volume, see Wiesel's address to the United Jewish Appeal, 14 December 1972, 134; and also Cargas, *Conversations with Elie Wiesel*, 34–35, 48.

44 Wiesel, *La Nuit*, 122–125 and Mauriac's preface, 28–29. For this line of interpretation, see Neher, *L'Exil de la parole*, 236; Ellen S. Fine, *Legacy of Night: The Literary Universe of Elie Wiesel* (Albany, 1982), 28.

45 Or Anne Franck as Mauriac misspells the name in his preface to Wiesel, *La Nuit*, 27.

46 Saint-Cheron, *Élie Wiesel*, 166.

47 For the quotations, see Wiesel, *La Nuit*, 64, 75; and for a discussion of the issue of believability, see Davis, *Elie Wiesel's Secretive Texts*, 33.

48 Wiesel, *La Nuit*, 95.

49 Cargas, *Conversations with Elie Wiesel*, 8, 56–57. See also: Rosenman, *Les Alphabets de la Shoah*, 129; Annette Wieviorka, *L'Ère du témoin* (Paris, 1998), 63.

50 Wiesel, review of Oskar Pincus, *The House of Ashes*, in the *New York Times Book Review*, 6 September 1964, reprinted in Abrahamson, ed., *Against Silence*, II: 278. Wiesel had used the term the year preceding in a *New York Review of Books* essay without elaborating on its meaning. See Wiesel, review of Joseph Bor, *The Terezin Requiem*, in *NYRB*, 27 October 1963, reprinted in Abrahamson, ed., *Against Silence*, II: 269. In later years, Wiesel was less sure that *Holocaust* was the best term to describe the genocide of the Jews. He preferred it to *Shoah* because it conjured images of fire; it had a poetic resonance and "a mystic religious density" that *Shoah* did not. That said, he was appalled by the American television series, *Holocaust*, first aired in 1978. For Wiesel, the show's vulgarity tarnished the integrity of the term and made him want to look for another. Saint-Cheron, *Élie Wiesel*, 246; interview with Helen Fine, Fall 1980, reprinted in Abrahamson, ed., *Against Silence*, I: 185–186.

51 Wiesel, *La Nuit*, 195.
52 Neher, *L'Exil de la parole*, 234; Francine Kaufmann, "Holocauste ou Shoah? Génocide ou '*Hourbane*'? Quels mots pour dire Auschwitz? Histoire et enjeux des choix et des rejets de mots désignant la Shoah," *Revue d'histoire de la Shoah*, no. 184 (January–June 2006), 354.
53 Cargas, *Conversations with Elie Wiesel*, 162.
54 See Wiesel's statement to the Niles Township Jewish Congregation, 7 December 1980, reprinted in Abrahamson, ed., *Against Silence*, I: 385. See also Cargas, *Conversations with Elie Wiesel*, 107, 126.
55 Ertel, "Écrits en yiddish," 34; Rosenman, *Les Alphabets de la Shoah*, 179–183.
56 Cohen, *Christ Killers*, 40.
57 Wiesel, *All Rivers Run to the Sea*, 272.
58 Michaël de Saint-Cheron, *Élie Wiesel*, 165.
59 Francine Kaufmann, *Pour Relire "Le Dernier des Justes"* (Paris, 1986), 13.
60 Francine Kaufmann, "Les enjeux de la polémique autour du premier best-seller français de la littérature de la Shoah," *Revue d'histoire de la Shoah*, no. 176 (September–December 2002), 69.
61 IMEC, Fonds Le Seuil, Dernier des Justes, E49, back cover text: "Shifting seamlessly from legend to chronicle, then to novel, André Schwarz-Bart goes far beyond testimony...." See also Rosenman, *Les Alphabets de la Shoah*, 171.
62 André Schwarz-Bart, *Le Dernier des Justes* (Paris, 1959), 12.
63 The point is made by Kaufmann in "Les enjeux de la polémique autour du premier best-seller français de la littérature de la Shoah," 70.
64 Paul-André Lesort, "Terrifiant Schwarz-Bart," *Les Nouvelles littéraires*, no. 2057 (2 février 1967), 7
65 Simone de Beauvoir, *La Force des choses* (Paris, 1963), 504–505.
66 For the quote from Mandel, see Kaufmann, "Holocauste ou Shoah? Génocide ou '*Hourbane*'? Quels mots pour dire Auschwitz? Histoire et enjeux des choix et des rejets des mots désignant Shoah," 368; for Poliakov, see idem, "Les enjeux de la polémique autour du premier best-seller français de la littérature de la Shoah," 89–92.
67 Lesort, "Terrifiant Schwarz-Bart," 7.
68 Jean Lacouture, *Paul Flamand, éditeur. La grande aventure des Éditions du Seuil* (Paris, 2010), 80, 106–109.
69 Personal communication from Véronique Chabrol, 26 March 2019.
70 Solzhenitsyn was drawn to Le Seuil because it was a "Christian house." See Lacouture, *Paul Flamand*, 154.
71 Wiesel, *All Rivers Run to the Sea*, 329.
72 Lacouture, *Paul Flamand*, 109.
73 For Father Guissard, see "Controverses: théâtre, roman, cinéma," *Recherches et Débats du Centre Catholique des Intellectuels Français*, cahier 32 (September 1960), 92–93. Domenach, *Esprit* (October 1959), as cited in Azouvi, *Le Mythe du grand silence*, 167.
74 Claire Toupin-Guyot, *Les Intellectuels catholiques dans la société française. Le Centre catholique des intellectuels français (1941–1976)* (Rennes, 2002), 38–43, 63–70.
75 Kaufmann, *Pour Relire "Le Dernier des Justes,"* 27.

76 Schwarz-Bart, *Le Dernier des Justes*, 153.
77 Ibid., 154–159. The English translation describes Ernie Levy as falling to the ground "his arms crossed," which doesn't quite capture the allusion to the Crucifixion. See Schwarz-Bart, *The Last of the Just*, tr. Stephen Becker (New York, 1973), 138.
78 Schwarz-Bart, *Le Dernier des Justes*, 153, 187, 195–196, 294.
79 Ibid., 407, 418–419. See also Annette Wieviorka, *L'Ère du témoin*, 108.
80 Schwarz-Bart, *Le Dernier des Justes*, 367–368.
81 See the discussion in Kaufmann, *Pour Relire "Le Dernier des justes,"* 192–194, 217.
82 Schwarz-Bart, *Le Dernier des Justes*, 69, 423–425.
83 See Schwarz-Bart's remarks in Kaufmann, "Entretien avec André Schwarz-Bart," *Pardès*, no. 6 (1987), 156. The interview dates from 29 August 1972.
84 Schwarz-Bart, *Le Dernier des Justes*, 49, 81. See also Kaufmann, *Pour Relire "Le Dernier des Justes,"* 72, 79.
85 Kaufmann, "Les enjeux de la polémique autour du premier best-seller français de la littérature de la Shoah," 74; IMEC, Fonds Le Seuil, Dernier des Justes, SEL2S2B726D5, which includes a folder containing photographs of four Chagall paintings, all dealing with themes of Jewish martyrdom and persecution.
86 For these scenes, see Schwarz-Bart, *Le Dernier des Justes*, 48, 84–85, 304–306, 397.
87 The interviewer is Francine Kaufmann, the most knowledgeable of Schwarz-Bart's interpreters. Kaufmann, "Entretien avec André Schwarz-Bart," 150.
88 Kaufmann, "Entretien avec André Schwarz-Bart," 153–154, 156.
89 Schwarz-Bart, *Le Dernier des Justes*, 425. For a similar but not identical interpretation, see Kaufmann, *Pour Relire "Le Dernier des Justes,"* 209.
90 De Beauvoir, *La Force des choses*, 507–508.
91 Schwarz-Bart, *La Mulâtresse Solitude* (Paris, 1972), 37.
92 Ibid., 147.
93 Ibid., 156.
94 Simone and André Schwarz-Bart, *Un Plat de porc aux bananes vertes* (Paris, 1967), 7. The protagonist is an aged woman named Mariotte, who is descended from Solitude. She has found her way to an old people's home in Paris, and the novel purports to be a transcription of Mariotte's diary. It is filled with memories of home and a deep longing to relive the sensual and emotional satisfactions that home had afforded. It is also full of wry commentary on her fellow "inmates," white French women, who are sometimes sympathetic souls but just as often vehicles of pettiness and prejudice. Among the white women is one Biquette, a monomaniac with a number tattooed on her arm. She is a mysterious figure who doesn't seem to have in fact been in the camps. She may not even be Jewish, but bangs her head whenever the word "Jew" is uttered. Ibid., 87–88.
95 Schwarz-Bart identified himself as a Zionist. Kaufmann, "Entretien avec André Schwarz-Bart," 156. For Schwarz-Bart's relations with Wiesel, see Wiesel, *All Rivers Run to the Sea*, 346; and idem, *And the Sea Is Never Full: Memoirs, 1969–* (New York, 1999), 56.

96 Saul Friedländer, *Kurt Gerstein ou l'ambiguité du bien* (Tournai, 1967), 143.
97 Friedländer, *Où mène le souvenir*, 118.
98 For Friedländer's remark to Flamand, see Lacouture, *Paul Flamand*, 164. See also Friedländer, "Pourquoi j'ai écrit 'Pie XII et le IIIe Reich,'" *L'Arche* (November 1964), 24; and idem, *Où mène le souvenir*, 119–120.
99 Friedländer, *Où mène la souvenir*, 122–123; idem, post-lecture question and answer period, "Pie XII and the Holocaust: A Reassessment," Princeton University, 12 April 2010; Wiesel, *All Rivers Run to the Sea*, 329.
100 Friedländer, post-lecture question and answer period, "Pie XII and the Holocaust: A Reassessment," Princeton University, 12 April 2010; idem, *Où mène le souvenir*, 124; "Pourquoi j'ai écrit 'Pie XII et le IIIe Reich,'" 24.
101 Friedländer, *Où mène le souvenir*, 124.
102 Grosser's afterword, Friedländer, *Pie XII et le IIIe Reich* (Paris, 1964), 221–232.
103 For these developments, see IMEC, Fonds Le Seuil, Pie XII et le IIIe Reich, SEL2077.9: Jean Lacouture, document titled "Friedländer," nd; letter from Simonne Lacouture to Friedländer, 26 August 1964; letter from the Abbé Pezeril to Madame [Lacouture], 30 August 1964; letter from Simonne Lacouture to the Abbé Pezeril, 8 September 1964. See also Lacouture, *Paul Flamand*, 164–165; and Friedländer, *Où mène le souvenir*, 123.
104 IMEC, Fonds Le Seuil, Pie XII et le IIIe Reich, SEL2S2B458D3, jacket copy.
105 Frideländer, *Où mène le souvenir*, 125; idem, "Pourquoi j'ai écrit 'Pie XII et le IIIe Reich,'" 24.
106 The book was also dedicated to Poliakov. Friedländer, *Où mène le souvenir*, 131; Poliakov afterword in idem, *Kurt Gerstein*, 193–203.
107 Friedländer, *Kurt Gerstein*, 191–192.
108 Friedländer, *Où mène le souvenir*, 114; idem, *Antisémitisme nazi: histoire d'une psychose collective* (1971) and *History and Psychoanalysis: An Inquiry into the Possibilities and Limits of Psychohistory* (1978).
109 Friedländer's search for a voice is recounted in *Où mène le souvenir*, 212.
110 The story of Friedländer's changing names is even more complicated than that: he was Pavel in Czechoslovakia, Paul in France, and then, when he entered boarding school, Paul-Henri Ferland. In Israel, he adopted a Hebrew name for a short time, Shaul, adapting it to Saül when he returned to France before eventually settling on Saul. See Friedländer, *Où mène le souvenir*, 33.
111 Saul Friedländer, *When Memory Comes*, tr. Helen R. Lane (New York, 1979), 78–80, 110, 135–139
112 Ibid., 185.

8 The Teaching of Contempt

1 Étienne Fouilloux, "L'étape Vatican II," in Annette Becker, Danielle Delmaire, and Frédéric Gugelot, *Juifs et Chrétiens: entre ignorance, hostilité et rapprochement (1898–1998)* (Lille, 2002), 209.

2 Paule Berger Marx, *Les Relations entre les juifs et les catholiques dans la France de l'après-guerre, 1945–1965* (Paris, 2009), 57–58.

3 Fadiey Lovsky, "Les premières années de l'Amité Judéo-Chrétienne," *Sens* (1998), 260.

4 Jacques Maritain, "Lettre à la Conférence de Seelisberg," 28 July 1947, in idem, *Oeuvres complètes* (Fribourg and Paris, 1992), XII: 637–645.

5 Rabbi Kaplan cited in Carol Iancu, "Le cheminement de Jules Isaac: de l'Affaire Dreyfus à *L'Enseignement du mépris*," in Becker, Delmaire, and Gugelot, *Juifs et Chrétiens*, 169. Pierre Pierrard, *Le Grand Rabbin Kaplan, justice pour la foi juive. Dialogue avec Pierre Pierrard* (Paris, 1995), 143–144.

6 Pierrard, *Le Grand Rabbin Kaplan*, 144.

7 For the Seelisberg theses, see "Les dix points de la rencontre de Seelisberg 1947)," in *Revue d'histoire de la Shoah*, no. 192 (January–June 2010), 360–362.

8 Berger Marx, *Les Relations entre les juifs et les catholiques*, 208–209; Iancu, "Le cheminement de Jules Isaac," 173; Michael Phayer, *The Catholic Church and the Holocaust, 1930–1965* (Bloomington, IN, 2000), 204–205; André Kaspi, *Jules Isaac. Historien, acteur du rapprochement judéo-chrétien* (Paris, 2002), 231.

9 See Norman C. Tobias, *Jewish Conscience of the Church: Jules Isaac and the Second Vatican Council* (New York, 2017).

10 The source to consult on Isaac's early years is Kaspi's biography, *Jules Isaac*, 41–42, 73, 93, 180, 247–250. See also Doris Bensimon, *Les Juifs de France et leurs relations avec Israël, 1945–1988* (Paris, 1989), 226.

11 For the preceding, see: Kaspi, *Jules Isaac*, 160–185; Iancu, "Le cheminement de Jules Isaac," 165–166; Berger Marx, *Les Relations entre les juifs et les catholiques*, 132; and Patrick Cabanel, "Le protestantisme français face à la Shoah et à l'antisémitisme, de 1945 à nos jours," *Revue d'histoire de la Shoah*, no. 192 (January–June 2010), 69.

12 Jules Isaac, *Jésus et Israël* (Paris, 1959), 572.

13 An argument fleshed out in Nina Valbousquet, "Conscience historique et mémorielle du genocide: Jules Isaac et *Jésus et Israël*, rescapés de la Shoah," *Archives Juives*, no. 51 (2018): 78–98.

14 Ibid., 81.

15 Isaac, *Jésus et Israël*, 418–420.

16 Ibid., 403.

17 Ibid., 274, 405–406, 457–458, 484.

18 Ibid., 508.

19 Ibid., 363, 368.

20 Isaac, *L'Enseignement du mépris*, 63, 105.

21 Isaac, *Jésus et Israël*, 459, 476, 560. So was *L'Enseignement du mépris*. Daniel-Rops, it will be recalled, treated biblical Judaism as dried up and exhausted, a parched desert that Jesus' teachings had made to bloom once more. In *L'Enseignement du mépris* (90–92), Isaac cited by way of riposte the findings of the archaeological team that had worked at Qumran in what is today Israel. Here, in 1947, had been found the Dead Sea Scrolls, dating from the first century BCE, which detailed the life of a Jewish sect, the Essenes. They were ascetics obsessed with a water-washed cleanliness, who professed an

apocalyptic brand of messianism. So perhaps, Isaac speculated, John the Baptist had Essene antecedents and Christian Messianism itself owed more than a little to messianic currents already coursing through Jewish life in the very era Jesus came to maturity. Jewish religion, in a word, was not the dead letter of Christian imagining but fertile soil from which Christianity itself had sprouted. See also Berger Marx, *Les Relations entre les juifs et les catholiques*, 349ff.; Phayer, *The Catholic Church*, 207.

22 Isaac, *L'Enseignement du mépris*, 137–139, Kaspi, *Jules Isaac*, 186–187.

23 Berger Marx, *Les Relations entre les juifs et les catholiques*, 188; Iancu, "Le cheminement de Jules Isaac," 166–167.

24 Berger Marx, "Jean Daniélou, les Juifs et la Shoah," *Revue d'histoire de la Shoah*, no. 192 (January–June 2010), 94–95; Kaspi, *Jules Isaac*, 212–213. .

25 The text of Marrou's review, titled "Trois Apostilles," is reprinted in *Revue d'histoire de la Shoah*, no. 192 (January–June 2010), 373–383. See also Berger Marx, *Les Relations entre les juifs et les catholiques*, 269–276.

26 Madaule was also prescient enough to recognize that the new state was creating problems for itself in the way it dealt with its Arab citizens. See Jacques Madaule, *Le Retour d'Israël* (Paris, 1951), 7, 167, 186, 190–194.

27 For a useful timeline, consult Catherine Poujol, "1945–1953: Petite chronique de l'affaire des enfants Finaly," *Archives juives*, no. 37 (2004), 7–15.

28 Michael Marrus, "The Vatican and the Custody of Jewish Child Survivors after the Holocaust," *Holocaust and Genocide Studies*, 21 (Winter 2007), 378–403.

29 Catherine Poujol, *Les Enfants cachés: l'affaire Finaly* (Paris, 2006), 41, 47, 80–81, 137–138.

30 Cited in Pierrard, *Le Grand Rabbin Kaplan*, 189–190. See also idem, 171–173; Poujol, *Les Enfants cachés*, 131–134; and Joyce Bloch Lazarus, *In the Shadow of Vichy: The Finaly Affair* (New York, 2008), 39.

31 Poujol, *Les Enfants cachés*, 159, 163, 165–166; Virginie Sansico, "L'Affaire Finaly: une controverse religieuse?" *Revue d'histoire de la Shoah*, no. 192 (January–June 2010), 312.

32 Lazarus, *In the Shadow of Vichy*, 63.

33 Poujol, *Les Enfants cachés*, 203–207, 253; Pierrard, *Le Grand Rabbin Kaplan*, 185–188; Lazarus, *In the Shadow of Vichy*, 44.

34 Lazarus, *In the Shadow of Vichy*, 111; Poujol, "Le grand rabbin Jacob Kaplan et l'affaire Finaly: guide, porte-parole et négociateur de la communauté juive de France," *Archives juives*, 37/2 (2004), 33, 42; idem, *Les Enfants cachés*, 163, 197, 253, 268–269.

35 Poujol, *Les Enfants cachés*, 189–190, 194.

36 Berger Marx, *Les Relations entre les juifs et les catholiques*, 247.

37 Ibid., 252; Mauriac cited in Poujol, *Les Enfants cachés*, 110, and see also 116–117 for Marrou's position.

38 APFSJ Fonds Riquet, L'Affaire Finaly 1953, 25, dossier Affaire Finaly, letter from Father Michel Riquet to Félix Goldschmidt, 17 April 1953. See also: clipping from *Le Monde*, 17 February 1953; letter from Father Michel Riquet to Monseigneur le Cardinal, 3 March 1953; clipping from unidentified

newspaper titled "Les déportés disent leur mot," 13 April 1953; and letter from Cardinal Gerlier to "Mon cher Père et Ami," 20 June 1953.

39 Sansico, "L'Affaire Finaly: une controverse religieuse?" 311, 314.

40 Keller had once belonged to the Party but was no longer a member. He remained, however, a *gauchiste* at heart close to Mapam, a Marxist-Zionist party on the Israeli Left. Poujol, *Les Enfants cachés*, 56–58, 260; idem, "Le grand rabbin Jacob Kaplan et l'affaire Finaly," 37–39.

41 Poujol, *Les Enfants cachés*, 113, 221, 269; idem, "Le grand rabbin Jacob Kaplan et l'affaire Finaly," 45–46; idem, "1945–1953: Petite chronique," 15.

42 Poujol, *Les Enfants cachés*, 126, 294–295; idem, "Le grand rabbin Jacob Kaplan et l'affaire Finaly," 48.

43 Poujol, "Le grand rabbin Jacob Kaplan et l'affaire Finaly," 48.

44 Berger Marx, *Les Relations entre les juifs et les catholiques*, 309–310, 494. See also Anne-Denise Rinckwald, "Affaire Finaly," in Becker, Delmaire, and Gugelot, *Juifs et Chrétiens*, 191.

45 Berger Marx, *Les Relations entre les juifs et les catholiques*, 407–408.

46 Iancu, "Le cheminement de Jules Isaac," 171; Pierrard, *Le Grand Rabbin Kaplan*, 212.

47 See John Connelly, *From Enemy to Brother: The Revolution in Catholic Teaching on the Jews, 1933–1965* (Cambridge, MA, 2012), passim.

48 Kaspi, *Jules Isaac*, 232; John W. O'Malley, *What Happened at Vatican II* (Cambridge, MA. 2008), 219; Rinckwald, "Affaire Finaly," 190.

49 The meeting is discussed in Iancu, "Le cheminement de Jules Isaac," 173–174.

50 Father Oesterreicher emigrated to the United States in 1940, entering on a visa that Maritain helped him to obtain. Jean-Luc Barré, *Jacques et Raïssa Maritain. Les mendiants du ciel* (Paris, 2009), 491.

51 Fouilloux, "L'étape Vatican II," 197; Connelly, *From Enemy to Brother*, 241.

52 Connelly, *From Enemy to Brother*, 249.

53 Phayer, *The Catholic Church*, 212–213.

54 Connelly, *From Enemy to Brother*, 251.

55 On the council's deliberations, see O'Malley, *What Happened at Vatican II*, 220–276.

56 Richard Francis Crane, *Passion of Israel: Jacques Maritain, Catholic Conscience and the Holocaust* (Scranton, PA, 2010), 126.

57 Pierrard, *Le Grand Rabbin Kaplan*, 213, 228; Berger Marx, *Les Relations entre les juifs et les catholiques*, 463–464, 468; Bensimon, *Les Juifs de France*, 230–231.

9 Witnesses

1 Annette Wieviorka, *L'Ère du témoin* (Paris, 1998), 81; see also idem, "Shoah. Les Étapes de la mémoire en France," in Pascal Blanchard and Isabelle Veyrat, eds., *Les Guerres de mémoire. France et son histoire* (Paris, 2008), 110.

2 Sylvie Lindeperg and Annette Wieviorka, *Univers concentrationnaire et génocide. Voir, savoir, comprendre* (Paris, 2008), 113; François Azouvi, *Le Mythe du grand silence. Auschwitz, les Français, la mémoire* (Paris, 2012), 187, 195.

3 See the superb discussion of Hurwitz's work in Lindeperg and Wieviorka, *Univers concentrationnaire et génocide*, ch. 3.

4 "Le professeur Wellers en face d'Eichmann," *Le Déporté*, nos. 155–156 (June–July 1961).

5 See Lindeperg and Wieviorka, eds., *Le Moment Eichmann* (Paris, 2016). This is an excellent collection, with strong articles on Israel, the United States, and Germany. The essay on France by Isabelle Delpla ("Chroniques judiciaires") is also excellent, but just deals with the press coverage of the trial.

6 "Les Écrivains devant le fait concentrationnaire," *L'Arche*, no. 50 (March 1961), 30. The eight were: Édouard Axelrad, Louis Martin-Chauffier, Pierre Gascar (the pen-name of Pierre Fournier), Anna Langfus, Robert Merle, David Rousset, Manès Sperber, and Elie Wiesel. Half the group were not Jewish: Martin-Chauffier, Gascar, Merle, and Rousset. Gascar, who has not been encountered before in these pages, was the author of a haunting and idiosyncratic text, *Le Temps des morts* (1953), which dealt with the author's experiences in the disciplinary camp of Rawa Ruska. Axelrad published *L'Arche ensevelie* in 1959, a chronicle of a fictional ghetto, Lewski, whose inhabitants are slated for eventual extermination in the equally fictional death camp of Trebibor.

7 Julie Maeck, *Montrer la Shoah à la télévision de 1960 à nos jours* (Paris, 2009), 57; André Pierre Colombat, *The Holocaust in French Film* (Metuchen, NJ, 1993), 367.

8 Lindeperg, *Clio de 5 à 7. Les actualités filmées de la Libération: archives du futur* (Paris, 2000), 182; Annette Insdorf, *Indelible Shadows: Film and the Holocaust*, Third Edition (New York, 1983), 375n18.

9 Maeck, *Montrer la Shoah à la télévision*, 54.

10 Cited in Jean-Yves Potel, *Les Disparitions d'Anna Langfus* (Paris, 2014), 110–111.

11 "Les Écrivains devant le fait concentrationnaire," 35.

12 Francine Kauffmann, "Les enjeux de la polémique autour du premier best-seller français de la littérature de la Shoah," *Revue d'histoire de la Shoah*, no. 176 (September–December 2002), 79–81.

13 Calmann-Lévy was the publisher. Sperber, *...qu'une larme dans l'océan* (Paris, 1952).

14 Annette Wieviorka, "Manès Sperber: le juif universaliste," *L'Histoire*, no. 417 (November 2015), 42–43.

15 Langfus cited in Alexandre Prstojevic, "La modernité littéraire de Piotr Rawicz," in Anny Dayan Rosenman and Fransiska Louwagie, eds., *Un Ciel de sang et des cendres. Piotr Rawicz et la solitude du témoin* (Paris, 2013), 314. See also "Les Écrivains devant le fait concentrationnaire," 33.

16 "Les Écrivains devant le fait concentrationnaire," 32–33.

17 Cited in Potel, *Les Disparitions*, 146.

18 See Langfus' remarks in "Les Écrivains devant le fait concentrationnaire," 33. See also Ellen S. Fine, "Le témoin comme romancier: Anna Langfus et le problème de la distance," *Pardès*, no. 17 (1993), 94; and Potel, *Les Disparitions*, 177.

19 Anna Langfus, *Le Sel et le soufre* (Paris, 1960), 212.

20 Ibid., 373. For the trunk as cradle, coffin, shipwreck, see the analysis of Anny Dayan Rosenman, *Les Alphabets de la Shoah. Survivre, témoigner, écrire* (Paris, 2007), 52.

21 Potel, *Les Disparitions*, 189.

22 Ibid., 188–189; Fine, "Le témoin comme romancier," 97.

23 Fine, "Le témoin comme romancier," 105; Potel, *Les Disparitions*, 191, 217; Myriam Ruszniewski-Dahan, *Romanciers de la Shoah. Si l'écho de leur voix faiblit…* (Paris, 1999), 111.

24 Langfus, *Les Bagages de sable* (Paris, 1962), 88, 126.

25 Ruszniewski-Dahan, *Romanciers de la Shoah*, 192–193; Potel, *Les Disparitions*, 213–218.

26 In fact, by Rabi in a review published in *L'Arche*. See Potel, *Les Disparitions*, 256.

27 Langfus, *Saute, Barbara* (Paris, 1965), 258.

28 Ibid., 25.

29 Ibid., 99.

30 For the quotes in the preceding paragraph, see Anna Langfus, "Conversation avec P. Rawicz," *L'Arche*, no. 61 (February 1962), 16–17.

31 Christoph Graf von Schwerin, "Je pense que je serai votre éditeur en allemand," in Rosenman and Louwagie, eds., *Un Ciel de sang et des cendres*, 32–33.

32 Anthony Rudolf, "Porter le fardeau de l'Histoire et de la souffrance," in Rosenman and Louwagie, eds., *Un Ciel de sang et des cendres*, 210, 212–213.

33 "Entretien avec André Bourin," in Rosenman and Louwagie, eds., *Un Ciel de sang et des cendres*, 90.

34 Rawicz, preface to Danilo Kiš, *Sablier* (1982), in Rosenman and Louwagie, eds., *Un Ciel de sang et des cendres*, 389.

35 Piotr Rawicz, *Le Sang du ciel* (Paris, 1961), 16.

36 Ibid., 132–139.

37 Ibid., 220.

38 See the preface to Rosenman and Louwagie, eds., *Un Ciel de sang et des cendres*, 12.

39 Rawicz, *Le Sang du ciel*, 54. This passage is discussed in Rosenman, "Piotr Rawicz: témoigner dans la blessure du texte," in idem, and Louwagie, eds., *Un Ciel de sang et des cendres*, 193–195.

40 Rawicz, *Le Sang du ciel*, 152–156. Jerzy Kosinski made use of a similar image in *The Painted Bird* (New York 1965), 23–26. The novel's hero, a parentless Jewish boy, wanders around wartime Poland. A superstitious old crone takes him in at one point. The boy falls ill with a high fever, and she buries him up to the neck by way of a cure. While buried, ravens come to peck at the boy's face, as they would peck at a head of cabbage. The old woman digs him out before he is eaten.

41 Rawicz, *Le Sang du ciel*, 217.

42 Rosenman, *Les Alphabets de la Shoah*, 213

43 Rawicz, *Le Sang du ciel*, 250–251. On this scene, see Alexandre Prstojevic, *Le Témoin et la Bibliothèque. Comment la Shoah est devenue un sujet romanesque* (Nantes, 2012), 74–76.

44 Rawicz, *Le Sang du ciel*, 277.
45 Ibid., 240.
46 Ibid., 227, 241.
47 Rawicz cited in Rosenman, *Les Alphabets de la Shoah*, 67; and in Catherine Coquio, "Rawicz. Le destructeur," in Rosenman and Louwagie, eds., *Un Ciel de sang et des cendres*, 250.
48 Rawicz, *Bloc-notes d'un contre-révolutionnaire ou La gueule de bois* (Paris, 1969), 90.
49 Ibid., 12.
50 Rawicz, "Une triple solitude" (1975), in Rosenman and Louwagie, eds., *Un Ciel de sang et des cendres*, 364–365.
51 Steven Jaron, "Ontologie et néantologie dans les écrits de Piotr Rawicz," in Rosenman and Louwagie, eds., *Un Ciel de sang et des cendres*, 341–342.
52 Ibid., 341. The quotation is from a 1979 text.
53 Rawicz, *Bloc-notes*, 42.
54 "Frédéric Rossif. Interview par Michel Capdenac," *Les Lettres françaises* (16–22 November 1961), 6.
55 Colombat, *The Holocaust in French Film*, 34; and Polanski cited in Insdorf, *Indelible Shadows*, 241.
56 Frédéric Rossif. Interview par Michel Capdenac," *Les Lettres françaises* (16–22 November 1961), 6.
57 On Rossif and Poliakov, see Claudine Drame, "*Le Temps du ghetto* ou 'L'invention' du témoignage mémoriel," *Revue d'histoire de la Shoah*, no. 195 (July–December 2011), 513; on Rossif and Leiser, see Georges Bensoussan, *Le Temps du ghetto* (Paris, 2008), 29. The Bensoussan text is a brochure included in the 2008 edition of the DVD.
58 As Rossif told an interviewer, what he was after was "the automatic tone of internal memory." See "Frédéric Rossif. Interview par Michel Capdenac," *Les Lettres françaises* (16–22 November 1961), 6.
59 Cited in Drame, "*Le Temps du ghetto*," 527.
60 Ibid., 515.
61 Ibid., 527.
62 Claude Lanzmann, *Le Lièvre de Patagonie. Mémoires* (Paris, 2009), 431.
63 "Frédéric Rossif. Interview par Michel Capdenac," *Les Lettres françaises* (16–22 November 1961), 6. See also Raphaël Basson, "*Le Temps du ghetto*. Représenter l'innommable," *La Revue du cinéma*, 431 (October 1987), 63; and Maeck, *Montrer la Shoah à la télévision*, 61.
64 Sarah Fishman, *From Vichy to the Sexual Revolution: Gender and Family Life in Postwar France* (New York, 2017), 152–153.
65 Drame, "*Le Temps du ghetto*," 530–531.

10 Generation

1 See http://fresques.ina.fr/de-gaulle/fiche-media/Gaulle00139/conference-de-presse-du-27-novembre-1967. Accessed 1 February 2018.
2 Doris Bensimon, *Les Juifs de la France et leurs relations avec Israël* (Paris, 1989), 168.

3 See the roundtable discussion in "Juifs, en France, aujourd'hui," *Esprit*, no. 370 (April 1968), 582.

4 Cited in Bensimon, *Les Juifs de la France*, 166.

5 Joan B. Wolf, *Harnessing the Holocaust: The Politics of Memory in France* (Stanford, CA, 2004), 17 ff. See also Pierre Nora, "Mémoire et identité juives dans la France contemporaine. Les grands déterminants," *Le Débat*, no. 131 (September–October 2004), 22; and Bensimon, *Les Juifs de la France*, 165.

6 Serge Klarsfeld, "Mes amis," *Bulletin de Liaison des Fils et Filles des Déportés Juifs de France*, no. 35 (November 1991), reprinted in *La Chronique des fils et filles: 25 années de militantisme de l'Association: les fils et les filles des déportés juifs de France, 1879–2004* (Paris, 2009)), 312. Hereinafter cited as *Chronique des FFDJF*.

7 The book to consult on the Steiner controversy is Samuel Moyn's *A Holocaust Controversy: The Treblinka Affair in Postwar France* (Waltham, MA, 2005). For Vidal-Naquet's *prise de position*, see idem, xv.

8 Susan Rubin Suleiman, "The 1.5 Generation: Thinking about Child Survivors and the Holocaust," *American Imago*, 59 (Fall 2002), 277–282.

9 Henry Rousso, *Le Syndrome de Vichy, 1944–198...* (Paris, 1987), ch. 3.

10 Klarsfeld himself has been insistent on this point, adding a date of his own to the list of Holocaust consciousness turning points: 1975. See Serge Klarsfeld and Henry Rousso, "Débat entre Serge Klarsfeld et Henry Rousso," *Esprit*, no. 181 (May 1992), 23; and Claude Bochurberg, *Entretiens avec Serge Klarsfeld* (Paris, 1997), 144.

11 For the preceding, see Moyn, *A Holocaust Controversy*, 20–22.

12 Jean-François Steiner, *Treblinka: la révolte d'un camp d'extermination* (Paris, 1966), 11, 137, 166, 284, 365.

13 François Azouvi, *Le Mythe du grand silence. Auschwitz, les Français, la mémoire* (Paris, 2012), 222.

14 Cited in Rousso, *Le Syndrome de Vichy*, 179.

15 Ibid., 179.

16 Levinas, cited in Azouvi, *Le Mythe du grand silence*, 221.

17 Vidal-Naquet, cited in Azouvi, *Le Mythe du grand silence*, 228–229.

18 *Le Nouvel Observateur*: "Eichmann et six millions de juifs," 5 October 1966, 14–19; "Eichmann et les 'conseils juifs'," 12 October 1966, 20–25; and "Hannah Arendt est-elle nazie?" 26 October 1966, 37–39.

19 Cited in Annette Wieviorka, *Eichmann de la traque au procès* (Paris, 2011), 217.

20 The Steiner controversy highlighted the distinction between concentration and extermination camps in a way that had not been done before. This critical point was first made by Moyn, *A Holocaust Controversy*, 82.

21 Steiner, *Treblinka*, 137.

22 On the Cercle Gaston Crémieux, see Judith Friedlander, *Vilna on the Seine: Jewish Intellectuals in France since 1968* (New Haven, CT, 1990), 14–16, 22; Wolf, *Harnessing the Holocaust*, 56. See also Shmuel Trigano's unkind remarks about Marienstras in idem, *La République et les juifs après Copernic* (Paris, 1982), 137ff.

23 Robert O. Paxton, *Vichy France: Old Guard and New Order* (New York, 1972). To this list of findings might be added two more: that Vichy did not act to protect the French against the Occupier's exactions but collaborated with the Germans to the extent the Germans allowed it; and that Vichy did not come to an end in 1944 full stop but left a significant technocratic legacy, hence the phrase "new order" in the book's title.

24 Marcel Ophuls, *Mémoires d'un fils à papa* (Paris, 2014), 176, 179.

25 Simone Veil, *Une Vie* (Paris, 2017 [orig. 2007]), 277–278.

26 See the interview with Ophuls published in *Télérama*, 9 July 2012, which can be found at: www.telerama.fr/television/marcel-ophuls-je-n-aime-pas-me-servir-d-une-camera-comme-d-une-arme,83377.php. Accessed 7 February 2018. This is Ophuls' version of events, and it does not appear to be accurate. It was the Gaullist TV executive Arthur Conte who was the author of these words, and what he in fact said was: "The film destroys myths that the French still need."

27 Ophuls, *Mémoires*, 186–187.

28 Rousso, *Le Syndrome de Vichy*, 125; Rebecca Clifford, *Commemorating the Holocaust: The Dilemmas of Remembrance in France and Italy* (Oxford, 2013), 55, 55n.

29 For the preceding, see the acute and moving review by Stanley Hoffmann, "On 'The Sorrow and the Pity'," *Commentary*, 54 (September 1972), 73–77.

30 Ophuls, *Mémoires*, 278.

31 For Ophuls' filmmaking technique, see the discussion and analysis in Vincent Lowy, *Marcel Ophuls* (Paris, 2008), 41–47, 195, 208. See also Julie Maeck, *Montrer la Shoah à la télévision de1960 à nos jours* (Paris, 2009), 88–92.

32 Marcel Ophuls, "Closely Watched Trains," in Stuart Liebman, ed., *Claude Lanzmann's Shoah Key Essays* (New York, 2007); 78; Annette Insdorf, *Indelible Shadows*, Third Edition (New York, 2009), 238.

33 Audrey Brunetaux, "La Rafle du Vél d'Hiv à la télévision française (1957–1995)," *French Historical Studies*, 41 (February 2018), 136.

34 Ophuls, *Mémoires*, 210–211, 220, 247–248. It was Navasky in fact who later persuaded Ophuls to cover the 1987 trial of Klaus Barbie, Gestapo chief in Lyon under the Occupation. Ophuls accepted the proposition and went on to make a film on the subject, *Hôtel Terminus: The Life and Times of Klaus Barbie* (1988), which won an Academy Award for best documentary.

35 See the analysis in Lowy, *Marcel Ophuls*, 89–90.

36 Ophuls, *Mémoires*, 211n; see also Lowy, *Marcel Ophuls*, 85–86, 102.

37 For the Kiesinger slap and its consequences, see Beate and Serge Klarsfeld, *Mémoires* (Paris, 2015), 99–190.

38 Serge Klarsfeld, "Mes amis," *Chronique des FFDJF*, no. 35 (November 1991), 312; Beate and Serge Klarsfeld, *Mémoires*, 83. David Bellos, *Georges Perec: A Life in Words* (London, 1993), 124.

39 Bochurberg, *Entretiens avec Serge Klarsfeld*, 215.

40 Beate and Serge Klarsfeld, *Mémoires*, 125.

41 Mahler was soon to be a founding member of the Red Army Faction, better known to Americans as the Baader-Meinhof gang. He went on to become a notorious Holocaust-denier.

42 Beate and Serge Klarsfeld, *Mémoires*, 258–262, 271–274, 288–289, 296–297, 373, 383, 386.

43 Serge Klarsfeld, "Évocation d'Henri Golub au cimetière de Kfar Samir à Haïfa, le 18 octobre 1983," *Chronique des FFDJF*, 179–180; idem, "Évocation de Gilbert Ermann au cimetière de Bagneux, le 19 octobre 1983," *Chroniques des FFDJF*, 184–185.

44 Serge Klarsfeld, *Le Mémorial de la Déportation des juifs de France* (Paris, 1978), from the unpaginated introduction.

45 Ibid., unpaginated "notice de technique"; see also Beate and Serge Klarsfeld, *Mémoires*, 412–413.

46 Bellos, *Georges Perec*, 125. See also Katy Hazan, *Les Orphelins de la Shaoh. Les maisons de l'espoir (1944–1960)* (Paris, 2000), 289.

47 See Annette Zaidman, "Julien, Raya, Henri, Glibert, Simon, Charlotte…" [2001] in *Chronique des FFDJF*, 610.

48 A. Zaidman, "Éditorial," *Bulletin*, no. 1 (June 1979), *Chronique des FFDJF*, 112.

49 "Déclaration de Me Klarsfled au Procès de Cologne, le 25 janvier 1980," in *Chronique des FFDJF*, 129–131; Beate and Serge Klarsfeld, *Mémoires*, 444–445.

50 Beate and Serge Klarsfeld, *Mémoires*, 448.

51 See Klarsfeld's speech at the 8 February 2001 flag ceremony of the FFDJF, *Chronique des FFDJF*, 574. For the FFDJF badge and much more, see Olivier Lalieu, *Histoire de la mémoire de la Shoah* (Paris, 2015), 114.

52 Bochurberg, *Entretiens avec Serge Klarsfeld*, 146, 150–151.

53 Ibid., 164.

54 Beate and Serge Klarsfeld, *Mémoires*, 319, 327–330. For much of what follows, see Serge Klarsfeld, *Les Enfants d'Izieu. Une tragédie juive* (Paris, 1984).

55 Klarsfeld, *Les Enfants d'Izieu*, 110.

56 Ibid., 116.

57 Beate and Serge Klarsfeld, *Mémoires*, 377.

58 See the November 2012 interview with Selinger, www.youtube.com/watch?v=EcPjj6p6_Ag, accessed 18 February 2018. See also Serge Barcellini and Annette Wieviorka, *Passant, souviens-toi! Les lieux du souvenir de la Seconde Guerre mondiale en France* (Paris, 1995), 462–465; and Caroline Wiedmer, *The Claims of Memory: Representations of the Holocaust in Contemporary Germany and France* (Ithaca, NY, 1999), 62–69

59 See the excellent discussion in Lalieu, *Histoire de la mémoire de la Shoah*, 100–102; and also Gérard Huber, *Henry Bulawko. Une vie après la vie* (Paris, 2012), 157, 165, 169–170.

60 Wiedmer, *Claims of Memory*, 62; Huber, *Bulawko*, 174.

61 Clifford, *Commemorating the Holocaust*, 67.

62 Klarsfeld is reported to have composed the text. Anna Senik, *L'Histoire mouvementée de la reconnaissance officielle des crimes de Vichy contre les Juifs. Autour de la cérémonie de commémoration de la rafle du Vél' d'Hiv'* (Paris, 2013), 52. My special thanks to Anna Senik for sharing her work with me. See also Bochurberg, *Entretiens avec Serge Klarsfeld*, 305–306.

63 For what follows, see the accounts in Eric Conan and Henry Rousso, *Vichy, un passé qui ne passe pas* (Paris, 1994), ch 1; and Clifford, *Commemorating the Holocaust*, 119–140. Clifford is more sympathetic to Senik's campaign than are Conan and Rousso.

64 Beate and Serge Klarsfeld, *Mémoires*, 549.

65 In English, "National day commemorating the racist and anti-Semitic persecutions committed under the de facto authority of the so-called 'government of the French State.'"

66 It is with this point that Clifford's book begins: idem, *Commemorating the Holocaust*, 1.

67 Barcellini and Wieviorka, *Passant, souviens-toi!* 478–479; Clifford, *Commemorating the Holocaust*, 187; *Maison d'Izieu. L'exposition permanente* (Lyon, 2015), 180–181.

68 Peter Carrier, *Holocaust Monuments and National Memory Cultures in France and Germany since 1989* (New York, 2005), 46, 155–156.

69 Clifford, *Commemorating the Holocaust*, 122; Senik, *L'Histoire mouvementée*, 40; Hervé Hamon and Patrick Rotman, *Génération. Les années de rêve* (Paris, 1987), I: 605–606.

70 Senik, *L'Histoire mouvementée*, 15, 40. See also Clifford, *Commemorating the Holocaust*, 122.

71 Cited from the Comité Vél d'hiv's 16 July 1992 manifesto in *Le Monde*. See Conan and Rousso, *Le Passé qui ne passe pas*, 43.

72 Senik, *L'Histoire mouvementée*, 40.

11 "The Return of the Repressed"

1 Olivier Lalieu, *Histoire de la mémoire de la Shoah* (Paris, 2015), 163–164, 182; Hasia R. Diner, "Origins and meanings of the myth of silence," in David Cesarini and Eric J. Sundquist, eds., *After the Holocaust: Challenging the Myth of Silence* (New York, 2012), 194–195.

2 Diner, *We Remember with Reverence and Love: American Jews and the Myth of Silence after the Holocaust, 1945-1962* (New York, 2009); François Azouvi, *Le Mythe du grand silence. Auschwitz, les Français, la mémoire* (Paris, 2012); Cesarini and Sundquist, eds. *After the Holocaust: Challenging the Myth of Silence*, passim.

3 Romain Gary, *Le Sens de ma vie. Entretien* (Paris, 2014), 53. This interview was conducted in 1980.

4 Ibid., 72–75.

5 Gary, *The Ski Bum* (New York, 1964), 33.

6 Gary, *Le Sens de ma vie*, 86–88.

7 Gary, *La Danse de Gengis Cohn* (Paris, 1967), 26.

8 Ibid., 166.

9 Ibid., 34.

10 Ibid., 95, 264–265.

11 Ibid., 252. Gary in fact sent a copy of the novel to General de Gaulle who replied with a note of thanks. The General remarked on Gary's irony, which spared no one, not even Jews, "scattered and persecuted as they have been for

centuries, then shamefully slaughtered, and among whom there is perhaps nowadays an imperialist tendency." De Gaulle's note is dated 7 August 1967, three months before the notorious news conference where he expressed the near identical views. Cited in David Bellos, *Romain Gary: A Tall Story* (London, 2010), 112.

12 Gary, *La Danse de Gengis Cohn*, 272

13 See David Bellos, "In the Worst Possible Taste: Romain Gary's *Dance of Genghis Cohn*," in J. Sherman and R. Robertson, eds., *The Yiddish Presence in European Literature* (Oxford, 2005), 20.

14 For the details of Gary's life, there is no better source than Bellos, *Romain Gary*, passim.

15 Gary, *Le Sens de ma vie*, 51.

16 Gary, *Les Racines du ciel* (Paris, 1980 [orig. 1956]), 437.

17 This is Bellos' characterization. Idem, "In the Worst Possible Taste: Romain Gary's *Dance of Genghis Cohn*," 17.

18 Henry Rousso, *Le Syndrome de Vichy, 1944-198...* (Paris, 1987), 141–142; Pierre Nora, "Mémoire et identité juives dans la France contemporaine. Les grands déterminants,"*Le Débat*, no. 131 (September–October 2004), 23.

19 Myriam Ruszniewski-Dahan, *Romanciers de la Shoah. Si l'écho de leurs voix faiblit...* (Paris, 1999), 137. Bellos also notes the commonalities between Gary's and Modiano's novels. Idem, "In the Worst Possible Taste: Romain Gary's *Dance of Genghis Cohn*," 19.

20 Patrick Modiano, *La Place de l'étoile* (Paris, 1985 [orig. 1968]), 187.

21 For this quote and the ones preceding, see ibid., 209–210.

22 Modiano discusses his childhood and developing vocation as a writer in *Un Pedigree* (Paris, 2005).

23 Ruszniewski-Dahan, *Romanciers de la Shoah*, 96–97; Maurice Samuels, *The Right to Difference: French Universalism and the Jews* (Chicago, 2016), 160.

24 Bellos, *Georges Perec: A Life in Words* (London, 1993), 562–563.

25 Ibid., 239, 278.

26 Ibid., 401.

27 Perec, *W ou le souvenir d'enfance* (Paris, 1975), 17–18.

28 Ibid., 211.

29 Ibid., 222.

30 Ibid., 222.

31 Ibid., 64.

32 Perec, *La Vie mode d'emploi* (Paris, 2010 [orig. 1978]), 168.

33 Dagmar Herzog, *Cold War Freud: Psychoanalysis in an Age of Catastrophes* (Cambridge, 2017), 109–113; Didier Fassin and Richard Rechtman, *The Empire of Trauma: An Inquiry into the Condition of Victimhood* (Princeton, NJ, 2009), 18, 71–74. The Mitscherlichs' book was also translated into English under the title, *The Inability to Mourn* (1967).

34 On this point and for much of what follows, I owe an obvious debt to Azouvi, *Le Mythe du grand silence*, 285–288.

35 Helen Epstein, *Le Traumatisme en héritage. Conversations avec des fils et filles de survivants de la Shoah* (Paris, 2005), 320. See also Katy Hazan, *Les Orphelins de la Shoah. Les maisons de l'espoir (1944-1960)* (Paris, 2000), 293.

36 Bruno Bettelheim, "The Fluctuating Price of Life," in idem, *The Informed Heart: Autonomy in a Mass Age* (New York, 1971 [orig. 1960]), 232–259.

37 From Bettelheim's postface, Claudine Vegh, *Je ne lui ai pas dit au revoir. Des enfants de déportés parlent* (Paris, 1979), 194.

38 See, for example, Henry Rousso, *Le Syndrome de Vichy: 1944-198...*; or Charles Maier, *The Unmasterable Past: History, Holocaust, and German National Identity* (Cambridge, MA, 1988). Rousso has since reconsidered and refined his borrowing from psychiatric vocabulary and concepts. See idem, *Face au passé. Essais sur la mémoire contemporaine* (Paris, 2016), 53–54.

39 For the expression, "black sun," see Claude Lanzmann, *Le Lièvre de Patagonie* (Paris, 2009), 536.

12 Shoah

1 François Azouvi, *Le Mythe du grand silence. Auschwitz, les Français, la mémoire* (Paris, 2012), 397.

2 *Bulletin de Liaison des Fils et Filles des Déportés Juifs de France*, no. 74 (10 April 2001), reprinted in *La Chronique des fils et filles: 25 années de militantisme, 1979-2004* (Paris, 2009), 576.

3 Rémy Besson, *Shoah, une double référence? Des faits au film, du film aux faits* (Paris, 2017), 131, 134. 139–140.

4 Claude Lanzmann, *Le Lièvre de Patagonie* (Paris, 2009), 31–32, 395–396.

5 Simone de Beauvoir, *La Force des choses* (Paris, 1963), 271, 304–305.

6 De Beauvoir, *La Force des choses*, 619; Lanzmann, *Le Lièvre de Patagonie*, 363.

7 Lanzmann, *Le Lièvre de Patagonie*, 364; interview with Lanzmann in Juliette Simont, ed., *Claude Lanzmann. Un voyant dans le siècle* (Paris, 2017), 256–259.

8 Jean-Pierre Martin, "La voix et la vie. À propos du *Lièvre de Patagonie*," in Simont, ed., *Claude Lanzmann*, 215.

9 Lanzmann, "La reconnaissance," *Les Temps modernes*, no. 429 (April 1982), 1711.

10 Claude Lanzmann, "L'héritage des 'Temps modernes': Éloge de l'engagement," *Le Nouvel Observateur*, 7 December 2000, 14.

11 Jonathan Judaken, *Jean-Paul Sartre and the Jewish Question: Anti-Antisemitism and the Politics of the French Intellectual* (Lincoln, NE, 2006), 139; Maurice Samuels, *The Right to Difference: French Universalism and the Jews* (Chicago, 2016), 144, 155.

12 Lanzmann, "Ce mot de 'Shoah'...Réponse à Henri Meschonnic," *Le Monde* (2005), reprinted in idem, *La Tombe du divin plongeur* (Paris, 2012), 497.

13 Lanzmann, *Le Lièvre de Patagonie*, 205; 243; interview with Lanzmann, in Simont, ed., *Claude Lanzmann*, 250, 255.

14 Interview with Lanzmann, cited in Shoshana Felman, "À l'âge du témoignage: Shoah de Claude Lanzmann," in *Au Sujet de Shoah. Le film de Claude Lanzmann* (Paris, 1990), 143.

15 Lanzmann, *Le Lièvre de Patagonie*, 240–241.

16 That Lanzmann had a romantic partner in Israel was also an incentive. Richard Brody, "Witness: Claude Lanzmann and the making of 'Shoah'," *The New Yorker* (19 March 2012), 80.

17 These two scenes are beautifully evoked in Juliette Simont's contribution to idem, ed., *Claude Lanzmann*, 42–43.

18 Lanzmann, "*Hazkarah.* La résurrection du nom," speech delivered at the Mémorial de la Shoah, reprinted in idem, *La Tombe du divin plongeur*, 578.

19 Lanzmann, *Le Lièvre de Patagonie*, 429–430.

20 In France, Holocaust denial goes by the name of negationism, and the people who espouse this view are known as negationists. The English language equivalents are revisionism and revisionists.

21 For the preceding, see Valérie Igounet, *Histoire du négationnisme en France* (Paris, 2000), passim. Chomsky had not intended for what he wrote about Faurisson to be used this way.

22 See Henry Rousso, *Le Syndrome de Vichy, 1944-198...* (Paris, 1987), 166, 168–169; Igounet, *Histoire du négationnisme*, 237; Nadine Fresco, "Les redresseurs de morts. Chambres à gaz: la bonne nouvelle. Comment on révise l'histoire," *Les Temps modernes*, no. 407 (June 1980), 2150–2211; Pierre Vidal-Naquet, "Un Eichmann de papier," *Esprit*, 45 (September 1980), 8–52.

23 From Klarsfeld's unpaginated introduction to idem, *The Auschwitz Album: Lili Jacob's Album* (New York, 1980).

24 Éditions Montparnasse released a DVD of *Auschwitz, l'album de la mémoire* in 2005. The disc includes an interview with the filmmaker by Sylvie Lindeperg. See also Lindeperg's own observations about the film in idem, *Cléo de 5 à 7. Les actualités filmées de la Libération: archives du futur* (Paris, 2000), 184–186.

25 From Klarsfeld's forward to David Olère and Alexandre Oler, *Un Génocide en héritage* (Paris, 1998), 34. Klarsfeld makes the same point in Beate and Serge Klarsfeld, *Mémoires* (Paris, 2015), 665.

26 David Olère and Alexandre Oler, *Witness: Images of Auschwitz* (New York, 1998), 108. In the French version, what killed Olère was the knowledge that "a French university professor dared to teach the young that what he had lived from 1943 to 1945, alongside millions of others, never happened." See Olère and Oler, *Un Génocide en héritage*, 119.

27 Lanzmann's preface to Filip Müller, *Trois Ans dans une chambre à gaz d'Auschwitz* (Paris, 1980), 10.

28 Julie Maeck, *Montrer la Shoah à la télévision de 1960 à nos jours* (Paris, 2009), 139.

29 Elie Wiesel, "Trivializing the Holocaust: Semi-Fact and Semi-Fiction," *The New York Times*, 16 April 1978.

30 There was not, of course, just a single American approach, but for the purposes of the French debate, it might have seemed so.

31 Joshua Hirsch, *Afterimage: Film, Trauma, and the Holocaust* (Philadelphia, 2004), 4.

32 Annette Insdorf, *Indelible Shadows: Film and the Holocaust*, Third Edition (New York, 2009), 4.

33 Igounet, *Histoire du négationnisme*, 243.

34 The Inathèque at the BNF has a recording of the 6 March 1979 edition of *Les Dossiers de l'écran* on file.

35 Joseph Rovan, "'Holocauste' et l'Allemagne," *Le Monde*, 14 February 1979; J.R., "Holocauste 1979," *Esprit*, 28 (April 1979), 116–118.

36 These observations were made well after the fact. See the reprint of an essay Ophuls published in 1985, "Closely Watched Trains," in Stuart Liebman, *Claude Lanzmann's* Shoah: *Key Essays* (New York, 2007), 84.

37 Charlotte Delbo, "Une marque indélébile," *Le Monde*, 27 February 1979; Pierre Vidal-Naquet, "Le navet et le spectacle," *Esprit*, 28 (April 1979), 121; P.T., "Se rappeler...," *Esprit*, 28 (April 1979), 121–122.

38 Claude Lanzmann, "De l'Holocauste à Holocauste ou comment s'en débarrasser," *Les Temps modernes*, no. 395 (June 1979), reprinted in *Au Sujet de la Shoah*, 426–442.

39 Lanzmann, *Le Lièvre de Patagonie*, 532.

40 Lanzmann, "Holocauste, la représentation impossible," *Le Monde*, 3 March 1994, reprinted in idem, *La Tombe du divin plongeur*, 534–540.

41 And to Rudolf Vrba who was an Auschwitz escapee. Lanzmann, *Le Lièvre de Patagonie*, 439–440.

42 André Pierre Colombat, *The Holocaust in French Film* (Metuchen, NJ, 1993), 301.

43 Lanzmann, *Le Lièvre de Patagonie*, 443, 502.

44 Patrice Maniglier, "Lanzmann philosophe," in Simont, ed., *Claude Lanzmann*, 69.

45 Interview with Claude Lanzmann in *Les Cahiers du Cinéma*, no. 374 (July–August 1985), reprinted as "Le lieu et la parole," in *Au Sujet de la Shoah*, 407–425.

46 Ophuls, "Closely Watched Trains," 79.

47 Ibid., 81–82.

48 Besson, *Shoah, une double référence?* 78.

49 Lanzmann, *Le Lièvre de Patagonie*, 444–450.

50 Jean-Charles Szurek, "*Shoah*: From the Jewish Question to the Polish Question," in Liebman, ed., *Claude Lanzmann's* Shoah, 152.

51 Leon Wieseltier, "*Shoah*," in Liebman, ed., *Claude Lanzmann's* Shoah, 91.

52 Marc Chevrie and Hervé Leroux, "Site and Speech: An Interview with Claude Lanzmann about *Shoah*," in Liebman, ed., *Claude Lanzmann's* Shoah, 44–45. See also Lanzmann, "Le lieu et la parole," 414–415.

53 Lanzmann does deal with ghetto life and the problem of the *Judenräte* in a later film, *Le Dernier des injustes* (2013). The subject is Rabbi Benjamin Murmelstein, a council elder at Theresienstadt. Lanzmann filmed Murmelstein in the making of *Shoah* but did not use the footage.

54 Lanzmann, *Le Lièvre de Patagonie*, 484.

55 For such omissions, see Dominick LaCapra, "Lanzmann's *Shoah*: 'Here There Is No Why'," in Liebman, ed., *Claude Lanzmann's* Shoah, 214.

56 Szurek, "*Shoah*: From the Jewish Question to the Polish Question," 153.

57 Lanzmann, "J'ai enquêté en Pologne," in *Au Sujet de la Shoah*, 292.

58 Chevrie and Leroux, "Site and Speech: An Interview with Claude Lanzmann about *Shoah*," 44; Besson, *Shoah, une double référence*, 86.
59 The interview exchange between Karski and Lanzmann was so emotion-charged that it was not just Karski who broke down but Lanzmann also. See Jan Karski, "*Shoah*," in Liebman, ed., *Claude Lanzmann's* Shoah, 174.
60 For "Zionist closure," see Tim Cole, *Selling the Holocaust from Auschwitz to Schindler. How History Is Bought, Packaged, and Sold* (New York, 1999), 85; for the second, more modulated citation, see LaCapra, "Lanzmann's *Shoah*: 'Here There Is No Why'," 207.
61 Lanzmann, *Le Lièvre de Patagonie*, 467.
62 Ibid., 446, 454.
63 See Lanzmann's preface to Müller, *Trois Ans dans une chambre à gaz d'Auschwitz*, 16; his preface to *La Tombe du divin plongeur*, 18; and his 1968 review of Albert Cohen's novel, *Belle du Seigneur*, reprinted in idem, 284–285. This point is also noted in LaCapra, "Lanzmann's *Shoah*: 'Here There Is No Why'," 215; and in more general terms, by Maniglier, "Lanzmann philosophe," 88.
64 On the funding question, see Lanzmann, *Le Lièvre de Patagonie*, 539.
65 Lanzmann, "La reconnaissance," 1709, 1712.
66 Lanzmann, *Le Lièvre de Patagonie*, 525.
67 For the movie's reception, see Besson, *Shoah, une double référence*, 127–144, 150–152. See also, Maeck, *Montrer la Shoah à la télévision de 1960 à nos jours*, 211, 334–340; and Ophuls as cited in Liebman, "Introduction," to idem, ed., *Claude Lanzmann's* Shoah, 4.

Epilogue and Conclusion

1 Olivier Wieviorka, *La Mémoire désunie. Le souvenir politique des années sombres, de la Libération à nos jours* (Paris, 2010), 209.
2 Danielle Tartakowsky, *Nous irons chanter sur vos tombes. Le Père-Lachaise, XIXe-XXe siècle* (Paris, 1999), 165.
3 For the text of Chirac's speech, see: https://fr.wikisource.org/wiki/Discours_prononc%C3%A9_lors_des_comm%C3%A9morations_de_la_Rafle_du_Vel%E2%80%99_d%E2%80%99Hiv%E2%80%99. Accessed 10 July 2018.
4 Henry Rousso, *Face au passé. Essais sur la mémoire contemporaine* (Paris, 2016), 256-258. See also Tony Judt, *Postwar. A History of Europe since 1945* (New York, 2005), 804.
5 Olivier Lalieu, *Histoire de la mémoire de la Shoah* (Paris, 2015), 148.
6 The book to read on this is: Sarah Gensburger, *Les Justes de France. Politiques publiques de la mémoire* (Paris, 2010).
7 Lalieu, *La Déportation fragmentée: les anciens déportés parlent de politique* (Paris, 1994); Wieviorka, *La Mémoire désunie*.
8 This is the theme, of course, of Michael Rothberg's pathbreaking book: *Multidirectional Memory: Remembering the Holocaust in the Age of Decolonization* (Stanford, 2009).

9 For the concept of a 1.5 generation, see Susan Rubin Suleiman, "The 1.5 Generation: Thinking about Child Survivors and the Holocaust," *American Imago*, 59 (Fall 2002), 277–282.

10 For one last time, see Samuel Moyn, *A Holocaust Controversy: The Treblinka Affair in Postwar France* (Waltham, MA, 2005), 82.

11 What about Lazarus, it might be asked? What about Jean Cayrol's exercises in Lazarean fiction and poetry? Lazarus, of course, was raised from the dead by Jesus, a miraculous resurrection that prefigured Jesus' own. There is no such miracle-working in Lanzmann's oeuvre who, need it be added, was not, as Cayrol was, a believing Christian.

12 The allusion is to Annette Becker, *Les Messagers du désastre* (Paris, 2018).

13 This question is addressed by Sébastien Ledoux in "Silence et oubli de la mémoire de la Shoah. Une 'illusion' historiographique?" *En Jeu. Histoire et mémoires vivantes*, no. 2 (December 2013), 81–93.

14 Emma Kuby, *Political Survivors: The Resistance, the Cold War, and the Fight against Concentration Camps after 1945* (Ithaca, NY, 2019).

15 Dominick LaCapra, "Lanzmann's *Shoah*: 'Here There Is No *Why*'," in Stuart Liebman, ed., *Claude Lanzmann's* Shoah *Key Essays* (New York, 2007), 194.

16 Semprun's *L'Écriture ou la vie* (Paris, 1994) in fact opens with reflections on how he looked in 1945, with a crazed, devastated expression imprinted on his face that Buchenwald's Allied liberators found terrifying.

17 Barbie Zelizer, *Remembering to Forget: Holocaust Memory through the Camera's Eye* (Chicago, 1998), ch. 4.

18 Carolyn J. Dean, *Aversion and Erasure: The Fate of the Victim after the Holocaust* (Ithaca, NY, 2010), 101.

19 Sidra DeKoven Ezrahi, *By Words Alone: The Holocaust in Literature* (Chicago, 1980), 14; James E. Young, *Writing and Rewriting the Holocaust: Narrative and the Consequences of Interpretation* (Bloomington, IN, 1988), 17; Michael Rothberg, *Traumatic Realism: The Demands of Holocaust Representation* (Minneapolis, MN, 2000), 99.

20 Lawrence L. Langer, *The Holocaust and the Literary Imagination* (New Haven, CT, 1975), 43; Alvin H. Rosenfeld, *A Double Dying: Reflections of Holocaust Literature* (Bloomington, IN, 1980), 54.

21 Anny Dayan Rosenman remarks on the imperative to "write but in a different key": *Les Alphabets de la Shoah. Survivre, témoigner, écrire* (Paris, 2007), 170.

22 The torch relay itself was very much a part of the Great War commemorative repertoire. See Daniel J. Sherman, *The Construction on Memory in Interwar France* (Chicago, 2000), 314.

23 Rémi Dalisson, *Histoire de la mémoire de la Grande Guerre* (Paris, 2015), passim.

24 As it was in framing memories of the Great War. See Becker, *La Guerre et la foi. De la mort à la mémoire, 1914-1930* (Paris, 1994).

25 Jay Winter, *Sites of Memory, Sites of Mourning: The Great War in European Cultural History* (Cambridge, 1995), 8–9.

26 Sherman, *The Construction of Memory*, 151–152; and idem, "Art, Commerce, and the Production of Memory in France after World War I," in John R. Gillis, ed., *Commemorations: The Politics of National Identity* (Princeton, 1994), 200–202. Sherman makes the case that critics of Great War memorial statuary preferred the realist mode to the allegorical but allowed for both, provided the allegorical didn't tend to excess.

27 See Antoine de Baecque who proposes that the encounter with images of the camps was foundational to modern cinema: "Premières images des camps: quel cinéma après Auschwitz?" *Cahiers du cinéma* (November 2000), hors série, Le Siècle du cinéma, 66.

Index